READINGS IN PRICE THEORY

THE SERIES OF REPUBLISHED
ARTICLES ON ECONOMICS
Volume VI

Selection Committee for This Volume

GEORGE J. STIGLER

KENNETH E. BOULDING

The participation of the American Economic Association in
the presentation of this series consists in the appointment of
a committee to determine the subjects of the volumes and
of special committees to select the articles for each volume.

READINGS IN

PRICE THEORY

Selected by a Committee of

THE AMERICAN ECONOMIC ASSOCIATION

1952

Published for the Association by

RICHARD D. IRWIN, INC.

CHICAGO · HOMEWOOD, ILLINOIS

INTRODUCTION

The editors of this volume have discovered no economist who has devoted himself to the Theory of the Anthology. The omission seems odd for a profession that ranges as widely as ours, because—as we have discovered by painful experience—constructing an anthology is an economic problem of some interest and difficulty—one might almost say hazard. Presumably an anthologist is maximizing something. He is faced with a problem of choice. He has limited space: if one item gets in, some other item must be left out. He has a problem of balance: he must equate the marginal utilities of pages devoted to various topics. He has problems of complementarity—article A does not make sense without article B—and of competitiveness—if article A is included, article C does not add much. And at the end of the process he knows that he will meet slightly raised eyebrows and slightly hurt feelings—why did he leave out this worthy item, or put in that not-so-worthy one? The feeling of dissatisfaction which most readers feel with anthologies arises out of a phenomenon which is never quite adequately dealt with in the literature of economics but which is of very general importance; it might be termed the Plateau Principle. The maximum of anthological virtue which the anthologist seeks is not a peak but a broad plateau: some of the items which got in just squeezed by; some of the items which were excluded were just fractionally below the threshold. Over a wide range of choice the selection is about equally good; consequently, the actual selection must be determined by rather personal and non-significant factors. To those who prefer another part of the plateau we offer no remonstrance; after all, it is not unusual for the contents of a book to be influenced by the particular men who fashion it.

There are one or two matters of policy, however, which it may be desirable to explain. We resolved at the outset to exclude articles dealing principally with welfare economics on the ground that this literature is so extensive that it may well form the subject of another volume of readings. That is to say, we have concentrated on what might be called the mechanics of the pricing process rather than on its evaluation. We have excluded articles which are more in the nature of applied economics and concentrated on those of general theoretical interest. We have followed the policy of not confining ourselves to the most recent literature but have taken a comprehensive view of the economic literature of the past forty years. We have been concerned with the usefulness of the collection as an adjunct to, rather than as a complete substitute for, the literature which is generally available in libraries. Consequently, we have been influenced not only by the merit but also by the relative availability of the articles under consideration. Our selection should not be regarded as a kind of prize list or award of merit but more as a device for making available and drawing to the attention of students articles of value which otherwise would less often be read.

Our task was rendered more difficult and its performance more satisfactory by the suggestions of economists too numerous to mention. We wish also to thank the publishers, authors, Lady Clapham, and Mr. Joseph H. Wicksteed for permission to reprint these articles. Professors Giorgio Fuà, Eric Lundberg, Oskar Morgenstern, and François Perroux generously contributed to the bibliography brief lists of important foreign language articles. Mr. H. Irving Forman redrew the charts.

KENNETH E. BOULDING
GEORGE J. STIGLER

May, 1951

CONTENTS

III. STOCKS IN THE THEORY OF PRICES

IV. THE RATIONALE OF THE FIRM

V. IMPERFECT COMPETITION

VI. SPATIAL COMPETITION

VII. THEORY OF GAMES

CONTENTS

PART I

UTILITY AND DEMAND

1

THE SCOPE AND METHOD OF
POLITICAL ECONOMY *¹

By Philip H. Wicksteed ‖

I

I address myself primarily to those who already accept the marginal theory of Value and Distribution, inviting their attention to the modifications it is already introducing into current conceptions of Political Economy and of its relation to other studies, and urging the necessity of accepting the change more frankly and pressing it further. But at the same time I think we shall find that the best approach to our proper subject is through a summary exposition, if not a defence, of the theory itself.

Let us begin by attempting to determine the characteristic of the economic field of investigation. Naturally there is no sharp line that marks off the economic life, and we must not expect to arrive at any rigid definition of it; but I take it that if I am doing a thing because I want it done for its own sake (not necessarily *my* own sake, in any restricted sense, for it may primarily concern some one else in whom I am interested out of pure goodwill), or am making a thing that I require for the supply of my own desires or the accomplishment of my own purposes; if, in fact, I am engaged in the direct pursuit of my own purposes, or expression of my own impulses, my action is not economic. But if I am making or doing anything not because I have any direct interest in it, but because some one else wants it, and that other person will either do what I want done or put me in command of it, then I am furthering his purposes as a means of furthering my own. I am indi-

---

* *The Economic Journal,* Vol. XXIV (1914), pp. 1–23. Reprinted, by the courtesy of the publisher and Mr. Joseph H. Wicksteed, with typographical corrections.

‖ Philip Wicksteed died in 1927.

¹ Presidential Address to Section F of the British Association, Birmingham, 1913.

rectly forwarding my purposes by directly forwarding his. This is the nature of the economic relation, and the mechanism or articulation of the whole complex of such economic relations is the proper subject of economic investigation. Thus, if a peasant adorns his ox-yoke with carving because he likes doing it and likes it when done, or if he carves a stool for his friend because he loves him and likes doing it for him and believes he will like it when done, the action is not economic; but if he gets a reputation for carving and other peasants want his work, he may become a professional carver and may carve a yoke or a stool because other people want them and he finds that supplying their wants is the easiest way for him to get food and clothes and leisure for his own art, and all things else that he desires. His artistic work now puts him into an economic relation with his fellows; but this example serves to remind us that there may be an indefinite area of coincidence between the economic and non-economic aspects of a man's occupations and relations. That man is happy indeed who finds that in expressing some part of his nature he is providing for all his natural wants; or that in rendering services to friends in which he delights he is putting himself in command of all the services he himself needs for the accomplishment of his own purposes. A perfect coincidence of this nature is the dream of modern Utopias; but my present subject is only the economic side of the shield.

The economic organism, then, of an industrial society represents the instrumentality whereby every man, by doing what he can for some of his fellows, gets what he wants from others. It is true, of course, that those for whom he makes or does something *may* be the same as those from whom he gets the particular things he wants. But this is not usual. In such a society as ours the persons whom a man serves are usually incapable of serving him in the way he desires, but they can put him in command of the services he requires, though they cannot render them. This is accomplished by the instrumentality of money, which is a generalised command of the services and commodities in the circle of exchange; "money" being at once a standard in which all market prices are expressed, and a universal commodity which every one who wishes to exchange what he has for what he·wants will accept as a medium, or middle term, by which to effect the transformation. Thus in most commercial transactions one party furthers a specific purpose of the other, and receives in exchange a command, defined in amount but not in kind, of services and commodities in general; the scale of equivalence being a publicly recognised thing announced in current market prices. Every member of the community who stands in economic relations with others alternately generalises his special resources and then specialises his general resources, first directly furthering some one else's purposes and then picking out the persons who can directly further his. Thus each of us puts in what he has at one point of the circle of exchange and takes out what he wants at another. Being out of work is being unable to find any one who values our special service enough to relinquish in our favour such a command of services in general as we are prepared to accept in return.

Our economic relations, therefore, are built up on a recognised scale of equivalences amongst the various commodities and services in the circle of exchange; or, in other words, upon market values. And our first step must be to formulate the "marginal" theory of exchange, or market, values. It is capable of very easy and precise formulation in mathematical language; for it simply regards value in exchange as the first derived or "differential" function of value in use; which is as much as to say, in ordinary language, that what a man will give for anything sooner than go without it is determined by a comparison of the *difference* which he conceives its possession will make to him, compared with the difference that anything he gives for it or could have had instead of it will or would make; and, further, that we are generally considering in our private budgets, and almost always in our general speculations, not the significance of a total supply of any commodity—coals, bread, or clothes, for instance—but the significance of the difference between, say, a good and a very good wheat harvest to the public, or the difference between ten and eleven loaves of bread per week to our own family, or perhaps between ten days and a fortnight spent at the seaside. In short, when we are considering whether we will contract or enlarge our expenditure upon this or that object, we are normally engaged in considering the difference to our satisfaction which differences of adjustment in our several supplies will make. We are normally engaged, then, not in the consideration of totals, either of supplies or of satisfactions, but of differences of satisfaction dependent upon differences of supplies.

According to this theory, then, what I am *willing* to give for an increase in my supply of anything is determined by the difference it will make to my satisfaction, but what I shall *have* to give for it is determined by the difference it would make to the satisfaction of certain other people; for if there is any one to whom it will make more difference than it will to me, he will be ready to give more for it, and he will get it, while I go without. But again, since the more he has the less difference will a still further increase make to him, and the less I have the more difference will a still further decrease make to me, we shall ultimately arrive at an equilibrium; what I am willing to give and what I am compelled to give will coincide, and the difference that a little more or a little less of any commodity which I habitually consume makes to my estimated satisfaction will be identical with a similar estimated difference to any other habitual consumer.

Or we may attack the problem from the point of view of the individual. We have pointed out that to any individual the differential significance of a unit of supply of any commodity or service declines as the supply increases. In our own expenditure, we find that current prices (our individual reaction on the market being insensible) fix the terms on which the various alternatives offered by the whole range of commodities and services in the circle of exchange are open to us. Obviously, so long as the differential satisfaction anticipated from one purchase exceeds that which the same money would procure from another, we shall take the preferable alternative (thereby reducing its differential superiority) until we have so regulated our expanding or contracting supplies that the differential satisfactions gained or lost from a given small increase or decrease of expenditure upon any one of our different objects of interest is identical. Into the practical difficulties that prevent our ever actually reaching this ideal equilibrium of expenditure I will not here enter; but I must call attention to the identity in principle of this analysis of the internal economy of our own choice between alternatives, tending to a subjective equilibrium between the differential significances of different supplies to the same person, and the corresponding analysis, just given, of the process by which an objective equilibrium is approached between the differential significances of the same supplies to different persons.

And this observation introduces another of extreme importance. In our private administration of resources we are concerned
both with things that are and with things that are not in the circle
of exchange, and the principle of distribution of resources is identical in both cases. The independent student who is apportioning
his time and energy between pursuing his own line of research and
keeping abreast of the literature of his subject is forming estimates
of differential significances and is equating them to each other just
as directly as the housewife who is hesitating between two stalls in
the market. And when we are considering whether we will live in
the country or the town, we may find, on examination, that we
are carefully equating increments and decrements of such apparently heterogeneous indulgences as those associated with fresh eggs
and friendship. Or, more generally, the inner core of our life
problems and the gratification of all our ultimate desires (which
are indeed inextricably interlaced with our command of exchangeable things, but are the ends to which the others are but means)
obey the same all-permeating law. Virtue, wisdom, sagacity, pru-
dence, success, imply different schemes of values, but thcy all submit to the law formulated by Aristotle with reference to virtue,
and analysed by modern writers with reference to business, for they
all consist in combining factors κατ' ὀρθὸν λόγον, *in the right proportion*, as fixed by that distribution of resources which estab-
lishes the equilibrium of their differential significances in securing
the object contemplated, whether that object be tranquillity of
mind, the indulgence of an overmastering passion or affection, the
command of things and services in the circle of exchange, or a
combination of all these, or of any other conceivable factors of life.

Now this dominating and universal principle of the distribution of resources, as we have seen, tends, by the instrumentality
of the market, to secure an identity in the relative positions of
increments of all exchangeable things upon the scales of all the
members of the community amongst whom they are distributed.
For if, amongst the things he possesses, *A* finds one, a given decrement in which would make less difference to him, as measured
in increments of other exchangeable things, than the corresponding increment would make to *B* (who is assumed to have a certain
command of exchangeable things in general), obviously there is a
mutual gain in *B* giving for the increment in question what is less

than worth it to him but more than worth it to A. There is equilibrium therefore only when a decrement in any man's stock of any exchangeable thing would make more difference to him, as measured in other exchangeable things, than the corresponding increment (measured in the same terms) would make to any one else. Hence all those who possess anything must, in equilibrium, value it more, differentially or incrementally, than any one who does not possess it, provided that this latter does possess something, and provided that "value" is measured in exchangeable things.

But this last qualification is all-important. The market tends to establish an identity of the place of the differential value of any commodity amongst all exchangeable things on everybody's scale of preferences, and further to secure that it is higher on the scale of every one that has it than on the scale of any one who has it not; so that to that extent, and in that sense, things must always tend to go and to stay where they are most significant. But then exchangeable things are never really the ultimately significant things at all. They are means. The ends, which are always subjective experiences of some kind, whether of the senses or the will or the emotions, are not in any direct way exchangeable; and there is no machinery to secure that increments and decrements of exchangeable things shall in industrial equilibrium take the same place and have the same differential significance on the scales of any two men when measured not in terms of other means, but in terms of ends. If two men habitually spend a portion of their resources on food and on books, there is a presumption that to both of them the differential significance of a shilling's-worth of food and of a volume of Everyman's or the Home University Library is equivalent. But there is no presumption whatever that the vital significance of either one or the other is identical to the two men as measured, not each in terms of the other, but each in the degree to which it ministers to the ultimate purposes of its possessor or consumer; in the pain that its absence or the pleasure that its presence would give him; or in its ultimate significance upon his life. Granted that x makes just as much difference, both to you and to me, as y does, it does not follow that either x or y makes the same difference to you that it does to me.

The ground is now clear for a step forward along the main line of our advance. The differential theory of exchange values carries with it a corresponding theory of distribution, whether we use this term in its technical sense of the division of a product amongst the factors that combine for its production, or whether we employ it as equivalent to "administration," and are thinking of the administration of our personal resources; that is to say, their distribution amongst the various objects that appeal to us; or again, the distribution, under economic pressures, of the sum of the industrial resources of a society amongst the objects that appeal to its members.

Land, manifold apparatus, various specialised faculties of hand, eye, and brain, are essential, let us say, to the production of some commodity valued by some one (it does not matter whom), for some purpose (it does not matter what). None of these hetero-geneous factors can be dispensed with, and therefore the product in its totality is dependent upon the co-operation of each one severally. But there is room for wide variety in the proportions in which they are combined, and whatever the existing proportion may be each factor has a differential significance, and all these differential significances can be expressed in a common unit; that is to say, all can be expressed in terms of each other, by noting the increment or decrement of any one that would be the equivalent of a given decrement or increment of any other; equivalence being measured by the neutralising of the effect upon the product, or rather, not upon the material product itself, but the command of generalised resources in the circle of exchange for the sake of which it is produced. The manager of a business is constantly engaged in considering, for instance, how much labour such-and-such a machine would save; how much raw material a man of such-and-such character would save; what equivalent an expansion or reconstruction of his premises would yield in ease and smooth-ness in the conduct of business; how much economy in the shop would be effected by a given addition to the staff in the office, and so on. This is considering differential significances and their equivalences as they affect his business. And all the time he is also considering the prices at which he can obtain these several factors, dependent upon their differential significances to other people in other businesses. His skill consists, like that of the housewife in the market, in expanding and contracting his expenditure on the several factors of production so as to bring their differential significances to himself into coincidence with their market prices. And note that the same principle can be applied without any difficulty to such immaterial factors of efficiency as "goodwill" or notoriety; but it would delay us too long to work this out or to anticipate possible objections. A hint must suffice.

Here, then, we have a firm theoretical basis for the study of distribution, independent of the particular form of organisation of a business. Whether those in command of the several factors of production meet and discuss the principles upon which the actual proceeds of the business shall be divided, when they are realised; or whether some one person takes the risks (on his own behalf or on behalf of a group of others), and discounts the estimated significance of the several factors, buying up their several interests in the product, by paying wages and salaries, interest, and rent, and by purchasing machinery and raw material, and so forth; or whatever other mechanism may be adopted, the underlying principle is the same. The differential equivalence of the factors of production reduces them to a common measure, and when they are all expressed in the same unit the problem of the division of the product amongst them is solved in principle.

Now I conceive that the application of this differential method to economics must tend to enlarge and to harmonise our conception of the scope of the study, and to keep it in constant touch with the wider ethical, social, and sociological problems and aspirations from which it must always draw its inspiration and derive its interest; for if we really understand and accept the principle of differential significances we shall realise, as already pointed out, that Aristotle's system of ethics and our reconstructed system of economics are twin applications of one identical principle or law, and that our conduct in business is but a phase or part of our conduct in life, both being determined by our sense, such as it is, of differential significances and their changing weights as the integrals of which they are the differences expand or contract. Cæsar, "that day he overcame the Nervii," being surprised by the enemy, contracted his exhortation to the troops, but did not omit it. In his distribution of the time at his disposal the differential significance of prompt movement was higher than usual in relation to the differential significance of stirring words from their beloved and trusted commander addressed to the soldiers as they entered upon action. An ardent lover may decline a business interview in order to keep an appointment with his lady-love, but there will be a point at which its estimated bearing upon his prospects of an early settlement will make him break his appointment with the lady in favour of the business interview. A man of leisure with a taste for literature and a taste for gardening will have to apportion time, money, and attention between them, and consciously or unconsciously will balance against each other the differential significances involved. All these, therefore, are making selections and choosing between alternatives on precisely the same principle and under precisely the same law as those which dominate the transactions of the housewife in the market, or the management of a great factory or ironworks, or the business of a bill-broker.

A full realisation of this will produce two effects. In the first place, it will put an end to all attempts to find "laws" proper to our conduct in economic relations. There are none. Hitherto economists for the most part have been vaguely conscious that the ultimate laws of economic conduct must be psychological, and, feeling the necessity of determining some defining boundaries of their study, have sought to make a selection of the motives and aims that are to be recognised by it. Hence the simplified psychology of the "economic man," now generally abandoned—but abandoned grudgingly, by piecemeal, under pressure, and with constant attempts to patch up what ought to be cast away. There is no occasion to define the economic motive, or the psychology of the economic man, for economics study a type of relation, not a type of motive, and the psychological law that dominates economics dominates life. We may either ignore all motives or admit all to our consideration, as occasion demands, but there is no rhyme or reason in selecting certain motives that shall and certain others that shall not be recognised by the economist.

In the second place, when taken off the wrong track we shall be able to find the right one, and shall understand that the proper field of economic study is, in the first instance, the type of relationship into which men spontaneously enter, when they find that they can best further their own purposes by approaching them indirectly. There is seldom a direct line by which a man can make his faculties and his specialised possessions minister continuously to all his purposes, or even to the greater part or the most importunate part of them. He must find some one else to whose purposes he can directly devote his powers or lend his resources in order that he may generalise his specific capacity or possession, and then again specialise this generalised command in the direction his tastes or needs dictate. The industrial world is a spontaneous organisation for transmuting what every man has into what he desires, wholly irrespective of what his desires may be.

And, in the third place, this truer conception of the economic field of investigation, coupled with the sense of the unity of fundamental law and fundamental motive that sways our economic and our non-economic action, will throw a constantly increasing emphasis upon the fact that our economic life is not and cannot be isolated, but is at every point combined with the direct expression of character and indulgence of taste, while the human relations into which it brings us are constantly waking in us a direct interest (whether of attraction or repulsion) in those purposes of others which we are directly furthering as an indirect means of furthering our own, purposes which we have indeed adopted, but beyond which we look whenever we reflect. There is no reason why means should not, to an undefined extent, be from the beginning, or become, in course of time, ends in themselves, while still continuing to be means; nor, alas, is there any guarantee that they will not be, or will not become, negative and repellent as ends, either through physical weariness or moral repulsion. Perhaps most men's "occupations" combine both characteristics.

Again, the realisation of the exact nature of the economic organisation as a machinery for combining in mutual helpfulness persons whose ends are diverse, will drive it home to our consciousness that one man's want is another man's opportunity, and that it may serve a man's turn to create a want or a passion in another in order that he may find his opportunity in it. All along the line, from a certain type of ingenious advertiser to the financier (if he really exists) who engineers a war in order that he may arrange a war loan, we may study the creation of wants and passions, destructive of general welfare, for the sake of securing wealth to individuals. And we may realise the deeply significant truth that to any individual the full discharge of his industrial function —that is to say, the complete satisfaction or disappearance, by whatever means, of the want which he is there to satisfy—must be, if he contemplates it, a nightmare; for it would mean that he would be "out of work," that because no one wants what he can give no one wants him, and neither will any one give him what he wants.

Yet again, in our industrial relations the thing we are doing is indeed an end, but it is some one else's end, not ours; and as far as the relation is really economic, the significance *to us* of what we are doing is measured not by its importance to the man for whom it is done, but by the degree to which it furthers our own ends. There can, therefore, be no presumption of any coincidence between the social significance of our work and the return we receive for it. We cannot say, "What men most care for they will pay most for, therefore what is most highly paid is most cared for," for (sometimes to our positive knowledge, and generally "for all we know") it is different men who express their eagerness for the different things we are comparing, by offering such-and-such prices, and those who offer little money for a thing may do so not because what they demand signifies so little, but because what they would have to give, or to forgo, for it signifies so much. They may offer little for a thing not because its possession matters so little but because their possession of anything, including this particular thing, matters so much.

These and other such considerations will not directly affect our exposition of the mechanism of the market, the central phenomenon of the industrial world, but they will profoundly affect the spirit in which we approach, and in which we conduct, our investigation of it. For we shall not only know but shall always feel that the economic machine is constructed and moved by individuals for individual ends, and that its social effect is incidental. It is a means and its whole value consists in the nature of the ends it subserves and its efficacy in subserving them. The collective wealth of a community ceases to be a matter of much direct significance to us, for if one man has a million pounds, and a hundred others have ten pounds each, the collective wealth is the same as if the hundred and one men had a thousand each. What are we to expect from a survey made from a point of view from which these two things are indistinguishable? The market does not tell us in any fruitful sense what are the "national," "social," or "collective" wants, or means of satisfaction, of a community, for it can only give us *sums,* and the significance of a sum varies indefinitely according to its distribution.

If we reflect on these things—and the study of differential significances forces us to reflect upon them—we shall never for a moment, in our economic investigations, be able to escape from the pressure of the consciousness that they derive their whole significance from their social and vital bearings, and that the categories under which we usually discuss them conceal rather than reveal their meaning. We shall understand that this ultimate significance is determined by ethical considerations; that the sanity of men's desires matters more than the abundance of their means of accomplishing them; that the chief dangers of poverty and wealth alike are to be found in degeneracy of desire, and that the final goal of education and of legislation alike must be to thwart corrupt and degrading ends, to stimulate worthy desires, to infect the mind with a wholesome scheme of values, and to direct means into the channels where they are likeliest to conduce to worthy ends.

To sum up this branch of our examination, the differential theory of economics will never allow us to forget that organised "production," which is the proper economic field, is a means only, and derives its whole significance from its relation to "consumption" or "fruition," which is the vital field, and covers all the ends to which production is a means; and, moreover, the economic laws must not be sought and cannot be found on the properly economic field. It is on the vital field, then, that the laws of economics must be discovered and studied, and the data of economics interpreted. To recognise this will be to humanise economics.

The merit of our present organisation of industry is to be found in the extent to which it is spontaneous, and lays every man, whatever his ends, under the necessity of seeking some other man whom he can serve, in order to accomplish them. So far it is social, for it compels the individual to relate himself to others. But the more we analyse the life of society the less can we rest upon the "economic harmonies"; and the better we understand the true function of the "market," in its widest sense, the more fully shall we realise that it never has been left to itself, and the more deeply shall we feel that it never must be. Economics must be the handmaid of sociology.

II

Let me now proceed to the consideration of a few points in which I think the traditional methods of technical exposition need reconsideration in the light of the differential theory.

At the root of all lies a profound modification of our conception of the nature and function of the "market" itself. The differential theory when applied to exchangeable things tells us that there is equilibrium only when an exchangeable commodity is so distributed that every one who possesses it assigns the same place to its differential value, amongst those of other commodities of which he has a supply; and that this place is a higher one than it occupies on the relative scale of any one who does not possess it. What this place is—that is to say, the differential equivalence of the commodity in terms of other commodities, when equilibrium is established—is fixed absolutely by two determinants. These are:—(1) The tastes, desires, and resources of the individuals constituting the society. When objectively measured and expressed, these individual desires for any one commodity can be represented by curves capable of being summed; and the resultant curve, objectively homogeneous but covering undefined differences of vital or subjective significance, is usually called, so far as it is understood and realised, the "curve of demand." This is one of the determinants we are examining, and it represents a series of hypothetically co-existing relations between given hypothetical supplies and corresponding differential significances. It is a curve representing a function. (2) The amount of the actual supply existing in the community. This is not a curve at all, but an actual quantity. It is not a series of co-existing relations, but one single fact, and it determines which of the series of hypothetical or potential relations represented by the curve shall be actually realised.

But what about the "supply curve" that usually figures as a determinant of price, co-ordinate with the demand curve? I say it boldly and baldly: There is no such thing. When we are speaking of a marketable commodity, what is usually called the supply curve is in reality the demand curve of those who possess the commodity; for it shows the exact place which every successive unit of the commodity holds in their relative scale of estimates. The so-called supply curve, therefore, is simply a part of the total demand curve which we have already described as factor (1). The separating out of this portion of the demand curve and reversing it in the diagram is a process which has its meaning and its legitimate function, as we shall see in a moment, but is wholly irrelevant to the determination of the price.

The intercourse of the market enables all the parties concerned to find their places with respect to each other on the general demand curve. Each individual, whether or not he possesses a stock of the commodity, brings his own individual curve of demand into the market, and there relates it to all the other individual curves of demand, thus constituting the collective curve, which (together

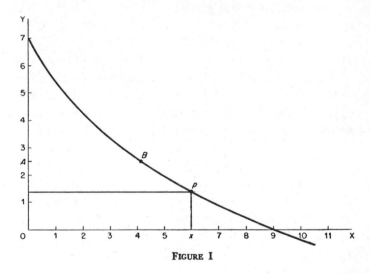

FIGURE I

with the amount of the commodity available) determines the price, *i.e.* the (objective) height of the lowest demand for a unit of the commodity which the available amount will suffice to reach.

The ordinary method of presenting the demand curve in two sections tells us the extent to which the present distribution of the commodity departs from that of equilibrium, and therefore the extent of the transactions that will be required to reach equilibrium. But it is the single combined curve alone that tells us what the equilibrium price will be. The customary representation of cross curves confounds the process by which the price is discovered with the ultimate facts that determine it.

Diagrams of intersecting curves (and corresponding tables) of

demand prices and supply prices are therefore profoundly misleading. They co-ordinate as two determinants what are really only two
separated portions of one; and they conceal altogether the existence
and operation of what is really the second determinant. For it will
be found on a careful analysis that the construction of a diagram
of intersecting demand and "supply" curves always involves, but
never reveals, a definite assumption as to the amount of the total
supply possessed by the supposed buyers and the supposed sellers
taken together as a single homogeneous body, and that if this total
is changed the emerging price changes too; whereas a change in its
initial distribution (if the collective curve is unaffected, while the

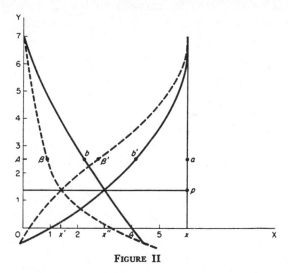

FIGURE II

component or intersecting curves change) will have no effect on
the market, or equilibrating price itself, which will come out
exactly the same. Naturally, for neither the one curve nor the one
quantity which determine the price has been changed.

The accompanying diagrams may suggest to the reader a
method of testing the validity of the argument in the text.

Ox in both figures represents the amount of the commodity,
and the curve in Fig. I represents the total demand curve. The
resultant price is *px*.

None of these data are altered in Fig. II, but the demand curves
of the possessors (collectively) and the non-possessors (collectively)
are separated out from each other, as representing the conditions

under which the market opens. Two different hypotheses as to this initial distribution of the stock are represented by the dotted and the continuous lines. But in each case, of course, the condition of preserving the data of Fig. I intact determines that at any price OA, the line AB (Fig. I) shall be equal to the sum $Ab + ab'$ or $A\beta + a\beta'$ (Fig. II). If this condition is observed, the intersection must be at the height xp, when AB or its equivalent sum in Fig. II equals Ox.

The dotted lines represent a market that opens with conditions nearer to equilibrium than those represented by the continuous lines; and in the one case only Ox' will change hands, whereas in the other Ox'' will do so. But this has nothing to do with the price.[2]

The curve of supply prices, then, is a mere *alias* of a portion of the demand curve. But so far we have only dealt with the market in the narrower sense. Our investigations throw sufficient light on the distribution of the hay harvest, for instance, or on the "catch" of a fishing fleet. But where the production is continuous, as in mining or in ironworks, will the same theory still suffice to guide us? Here again we encounter the attempt to establish two co-ordinate principles, diagrammatically represented by two inter-secting curves; for though the "cost of production" theory of value is generally repudiated, we are still too often taught to look for the forces that determine the stream of supply along two lines, the value of the product, regulated by the law of the market, and the cost of production. But what is cost of production? In the market of commodities I am ready to give as much as the article is worth to me, and I cannot get it unless I give as much as it is worth to others. In the same way, if I employ land or labour or tools to produce something, I shall be ready to give as much as they are worth to me, and I shall have to give as much as they are worth to others—always, of course, differentially. Their worth to me is de-termined by their differential effect upon *my* product, their worth to others by the like effect upon *their* products (or direct fruitions, if they do not apply them industrially). Again we have an *alias* merely. Cost of production is merely the form in which the desired-

---

[2] For further details and the treatment of possible objections, see my *Common Sense of Political Economy*, Book II, Chap. IV.

ness a thing possesses for some one else presents itself to me.[3] When we take the collective curve of demand for any factor of production we see again that it is entirely composed of demands, and my adjustment of my own demands to the conditions imposed by the demands of others is of exactly the same nature whether I am buying cabbages or factors for the production of steel plates. I have to adjust my desire for a thing to the desires of others for the same thing, not to find some principle other than that of desiredness, co-ordinate with it as a second determinant of market price. The second determinant, here as everywhere, is the supply. It is not until we have perfectly grasped the truth that costs of production of one thing are nothing whatever but an *alias* of efficiencies in production of other things that we shall be finally emancipated from the ancient fallacy we have so often thrust out at the door, while always leaving the window open for its return.

I now turn to some of the most obvious consequences of the differential theory of distribution. They are all included in the one statement that when fully grasped this theory must destroy the very conception of separate laws of distribution such as the law of rent, the law of interest, or the law of wages. It is by determining the differential equivalence of all the factors of production, however heterogeneous, that we reduce them to a common measure and establish the theory of distribution; just as it is by determining the differential equivalence of all our pursuits and possessions that we attempt to place a shilling or an hour or an effort of the mind where it will tell best, and so distribute our money or time or mental energy well. There can no more be a law of rent than there can be a law of the price of shoes distinct from the general

---

[3] I do not deny that, as we recede from the market and deal with long periods and the ultimate conditions on which nature yields her stores, cases may arise in which something like a "supply curve" seems legitimate. The terms on which nature yields increasing supplies of some raw material, for instance, cannot legitimately be regarded as the reserve prices in which she expresses her own demand! But even here in the last analysis, and when we consider the enormous range of the principle of "substitution" and the pressures that determine the directions taken by inventive genius, I believe we shall be thrown back in all important cases upon modifications in the demands upon human energy and expressions of human vitality and their distribution amongst all the utilities and fruitions that appeal to them.

law of the market. The way in which the several factors render
their service to production differs, but the differential service they
render is in every case identical, and it is on this identity or equivalence of service that the possibility of co-ordinate distribution rests.
So the economist, though he may begin by giving precision to the
student's idea of *how* "waiting," for example, or tools, or mere
command of "extension" in space, or manual skill, or experience,
or honesty, may affect the value of the product, must end by
showing him that their distributive share of the product depends
not upon *the way in which* they affect the product (wherein they
are all heterogeneous), but on the differential *amount* of their
effect (wherein they are all alike). The law of distribution, then,
is one, and is governed not by the differences of nature in the
factors, but by the identity of their differential effect. With this
searchlight we must scrutinise the body of current economic teaching, and must cast out the mischievous survivals that deform it.

On the present occasion severe selection and limitation is, of
course, necessary, and I think we cannot do better than take up
a few of the current phrases, or conceptions and diagrammatic
illustrations connected with the phenomenon of rent. Antece-
dently we must expect that as there is no theoretical difference
between the part played by land and that played by other factors
of production (or more direct ministrants to enjoyment), so there
can be no general assertion about rent and land which is at once
true and distinctive; for, if true, it must be based on that aspect
of land which expresses its function in a unit common, say, to
capital, and which brings its differential significance, upon which
all depends, under the same law; and therefore it cannot be distinctive of land.

Let us test the truth of these anticipations. Ricardo's celebrated
law of rent really asserts nothing except that the superior article
fetches the superior price, in proportion to its superiority; and it
is obvious that all "superiorities" in land, whether arising from
"inalienable" properties or from expenditure of capital, tell in
exactly the same way upon the rent.

Again, a diagram may easily be constructed in which different
qualities of land are represented along the axis of X and their
supposed relative fertilities to a fixed application of labour and
capital along the axis of Y. The "marginal" land will occupy the

extreme place to the right. This is not a functional curve; for the height of y does not depend upon the length of x, the units being expressly so placed on OX as to produce a declining y. It is applicable to land or to anything else of which typical units can be arranged in ascending or descending order of efficiency.

But the same figure has been used as a functional curve in connection with the theory of rent. Take a given fixed area of land of a certain quality and consider what would be its yield if it were "dosed" with a certain quantity of labour and capital represented by a unit on the axis of X. Increase the doses till a further increment of labour and capital would not produce as large an increment in the yield of this land as it would if applied to some other piece of land of the same or different quality, or if turned to some non-agricultural business. The last increment actually applied is the "marginal" increment, and it measures the distributive share of a unit "dose" in the product. The figure and the details of the argument are too familiar to need elaboration; nor can I stay to show that such a curve ought really to pass through the origin, for important as the point is, it does not affect our present investigation; but it is essential to point out that the descriptive and the functional curves just described both present the same appearance, both represent "rent" by a curvilinear surface, both use the term "margin," though in entirely different senses, as determining rent, and are both just as applicable to anything else as to land, and (specifically) ignore the difference between "economic" and "commercial" rent, being just as applicable to one as to the other.

The ambiguous use of "marginal" has naturally caused some confusion (a point to which I shall soon revert), but at present the descriptive curve and "margin" have only been introduced to be dismissed. In the discussion of the functional curve, which we must now continue, I have used the term "marginal" in the sense of "differential" as applied throughout our whole investigation. It is not any peculiarity of the "marginal" increment that makes it yield less than the others. It does not. They all have exactly the same differential effect on the yield, as to which none is after or afore the other. The height of this differential or marginal yield is dependent not upon the nature of each several dose, but upon their aggregate number. What we have here, then, is not a law or theory of rent at all, but the tacit assumption that the differential theory of distribution is true of every factor of production except land, and that rent is what is left after everything that is not rent is taken away. For, observe, land-and-labour is treated as a homogeneous quantity, so that the reduction of heterogeneous factors to a common unit is assumed, and how is this to be done except by comparing their several efficiencies on the product, and so combining them as to keep those efficiencies in differential equivalence to their market prices, *i.e.* their efficiencies on other land or in other industries? And thus the principle of marginal or differential efficiency as determining distributive shares in the product has long been quite definitely, though naïvely and unconsciously, asserted in saying that the "marginal" efficiency of this compound factor of production will find the same level in the specified industry and out of it, and will determine its remuneration.

This so-called statement of the law of rent, then, assumes our differential laws of exchange value and distribution, with all their implications, as ruling everywhere *except* in land and rent. Rent is merely what is left when everything except rent is taken away. This can hardly be called a "law," but, such as it is, it is again common to all factors of production. Wages are all that is left when everything that is not wages is taken out. And this is actually the statement of Walker's "law of wages." And so with the rest.

But this is not all. In the treatment of rent that we are examining the differential theory of distribution is avowed with respect to every factor except land; but it is implied with respect to land also. This can be rigidly proved mathematically, as is now beginning to be acknowledged; and even the non-mathematical student can easily perceive that the forms of the figures representing the shares of "land" and "labour-and-capital" respectively are determined not by any peculiarity of land, but by the fact that land is supposed to remain constant, while labour-and-capital vary. But three pounds sterling applied to one acre is the same thing as a third of an acre coming under one pound's worth of culture, and five pounds per acre is a fifth of an acre per pound. Instead of taking an acre, therefore, and considering the difference of yield, as two, three, four, five pounds are expended upon it, let us take one pound and consider the differences of yield, as one-fifth, one-fourth, one-third, one-half of an acre come under it, or in other words, as it spreads itself over these different areas. You will then find that you have a figure in which the same identical data are presented and the same identical results obtained, but the return to land is represented as a rectangle cut off by a line parallel to OX, and the return to labour-and-capital by a curvilinear "surplus" or residuum. So that the supposed law of rent again turns out, in so far as it is true of land, to be true of all the other factors of production. But the unhappy confusion between the geometric properties of an arbitrarily selected constant factor in a diagram and the economic properties of land has brought dire confusion into economic thought and economic terminology. The Augean stables must be cleansed. We must understand that when the differential distribution is effected there is no surplus or residuum at all; and that any diagram of distribution that represents the shares of the different factors under different geometrical forms is sure to be misleading, and is likely to be particularly mischievous in its misdirection of social imagination and aspiration.

And note, finally, that even in practical problems the supposed peculiar conditions introduced by the rigidly determined quantity of land in existence are non-existent. Any individual can have as much land as he likes if he will pay the price, and he is conscious of no difference in principle whether he is bidding for a certain quality and site of land, or a certain grade of labour or kind of ability, unless it be that in the latter case he is *more* conscious of the limits of supply that no offer of remuneration can stretch.

In conclusion, I will revert to the point, incidentally raised in connection with rent, of the difficulties and confusions connected with terminology.

. I have throughout spoken of *differential*, rather than *marginal* significances; for there is a fatal ambiguity in the use of the word "marginal." And yet, after all, I have felt like the man who "did flee from a lion and a bear met him; or went into the house and leaned his hand on the wall, and a serpent bit him," for by a singular perversity of fate or fashion a closely similar ambiguity besets the word "differential" itself, and yet another and equally appropriate term "incremental." All these words have been preoccupied; and curiously enough it is speculations on the nature of rent or projects concerning land that have done the mischief in every case. "Increment," instead of suggesting a small homogeneous addition to any magnitude whatever, at once suggests to the reader of economic literature the "unearned increment of land," so that the "incremental value," "efficacy," or "significance" of anything cannot conveniently carry its proper meaning of the value attached to a small increment or decrement of anything, varying with the expansion or contraction of the supply. This is the conception I have indicated by the term "differential." But here again we are forestalled. "Differential payment," for instance, would generally be understood by readers of economic literature to mean payment made for some articles in excess of that made for others, in consideration of their superiority. Thus, if I were to say that "rent is a differential charge," I should be supposed to mean that what you pay for a certain piece of land as rent represents the superiority of that piece of land to another that you can get for nothing. In this use of the word everything depends upon the different *quality* of the things compared. But what we want is a word which shall always carry the underlying assumption that we are considering the expansion and contraction of a *homogeneous* supply, the "differential" value of that supply being a function of its breadth or magnitude.

Again, the same theory of rent which regards it as a differential charge, in the sense of a charge due to an inherent difference of quality in the things charged for, assumes that there is some land which bears no rent at all. This is the land on the "margin" of cultivation. Hence "marginal" has come to be used in economic literature to signify the lowest grade or quality of any commodity, or service, or the least favourable set of conditions, that just hold their footing in any industry. Thus the marginal land would mean the worst land under cultivation, the marginal workman the least efficient man in actual employment, the marginal conditions of an industry the least advantageous conditions under which it is actually conducted, and, I suppose, the marginal grade of potatoes or wheat the worst quality actually in the market; or to the hungry individual the marginal mouthful of beef would be the one just not rejected and left on the plate because too largely composed of "veins" to be eaten, even if no more of any kind were to be had.

Now attempts have been made to erect a theory of distribution upon the consideration of "margins" in this sense. The "marginal" man, working on the "marginal" land, under the "marginal" conditions, and with the "marginal" appliances, is taken as the ultimate basis of the pile, and wages, rent and interest are explained as "differential" in their nature; that is to say, as due to the superiority in quality, position, or point of application, of such-and-such work, land, or apparatus, over the "marginal" specimens.

I do not stay to examine this theory on its merits; but it is necessary to insist on the almost incredible fact that there is constant confusion between it and what I have tried to expound as the "differential" theory of distribution, simply because they can both be described as "marginal," and the term "differential," though in quite divergent senses, may be introduced in the exposition of either.

Once again, then, if I speak of the differential or marginal significance of my supply of bread and milk, and say that it depends, *ceteris paribus,* upon how many loaves of bread and how many pints of milk I take, I am supposing all the bread and milk to be of the same quality. And if I speak of the differential or marginal significance of labour in a particular industry, I am either speaking of a uniform grade of labour or of different grades reduced to some common measure and expressed in one and the same unit, and I mean the significance which such a unit has when it is one out of so many others like itself. Thus, in my use of the word, there is no ear-marked marginal unit, which is such in virtue of its special quality. Any one of 100 units has exactly the same marginal value; but as soon as one unit is withdrawn, all the remaining 99 have a higher marginal value; and when one is added, all the 101 a lower.

The only word I can think of free from misleading associations would be "quotal"; for *quotus* means (amongst other things) "one out of how many," and so *quotal* significance might mean the significance which a unit has when associated with such-and-such a number of others *homogeneous with itself.*

Here I must close these almost random indications of some of the directions in which I think that convinced apostles of the differential economics should revise the methods of economic exposition. For myself I cannot but believe that if this were accomplished, all serious opposition to the doctrine would cease, that there would once again be a body of accepted economic doctrine, and that Jevons's dream would be accomplished and economic science re-established "on a sensible basis."

It is impossible to exaggerate the importance of such a consummation. Social reformers and legislators will never be economists, and they will always work on economic theory of one kind or another. They will quote and apply such dicta as they can assimilate, and such acknowledged principles as seem to serve their turn. Let us suppose there were a recognised body of economic doctrine the truth and relevancy of which perpetually revealed itself to all who looked below the surface, which taught men what to expect and how to analyse their experience; which insisted at every turn on the illuminating relation between our conduct in life and our conduct in business; which drove the analysis of our daily administration of our individual resources deeper, and thereby dissipated the mist that hangs about our economic relations, and concentrated attention upon the uniting and all-penetrating principles of our study. Economics might even then be no more than a feeble barrier against passion, and might afford but a feeble light to guide honest enthusiasm, but it would exert a steady and a cumulative pressure, making for the truth. While the experts worked on severer methods than ever, popularisers would be found to drive homely illustrations and analogies into the general consciousness; and the roughly understood dicta bandied about in the name of Political Economy would at any rate stand in some relation to truth and to experience, instead of being, as they too often are at present, a mere armoury of consecrated paradoxes that cannot be understood because they are not true, that every one uses as weapons while no one grasps them as principles.

2

ON THE THEORY OF
THE BUDGET OF THE CONSUMER *

By Eugen E. Slutsky ||

1. Preliminary Considerations

At first the modern theory of value seemed almost a branch of psychology, and this helped to complicate the question of the applicability of mathematical methods to economic science. For, since the solution of all problems related to the measurableness of psychic phenomena is quite uncertain, a wide field remains subject to controversy. Even aside from the differences of opinion among the followers of the hedonistic school, the very bases of the edifice constructed by this school have been shaken by violent attacks. Thus it is doubtful whether the hedonistic school today still preserves its predominance, although agreement among its opponents is far from universal. Therefore, if we assume the concept of pleasure and pain, or that of desire, as basis of the theory, we remain in a realm open to lively discussions. For the study of such problems we would have to conduct our inquiry in the vast sphere of psychology and of philosophy, without hope of reaching at present, nor in a more or less distant future, results capable of leading to the elimination of today's profound divergence of opinions. From this it follows that, if we wish to place economic science upon a solid basis, we must make it completely independent of psychological assumptions and philosophical hypotheses. On the other hand, since the fundamental concept of modern economics is that of utility, it does not seem opportune to disregard all connections existing between the visible and measurable facts of human conduct and the psychic phenomena by which they seem to be regulated. Utility must therefore be defined in

* *Giornale degli Economisti,* Vol. LI (1915), pp. 1–26. Reprinted, by the courtesy of the publisher. The translation is by Olga Ragusa.

|| Professor Slutsky was at the Institute of Commerce at Kiev when this article was published; he died in Moscow in 1948.

such a way as to make it logically independent of every disputable hypothesis or concept, without however excluding the possibility of further research regarding the relations between the individual's conduct and his psychic life.

The strictest conception of utility is the one formulated by Pareto. Its purely formal character and its complete independence of all psychological and philosophical hypotheses recommend it as a solid basis for the construction of our own theory. However, Pareto's conception cannot be considered to be well defined. Strictly speaking, it is not composed of only one concept, but of two different ones, which do not seem to us to be closely related. The first is the concept of utility (ophelimity) as that pleasure which an individual receives through an additional quantity of a certain good.[1] This is a purely psychological concept and in no way differs from the usual, rather disputable, hedonistic concept of Gossen, Jevons, and others. In Pareto's theory, however, this first concept is rarely applied. The other concept, that of a function index of utility, is quite a different matter. It is a happy construction, completely strict and abstract in all its aspects. We shall make use of it as the point of departure of our discussion. But it must be noted, that should we limit ourselves to Pareto's definition, *we would not succeed in finding any point of contact whatsoever* between economics and psychology; because from a function determined by empirical data it is impossible to derive Pareto's function uniquely.[2] Nevertheless, we shall start from this concept. We shall see later how it is possible to arrive at another, better defined concept.

2. The Utility Function

Let us start from the following definition: *The utility of a combination of goods is a quantity, which has the property that its value is the greater the more the given combination is desired by the individual whom one considers.*

The more desirable combination must be understood to be the one the individual chooses in preference to another when he has the possibility of choice between the two. Only if an individual, possessing combination A, does not pass over to com-

---

[1] Pareto, *Manuel d'économie politique* (1909), pp. 158–159.
[2] *Ibid.*, pp. 539–557.

bination B, and vice versa, possessing B, does not pass over to A, must the utility of the two combinations be considered of equal value.

The analysis of the definition of utility leads us to the following conclusions. First of all, it is clear that the subject always tends to relinquish one combination to pass on to another of greater utility. This proposition, an obvious deduction from the definition, can be regarded as a theory without exceptions. It is clear, besides, that the one possible state in which an individual's budget could remain unchanged, even for a short time, is that whose present utility is equal to or greater than that of all states immediately proximate. Such a state can be called a state of equilibrium. It is *stable* if any divergence from it tends to diminish utility, *unstable* in the contrary case. But in practice, every individual's budget being subject to innumerable influences incessantly perturbing its equilibrium, it is evident that there can in actuality exist *only stable budgets*. Therefore, the discovery of the conditions of stability is a problem of the greatest importance in the theory of consumer budgets.

As to the utility function, we must remember that it can be regarded as empirically given, even though the experiments by means of which it should be construed cannot be carried out in practice. Only after the theory of the consumer's budget will have been completely developed, will one be able to face and solve the problem of the determination of the utility function by means that are practicably attainable, such as the variations of demand as a function of income and of prices.

Whatever be the data used for constructing the function of utility, there are cases (and they are the most frequent ones) in which it cannot be unequivocally determined. The question has been studied by Pareto, and we do not intend proceeding to a complete revision of his conclusions; we shall attempt only to establish the conditions of the second derivatives of the utility function in order that it be uniquely determined. As we shall see, this problem is intimately connected with that of the possibility of an agreement between the formal and the psychological aspects of the problem of utility.

Let us now formulate the hypotheses upon which the theory of the budget is constructed:

(1) The hypothesis of the continuity of the utility function and of its derivatives of at least the first two orders.

(2) The hypothesis that the character of the utility function undergoes no variation during the period considered.

(Both hypotheses would probably find approximate confirmation in experience, if, instead of considering a single individual, we were to consider a group, applying statistical methods in the investigation.)

(3) The hypothesis that the increment of utility obtained in passing from one combination of goods to another does not depend upon the mode of passage. In mathematical language this leads to the condition:

$$\frac{\delta^2 U}{\delta x_1 \delta x_2} = \frac{\delta^2 U}{\delta x_2 \delta x_1}$$

We shall see later how this can be verified empirically.

Since we intend to treat the problem in the most general manner, the utility function should not be subjected to further restrictions. If we put

$$U = \Psi(x_1, x_2, \cdots, x_n),$$

($x_1, x_2, \ldots, x_n$ being the quantities of the various goods bought by the subject in a given interval of time, and U the utility gained by the subject by means of that combination of goods), the marginal utility of a good, for example of the good i, is represented by the partial derivative,

$$u_i = \frac{\delta \Psi}{\delta x_i}.$$

We can regard it as always positive, if, as in this study, we limit ourselves to the budgets of consumers, and hence consider only goods which are positively desirable. By desirability of a good we mean the fact that the individual would rather have the good itself or one of its increments, than not have it.

The second derivatives of the same function indicate the dependence of the marginal utilities of a good upon the quantity of this good or other goods:

$$u_{ii} = \frac{\delta^2 \Psi}{\delta x_i^2}; \qquad u_{ij} = \frac{\delta^2 \Psi}{\delta x_i \delta x_j}.$$

As to Gossen's law of the satiability of needs, we must regard it simply as an empirical generalization, which as yet lacks rigorous demonstration. On that account, we will disregard it and consider two kinds of goods: those whose marginal utility decreases with the increase of their quantity ($u_{ii} < 0$), which we shall call *satiating* goods, and those whose marginal utility increases in the same situation ($u_{ii} > 0$), which we shall call *non-satiating* goods.

3. On the Stability of the Equilibrium of the Consumer Budget

Let s be the income of an individual, p_1, p_2, . . . , p_n the prices of n goods which he buys, x_1, x_2, . . . , x_n the quantities bought. We have then

(1) $$p_1x_1 + p_2x_2 + \cdots + p_nx_n = s.$$

We have seen that in order for the budget to be stable, the utility function must have a maximum value; evidently we are concerned with a maximum consistent with equation (1). It is known, however, that this condition resolves itself into:

1. the equations:

(2) $$\frac{u_1}{p_1} = \frac{u_2}{p_2} = \cdots = \frac{u_n}{p_n} = u',$$

where u' is the marginal utility of money;

2. the inequality:

(3) $d^2U = u_{11}dx_1^2 + u_{22}dx_2^2 + \cdots + 2u_{12}dx_1dx_2 + \cdots < 0.$

If we put

(4) $$dx_i = c_{i1}d\xi_1 + c_{i2}d\xi_2 + \cdots + c_{in}d\xi_n,$$

where

(5) $$c_{ik} = 0 \quad \text{if } i > k$$
$$c_{ik} = 1 \quad \text{if } i = k,$$

and substitute these values in (4) and in (3), the coefficients c_{ik} can be determined in such a way as to render the coefficients of all the products equal to 0. In this manner we shall obtain:

(6) $$d^2U = A_1 d\xi_1^2 + A_2 d\xi_2^2 + \cdots + A_n d\xi_n^2,$$

where the values, $d\xi_1$, $d\xi_2$, · · · , $d\xi_n$ are related by the linear equation:

(7) $$B_1 d\xi_1 + B_2 d\xi_2 + \cdots + B_n d\xi_n = 0.$$

In order to determine the coefficients B_1, B_2, . . . , B_n, as functions of c_{ik}, let us differentiate equation (1) and substitute for dx_1, $dx_2, \ldots$ the expressions for them resulting from (4).

Taking account of the conditions (5) we obtain:

$$(8) \quad \begin{cases} B_1 = p_1 \\ B_2 = p_1 c_{12} + p_2 \\ B_3 = p_1 c_{13} + p_2 c_{23} + p_3 \\ \cdot \cdot \cdot \cdot \cdot \cdot \cdot \cdot \cdot \cdot \cdot \cdot \\ B_n = p_1 c_{1n} + p_2 c_{2n} + \cdots + p_{n-1} c_{n-1 n} + p_n. \end{cases}$$

The determination of c_{ik} will be indicated in the following paragraph. From the analysis of equation (6) one can easily draw the following conclusions:

1. *If all the values $A_1, A_2, \ldots, A_n$ are negative, d^2U is negative definite.*

2. *If two or more quantities among $A_1, A_2, \ldots, A_n$ are positive, d^2U cannot be negative for all the values of $d\xi_1, d\xi_2, \ldots, d\xi_n$.*

3. *Further investigation is necessary for the case in which only one of the quantities $A_1, A_2, \ldots, A_n$ is positive.*

Let us suppose:

$A_i > 0, A_1 < 0, A_2 < 0, \cdots, A_{i-1} < 0, A_{i+1} < 0, \cdots, A_n < 0$. If $d\xi_i = 0$, $d^2U < 0$; and therefore there remains to be considered only the case in which $d\xi_i$ is different from zero.

The expressions (6) and (7) can now be divided, respectively, by $d\xi_i^2$ and by $d\xi_i$, and we obtain:

$$(9) \quad d^2U = d\xi_i^2(A_1\eta_1^2 + A_2\eta_2^2 + \cdots + A_{i-1}\eta_{i-1}^2 + A_i + A_{i+1}\eta_{i+1}^2 + \cdots + A_n\eta_n^2) < 0,$$

and

$$(10) \quad B_1\eta_1 + B_2\eta_2 + \cdots + B_{i-1}\eta_{i-1} + B_i + B_{i+1}\eta_{i+1} + \cdots + B_n\eta_n = 0,$$

where

$$\eta_k = \frac{d\xi_k}{d\xi_i}.$$

We deduce from (9) that d^2U can always remain negative only if the maximum value of the quantity

$$(11) \quad A_1\eta_1^2 + A_2\eta_2^2 + \cdots + A_{i-1}\eta_{i-1}^2 + A_i + A_{i+1}\eta_{i+1}^2 + \cdots + A_n\eta_n^2$$

is negative. Indicating for brevity's sake this quantity by the letter Y, and differentiating the auxiliary expression:

$$Z = Y - 2\lambda(B_1\eta_1 + B_2\eta_2 + \cdots + B_{i-1}\eta_{i-1} +$$
$$B_i + B_{i+1}\eta_{i+1} + \cdots + B_n\eta_n),$$

we obtain:

$$\frac{1}{2}\frac{dZ}{d\eta_1} = A_1\eta_1 - \lambda B_1 = 0,$$

$$\frac{1}{2}\frac{dZ}{d\eta_2} = A_2\eta_2 - \lambda B_2 = 0, \text{ etc.};$$

and hence:

$$(12) \qquad \eta_1 = \lambda\frac{B_1}{A_1}, \quad \eta_2 = \lambda\frac{B_2}{A_2}, \cdots, \quad \eta_{i-1} = \lambda\frac{B_{i-1}}{A_{i-1}},$$

$$\eta_{i+1} = \lambda\frac{B_{i+1}}{A_{i+1}}, \cdots, \eta_n = \lambda\frac{B_n}{A_n}.$$

Substituting these values into (10), we find λ:

$$(13) \qquad \lambda = -\frac{B_i}{\dfrac{B_1^2}{A_1} + \dfrac{B_2^2}{A_2} + \cdots + \dfrac{B_{i-1}^2}{A_{i-1}} + \dfrac{B_{i+1}^2}{A_{i+1}} + \cdots + \dfrac{B_n^2}{A_n}}.$$

Substituting (12) and (13) in (11), the maximum value of Y is given by:

$$(14) \qquad Y_{max.} = A_i + \lambda^2\left(\frac{B_1^2}{A_1} + \frac{B_2^2}{A_2} + \cdots + \frac{B_{i-1}^2}{A_{i-1}} + \frac{B_{i+1}^2}{A_{i+1}} + \cdots + \frac{B_n^2}{A_n}\right)$$

$$= A_i \frac{\dfrac{B_1^2}{A_1} + \dfrac{B_2^2}{A_2} + \cdots\cdots\cdots\cdots\cdots + \dfrac{B_n^2}{A_n}}{\dfrac{B_1^2}{A_1} + \dfrac{B_2^2}{A_2} + \cdots + \dfrac{B_{i-1}^2}{A_{i-1}} + \dfrac{B_{i+1}}{A_{i+1}} + \cdots\cdots + \dfrac{B_n^2}{A_n}}.$$

It can easily be seen that, A_i being positive, $Y_{max.}$ can be negative only if:

$$(15) \qquad \Omega = \frac{B_1^2}{A_1} + \frac{B_2^2}{A_2} + \cdots\cdots + \frac{B_n^2}{A_n} > 0.$$

We have thus determined all the conditions for the stability of a budget. I propose to call a budget *normal* if all the A_i are < 0. It is always stable if the first condition of equilibrium (2) is verified and $\Omega < 0$.

On the contrary I call a budget *abnormal* if only one of the quantities A_i is positive. The conditions for its stability are furnished by (2) and (15), that is by the first condition of equilibrium and by the inequality $\Omega > 0$.

Finally, if two or more of the quantities A_i are positive the budget can in no case be stable.

4. Determination of the Values c_{ik}, A_i, and B_i

From (4) it follows that:

$$dx_i^2 = \Sigma(c_{ik}^2 d\xi_k^2) + \underset{k\angle l}{\Sigma \;\; \Sigma} (c_{ik}c_{il}d\xi_k d\xi_l),$$

$$dx_i dx_j = \underset{k}{\Sigma}(c_{ik}c_{jk}d\xi_k^2) + \underset{k\angle l}{\Sigma \;\; \Sigma} (c_{ik}c_{jl}d\xi_k d\xi_l).$$

Substituting these expressions in (3), we obtain the coefficient of $d\xi_1^2$:

$$\begin{aligned}
\text{(16)} \quad A_i = \; & c_{1i}(u_{11}c_{1i} + u_{12}c_{2i} + \cdots + u_{1n}c_{ni}) \\
+ \; & c_{2i}(u_{21}c_{1i} + u_{22}c_{2i} + \cdots + u_{2n}c_{ni}) \\
+ \; & \cdots\cdots\cdots\cdots\cdots\cdots\cdots\cdots \\
+ \; & c_{ni}(u_{ni}c_{1i} + u_{n2}c_{2i} + \cdots + u_{nn}c_{ni}),
\end{aligned}$$

and half of the coefficient of $d\xi_i d\xi_j$:

$$\begin{aligned}
\text{(17)} \quad A_{ij} = \; & c_{1i}(u_{11}c_{1j} + u_{12}c_{2j} + \cdots + u_{1n}c_{nj}) \\
+ \; & c_{2i}(u_{21}c_{1j} + u_{22}c_{2j} + \cdots + u_{2n}c_{nj}) \\
+ \; & \cdots\cdots\cdots\cdots\cdots\cdots\cdots\cdots \\
+ \; & c_{ni}(u_{n1}c_{1j} + u_{n2}c_{2j} + \cdots + u_{nn}c_{nj}) = 0.
\end{aligned}$$

Remembering conditions (5), we obtain from (17) the following system of $\dfrac{n(n-1)}{2}$ equations:

$$\text{(18)} \quad \begin{cases}
u_{11}c_{12} + u_{12} = 0 & \text{from } A_{12} = 0 \\
u_{11}c_{13} + u_{12}c_{23} + u_{13} = 0 & \text{from } A_{13} = 0 \\
\cdots\cdots\cdots\cdots\cdots & \cdots\cdots \\
u_{11}c_{1n} + u_{12}c_{2n} + u_{13}c_{3n} + \cdots + u_{1n} = 0 & \text{from } A_{1n} = 0
\end{cases}$$

(18)
(*Cont.*)

$$\begin{cases} u_{21}c_{13} + u_{22}c_{23} + u_{23} = 0 \qquad \text{from } A_{23} = 0 \\ u_{21}c_{14} + u_{22}c_{24} + u_{23}c_{34} + u_{24} = 0 \qquad \text{from } A_{24} = 0 \\ \cdots \cdots \cdots \cdots \qquad\qquad \cdots \cdots \cdots \\ u_{21}c_{1n} + u_{22}c_{2n} + u_{23}c_{3n} + \cdots + u_{2n} = 0 \text{ from } A_{2n} = 0 \end{cases}$$

$$\cdots \cdots \cdots \cdots \cdots \cdots \cdots \cdots$$

$$\begin{cases} u_{n-2,1}c_{1,n-1} + u_{n-2,2}c_{2,n-1} + \cdots \\ \qquad + u_{n-2,n-2}c_{n-2,n-1} + u_{n-2,n-1} = 0 \quad \text{from } A_{n-2,n-1} = 0 \\ u_{n-2,1}c_{1,n} + u_{n-2,2}c_{2n} + \cdots \\ \qquad + u_{n-2,n-1}c_{n-1,n} + u_{n-2,n} = 0 \qquad \text{from } A_{n-2,n} = 0 \\ u_{n-1,1}c_{1n} + u_{n-1,2}c_{2n} + \cdots \\ \qquad + u_{n-1,n-1}c_{n-1,n} + u_{n-1,n} = 0 \qquad \text{from } A_{n-1,n} = 0 \end{cases}$$

This system is formed by various independent linear systems (I, $A_{12} = 0$; II, $A_{13} = 0$, $A_{22} = 0$; III, $A_{14} = 0$, $A_{24} = 0$, $A_{34} = 0$; etc.), which could easily be solved.

Let:

(19)
$$R_i = \begin{vmatrix} u_{11} & u_{12} & \cdots & u_{1i} \\ u_{21} & u_{22} & \cdots & u_{2i} \\ \cdots & \cdots & \cdots & \cdots \\ u_{i1} & u_{i2} & \cdots & u_{ii} \end{vmatrix}$$

where $u_{kl} = u_{lk}$; and $R_{i(kl)} = R_{i(lk)}$ are the cofactors of R_i. From (18) we obtain:

(20)
$$c_{ij} = \frac{R_{j(ii)}}{R_{j(jj)}} = \frac{R_{j(ij)}}{R_{j-1}} .$$

Returning to (16), we observe that in consequence of conditions (5), the lines from $(i + 1)$ to n cancel, and in consequence of (18) the lines from 1 to $(i - 1)$ also cancel. Hence we have

(21)
$$\begin{aligned} A_i &= u_{i1}c_{1i} + u_{i2}c_{2i} + \cdots + u_{ii} \\ &= \frac{1}{R_{i-1}} (u_{i1}R_{i(i1)} + u_{i2}R_{i(i2)} + \cdots + u_{ii}R_{i(ii)}) \\ &= \frac{R_i}{R_{i-1}} . \end{aligned}$$

If now we put

(22)
$$H_{i(j)} = \begin{vmatrix} u_{11} & u_{12} & \cdots & u_{1,j-1} & p_1 & u_{1,j+1} & \cdots & u_{1i} \\ u_{21} & u_{22} & \cdots & u_{2,j-1} & p_2 & u_{2,j+1} & \cdots & u_{2i} \\ \cdots & \cdots & \cdots & \cdots & \cdots & \cdots & \cdots & \cdots \\ u_{i1} & u_{i2} & \cdots & u_{i,j-1} & p_i & u_{i,j+1} & \cdots & u_{ii} \end{vmatrix} = p_1 R_{i(1j)} + \\ p_2 R_{i(2j)} + \cdot \\ + p_i R_{i(ij)},$$

we find, by means of (8):

$$(23) \quad B_i = \frac{1}{R_{i-1}} (p_1 R_{i(1i)} + p_2 R_{i(2i)} + \cdots + p_i R_{i(ii)}) = \frac{H_{i(i)}}{R_{i-1}} .$$

The formulas (21) and (23) can be considered absolutely general if we put $1 = R_o$; in this case (as also results directly from (8) and (16)), $A_1 = \dfrac{R_1}{R_0} = u_{11}$ and $B_1 = \dfrac{H_{1(1)}}{R_0} = p_1.$

5. Determination of the Value of Ω

Substituting expressions (21) and (23) into (15), we obtain:

$$(24) \quad \Omega = \frac{H_{1(1)}^2}{R_0 R_1} + \frac{H_{2(2)}^2}{R_1 R_2} + \cdots + \frac{H_{n(n)}^2}{R_{n-1} R_n} .$$

Indicating the same quantity by the symbol Ω_n, we shall show that it can be reduced to a more symmetrical form. Let us begin by putting:

$$(25) \quad M_i = \begin{vmatrix} o & p_1 & p_2 & \cdots & p_i \\ p_1 & u_{11} & u_{12} & \cdots & u_{1i} \\ p_2 & u_{21} & u_{22} & \cdots & u_{2i} \\ \cdots & \cdots & \cdots & \cdots & \cdots \\ p_i & u_{i1} & u_{i2} & \cdots & u_{ii} \end{vmatrix} = \begin{matrix} (p_1 H_{i(1)} + p_2 H_{i(2)} \\ + \cdots + p_i H_{i(i)}) . \end{matrix}$$

We now have

$$(26) \quad \Omega_2 = \frac{H_{1(1)}^2}{R_o R_1} + \frac{H_{2(2)}^2}{R_1 R_2} = \frac{p_1^2}{u_{11}} + \frac{(p_2 u_{11} - p_1 u_{12})^2}{u_{11}(u_{11} u_{22} - u_{12}^2)}$$

$$= \frac{p_1^2 u_{22} + p_2^2 u_{11} - 2 p_1 p_2 u_{12}}{u_{11} u_{22} - u_{12}^2} = - \frac{M_2}{R_2} .$$

The foregoing result can be generalized. For this purpose it suffices to demonstrate that if it is valid for Ω_i, it is also valid for Ω_{i+1}; or that

$$(27) \quad \Omega_{i+1} = \frac{H_{1(1)}^2}{R_0 R_1} + \frac{H_{2(2)}^2}{R_1 R_2} + \cdots + \frac{H_{i(i)}^2}{R_{i-1} R_i} + \frac{H_{i+1(i+1)}^2}{R_i R_{i+1}}$$

$$= - \frac{M_i}{R_i} + \frac{H_{i+1(i+1)}^2}{R_i R_{i+1}} = - \frac{M_i R_{i+1} - H_{i+1(i+1)}^2}{R_i R_{i+1}}$$

To reduce the numerator to a different form we shall make use of the well-known formula of the theory of determinants:

$$(28) \qquad \Delta_{ij}\,\Delta_{kl} - \Delta_{ik}\,\Delta_{jl} = \Delta\Delta_{(ij)\,(kl)},$$

where the quantities of the first member are cofactors of the first order of the determinant Δ (the first index corresponds to the suppressed row and the second to the suppressed column); and $\Delta_{(ij)\,(kl)}$ is the cofactor of the second order obtained by suppressing rows i and k and columns j and l.

Let us indicate, then, by $M_{i(kk)}$ and by $M_{i(kl)}$ the cofactors of M_i corresponding respectively to the elements u_{kk} and u_{kl}; and by $M_{i(01)}, M_{i(02)}, \ldots,$ and $M_{i(00)}, M_{i(10)}, M_{i(20)}, \ldots$ the cofactors of the first row and the first column.

We have:

$$(29) \qquad \begin{cases} M_i & = M_{i+1\ (i+1\ i\ |\ 1)} \\ R_i & = M_{i(00)} = M_{i+1\ (i+1\ i+1)\ (00)} \\ H_{i+1(i+1)} & = -M_{i+1(0\ i+1)} = -M_{i+1(i+1\ 0)}\,. \end{cases}$$

Using this notation, and remembering (28), we easily find:

$$(30) \qquad \begin{aligned} M_i R_{i+1} - H^2_{i+1(i+1)} &= M_{i+1(i+1\ i+1)}\,M_{i+1(00)} \\ -M_{i+1(i+1\ 0)}\,M_{i+1(i+1\ 0)} &= M_{i+1}M_{i+1(i+1\ i+1)(00)} \\ &= M_{i+1}R_i; \end{aligned}$$

and hence, substituting into (27) the preceding value:

$$(31) \qquad \Omega_{i+1} = -\frac{M_{i+1}}{R_{i+1}}.$$

We have seen that this formula is valid for Ω_2; therefore its general validity is demonstrated. Hence:

$$(32) \qquad \Omega_n = -\frac{M_n}{R_n},$$

or, more simply:

$$(32') \qquad \Omega = -\frac{M}{R}\,.$$

6. Variations of the Individual's Demand as a Function of Income

It follows from (2) that:

$$(33) \qquad u_1 = p_1 u', \quad u_2 = p_2 u', \quad \cdots, \quad u_n = p_n u'.$$

Differentiating with respect to s, we obtain:

$$(34) \begin{cases} u_{11} \dfrac{\delta x_1}{\delta s} + u_{12} \dfrac{\delta x_2}{\delta s} + \cdots\cdots + u_{1n} \dfrac{\delta x_n}{\delta s} = p_1 \dfrac{\delta u'}{\delta s} \\[2ex] u_{21} \dfrac{\delta x_1}{\delta s} + u_{22} \dfrac{\delta x_2}{\delta s} + \cdots\cdots + u_{2n} \dfrac{\delta x_n}{\delta s} = p_2 \dfrac{\delta u'}{\delta s} \\[1ex] \cdots\cdots\cdots\cdots\cdots\cdots\cdots\cdots\cdots\cdots\cdots\cdots\cdots \\[1ex] u_{n1} \dfrac{\delta x_1}{\delta s} + u_{n2} \dfrac{\delta x_2}{\delta s} + \cdots\cdots + u_{nn} \dfrac{\delta x_n}{\delta s} = p_n \dfrac{\delta u'}{\delta s} \end{cases}$$

Solving this system, we may write:

$$(35) \qquad \frac{\delta x_i}{\delta s} = \frac{H_{n(i)}}{R_n} \frac{\delta u'}{\delta s}$$

Differentiating now the equation (1) with respect to s, we have:

$$(36) \qquad p_1 \frac{\delta x_1}{\delta s} + p_2 \frac{\delta x_2}{\delta s} + \cdots + p_n \frac{\delta x_n}{\delta s} = 1;$$

and hence substituting for $\dfrac{\delta x_1}{\delta s}$, $\dfrac{\delta x_2}{\delta s}$, etc., their expressions taken from (35):

(37)
$$\frac{\delta u'}{\delta s} = \frac{R_n}{p_1 H_{n(1)} + p_2 H_{n(2)} + \cdots + p_n H_{n(n)}} = -\frac{R_n}{M_n} = \frac{1}{\Omega}.$$

Making use of this, we have:

$$(38) \qquad \frac{\delta x_i}{\delta s} = -\frac{H_{n(i)}}{M_n} = \frac{M_{n(0i)}}{M_n}$$

It is impossible to formulate any one specific proposition, true in all cases, about the sign of this expression. We only know that the value of $\dfrac{\delta x_1}{\delta s}$ can be positive as well as negative; and observation confirms the fact that both cases actually occur. It is therefore necessary to proceed to a classification of goods: those whose quantity increases with the increase of income can be said to be *relatively indispensable;* those whose quantity diminishes with the increase of income, *relatively dispensable.*

For example, suppose that a poor family in consequence of a slight increase of income consumes more meat, more sugar, more tea, and less bread and potatoes. The first victuals should then be considered relatively indispensable, the others relatively dispensable, for the family.

Keeping in mind formula (37), and remembering the discussion of the problem of stability, we immediately deduce that in the case of a normal budget the marginal utility of money should decrease with the increase of income and increase with its decrease. In the case of an abnormal budget the contrary occurs.

7. VARIATIONS OF DEMAND AS A FUNCTION OF PRICE

Differentiating equations (33) with respect to p_i, we obtain:

(39)
$$\begin{cases} u_{11} \dfrac{\delta x_1}{\delta p_i} + u_{12} \dfrac{\delta x_2}{\delta p_i} + \cdots + u_{1n} \dfrac{\delta x_n}{\delta p_i} = p_1 \dfrac{\delta u'}{\delta p_i} \\[2ex] u_{21} \dfrac{\delta x_1}{\delta p_i} + u_{22} \dfrac{\delta x_2}{\delta p_i} + \cdots + u_{2n} \dfrac{\delta x_n}{\delta p_i} = p_2 \dfrac{\delta u'}{\delta p_i} \\[2ex] \cdots\cdots\cdots\cdots\cdots\cdots\cdots\cdots\cdots\cdots\cdots\cdots \\[1ex] u_{i1} \dfrac{\delta x_1}{\delta p_i} + u_{i2} \dfrac{\delta x_2}{\delta p_i} + \cdots + u_{in} \dfrac{\delta x_n}{\delta p_i} = p_i \dfrac{\delta u'}{\delta p_i} + u \\[2ex] \cdots\cdots\cdots\cdots\cdots\cdots\cdots\cdots\cdots\cdots\cdots\cdots \\[1ex] u_{n1} \dfrac{\delta x_1}{\delta p_i} + u_{n2} \dfrac{\delta x_2}{\delta p_i} + \cdots + u_{nn} \dfrac{\delta x_n}{\delta p_i} = p_n \dfrac{\delta u'}{\delta p_i}, \end{cases}$$

and hence:

(40)
$$\begin{cases} R_n \dfrac{\delta x_i}{\delta p_i} = H_{n(i)} \dfrac{\delta u'}{\delta p_i} + u' R_{n(ii)} \\[2ex] R_n \dfrac{\delta x_j}{\delta p_i} = H_{n(j)} \dfrac{\delta u'}{\delta p_i} + u' R_{n(ij)} \, . \end{cases}$$

Then, differentiating (1) with respect to p_i, we have:

(41)
$$p_1 \frac{\delta x_1}{\delta p_i} + p_2 \frac{\delta x_2}{\delta p_i} + \cdots + p_n \frac{\delta x_n}{\delta p_i} = - x_i \, ;$$

and substituting (40) into (41), and writing $- M_{n(0i)}$ instead of $H_{n(i)}$, we obtain:

(42)
$$\frac{\delta u'}{\delta p_i} = \frac{- u' M_{n(0i)} + x_i R_n}{M_n}.$$

Now, substituting the preceding expression in (40), we obtain:[3]

(43)
$$\frac{\delta x_i}{\delta p_i} = u' \frac{R_{n(ii)} M_n + M_{n(0i)}^2}{R_n M_n} - x_i \frac{M_{n(0i)}}{M_n} \, ;$$

___

[3] The formulas in the text were deduced by Pareto, and published in this *Giornale*, August 1892 (see also the *Manuel d' économie politique*, 1909, p. 581). The differences in notation and form between our formulas and Pareto's are so unimportant that they can be considered identical.

Our attempt at developing the formulas aims only at putting them in more convenient form for mathematical analysis.

(44) $$\frac{\delta x_j}{\delta p_i} = u' \frac{R_{n(ij)}M_n + M_{n(0i)}M_{n(0j)}}{R_n M_n} - x_i \frac{M_{n(0j)}}{M_n} .$$

By a procedure analogous to that employed in Section 5, we can simplify these expressions considerably. In fact:

$$R_{n(ii)}M_n + M_{n(0i)}^2 = M_{n(00)(ii)}M_n + M_{n(0i)}M_{n(0i)}$$
$$= M_{n(00)}M_{n(ii)} = R_n M_{n(ii)},$$
$$R_{n(ij)}M_n + M_{n(0i)}M_{n(0j)} = M_{n(00)(ij)}M_n + M_{n(0i)}M_{n(0j)}$$
$$= M_{n(00)}M_{n(ij)} = R_n M_{n(ij)},$$

whence we obtain from (43) and (44):[4]

(45) $$\begin{cases} \dfrac{\delta x_i}{\delta p_i} = u' \dfrac{M_{ii}}{M} - x_i \dfrac{M_{0i}}{M} , \\[2mm] \dfrac{\delta x_j}{\delta p_i} = u' \dfrac{M_{ij}}{M} - x_i \dfrac{M_{0j}}{M} . \end{cases}$$

Or, using (38):

(46) $$\frac{\delta x_i}{\delta p_i} = u' \frac{M_{ii}}{M} - x_i \frac{\delta x_i}{\delta s} ;$$

(47) $$\frac{\delta x_j}{\delta p_i} = u' \frac{M_{ij}}{M} - x_i \frac{\delta x_j}{\delta s} .$$

8. DEPENDENCE OF THE DEMAND FOR A GOOD ON ITS PRICE

Let us now study formula (46); and let us begin by demonstrating that there always exists the inequality:

(48) $$\frac{M_{ii}}{M} < 0 .$$

For this purpose we must analyze the two cases of normal and abnormal budgets separately.

I. NORMAL BUDGETS. Using the notation of Section 5, we have:

$$\frac{\Omega_{n-1}}{\Omega_n} = \frac{M_{n-1}}{M_n} \frac{R_n}{R_{n-1}} = \frac{M_{n-1}}{M_n} A_n .$$

All the A_i being negative, Ω_{n-1} and Ω_n are also negative and hence:

$$\frac{M_{n-1}}{M_n} < 0 .$$

---

[4] Here and in the following differentiations the index n in $M_{n(ii)}$, $M_{n(ij)}$, $M_{n(0i)}$, etc., is omitted in each case where the omission does not lead to misunderstanding.

II. ABNORMAL BUDGETS. We distinguish two cases:

(a) If $A_n > 0$, then $\Omega_{n-1} < 0$, $\Omega_n > 0$; and hence $\dfrac{M_{n-1}}{M_n} < 0$.

(β) If $A_n < 0$, then $\Omega_{n-1} > 0$, $\Omega_n > 0$; and hence $\dfrac{M_{n-1}}{M_n} < 0$.

It is clear that the order in which the goods are considered is indifferent; the i-th good can hence be put after the n-th. We now have:

$$M_n = (0, u_{11}, u_{22}, \cdots, u_{nn})$$
$$= (0, u_{11}, \cdots, u_{i-1\ i-1}, u_{i+1\ i+1}, \cdots u_{nn}, u_{ii})$$
$$M_{n(ii)} = (0, u_{11}, u_{22}, \cdots, u_{i-1\ i-1}, u_{i+1\ i+1}, \cdots, u_{nn});$$

for the value which, in the new arrangement of the system, takes

the place of M_{n-1}. Therefore $\dfrac{M_{ii}}{M} < 0$.

We can now easily deduce from (46) the following *laws of demand:*

I. *The demand for a relatively indispensable good* $\left(\dfrac{x\delta_i}{\delta s} > 0\right)$

is necessarily always normal, that is, it diminishes if its price increases, and increases if its price decreases.

II. *The demand for a relatively dispensable good* $\left(\dfrac{\delta x_i}{\delta s} < 0\right)$

can be abnormal in certain cases, that is, it can increase with the increase of price and diminish with the decrease of price.

We now put:

(49) $$k_{ii} = u' \frac{M_{ii}}{M} = \frac{\delta x_i}{\delta p_i} + x_i \frac{\delta x_i}{\delta s},$$

(50) $$k_{ij} = u' \frac{M_{ij}}{M} = \frac{\delta x_j}{\delta p_i} + x_i \frac{\delta x_j}{\delta s}.$$

We can demonstrate that the inequality (48) has a well-defined economic significance. In fact, if price increases by dp_i, the value $x_i dp_i$ can be said to be an *apparent loss*, since, in order to make possible the purchase of the same quantities of all the goods that had formerly been bought, the income should have to increase by $ds = x_i dp_i$. But the individual, though having the possibility of preserving unchanged the preceding budget, will no longer consider it preferable to any other, and there will take place some kind of *residual variations* of demand:

$$(51) \begin{cases} dx_i = \dfrac{\delta x_i}{\delta p_i}\, dp_i + \dfrac{\delta x_i}{\delta s}\, ds \;-\; \left(u'\, \dfrac{M_{ii}}{M} - x_i\, \dfrac{\delta x_i}{\delta s} \right) dp_i \\[2mm] \qquad + \dfrac{\delta x_i}{\delta s}\, (x_i dp_i) = u'\, \dfrac{M_{ii}}{M}\, dp_i = k_{ii} dp_i; \\[3mm] dx_j = \dfrac{\delta x_j}{\delta p_i}\, dp_i + \dfrac{\delta x_j}{\delta s}\, ds = \left(u'\, \dfrac{M_{ij}}{M} - x_i\, \dfrac{\delta x_i}{\delta s} \right) dp_i \\[2mm] \qquad + \dfrac{\delta x_i}{\delta s}\, (x_i dp_i) = u'\, \dfrac{M_{ij}}{M}\, dp_i = k_{ij} dp_i. \end{cases}$$

The increment dp_i of price, accompanied by an increment of income equal to the apparent loss, can be said to be the *compensated variation* of price. In such a case k_{ii} and k_{ij} can be regarded as residual variations of the demand for each unit of the compensated increment of price, and can be called the *residual variability* of x_i and x_j respectively.

Using this terminology, the inequality (48) can be expressed thus:

III. *The residual variability of a good in the case of a compensated variation of its price, is always negative.* Or:

$$(52) \qquad k_{ii} = u'\, \frac{M_{ii}}{M} = \frac{\delta x_i}{\delta p_i} + x_i\, \frac{\delta x_i}{\delta s} < 0.$$

For example, if after an increase of the price of bread, wages increase only by the amount of the apparent loss, the demand for bread on the part of the wage-earners will not be maintained at the original level; on the contrary, it will fall.

Concluding, we note that if $\dfrac{\delta x_i}{\delta p_i}$ and $\dfrac{\delta x_i}{\delta s}$ are of opposite sign, the formula (52) resolves itself into the following inequalities between the numerical values of the derivatives:

Case I	Case II
$\dfrac{\delta x_i}{\delta s} > 0,\ \dfrac{\delta x_i}{\delta p_i} < 0;$	$\dfrac{\delta x_i}{\delta s} < 0,\ \dfrac{\delta x_i}{\delta p_i} > 0.$

$$(53) \qquad \frac{\left|\dfrac{\delta x_i}{\delta p_i}\right|}{\left|\dfrac{\delta x_i}{\delta s}\right|} > x_i; \qquad\qquad (54) \qquad \frac{\left|\dfrac{\delta x_i}{\delta p_i}\right|}{\left|\dfrac{\delta x_i}{\delta s}\right|} < x_i.$$

The foregoing formulas belong to the category of relations which to date have never been the object of research in social science; that is, they belong to relations quantitatively defined between empirical, measurable facts; therefore they can be *verified* by means of observation of real budgets.

9. Dependence of the Demand for One Good on the Price of Another

It follows from (47) that:

$$\frac{\delta x_j}{\delta p_i} = u' \frac{M_{ij}}{M} - x_i \frac{\delta x_j}{\delta s} \; ; \quad \frac{\delta x_i}{\delta p_j} = u' \frac{M_{ji}}{M} - x_j \frac{\delta x_i}{\delta s} \; .$$

M_{ij} being equal to M_{ji}, and so $k_{ij} = k_{ji}$; or

$$(55) \qquad \frac{\delta x_j}{\delta p_i} + x_i \frac{\delta x_j}{\delta s} = \frac{\delta x_i}{\delta p_j} + x_j \frac{\delta x_i}{\delta s} \; .$$

This important relation can be called the *law of reversibility* of residual variations, and expressed thus:

The residual variability of the j-th good in the case of a compensated variation of the price p_i is equal to the residual variability of the i-th good in the case of a compensated variation of the price p_j.

Equation (55) belongs to the previously mentioned category of quantitatively defined relations between observable quantities. Empirical confirmation is highly desirable, inasmuch as it would demonstrate the correspondence to the truth, or at least the plausibility, of the hypothesis that the increments of utility do not depend upon the mode of variation. It is clear, in fact, that if this hypothesis were not to correspond to the real phenomena of budgets, u_{ij} would not be equal to u_{ji} nor M_{ij} to M_{ji}, and the law of reversibility would not have been verified.

Continuing, we write:

$$\frac{\delta x_i}{\delta p_1} = u' \frac{M_{1i}}{M} - x_1 \frac{\delta x_i}{\delta s}$$

$$\frac{\delta x_i}{\delta p_2} = u' \frac{M_{2i}}{M} - x_2 \frac{\delta x_i}{\delta s}$$

$$\cdots\cdots\cdots\cdots\cdots$$

$$\frac{\delta x_i}{\delta p_n} = u' \frac{M_{ni}}{M} - x_n \frac{\delta x_i}{\delta s}$$

Multiplying the foregoing equalities by p_1, p_2, . . . , p_n, respectively, and adding them, we have:

$$p_1 \frac{\delta x_i}{\delta p_1} + p_2 \frac{\delta x_i}{\delta p_2} + \cdots + p_n \frac{\delta x_i}{\delta p_n} =$$

$$\frac{u'}{M} (p_1 M_{1i} + p_2 M_{2i} + \cdots + p_n M_{ni})$$

$$- (p_1 x_1 + p_2 x_2 + \cdots + p_n x_n) \frac{\delta x_i}{\delta s}$$

Adding $0\, M_{0i}$ to the polynomial in the first parentheses, we obtain the sum of the cofactors of the determinant M corresponding to the elements of column (i), multiplied by the elements of column (0). The sum is therefore zero; and we have the interesting relation:

$$(56) \quad p_1 \frac{\delta x_i}{\delta p_1} + p_2 \frac{\delta x_i}{\delta p_2} + \cdots \cdots + p_n \frac{\delta x_i}{\delta p_n} = -s \frac{\delta x_i}{\delta s}$$

We write, then, on the basis of (55):

$$\frac{\delta x_i}{\delta p_j} - \frac{\delta x_j}{\delta p_i} = x_i \frac{\delta x_j}{\delta s} - x_j \frac{\delta x_i}{\delta s} ;$$

$$\frac{\delta x_i}{\delta p_k} - \frac{\delta x_k}{\delta p_i} = x_i \frac{\delta x_k}{\delta s} - x_k \frac{\delta x_i}{\delta s}$$

Multiplying the first equation by x_k and the second by x_j, and subtracting the second product from the first, we obtain:

$$x_k \left(\frac{\delta x_i}{\delta p_j} - \frac{\delta x_j}{\delta p_i} \right) - x_j \left(\frac{\delta x_i}{\delta p_k} - \frac{\delta x_k}{\delta p_i} \right) = x_i \left(x_k \frac{\delta x_j}{\delta s} - x_j \frac{\delta x_k}{\delta s} \right)$$

$$= x_i \left(\frac{\delta x_k}{\delta p_j} - \frac{\delta x_j}{\delta p_k} \right) ;$$

from which we have:

$$(57) \quad \frac{1}{x_i x_j} \frac{\delta x_i}{\delta p_j} + \frac{1}{x_j x_k} \frac{\delta x_j}{\delta p_k} + \frac{1}{x_k x_i} \frac{\delta x_k}{\delta p_i}$$

$$= \frac{1}{x_i x_k} \frac{\delta x_i}{\delta p_k} + \frac{1}{x_k x_j} \frac{\delta x_k}{\delta p_j} + \frac{1}{x_j x_i} \frac{\delta x_j}{\delta p_i}.$$

This *cyclic relation* can be extended to the general case of any number of goods. Putting, in fact, $\xi_{ij} = \dfrac{\frac{\delta x_i}{\delta p_j}}{x_i x_j}$; and writing:

$$\xi_{12} \ + \ \xi_{23} \ + \ \xi_{31} = \xi_{13} + \xi_{32} \ + \ \xi_{21}$$
$$\xi_{13} \ + \ \xi_{34} \ + \ \xi_{41} = \xi_{14} + \xi_{43} \ + \ \xi_{31}$$
$$\cdots\cdots\cdots\cdots\cdots\cdots\cdots\cdots\cdots\cdots$$
$$\xi_{1\,n-1} + \ \xi_{n-1\,n} + \ \xi_{n1} = \ \xi_{1n} + \ \xi_{n\,n-1} + \ \xi_{n-1\,1},$$

by adding the preceding equalities we find:

$$(58) \qquad \xi_{12} + \xi_{23} + \xi_{34} + \cdots + \xi_{n-1\,n} + \xi_{n1}$$
$$= \xi_{1n} + \xi_{n\,n-1} + \cdots + \xi_{32} + \xi_{21} \ .$$

10. Theory of the Budget in the Case in Which the Marginal Utility of Any One Good Is a Function Only of Its Quantity

This particular case has special importance in the history of economic science, having furnished the first basis for the theory of marginal utility. None of the authors who elaborated the theory of the budget, because they regarded it necessary to accept the so-called law of satiability of needs (Gossen's law), could reach results of general validity. Gossen's law itself remains what it always was, that is, an empirical proposition, not a rigorously demonstrated truth; and several authors have had occasion to express doubts on its general validity.[5]

It is common opinion that if there are exceptions to this law, they are rare; but one can point out that natural laws, if they admit of exceptions, become things but slightly different from the rules of grammar. Speaking from the logical viewpoint, one cannot call *law* any rule which admits of exceptions—it matters not whether they are few or many—in *unknown* conditions or circumstances. In our case, moreover, it is doubtful whether the exceptions are indeed so few as one is wont to believe, since the question was never tested on the basis of scientifically arranged, empirical observations. And we hold that specialized research,

---

[5] Gossen himself was the first to express doubts in that respect. See *Entwickelung der Gesetze des menschlichen Verkehrs* (N. Augs., 1889), pp. 47–48. See also: Edgeworth, *Mathematical Psychics* (1881), pp. 34–35; Pantaleoni, *Principii di economia pura* (1889), pp. 40, 87; Pareto, *Proprietà fondamentale dei gradi finali d'utilità* (in this *Giornale* [1893], Vol. I, pp. 1, 2) and *Manuel d'économie politique* (1909), p. 266; Marshall, *Principles of Economics* (1895), p. 169, n. 2; von Schubert-Soldern, *Das menschliche Glück und die soziale Frage, Tueb. Zeitschr.* (1896), Vol. I, p. 68, Vol. III, p. 512; Cuhel, *Zur Lehre von den Bedürfnissen* (1907), pp. 238–239.

directed above all toward the life and labor of the poorer classes, will be rewarded by unexpected results.[6]

To carry out such research one needs as a basis a theory which to this day has been almost completely lacking. As far as we know, only one author has studied the theory of demand of a non-satiating good: Umberto Ricci.[7] Using mathematical analysis, he has reached the conclusion that the demand for a non-satiating good increases with the increase of its price, if:

$$\frac{p_1^2}{u_{11}} + \frac{p_2^2}{u_{22}} + \cdots\cdots\cdots + \frac{p_n^2}{u_{nn}} < 0.$$

But since, as we shall see, the first member of the preceding inequality is nothing but our criterion of stability, it is obvious how unstable Ricci's budget is. Hence in consequence of the increase of price and of the disturbance of equilibrium, it will not tend to approach the displaced point of minimum [maximum] utility, but to move away from it. It follows from the theory of equilibrium that Ricci's result, which refers to a case which cannot occur in reality, does not correspond to the truth.

Having developed the general theory, we will now easily obtain the theory for the case under examination. From the fundamental form of the condition of stability:

$$d^2U = u_{11}dx_1^2 + u_{22}dx_2^2 + \cdots\cdots + u_{nn}dx_n^2 < 0 ,$$

it follows that:

I. The budget is stable if all the u_{ii} are negative.

II. If only one of the u_{ii} is positive, the budget is stable if $\Omega > 0$, unstable if $\Omega < 0$.

III. The budget can never be stable if more than one of the u_{ii} is positive.

Let us apply the method of Section 5 to the determination of Ω; the deduction of the general formula will be facilitated here by remembering the fact that all the $u_{ij} = 0$. We have, hence:

$$M = \begin{vmatrix} 0 & p_1 & p_2 & \cdots & p_n \\ p_1 & u_{11} & 0 & \cdots & 0 \\ p_2 & 0 & u_{22} & \cdots & 0 \\ \cdots & \cdots & \cdots & \cdots & \cdots \\ p_n & 0 & 0 & \cdots & u_{nn} \end{vmatrix} = u_{11}u_{22}\cdots u_{nn}\left(\frac{p_1^2}{u_{11}} + \frac{p_2^2}{u_{22}} + \cdots + \frac{p_n^2}{u_{nn}}\right)$$

[6] Marshall, *op. cit.*, p. 208.

[7] *Curve crescenti di ofelimità e di domanda* (in this *Giornale* [1904, August], pp. 112–138).

$$R = \begin{vmatrix} u_{11} & 0 & 0 & \cdots & 0 \\ 0 & u_{22} & 0 & \cdots & 0 \\ 0 & 0 & u_{33} & \cdots & 0 \\ \cdots & \cdots & \cdots & \cdots & \cdots \\ 0 & 0 & 0 & \cdots & u_{nn} \end{vmatrix} = u_{11}u_{22} \cdots u_{nn}$$

and consequently:

$$(59) \qquad \Omega = \frac{M}{R} = \frac{p_1^2}{u_{11}} + \frac{p_2^2}{u_{22}} + \cdots\cdots + \frac{p_n^2}{u_{nn}} \, .$$

Similarly we obtain:

$$H_i = - M_{0i} = u_{11}u_{22} \cdots u_{nn} \frac{p_i}{u_{ii}}$$

$$M_{ii} = - u_{11}u_{22} \cdots u_{nn} \frac{\Omega - \dfrac{p_i^2}{u_{ii}}}{u_{ii}}$$

$$M_{ij} = u_{11}u_{22} \cdots u_{nn} \frac{p_1 p_2}{u_{ii}u_{jj}}$$

and hence:

$$(60) \qquad \begin{cases} \dfrac{\delta x_i}{\delta s} = \dfrac{p_i}{u_{ii}\Omega} \\[3mm] \dfrac{\delta x_i}{\delta p_i} = \dfrac{u'\left(\Omega - \dfrac{p_i^2}{u_{ii}}\right) - p_i x_i}{u_{ii}\,\Omega} \\[3mm] \dfrac{\delta x_j}{\delta p_i} = - \dfrac{p_j(u_i + x_i u_{ii})}{u_{ii}u_{jj}\,\Omega} \, . \end{cases}$$

The analysis of the preceding formulas leads to the following conclusions:

If the budget is *normal,* the demand for any one good increases with the increase of the income and diminishes with the increase of the price of that good. If the budget is *abnormal,* the increase of income causes an increase in the demand for the non-satiating goods, and a decrease in that for the satiating goods. Moreover, with the increase of price of a non-satiating good, its demand should always decrease; the contrary can happen only in the case of a satiating good. The satiating goods being, in the case considered, relatively dispensable, the result is in accord with the previously deduced laws of demand.

11. Determination (Possibly by Means of Empirical, Quantitative Data) of the Second Derivatives of the Utility Function

The values of $\dfrac{\delta x_1}{\delta s}$, $\dfrac{\delta x_2}{\delta s}$, ... , $\dfrac{\delta x_n}{\delta s}$ and of all the quantities

of the type $\dfrac{\delta x_i}{\delta p_i}$ and $\dfrac{\delta x_i}{\delta p_j}$ can be determined by virtue of the observation of real budgets; on that account we shall consider them as empirically measurable data and we shall make use of them to determine u_{ii} and u_{ij}. Using the usual notation, and remembering the formulas (38), (49), and (50), we find:

$$(61) \qquad \begin{cases} M_{0i} = M \dfrac{\delta x_i}{\delta s} \\[2ex] M_{ii} = k_{ii} \dfrac{M}{u'} \\[2ex] M_{ij} = k_{ij} \dfrac{M}{u'}. \end{cases}$$

Indicating then by Δ the determinant formed by means of the cofactors of M, we obtain from the well-known formulas of the theory of determinants:

$$(62) \qquad \Delta = \begin{vmatrix} R & M_{01} & M_{02} & \cdots & M_{0n} \\ M_{10} & M_{11} & M_{12} & \cdots & M_{1n} \\ \multicolumn{5}{c}{\dotfill} \\ M_{n0} & M_{n1} & M_{n2} & \cdots & M_{nn} \end{vmatrix} = M^n$$

and

$$(63) \qquad 0 = \frac{\Delta_{00}}{M^{n-1}}, \; p_i = \frac{\Delta_{0i}}{M^{n-1}}, \; u_{ii} = \frac{\Delta_{ii}}{M^{n-1}}, \; u_{ij} = \frac{\Delta_{ij}}{M^{n-1}}.$$

Let us substitute in Δ the expressions for the cofactors obtained in (61):

$$(64) \qquad \Delta = \begin{vmatrix} R & M \dfrac{\delta x_1}{\delta s} & M \dfrac{\delta x_2}{\delta s} & \cdots\cdots & M \dfrac{\delta x_n}{\delta s} \\[2ex] M \dfrac{\delta x_1}{\delta s} & \dfrac{M}{u'} k_{11} & \dfrac{M}{u'} k_{12} & \cdots\cdots & \dfrac{M}{u'} k_{1n} \\[2ex] \multicolumn{5}{c}{\dotfill} \\[1ex] M \dfrac{\delta x_n}{\delta s} & \dfrac{M}{u'} k_{n1} & \dfrac{M}{u'} k_{n2} & \cdots\cdots & \dfrac{M}{u'} k_{nn} \end{vmatrix}$$

$$= \frac{M^{n+1}}{u'^{n-1}} \begin{vmatrix} \frac{R}{u'M} & \frac{\delta x_1}{\delta s} & \frac{\delta x_2}{\delta s} & \cdots\cdots & \frac{\delta x_n}{\delta s} \\ \frac{\delta x_1}{\delta s} & k_{11} & k_{12} & \cdots\cdots & k_{1n} \\ \cdots\cdots\cdots\cdots\cdots\cdots\cdots \\ \frac{\delta x_n}{\delta s} & k_{n1} & k_{n2} & \cdots\cdots & k_{nn} \end{vmatrix}$$

Putting for brevity's sake:

$$(65) \qquad \theta = \frac{R}{u'M} = \frac{1}{u'\Omega} ,$$

$$(66) \qquad N = \begin{vmatrix} \theta & \frac{\delta x_1}{\delta s} & \frac{\delta x_2}{\delta s} & \cdots\cdots & \frac{\delta x_n}{\delta s} \\ \frac{\delta x_1}{\delta s} & k_{11} & k_{12} & \cdots\cdots & k_{1n} \\ \cdots\cdots\cdots\cdots\cdots\cdots\cdots \\ \frac{\delta x_n}{\delta s} & k_{n1} & k_{n2} & \cdots\cdots & k_{nn} \end{vmatrix}$$

we obtain from (62) and (64):

$$\Delta = \frac{M^{n+1}}{u'^{n-1}} N = M^n ;$$

and hence:

$$(67) \qquad M = \frac{u'^{n-1}}{N} .$$

Applying the same procedure to the cofactors of Δ, we **find**:

$$\Delta_{00} = \frac{M^n}{u'^n} N_{00} , \quad \Delta_{0i} = \frac{M^n}{u'^{n-1}} N_{0i} ,$$

$$\Delta_{ii} = \frac{M^n}{u'^{n-2}} N_{ii} , \quad \Delta_{ij} = \frac{M^n}{u'^{n-2}} N_{ij} .$$

Substituting these values in (63), and taking account of (67), we have:

$$(68) \quad 0 = \frac{N_{00}}{u'N} , \; p_i = \frac{N_{0i}}{N} , \; u_{ii} = u' \frac{N_{ii}}{N} , \; u_{ij} = u' \frac{N_{ij}}{N} .$$

Let us introduce the quantities:

$$(69)\quad P = \begin{vmatrix} 0 & \dfrac{\delta x_1}{\delta s} & \dfrac{\delta x_2}{\delta s} & \cdots & \dfrac{\delta x_n}{\delta s} \\ \dfrac{\delta x_1}{\delta s} & k_{11} & k_{12} & \cdots & k_{1n} \\ \cdots & \cdots & \cdots & \cdots & \cdots \\ \dfrac{\delta x_n}{\delta s} & k_{n1} & k_{n2} & \cdots & k_{nn} \end{vmatrix} \text{ and } Q = \begin{vmatrix} k_{11} & k_{12} & \cdots & k_{1n} \\ k_{21} & k_{22} & \cdots & k_{2n} \\ \cdots & \cdots & \cdots & \cdots \\ k_{n1} & k_{n2} & \cdots & k_{nn} \end{vmatrix}$$

which can be expressed entirely by means of empirical data. If $Q = N_{00} = 0$, as appears from (68), we find the following definitive formulas:

$$(70)\qquad u_{ii} = u' \left(\frac{P_{ii}}{P} - \theta \frac{Q_{ii}}{P} \right),$$

$$(71)\qquad u_{ij} = u' \left(\frac{P_{ij}}{P} - \theta \frac{Q_{ij}}{P} \right).$$

To demonstrate that this solution is definitive, we must prove the impossibility of obtaining θ as a function of empirical data.

For this purpose, let us begin by supposing the contrary thesis is true. Then the second derivatives of the utility function could be expressed as functions of u' and of the quantities of goods $x_1, x_2, \ldots, x_n$; and we would have:

$$u_{i1} = u' \; \varphi_1(x_1, x_2, \cdots, x_n)$$
$$u_{i2} = u' \; \varphi_2(x_1, x_2, \cdots, x_n)$$
$$\cdots \cdots \cdots \cdots \cdots \cdots \cdots$$
$$u_{in} = u' \; \varphi_n(x_1, x_2, \cdots, x_n) .$$

Moreover, it being always possible (at least in principle) to find the individual demand functions, the prices could be expressed as empirical functions of the quantities $x_1, x_2, \ldots, x_n$. And we could write:

$$(72)\qquad u_i = u' p_i = u' f(x_1, x_2, \cdots, x_n) \cdot$$

Indicating, then, by ψ_k the quotient $\dfrac{\varphi_k(x_1, x_2, \cdots, x_n)}{f(x_1, x_2, \cdots, x_n)},$

we will obtain:

$$(73)\quad\begin{cases}\dfrac{u_{i1}}{u_i} = \dfrac{\dfrac{\delta u_i}{\delta x_1}}{u_i} = \dfrac{\delta(\log u_i)}{\delta x_1} = \psi_1 \\[2em] \dfrac{u_{i2}}{u_i} = \dfrac{\dfrac{\delta u_i}{\delta x_2}}{u_i} = \dfrac{\delta(\log u_i)}{\delta x_2} = \psi_2 \\[2em] \cdots\cdots\cdots\cdots\cdots\cdots\cdots\cdots \\[1em] \dfrac{u_{in}}{u_i} = \dfrac{\dfrac{\delta u_i}{\delta x_n}}{u_i} = \dfrac{\delta(\log u_i)}{\delta x_n} = \psi_n. \end{cases}$$

If our hypothesis that the utility is independent of the mode of variation corresponds to the truth, it is easy to demonstrate that there should exist equalities of the type, $\dfrac{\delta\psi_1}{\delta x_2} = \dfrac{\delta\psi_2}{\delta x_1}$, etc.; and the function $\log u_1$ can be determined by the well-known procedure of integrating the total differential:

$$d(\log u_i) = \psi_1 dx_1 + \psi_2 dx_2 + \cdots\cdots + \psi_n dx_n.$$

We thus have: $\log u_1 = \Psi(x_1, x_2, \ldots\ldots\ldots, x_n) + \log C$;

$$(74)\qquad\qquad u_i = C e^{\Psi},$$

C being a constant of integration independent of $x_1, x_2, \ldots, x_n$.

If we take as our unit of measure the marginal utility of money, corresponding to a certain state of the budget, for example to that in which $x_1 = a_1, x_2 = a_2, \ldots\ldots\ldots, x_n = a_n$; and if we put:

$$\Psi_0 = \Psi(a_1, a_2, \cdots\cdots, a_n), \qquad f_0 = f(a_1, a_2, \cdots\cdots, a_n),$$

we shall have:

$$u' = \frac{u_i}{p_i} = \frac{C e^{\Psi_0}}{f_0} = 1;$$

and hence $C = f_0 e^{-\Psi_0}$. We thus obtain the solution:

$$(75)\qquad\qquad u_i = f_0\, e^{\Psi - \Psi_0}$$

Knowing, besides, all the marginal utilities as functions of

$x_1, x_2, \ldots\ldots\ldots, x_n$, it would be possible to find the total utility by the application of the same method to the equations:

$$\frac{\delta U}{\delta x_1} = u_1, \ \frac{\delta U}{\delta x_2} = u_2, \ \ldots\ldots\ldots, \ \frac{\delta U}{\delta x_n} = u_n \ .$$

The constant of integration would be given by the equation:

$$U_0 = \Phi(0,0, \ \ldots\ldots, 0) = 0 \ .$$

We see therefore that, if θ is known, all the marginal utilities and the utility function itself can be unequivocally determined as functions of the empirical data. But, the question having been completely clarified by V. Pareto's researches,[8] we know that when all the marginal utilities are assumed to be functions of the quantities of all the goods, unequivocal determination becomes impossible. We conclude, therefore, that θ also is not determinable, and that it should be considered an entirely arbitrary function of $x_1, x_2, \ldots\ldots\ldots, x_n$.

12. On the Concept of Utility

The definition of utility given in Section 2, being governed by a completely empirical concept, can serve as basis for the entire theory of the budget. But since the values of the marginal utilities and their variations connected with variations in the quantities of goods remain undetermined, obviously an irreconcilable conflict exists between the two aspects of the problem of utility. The value of θ being, in fact, arbitrary, we can explain observable and measurable facts of human conduct by attributing to the quantity

$$u_{ij} = \frac{P_{ij}}{P} - \theta \, \frac{Q_{ij}}{P} \, ,$$

or to the quantity:

$$u_{ii} = \frac{P_{ii}}{P} - \theta \, \frac{Q_{ii}}{P} \, ,$$

any value whatsoever: great or small, positive or negative, at our pleasure. It will be permissible, therefore, to attribute all the facts of my economic conduct to any hypotheses whatsoever on dependence, for example, between the quantity of apples I consume and the marginal utility of the paper upon which I am writing; and to suppose that with the consuming of one apple more per month the utility of a sheet of paper becomes 1000 times greater or 1000

[8] *Manuel d'économie politique* (1909), pp. 539–557.

times smaller. Both hypotheses would attribute determinate values to all the quantities u_{ii}, u_{ij}, and no contradiction need exist between either of the two modes of *explanation* and the real facts of my conduct.

Nor will a contradiction exist between the psychological concept of utility and the results at which we have arrived, it being clear that our definition of utility (the *index of ophelimity* of Pareto) is completely foreign to psychology. Nevertheless, the conclusion is not satisfactory; because, even though attaching great importance to the absolute logical independence of the methods of economic science from those of psychology, we could not ignore the existence of a very complicated interdependence between the *facts* studied by the two sciences.

We therefore consider it necessary to complete the formal concept of utility in such a manner as to put the economic aspect of the problem of utility in close relation with the psychological one. Specifically, we propose to investigate whether the following definition is admissible:

The utility of a combination of goods is a quantity which possesses the following properties: it is greater the more the combination is desired by the individual; and *its variations are immediately perceptible by the subject.*

For our present purpose a more profound investigation with respect to the character of the manifestations of utility in the consciousness of the individual is superfluous; therefore, we leave the task to future studies. On the basis of the preceding definition it can be said that, if after an increment in the quantity of good a has occurred, an individual does not observe any modification in his subjective relations with the good β, the marginal utility of the latter has not noticeably changed and there exists the approximate equality:

$$u_{\alpha\beta} = 0.$$

By "lack of modification in the subjective relations with the good" we mean to indicate all possible psychic phenomena: pleasure obtained by means of consumption, pain through loss, intensity of desire for possession, etc. Only if it could be verified that there exist no modifications of this kind, would it be permissible to assert the complete independence of the marginal utility of one good from the quantity of another.

The foregoing addition to the definition of utility notably modifies this definition from the mathematical point of view; because it determines all the values in question. In fact, solving the equation $u_{\alpha\beta} = 0$ for θ, and substituting this value in the expressions for all the other second derivatives, we find, by the method of the preceding section, the marginal utility and the utility function.

It is doubtful, however, whether the proposed definition is admissible. For, if one assumes that an individual observes no dependence, not only between the good a and the good β, but also between the goods γ and δ, ϵ and ζ, etc., we have:

$$(76) \quad \begin{cases} u_{\alpha\beta} = \dfrac{u'}{P} \left(P_{\alpha\beta} - \theta\, Q_{\alpha\beta} \right) = 0 \\[2ex] u_{\gamma\delta} = \dfrac{u'}{P} \left(P_{\gamma\delta} - \theta\, Q_{\gamma\delta} \right) = 0 \\[2ex] u_{\epsilon\zeta} = \dfrac{u'}{P} \left(P_{\epsilon\zeta} - \theta\, Q_{\epsilon\zeta} \right) = 0 \end{cases}$$

whence it follows:

$$\theta = \frac{P_{\alpha\beta}}{Q_{\alpha\beta}} = \frac{P_{\gamma\delta}}{Q_{\gamma\delta}} = \frac{P_{\epsilon\zeta}}{Q_{\epsilon\zeta}} = \cdots .$$

But will experience confirm these relations? That is the problem.

13. On the Consciousness of Economic Conduct

Let us try to penetrate into the meaning of the question. All the economists who discussed it have thought it possible to consider marginal utilities (at least in the greater number of instances) as obeying Gossen's law as much in the case of dependence on, as in the case of independence of, the quantities of other goods; and they have classified the cases of dependence by distinguishing complementary and competing goods. This whole edifice falls if one remains loyal to the formal definition of utility, for it is impossible to deduce from the facts of conduct the character (that is, the sign) of the second derivatives of utility.

If, instead, we are convinced that the marginal utility of any one good decreases with an increase of its quantity; that, moreover, for example, sugar and tea, salt and meat, etc., are complementary, while pork and mutton are normally competing, etc., it is obvious that this conviction can be founded only upon some sort of *inter-*

nal evidence, not on facts of economic conduct. The generality of this conviction authorizes us to call it *faith in the consciousness of economic conduct.* It is in fact common opinion that the motives by which we are guided, or at least factors parallel to these, manifest themselves, more or less clearly, in our consciousness, so as to enable us to perceive the increase and decrease in their intensity.

If we admit, by way of hypothesis, such a proposition as true, our formulas permit the derivation of the following laws:

I. *If an individual does not perceive any modification in his subjective relation with the good α when the quantity of the good β varies, nor in that with γ when the quantity of δ varies, nor in that with ε when the quantity of ζ varies, etc., the following equalities must exist:*

$$\frac{P_{\alpha\beta}}{Q_{\alpha\beta}} = \frac{P_{\gamma\delta}}{Q_{\gamma\delta}} = \frac{P_{\epsilon\zeta}}{Q_{\epsilon\zeta}} = \cdots$$

II. If this proposition is true, one can calculate θ and substitute its value in the formulas for u_{ii} and u_{ij}. Then, *in the case of goods which on the basis of internal evidence must be considered satiating, the following relations must hold:*

$$\frac{P_{ii}}{P} - \theta\,\frac{Q_{ii}}{P} < 0, \text{ or } \qquad \frac{P_{jj}}{P} - \theta\,\frac{Q_{jj}}{P} > 0.$$

III. *In the case of two goods which on the basis of internal evidence are regarded as complementary or competing, there must be, respectively:*

$$\frac{P_{ij}}{P} - \theta\,\frac{Q_{ij}}{P} > 0, \text{ or } \qquad \frac{P_{kl}}{P} - \theta\,\frac{Q_{kl}}{P} < 0.$$

Since the foregoing propositions can be treated empirically, we find ourselves again compelled to insist upon the urgent necessity for passing from abstract schemes to positive research, in the field embraced by the theory of the budget. Only thus could certain problems be solved, only thus certain formulas verified. But as to other problems (like those to which the propositions last propounded refer) it cannot be hoped that the empirical data required for their solution will be obtained. The calculation of the value of the determinants P and Q and of their cofactors would be possible only if we knew the quantities of *all* goods consumed by the individual and *all* the variations in the demand of *any one* good due to changes in income and in the prices of *all* goods.

It is evidently impossible to obtain all these values by observation of existing budgets; therefore, the only way that remains open is that of *experiment,* by means of which a totality of conditions similar to the budget could be created, and hence, the laws we have propounded could be confirmed or confuted.

It is worth the effort to attempt the enterprise, because if the experimental results were to lead to a confirmation of the laws, we shall have obtained in addition to this direct advantage also the ability to proceed further in investigations of the psychological aspect of utility. If, instead, the laws were not to find experimental verification, we would come to very important conclusions, not so much for the economic as for the psychic and moral sciences, for it would have been demonstrated that the variations in the value of utility were not perceptible by the subject, so the motives which govern human conduct not only by their nature escape from our consciousness but do not even indirectly become manifest to it.

These problems are much too complicated for us to attempt here not only to solve but even to present in an adequate manner. But we hope to have succeeded in bringing to light how they are connected with the theory of the budget, and in demonstrating the necessity for developing this theory further by employing the procedures proper to experimental science.

3

THE UTILITY ANALYSIS OF CHOICES
INVOLVING RISK [*][1]

By Milton Friedman and L. J. Savage ||

1. The Problem and Its Background

The purpose of this paper is to suggest that an important class of reactions of individuals to risk can be rationalized by a rather simple extension of orthodox utility analysis.

Individuals frequently must, or can, choose among alternatives that differ, among other things, in the degree of risk to which the individual will be subject. The clearest examples are provided by insurance and gambling. An individual who buys fire insurance on a house he owns is accepting the certain loss of a small sum (the insurance premium) in preference to the combination of a small chance of a much larger loss (the value of the house) and a large chance of no loss. That is, he is choosing certainty in preference to uncertainty. An individual who buys a lottery ticket is subjecting himself to a large chance of losing a small amount (the price of the lottery ticket) plus a small chance of winning a large amount (a prize) in preference to avoiding both risks. He is choosing uncertainty in preference to certainty.

This choice among different degrees of risk so prominent in insurance and gambling, is clearly present and important in a much broader range of economic choices. Occupations differ greatly in the variability of the income they promise: in some, for example, civil service employment, the prospective income is rather clearly defined and is almost certain to be within rather narrow limits; in others, for example, salaried employment as an accountant, there is somewhat more variability yet almost no chance of either

---

* *The Journal of Political Economy,* Vol. LVI (1948), pp. 279–304. Reprinted, by the courtesy of The University of Chicago Press and the authors, with one indicated change.

|| The University of Chicago.

[1] The fundamental ideas of this paper were worked out jointly by the two authors. The paper was written primarily by the senior author.

an extremely high or an extremely low income; in still others, for example, motion-picture acting, there is extreme variability, with a small chance of an extremely high income and a larger chance of an extremely low income. Securities vary similarly, from government bonds and industrial "blue chips" to "blue-sky" common stocks; and so do business enterprises or lines of business activity. Whether or not they realize it and whether or not they take explicit account of the varying degree of risk involved, individuals choosing among occupations, securities, or lines of business activity are making choices analogous to those that they make when they decide whether to buy insurance or to gamble. Is there any consistency among the choices of this kind that individuals make? Do they neglect the element of risk? Or does it play a central role? If so, what is that role?

These problems have, of course, been considered by economic theorists, particularly in their discussions of earnings in different occupations and of profits in different lines of business.[2] Their treatment of these problems has, however, never been integrated with their explanation of choices among riskless alternatives. Choices among riskless alternatives are explained in terms of maximization of utility: individuals are supposed to choose as they would if they attributed some common quantitative characteristic —designated utility—to various goods and then selected the combination of goods that yielded the largest total amount of this common characteristic. Choices among alternatives involving different degrees of risk, for example, among different occupations, are explained in utterly different terms—by ignorance of the odds or by the fact that "young men of an adventurous disposition are more attracted by the prospects of a great success than they are deterred by the fear of failure," by "the overweening conceit which the greater part of men have of their own abilities," by "their absurd presumption in their own good fortune," or by some similar *deus ex machina.*[3]

---

[2] E.g., see Adam Smith, *The Wealth of Nations,* Book I, Chap. X (Modern Library reprint of Cannan ed.), pp. 106–111; Alfred Marshall, *Principles of Economics* (8th ed.; London, Macmillan & Co., Ltd., 1920), pp. 398–400, 554–555, 613.

[3] Marshall, *op. cit.,* p. 554 (first quotation); Smith, *op. cit.,* p. 107 (last two quotations).

The rejection of utility maximization as an explanation of choices among different degrees of risk was a direct consequence of the belief in diminishing marginal utility. If the marginal utility of money diminishes, an individual seeking to maximize utility will never participate in a "fair" game of chance, for example, a game in which he has an equal chance of winning or losing a dollar. The gain in utility from winning a dollar will be less than the loss in utility from losing a dollar, so that the expected utility from participation in the game is negative. Diminishing marginal utility plus maximization of expected utility would thus imply that individuals would always have to be paid to induce them to bear risk.[4] But this implication is clearly contradicted by actual behavior. People not only engage in fair games of chance, they engage freely and often eagerly in such unfair games as lotteries. Not only do risky occupations and risky investments not always yield a higher average return than relatively safe occupations or investments, they frequently yield a much lower average return.

Marshall resolved this contradiction by rejecting utility maximization as an explanation of choices involving risk. He need not have done so, since he did not need diminishing marginal utility —or, indeed, any quantitative concept of utility—for the analysis of riskless choices. The shift from the kind of utility analysis employed by Marshall to the indifference-curve analysis of F. Y. Edgeworth, Irving Fisher, and Vilfredo Pareto revealed that to rationalize riskless choices, it is sufficient to suppose that individuals can rank baskets of goods by total utility. It is unnecessary to suppose that they can compare differences between utilities.

---

[4] See Marshall, *op. cit.,* p. 135 n.; Mathematical Appendix, n. IX (p. 843). "Gambling involves an economic loss, even when conducted on perfectly fair and even terms. . . . A theoretically fair insurance against risks is always an economic gain" (p. 135). "The argument that fair gambling is an economic blunder . . . requires no further assumption than that, firstly the pleasures of gambling may be neglected; and, secondly $\phi''(x)$ is negative for all values of x, where $\phi(x)$ is the pleasure derived from wealth equal to x. . . . It is true that this loss of probable happiness need not be greater than the pleasure derived from the excitement of gambling, and we are then thrown back upon the induction that pleasures of gambling are in Bentham's phrase 'impure'; since experience shows that they are likely to engender a restless, feverish character, unsuited for steady work as well as for the higher and more solid pleasures of life" (p. 843).

But diminishing, or increasing, marginal utility implies a comparison of differences between utilities and hence is an entirely gratuitous assumption in interpreting riskless choices.

The idea that choices among alternatives involving risk can be explained by the maximization of expected utility is ancient, dating back at least to D. Bernoulli's celebrated analysis of the St. Petersburg paradox.[5] It has been repeatedly referred to since then but almost invariably rejected as the correct explanation—commonly bcause the prevailing belief in diminishing marginal utility made it appear that the existence of gambling could not be so explained. Even since the widespread recognition that the assumption of diminishing marginal utility is unnecessary to explain riskless choices, writers have continued to reject maximization of expected utility as "unrealistic."[6] This rejection of maximization

---

[5] See Daniel Bernoulli, *Versuch einer neuen Theorie der Wertbestimmung von Glücksfällen* (Leipzig, 1896), translated by A. Pringsheim from "Specimen theoriae novae de mensura sortis," *Commentarii academiae scientiarum imperialis Petropolitanae,* Vol. V, for the years 1730 and 1731, published in 1738.

In an interesting note appended to his paper Bernoulli points out that Cramer (presumably Gabriel Cramer [1704–1752]), a famous mathematician of the time, had anticipated some of his own views by a few years. The passages that he quotes from a letter in French by Cramer contain what, to us, is the truly essential point in Bernoulli's paper, namely, the idea of using the mathematical expectation of utility (the "moral expectation") instead of the mathematical expectation of income to compare alternatives involving risk. Cramer has not in general been attributed this much credit, apparently because the essential point in Bernoulli's paper has been taken to be the suggestion that the logarithm of income is an appropriate utility function.

[6] "It has been the assumption in the classical literature on this subject that the individual in question will always try to maximize the mathematical expectation of his gain or utility. . . . This may appear plausible, but it is certainly not an assumption which must hold true in all cases. It has been pointed out that the individual may also be interested in, and influenced by, the range or the standard deviation of the different possible utilities derived or some other measure of dispersion. It appears pretty evident from the behavior of people in lotteries or football pools that they are not a little influenced by the skewness of the probability distribution" (Gerhard Tintner, "A Contribution to the Non-Static Theory of Choice," *The Quarterly Journal of Economics,* Vol. LVI [February, 1942], p. 278).

"It would be definitely unrealistic . . . to confine ourselves to the mathematical expectation only, which is the usual but not justifiable practice of the

of expected utility has been challenged by John von Neumann and Oskar Morgenstern in their recent book, *Theory of Games and Economic Behavior*.[7] They argue that "under the conditions on which the indifference curve analysis is based very little extra effort is needed to reach a numerical utility," the expected value of which is maximized in choosing among alternatives involving risk.[8] The present paper is based on their treatment but has been made self-contained by the paraphrasing of essential parts of their argument.

If an individual shows by his market behavior that he prefers *A* to *B* and *B* to *C*, it is traditional to rationalize this behavior by supposing that he attaches more utility to *A* than to *B* and more utility to *B* than to *C*. All utility functions that give the same ranking to possible alternatives will provide equally good rationalizations of such choices, and it will make no difference which particular one is used. If, in addition, the individual should show by his market behavior that he prefers a 50-50 chance of *A* or *C* to the certainty of *B*, it seems natural to rationalize this behavior by supposing that the *difference* between the utilities he attaches to *A* and *B* is greater than the *difference* between the utilities he attaches to *B* and *C*, so that the *expected* utility of the preferred combination is greater than the utility of *B*. The class of utility functions, if there be any, that can provide the same ranking of alternatives that involve risk is much more restricted than the class that can provide the same ranking of alternatives that are certain. It consists of utility functions that differ only in origin and unit of measure (i.e., the utility functions in the class are linear functions of one another).[9] Thus, in effect, the ordinal properties

---

traditional calculus of 'moral probabilities'" (J. Marschak, "Money and the Theory of Assets," *Econometrica*, Vol. VI [1938], p. 320).

Tintner's inference, apparently also shared by Marschak, that the facts he cites are necessarily inconsistent with maximization of expected utility is erroneous (see sections 3 and 4 below). He is led to consider a formally more general solution because of his failure to appreciate the real generality of the kinds of behavior explicable by the maximization of expected utility.

[7] Princeton University Press, 1st ed., 1944; 2d ed., 1947; pp. 15–31 (both eds.), pp. 617–632 (2d ed. only); succeeding references are to 2d ed.

[8] *Ibid.*, p. 17.

[9] *Ibid.*, pp. 15–31, especially p. 25.

of utility functions can be used to rationalize riskless choices, the numerical properties to rationalize choices involving risk.

It does not, of course, follow that there will exist a utility function that will rationalize in this way the reactions of individuals to risk. It may be that individuals behave inconsistently—sometimes choosing a 50-50 chance of A or C instead of B and sometimes the reverse; or sometimes choosing A instead of B, B instead of C, and C instead of A—or that in some other way their behavior is different from what it would be if they were seeking rationally to maximize expected utility in accordance with a given utility function. Or it may be that some types of reactions to risk can be rationalized in this way while others cannot. Whether a numerical utility function will in fact serve to rationalize any particular class of reactions to risk is an empirical question to be tested; there is no obvious contradiction such as was once thought to exist.

This paper attempts to provide a crude empirical test by bringing together a few broad observations about the behavior of individuals in choosing among alternatives involving risk (section 2) and investigating whether these observations are consistent with the hypothesis revived by von Neumann and Morgenstern (sections 3 and 4). It turns out that these empirical observations are entirely consistent with the hypothesis if a rather special shape is given to the total utility curve of money (section 4). This special shape, which can be given a tolerably satisfactory interpretation (section 5), not only brings under the aegis of rational utility maximization much behavior that is ordinarily explained in other terms but also has implications about observable behavior not used in deriving it (section 6). Further empirical work should make it possible to determine whether or not these implications conform to reality.

It is a testimony to the strength of the belief in diminishing marginal utility that it has taken so long for the possibility of interpreting gambling and similar phenomena as a contradiction of universal diminishing marginal utility, rather than of utility maximization, to be recognized. The initial mistake must have been at least partly a product of a strong introspective belief in diminishing marginal utility: a dollar must mean less to a rich man than to a poor man; see how much more a man will spend when he is rich than when he is poor to avoid any given amount of pain or discomfort.[10] Some of the comments that have been published by competent economists on the utility analysis of von Neumann and Morgenstern are even more remarkable testimony to the hold that diminishing marginal utility has on economists. Vickrey remarks: "There is abundant evidence that individual decisions in situations involving risk are not always made in ways that are compatible with the assumption that the decisions are made rationally with a view to maximizing the mathematical expectation of a utility function. The purchase of tickets in lotteries, sweepstakes, and 'numbers' pools would imply, on such a basis, that the marginal utility of money is an increasing rather than a decreasing function of income. Such a conclusion is obviously unacceptable as a guide to social policy."[11] Kaysen remarks, "Unfortunately, these postulates [underlying the von Neumann and Morgenstern discussion of utility measurement] involve an assumption about economic behavior which is contrary to experience. . . . That this assumption is contradicted by experience can easily be shown by hundreds of examples [including] the participation of individuals in lotteries in which their mathematical expectation of gain (utility) is negative."[12]

2. Observable Behavior to Be Rationalized

The economic phenomena to which the hypothesis revived by von Neumann and Morgenstern is relevant can be divided into,

[10] This elemental argument seems so clearly to justify diminishing marginal utility that it may be desirable even now to state explicitly how this phenomenon can be rationalized equally well on the assumption of increasing marginal utility of money. It is only necessary to suppose that the avoidance of pain and the other goods that can be bought with money are related goods and that, while the marginal utility of money increases as the amount of money increases, the marginal utility of avoiding pain increases even faster.

[11] William Vickrey, "Measuring Marginal Utility by Reactions to Risk," *Econometrica*, Vol. XIII (1945), pp. 319–333. The quotation is from pp. 327 and 328. "The purchase of tickets in lotteries, sweepstakes, and 'numbers' pools" does not imply that marginal utility of money increases with income everywhere (see section 4 below). Moreover, it is entirely unnecessary to identify the quantity that individuals are to be interpreted as maximizing with a quantity that should be given special importance in public policy.

[12] C. Kaysen, "A Revolution in Economic Theory?" *Review of Economic Studies,* Vol. XIV, No. 35 (1946–47), pp. 1–15; quotation is from p. 13.

first, the phenomena ordinarily regarded as gambling and insurance; second, other economic phenomena involving risk. The latter are clearly the more important, and the ultimate significance of the hypothesis will depend primarily on the contribution it makes to an understanding of them. At the same time, the influence of risk is revealed most markedly in gambling and insurance, so that these phenomena have a significance for testing and elaborating the hypothesis out of proportion to their importance in actual economic behavior.

At the outset it should be confessed that we have conducted no extensive empirical investigation of either class of phenomena. For the present, we are content to use what is already available in the literature, or obvious from casual observation, to provide a first test of the hypothesis and to impose significant substantive restrictions on it.

The major economic decisions of an individual in which risk plays an important role concern the employment of the resources he controls: what occupation to follow, what entrepreneurial activity to engage in, how to invest (nonhuman) capital. Alternative possible uses of resources can be classified into three broad groups according to the degree of risk involved: (a) those involving little or no risk about the money return to be received—occupations like schoolteaching, other civil service employment, clerical work; business undertakings of a standard, predictable type like many public utilities; securities like government bonds, high-grade industrial bonds; some real property, particularly owner-occupied housing; (b) those involving a moderate degree of risk but unlikely to lead to either extreme gains or extreme losses—occupations like dentistry, accountancy, some kinds of managerial work; business undertakings of fairly standard kinds in which, however, there is sufficient competition to make the outcome fairly uncertain; securities like lower-grade bonds, preferred stocks, higher-grade common stocks; (c) those involving much risk, with some possibility of extremely large gains and some of extremely large losses—occupations involving physical risks, like piloting aircraft, automobile racing, or professions like medicine and law; business undertakings in untried fields; securities like highly speculative stocks; some types of real property.

The most significant generalization in the literature about

choices among these three uses of resources is that, other things the same, uses *a* or *c* tend in general to be preferred to use *b;* that is, people must in general be paid a premium to induce them to undertake moderate risks instead of subjecting themselves to either small or large risks. Thus Marshall says: "There are many people of a sober steady-going temper, who like to know what is before them, and who would far rather have an appointment which offered a certain income of say £400 a year than one which was not unlikely to yield £600, but had an equal chance of affording only £200. Uncertainty, therefore, which does not appeal to great ambitions and lofty aspirations, has special attractions for very few; while it acts as a deterrent to many of those who are making their choice of a career. And as a rule the certainty of moderate success attracts more than an expectation of an uncertain success that has an equal actuarial value.

"But on the other hand, if an occupation offers a few extremely high prizes, its attractiveness is increased out of all proportion to their aggregate value."[13]

Adam Smith comments similarly about occupational choices and, in addition, says of entrepreneurial undertakings: "The ordinary rate of profits always rises more or less with the risk. It does not, however, seem to rise in proportion to it, or so as to compensate it completely. . . . The presumptuous hope of success seems to act here as upon all other occasions, and to entice so many adventurers into those hazardous trades, that their competition reduces the profit below what is sufficient to compensate the risk."[14]

Edwin Cannan, in discussing the rate of return on investments, concludes that "the probability is that the classes of investments which on the average return most to the investor are neither the very safest of all nor the very riskiest, but the intermediate classes which do not appeal either to timidity or to the gambling instinct."[15]

---

[13] *Op. cit.,* pp. 554–555.

[14] *Op. cit.,* p. 111.

[15] Article on "Profit," in *Dictionary of Political Economy,* ed. R. H. Inglis Palgrave (new edition, ed. Henry Higgs; London, 1926); see also the summary of the views of different writers on risk-taking in F. H. Knight, *Risk, Uncertainty, and Profit* (New York, 1921; reprint London School of Economics and Political Science, 1933), pp. 362–367.

This asserted preference for extremely safe or extremely risky investments over investments with an intermediate degree of risk has its direct counterpart in the willingness of persons to buy insurance and also to buy lottery tickets or engage in other forms of gambling involving a small chance of a large gain. The extensive market for highly speculative stocks—the kind of stocks that "blue-sky" laws are intended to control—is a border-line case that could equally well be designated as investment or gambling.

The empirical evidence for the willingness of persons of all income classes to buy insurance is extensive.[16] Since insurance companies have costs of operation that are covered by their pre-

---

[16] E.g., see U. S. Bureau of Labor Statistics, *Bulletin 648: Family Expenditures in Selected Cities, 1935–36,* Vol. I: *Family Expenditures for Housing, 1935–36;* Vol. VI: *Family Expenditures for Transportation, 1935–36;* and Vol. VIII: *Changes in Assets and Liabilities, 1935–36.*

Table 6 of the Tabular Summary of Vol. I gives the percentage of home-owning families reporting the payment of premiums for insurance on the house. These percentages are given separately for each income class in each of a number of cities or groups of cities. Since premiums are often paid less frequently than once a year, the percentages given definitely understate the percentage of families carrying insurance. Yet the bulk of the percentages are well over 40.

Table 5 of the Tabular Summary of Vol. VI gives the percentage of families (again by income classes and cities or groups of cities) reporting expenditures for automobile insurance. These figures show a very rapid increase in the percentage of automobile operators that had insurance (this figure is derived by dividing the percentage of families reporting automobile insurance by the percentage of families operating cars) as income increases. In the bottom income classes, where operation of a car is infrequent, only a minority of those who operate cars carry insurance. In the upper income classes, where most families operate cars, the majority of operators carry insurance. A convenient summary of these percentages for selected income classes in six large cities, given in text Table 10 (p. 26), has forty-two entries. These vary from 4 per cent to 98 per cent and twenty-three are over 50 per cent.

Table 3 of the Tabular Summary of Vol. VIII gives the percentage of families in each income class in various cities or groups of cities reporting the payment of life, endowment, or annuity insurance premiums. The percentages are uniformly high. For example, for New York City the percentage of white families reporting the payment of insurance premiums is 75 per cent or higher for every income class listed and varies from 75 per cent in the income class $500–$749 to over 95 per cent in the upper-income classes; the percentage of Negro families purchasing insurance was 38 per cent for the $1,000–$1,249 class but 60 per cent or higher for every other class. This story is repeated for

mium receipts, the purchaser is obviously paying a larger premium than the average compensation he can expect to receive for the losses against which he carries insurance. That is, he is paying something to escape risk.

The empirical evidence for the willingness of individuals to purchase lottery tickets, or engage in similar forms of gambling, is also extensive. Many governments find, and more governments

---

city after city, the bulk of the entries in the table for the percentage of families purchasing insurance being above 80 per cent.

These figures cannot be regarded as direct estimates of the percentage of families willing to pay something—that is, to accept a smaller actuarial value—in order to escape risk, the technical meaning of the purchase of insurance that is relevant for our purpose. (1) The purchase of automobile and housing insurance may not be a matter of choice. Most owned homes have mortgages (see I, 361, Table L) and the mortgage may require that insurance be carried. The relevant figure for mortgaged homes would be the fraction of owners carrying a larger amount of insurance than is required by the mortgage. Similarly, finance companies generally require that insurance be carried on automobiles purchased on the instalment plan and not fully paid for, and the purchase of automobile insurance is compulsory in some states. (2) For automobile property damage and liability insurance (but not collision insurance) the risks to the operator and to the insurance company may not be the same, particularly to persons in the lower-income classes. The loss to the uninsured operator is limited by his wealth and borrowing power, and the maximum amount that he can lose may be well below the face value of the policy that he would purchase. The excess of the premium over the expected loss is thus greater for him than for a person with more wealth or borrowing power. The rise in the percentage of persons carrying automobile insurance as income rises may therefore reflect not an increased willingness to carry insurance but a reduction in the effective price that must be paid for insurance. (3) This tendency may be reversed for the relatively high-income classes for both automobile and housing insurance by the operation of the income tax. Uninsured losses are in many instances deductible from income before computation of income tax under the United States federal income tax, while insurance premiums are not. This tends to make the net expected loss less for the individual than for the insurance company. This effect is almost certainly negligible for the figures cited above, both because they do not effectively cover very high incomes and because the federal income tax was relatively low in 1935–36. (4) Life insurance at times comes closer to gambling (the choice of an uncertain alternative in preference to a certain alternative with a higher expected value) than to the payment of a premium to escape risk. For example, special life-insurance policies purchased to cover a single railroad or airplane trip are probably more nearly comparable to a lottery ticket than a means of achieving certainty. (5) Even aside from these qualifications, actual purchase of insurance

have found, lotteries an effective means of raising revenue.[17] Though illegal, the "numbers" game and similar forms of gambling are reported to flourish in the United States,[18] particularly among the lower income classes.

It seems highly unlikely that there is a sharp dichotomy between the individuals who purchase insurance and those who gamble. It seems much more likely that many do both or, at any rate, would be willing to. We can cite no direct evidence for this asserted fact, though indirect evidence and casual observation give us considerable confidence that it is correct. Its validity is suggested by the extensiveness of both gambling and the purchase of insurance. It is also suggested by some of the available evidence on how people invest their funds. The widespread legislation against "bucket shops" suggests that relatively poor people must have been willing to buy extremely speculative stocks of a "blue-sky" variety. Yet the bulk of the property income of the lower-income classes consists of interest and rents and relatively little

---

would give at best a lower limit to the number willing to buy insurance, since there will always be some who will regard the price asked as too high.

These qualifications offset one another to some extent. It seems highly unlikely that their net effect could be sufficient to reverse the conclusion suggested by the evidence cited that a large fraction of people in all income classes are willing to buy insurance.

[17] France, Spain, and Mexico, to name but three examples, currently conduct lotteries for revenue. Russia attaches a lottery feature to bonds sold to the public. Great Britain conducted lotteries from 1694 to 1826. In the United States lotteries were used extensively before the Revolution and for some time thereafter, both directly by state governments and under state charters granted to further specific projects deemed to have a state interest. For the history of lotteries in Great Britain see C. L'Estrange Ewen, *Lotteries and Sweepstakes* (London, 1932); in New York State, A. F. Ross, "History of Lotteries in New York," *Magazine of History,* Vol. V (New York, 1907). There seem to be no direct estimates of the fraction of the people who purchase tickets in state or other legal lotteries, and it is clear that such figures would be difficult to get from data obtained in connection with running the lotteries. The receipts from legal lotteries, and casual impressions of observers, suggest that a substantial fraction of the relevant units (families or, alternatively, individual income recipients) purchase tickets.

[18] Evidence from wagering on horse races, where this has been legalized, is too ambiguous to be of much value. Since most legal wagering is at the track, gambling is available only to those who go to watch the races and is combined with participation in the mechanics of the game of chance.

of dividends, whereas the reverse is true for the upper-income classes.[19] Rents and interest are types of receipts that tend to be derived from investments with relatively little risk, and so correspond to the purchase of insurance, whereas investment in speculative stocks corresponds to the purchase of lottery tickets.

Offhand it appears inconsistent for the same person both to buy insurance and to gamble: he is willing to pay a premium, in the one case, to avoid risk, in the other, to bear risk. And indeed it would be inconsistent for a person to be willing to pay something (no matter how little) in excess of actuarial value to avoid every possible risk and also something in excess of actuarial value to assume every possible risk. One must distinguish among different kinds of insurance and different kinds of gambling, since a willingness to pay something for only some kinds of insurance would not necessarily be inconsistent with a willingness to engage in only some kinds of gambling. Unfortunately, very little empirical evidence is readily available on the kinds of insurance that people are willing to buy and the kinds of gambling that they are willing to engage in. About the only clear indication is that people are willing to enter into gambles that offer a small chance of a large gain—as in lotteries and "speculative" securities.

Lotteries seem to be an extremely fruitful, and much neglected, source of information about reactions of individuals to risk. They present risk in relatively pure form, with little admixture of other factors; they have been conducted in many countries and for many centuries, so that a great deal of evidence is available about them; there has been extensive experimentation with the terms and conditions that would make them attractive, and much competition in conducting them, so that any regularities they may show would have to be interpreted as reflecting corresponding regularities in human behavior.[20] It is, of course, not certain that inferences from

---

[19] *Delaware Income Statistics,* Vol. I (Bureau of Economic and Business Research, University of Delaware, 1941, Table 1; *Minnesota Incomes, 1938–39,* Vol. II (Minnesota Resources Commission, 1942), Table 27; F. A. Hanna, J. A. Pechman, S. M. Lerner, *Analysis of Wisconsin Income* ("Studies in Income and Wealth," Vol. IX [National Bureau of Economic Research, 1948]), Part II, Table 1.

[20] Aside from their value in providing information about reactions to risk, data from lotteries may be of broader interest in providing evidence about the

lotteries would carry over to other choices involving risk. There would, however, seem to be some presumption that they would do so, though of course the validity of this presumption would have to be tested.[21]

The one general feature of lotteries that is worth noting in this preliminary survey, in addition to the general willingness of people to participate in them, is the structure of prizes that seems to have developed. Lotteries rarely have just a single prize equal to the total sum to be paid out as prizes. Instead, they tend to have several or many prizes. The largest prize is ordinarily not very much larger than the next largest, and often there is not one largest prize but several of the same size.[22] This tendency is so general that one would expect it to reflect some consistent feature of individual reactions, and any hypothesis designed to explain reactions to uncertainty should explain it.

3. THE FORMAL HYPOTHESIS

The hypothesis that is proposed for rationalizing the behavior just summarized can be stated compactly as follows: In choosing among alternatives open to it, whether or not these alternatives involve risk, a consumer unit (generally a family, sometimes an individual) behaves as if (a) it had a consistent set of preferences; (b) these preferences could be completely described by a function attaching a numerical value—to be designated "utility"—to alternatives each of which is regarded as certain; (c) its objective were to make its expected utility as large as possible. It is the contribution of von Neumann and Morgenstern to have shown that an alternative statement of the same hypothesis is: An individual chooses in accordance with a system of preferences which has the following properties:

---

stability of tastes and preferences over time and their similarity in different parts of the world. Here is a "commodity" which has remained unchanged over centuries, which is the same all over the globe, and which has been dealt in widely for the entire period and over much of the globe. It is hard to conceive of any other commodity for which this is true.

[21] See Smith, *op. cit.*, p. 108, for a precedent.

[22] See Ewen, *op. cit., passim,* but especially descriptions of state lotteries in Chap. VII, pp. 199–244; see also the large numbers of bills advertising lotteries in John Ashton, *A History of English Lotteries* (London, Leadenhall Press, 1893).

1. The system is complete and consistent; that is, an individual can tell which of two objects he prefers or whether he is indifferent between them, and if he does not prefer C to B and does not prefer B to A, then he does not prefer C to A.[23] (In this context, the word "object" includes combinations of objects with stated probabilities; for example, if A and B are objects, a 40-60 chance of A or B is also an object.)

2. If the object A is preferred to the object B, then a combination of A and any object C with stated probabilities is preferred to a combination of B and C with the same probabilities, provided that the probability attached to C is less than unity. Conversely, if a combination of A and C with stated probabilities is preferred to a combination of B and C with the same probabilities, then A is preferred to B.

3. If the object A is preferred to the object B and B to the object C, there will be some probability combination of A and C such that the individual is indifferent between it and B.[24]

This form of statement is designed to show that there is little difference between the plausibility of this hypothesis and the usual indifference-curve explanation of riskless choices.

These statements of the hypothesis conceal by their very compactness most of its implications. It will pay us, therefore, to elaborate them. It simplifies matters, and involves no loss in generality, to regard the alternatives open to the consumer unit as capable

---

[23] The transitivity of the relation of indifference assumed in this postulate is, of course, an idealization. It is clearly possible that the difference between successive pairs of alternatives in a series might be imperceptible to an individual, yet the first of the series definitely preferable to the last. This idealization, which is but a special case of the idealization involved in the geometric concept of a dimensionless point, seems to us unobjectionable. However, the use of this idealization in indifference-curve analysis is the major criticism offered by W. E. Armstrong in an attack on indifference-curve analysis in his article "The Determinateness of the Utility Function," *The Economic Journal*, Vol. XLIX (September, 1939), pp. 453–467. In a more recent article ("Uncertainty and the Utility Function," *The Economic Journal*, Vol. LVIII [March, 1948], pp. 1–10) Armstrong repeats this criticism and adds to it the criticism that choices involving risk cannot be rationalized by the ordinal properties of utility functions.

[24] For a rigorous presentation of the second statement and a rigorous proof that the statements are equivalent see von Neumann and Morgenstern, *op. cit.*, pp. 26–27, 617–632.

In this reprint, the authors have revised point 2 of the second statement. We are grateful to Paul A. Samuelson for having called our attention to the fact that the original point 2 was inadequate to assure the equivalence of the two statements.

of being expressed entirely in terms of money or money income. Actual alternatives are not, of course, capable of being so expressed: the same money income may be valued very differently according to the terms under which it is to be received, the nonpecuniary advantages or disadvantages associated with it, and so on. We can abstract from these factors, which play no role in the present problem, by supposing either that they are the same for different incomes compared or that they can be converted into equivalent sums of money income.[25] This permits us to consider total utility a function of money income alone.

Let I represent the income of a consumer unit per unit time, and $U(I)$ the utility attached to that income if it is regarded as certain. Measure I along the horizontal axis of a graph and U along the vertical. In general, $U(I)$ will not be defined for all values of I, since there will be a lower limit to the income a consumer unit can receive, namely, a negative income equal (in absolute value) to the maximum amount that the consumer unit can lose per unit time for the period to which the utility curve refers.

Alternatives open to the consumer unit that involve no risk consist of possible incomes, say I', I'', ... The hypothesis then implies simply that the consumer unit will choose the income to which it attaches the most utility. Other things the same, we know from even casual observation that the consumer unit will in general choose the largest income: put differently, we consider it pathological for an individual literally to throw money away, yet this means of choosing a smaller income is always available. It follows that the hypothesis can rationalize riskless choices of the limited kind considered here if, and only if, the utility of money income is larger, the higher the income. Consideration of riskless choices imposes no further requirements on the utility function.

___

[25] The other factors abstracted from must not, of course, include any that cannot in fact be held constant while money income varies. For example, a higher income is desired because it enables a consumer unit to purchase a wider variety of commodities. The consumption pattern of the consumer unit must not therefore be supposed to be the same at different incomes. As another example, a higher income may mean that a consumer unit must pay a higher price for a particular commodity (e.g., medical service). Such variation in price should not be impounded in *ceteris paribus*, though price changes not necessarily associated with changes in the consumer unit's income should be.

Alternatives involving risk consist of probability distributions of possible incomes. Fortunately, it will suffice for our purpose to consider only a particularly simple kind of alternative involving risk, namely (A) a chance $a(0 < a < 1)$ of an income I_1, and a chance $(1 - a)$ of an income I_2, where for simplicity I_2 is supposed always greater than I_1. This simplification is possible because, as we shall see later, the original hypothesis implies that choices of consumer units among more complicated alternatives can be predicted from complete knowledge of their preferences among alternatives like A and a riskless alternative (B) consisting of a certain income I_0.

Since "other things" are supposed the same for alternatives A and B, the utility of the two alternatives may be taken to be functions solely of the incomes and probabilities involved and not also of attendant circumstances. The utility of alternative B is $U(I_0)$. The expected utility of A is given by

$$\bar{U}(A) = aU(I_1) + (1 - a) U(I_2).$$

According to the hypothesis, a consumer unit will choose A if $U > \bar{U}(I_0)$, will choose B if $\bar{U} < U(I_0)$, and will be indifferent between A and B if $\bar{U} = U(I_0)$.

Let $\bar{I}(A)$ be the actuarial value of A, i.e., $\bar{I}(A) = aI_1 + (1 - a)I_2$. If I_0 is equal to $\bar{I}$, the "gamble" or "insurance" is said to be "fair" since the consumer unit gets the same actuarial value whichever alternative it chooses. If, under these circumstances, the consumer unit chooses A, it shows a preference for this risk. This is to be interpreted as meaning that $\bar{U} > U(\bar{I})$ and indeed $\bar{U} - U(\bar{I})$ may be taken to measure the utility it attaches to this particular risk.[26] If the consumer unit chooses B, it shows a preference for certainty. This is to be interpreted as meaning that $\bar{U} < U(\bar{I})$. Indifference between A and B is to be interpreted as meaning that $\bar{U} = U(\bar{I})$.

---

[26] This interpretation of $\bar{U} - U(\bar{I})$ as the utility attached to a particular risk is directly relevant to a point to which von Neumann and Morgenstern and commentators on their work have given a good deal of attention, namely, whether there may "not exist in an individual a (positive or negative) utility of the mere act of 'taking a chance,' of gambling, which the use of the mathematical expectation obliterates" (von Neumann and Morgenstern, *op. cit.*, p. 28). In our view the hypothesis is better interpreted as a rather special explanation why gambling has utility or disutility to a consumer unit, and as providing a particular measure of the utility or disutility, than as a denial that gambling has utility (see *ibid.*, pp. 28, 629–632).

Let I^* be the certain income that has the same utility as A, that is, $U(I^*) = \bar{U}.$[27] Call I^* the income equivalent to A. The requirement, derived from consideration of riskless choices, that utility increase with income means that

$$\bar{U} \gtreqless U(\bar{I})$$

implies

$$I^* \gtreqless \bar{I}.$$

If I^* is greater than $\bar{I}$, the consumer unit prefers this particular risk to a certain income of the same actuarial value and would be willing to pay a maximum of $I^* - \bar{I}$ for the privilege of "gam-

Illustration of Utility Analysis of Choices Involving Risk
a, Preference for Certainty; b, Preference for Risk

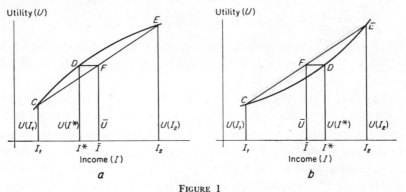

FIGURE 1

bling." If I^* is less than $\bar{I}$, the consumer unit prefers certainty and is willing to pay a maximum of $\bar{I} - I^*$ for "insurance" against this risk.

These concepts are illustrated for a consumer unit who is willing to pay for insurance $(\bar{I} > I^*)$ in Fig. 1, a, and for a consumer unit who is willing to pay for the privilege of gambling $(\bar{I} < I^*)$ in Fig. 1, b. In both figures, money income is measured along the horizontal axis, and utility along the vertical. On the

---

[27] Since U has been assumed strictly monotonic to rationalize riskless choices, there will be only one income, if any, that has the same utility as A. There will be one if U is continuous which, for simplicity, we assume to be the case throughout this paper.

horizontal axis, designate I_1 and I_2. $\bar{I}$, the actuarial value of I_1 and I_2, is then represented by a point that divides the interval I_1 to I_2 in the proportion

$$\frac{1-a}{a}\left(\text{i.e., } \frac{\bar{I}-I_1}{I_2-\bar{I}} = \frac{1-a}{a}\right).$$

Draw the utility curve (*CDE* in both figures). Connect the points $(I_1, U[I_1])$, $(I_2\ U[I_2])$ by a straight line (*CFE*). The vertical distance of this line from the horizontal axis at $\bar{I}$ is then equal to $\bar{U}$. (Since $\bar{I}$ divides the distance between I_1 and I_2 in the proportion $[1-a]/a$, F divides the vertical distance between C and E in the same proportion, so the vertical distance from F to the horizontal axis is the expected value of $U[I_1]$ and $U[I_2]$). Draw a horizontal line through F and find the income corresponding to its intersection with the utility curve (point D). This is the income the utility of which is the same as the expected utility of A, hence by definition is I^*.

In Fig. 1, *a*, the utility curve is so drawn as to make I^* less than $\bar{I}$. If the consumer unit is offered a choice between A and a certain income I_0 greater than I^*, it will choose the certain income. If this certain income I_0 were less than $\bar{I}$, the consumer unit would be paying $\bar{I}-I_0$ for certainty—in ordinary parlance it would be "buying insurance"; if the certain income were greater than $\bar{I}$, it would be being paid $I_0-\bar{I}$ for accepting certainty, even though it is willing to pay for certainty—we might say that it is "selling a gamble" rather than "buying insurance." If the consumer unit were offered a choice between A and a certain income I_0 less than I^*, it would choose A because, while it is willing to pay a price for certainty, it is being asked to pay more than the maximum amount $(\bar{I}-I^*)$ that it is willing to pay. The price of insurance has become so high that it has, as it were, been converted into a seller rather than a buyer of insurance.

In Fig. 1, *b*, the utility curve is so drawn as to make I^* greater than $\bar{I}$. If the consumer unit is offered a choice between A and a certain income I_0 less than I^*, it will choose A. If this certain income I_0 were greater than $\bar{I}$, the consumer unit would be paying $I_0-\bar{I}$ for this risk—in ordinary parlance, it would be choosing to gamble or, one might say, "to buy a gamble"; if the certain income were less than $\bar{I}$, it would be being paid $\bar{I}-I_0$ for accepting this risk even though it is willing to pay for the risk—we might say that it is "selling insurance" rather than "buying a gamble." If the consumer unit is offered a choice between A and a certain income I_0 greater than I^*, it will choose the certain income because, while it is willing to pay something for a gamble, it is not willing to pay more than $I^* - \bar{I}$. The price of the gamble has become so high that it is converted into a seller, rather than a buyer, of gambles.

It is clear that the graphical condition for a consumer unit to be willing to pay something for certainty is that the utility function be above its chord at $\bar{I}$. This is simply a direct translation of the condition that $U(\bar{I}) > \bar{U}$. Similarly, a consumer unit will be willing to pay something for a risk if the utility function is below its chord at $\bar{I}$.

The relationship between these formalized "insurance" and "gambling" situations and what are ordinarily called insurance and gambling is fairly straightforward. A consumer unit contemplating buying insurance is to be regarded as having a current income of I_2 and as being subject to a chance of losing a sum equal to $I_2 - I_1$, so that if this loss should occur its income would be reduced to I_1. It can insure against this loss by paying a premium equal to $I_2 - I_0$. The premium, in general, will be larger than $I_2 - \bar{I}$, the "loading" being equal to $\bar{I} - I_0$. Purchase of insurance therefore means accepting the certainty of an income equal to I_0 instead of a pair of alternative incomes having a higher expected value. Similarly, a consumer unit deciding whether to gamble (e.g., to purchase a lottery ticket) can be interpreted as having a current income equal to I_0. It can have a chance $(1 - a)$ of a gain equal to $I_2 - I_0$ by subjecting itself to a chance a of losing a sum equal to $I_0 - I_1$. If it gambles, the actuarial value of its income is $\bar{I}$, which in general is less than I_0. $I_0 - \bar{I}$ is the premium it is paying for the chance to gamble (the "take" of the house, or the "banker's cut").

It should be emphasized that this analysis is all an elaboration of a particular hypothesis about the way consumer units choose among alternatives involving risk. This hypothesis describes the reactions of consumer units in terms of a utility function, unique except for origin and unit of measure, which gives the utility assigned to certain incomes and which has so far been taken for

granted. Yet for choices among certain incomes only a trivial characteristic of this function is relevant, namely, that it rises with
income. The remaining characteristics of the function are relevant
only to choices among alternatives involving risk and can therefore
be inferred only from observation of such choices. The precise
manner in which these characteristics are implicit in the consumer
unit's preferences among alternatives involving risk can be indicated most easily by describing a conceptual experiment for determining the utility function.

Select any two incomes, say $500 and $1,000. Assign any arbitrary utilities to these incomes, say 0 utiles and 1 utile, respectively.
This corresponds to an arbitrary choice of origin and unit of measure. Select any intermediate income, say $600. Offer the consumer
unit the choice between (A) a chance a of $500 and $(1 - a)$ of
$1,000 or (B) a certainty of $600, varying a until the consumer unit
is indifferent between the two (i.e., until $I^* = 600). Suppose this
indifference value of a is $\frac{2}{5}$. If the hypothesis is correct, it follows
that

$$U(600) = \tfrac{2}{5}U(500) + \tfrac{3}{5}U(1000) = \tfrac{2}{5} 0 + \tfrac{3}{5} \cdot 1 = \tfrac{3}{5} = .60.$$

In this way the utility attached to every income between $500 and
$1,000 can be determined. To get the utility attached to any in-
come outside the interval $500 to $1,000, say $10,000, offer the
consumer unit a choice between (A) a chance a of $500 and
$(1 - a)$ of $10,000 or (B) a certainty of $1,000, varying a until the
consumer unit is indifferent between the two (i.e., until $I^* =$
$1,000). Suppose this indifference value of a is $\frac{4}{5}$. If the hypothesis
is correct, it follows that

$$\tfrac{4}{5}U(500) + \tfrac{1}{5}U(10,000) = U(1000),$$

or

$$\tfrac{4}{5} \cdot 0 + \tfrac{1}{5}U(10,000) = 1,$$

or

$$U(10,000) = 5.$$

In principle, the possibility of carrying out this experiment, and
the reproducibility of the results, would provide a test of the
hypothesis. For example, the consistency of behavior assumed by

the hypothesis would be contradicted if a repetition of the experiment using two initial incomes other than $500 and $1,000 yielded a utility function differing in more than origin and unit of measure from the one initially obtained.

Given a utility function obtained in this way, it is possible, if the hypothesis is correct, to compute the utility attached to (that is, the expected utility of) any set or sets of possible incomes and associated probabilities and thereby to predict which of a number of such sets will be chosen. This is the precise meaning of the statement made toward the beginning of this section that, if the hypothesis were correct, complete knowledge of the preferences of consumer units among alternatives like A and B would make it possible to predict their reactions to any other choices involving risk.

The choices a consumer unit makes that involve risk are typically far more complicated than the simple choice between A and B that we have used to elaborate the hypothesis. There are two chief sources of complication: Any particular alternative typically offers an indefinitely large number of possible incomes, and "other things" are generally not the same.

The multiplicity of possible incomes is very general: losses insured against ordinarily have more than one possible value; lotteries ordinarily have more than one prize; the possible income from a particular occupation, investment, or business enterprise may be equal to any of an indefinitely large number of values. A hypothesis that the essence of choices among the degrees of risk involved in such complex alternatives is contained in such simple choices as the choice between A and B is by no means tautological.

The hypothesis does not, of course, pretend to say anything about how consumer choices will be affected by differences in things other than degree of risk. The significance for our purposes of such differences is rather that they greatly increase the difficulty of getting evidence about reactions to differences in risk alone. Much casual experience, particularly experience bearing on what is ordinarily regarded as gambling, is likely to be misinterpreted, and erroneously regarded as contradictory to the hypothesis, if this difficulty is not explicitly recognized. In much so-called gambling the individual chooses not only to bear risk but also to participate in the mechanics of a game of chance; he buys, that is, a gamble, in our technical sense, and entertainment. We can conceive of separating these two commodities: he could buy entertainment alone by paying admission to participate in a game using valueless chips; he could buy the gamble alone by having an agent play the game of chance for him according to detailed instructions.[28] Further, insurance and gambles are often purchased in almost pure form. This is notably true of insurance. It is true also of gambling by the purchase of lottery tickets when the purchaser is not a spectator to the drawing of the winners (i.e., Irish sweepstakes tickets bought in this country or the "numbers" game), and of much stock-market speculation.

An example of behavior that would definitely contradict the assertion, contained in the hypothesis, that the same utility function can be used to explain choices that do and do not involve risk would be willingness by an individual to pay more for a gamble than the maximum amount he could win. In order to explain riskless choices it is necessary to suppose that utility increases with income. It follows that the average utility of two incomes can never exceed the utility of the larger income and hence that an individual will never be willing to pay, for example, a dollar for a chance of winning, at most, 99 cents.

More subtle observation would be required to contradict the assertion that the reactions of persons to complicated gambles can be inferred from their reactions to simple gambles. For example, suppose an individual refuses an opportunity to toss a coin for a dollar and also to toss a coin for two dollars but then accepts an opportunity to toss two coins in succession, the first to determine whether the second toss is to be for one dollar or for two dollars. This behavior would definitely contradict the hypothesis. On the hypothesis, the utility of the third gamble is an average of the utility of the first two. His refusal of the first two indicates that

---

[28] It does not, of course, follow that the price an individual is willing to pay for the joint commodity is simply the sum of the prices he is willing to pay for them separately. Indeed, it may well be the possible existence of such a difference that people have in mind when they speak of a "specific utility of gambling."

each of them has a lower utility than the alternative of not gambling; hence, if the hypothesis were correct, the third should have a lower utility than the same alternative, and he should refuse it.

4. Restrictions on Utility Function Required to Rationalize Observable Behavior

The one restriction imposed on the utility function in the preceding section is that total utility increase with the size of money income. This restriction was imposed to rationalize the first of the facts listed below. We are now ready to see whether the behavior described in section 2 can be rationalized by the hypothesis, and, if so, what additional restrictions this behavior imposes on the utility function. To simplify the task, we shall take as a summary of the essential features of the behavior described in section 2 the following five statements, alleged to be facts: (1) consumer units prefer larger to smaller certain incomes; (2) low-income consumer units buy, or are willing to buy, insurance; (3) low-income consumer units buy, or are willing to buy, lottery tickets; (4) many low-income consumer units buy, or are willing to buy, both insurance and lottery tickets; (5) lotteries typically have more than one prize.

These particular statements are selected not because they are the most important in and of themselves but because they are convenient to handle and the restrictions imposed to rationalize them turn out to be sufficient to rationalize all the behavior described in section 2.

It is obvious from Fig. 1 and our discussion of it that if the utility function were everywhere convex from above (for utility functions with a continuous derivative, if the marginal utility of money does not increase for any income), the consumer unit, on our hypothesis, would be willing to enter into any fair insurance plan but would be unwilling to pay anything in excess of the actuarial value for any gamble. If the utility function were everywhere concave from above (for functions with a continuous derivative, if the marginal utility of money does not diminish for any income), the consumer unit would be willing to enter into any fair gamble but would be unwilling to pay anything in excess of the actuarial value for insurance against any risk.

It follows that our hypothesis can rationalize statement 2, the

purchase of insurance by low-income consumer units, only if the
utility functions of the corresponding units are not everywhere
concave from above; that it can rationalize statement 3, the purchase of lottery tickets by low-income consumer units, only if the
utility functions of the corresponding units are not everywhere
convex from above; and that it can rationalize statement 4, the
purchase of both insurance and lottery tickets by low-income consumer units, only if the utility functions of the corresponding units
are neither everywhere concave from above nor everywhere convex
from above.

The simplest utility function (with a continuous derivative)
that can rationalize all three statements simultaneously is one that
has a segment convex from above followed by a segment concave
from above and no other segments.[29] The convex segment must
precede the concave segment because of the kind of insurance and
of gambling the low-income consumer units are said to engage in:
a chord from the existing income to a lower income must be below
the utility function to rationalize the purchase of insurance against
the risk of loss; a chord from the immediate neighborhood of the
existing income to a higher income must be above the utility function at the existing income to rationalize the purchase for a small
sum of a small chance of a large gain.[30]

Figure 2 illustrates a utility function satisfying these requirements. Let this utility function be for a low-income consumer unit
whose current income is in the initial convex segment, say at the
point designated I^* If some risk should arise of incurring a loss,
the consumer unit would clearly (on our hypothesis) be willing
to insure against the loss (if it did not have to pay too much
"loading") since a chord from the utility curve at I^* to the utility
curve at the lower income that would be the consequence of the
actual occurrence of the loss would everywhere be below the utility
function. The consumer unit would not be willing to engage in

---

[29] A kink or a jump in the utility function could rationalize either the
gambling or the insurance. For example, the utility function could be composed of two convex or two concave segments joined in a kink. There is no
essential loss in generality in neglecting such cases, as we shall do from here on,
since one can always think of rounding the kink ever so slightly.

[30] If there are more than two segments and a continuous derivative, a
convex segment necessarily precedes a concave segment.

small gambling. But suppose it is offered a fair gamble of the kind represented by a lottery involving a small chance of winning a relatively large sum equal to $I_2 - I^*$ and a large chance of losing a relatively small sum equal to $I^* - I_1$. The consumer unit would clearly prefer the gamble, since the expected utility (I^*G) is greater than the utility of I^*. Indeed it would be willing to pay any premium up to $I^* - \bar{I}$ for the privilege of gambling; that is, even if the expected value of the gamble were almost as low as $\bar{I}$, it would accept the gamble in preference to a certainty of receiving I^*. The

Illustration of Utility Function Consistent with
Willingness of a Low-Income Consumer Unit
Both to Purchase Insurance and to Gamble

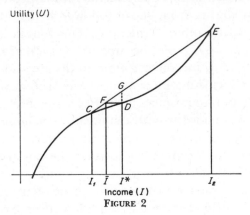

Utility (U)

Income (I)

FIGURE 2

utility curve in Fig. 2 is therefore clearly consistent with statements 2, 3, and 4.

These statements refer solely to the behavior of relatively low-income consumer units. It is tempting to seek to restrict further the shape of the utility function, and to test the restrictions so far imposed, by appealing to casual observation of the behavior of relatively high-income consumer units.[31] It does not seem desirable

[31] For example, a high-income consumer unit that had a utility function like that in Fig. 2 and a current income of I_2 would be willing to participate in a wide variety of gambling, including the purchase of lottery tickets; it would be unwilling to insure against losses that had a small expected value (i.e., involved payment of a small premium) though it might be willing to insure against losses that had a large expected value. Consequently, unwillingness of relatively high-income consumer units to purchase lottery tickets, or willingness to purchase low-premium insurance, would contradict the utility function of Fig. 2 and require the imposition of further restrictions.

to do so, however, for two major reasons: (1) it is far more difficult to accumulate reliable information about the behavior of relatively high-income consumer units than about the behavior of the more numerous low-income units; (2) perhaps even more important, the progressive income tax so affects the terms under which the relatively high-income consumer units purchase insurance or gamble as to make evidence on their behavior hard to interpret for our purposes.[32] Therefore, instead of using observations about the behavior of relatively high-income consumer units, we shall seek to learn more about the upper end of the curve by using statement 5, the tendency for lotteries to have more than one prize.

In order to determine the implications of this statement for the utility function, we must investigate briefly the economics of lotteries. Consider an entrepreneur conducting a lottery and seek-

---

[32] The effect of the income tax, already referred to in n. 16 above, depends greatly on the specific provisions of the tax law and of the insurance or gambling plan. For example, if an uninsured loss is deductible in computing taxable income (as is loss of an owned home by fire under the federal income tax) while the premium for insuring against the loss is not (as a fire-insurance premium on an owned home is not), the expected value of the loss is less to the consumer unit than to the firm selling insurance. A premium equal to the actuarial value of the loss to the insurance company then exceeds the actuarial value of the loss to the consumer unit. That is, the government in effect pays part of the loss but none of the premium. On the other hand, if the premium is deductible (as a health-insurance premium may be), while an uninsured loss is not (as the excess of medical bills over $2,500 for a family is not), the net premium to the consumer unit is less than the premium received by the insurance company. Similarly, gambling gains in excess of gambling losses are taxable under the federal income tax, while gambling losses in excess of gambling gains are not deductible. The special treatment of capital gains and losses under the existing United States federal income tax adds still further complications.

Even if both the premium and the uninsured loss are deductible, or a gain taxable and the corresponding loss deductible, the income tax may change the terms because of the progressive rates. The tax-saving from a large loss may be a smaller fraction of the loss than the tax payable on the gain is of the gain.

These comments clearly apply not only to insurance and gambling proper but also to other economic decisions involving risk—the purchase of securities, choice of occupation or business, etc. The neglect of these considerations has frequently led to the erroneous belief that a progressive income tax does not affect the allocation of resources and is in this way fundamentally different from excise taxes.

ing to maximize his income from it. For simplicity, suppose that
he conducts the lottery by deciding in advance the number of
tickets to offer and then auctioning them off at the highest price
he can get.[33] Aside from advertising and the like, the variables at
his disposal are the terms of the lottery: the number of tickets to
sell, the total amount to offer as prizes (which together, of course,
determine the actuarial value of a ticket), and the structure of
prizes to offer. For any given values of the first two, the optimum
structure of prizes is clearly that which maximizes the price he can
get per ticket or, what is the same thing, the excess of the price of
a ticket over its actuarial value—the "loading" per ticket.

In the discussion of Fig. 2, it was noted that $I^* - \bar{I}$ was the
maximum amount in excess of the actuarial value that the corresponding consumer unit would pay for a gamble involving a
chance $(1 - a)$ of winning $I_2 - I^*$ and a chance a of losing $I^* - I_1$.
This gamble is equivalent to a lottery offering a chance $(1 - a)$ of a
prize $I_2 - I_1$ in return for the purchase of a ticket at a price of
$I^* - I_1$, the chance of winning the prize being such that $\bar{I} - I_1$ is
the actuarial worth of a ticket (i.e., is equal to $[1 - a] \times [I_2 - I_1]$).
If the consumer unit won the prize, its net winnings would be
$I_2 - I^*$, since it would have to subtract the cost of the ticket from
the gross prize. The problem of the entrepreneur, then, is to choose
the structure of prizes that will maximize $I^* - \bar{I}$ for a given actuarial value of a ticket, that is, for a given value of $\bar{I} - I_1$. Changes
in the structure of prizes involve changes in $I_2 - I_1$. If there is a
single prize, $I_2 - I_1$ is equal to the total amount to be distributed
($[1 - a]$ is equal to the reciprocal of the number of tickets). If there
are two equal prizes, $I_2 - I_1$ is cut in half ($[1 - a]$ is then equal to
twice the reciprocal of the number of tickets). Suppose Fig. 2
referred to this latter situation in which there were two equal
prizes, I^* on the diagram designating both the current income of
the consumer unit and the income equivalent to the lottery. If the
price and actuarial worth of the ticket were kept unchanged, but
a single prize was substituted for the two prizes (and $[1 - a]$ correspondingly reduced), the gamble would clearly become more

---

[33] This was, in fact, the way in which the British government conducted
many of its official lotteries. It frequently auctioned off the tickets to lottery
dealers, who served as the means of distributing the tickets to the public (see
Ewen, *op. cit.*, pp. 234–240).

attractive to the consumer unit. I_2 would move to the right, the chord connecting $U(I_1)$ and $U(I_2)$ would rotate upward, U would increase, and the consumer unit would be paying less than the maximum amount it was willing to pay. The price of the ticket could accordingly be increased; that is, I_2, $\bar{I}$, and I_1 could be moved to the left until the I^* for the new gamble were equal to the consumer unit's current income (the I^* for the old gamble). The optimum structure of prizes clearly consists therefore of a single prize, since this makes $I_2 - I_1$ as large as possible.

Statement 5, that lotteries typically have more than one prize, is

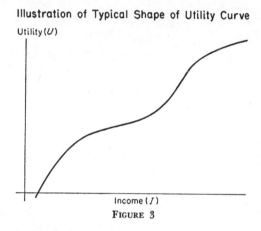

Illustration of Typical Shape of Utility Curve

FIGURE 3

therefore inconsistent with the utility function of Fig. 2. This additional fact can be rationalized by terminating the utility curve with a suitable convex segment. This yields a utility curve like that drawn in Fig. 3. With such a utility curve, $I^* - I$ would be a maximum at the point at which a chord from $U(I_1)$ was tangent to the utility curve, and a larger prize would yield a smaller value of $I^* - \bar{I}$.[34]

---

[34] An additional convex segment guarantees that there will always exist current incomes of the consumer unit for which (a) attractive gambles exist and (b) the optimum prize for attractive gambles has a maximum. It does not guarantee that b will be true for every income for which attractive gambles exist. The condition on the current income that attractive gambles exist is that the tangent to the utility curve at the current income be below the utility curve for some income (this argument, like many in later technical footnotes, holds not only for the utility function of Fig. 3 but for any differentiable utility function). A single prize will be the optimum, no matter what the amount distributed in prizes or the fixed actuarial worth of the prize if, and

A utility curve like that drawn in Fig. 3 is the simplest one consistent with the five statements listed at the outset of this section.

5. A DIGRESSION

It seems well to digress at this point to consider two questions that, while not strictly relevant to our main theme, are likely to occur to many readers: first, is not the hypothesis patently unrealistic; second, can any plausible interpretation be given to the rather peculiar utility function of Fig. 3?

a. The Descriptive "Realism" of the Hypothesis

An objection to the hypothesis just presented that is likely to be raised by many, if not most, readers is that it conflicts with the way human beings actually behave and choose. Is it not patently unrealistic to suppose that individuals consult a wiggly utility curve before gambling or buying insurance, that they know the odds involved in the gambles or insurance plans open to them, that they can compute the expected utility of a gamble or insurance plan, and that they base their decision on the size of the expected utility?

While entirely natural and understandable, this objection is not strictly relevant. The hypothesis does not assert that individuals explicitly or consciously calculate and compare expected utilities. Indeed, it is not at all clear what such an assertion would mean or how it could be tested. The hypothesis asserts rather that, in making a particular class of decisions, individuals behave *as if* they calculated and compared expected utility and *as if* they knew the odds. The validity of this assertion does not depend on whether individuals know the precise odds, much less on whether they say that they calculate and compare expected utilities or think that they do, or whether it appears to others that they do, or whether psychologists can uncover any evidence that they do, but solely on whether it yields sufficiently accurate predictions about the class of decisions with which the hypothesis deals. Stated

---

only if, every chord from the utility curve at the current income to the utility of a higher income is everywhere above the utility curve. A particular, and somewhat interesting, class of utility functions for which *b* will be true for every income for which *a* is true is the class for which utility approaches a finite limit as income increases.

differently, the test by results is the only possible method of determining whether the *as if* statement is or is not a sufficiently good approximation to reality for the purpose at hand.

A simple example may help to clarify the point at issue. Consider the problem of predicting, before each shot, the direction of travel of a billiard ball hit by an expert billiard player. It would be possible to construct one or more mathematical formulas that would give the directions of travel that would score points and, among these, would indicate the one (or more) that would leave the balls in the best positions. The formulas might, of course, be extremely complicated, since they would necessarily take account of the location of the balls in relation to one another and to the cushions and of the complicated phenomena introduced by "english." Nonetheless, it seems not at all unreasonable that excellent predictions would be yielded by the hypothesis that the billiard player made his shots *as if* he knew the formulas, could estimate accurately by eye the angles, etc., describing the location of the balls, could make lightning calculations from the formulas, and could then make the ball travel in the direction indicated by the formulas. It would in no way disprove or contradict the hypothesis, or weaken our confidence in it, if it should turn out that the billiard player had never studied any branch of mathematics and was utterly incapable of making the necessary calculations: unless he was capable in some way of reaching approximately the same result as that obtained from the formulas, he would not in fact be likely to be an expert billiard player.

The same considerations are relevant to our utility hypothesis. Whatever the psychological mechanism whereby individuals make choices, these choices appear to display some consistency, which can apparently be described by our utility hypothesis. This hypothesis enables predictions to be made about phenomena on which there is not yet reliable evidence. The hypothesis cannot be declared invalid for a particular class of behavior until a prediction about that class proves false. No other test of its validity is decisive.

b. A Possible Interpretation of the Utility Function

A possible interpretation of the utility function of Fig. 3 is to regard the two convex segments as corresponding to qualitatively different socioeconomic levels, and the concave segment to the transition between the two levels. On this interpretation, increases in income that raise the relative position of the consumer unit in its own class but do not shift the unit out of its class yield diminishing marginal utility, while increases that shift it into a new class, that give it a new social and economic status, yield increasing marginal utility. An unskilled worker may prefer the certainty of an income about the same as that of the majority of unskilled workers to an actuarially fair gamble that at best would make him one of the most prosperous unskilled workers and at worst one of the least prosperous. Yet he may jump at an actuarially fair gamble that offers a small chance of lifting him out of the class of unskilled workers and into the "middle" or "upper" class, even though it is far more likely than the preceding gamble to make him one of the least prosperous unskilled workers. Men will and do take great risks to distinguish themselves, even when they know what the risks are. May not the concave segment of the utility curve of Fig. 3 translate the economic counterpart of this phenomenon appropriately?

A number of additions to the hypothesis are suggested by this interpretation. In the first place, may there not be more than two qualitatively distinguishable socioeconomic classes? If so, might not each be reflected by a convex segment in the utility function? At the moment, there seems to be no observed behavior that requires the introduction of additional convex segments, so it seems undesirable and unnecessary to complicate the hypothesis further. It may well be, however, that it will be necessary to add such segments to account for behavior revealed by further empirical evidence. In the second place, if different segments of the curve correspond to different socioeconomic classes, should not the dividing points between the segments occur at roughly the same income for different consumer units in the same community? If they did, the fruitfulness of the hypothesis would be greatly extended. Not only could the general shape of the utility function be supposed typical; so also could the actual income separating the various segments. The initial convex segment could be described as applicable to "relatively low-income consumer units" and the terminal convex segment as applicable to "relatively high-income consumer units"; and the groups so designated could be identified by the actual income or wealth of different consumer units.

Interpreting the different segments of the curve as corresponding to different socioeconomic classes would, of course, still permit wide variation among consumer units in the exact shape and height of the curve. In addition, it would not be necessary to suppose anything more than rough similarity in the location of the incomes separating the various segments. Different socioeconomic classes are not sharply demarcated from one another; each merges into the next by imperceptible gradations (which, of course, accounts for the income range encompassed by the concave segment); and the generally accepted dividing line between classes will vary from time to time, place to place, and consumer unit to consumer unit. Finally, it is not necessary that every consumer unit have a utility curve like that in Fig. 3. Some may be inveterate gamblers; others, inveterately cautious. It is enough that many consumer units have such a utility curve.

6. Further Implications of Hypothesis

To return to our main theme, we have two tasks yet to perform: first, to show that the utility function of Fig. 3 is consistent with those features of the behavior described in section 2 not used in deriving it; second, to suggest additional implications of the hypothesis capable of providing a test of it.

The chief generalization of section 2 not so far used is that people must in general be paid a premium to induce them to bear moderate risks instead of either small or large risks. Is this generalization consistent with the utility function of Fig. 3?

It clearly is for a consumer unit whose income places it in the initial convex segment. Such a relatively low-income consumer unit will be willing to pay something more than the actuarial value for insurance against any kind of risk that may arise; it will be averse to small fair gambles; it may be averse to all fair gambles; if not, it will be attracted by fair gambles that offer a small chance of a large gain; the attractiveness of such gambles, with a given possible loss and actuarial value, will initially increase as the size of the possible gain increases and will eventually decrease.[35] Such

---

[35] The willingness of a consumer unit in the initial convex segment to pay something more than the actuarial value for insurance against any kind of risk follows from the fact that a chord connecting the utility of its current income with the utility of any lower income to which it might be reduced by

consumer units therefore prefer either certainty or a risk that offers a small chance of a large gain to a risk that offers the possibility of moderate gains or losses. They will therefore have to be paid a premium to induce them to undertake such moderate risks.

The generalization is clearly false for a consumer unit whose income places it in the concave segment. Such an "intermediate-income" consumer unit will be attracted by every small fair gamble; it may be attracted by every fair gamble; it may be averse to all fair insurance; if not, it will be attracted by insurance against relatively large losses.[36] Such consumer units will therefore be willing to pay a premium in order to assume moderate risks.

---

the risk in question will everywhere be below the utility curve. The expected utility is therefore less than the utility of the expected income.

To analyze the reaction of such a consumer unit to different gambles, consider the limiting case in which the gamble is fair, i.e., $\bar{I} = I_0$. $\bar{I}$ then is both the expected income of the consumer unit if it takes the gamble and its actual income if it does not (i.e., its current income). The possible gains (and associated probabilities) that will be attractive to the unit for a given value of I_1 (i.e., a given possible loss) can be determined by drawing a straight line through $U(I_1)$ and $U(\bar{I})$. All values of $I_2 > \bar{I}$ for which $U(I_2)$ is greater than the ordinate of the extended straight line will be attractive; no others will be.

Since $\bar{I}$ is assumed to be in the first convex segment, there will always exist some values of $I_2 > \bar{I}$ for which $U(I_2)$ is less than the ordinate of the extended straight line. This is the basis for the statement that the consumer unit will be averse to small gambles.

Consider the line that touches the curve at only two points and is nowhere below the utility curve. Call the income at the first of the points at which it touches the curve, which may be the lowest possible income, I', and the income at the second point, I''. The consumer unit will be averse to all gambles if its income $(I_0 = \bar{I})$ is equal to or less than I'. This follows from the fact that a tangent to the curve at $\bar{I}$ will then be steeper than the "double tangent" and will intersect the latter prior to I'; a chord from $\bar{I}$ to a lower income will be even steeper. This is the basis for the statement that the consumer unit may be averse to all gambles.

If the income is above I', there will always be some attractive gambles. These will offer a small chance of a large gain. The statement about the changing attractiveness of the gamble as the size of the possible gain changes follows from the analysis in section 4 of the conditions under which it would be advantageous to have a single prize in a lottery.

[36] Consider the tangent to the utility curve at the income the consumer unit would have if it did not take the gamble $(\bar{I} = I_0)$. If this income is in the concave section, the tangent will be below the utility curve at least for an interval of incomes surrounding $\bar{I}$. A chord connecting any two points of

The generalization is partly true, partly false, for a consumer unit whose income places it in the terminal convex segment. Such a relatively high-income consumer unit will be willing to insure against any small possible loss and may be attracted to every fair insurance plan; the only insurance plans it may be averse to are plans involving rather large losses; it may be averse to all fair gambles; if not, it will be attracted by gambles that involve a reasonably sure, though fairly small, gain, with a small possibility of a sizable loss; it will be averse to gambles of the lottery variety.[37] These consumer units therefore prefer certainty to moderate risks; in this respect they conform to the generalization. However, they may prefer moderate risks to extreme risks, though these adjectives hardly suffice to characterize the rather complex pattern of risk preferences implied for high-income consumer units by a utility curve like that of Fig. 3. Nonetheless, in this respect the implied behavior of the high-income consumer units is either neutral or contrary to the generalization.

Our hypothesis does not therefore lead inevitably to a rate of return higher to uses of resources involving moderate risk than to uses involving little or much risk. It leads to a rate of return higher for uses involving moderate risk than for uses involving little risk only if consumer units in the two convex segments outweigh in importance, for the resource use in question, consumer units in the concave segment.[38] Similarly, it leads to a rate of return higher for uses involving moderate risk than for uses

---

the utility curve on opposite sides of $\bar{I}$ and within this interval will always be above the utility curve at $\bar{I}$ (i.e., the expected utility will be above the utility of the expected income), so these gambles will be attractive. The tangent may lie below the utility curve for all incomes. In this case, every fair gamble will be attractive. The unit will be averse to insuring against a loss, whatever the chance of its occurring, if a chord from the current income to the lower income to which it would be reduced by the loss is everywhere above the utility curve. This will surely be true for small losses and may be true for all possible losses.

[37] These statements follow directly from considerations like those in the two preceding footnotes.

[38] This statement is deliberately vague. The actual relative rates of return will depend not only on the conditions of demand for risks of different kinds but also on the conditions of supply, and both would have to be taken into account in a comprehensive statement.

involving much risk only if consumer units in the initial convex segment outweigh in importance consumer units in both the concave and the terminal convex segments—though this may be a more stringent condition than is necessary in view of the uncertainty about the exact role of consumer units in the terminal convex segment.

This relative distribution of consumer units among the various segments could be considered an additional restriction that would have to be imposed to rationalize the alleged higher rate of return to moderately risky uses of resources. It is not clear, however, that it need be so considered, since there are two independent lines of reasoning that, taken together, establish something of a presumption that relatively few consumer units are in the concave segment.

One line of reasoning is based on the interpretation of the utility function suggested in section 5b above. If the concave segment is a border line between two qualitatively different social classes, one would expect relatively few consumer units to be between the two classes.

The other line of reasoning is based on the implications of the hypothesis for the relative stability of the economic status of consumer units in the different segments. Units in the intermediate segment are tempted by every small gamble and at least some large ones. If opportunities are available, they will be continually subjecting themselves to risk. In consequence, they are likely to move out of the segment; upwards, if they are lucky; downwards, if they are not. Consumer units in the two convex segments, on the other hand, are less likely to move into the intermediate segment. The gambles that units in the initial segment accept will rarely pay off and, when they do, are likely to shift them all the way into the terminal convex segment. The gambles that units in the terminal segment accept will rarely involve losses and, when they do, may shift them all the way into the lower segment. Under these conditions, maintenance of a stable distribution of the population among the three segments would require that the two convex segments contain many more individuals than the concave segment. These considerations, while persuasive, are not, of course, conclusive. Opportunities to assume risks may not exist. More important, the status of consumer units is determined not alone by the outcome of risks deliberately assumed but also by random events over which they cannot choose and have no control; and it is conceivable that these random events might be distributed in such a way that their main effect was to multiply the number in the concave segment.

The absolute number of persons in the various segments will count most for choices among the uses of human resources; wealth will count most for choices among uses of nonhuman resources.[39] In consequence, one might expect that the premium for bearing moderate risks instead of large risks would be greater for occupations than for investments. Indeed, for investments, the differential might in some cases be reversed, since the relatively high-income consumer units (those in the terminal segment) count for more in wealth than in numbers and they may prefer moderate to extreme risks.

In judging the implications of our hypothesis for the market as a whole, we have found it necessary to consider separately its implications for different income groups. These offer additional possibilities of empirical test. Perhaps the most fruitful source of data would be the investment policies of different income groups.

It was noted in section 2 that, although many persons with low incomes are apparently willing to buy extremely speculative stocks, the low-income group receives the bulk of its property income in the form of interest and rents. These observations are clearly consistent with our hypothesis. Relatively high-income groups might be expected, on our hypothesis, to prefer bonds and relatively safe stocks. They might be expected to avoid the more speculative common stocks but to be attracted to higher-grade preferred stocks, which pay a higher nominal rate of return than high-grade bonds to compensate for a small risk of capital loss. Intermediate income groups might be expected to hold relatively large shares of their assets in moderately speculative common stocks and to furnish a disproportionate fraction of entrepreneurs.

Of course, any empirical study along these lines will have to take into account, as noted above, the effect of the progressive

---

[39] This distinction requires qualification because of the need for capital to enter some types of occupations and the consequent existence of "noncompeting groups"; see Milton Friedman and Simon Kuznets, *Income from Independent Professional Practice* (New York, National Bureau of Economic Research, 1945), Chap. III, Sec. 3; Chap. IV, Sec. 2.

income tax in modifying the terms of investment. The current United States federal income tax has conflicting effects: the progressive rates discourage risky investments; the favored treatment of capital gains encourages them. In addition, such a study will have to consider the risk of investments as a group, rather than of individual investments, since the rich may be in a position to "average" risks.

Another implication referred to above that may be susceptible of empirical test, and the last one we shall cite, is the implied difference in the stability of the relative income status of various economic groups. The unattractiveness of small risks to both high- and low-income consumer units would tend to give them a relatively stable status. By contrast, suppose the utility curve had no terminal convex segment but was like the curve of Fig. 2. Low-income consumer units would still have a relatively stable status: their willingness to take gambles at long odds would pay off too seldom to shift many from one class to another. High-income consumer units would not. They would then take almost any gamble, and those who had high incomes today almost certainly would not have high incomes tomorrow. The average period from "shirt sleeves to shirt sleeves" would be far shorter than "three generations."[40] Unlike the other two groups, the middle-income class might be expected to display considerable instability of relative income status.[41]

7. Conclusion

A plausible generalization of the available empirical evidence on the behavior of consumer units in choosing among alternatives

---

[40] We did not use the absence of such instability to derive the upper convex segment because of the difficulty of allowing for the effect of the income tax.

[41] The existing data on stability of relative income status are too meager to contradict or to confirm this implication. In their study of professional incomes Friedman and Kuznets found that relative income status was about equally stable at all income levels. However, this study is hardly relevant, since it was for homogeneous occupational groups that would tend to fall in a single one of the classes considered here. Mendershausen's analysis along similar lines for family incomes in 1929 and 1933 is inconclusive. See Friedman and Kuznets, *op. cit.*, Chap. VII; Horst Mendershausen, *Changes in Income Distribution during the Great Depression* (New York, National Bureau of Economic Research, 1946), Chap. III.

open to them is provided by the hypothesis that a consumer unit (generally a family, sometimes an individual) behaves as if

1. It had a consistent set of preferences;

2. These preferences could be completely described by attaching a numerical value—to be designated "utility"—to alternatives each of which is regarded as certain;

3. The consumer unit chose among alternatives not involving risk that one which has the largest utility;

4. It chose among alternatives involving risk that one for which the expected utility (as contrasted with the utility of the expected income) is largest;

5. The function describing the utility of money income had in general the following properties:

a) Utility rises with income, i.e., marginal utility of money income everywhere positive;

b) It is convex from above below some income, concave between that income and some larger income, and convex for all higher incomes, i.e., diminishing marginal utility of money income for incomes below some income, increasing marginal utility of money income for incomes between that income and some larger income, and diminishing marginal utility of money income for all higher incomes;

6. Most consumer units tend to have incomes that place them in the segments of the utility function for which marginal utility of money income diminishes.

Points 1, 2, 3, and 5a of this hypothesis arc implicit in the orthodox theory of choice; point 4 is an ancient idea recently revived and given new content by von Neumann and Morgenstern; and points 5b and 6 are the consequence of the attempt in this paper to use this idea to rationalize existing knowledge about the choices people make among alternatives involving risk.

Point 5b is inferred from the following phenomena: (a) low-income consumer units buy, or are willing to buy, insurance; (b) low-income consumer units buy, or are willing to buy, lottery tickets; (c) many consumer units buy, or are willing to buy, both insurance and lottery tickets; (d) lotteries typically have more than one prize. These statements are taken as a summary of the essential features of observed behavior not because they are the most important features in and of themselves but because they are convenient to handle and the restrictions imposed to rationalize them turn out to be sufficient to rationalize all the behavior described in section 2 of this paper.

A possible interpretation of the various segments of the utility curve specified in 5b is that the segments of diminishing marginal utility correspond to socioeconomic classes, the segment of increasing marginal utility to a transitional stage between a lower and a higher socioeconomic class. On this interpretation the boundaries of the segments should be roughly similar for different people in the same community; and this is one of several independent lines of reasoning leading to point 6.

This hypothesis has implications for behavior, in addition to those used in deriving it, that are capable of being contradicted by observable data. In particular, the fundamental supposition that a single utility curve can generalize both riskless choices and choices involving risk would be contradicted if (a) individuals were observed to choose the larger of two certain incomes offered to them but (b) individuals were willing to pay more than the largest possible gain for the privilege of bearing risk. The supposition that individuals seek to maximize expected utility would be contradicted if individuals' reactions to complicated gambles could not be inferred from their reactions to simple ones. The particular shape of the utility curve specified in 5b would be contradicted by any of a large number of observations, for example, (a) general willingness of individuals, whatever their income, who buy insurance against small risks to enter into small fair gambles under circumstances under which they are not also buying "entertainment," (b) the converse of a, namely an unwillingness to engage in small fair gambles by individuals who are not willing to buy fair insurance against small risks, (c) a higher average rate of return to uses of resources involving little risk than to uses involving a moderate amount of risk when other things are the same, (d) a concentration of investment portfolios of relatively low-income groups on speculative (but not highly speculative) investments or of relatively high-income groups on either moderately or highly speculative investments, (e) great instability in the relative income status of high-income groups or of low-income groups as a consequence of a propensity to engage in speculative activities.

4

WHAT DO STATISTICAL "DEMAND CURVES" SHOW? [*][1]

By E. J. Working||

Many questions of practical importance hinge upon the elasticity of demand, or of demand and supply. The economist can answer them only in a vague and indefinite manner, because he does not know the nature of the demand curve. What will be the effect of a five-million-bushel increase in the corn crop upon the price of corn and of hogs? What will be the effect of a tariff on imports and prices; on the protected industry; on the balance of international payments? How large an indemnity can Germany pay? The answers all depend in greater or less measure upon the elasticity of demand of the various commodities in question.

Such are the needs of the theorist, and in recent years a great deal of attention has been turned to the construction of statistical demand curves. Beef, corn, cotton, hay, hogs, pig iron, oats, potatoes, sweet potatoes, sugar, and wheat are on the list of commodities for which we have statements of the "law of demand." Many economists have been skeptical, while others have been enthusiastic, on the significance of such demand curves. In consequence of this divergence of opinion, it may be well to consider some of the theoretical aspects of what the demand curves con-

---

* The Quarterly Journal of Economics, Vol. XLI (1927), pp. 212–235. Reprinted, by the courtesy of Harvard University Press and the author, with typographical corrections.

|| University of Illinois.

[1] The author is indebted to those who have read the manuscript while it was in various stages of completion. The criticisms of Professors Allyn A. Young, F. W. Taussig, and W. L. Crum of Harvard University, of Dr. C. O. Hardy of the Institute of Economics, and of Dr. H. Working of the Food Research Institute, have been particularly helpful. The original charts were drawn by Mr. R. P. Ward of the Institute of Economics.

structed by our statistical experts may be expected to show. Do
they correspond to the demand curves of economic theory? If so,
it would seem that they represent something tangible by which
our theories may be tested and turned to better account.[2]

Among the statistical studies of demand that have been made,
there are cases in which the same commodity has been studied by
more than one investigator, and their results indicate varying degrees of elasticity of demand. But despite this, in all but one of
the cases the demand curves have been negatively inclined—they
have been in accord with Marshall's "one general *law of demand.*"[3]

In the case of pig iron, however, Professor H. L. Moore finds
a "law of demand" which is not in accord with Marshall's universal rule. He finds that the greater the quantity of pig iron sold,
the higher will be the prices.[4] If this is the nature of the statistical
demand curve for pig iron, surely statistical demand curves must

---

[2] Among the leading discussions of the subject, the following may be noted:

Lehfeldt, R. A., "The Elasticity of Demand for Wheat," *The Economic
Journal,* June 1914, pp. 212–217.

Moore, Henry L., *Economic Cycles: Their Law and Cause* (1914), Chaps.
4 and 5; *Forecasting the Yield and Price of Cotton* (1917), Chap. 5; "Empirical
Laws of Demand and Supply and the Flexibility of Prices," *Political Science
Quarterly,* December 1919; "Elasticity of Demand and Flexibility of Prices,"
Journal of the American Statistical Association, March 1922; "Partial Elasticity
of Demand," *The Quarterly Journal of Economics,* May 1926; "A Moving
Equilibrium of Demand and Supply," *The Quarterly Journal of Economics,*
May 1925.

Persons, Warren M., "The Correlation of Economic Statistics," *Publications of the American Statistical Association,* December 1910, pp. 287–322.

Schultz, Henry, "The Statistical Law of Demand," *The Journal of Political
Economy,* October and December 1925.

Working, Holbrook, "The Statistical Determination of Demand Curves,"
The Quarterly Journal of Economics, August 1925.

In this list no attempt is made to include the many studies of demand of
specific articles. A bibliography of the latter is given by Holbrook Working,
The Quarterly Journal of Economics, August 1925, pp. 539–543.

[3] "There is then one general *law of demand:*—The greater the amount to
be sold, the smaller must be the price at which it is offered in order to find
purchasers; or, in other words, the amount demanded increases with a fall in
price and diminishes with a rise in price." Alfred Marshall, *Principles of
Economics* (8th ed.), p. 99.

[4] Henry Ludwell Moore, *Economic Cycles: Their Law and Cause* (1914),
p. 114.

be of a very different sort from the demand curves of traditional economic theory!

Professor Moore holds that the statistical "law of demand" at which he arrives is a *dynamic* law, while that of theory is a *static* law. He says in part: "The doctrine of the uniformity of the demand function is an idol of the static state—the method of *cæteris paribus*—which has stood in the way of the successful treatment of dynamic problems." If it be true that statistical demand curves and the demand curves of theory differ so utterly from each other, of what value is statistical analysis to the theorist—of what value is economic theory to the statistical analyst? It would seem that so far as the study of demand is concerned, the statistical analyst and the economic theorist are on paths so divergent as to be wholly out of touch with each other. Before we accede to such a discouraging thought, let us examine a little more closely the nature of statistical demand curves as they may be viewed in the light of economic theory.

Let us first consider in what way statistical demand curves are constructed. While both the nature of the data used and the technique of analysis vary, the basic data consist of corresponding prices and quantities. That is, if a given quantity refers to the amount of a commodity sold, produced, or consumed in the year 1910, the corresponding price is the price which is taken to be typical for the year 1910. These corresponding quantities and prices may be for a period of a month, a year, or any other length of time which is feasible; and, as has already been indicated, the quantities may refer to amounts produced, sold, or consumed. The technique of analysis consists of such operations as fitting the demand curve, and adjusting the original data to remove, in so far as is possible, the effect of disturbing influences. For a preliminary understanding of the way in which curves are constructed, we need not be concerned with the differences in technique; but whether the quantities used are the amounts produced, sold, or consumed is a matter of greater significance, which must be kept in mind.

For the present, let us confine our attention to the type of study which uses for its data the quantities which have been sold in the market. In general, the method of constructing demand curves of this sort is to take corresponding prices and quantities, plot them, and draw a curve which will fit as nearly as possible all the plotted points. Suppose, for example, we wish to determine the demand curve for beef. First, we find out how many pounds of beef were sold in a given month and what was the average price. We do the same for all the other months of the period over which our study is to extend, and plot our data with quantities as abscissas and corresponding prices as ordinates. Next we draw a curve to fit the points. This is our demand curve.

In the actual construction of demand curves, certain refinements necessary in order to get satisfactory results are introduced.[5] The purpose of these is to correct the data so as to remove the effect of various extraneous and complicating factors. For example, adjustments are usually made for changes in the purchasing power of money, and for changes in population and in consumption habits. Corrections may be made directly by such means as dividing all original price data by "an index of the general level of prices." They may be made indirectly by correction for trends of the two time series of prices and of quantities. Whatever the corrections and refinements, however, the essence of the method is that certain prices are taken as representing the prices at which certain quantities of the product in question were sold.

With this in mind, we may now turn to the theory of the demand-and-supply curve analysis of market prices. The conventional theory runs in terms substantially as follows.[6] At any given time all individuals within the scope of the market may be considered as being within two groups—potential buyers and potential sellers.[7] The higher the price, the more the sellers will be ready to sell and the less the buyers will be willing to take. We may assume a demand schedule of the potential buyers and a supply

---

[5] Instead of using actual prices and quantities, percentage changes or link relatives of prices and quantities may be used. In note 2 on page 98 will be found references to various discussions of the details of statistical procedure used in the consideration of demand curves and also of the theory of statistical analysis of demand curves.

[6] Alfred Marshall, *Principles*, Book V, Chap. 2. F. W. Taussig, *Principles*, Chap. 10; "Is Market Price Determinate?" *The Quarterly Journal of Economics*, May 1921, p. 204.

[7] This does not mean that the same individual may not be in both groups. He may be a potential seller at any price above a certain level and a potential buyer at any price below.

schedule of the potential sellers which express the amounts that these groups are ready to buy and sell at different prices. From these schedules supply and demand curves may be made. Thus we have our supply and demand curves showing the market situation at any given time, and the price which results from this situation will be represented by the height of the point where the curves intersect.

This, however, represents the situation as it obtains at any given moment only. It may change; indeed, it is almost certain to change. The supply and demand curves which accurately represent the market situation of to-day will not represent that of a week hence. The curves which represent the average or aggregate of conditions this month will not hold true for the corresponding month of next year. In the case of the wheat market, for example, the effect of news that wheat which is growing in Kansas has been damaged by rust will cause a shift in both demand and supply schedules of the traders in the grain markets. The same amount of wheat, or a greater, will command a higher price than would have been the case if the news had failed to reach the traders. Since much of the buying and selling is speculative, changes in the market price itself may result in shifts of the demand and supply schedules.

If, then, our market demand and supply curves are to indicate conditions which extend over a period of time, we must represent them as shifting.[8] A diagram such as the following, Fig. 1, may be used to indicate them. The demand and supply curves may meet at any point within the area a, b, c, d, and over a period of time points of equilibrium will occur at many different places within it.

But what of statistical demand curves in the light of this analysis? If we construct a statistical demand curve from data of quantities sold and corresponding prices, our original data consist, in effect, of observations of points at which the demand and supply curves have met. Altho we may wish to reduce our data to static conditions, we must remember that they originate in the market

---

[8] Compare Taussig, "Is Market Price Determinate?" *The Quarterly Journal of Economics,* May 1921, p. 204. This article illustrates a somewhat different way of representing market conditions. It represents the curves as being of uncertain conformation rather than as shifting.

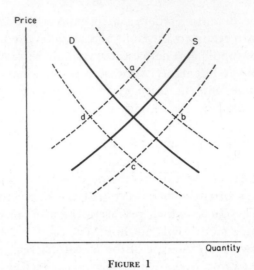

FIGURE 1

itself. The market is dynamic and our data extend over a period of time; consequently our data are of changing conditions and must be considered as the result of shifting demand and supply schedules.

Let us assume that conditions are such as those illustrated in Fig. 2, the demand curve shifting from D1 to D2, and the supply curve shifting in similar manner from S1 to S2. It is to be noted that the chart shows approximately equal shifting of the demand and supply curves.

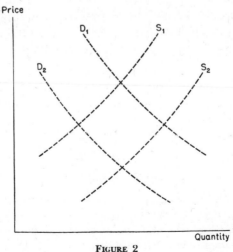

FIGURE 2

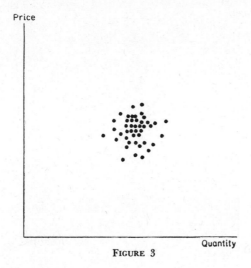

FIGURE 3

Under such conditions there will result a series of prices which may be graphically represented by Fig. 3. It is from data such as those represented by the dots that we are to construct a demand curve, but evidently no satisfactory fit can be obtained. A line of one slope will give substantially as good a fit as will a line of any other slope.

But what happens if we alter our assumptions as to the relative shifting of the demand and supply curves? Suppose the supply curve shifts in some such manner as is indicated by Fig. 4, that

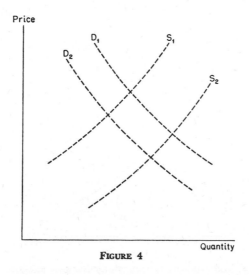

FIGURE 4

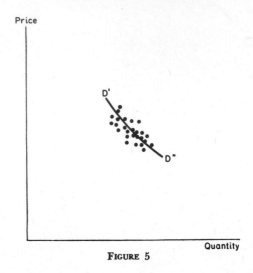

FIGURE 5

is, so that the shifting of the supply curve is greater than the shifting of the demand curve. We shall then obtain a very different set of observations—a set which may be represented by the dots of Fig. 5. To these points we may fit a curve which will have the elasticity of the demand curve that we originally assumed, and whose position will approximate the central position about which the demand curve shifted. We may consider this to be a sort of typical demand curve, and from it we may determine the elasticity of demand.

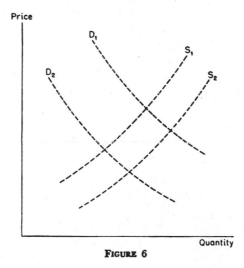

FIGURE 6

If, on the other hand, the demand schedules of buyers fluctuate more than do the supply schedules of sellers, we shall obtain a different result. This situation is illustrated by Fig. 6. The resulting array of prices and quantities is of a very different sort from the previous case, and its nature is indicated by Fig. 7. A line drawn so as most nearly to fit these points will approximate a supply curve instead of a demand curve.

If this analysis is in accord with the facts, is it not evident that

FIGURE 7

Professor Moore's "law of demand" for pig iron is in reality a "law of supply" instead?[9] The original observations of prices and

---

[9] P. G. Wright (*The Quarterly Journal of Economics*, May, 1915, p. 638) comes to the same conclusion, in a review of Moore's *Economic Cycles*. Furthermore, his analysis bears some resemblance to that above. However, his specific argument is unfortunate in that he says "the conditions of demand are changed (very probably by improved business conditions) in the direction of a rapid and continuous increase." Apparently Mr. Wright had in mind the results which would be obtained by the use of absolute quantities and prices instead of relative changes in quantities and prices. The trend inherent in the production figures due to a continuous increase in demand would tend to be eliminated by Moore's use of *relative* changes in quantities unless there were a distinctly progressive increase. Mr. Wright's contention that the peculiar result was due to a shifting of the demand curve is quite correct. Mr. Wright, to whom the present paper has been submitted, now concurs that the result is due to a shifting back and forth rather than to a continuous shift of the demand curve to the right.

corresponding quantities are the resultant of both supply and demand. Consequently, they do not necessarily reflect the influence of demand any more than that of supply. The methods used in constructing demand curves (particularly if the quantity data are of quantities sold) may, under some conditions, yield a demand curve, under others, a supply curve, and, under still different conditions, no satisfactory result may be obtained.

In the case of agricultural commodities, where production for any given year is largely influenced by weather conditions, and where farmers sell practically their entire crop regardless of price, there is likely to be a much greater shifting of the supply schedules of sellers than of the demand schedules of buyers. This is particularly true of perishable commodities, which cannot be withheld from the market without spoilage, and in case the farmers themselves can under no conditions use more than a very small proportion of their entire production. Such a condition results in the supply curve shifting within very wide limits. The demand curve, on the other hand, may shift but little. The quantities which are consumed may be dependent almost entirely upon price, so that the only way to have a much larger amount taken off the market is to reduce the price, and any considerable curtailment of supply is sure to result in a higher price.

With other commodities, the situation may be entirely different. Where a manufacturer has complete control over the supply of the article which he produces, the price at which he sells may be quite definitely fixed, and the amount of his production will vary, depending upon how large an amount of the article is bought at the fixed price. The extent to which there is a similar tendency to adjust sales to the shifts of demand varies with different commodities, depending upon how large overhead costs are and upon the extent to which trade agreements or other means are used to limit competition between different manufacturers. In general, however, there is a marked tendency for the prices of manufactured articles to conform to their expenses of production, the amount of the articles sold varying with the intensity of demand at that price which equals the expenses of production. Under such conditions, the supply curve does not shift greatly, but rather approximates an expenses-of-production curve, which does not vary much from month to month or from year to year. If this condition is combined with a fluctuating demand for the product, we shall have a situation such as that shown in Figs. 6 and 7, where the demand curves shift widely and the supply curves only a little.

From this, it would seem that, whether we obtain a demand curve or a supply curve, by fitting a curve to a series of points which represent the quantities of an article sold at various prices, depends upon the fundamental nature of the supply and demand conditions. It implies the need of some term in addition to that of elasticity in order to describe the nature of supply and demand. The term "variability" may be used for this purpose. For example, the demand for an article may be said to be "elastic" if, at a given time, a small reduction in price would result in a much greater quantity being sold, while it may be said to be "variable" if the demand curve shows a tendency to shift markedly. To be called variable, the demand curve should have the tendency to shift back and forth, and not merely to shift gradually and consistently to the right or left because of changes of population or consuming habits.

Whether a demand or a supply curve is obtained may also be affected by the nature of the corrections applied to the original data. The corrections may be such as to reduce the effect of the shifting of the demand schedules without reducing the effect of the shifting of the supply schedules. In such a case the curve obtained will approximate a demand curve, even tho the original demand schedules fluctuated fully as much as did the supply schedules.

By intelligently applying proper refinements, and making corrections to eliminate separately those factors which cause demand curves to shift and those factors which cause supply curves to shift, it may be possible even to obtain both a demand curve and a supply curve for the same product and from the same original data. Certainly it may be possible, in many cases where satisfactory demand curves have not been obtained, to find instead the supply curves of the articles in question. The supply curve obtained by such methods, it is to be noted, would be a market supply curve rather than a normal supply curve.

Thus far it has been assumed that the supply and demand curves shift quite independently and at random; but such need

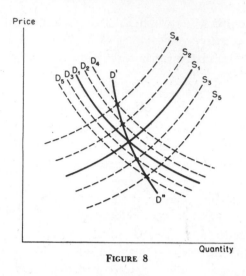

FIGURE 8

not be the case. It is altogether possible that a shift of the demand
curve to the right may, as a rule, be accompanied by a shift of
the supply curve to the left, and vice versa. Let us see what result
is to be expected under such conditions. If successive positions of
the demand curve are represented by the curves D_1, D_2, D_3, D_4,
and D_5 of Fig. 8, while the curves S_1, S_2, S_3, S_4, and S_5 represent
corresponding positions of the supply curves, then a series of prices
will result from the intersection of D_1 with S_1, D_2 with S_2, and so
on. If a curve be fitted to these points, it will not conform to the

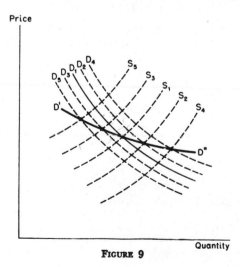

FIGURE 9

theoretical demand curve. It will have a smaller elasticity, as is shown by D′ D″ of Fig. 8. If, on the other hand, a shift of the demand curve to the right is accompanied by a shift of the supply curve to the right, we shall obtain a result such as that indicated by D′ D″ in Fig. 9. The fitted curve again fails to conform to the theoretical one, but in this case it is more elastic.

Without carrying the illustrations further, it will be apparent that similar reasoning applies to the fitted "supply curve" in case conditions are such that the demand curve shifts more than does the supply curve.

If there is a change in the range through which the supply curve shifts, as might occur through the imposition of a tariff on an imported good, a new fitted curve will result, which will not be a continuation of the former one—this because the fitted curve does not correspond to the true demand curve. In case, then, of correlated shifts of the demand and supply curves, a fitted curve cannot be considered to be the demand curve for the article. It cannot be used, for example, to estimate what change in price would result from the levying of a tariff upon the commodity.

Perhaps a word of caution is needed here. It does not follow from the foregoing analysis that, when conditions are such that shifts of the supply and demand curves are correlated, an attempt to construct a demand curve will give a result which will be useless. Even tho shifts of the supply and demand curves are correlated, a curve which is fitted to the points of intersection will be useful for purposes of price forecasting, provided no new factors are introduced which did not affect the price during the period of the study. Thus, so long as the shifts of the supply and demand curves remain correlated in the same way, and so long as they shift through approximately the same range, the curve of regression of price upon quantity can be used as a means of estimating price from quantity.

In cases where it is impossible to show that the shifts of the demand and supply curves are not correlated, much confusion would probably be avoided if the fitted curves were not called demand curves (or supply curves), but if, instead, they were called merely lines of regression. Such curves may be useful, but we must be extremely careful in our interpretation of them. We must also make every effort to discover whether the shifts of the supply and demand curves are correlated before interpreting the results of any fitted curve.

In assuming that we are dealing with quantities actually sold in the market, and in disregarding the fact that for many commodities there is a whole series of markets at various points in the marketing chain, we have simplified our problem. But it has been more than mere simplification, for the interpretation which is to be placed on statistical demand curves depends in large measure upon these matters. Whether the demand curve is a "particular" or a "general" demand curve, depends upon whether or not we use quantities sold. Whether it represents consumer or dealer demand, depends upon the point in the marketing chain to which the quantities sold refer.

Most theorists are acquainted with the concept of the general demand curve as it is presented by Wicksteed and Davenport.[10] Briefly, the idea is that demand should be considered as including not merely the quantities that are bought, but rather all those in existence. The general demand curve, then, includes the possessors of a commodity as having a demand for it at any price below their reservation price, even if they are prospective sellers. Instead of showing the amounts that will be bought at various prices, it shows the marginal money valuation which will be placed upon varying quantities of an existing supply.

Wicksteed even indicates that the supply curve ought not to be considered at all. The following gives an intimation of his viewpoint:

But what about the "supply curve" that usually figures as a determinant of price, coördinate with the demand curve? I say it boldly and baldly: There is no such thing. When we are speaking of a marketable commodity, what is usually called a supply curve is in reality a demand curve of those who possess the commodity; for it shows the exact place which every successive unit of the commodity holds in their relative scale of estimates. The so-called supply curve, therefore, is simply a part of the total demand curve.[11]

Thus the general demand curve is an expression of the rela-

---

[10] P. H. Wicksteed, "The Scope and Method of Political Economy in the Light of the 'Marginal' Theory of Value," *The Economic Journal*, March 1914, p. 1. See also H. J. Davenport, *Economics of Enterprise*, pp. 47–51.

[11] Wicksteed, *ibid.*, p. 13.

tion between the supply of a commodity and its valuation. In other words, to put it in more familiar terms, it expresses the marginal valuation of different supplies. It is the same sort of. thing as a curve of marginal utility, except that it uses monetary valuations instead of abstract "satisfactions" as its ordinate. This raises the question, if, instead of quantities sold, we use quantities produced (or total supply) when we construct a statistical demand curve, do we not obtain a general demand curve, and does not this preclude the possibility of obtaining a supply curve? Let us examine the matter a little further.

As it is usually applied, the idea of the general demand curve refers to valuations of an existing stock of durable goods, such as paintings, diamonds, or hats. If it is applied to a stock of nondurable goods, it is of less significance; and in case this stock is replenished periodically, the demand curve must be considered as changing greatly from period to period. For example, in the case of wheat the stock varies greatly, being large just after harvest and gradually dwindling until it becomes very small just before the next harvest. The general demand curve, as applied to an existing stock, would exhibit correspondingly large shifts.

An idea similar to that of the general demand curve is that which is used in regard to *rate* of supply. If, instead of using the rates at which quantities are sold in the market, we use rate of production, which we relate to the unit value of the commodity, we obtain a curve which is analogous to the general demand curve. It gives the marginal valuation which would be placed upon various rates of supply, that is, of supplies produced, not of supplies sold. This sort of a demand curve has been called a "general" demand curve, but it is to be noted that the general demand curve which uses total stocks as its abscissa cannot be placed as coördinate with a supply curve; whereas the demand curve which uses as abscissa total quantities produced can be used in connection with a supply curve of quantities produced.

The use of quantities produced, then, does not give us a general demand curve in the usual sense of the word. Instead, it gives us a demand curve which we may consider as being coordinate with a supply curve, tho we must keep in mind that our supply curve in this case is of supplies produced rather than of supplies sold in the market. The demand curve is of demand for storage and consumption by producers as well as for storage and consumption by buyers. There is no reason why we may not obtain a supply curve instead of a demand curve, even tho we use quantities produced. To do so requires only that shifts in the demand curve be very large relative to those of the supply curve, and that amounts sold differ but little from amounts produced. The scatter of the points will, of course, be greater than if amounts sold had been used.

The question of the difference between consumer and dealer demand presents a problem somewhat analogous to that just discussed. The amount of a commodity sold at one point in the marketing chain may differ from that sold at another in much the same way that the amount produced may differ from the amount sold. This is particularly true if monthly data are used. A case in point would be the demand for eggs. The amount of eggs sold by farmers in the spring of the year is greatly in excess of the amount sold by retail dealers, while in the winter months it is much less. Since differentials between the prices received by farmers and those received by retail dealers remain fairly constant, very different demand curves would be obtained. The consumers' demand curve would be very much less elastic than that of the dealers who buy from farmers.

Differences between dealer demand and consumer demand are largely dependent upon whether we are considering short or long periods. Over long periods of time, dealer demand tends to conform to consumer demand. This difference, however, is not a thing which depends upon the length of period over which the data extend, but of the length of period to which the individual observations of prices and quantities refer. In the case of eggs, if yearly data were used, the principal difference which would be found between the elasticity of consumer and dealer demands would be due to price differentials alone.

The question whether statistical demand curves are static or dynamic is a perplexing one and rather difficult to deal with. This is largely due to uncertainty as to just what is meant by the terms "static" and "dynamic." Moore holds that his "laws of demand" are dynamic,[12] and that this is an eminently desirable feature.

---

[12] *Economic Cycles*, pp. 64–67, 113.

Schultz, while considering it most desirable to obtain both a static and a dynamic law by means of multiple correlation, holds that the statistical devices of relative changes and of trend ratios give a static "law of demand."[13]

Conditions are often defined as being static or dynamic on two different grounds. They may be called static if they refer to a point of time; or else they may be said to be static if all other things are held equal. Statements such as these, however, lack much in clarity and accuracy. How can a statement be made as to prices at which different quantities of a commodity will sell at a *point* of time? Is it really supposed that *all* other things must be held equal in order to study the demand of the commodity? Rather, the real supposition, tho it may not be accurately expressed, is that the relationships between the various economic factors should be the same as those which exist at a given point of time, or that the relationships between these factors should remain constant.

The data used in a statistical study of demand must, of course, extend over a period of time, but they may in effect conform to conditions at a point of time if trend is removed and if there is no other change in the relationship between quantity and price. Of course, the shifting of the demand and supply curves constitutes a change in the relationship between the quantity and price, but the process of curve-fitting corresponds to that of averaging. Consequently, the fitted curve may be considered to depict the average relationship between quantity and price. This amounts to the same thing as representing the relationship at a point of time which is typical for the period studied. In this sense, then, of relating to a point of time, Moore's "laws of demand" are static instead of dynamic.

Holding "all other things equal," however, is a different matter. Schultz states the difficulty in the following manner:

In *theory* the law of demand for any one commodity is given only on the assumption that the prices of all other commodities remain constant (the old *ceteris paribus* assumption). This postulate fails in the case of commodities for which substitutes are available. Thus when the price of beef is changed markedly, the prices of such rival commodities as mutton, veal, and pork cannot be supposed to remain constant. Likewise, the price of sugar cannot

---

[13] Henry Schultz, "The Statistical Law of Demand," *The Journal of Political Economy,* October and December 1925. See pp. 498–502 of October issue.

be increased beyond a certain point without affecting the prices of glucose, corn sugar, and honey.[14]

Marshall makes similar restrictions as to the need for other things to be held equal, and suggests that in some cases it may be best to "group together commodities as distinct as beef and mutton,"[15] in order to obtain a demand curve which will not be too restricted because of other things being equal.

The question arises, however, whether it is desirable to hold all other things equal in any case. Is it not better to have a demand curve for beef which expresses the relation between the price and quantity of beef while the prices of pork, mutton, and veal, vary as they normally do, with different prices of beef? Furthermore, may not this be called a static condition? The point can perhaps be made clearer if we take an extreme example. If we are studying the demand for wheat, it would be almost meaningless to get the demand curve for No. 2 Winter wheat while holding the price of all other grades of wheat constant. Other grades of wheat can be so readily substituted that the demand would be almost completely elastic. The difference between this and holding the prices of pork, mutton, and veal constant, while the price of beef varies, is only one of degree—a difference which depends upon the ease with which substitutes can be used in place of the article whose demand is being studied.

All other things being held equal is not a condition represented by a statistical law of demand or, strictly interpreted, of any useful demand curve theory. Some of the things that are correlated with the price of the commodity in question may be held equal, but it is impossible for all things to be held equal. However, a statistical law of demand represents a condition under which the relationships between factors may be considered to have remained the same, or, to put it more accurately, a condition which is an average of the relationships during the period studied.

In conclusion, then, it is evident that the mere statement that the demand for a commodity has a given elasticity is meaningless. As with the results of all other statistical analysis, statistical demand

---

[14] *Ibid.*, pp. 498–499.

[15] Alfred Marshall, *Principles* (8th ed.), p. 100 n.

curves must be interpreted in the light of the nature of the original data and of the methods of analysis used. There are four questions, the answers to which it is particularly important to know. They concern (1) whether the supply or demand curve is more variable, (2) the market to which the price and quantity data refer, (3) the extent to which "other things are held equal," and (4) whether the shifting of the supply and demand curves is correlated or random.

For precision, it is preferable that the data of price and quantity should refer to the same market. Yet this may be out of the question. In a study of the demand for wheat, for example, if we want to obtain a demand curve of the quantity demanded by the entire country, we cannot use prices for all different points and for all different grades. Instead, the price at one market and for one grade may be used as representative, and the demand of the entire country determined for various prices at the one market-place. If the price at any other market or for any other grade were used, the elasticity of demand might be different.

Furthermore, the point in the market chain must be specified and the results interpreted accordingly. As is the case with geographical points, it is preferable that the quantities and prices should refer to the same stage in the marketing process. If this is not the case, the interpretation should be made with the situation in view.

It is to be expected that the methods used in constructing statistical demand curves should be such as to give a demand curve which represents a point of time, that is, that trends in both quantities and prices are removed, or else multiple correlation is used to effect the same result. If, in addition to this, other things are held constant, the fact should be noted and the elasticity of demand should be stated as referring to a condition where these other things are held constant.

The matter of correlation between shifts of the demand and supply curves is a more difficult problem to deal with. Every effort should be made to discover whether there is a tendency for the shifting of these to be interdependent. In case it is impossible to determine this, it should be carefully noted that the demand curve which is obtained is quite likely not to hold true for periods other than the one studied, and cannot be treated as corresponding to the demand curve of economic theory.

II. COSTS AND RETURNS

5

OF EMPTY ECONOMIC BOXES *

By J. H. Clapham ‖

Picture an economist, well-educated in the dominant British school, going over a hat-factory. On the shelves of the store, the first room he enters, are boxes containing hats. On the shelves of his mind are also boxes. There is a row labelled Diminishing Return Industries, Constant Return Industries, Increasing Return Industries. Above that a dustier row labelled Monopolies (with discrimination of three degrees) in Diminishing Return Industries, Constant Return Industries, Increasing Return Industries. On top again he can just read the dockets, Taxes on Monopolies in Diminishing Return Industries—and so on. He is aware that these boxes are not very prominent on the shelves of some economists of whose mental furniture he generally approves; but he received them from his masters and he has seen them handled with beautiful ingenuity by his friends. Yet from all his reading and conversations he cannot recall a scene in which anyone opened the boxes and said, with authority and convincing evidence, "Constant Return Industry, hosen; Increasing Return Industry, hats," or used any like words. Nor can he think of an industrial monograph in which profitable use was made of the Laws of Returns in commenting on the things of life. Perhaps he has himself tried to write a little monograph and remembers how, doubtless for lack of wit, he made of them no use; but how for this no one ever blamed him.

He takes down, in memory and when he gets home from his shelves, *Industry and Trade: A Study of Industrial Technique and Business Organisation,* with its nearly nine hundred pages

* *The Economic Journal,* Vol. XXXII (1922), pp. 305–314. Reprinted, by the courtesy of the publisher and Lady Clapham, without change from the original text.

‖ Sir John Clapham died in 1946. He was formerly of King's College, Cambridge University, England.

packed full of the things of life. Two references to Constant Returns—one in a footnote—and a handful of references to Diminishing and Increasing Returns *im Allgemeinen,* not so far as he can find in close relation to the facts of those British, French, German and American Industries of which the great book has taught him so much: these seem to be all. He tries *The Economics of Welfare* to find that, in nearly a thousand pages, there is not even one illustration of what industries are in which boxes, though many an argument begins—"when conditions of diminishing returns prevail" or "when conditions of increasing returns prevail," as if everyone knew when that was.

The difficulty of supplying illustrations had been brought home to him that day in the hat-factory. Whilst wandering among hollow copper cones to which hat-stuff miraculously adhered, shaping and pressing appliances, and dye vats, he had wondered— recalling the words with difficulty—whether "the increment of product due to the increase by a unit in the quantity of resources occupied in producing" hats is smaller (diminishing returns), or greater (increasing returns), "the greater is the quantity of resources so employed."[1] How should he conceive his unit of resources? How his increment of product? No one had given him any help here. Must he fix on a standard hat or a standard quantity of standard hat-stuff? It is physical output, the Great Analytics repeat, with which these Laws deal; so something of the sort seems necessary. He appreciates the wisdom of talking not of hats but of commodities.

Or how is he to conceive of "an industry"? Is it a national industry? The Great Analytics seem to assume this; though they are not perfectly explicit. But are they entitled to assume it? Ought he not somehow to take into account conditions in that place— now in Czecho-Slovakia—whence came the "Austrian velours hats" of which he hears so much among the hat-factories of Denton? Discouraged, he falls back, most reluctantly, on generalities. As the world's population is still growing, presumably more units of resources, however conceived, are in fact being turned to hat-making. But only the most searching and difficult realistic inquiry could, he feels sure, even suggest the conclusion that, in

---

[1] *The Economics of Welfare,* p. 120.

this industry at this time, each "dose" of manufacturing resources means more standard hats.

Can the diminishing returns side help? Hats; chief raw materials, coal, rabbits' fur, shellac, leather for the inside band and pulp for the box. Coal seems easy; and an approximate solution there will help in so many other industries, in some of which the value of the product is thirty per cent. fuel cost, or more. To assert that the produce of mines conforms to the Law of Diminishing Returns is, he knows, "misleading."[2] But if the one raw material common to all industries is not to be brought within the scope of the Laws, all hope of dragging them out of the realm of the categories must be abandoned *in limine*. So the risk of misleading must be shouldered.

Nature's response to the miner is notoriously reluctant. A time must come in the history of the planet, as a time comes in the history of every pit, when equal successive "doses" of resources will yield smaller physical returns. Economics, however, is not concerned with geological time; nor the Laws of Returns, if he has rightly apprehended them, with individual pits. The industry is the unit. For the moment he will think of a national industry, an old national industry, that of Britain. Have the new large-scale applications of resources, those great pit-sinkings on the Doncaster extension of the Yorkshire coal-field which the war interrupted, have they the effect of increasing or of only keeping constant the yield of coal "per unit of resources" in Britain? Or, in spite of their undoubted efficiency, is the return per unit for the whole industry actually diminishing, because elsewhere the working out of pits is rendering the successive "doses" applied to them less efficient? He does not know; but it seems not impossible that an approximate answer might be worked out—with a gigantic reservation which he sets aside for further thought.

That coal in Britain is being produced under conditions of diminishing returns is quite possible; but this is one of the cases in which we are least entitled to adopt a narrow national standpoint. One could hardly err in assuming that in Upper Silesia, or in the Transvaal, or in many parts of the United States the reverse is true; and as the world is fast becoming a single market for coal,

[2] Marshall, *Principles*, p. 168.

and coal-mining a single world-industry like wheat-growing, any thorough inquiry would have not only to balance the virgin coal of Doncaster against the well-worked Lancashire field, but Britain against America or even against that wonderful coal-field through which, they say, the upper Yangtse-Kiang cuts its gorges. So far as our economist knows the work is not yet begun.

After coal, rabbits' fur: an awkward case: a joint-product too. Nature shows no reluctance to supply mankind with rabbits; but as a crop they compete with others. The rabbit-skin industry is distributed between Hampshire warrens, Belgian hutches, and Australian back-blocks. There is system in it, at least in the hutches and on the back-blocks; but its organisation, its internal and external economies, are elusive. The puzzled economist has no idea, and no notion how he shall begin to form an idea, whether it is or is not carried on under conditions of diminishing returns. Of the leather for the hat-bands he is more disposed to hazard a guess that diminishing returns prevail; but it is a guess, and there are all the problems of the joint-product and the sources of supply (some in old countries and some in new) which faced him when considering the rabbits.

Shellac and pulp for the boxes are more hopeful. From what he has read of the shellac "industry" and the lac insect he suspects diminishing returns. Things picked up in forests are apt to elude with greater and greater success intensive efforts to pick them up. But stay—is there any "cultured" shellac? That is a thing to be looked into; for, in the slightly similar case of wild and plantation rubber, he suspects that the transition from the wild to the cultured product marked a transition from diminishing to increasing returns upon each "unit of resources" devoted to rubber production. It looks almost as if a proof of increasing returns in rubber planting might be established statistically for the period 1905–22: it is, of course, the simple case of an organised large-scale industry on virgin soil, a Ricardian, or perhaps we should say a Careyite, rudiment. Shellac is not so easy. With a confession of ignorance, coupled with a strong guess of diminishing returns, he passes to pulp, the most hopeful of all his raw materials.

Common knowledge of the wastage of the world's timber—which was being treated rather as a stock, like coal, than as a crop, like rubber—supported by some study of timber price move-

ments as compared with other price movements before 1914, did
suggest definitely that "units of resources" applied to forest exploitation were yielding smaller physical returns. Whether this
is true of wood-pulp is less certain. There the economies of an
organised industry, the increasing returns tendency, have to be
set against Nature's very obvious reluctance to supply mankind
with timber indefinitely on the stock system. But it is likely that
the pulp industry also, thanks more to human carelessness than
to the niggardliness of Nature, is working under conditions of
diminishing returns. Provisionally, and with hesitation, our economist was just about to conclude that the cardboard of his hat-boxes
shows clear signs of Nature's reluctance to meet man half-way,
when someone reminded him that this particular cardboard was
made not of wood-pulp but of straw, ropes' ends, and the worn-
out covers of railway wagons. Vegetable materials, no doubt, and
against all such a suspicion of diminishing returns lies; but may
not the improving organisation of the marine-store dealers and
other handlers of "junk" come in on the other side? New processes
have got between him and Nature: a new, long and none too
hopeful inquiry into fact lies before him. He must, if honest,
admit ignorance of the class of "returns" under which this cardboard is made. Finally he must balance all these uncertainties and
ignorances on the "diminishing" side against the equally stubborn
ignorances—all of which there has not been space here to tabulate—
on the "increasing" side. He leaves the factory with no formed
opinion about the proper economic box for hats.

It may be said that the industry is not typical of industries
generally. Certainly there is a special lack of decent organisation
for the production of some of its raw materials and great difficulty
in hitting on a representative finished product. But the same is
true of many other trades; and incidentally it has been shown, or
suggested, that coal itself cannot be boxed confidently. No doubt
it is easy to take extreme cases on the "increasing" side and box
them. Meccano Ltd., no doubt, are working under conditions of
increasing returns. So, one supposes, are the Ford establishments
and probably the car industry generally; but whether or not well-
established industries, say textile machinery or locomotives, are
working under decided conditions of increasing returns would
be very difficult to determine. True, it seems most unlikely that

mechanical industries with mineral raw materials, in the present state of the world's mineral resources, are producing under "diminishing" conditions; but no more can be said with any confidence. Wherever animal or vegetable materials are involved the element of uncertainty is greatly increased. And it was for these cases in particular that the conception of the balance of forces, man's organisation *versus* Nature's reluctance, was worked out. A strict interpretation of diminishing returns, as we know, excludes the mineral stocks. Then consider wool.

It is no use discussing "woollen cloth"; for there is no such thing. You might as well discuss a commodity. But there are standard products of the industry, reasonably uniform and regularly quoted. Take combed wool, "tops." If any problem in "returns" involving organic matter is soluble, that of 64's Botany tops should be. The wool is, by definition, all Australian; and if perhaps now and then some River Plate or New Zealand wool gets into the tops, that too is new country wool. "In the production of wheat and wool" (the tendency towards diminishing returns) "has almost exclusive sway in an old country."[3] The converse is no doubt true of a new one. But is Australia still "new"? There is keen competition between agricultural and pastoral interests and, in some districts, between sheep and cattle. The districts in which the fine merino wool used for 64's can be produced to perfection are limited; and as the supply has grown but little, in spite of steady demand, it is likely enough that "conditions of diminishing returns" prevail. But just how the situation is now to be described, I do not know. A monograph, as yet unwritten, would be illuminating but might not be decisive. At present we are not justified in stating that Botany (i.e. fine merino) wool is being produced under the sway of either of the returns tendencies. On the other hand we are, I think, justified in stating that the tendency to increasing returns is not working strongly on the manufacturing side. The combing industry is highly organised and localised to an astonishing degree. Apart from combs run by some spinners, the combing plants are mostly large. Fresh ones are seldom set up, and it is unlikely that the building of new mills or the extension of those now existing would increase the

[3] Marshall, *Principles*, p. 319.

efficiency of the industry disproportionately to the effort expended. This is almost a verbal repetition of what Dr. Marshall wrote long ago about the production of blankets. Supposing that Botany wool is, in fact, produced to-day under conditions of slightly diminishing returns, it is conceivable that 64's Botany tops are being turned out very near the mathematical point of constant returns. But we do not know.

Constant returns, it may be observed in passing, must always remain a mathematical point, their box an empty one. It is inconceivable that a method can ever be devised for so measuring these real but infinitely subtle and imponderable tendencies towards diminishing and increasing returns that someone will be able to say, Lo, here a perfect balance. If this is so, constant returns industries may be relegated finally to the limbo of the categories, in company for the present with such still disembodied phantoms as the "commodity whose elasticity of demand is unity."

In the passage where Dr. Marshall discusses blankets occurs the reservation referred to above as gigantic and set aside for further thought. The improvements in efficiency arising from the increasing size of an industry, to which Dr. Marshall attributes increasing returns, are, as I read him, not to include notable inventions, perhaps not inventions at all. They are improvements in organisation only. Referring to the blanket trade he writes, "an increase in the aggregate volume of production brings some new economics, but not many," because the trade is "already on so great a scale that any new economics that (it) may attain are more likely to be the result of new inventions than of improved organisation." I think Professor Pigou endorses this distinction between invention and organisation, but I am not quite sure; he is less concrete in his treatment than Dr. Marshall, further from the clod and much further from machinery. The distinction, important as it is and clarifying of pure thought, discourages the student not of categories but of things. For, when trying to box an industry with the increasing docket, he must strive to think away that part of any additional output, coinciding with a fresh "dose of resources," which is due to invention, and concentrate on the part due to size and organisation only. Suppose he has just found out—it would be hard enough, perhaps not possible, but conceivable—that the returns to the expenditure of resources in sinking of coal-pits near Doncaster are such as to show that even the British coal industry is still in the "increasing" stage; and that then someone tells him (I fancy it is true) that these pits would never have been sunk at the price in "resources" but for the modern invention by which loose and water-logged strata above the coal-measures are frozen artificially to facilitate sinking. Can he, like a schoolman, put this aside as an *accidens* and concentrate on the pure *substantia* of the growing industry apart from the invention? He is not tempted to try. If he were, quite certainly the boxes would always remain empty. Should the laws ever be rescued from the limbo of the categories, it could only be by treating industries as they are and lumping in inventions. Professor Pigou's definition quoted above would, I think, permit of this. You can pack much into the phrase, "a unit in the quantity of resources." It may prove difficult to suggest a concrete measure for the "unit of inventiveness," but it should not be much more difficult than measurement of the "unit of normal managerial capacity," which is obviously included in Professor Pigou's composite unit.

Perhaps some analytic, great or small, having read so far with impatience will be muttering quite loud, *connu, farceur!* Was it not obvious to you that we did not pretend to have set up measured units of managerial capacity, units of capital, and units of labour, compounded into a joint-unit of resources? Of course there are endless practical difficulties in fixing on standard units of product for particular industries and correlating them with the application of units of resources. Did not the rarity of illustrations in our discussion of "returns" indicate what we were doing? A standard hat is not a mathematical concept. We are generalising the bewildering detail of industry. Do you admit the logic of the conception of the laws of returns? Yes? Well, we are building a framework into which we hope facts may in time be fitted. If those who know the facts cannot do the fitting, we shall regret it. But our doctrine will retain its logical—and, may we add, its pedagogic—value. And then you know it goes so prettily into graphs and equations. Besides, in the history of thought analysis has often outrun verification.

The answer to such a statement of the case depends, *first,* upon the measure of hopefulness or despondency with which one contemplates the task of translating the theory into the facts of those industries which one knows best; *secondly,* upon one's estimate of the final utility of such a translation if it could be made; and *thirdly,* upon one's personal opinion of the consequences of the outrunning of verification by analysis in Economics. Taking the last point first and speaking in the first person, as in such a case one must, I think a good deal of harm has been done through omission to make it quite clear that the Laws of Returns have never been attached to specific industries; that the boxes are, in fact, empty; that we do not, for instance, at this moment *know* under what conditions of returns coal or boots are being produced. If unwary, one might read *The Economics of Welfare,* a book which from its title would not appear to be an essay in "pure economics," without apprehending this; and I suspect that many students do so. I myself did not appreciate how completely empty the boxes were until I had given a number of public demonstrations with them. And if more acute minds are not likely so to be misled, the rank and file surely are. Unless we have a good prospect in the near future of filling the boxes reasonably full, there is, I hold, grave danger to an essentially practical science such as Economics in the elaboration of hypothetical conclusions about, say, human welfare and taxes in relation to industries which cannot be specified.

Next, supposing we did, after much labour, ascertain definitely that coal in England was being produced under conditions of slightly diminishing and 64's Botany tops under conditions of slightly increasing returns—what would be the utility of the knowledge, apart from the satisfaction of a legitimate scientific curiosity? Professor Marshall has stated that *"other things being equal,* the Finance Minister should press on products of Decreasing Return industries rather than on products of Increasing Return industries,"[4] and there is a considerable literature, with few illustrations, on the working of taxes upon commodities under different assumptions as to returns. But I think we may take it that the italicising of the "other things being equal" is a scholarly reminder that this is not a bit of political advice; for it is hard to think of

---

[4] *Industry and Trade,* p. 405 n

cases in which other things would be equal, since Diminishing Return industries, if we can lay them by the heels, are likely to prove nearer the raw material, so to speak, and so less eligible for taxation, than Increasing Return industries. If not a safe guide to taxation, would the knowledge affect social, industrial or commercial policy? At the moment I can think of no advice which I should give to a working wool-comber, top-maker, spinner, merchant or reformer of social conditions in the worsted trade, as a result of the decision that 64's Botany tops were being produced under conditions of slightly increasing returns. Long before scholars had established that British coal was being produced under conditions of slightly diminishing returns, the resultant price rise relative to the price in increasing return areas would have stimulated organisation and invention to restore at least a state of constant returns, were that in any way possible. In all these matters the economist is, willy-nilly, an historian. The world has moved on before his conclusions are ripe.

And with how much hope does one face the establishing of these conclusions? The instances referred to so far have not been very encouraging. Looking backwards over long periods the task can be approached with some hope, provided one does not seek too great precision, does not, for instance, try to separate the effects of organisation from those of invention. The fact that the iron-work required to build a church cost about as much in sterling in 1913 as when Sir Christopher Wren was estimating for City churches, after the great fire of London,[5] alone indicates an enormously increased return to invention and organisation combined during the intervening two centuries and a half. But to prove that any standard grade of iron—No. 3 Cleveland pig or crown bars, let us say—has been turned out since the war under any particular condition of returns is a different matter. I can at present see no way of giving reality to the "unit of resources": though that by no means proves that there is no way. If it were given reality, some appreciable period of time would be necessary during which successive "units" would have to be applied to the industry, and the physical outputs measured. The allowance of time might have to be so long as to "make history" of the inquiry:

---

[5] W. G. Bell, *The Great Fire of London*, p. 282.

its results might be true only of yesterday. Again the experimental difficulties appear, though they may not prove to be, insurmountable. No one, so far as I know, has begun to attempt to surmount them.

If it is judged worth while to make a serious and concerted effort to fill the boxes—of which I am doubtful—a beginning might be made with some of the simple industries which it is customary to assume are working under conditions of diminishing returns. Do we really know that wheat, world wheat, is produced under those conditions? Or wool, or cotton? Some rough suggestions have been thrown out above as to timber, rubber and coal: the two first are the most hopeful. Before we know how much reluctance on the part of Nature we have to overcome, it is rather vain to speculate on the extent of our achievement in overcoming it and establishing conditions of increasing returns. Nature's reluctance varies presumably with the proportions of virgin and non-virgin soil, forests, coal measures and so forth to the total quantity of each being exploited at a given time for the production of a given raw material or food-stuff. In special cases, of which rubber may be one, she may for the time being be not reluctant at all. Easy generalisations about the Law of Diminishing Returns being necessarily true, because if it is not you might feed the world from a square yard, will help little in the discussion of these world-problems.

As to Increasing Returns: if we are to restrict the conception as, I believe, Dr. Marshall does, to the increased efficiency resulting from the improved organisation which generally accompanies an increase of capital and labour in any industry, or in industries in general,[6] to the exclusion of the efficiency flowing from invention—and a very good case can be made out for such restriction—then, I think, we should on principle avoid even the suggestion that we know that particular industries come into the "increasing" category, because we never can know what proportion of their efficiency is due to organisation resulting from mere size and what to invention. This is not a denial of the reality of increasing returns in this sense, only a denial of their measurability. If, on the other hand, we widen the conception as suggested above so

---

[6] See the definition in *Principles*, p. 319.

as to cover all inventions, we can arrive at certain tolerable historical results; but, as I think, we shall be permanently held up by "experimental" difficulties in dealing with the present and, *a fortiori*, with that near future which is so particularly interesting to the working economist. If I am wrong, and there are ways over any or all of the difficulties, which someone can point out, these mainly destructive notes may have constructive uses.

6

EMPTY ECONOMIC BOXES: A REPLY *

By A. C. Pigou‖

Dr. Clapham's entertaining paper on *Empty Economic Boxes* in the September issue of THE ECONOMIC JOURNAL is evidently designed to provoke one of his friends, "some analytic great or small," to reply. For myself I am inclined to suspect that the boxes labelled "analytic" and "realitic"—if that is the corresponding term —among economists are themselves empty, and that nobody in the world really falls into either category. Still "analytic" is a charming word and, for the purposes of this paper, I am ready to accept it as a label. In revenge, however, for letting myself be boxed in this way I claim the right, proper among friends, to indulge in whatever "brilliances" at Dr. Clapham's expense the spirit of controversy may whisper to me.

The substantial content of his paper is contained in the following propositions. (1) There are difficulties in the *conception* of a rate of returns in industry, particularly of a rate of increasing returns. (2) There are difficulties in deciding which particular industries are at the present time being conducted under conditions of increasing or conditions of diminishing returns—difficulties which keep these economic boxes empty. (3) If we could fill the boxes, very little practical good would come of it. (4) Therefore the said boxes are useless, dangerous and ought to be abolished. The first of these propositions is obviously true. Since, however, Dr. Clapham does not display, or profess to display, any difficulties in the conception of returns additional to those that have been familiar to economists for the past quarter of a century, nothing further need be said about it. In the following pages, therefore, I shall confine attention to the other parts of his paper.

---

* *The Economic Journal*, Vol. XXXII (1922), pp. 458–465. Reprinted, by the courtesy of the publisher and the author, without change from the original text, with a reply by J. H. Clapham.

‖ King's College, Cambridge University, England.

Let us begin by clearing the ground. There are two broadly distinguished sorts of knowledge: "pure" knowledge about implications, such as is sought in mathematics and logic; and realistic knowledge concerned with a subject-matter presumed to be actual, such as is sought by physicists. Within that second sort of knowledge must be further distinguished knowledge that cannot, and knowledge that can, give us direct help in the practical conduct of affairs. This second distinction seems to be somewhat blurred in Dr. Clapham's mind: with the result that it is not clear how far his antipathy to the categories of increasing and diminishing returns is due to his belief that they cannot be given a concrete filling, and how far to his belief that they cannot show us the way to card wool or impose taxes. Thus, I cannot gather from his article whether or not he would enjoy the contemplation of these categories, provided they were given a complete concrete filling *and yet* could not help practice at all. This woolliness in his critique makes the task of reply a little embarrassing.

If he is to be interpreted literally, his argument is that the analysis of increasing and diminishing returns is not worth pursuing, because, even if these economic boxes could be filled, no help would be given thereby to practice. Let us grant, for the sake of argument, that the analysis does not touch practice at all. The conclusion that it is not worth pursuing does not follow. Dr. Clapham, as a historian, is debarred from contending that the only knowledge which has value is knowledge which can guide practice; for by far the greater part of the knowledge which history aims at is totally irrelevant to practice. Hence, knowledge may have a value for its own sake. But knowledge of *implications* is just as much knowledge as knowledge of *matters of fact*. That, *if* certain conditions as to increasing or diminishing returns prevail, and *if* a tax of so much is imposed on a given article, such and such an effect will follow, is a piece of truth, just as it is a piece of truth—if it is one—that a certain English king died from a surfeit of lampreys. The historian is interested in matters of fact; but the logician is interested in implications. What right has the one to condemn the other? On what metaphysical or other basis is he entitled to lay it down, that knowledge of the form, "If X, then Y," is inferior to the knowledge of the form, "In the year 1600, X"? There are many empty boxes, in Dr. Clapham's sense, in the kingdom of pure mathematics: will he invite the mathematicians to abandon them and join in his researches about lampreys? This kind of answer to the contemner of "useless knowledge"—as followed by other people—is, I think, a perfectly legitimate one. Nevertheless, it is not one that, in the present connection, I wish specially to stress. For I do not myself judge that a knowledge of implications *of the type that pure economics can provide* has, in and for itself, any large value. To this extent I am really at one with Dr. Clapham, though, since I see no way in which a person who takes a different view can possibly be confuted, I am less willing than he appears to be to dogmatise on the matter.

I suspect, however, that, though Dr. Clapham in words makes his valuation of different parts of economics depend on their practical usefulness, he would, in thought, be content with any *schema*, whether it had a bearing on practice or not, provided it could be given a realistic content. For I cannot imagine that a person, who thinks it worth while to study the economic conditions of the past for their own sake, should think it not worth while to study these conditions in the present except where it can be shown that practical applications result. Moreover, I am confirmed in this view by the curious complex from which Dr. Clapham appears to suffer in connection with general terms. The word "commodity," for instance, is a red rag to him. He prefers to talk of hats, not appearing to realise that, if I wish to say something which is true, not only of hats, but also of gold watches and of onions, to express the proposition in terms of hats alone is not to express it fully. When this complex is developed a little further, he will probably rebel at the statement that two and two make four, and will insist on substituting for it the statement, which is also true but is not the same statement, that two hats and two hats make four hats! This, however, is by the way. I merely refer to it because it strengthens a little my view that, in spite of his words, it is realism rather than practical usefulness that Dr. Clapham wishes to extol.

If I am right in this view, the point at issue is whether the concepts of increasing and diminishing returns are instruments of service in the construction of a realistic economic science. Dr. Clapham appears to hold that, provided, as boxes, they cannot be filled, it is self-evident they can serve no purpose of this kind. In that I venture to suggest that he is mistaken, that he has, in fact,

misunderstood altogether the nature of the work that he is belittling. A central problem of economics, from the time of Adam
Smith downward, has been to disentangle and analyse the causes
by which the values of different things are determined. In the
course of the prolonged attack that economists have made upon
this problem it has been found convenient to distinguish influences
acting from the side of demand and influences acting from the side
of supply; and it has been found further, on the side of supply,
that the relations between changes in aggregate output and changes
in cost per unit differ according to the nature of the article and
the period of time that we have in view. In studying the relation
between aggregate output and cost we naturally distinguish the
group of conditions under which cost increases as aggregate output
increases from the group of conditions under which it diminishes
as aggregate output increases. Since it so happens that alterations
in demand will produce effects of a different kind, and not merely
of a different degree, according as one or other of these groups of
conditions prevail, we are led to give the distinction between them
a certain prominence. But the distinction itself is not the fruit for
which we have been labouring. It is a mere incident in our general
analysis of the problem of value—an analysis in which are brought
to light the complex inter-relations of internal and external economies and those deep-seated difficulties, obscure to all economists
before Dr. Marshall wrote, connected with the element of time.
It is not to be judged by itself in isolation from the general analysis.
To take the categories of increasing and diminishing returns out
of their setting and to speak of them as though they were a thing
that could be swept away without injury to the whole *corpus* of
economics is a very perverse proceeding. It would be easy enough
to drop the names; but does anybody seriously imagine that we
could have any understanding at all of the influences governing
economic values if the *fact* that aggregate output and supply cost
have varying relations to one another were ignored?

But I am anxious to return to the question of practical usefulness, because I personally am inclined to go further in this
matter than I think Dr. Clapham himself would go. Even a thoroughly realistic economic science would not, in and for itself, make
any great appeal to me. Practical usefulness, not necessarily, of
course, immediate and direct, but still practical usefulness of some

sort, is what I look for from this particular department of knowledge. Without that, if there were hope of light alone, and not of fruit, from economic investigation, I should not trouble much about it. It is here, therefore, that Dr. Clapham's paper chiefly interests me. He maintains three separate things: first, that his economic boxes, so long as they are empty, cannot have practical usefulness; secondly, that, even if they were filled, they would not have practical usefulness; thirdly, that they cannot be filled. I proceed to consider these three contentions in turn.

The first of them I have already partly answered. These boxes, as he calls them, are not merely boxes; they are also elements in the intellectual machinery by which the main part of modern economic thought functions. If then it be granted that this thought as a whole is able to render any practical service—and, in face of the enormous range of problems now confronting Europe in which the issues involved are largely economic, this will scarcely be disputed—these particular elements in that machinery cannot be singled out from the rest and condemned as useless; they are an organic and inseparable part of that machinery. But there is a further consideration of a more direct kind. Even regarded as boxes, and empty ones at that, the categories of increasing and diminishing returns are not mere ornaments. Knowledge about them cannot, indeed, on the hypothesis of their eternal emptiness, help us in a positive way, but it can help us a great deal in a negative one. It enables us to discover with absolute precision what assumptions are implicit in the statements about economic causation (upon which action is often based) that politicians and other such persons are accustomed to make for the guidance of the public. When we are informed that a tax always raises the price of the taxed article by the amount of the tax, we know that our informant, though himself probably unaware of it, is tacitly assuming that all articles are produced under conditions of constant return. We know, therefore, that his statement is almost certainly untrue, and we also know what information we should need to have about any article subject to tax, in order to prophesy what the result on the price, at various intervals after the tax was imposed, would be. Dr. Clapham will hardly contend that this is unimportant. He will hardly deny that science may help practice by exposing the falsehoods of charlatanry as well as by itself discovering truths.

The second contention is that, even if they could be filled,
knowledge about these boxes would have no practical usefulness.
In discussing this contention I am again placed in something of
a difficulty by Dr. Clapham's failure to clarify his own meaning.
Of course, merely to know that a particular article—article, being
a term used by shopkeepers, sounds more "realistic" than commodity—is being produced under conditions of increasing or diminishing returns is to know very little indeed about it. It is on
a par with knowing merely that a man's temperature is above or
below normal. To get any large and important guidance for practice we must know, or, at all events, we must have some rough
general idea, as to *how much* above or below the normal it is. If
we knew that the hat industry was being conducted under conditions of increasing or of diminishing returns, we should be able,
it is true, to say *something* more about the effect to be expected
from the imposition of a tax on hats than we can say now; we
should be able to say, that is, whether, *other things being equal,*
a given tax would cause the price to go up by more or by less than
the amount of the tax. But this is all we should be able to say. In
order to get a definite result—to be able to say by how much, in
actual pounds, shillings and pence, prices would go up,—we must
know a great deal more than this. We must know the exact shape
of the relevant part of the supply curve for hats and also the exact
shape of the relevant part of the demand curve; in more general,
if less exact, terms, we must know the numerical values of the
elasticities of supply and demand for quantities of hats in the
neighbourhood of the quantity that is actually being produced,
and the relation of these elasticities to the passage of various intervals of time. Had Dr. Clapham pointed out that to know that a
particular article is being produced under conditions of increasing
or diminishing returns is not to know these things, and is, therefore, of little practical use, I should have agreed with him. But this
is not his line of argument at all. He speaks as though increasing
returns is one definite thing and diminishing returns another,
whereas, in fact, each of these terms covers an infinite number of
different things. The boxes between which the "analytics" are interested to draw distinctions are not, as he evidently supposes, the
bulky valises displayed in their shop windows, but an intricate collection of little cases inside these, each labelled with a legend of

the form "η lies between a and $(a + \Delta\, a)$ and e lies between b and $(b + \Delta\, b)$." Dr. Clapham does not say in so many words that the filling of these little cases would have no usefulness for practice, because he does not seem to realise that, inside the valises, there are any little cases. But the form of his argument suggests that, if he had realised that fact, he would have said this. At all events, in rebuttal of his view I wish to argue, not that the filling of the boxes would serve practice a great deal, but only that the filling of the little cases would do so.

Consider then his argument. For believing that the filling of the boxes would be of no appreciable use he adduces two reasons. First, he would not thereby be enabled to give any more advice than he can offer now to a manufacturer of woollen goods in the conduct of his business. Secondly, the information available to governments through the filling of the boxes would not, *by itself,* enable them to reach any political decisions. To the first of these reasons the answer is that it is not the business of economists to teach woollen manufacturers how to make and sell wool, or brewers how to make and sell beer, or any other business men how to do their job. If that was what we were out for, we should, I imagine, immediately quit our desks and get somebody—doubtless at a heavy premium, for we should be thoroughly inefficient—to take us into his woollen mill or his brewery. The second reason is a remarkable one. Dr. Clapham has learnt from the *Principles of Economics* that, if we knew, as between two articles, that one was being produced under conditions of increasing and the other under conditions of diminishing returns, we could draw inferences that were relevant to the comparative effects on social welfare of putting taxes on the one or the other of them. Because there are also other considerations relevant to that problem, Dr. Clapham considers that this knowledge would be useless! What is there to say of reasoning of this quality? It is as though Dr. Clapham, in choosing between two suits of clothes (he will forgive the horrible suggestion that he might buy such things ready-made!), should refuse to inquire which of them will fit him best, because there is another consideration also relevant to his choice, namely, the amount of money that they respectively cost!

There remains the contention that the empty boxes cannot, in fact, be filled. Here I must point out that, had Dr. Clapham realised what the issue really was, he would have been able to strengthen his case very considerably. For, if it is difficult to decide whether a particular article falls into the increasing returns box or the diminishing returns box, *a fortiori* it is difficult to decide into which of the little cases inside these boxes it falls. I am very far from wishing to underrate the difficulty of this task: indeed I have myself more than once discussed and emphasised it.[1] None the less to declare, of a piece of work that has not yet been seriously tackled, that it is impossible, is, in my judgment, at least premature. Something, I believe, might be accomplished if economists would take counsel with leaders of business, expert in particular branches of production. Of course, if Dr. Clapham, or anybody else, goes to them and says, "My dear fellows, an 'analytic' up at Cambridge wants to know if your industries obey the laws of diminishing, constant or increasing returns," no great illumination is likely to result. But, if he were to ask them to discuss the conditions, as regards the relation between aggregate output and cost, under which various important articles have been and are being produced,—which is really asking a great deal more—I for one do not believe that he would always come empty away. Nor need we rely only on the general judgment of people expert in particular industries. There is already available a certain amount of statistical material—and we may reasonably hope that this material will both grow in quantity and improve in quality—from which students with the requisite mathematical equipment may make rough deductions about the shapes of certain supply schedules. On the side of demand something on these lines has already been accomplished. On the side of supply the task is undoubtedly more difficult. But we need not conclude that it is impossible. The hope of which I have just spoken, that better statistical material may presently be available for study, thus making the inquiry more feasible than it has been hitherto, should itself forbid that. There is, indeed, a lion in the path; the fact that those people—with the towering exception of Jevons—who have the qualities required for conducting a detailed intensive study of particular industries and writing monographs about them, are not usually well versed either in the more intricate parts of economic analysis or in modern sta-

---

[1] Cf., e.g., *The Economics of Welfare*, pp. 8–10.

tistical technique; while the "analytics" lack alike capacity and inclination for these detailed studies. For this there is only one real remedy. We must endeavour to train up more men of the calibre of Jevons, who are equally at home in both fields. Till we can accomplish that, the next best thing, for those lesser persons who are moderately qualified for the one sort of inquiry and for the other, is to work together in combination, and not to waste time in quarrelling, perhaps on the basis of an imperfect understanding, with the deficiencies of one another's methods.

THE ECONOMIC BOXES: A REJOINDER *

By J. H. Clapham

By the courtesy of the Editor and of Professor Pigou I am allowed to append a few notes and comments. My object having been to elicit a reply, I am content to have succeeded and so will be brief. The preliminary sparring before the big blows are hit I will pass over, without denying that so good a sparrer as Professor Pigou "gets in." Neither he nor I think very highly of "pure" economic knowledge which is likely to remain "pure" indefinitely. We agree that a mere study of implications which is fully justifiable "in the kingdom of pure mathematics," or a mere study of facts in succession which may be justifiable in the kingdom of history, would not be justifiable as the main business of economics. I cannot tell him—nor in a similar case, I should imagine, could he tell himself—how much of my rudeness towards the boxes is due to (a) their emptiness and (b) their possible uselessness is filled. The emptiness is ground common to us both; an important fact, I think.

A word about "complexes." In form Professor Pigou's reference to them is only a sparring point, but I think it has importance. I admit the anti-commodity complex: Professor Pigou has found the right name for my complaint. I know that the term commodity is used in order that it may cover hats and gold watches and onions,

---

* *The Economic Journal*, Vol. XXXII (1922), pp. 560–563. Reprinted, by the courtesy of the publisher and Lady Clapham, without change from the original text.

and I constantly suspect that the user does not know whether the propositions which he is affirming as to commodities are true of either onions or gold watches or hats. The oftener he does it without an illustration the stronger grow my suspicion and my complex. The cure—in a friend's hands—is a series of illustrative footnotes.

This leads to a point of more general interest. "Dr. Clapham appears to hold that, provided as boxes they cannot be filled, it is self-evident that they can serve no purpose"—"as instruments in the construction of a realistic economic science." "In that I venture to suggest . . . that he has, in fact, misunderstood altogether the nature of the work that he is belittling." Professor Pigou then goes on to show the importance of the laws of returns, or some equivalent, in the whole theory of value, and says that to take them out of their setting is "a very perverse proceeding." I see no perversity in criticising part of a theory; but I was at first disposed to search for empty boxes in more parts than one. This space forbade. I have a fear lest a theory of value which should prove permanently unable to state of what particular and individual values some of its more important conclusions were true might in the long run be neglected by mankind. I fear also that a too constant thinking in terms of commodities may tend to blind "analytics"—to use the nickname as to whose imperfect applicability Professor Pigou and I are in fact at one—to this danger. It was solicitude for the theory of value, not indifference to its complex beauties, which urged me on.

Professor Pigou's argument about the negative use of the boxes, even if empty, is decisive within its range. It is one of the considerations which I had overlooked and which I am glad to have pointed out. "Dr. Clapham will hardly deny that science may help practice by exposing the falsehoods of charlatanry as well as by itself discovering truths." He will not; but he is very anxious that economic science should be able to do more, and that, where and in so far as it is at present unable to do more, it should make the fact quite clear.

I believe I was aware of the "intricate collection of little cases inside" my big boxes; although I seem to have written so carelessly that Professor Pigou can tell people that I "evidently suppose" that "analytics" are only interested in the question whether hats or onions are in big box D.R. or in big box I.R. My natural, and not unscientific, wish was to learn about the big boxes first. When I know that my Botany tops are in I.R. it will be time enough to examine further. Professor Pigou will find a reference to tops which shows that I was not entirely blind to the subdivisions of the big boxes, though I know well enough that he and not I should be entrusted with the labelling of some of the little ones. He has shown, that had I "realised what the issue really was," I could have made this part of my argument much stronger. I always thought I could.

I accept the rebuke, whose point is sharpened by references to ready-made clothes and "a certain *naïveté*." My statements in the section criticised were exceedingly incomplete. I was not writing a treatise. I was merely anxious to indicate that we have had hitherto, even from the very greatest economists, rather sketchy indications of the probable uses of the big and little cases, when filled. I was not anxious to suggest that it is Professor Pigou's business to teach a brewer to brew; but I think it may be his business, when he says that such and such social consequences will result from a tax on, or a monopoly in, commodities of such and such a type, to be able to tell the brewer whether in this context "commodity" covers beer as well as hats, onions and gold watches.

Professor Pigou does not say whether or not inventions are to be included in that general progress in the efficiency of an industry which tends towards increasing returns. I assume, therefore, that he agrees with me that exclusion will condemn the boxes to perpetual emptiness. His suggestions towards filling the boxes are much scantier than I had thought possible. I made my treatment a trifle crude partly in the hope of provoking someone to say—Give me these and those facts and series of statistics about, say, pig-iron and I will box it for you. I had anticipated that the facts and statistics demanded might be, by common consent, at present unprocurable; but I had hoped that they might be specified. And now I am paid with a cheque drawn on the bank of an unborn Jevons. Can no one give us more current coin? I do not deny that a second Jevons may do this thing; but I do not think that Professor Pigou's reply has given him much help.

Finally, I do not agree that discussions about method are "time wasted in quarrelling," even if, as Professor Pigou suggests, we may have an imperfect understanding of one another's methods. Public discussion elucidates the methods and improves the understanding. There has for some years been too much abstention from it among economists, due in part to a certain very natural piety. Things are constantly said in conversation which never get into print, and we need, as one of us would say, to bring inside and outside opinion into line. Mounted on the smoothly running machine which he handles with such incomparable skill, Professor Pigou may be a trifle impatient of suggestions that a rather differently constructed model might have a longer and more useful life; but that is no reason why the suggestion should not be made, even by a much less expert driver.

7

THOSE EMPTY BOXES *

By D. H. Robertson ‖ **

§ 1. A year ago the pages of this Journal were enlivened by a battle of giants. The contest raged over the practical utility of certain refinements of analytical economics: in particular it was debated whether the theoretical sorting of industries into boxes labelled "diminishing return" and "increasing return" could be turned to practical account. Into that mêlée it is not my purpose to enter directly, though I think that my suggestions, if correct, may have some bearing upon its issue. My purpose is an even more presumptuous one—to engage, albeit armed with an apparatus as defective as David's, one of the giants upon his own ground, and to cast a pebble which, if it glances innocuous from that august brow, may perhaps at least elicit an explanatory roar.

My aim then is to echo, and I hope to expand, certain criticisms which have been wafted across the Atlantic of the analytical mechanism elaborated by Professor Pigou in his *Economics of Welfare*

---

* *The Economic Journal,* Vol. XXXIV (1924), pp. 16–30. Reprinted, by the courtesy of the publisher and the author, with typographical corrections.

‖ Trinity College, Cambridge University, England.

** Professor Robertson adds the following note, written in November, 1950:

"The reader is begged to remember that this 26-year-old article belongs to the pre-Sraffa, pre-Chamberlin age. In gratefully giving my consent to its reprint, I must not be thought to be offering any defense either of its style or of its content. In particular, I have long since acquiesced in the concept of a true or 'hypothetical' long period falling supply curve, provided it is used with the caution which Marshall enjoins; and I would agree that in any attempt to distil such a curve from recorded facts, it would be proper to attempt to eliminate the effect of major inventions which were clearly not dependent on the size of the industry.

"Nevertheless, however unconvincingly formulated, I think that my instincts to cry out against the excesses of 'marginal cost pricing,' and to appeal for a more 'workable' concept of competition, were sound, and even look rather surprisingly up-to-date!"

for dealing with these conceptions of diminishing and increasing return. I desire to suggest that the character of that mechanism (1) renders the "filling of the boxes" unnecessarily difficult; (2) prompts to a use of the boxes, if filled, which under certain conditions of political and economic development might become positively misleading and dangerous. And I desire to suggest that this unfortunate result has its roots—I will not say in an unhappy choice of terminology (there are limits even to David's presumption), but in a tendency to discover a simplicity of parallelism where none exists, and to submit disparate materials to an identical logical process. The boxes, if I may make free with the metaphor, are not in my view properly to be loaded upon the same cab. It is almost as though one were a hat-box, and the other a monstrous compound of a box at the opera and a box growing alongside a garden path.

§ 2. Now first, while far from insisting that this question of terminology is fundamental, I must be allowed my private grumble about it. By industries which obey the laws respectively of diminishing and increasing return I take to be meant those in which the average full expenses per unit of product respectively increase and diminish as the scale of production is expanded.[1] In spite of Dr. Marshall's arguments to the contrary,[2] I wish heartily that English-speaking writers could agree to speak of such industries as obeying respectively the laws of increasing and decreasing cost.[3] What superfluous confusions about the emergence of rent in manufacturing industries, what regrettable misunderstandings of the teaching of economic science about the relation of agricultural progress to the problem of population,[4] could have been avoided if the phrase "the law of diminishing return" could have been tied down to denoting the results of either (a) applying successive

---

[1] Professor Pigou does not himself use this definition; but it appears consistent with, and is indeed derived from, the definition and properties of his "supply-curve" (*Economics of Welfare*, p. 933).

[2] *Principles*, p. 319 n.

[3] See Professor Bullock's most valuable article, "The Variation of Productive Forces," *The Quarterly Journal of Economics*, August 1902.

[4] A distinguished Colonial professor still, I believe, boasts publicly of his intention of disproving the existence of the law of diminishing return from land.

doses of one factor to a fixed quantity of all the others, or (*b*) applying successive doses of all the factors but one to a fixed quantity of that one! And even that much duplicity of function would seem to entitle it to extra pay! I look forward to the time when this hard-worked phrase, relieved of all other duties, shall thus be confined to expressing the great unifying principle which runs through the whole theory of distribution—surely a sufficient honour to content the most ambitious company of words.

I propose, therefore, to speak of "decreasing cost" industries and "increasing cost" industries; but I repeat that I do not intend that this choice of phrasing shall alter the substance of my argument.

§ 3. And now to business. Professor Pigou's most momentous conclusion is that under conditions of free competition production in "increasing cost" industries is carried further, and in "decreasing cost" industries less far than the true interests of society require. I shall not attempt to summarise his argument, but shall give such references as will enable the reader to refresh his memory of it.

Let us confine ourselves at present to "long-period" conditions, in the sense that we are not concerned with the effects of cyclical or other temporary fluctuations of demand. And let us deal first with "decreasing cost" industries in the sense defined. Now the first point is that, so far as I can see, this apparently harmless phrase covers two sets of analytically quite distinct phenomena. As the scale of output of an industry is increased, the average cost[5] per unit may. fall for either of the two following reasons. (I) in some branches of production the process of investment of fixed capital is, from the nature of the case, lumpy and discontinuous; and once such a process is completed, the larger the number of units of output produced (or, to put the same thing in a different way, the larger the number of units of floating resources of all kinds employed) the smaller the share of fixed capital charges which each unit has to bear, and the less therefore, in general, its full cost. "We may take the production of a medal as a type of such a supply. For we may suppose that it costs a manu-

---

[5] I use this word henceforth as an abbreviation for "full expenses of production."

facturer of medals £20 to produce a steel die, and after that has
been made it costs him 5s. for the metal and stamping of each
medal. If then he produced only one medal the cost would be
£20 5s. If he produced two medals, £10 5s. each. If he produced
fifty medals, the cost would be 13s. each; and so on."[6] Note first
that such a statement may well represent, not an evanescent state
of affairs, but the permanent conditions under which an industry
(such as newspaper enterprise?) is operated. Note secondly that
the element of time, so often the source of all our troubles, is here
as nearly as possible innocent: a raising of the demand schedule
for the medals (occasioned, say, by the establishment of a permanent state of war) will instantaneously lower their average cost.

But (II) decreased average cost may accompany expanded output for another reason, namely, because, *given time*, methods of
technique and of organisation are capable of improvement in any
one of a myriad different ways, so that ultimately a larger output
can be produced at a lower cost per unit than that at which a
smaller output was previously produced. I do not pretend that
this class of cases is entirely unconnected with the first class; for
the "economies of large-scale production," and among them the
installation of large and specialised pieces of plant, are among
the causes of the prevalence of decreasing cost in my sense (II).
But the difference between the classes can be seen by reflecting
that *nothing but a raising of the demand schedule* can be relied
upon to establish a lowered cost in Class (I), while the progress
of time, the enterprise of producers and the occurrence of invention[7] are expected, without necessarily any alteration of normal
demand, to produce this result in Class (II).

§ 4. But already I seem to myself to hear a triple growl from
the giant. (A) First, "Have I not made it clear," I hear him ask,
"that for simplicity's sake I conceive of the resources applied to
industry as a homogeneous flow (*Economics of Welfare*, p. 114)?
And how am I touched then by that discontinuous £20 steel die,
or by your distinction between fixed and floating resources, which

---

[6] Cunynghame, *A Geometrical Political Economy*, p. 57.

[7] Dr. Clapham's query whether invention is to be classed among the causes
of "decreasing cost" must clearly, on my definition, be answered in the
affirmative (*The Economic Journal*, 1922, pp. 314, 562). (See pages 129 and 141
of the present volume.)

I have decided to ignore?" And I can only reply, Yes, he seems to have made that clear. But I shall go on to urge three things. (1) There is no doubt that, in ordinary discussions of the phenomenon of decreasing cost, industries of my set (I) play a very large part. It seems to be of such cases that Prof. Edgeworth[8] speaks as "so important as often to obtain the title of Increasing Return *par excellence*," and of the five sets of conditions which he distinguishes as "attended with the attribute Increasing Return," two indubitably turn on this principle of the discontinuity of investment and the economy of multiplication.[9] (2) The case is covered by Professor Pigou's diagrams in so far that while, in the case of our medal-manufacturer, the "curve of marginal supply prices" (*Economics of Welfare*, p. 931) would become horizontal after the second medal, it would remain continuously below the supply-curve, and cut the demand-curve further to the right than the supply-curve does. (3) But I can appeal more directly to Professor Pigou. He states specifically (*op. cit.*, pp. 275–276) that "among railways there is ground for believing that, at all events until considerable development has been reached, this condition [strong action of the law of increasing returns] is generally satisfied. The reason is that the fixed plant of a railway cannot, in practice, be so made as to be capable of effecting less than a considerable minimum of transportation. The aggregate costs of arranging for rail transport for one ounce per week are very nearly as great as those of arranging for the transport of many thousand tons. . . . This implies increasing returns acting strongly till a large investment has been made, and afterwards less strongly." There can indeed be no question that Professor Pigou's analysis is intended to apply to railways; nor that, in Ripley's words,[10] "from this fact [discontinuity of investment], therefore, rather than because of any marked economies of large-scale production, may it be affirmed that railroads offer a notable example of the law of increasing

---

[8] "Contributions to the Theory of Railway Rates," *The Economic Journal*, 1911, p. 370.

[9] *Ibid.*, pp. 553–555.

[10] Quoted by Edgeworth, "Contributions," etc., *The Economic Journal*, 1913, p. 217; who, while holding that other conditions generating "increasing return" have been too much ignored by writers on Railway Economics (*ibid.*, 1911, p. 553), seems to concur in giving such considerations the primacy.

returns." If, therefore, Professor Pigou tells me that his apparatus of a homogeneous flow of resources is not a suitable one for dealing with my Class (I) industries, I shall joyfully agree; but if he forbids me on that account to discuss them with him, I shall decline to obey.

§ 5. (B) But there is another door of escape for the wounded giant which I think it prudent to bar. We are dealing so far with a regime of competition; and he may tell me that my adopted medal-maker is not a true subject of that regime. If he were, and if he found that £10 5s. were the ruling price for medals, he would produce not two, but ever such a large number. The fact that an output of two is associated with a price of £10 5s. indicates that he is regulating output with an eye to the effect of his actions upon the price of his product, which is improper conduct in a denizen of the realm of competition, even though to act otherwise would, by preventing him covering his total costs of production, drive him out of business. Now poor David has no weapons with which to attack this mathematical conception of pure competition. But he knows, or thinks he knows, that his Class (I) industries exist, and that they do not all exercise monopoly powers, but that in their case, as in others, normal competitive price must in the long run cover supplementary as well as prime costs. He is even prepared to invent for his own use a meaning of the term "competition," which shall imply that producers are not in a position to make monopoly profits, but *are* free, and determined, in the long run to cover their standing charges. He suspects that printing, and in most countries in normal times railways, are conducted permanently on these lines, and he is tempted (but without falling) to hazard further attempts at filling this particular sub-box. He suspects too—a point to which he will return—that it is "competitive" conditions of this kind that the State, if it takes over an industry, should (unless for good reason to the contrary) seek to emulate.

(C) There is one more loophole—will the giant make for it? Will he charge me with neglecting his warning (*op. cit.,* p. 115 and p. 931, note) that whatever the scale of output, the flow of resources must be conceived of as organised appropriately to that scale? I shall not plead guilty; for whether my medal-maker is turning out two medals or fifty, he must be assumed to be acting in the most sensible way open to him. The relatively high cost per unit of the smaller output is due, not to any lack of judgment on his part in combining his factors, but to technical facts beyond his control.

§ 6. I shall assume, therefore, that I am entitled to discuss with Professor Pigou both my types of "decreasing cost" industry, and to discuss them separately. Let us take Group (I) first.

Let us suppose that m units of fixed resources (typified by the steel die) have been sunk in the industry, and that n units of running resources (typified by metal and labour for stamping) are being employed in conjunction with them, and that p units of output are being produced. Professor Pigou's analysis (*op. cit.*, p. 937) leads us to suppose that, in the social interest, p should be such that the additional units of output specifically attributable to the addition of the nth unit of running resources should sell for a price which adequately remunerates that nth unit of running resources. In our concrete case, if demand is such that fifty medals can be disposed of at 5s. each, fifty medals should be produced, since the fiftieth medal is the "net product" of the marginal 5s. worth of resources, and 5s. is the "marginal supply price" for an output of fifty—the difference made to aggregate expenses of production by organising production so as to produce fifty instead of forty-nine (*op. cit.*, p. 931).

Now I deny that this pth unit of output is in any significant sense the net product of the nth unit of running resources.[11] It is the net product of [that unit $+ \dfrac{m}{p}$ units of fixed resources]. The fact is that these m units of fixed resources yield *no* product unless at least one unit of running resources is applied in conjunction with them, and that in order to make sense at all we must credit them with a part of any additional output which appears at first sight to be specifically attributable to the addition of any nth unit of running resources. Professor Pigou's statement (*op. cit.*, p. 190) that when any given aggregate of resources is devoted to an occupation, any one unit of those resources must be conceived

---

[11] In our concrete case, we can choose our units so that p always $= n$. If the special costs per medal for labour and materials either increase or diminish as output is expanded, the argument becomes slightly more complex in form, but is unaltered in substance.

of as yielding the same net product as any other, leads me to suppose that he would agree with this view; but, on the other hand, the rest of his analysis, and especially his treatment of the railway problem, leads me to suppose that he would not. For if the view is correct, the whole case for carrying production in this group of "decreasing cost" industries beyond the competitive point seems to me to vanish. And consider how paradoxical that case is! For if it is sound, the logical outcome seems to be that the State, if it takes over an industry of this type, is entitled to neglect altogether, in determining its price-and-output policy, the costs of the fixed capital embarked, paying for them presumably out of taxation, and pushing production to such a point that price covers only the special costs of the pth unit of output. Whereas, if my view is correct, the State (unless for clear cause shown) ought so to regulate output that aggregate receipts cover aggregate costs without yielding monopoly profits. Even if through want of capacity I have misunderstood the giant's analysis, let me try to pin him down to this supremely important point of practical policy. Suppose discrimination to be ruled out, as in the sale of Government publications (for I see an avenue of escape for him along the road of discrimination), how should such a nationalised enterprise (any broader social reasons for subsidisation being disregarded) fix the scale of its output and its charges? Does his analysis or does it not lead directly to the conclusion that it should claim to be subsidised to the extent of the whole burden of the charges of the fixed original plant? And can this conclusion possibly be sound? And if not, what logical half-way house is there between this procedure and charging so as to cover total costs, i.e. simulating the conditions of free competition?

§ 7. Now let us turn to my second group of "decreasing cost" industries—those in which an enlarged output is associated with a decreased cost per unit of output as a result of the introduction of improvements in technique and organisation. How far is it true that in these industries output is smaller than is socially desirable, and might be brought to a socially more desirable level by some form or other of State intervention?

Now it is these industries that, at any rate in the prelude (*op. cit.* pp. 189–192) to his discussion of the whole matter, Professor Pigou seems to me to have uppermost in his mind. His explanation there given of the failure of competition to produce the best results must therefore be carefully noted. The employment of an additional unit of resources in any industry may, it appears, so modify the general organisation of the industry as to make each of the units of resources employed in it yield a different net product from what it otherwise would have done; but since, under pure competition, the individual who has made the extra investment experiences only a very small part of the effects of this indirect impact upon general organisation, it is not to be expected that the probable nature and total magnitude of these effects should appreciably influence his actions. The relevance of this doctrine to "increasing cost" industries does not concern us here: as applied to "decreasing cost" industries, it can only mean that all the improvements in organisation from which "decreasing cost" arises are of the nature of "external economies"—"those dependent on the general development of the industry"[12]—, the familiar "internal economies"—"those dependent on the resources of the individual houses of business engaged in it, on their organisation and the efficiency of their management"[12]—having vanished into thin air.[13]

Now once again I am conscious of being up against the mathematical theory of pure competition, and aware that that is so much the worse for me. But I cannot let it rest at that. I recall to mind the "representative firm," which "has its fair share of those *internal and* external economies, which appertain to the aggregate scale of production in the industry to which it belongs";[14] whose size, "while partly dependent on changes in technique and in the costs of transport, is governed, other things being equal, by the general expansion of the industry," and is therefore clearly to be regarded

---

[12] Marshall, *Principles,* p. 266.

[13] So determined is the Professor to banish these old friends that, disturbed by the apparent theoretical incompatibility of pure competition with the prevalence of decreasing cost at all, he seems to hold (p. 192) that each firm is (? or would be if it were isolated) working under conditions of increasing cost while the industry as a whole is working under conditions of decreasing cost. I would prefer to offend the mathematical theory of competition than to follow him through this logical hole in his own logical net; therein agreeing with Professor Allyn Young, who "cannot imagine 'external economies' adequate to bring about this result" (*The Quarterly Journal of Economics,* August 1913, p. 678, note).

[14] Marshall, *Principles,* p. 459. My italics.

as capable of significant variation:[14] and which is nevertheless certainly a denizen of the realm of competition, and indeed plays a commanding part in the theory of normal competitive price. I even take the supreme risk of starting to fill the sub-box under consideration, by flinging into it at a venture electrical engineering and cinema-film manufacture, in order to confirm my impression that any likely occupant of the sub-box is almost sure to be carried on by firms who *are* capable of introducing and appropriating internal improvements in organisation and technique. I cannot, therefore, bring myself to believe that, under any conception of competition which is appropriate to the matter in hand, the phenomenon of decreasing cost can be explained entirely in terms of external economies: nor, therefore, that if the rigid mathematical disharmony which Professor Pigou predicates (*op. cit.* p. 938) between competitive and socially desirable output really exists, it is to be explained on this ground of the certainty that the individual producer will not reap the reward of his own improvements. And in order to test this conclusion, I make my old supposition. Suppose an industry of this character to be administered in trust by a National Guild. Since the disharmony of interest due to the externalisation of economies is removed—since the Guild can be certain that the full advantages of any improvement which it makes in organisation will be enjoyed by itself alone—it would be natural to infer from Professor Pigou's analysis that such a Guild will produce what he holds to be the socially most desirable output— that is, will push production to a point at which the product of the marginal unit of resources is sold for a price which just affords adequate remuneration to that marginal unit. But of course it will do no such thing, for that would be to carry on production at a loss. It will regulate output in such a way that total receipts cover total costs—that is, it will seek to establish deliberately the equilibrium which tends to be established automatically under conditions of competition.

§ 8. If, therefore, competition really offends in the rigid mathematical manner asserted, we must look for some other explanation. And I can find none. I am led on to question the relevance of Professor Pigou's whole apparatus to this group of "decreasing cost" industries as well as to the other. Is not the body (whether private monopolist or State) which seeks to improve substantially[15] on competitive output in such cases seeking to voyage *pennis non homini datis,* and not merely to penetrate the secrets of Time, but to do that leisurely old gentleman's work for him? I struggle out of the giant's embraces into the peaceful enclave of my hard-won prejudices about the nature of decreasing cost of this type:– that it only means that, given time and the progress of organisation, a larger output can be produced at a lower cost per unit than a smaller output used to be. We used not to dare conceive of falling cost per unit as a determinant of increased output, but only as resulting from it, or at the rashest as "being associated with it."[16] Dare we, therefore, conceive of falling "marginal supply price" as a potential determinant of increased output, as Professor Pigou seems to do when he comes to discuss the actions of a monopolist with powers of discrimination (*op. cit.* pp. 248, 950)? Let me make my full confession. I do not believe the "curve of marginal supply prices" has any message for us at all in connection with my "decreasing cost" industries of Group (II). I can attach a meaning to him in connection with my Group (I), and though I do not regard him as such a socially desirable character as Professor Pigou does, I can see his bearing on certain problems of price-discrimination. But in our present surroundings I do not want him at all. I am content with an old-fashioned supply-curve, the locus through time of the end-points of a number of "particular expenses curves," each of them indicating the conditions of production in a given state of organisation. And I am content to suppose that at each point on the locus competition, by producing just so much that total receipts cover total costs, is *on the whole* securing the best results at that time and in that stage of organisation attainable.

§ 9. *On the whole,* for having cleared away the alleged rigidly mathematical sins of competition, we are now free to consider its not precisely measurable peccadilloes. For I have no wish to deny that the State, by well-devised intervention, can in certain cases accelerate the improvements in organisation from which decreasing cost arises. It can artificially raise the demand-curve by pro-

---

[15] For I have some qualifications to make, below, § 9.

[16] Cp. Marshall, *Principles,* p. 45, note. "But in real life the cost of production per unit is deduced from the amount expected to be produced, and not vice versa. Economists commonly follow this practice."

tective tariffs; it can artificially lower the particular expenses curve in force for the time being by the grant of well-administered subsidies; and in either way it may enable any given point on the original supply-curve to be reached earlier than it otherwise would have been. This would be true even if all economies were "internal"; but the admitted fact that some of them are "external" strengthens the point; for I have no wish to deny that the uncertainty of enjoying the full fruits of one's labours retards progress.[17] I have no theoretical quarrel, therefore, with the old-fashioned "infant industry" argument for protection or subsidisation, which it seems to me would remain intact even if Professor Pigou's constructions were to collapse, and which indeed is supported by him without the aid of their more intricate scaffolds (*op. cit.* p. 122). But the aim of such State intervention must be clearly conceived. It is not to maintain permanently a production which is "uneconomic" in the old-fashioned sense that receipts do not cover costs, but, at the expense of temporary loss, to bring about more quickly a state of affairs where production is still "economic," though larger than before. Such a policy of subsidy is, therefore, quite different in nature from the policy of *permanent* subsidy to "decreasing cost" industries recommended, at least in theory, by Professor Pigou (*op. cit.* p. 193).

§ 10. Has David grown bolder? Or is the giant really an easier mark when he stalks through the pastures of "increasing cost"? At any rate I take up my sling with alacrity.

What meaning are we to attach to the curves which exhibit the disharmony between competitive output and socially desirable output under conditions of increasing cost? We must return to the already-quoted prelude (*op. cit.* pp. 190–191) for Professor Pigou's answer. We find there that the employment of an additional unit of resources in an industry may modify *unfavourably* the general organisation of the industry, so as to make each unit of resources there employed yield a *smaller* net product than it would other-

---

[17] But it might, I think, be argued that under competition, since each supplier is chronically tempted to cater for a larger part of the market than is in fact likely to fall to his share, those experimental enlargements and improvements in which some of the roots of "decreasing cost" are found are more likely to take place than under a regime of single supply, even if the latter does not seek monopoly profits.

wise have done. And since, as we have seen, Professor Pigou conceives of each supplier as producing an indefinitely small proportion of the total output, these unfavourable results are felt almost entirely by other suppliers. In other words, we are asked to recognise the existence of "external diseconomies"[18] arising from the increase in output, and sufficient to produce the rigid mathematical defect of competitive output from the output socially desirable.

Now external economies we know, even if we refuse to yield them exclusive homage: transport developments, the telephone and the trade journal, the shop of the club and the market-price, subsidiary industries, a skilled labour supply,—we have all at some time tried to memorise and to reproduce the formidable list. But these external diseconomies, mathematically no less powerful, who in the world are they? Can we not be told at least one of their names? We are told in an appendix that "the reason why diminishing returns in terms of money appear where they do appear is, in general . . . that that proportionate combination of factors which it is most economical to employ when $(x + \Delta x)$ units of commodities are being produced is in general a less efficient proportionate combination than that which it is most economical to employ when x units are being produced" (*op. cit.* p. 936); but we seek in vain for a further word of explanation, or for any word at all of illustration. Out with your pebble, David, and get it over! You do not believe that there are "no sich persons."

It is natural that we should fall back on what we learnt long ago about the phenomenon of increasing cost. We know that additional applications of capital and labour to a given piece of land yield after a point a diminishing return of product; we know that the supply of land, and still more the supply of land of any particular quality, is limited; and we know that in industries making, directly or indirectly, a large use of land, the influence of these facts may overbear the influence of improvements in technique and organisation, and bring it about that, even if we allow for the progress of time, a larger volume of output is produced at a greater cost per unit than that at which a smaller volume of output used

---

[18] I am not attempting to father the actual phrase on Professor Pigou, but must ask him to admit parentage of the conception.

to be produced. Herein I am content to find the sole and sufficient explanation of the phenomenon of increasing cost. But I see no reason at all to infer from this state of affairs that production in such industries is being carried further than the social interest dictates. The land itself, and the other factors employed with it, are presumably each being employed up to, but not beyond, the point at which any further application would be less advantageous to the individuals concerned than application in some other field; and I see no cause for suspecting in this matter any but special and incidental disharmonies, of varying and indefinite magnitudes, between the interests of the individual and of society.

§ 11. But this, the giant may say, is to evade his fortifications, not to overthrow them by frontal attack. I must reply that that task, in my judgment, has been performed. Professor Allyn Young, accepting the twin curves but not the inferences drawn from them, argues that the reason for the excess of the "marginal supply price" of any given volume of output over its average cost per unit, lies in the necessity which increased output entails of paying higher prices for the land employed in yielding every unit of output, and not in any attraction of real resources to the industry beyond those specifically employed in producing the additional units of output.[19] I am convinced by this, and unshaken by the Professor's reply (*op. cit.* pp. 934–6), which turns once more on the negligibility of the relatively small. Any given industry, he states (a generous exception is made for "dominant crops" such as wheat), uses so small a proportion of the community's whole supply of land that it can obtain additional supplies of land without driving up against itself the price of land per unit. Yet I cannot unlearn all at once that the rent of land in any use depends on its productivity in that use, and not in some other use; I recall that farmer who has no doubt at all that it is best to grow hops on his land,[20] and therefore pre-

---

[19] Review of *Wealth and Welfare* in *The Quarterly Journal of Economics,* August 1913, p. 683.

[20] Marshall, *Principles,* p. 436. Cf. the note on the following page: "And if for the purposes of any particular argument we take together the whole expenses of the production on that land, and divide these among the whole of the commodity produced, then the rent which we ought to count in is not that which the land would pay if used for producing the first commodity. but that which it does pay when used for producing the second."

sumably under competition has to pay a rent appropriate to hop-growing; and I feel convinced that if there is a large expansion in the scale of production, say, of the cinema industry in any town, its effect will be felt on the rental value of the sites which that industry occupies.

And if Professor Pigou is right, how does it come about that when output is expanded a "less efficient proportionate combination of factors" has to be employed than was previously the case? I can see no reason for such a drop in efficiency, except that the margin of application of capital and labour has had to be pushed further, owing to the impossibility of obtaining indefinitely increased supplies of land at the old rent. Will Professor Pigou tell us clearly whether he conceives this drop in efficiency to be due to the operation of the law of diminishing return from land, or to some other "external diseconomy"? If the former, why should this law be brought into play if the industry can obtain the use of increased quantities of land at the old rent? And if the latter, what, once more, are these "external diseconomies"?

Meanwhile I conclude provisionally that, under increasing as under decreasing cost, competitive output, whilst doubtless not impeccable, commits no such rigid mathematical sin as that which has been laid to its charge.

§ 12. There remains a word to be said about "short periods," with reference to my Group (I) of "decreasing cost" industries. Such industries are, as has long been recognised, liable to terrible disorganisation in times of temporary depression of demand, since any hope of covering standing charges is apt to be temporarily abandoned, and slaughter prices accepted. If sellers "pursue this policy constantly and without moderation . . . they might ruin many of those in the trade, themselves perhaps among the number; and in that case a revival of demand would find very little response in supply, and would raise violently the prices of the goods produced by the trade."[21] Further, as I have argued elsewhere,[22] such a policy may be disadvantageous to output in other trades, since if the demand for the product becomes inelastic (as it may, for instance, in such circumstances for machinery or for railway transport) the incentive to output in other trades is reduced. Restriction

[21] Marshall, *Principles*, p. 375.
[22] *A Study of Industrial Fluctuation*, pp. 203–205.

of output is the remedy now normally proposed and frequently adopted in such circumstances, and is in harmony with the general presumption (§ 6) that price should be made to cover full costs; but it does not follow that, *if we confine our view to temporary results,* there are not other better ways of dealing with the situation. Discrimination may be practised (as in the dumping policy of cartells), or a State subsidy may be given (as in effect proposed recently by the Industrial Group of Members of Parliament, and to some extent already done under the Trade Facilities Act), or, perhaps better still, the State might assist in storing the results of continued output clear of the market until demand revives once more.[23] I am far from denying that such devices have their place in dealing with emergencies; and I concede, therefore, that in such cases it may be right to push production in these industries beyond what is at the moment the "economic" point (in my sense of receipts covering costs). But I suggest that this is a wholly different matter from a permanent policy of subsidisation; and I would urge further that in all such emergency measures the urgency of the immediate necessity must be weighed against the danger of encouraging *over-investment* in these industries in the future, by relieving them from the responsibility for the consequences of any excesses in investment policy in which they may choose to indulge.

§ 13. Have I fulfilled either of my remoter hopes? Have I, by attempting a further analysis of the boxes, contributed at all either towards making them easier to fill, or towards making any good use of them when filled? As to the latter, at all events, I fear that I have been destructive rather than helpful; for if I am right, the uses that can be made of them are more modest, even in theory, than has been claimed. But I have, to console me, Professor Pigou's contention, and Dr. Clapham's admission, that even negative conclusions may be of use.[24]

And yet at the end I am a little despondent. Clad in the cuirass of the calculus, the vizard of unverified probability, and greaves of the second order of smalls, perhaps the giant is still unscathed and derisory. But will he at least—for he is a gentle giant—deign to pick up David's pebbles and fling them back at him? For David

---

[23] See *A Study of Industrial Fluctuation,* p. 251.

[24] *The Economic Journal,* 1922, pp. 462, 561. (Reprinted in the present volume, pages 135 and 140.)

is humble at heart, and would like to sing new songs to his sheep if only he really understood the tunes. And further, being of a mischievous disposition, he would rather enjoy telling the chieftains that the stern science of economics, who has so often enjoined the contrary, now actually urges them to supply many things to the people—Ford chariots perhaps, perhaps even copies of the Psalms—at almost nominal prices.

8

SOME FALLACIES IN THE INTERPRETATION
OF SOCIAL COST*

By F. H. Knight ||

In two recent articles in this Journal,[1] Professor F. D. Graham of Princeton University has developed an ingenious argument to prove that the classical theory of comparative cost as a demonstration of the economic advantage of trade between nations is "all wrong." He contends that a protective tariff may, after all, be a wise national policy in that it may enable the nation which adopts it to secure a larger product from its resources than would be secured if free trade were permitted. It is the opinion of the present writer, and the contention of this paper, that it is Professor Graham's argument which is fallacious, tho the way in which the classical theory has been formulated in many instances leaves much to be desired. The matter is of the greater importance because the most important argument, from the standpoint of general theory, in Professor A. C. Pigou's monumental work on *The Economics of Welfare*[2] is, as I shall also try to show, marred by the same, or a very similar, fallacy.

* *The Quarterly Journal of Economics,* Vol. XXXVIII (1924), pp. 582–606. Reprinted, by the courtesy of Harvard University Press and the author, without change from the original text.

|| The University of Chicago.

[1] *The Quarterly Journal of Economics,* February 1923, November 1923.

[2] The Macmillan Co., 1918. This paper was written and submitted to the editor of *The Quarterly Journal* before the appearance of the March number of *The Economic Journal.* In that number, Professor D. H. Robertson has an article covering some of the same ground and treating it with his usual analytic penetration and stylistic brilliancy. Moreover, in a rejoinder appended to that article, Professor Pigou admits the particular error in his analysis and states that it is to be eradicated in a forthcoming revised edition of his book. It seems inadvisable to recast and enlarge the present paper so as to include a discussion of Professor Robertson's argument, which is notably divergent from that presented herewith. I trust it will not be thought presumptuous to print without change the few pages which in some sense cover ground already covered by Professor Robertson.

If economic theory is interpreted as a critique of the competitive system of organization, its first and most general problem is that of determining whether the fundamental tendencies of free contractual relations under competitive control lead to the maximum production of value as measured in price terms. The problems of the validity of the price measure of "real value," and of the distribution of the value produced, are larger but subsequent problems, and belong to ethics as much as to economics; while the detailed comparison of the theoretical tendencies of perfect competition with the facts of any actual competitive society lie in the field of applied economics rather than that of theory. The theory of international or inter-regional trade is a special case under the more general problem, whether "society" can increase the production of exchange value by interfering with free bargaining relations: the case, namely, of bargains between its own members and members of some other society possessing a distinct body of productive resources. The peculiarity of international trade as compared with domestic lies in the immobility of population viewed as labor power. Natural resources are immobile even within a country, and capital goods enter into international commerce in the same way as goods ready for consumption.

Both Professor Graham and Professor Pigou reason to the conclusion that freedom of trade between regions may reduce the production of wealth in one or even both; and Professor Pigou extends essentially the same logic to cover the relations between different industries, irrespective of regional separation. The contention is that individual profit-seeking leads to an excessive investment of resources in industries of increasing cost (decreasing returns), part of which would yield more product if transferred by social action in some form to industries of constant or decreasing cost. The fallacy to be exposed is a misinterpretation of the relation between social cost and *entrepreneur's* cost. It will be convenient to take up first Professor Pigou's argument, which presents the more general problem.

I

In Professor Pigou's study the argument that free enterprise leads to excessive investment in industries having relatively upward-sloping cost curves is developed with the aid of a concrete example, the case of two roads.[3] Suppose that between two points there are two highways, one of which is broad enough to accommodate without crowding all the traffic which may care to use it, but is poorly graded and surfaced, while the other is a much better road but narrow and quite limited in capacity.[4] If a large number of trucks operate between the two termini and are free to choose either of the two routes, they will tend to distribute themselves between the roads in such proportions that the cost per unit of transportation, or effective result per unit of investment, will be the same for every truck on both routes. As more trucks use the narrower and better road, congestion develops, until at a certain point it becomes equally profitable to use the broader but poorer highway. The congestion and interference resulting from the addition of any particular truck to the stream of traffic on the narrow but good road affects in the same way the cost and output of all the trucks using that road. It is evident that if, after equilibrium is established, a few trucks should be arbitrarily transferred to the broad road, the reduction in cost, or increase in output, to those remaining on the narrow road would be a clear gain to the traffic as a whole. The trucks so transferred would incur no loss, for any one of them on the narrow road is a marginal truck, subject to the same relation between cost and output as any truck using the broad road. Yet whenever there is a difference in the cost, to an additional truck, of using the two roads, the driver of any truck has an incentive to use the narrow road, until the advantage is reduced to zero for all the trucks. Thus, as the author contends, individual freedom results in a bad distribution of investment between industries of constant and industries of increasing cost.

In such a case social interference seems to be clearly justified. If the government should levy a small tax on each truck using

---

[3] *Economics of Welfare,* p. 194.

[4] For simplicity, no account is taken of costs involved in *constructing* the two roads. The aim is to study the effects of the two types of "cost"—that which represents a consumption of productive power which might have been put to some other use, and pure rent or the payment for situation and opportunity. The assumption adopted is the simplest way of making the separation. The conclusion will not be changed if various types of cost are taken into account, so long as one of the roads has a definite situation advantage while the investment in the other can be repeated to any desirable extent with equivalent results in other locations.

the narrow road, the tax would be considered by the trucker as an element in his cost, and would cause the number of trucks on the narrow road to be reduced to the point where the *ordinary cost, plus the tax,* became equal to the cost on the broad road, assumed to be left tax free. The tax could be so adjusted that the number of trucks on the narrow road would be such as to secure the maximum efficiency in the use of the two roads taken together. The revenue obtained from such a tax would be a clear gain to the society, since no individual truck would incur higher costs than if no tax had been levied.

It is implied that the same argument holds good over the whole field of investment wherever investment is free to choose between uses subject to cost curves of different slope. Take, for example, two farms, one of superior quality, the other marginal or free land. Would not labor and capital go to the better farm, until the product per man became equal to the product to be obtained from the marginal land? If so, it is clear that the total product of all the labor and capital could be increased, as in the case of the roads, by transferring some of it from the superior to the inferior farm. This application of the reasoning will probably suggest the fallacy to any one familiar with conventional economic theory. The statement does in fact indicate what would happen *if no one owned the superior farm.* But under private appropriation and self-seeking exploitation of the land the course of events is very different. It is in fact the social function of ownership to prevent this excessive investment in superior situations.

Professor Pigou's logic in regard to the roads is, as logic, quite unexceptionable. Its weakness is one frequently met with in economic theorizing, namely that the assumptions diverge in essential respects from the facts of real economic situations.[5] The most essential feature of competitive conditions is reversed, the feature namely, of the private ownership of the factors practically significant for production. If the roads are assumed to be subject to private appropriation and exploitation, precisely the ideal situa-

---

[5] For the edification of the advocates of "inductive economics" it may be observed that the "facts" are not in dispute; that what is needed in the case is not more refined observation or the gathering of "statistics," but simply correct theorizing. There is, of course, also a large field in which the crucial facts are *not* obvious.

tion which would be established by the imaginary tax will be brought about through the operation of ordinary economic motives. The owner of the broad road could not under effective competition charge anything for its use. If an agency of production is not subject to diminishing returns, and cannot be monopolized, there is, in fact, no incentive to its appropriation, and it will remain a free good. But the owner of the narrow road can charge for its use a toll representing its "superiority" over the free road, in accordance with the theory of rent, which is as old as Ricardian economics. An application of the familiar reasoning to this case will show that the toll will exactly equal the ideal tax above considered,—tho the application may need to be more careful and complete than that made by many of the expositors of the classical theory.

The owner of a superior opportunity for investment can set the charge for its use at any amount not greater than the excess of the product of the first unit of investment above what that unit could produce on the free opportunity. Under this charge investment will flow into the superior road up to the point where congestion and diminishing returns set in. (It is better in such a simple case to use the notion of diminishing returns than to use that of diminishing costs, since in the large the practical objective is to maximize the product of given resources and not to minimize the expenditure of resources in producing a given product.) By reducing the charge, the owner will increase the amount of traffic using his road (or in general the amount of investment of labor and capital in any opportunity). But obviously the owner of the road will not set the charge so low that the last truck which uses the road secures a return in excess of the amount which it adds to the total product of the road (that is, of all the trucks which use it). This is clearer if we think of the owner of the road hiring the trucks instead of their hiring the use of the road. The effect is the same either way; it is still the same if some third party hires the use of both. The toll or rent will be so adjusted that *added* product of the last truck which uses the narrow road is just equal to what it could produce on the broad road. No truck will pay a higher charge, and it is not to the interest of the owner of the road to accept a lower fee. And this adjustment is exactly that which maximizes the total product of both roads.

The argument may be made clearer by the use of simple diagrams.[6]

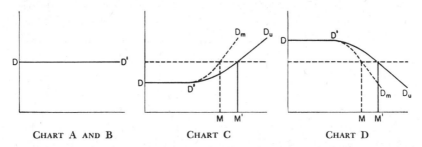

| CHART A AND B | CHART C | CHART D |

Chart A and B represents the case of constant cost or constant returns, the cost of successive units of output or the return from successive units of investment on the broad road. In Chart C, the curve $DD'D_u$ is a *cost* curve for the narrow road, showing the cost of successive units of output. It starts at a lower level than the cost on the broad road, but at a certain point D', congestion sets in and increasing cost appears. Curve $DD'D_m$ is a curve of *marginal* costs on the narrow road, as Professor Pigou uses the term marginal cost; the marginal cost of the nth unit of product is the difference between the total cost of producing n units and the total cost of producing $n + 1$ units. When costs begin to increase, the marginal cost will increase more rapidly than the cost of the added unit, since the production of each additional unit raises the cost of the earlier units to a level with that of the new unit. It must be observed that the cost of the additional unit is always the same as the cost per unit of the whole supply produced; much economic analysis is vitiated by a spurious separation of these two conceptions of cost.

Chart D represents the same facts as Chart C, but in terms of the product of successive units of investment instead of the cost of successive units of output, that is, as curves of "diminishing returns" instead of "increasing costs." The output begins at a higher level than on the broad road, but at the point D', which corresponds to the point of the same designation on Chart C, the return from investment begins to fall off. The curve $D'D_u$ shows the actual product of the added unit of investment, and the curve

---

[6] Cf. Pigou, *op. cit.*, Appendix iii, pp. 931–938.

$D'D_m$ its marginal product, its addition to the total. The latter decreases more rapidly, because the application of the additional unit reduces the yield of the earlier ones to equality with its own. The argument is the same, but stated in inverse or reciprocal form. As indicated, the viewpoint of Chart D is to be preferred, and it may be surmised that, if Professor Pigou had put his argument in this form, he would probably have avoided the error into which he was very likely misled by measuring efficiency in terms of cost of output instead of output of resources.[7]

The owner of the road will adjust his toll so that the traffic will take his road out to the point M in Chart C or D. It will *not*, under conditions of profit-seeking exploitation, be continued to M', as argued by Professor Pigou. The actual output is the same as the "ideal" output, but it is the "ideal" output which is wrongly defined in Pigou's treatment (p. 937). Evidently, the adjustment is correct when the *marginal* product of the last unit of investment on the superior road is equal to the product of a similar unit on the free road. Confusion arises in translating this condition into terms of cost and selling price of product. Selling price will be determined by cost on the free road, or at least these two will be equal, however the causal relation is conceived. That is, the *money* cost of any unit of product is the value of the investment which is necessary to produce it on the free opportunity, where cost is constant, or, in general, at an opportunity margin where rent does not enter. Comparison of the two viewpoints shown by our Charts C and D above shows that under competitive conditions the application of investment to the superior opportunity will be stopped at the point where *marginal real cost* (cost in terms of the transferable investment) is equal to real cost on the free opportunity. When equal additions to investment make equal additions to output, equal units of output have the same cost. But the condition of equilibrium cannot be stated in terms of money cost and money selling price of product on the superior opportunity, *because these*

---

[7] It may be noted that Robertson makes the opposite contention, that the concepts of increasing and decreasing costs are to be preferred to those of decreasing and increasing returns. *Loc. cit.,* p. 17. He gives no argument for this position. It seems to me that this is the entrepreneur's point of view, while that of either the investor or society is the inverse one advocated in the text above, and is distinctly to be preferred for general analysis.

would be equal however the investment might be distributed, whatever rent were charged, or whether the opportunity were appropriated and exploited at all. The condition of equilibrium is that the rent on the superior opportunity is maximized as an aggregate. The rent per unit of output is a variable portion of a total unit cost which is fixed.

Extension of the foregoing argument to the general case of land rent involves no difficulties and will not be carried out in detail. The point is that any opportunity, whether or not it represents a previous investment of any sort, is a productive factor if there is sufficient demand for its use to carry into the stage of diminishing returns the application to it of transferable investment. The charge made by a private owner for the use of such an opportunity serves the socially useful purpose of limiting the application of investment to the point where *marginal* product instead of product per unit is equal to the product of investment in free (rentless) opportunities; and under competitive conditions this charge will be fixed at the level which does make marginal products equal, and thus maximizes productivity on the whole.[8]

It is pertinent to add that in real life, the original "appropria-

---

[8] It is a theoretically interesting fact that the rent on an opportunity which maximizes the return to its owner and brings about the socially correct investment in it is its "marginal product," in the same sense as used to describe the competitive remuneration of other productive factors transferable from one use to another or ultimately derived from labor and waiting. It is exactly the amount by which the product of the whole competitive system would be reduced if the opportunity were held out of use or destroyed, and the investment which would be combined with it were put to the next best possible use. This point is brought out in Professor Young's chapter on Rent in Ely's *Outlines of Economics* (pp. 409, 410, 4th ed.). Professor Young also pointed out the essential fallacy in Professor Pigou's argument, in a review of the latter's earlier work on *Wealth and Welfare* (*The Quarterly Journal of Economics,* August 1913).

The relation between "investment" and "opportunity" is an interesting question, by no means so simple as it is commonly assumed to be. In the writer's view there is little basis for the common distinction in this regard between "natural resources" and labor or capital. The qualities of real significance for economic theory are the conditions of supply and the degree of fluidity or its opposite, specialization to a particular use. In a critical examination neither attribute forms a basis for erecting natural agents into a separate class.

tion" of such opportunities by private owners involves investment in exploration, in detailed investigation and appraisal by trial and error of the findings, in development work of many kinds necessary to secure and market a product—besides the cost of buying off or killing or driving off previous claimants. Under competitive conditions, again, investment in such activities of "appropriation" would not yield a greater return than investment in any other field. These activities are indeed subject to a large "aleatory element"; they are much affected by luck. But there is no evidence proving either that the luck element is greater than in other activities relating to economic progress, or that in fact the average reward has been greater than that which might have been had from conservative investments.

II

While Professor Pigou constantly refers to industries of decreasing cost, or increasing returns, the principles at issue do not necessarily imply more than a *difference* in the way in which efficiency varies with size from one industry to another. Some of Professor Graham's reasoning in regard to international trade and international value depends upon decreasing cost as such. It seems advisable, before taking up his argument concretely, to devote a few paragraphs to this conception, which the writer believes to involve serious fallacies, and to the meaning of cost and its variation.

Valuation is an aspect of conscious choice. Apart from a necessity of choosing, values have no meaning or existence. Valuation *is* a comparison of values. A single value, existing in isolation, can no more be imagined than can a single force without some other force opposed to it as a "reaction" to its "action." Value is in fact the complete analogue of force in the interpretation of human activity, and in a behavioristic formulation is identical with force —which is to say, it is an instrumental idea, metaphysically nonexistent. Fundamentally, then, the cost of any value is simply the value that is given up when it is chosen; it is just the reaction or resistance to choice which makes it choice. Ordinarily we speak of cost as a consumption of "resources" of some kind, but everyone recognizes that resources have no value in themselves; that they simply represent the products which could have been had by their use in some other direction than the one chosen.

The notion of cost suffers greatly in logical clearness from confusion with the vague and ambiguous term "pain." In the broad true sense every cost is a pain, and the two are identical. Little or nothing can be made of the distinction between pain and the sacrifice of pleasure, or between pleasure and escape from pain. The subject cannot be gone into here from the point of view of psychology; it is enough to point out that the way in which a particular person regards a particular sacrifice depends mainly upon the direction of *change* in the affective tone of his consciousness or upon the established level of expectations. The essential thing is that the pleasure-pain character of a value is irrelevant, that the universal meaning of cost is the sacrifice of a value-alternative. This is just as true of the "irksomeness" of labor, as of a payment of money. The irksomeness of digging a ditch reflects the value of the loafing or playing which might be done instead. And there is no significant difference between this irksomeness or pain and that of using the proceeds of the sale of a Liberty bond to pay a doctor's bill when it might have been used to procure a fortnight's vacation.[9]

The natural and common rule in choice is necessarily that of increasing cost. In the exchange of one good for another at a fixed ratio, the further the exchange is carried, the more "utility" is given up and the less is secured. This is merely the law of diminishing utility. It is only when one commodity is given up in order that another may be produced by the use of the common and divertible productive energy that we ordinarily think of the variation of cost. If two commodities are produced by a single homogeneous productive factor, there is no variation of cost as

---

[9] Besides confusion with the notion of pain, which has at last obtained in, psychology a definite meaning independent of unpleasantness, the notion of cost encounters in economics another source of obscurity. This is in the relation between those values which do not pass through the market and receive prices and those which do. The "loafing" which underlies the irksomeness of labor is such a value, and there is a tendency to associate the notion of cost with these non-pecuniary values. In this connection it should be noted that not merely labor but all types of productive service are subject to the competition of uses which yield their satisfactions directly and not through the channel of a marketable product. Thus land is used for lawns as well as for fields, and examples could be multiplied at will.

successive portions of one are given up to procure more of the other by shifting that factor—except in the sense of increasing utility cost as met with in the case of exchange. Ordinarily, however, new considerations enter, as a matter of fact. If we wish to produce more wheat by producing less corn, we find that the further the shift of production is carried, the more *bushels* of corn (as well as corn value) have to be given up to produce a *bushel* of wheat (and still more for a given amount of wheat value). This is the economic principle of increasing cost (decreasing returns) as generally understood, reduced to its lowest terms and freed from ambiguity.

When costs are measured in value terms and product in physical units there are two sorts of reasons for increasing cost, one reflecting value changes and the other technological changes. The first would be operative if all productive resources were perfectly homogeneous and perfectly fluid. But this is not, in general, the case, and technological changes supervene which work in the same direction and add to the increase which would otherwise take place in the cost of a unit of the product which is being produced in larger volume. Principal among these technological changes is the fact that some of the resources used to produce the commodity being sacrificed are not useful in the production of that whose output is being increased, and in consequence the resources which are transferred are used in progressively larger proportions in the second industry and in smaller proportions in the first, in combination with certain other resources which are specialized to the two industries respectively. The consequent reduction in the physical productive effect of the transferred factors is what is meant by diminishing returns in one of the many narrower uses of that highly ambiguous expression. Another technological cause still further aggravating the tendency to increasing costs arises from the fact that productive factors are not really homogeneous or uniform in quality. As productive power is transferred from corn to wheat, it will be found that the concrete men, acres, and implements transferred are those progressively more suitable for corn-growing and less suitable for wheat. Thus each unit suffers a progressively greater reduction in its value in terms of units of either commodity, or it takes more units to represent in the wheat industry the value of a single unit in the corn industry, and value costs of wheat mount still higher for this third reason.

All three changes so far noted clearly involve increasing cost in the real sense, the amount of value[10] outlay or sacrifice necessary to produce an additional physical unit of the commodity whose production is increased. In addition to these we have to consider two further possible sources of increased cost. The first is that, when an additional unit of, say, wheat is produced, and the factors transferable from other industries to wheat are raised in price, the quantities of these factors already used to produce wheat will rise in price along with those added to the industry. Should all this increase in cost be charged up to the production of the last unit of wheat produced, which causes it to appear? In a sense, this is in truth a social cost of this last unit. Yet the transfer of productive energy will not take place unless there has been a shift in the market estimate of wheat in comparison with competing commodities such as to justify it. That is, as the exchange system measures values, making all units of the same good equal in value, the increase in the total value of the wheat must be greater than the decrease in the value of the output of competing commodities. (A discrepancy—*in either direction*—may result from considering the potential significances of infra-marginal units commonly designated as consumers' surplus.) The second additional possible source of increased cost is the increased payments which will be made for the specialized factors used in producing wheat,[11] the cost elements which are of the nature of rent or surplus. These payments evidently do not represent social costs at all, but redistributions of product merely. Such redistributions may be "good," or "bad," depending on the moral position, according to some standard, of the owners of the two classes of factors respectively.

Decreasing cost (or increasing returns) is alleged to result in several ways, which can be dealt with but briefly. The most important is the technological economy of large-scale production. When

---

[10] Value as used in this discussion means "real" value, relative significance or utility. No assertion as to exchange value or price is implied.

[11] The fallacy of identifying specialized factors with natural agents and transferable factors with labor and capital has been referred to above. It will not be elaborated in this paper.

the output of a commodity is increased, the cost of the productive services used to produce it will be higher; but this increase in their cost per unit may, it is held, be more than offset by economies in utilization, made possible by larger-scale operations, which increase the amount of product obtained from given quantities of materials and resources consumed.[12] But technological economies arise from increasing the size of the productive unit, not from increasing the total output of the industry as a whole. The possibility of realizing such economies—by the distribution of "overhead," or more elaborate division of labor, or use of machinery —tends to bring about an increase in the *scale* of production, but this may happen independently of any change in the output of the industry. If competition is effective, the size of the productive unit will tend to grow until *either* no further economies are obtainable, *or* there is only one establishment left and the industry is a monopoly. When all establishments have been brought to the most efficient size, variation in total output is a matter of changing their *number,* in which no technical economies are involved.

The rejoinder to the above argument is the doctrine of "external economies," which surely rests upon a misconception. Economies may be "external" to a particular establishment or technical production unit, but they are not external to the industry if they affect its efficiency. The portion of the productive process carried on in a particular unit is an accidental consideration. External economies in one business unit are internal economies in some other, within the industry. Any branch or stage in the creation of a product which offers continuously a chance for technical economies with increase in the scale of operations must eventuate either in monopoly or in leaving the tendency behind and establishing the normal relation of increasing cost with increasing size. If the organization unit is not small in comparison with the industry as a whole, a totally different law must be applied to the relation between output, cost, and price.

Two other alleged sources of decreasing cost are the stimulation

---

[12] Professor Graham says (p. 203, note) that decreasing cost is an "aspect of the law of proportionality." This is a form of statement frequently met with, but rests on a misconception sufficiently refuted in the text. It is true only accidentally, if it is true in any general sense at all, that a more elaborate technology is associated with a change in the proportions of the factors.

of demand and the stimulation of invention. Neither can properly be regarded as an effect of increasing output, other things being equal. Producing a commodity and distributing it at a loss might result in developing a taste for it, but would be no different in principle from any other method of spending money to produce this result. Inventions tend to enlarge the scale of production rather than large-scale production to cause inventions. It is true that an increase in demand from some outside cause may stimulate invention, but the action takes place through first making the industry highly profitable. The result is not uniform or dependable, nor is it due to increased production as such.

These brief statements form a mere summary of the argument that, with reference to long-run tendencies under given general conditions, increasing the output of a commodity must increase its cost of production unless the industry is, or becomes, a monopoly. They also indicate the nature of the relation between social cost and entrepreneur's money cost. Under competition, transferable resources are distributed among alternative uses in such a way as to yield equal marginal[13] value product everywhere, which is the arrangement that maximizes production, as measured by value, on the whole. Non-transferable resources secure "rents" which equalize money costs to all producers and for all units of product under the foregoing condition; or, better, the rents bring about that allocation of resources which maximizes production, under the condition that money costs are equalized.

A further major fallacy in value theory which suffuses Professor Graham's argument will be pointed out in general terms before proceeding with detailed criticism. The reference is to the notorious "law of reciprocal demand." This so-called law, that the prices of commodities exchanged internationally are so adjusted that a country's exports pay for its imports, is at best a truism. To say that what one gives in exchange pays for what one gets is merely a statement of the fact that one is exchanged for the other. What calls for explanation in the case is the process which fixes *how much* of one thing will be parted with, and *how much* of the other received in return.

---

[13] "Differential" is the term in use in other sciences for the idea commonly referred to as a marginal unit in economics.

III

We are now ready to take up concretely the proposed refutation of the law of comparative advantage. Professor Graham begins by assuming two countries, which he calls A and B, but which it appears simpler to designate as England and America respectively. Suppose then that in England

> 10 days' labor produces 40 units of wheat
> 10 days' labor produces 40 watches;

in America

> 10 days' labor produces 40 units of wheat
> 10 days' labor produces 30 watches.

America has a comparative advantage in wheat, England in watches.[14] According to the accepted theory, trade at any ratio intermediate between the two cost ratios will be of advantage to both countries. Our author assumes it to begin at the ratio of 35 watches for 40 units of wheat. Then, for each ten days' labor devoted to producing wheat and exchanging for watches, America can get 35 watches instead of the 30 which could be produced by using the same labor in producing the watches. England, for each ten days' labor devoted to producing watches and exchanging for wheat can secure $\frac{40}{35} \times 40$ ($= 45\frac{5}{7}$) units of wheat, instead of the 40 units which could be directly produced with the same labor.

So far, well and good for the theory. But at this point Professor Graham's blows begin to fall. Assuming that wheat-growing is an industry of increasing, and watch-making one of decreasing costs, it will come to pass, as the two countries progressively specialize, that the cost of both commodities is decreased for England and increased for America. It clearly follows, first, that if the process goes on long enough, America will begin to lose, and just as clearly, from the assumptions of the article, that the process will go on forever! For the further it is carried, the greater becomes England's comparative advantage in the production of watches and the

---

[14] The use of labor as equivalent to productive power, or the treatment of labor as the only factor which may be transferred from one industry to the other, is a simplification likely to mislead the unwary, but it will not be criticized here. It is of interest to note, however, that historically the whole doctrine of comparative cost was a prop for a labor cost theory of value.

greater becomes America's comparative advantage in the production of wheat. Yet this conclusion must arouse a suspicion that there is something wrong in Denmark.

First, in accordance with the argument above, drop the assumption of decreasing cost as a permanent condition in the watch-making industry; then the two cost ratios in the two countries must come together instead of separating as the specialization of productive efforts progresses. Under any assumption whatever, *either* this must happen, *or else* one country must entirely cease to produce one of the commodities. In the first event, the exchange ratio will be the common cost ratio of the two countries (transportation costs being neglected, as usual in these discussions). If the second result ensues,—that one country abandons one of the industries,—*the exchange ratio will be the cost ratio in the country which still produces both commodities* (assuming, always, that monopoly is absent). Professor Graham "assumes" that the comparative advantage has become progressively greater as the result of specialization and then "assumes" (p. 210) that, with the cost ratio in one country half what it is in the other, the market price may be established at any ratio between the two. In reality the only possible result under the cost conditions he states would be that America would stop producing watches at once and would exchange wheat for watches at the ratio of 40 for 40 (the cost ratio in England), thus making a *gain* of 20 watches on each ten days' labor so employed as compared with using it to produce the watches in America.

Next, the author proposes to consider the effect of interpreting his cost figures as representing marginal cost instead of cost per unit. He gets no further, however, than to average up the marginal with assumed infra-marginal costs, which amounts merely to a slight change in the numbers assumed for cost per unit. He nowhere gives an explicit statement of what he means by cost, and must be suspected of not having clearly faced the difficulties and ambiguities in the notion, as brought out in the argument of the first and second parts of this paper. Certainly it will not do to recognize a possible permanent difference under competition in the money cost of different units of a supply, or in their marginal real cost. The money costs which represent real costs differ in different situations, but the rent element always equalizes them, or produces *coincidence* between equality of money cost, which would result in any case, and equality of marginal real cost, which is the social desideratum. Value and cost are like action and reaction, axiomatically equal, and as in an exchange system the value of all similar units must be equal, so must their costs.

In the writer's opinion this also is socially and morally correct. We do not, and should not, value the first slice of bread more highly than the last, nor systematically value anything at more or less than its necessary cost. As between units of supply consumed by different persons, the case is different, because different persons do not come into the market with equal exchange power in the form of productive capacity. But the question is one of ethics, entirely outside the field of exchange as a mechanical problem. The famous surpluses have the same kind of significance as potential energy in physics. They relate to possible changes in fundamental conditions, but have nothing to do with the conditions of equilibrium in any particular situation. With reference to relations among actual magnitudes, cost curves and utility curves should always be interpreted to mean that, as supply varies, the cost, or utility, of every unit changes in the manner shown by the curve.

Marginal money cost, in the sense in which it is used by Professor Pigou, is meaningless with relation to competitive conditions. It is true that under monopoly the supply is so adjusted that the contribution of the last unit to total selling price (marginal demand price) is equal to the addition to total cost incurred in consequence of producing it (marginal supply price); but this is a mere equivalent of the statement that the difference between total cost and total selling price is made a maximum. Professor Graham seems to use the expression marginal cost to mean the particular money expense of producing the last unit of supply; but, as already stated, there cannot in the long run under competitive conditions be a difference between the cost of this unit and that of any other, or the cost per unit of producing the whole supply.

Professor Graham's article makes use at several points of the effects of different elasticities of demand for different goods, especially as between agricultural products and manufactures. He fails to recognize that, with reference to large and inclusive groups of commodities, demand, which is an exchange *ratio,* is merely a different view of a production ratio, and hence of a cost ratio. In discussing the sale of a single commodity in a complicated economic society and with reference to small changes, it is permissible to treat money as an absolute; but in reducing all exchange to barter between two classes of goods, this procedure is quite inadmissible.

Moreover, consideration of the actual course of events when trade is opened up will show that elasticity of demand has little to do with the special theory of international trade or international value. Each country continues to specialize in the commodities in which it has a comparative advantage, until there is no gain to be secured from further specialization; that is, until it will cost as much to secure the next unit of the imported good by exchange as it will to produce it within the country. Now at a certain point, a country will obtain as much of the imported good as it would have produced for itself under an equilibrium adjustment within itself if foreign trade had been prohibited; and in consequence of the saving of productive power effected by the trade, a part of the resources which in its absence would be used to produce that commodity will be left to be disposed of. *Beyond this point,* that is, in the disposition of the saved productive power, elasticities of demand come into operation. This fund of saved productive power will not all be used to produce either of the commodities concerned in the exchange with the foreign nation, but will be distributed over the whole field of production in accordance with the ordinary laws of supply and demand.

The foregoing paragraphs are believed to cover the main points in the writings criticized which involve fallacies in the interpretation of cost and so come under the title of this paper. The entire argument of Professor Graham's second article falls to the ground, as he has stated it, as soon as the principles of cost are applied to the determination of international values instead of "assuming" the latter. Many further points in his first article are especially inviting to criticism, but fall outside the scope of the present paper. It suffices for the solution of the essential problem of international trade to recognize that the production of one good to exchange for another is an *alternative method of producing* the second commodity. Under competitive conditions, productive resources will not be used in this indirect process of production unless the yield is greater than that obtained by the use of the direct method. The task of economic analysis is to show why the profit-seeking motive impels the private producer to put resources to the use which brings the largest yield. Now to the entrepreneur producers of wheat and watches, in a case like that used in the illustration, the choice is not a question of comparative advantage, but of absolute profit or loss. If ten days' labor will produce a quantity of wheat which can be exchanged for more than 40 watches, then that amount of labor will be *worth more* than 40 watches, and the business enterprise which uses it to produce the watches will simply lose money. It is an example of the common fallacy of thinking in terms of physical efficiency, whereas efficiency is in the nature of the case a relation between value magnitudes.

That free enterprise is not a perfectly ideal system of social organization is a proposition not to be gainsaid, and nothing is further from the aims of the present writer than to set up the contention that it is. But in his opinion the weaknesses and failures of the system lie outside the field of the mechanics of exchange under the theoretical conditions of perfect competition. It is probable that *all* efforts to prove a continued bias in the workings of competition as such, along the lines followed by Professors Pigou and Graham, are doomed to failure. Under certain theoretical conditions, more or less consciously and definitely assumed in general by economic theorists, the system would be ideal. The correct form of the problem of general criticism referred to at the outset of this paper is, therefore, that of bringing these lurking assumptions above the threshold into the realm of the explicit and of contrasting them with the facts of life—the conditions under which competitive dealings are actually carried on.[15]

When the problem is attacked from this point of view, the critic finds himself moving among considerations very different from the logical quantitative relations of such discussions as the foregoing. Human beings are not "individuals," to begin with; a large majority of them are not even legally competent to contract. The values of life are not, in the main, reducible to satisfactions obtained from the consumption of exchangeable goods and services. Such desires as people have for goods and services are not

---

[15] The great bulk of the critical material in Professor Pigou's *Wealth and Welfare* is of this character.

their own in any original sense, but are the product of social influence of innumerable kinds and of every moral grade, largely manufactured by the competitive system itself. The productive capacities in their own persons and in owned external things which form the ultimate stock in trade of the human being are derived from an uncertain mixture of conscientious effort, inheritance, pure luck, and outright force and fraud. He cannot be well or truly informed regarding the markets for the productive power he possesses, and the information which he gets has a way of coming to him after the time when it would be of use. The business organizations which are the directing divinities of the system are but groups of ignorant and frail beings like the individuals with whom they deal. (In the perfectly ideal order of theory the problem of management would be non-existent!) The system as a whole is dependent upon an outside organization, an authoritarian state, made up also of ignorant and frail human beings, to provide a setting in which it can operate at all. Besides watching over the dependent and non-contracting, the state must define and protect property rights, enforce contract and prevent non-contractual (compulsory) transactions, maintain a circulating medium, and most especially prevent that collusion and monopoly, the antithesis of competition, into which competitive relations constantly tend to gravitate. It is in the field indicated by this summary list of postulates, rather than in that of the mechanics of exchange relations, that we must work out the ultimate critique of free enterprise.

9

THE LAWS OF RETURNS
UNDER COMPETITIVE CONDITIONS [*][1]

By Piero Sraffa ||

A striking feature of the present position of economic science is the almost unanimous agreement at which economists have arrived regarding the theory of competitive value, which is inspired by the fundamental symmetry existing between the forces of demand and those of supply, and is based upon the assumption that the essential causes determining the price of particular commodities may be simplified and grouped together so as to be represented by a pair of intersecting curves of collective demand and supply. This state of things is in such marked contrast with the controversies on the theory of value by which political economy was characterised during the past century, that it might almost be thought that from these clashes of thought the spark of an ultimate truth had at length been struck. Sceptics might perhaps think that the agreement in question is due, not so much to everyone being convinced, as to the indifference felt by the majority nowadays in regard to the theory of value—an indifference which is justified by the fact that this theory, more than any other part of economic theory, has lost much of its direct bearing upon practical politics, and particularly in regard to doctrines of social changes, which had formerly been conferred upon it by Ricardo and afterwards by Marx, and in opposition to them by the bourgeois economists. It has been transformed more and more into "an apparatus of the mind, a technique of thinking" which does

* *The Economic Journal*, Vol. XXXVI (1926), pp. 535–550. Reprinted, by the courtesy of the publisher and the author, without change from the original text.

|| Trinity College, Cambridge University, England.

[1] The opening pages of this article contain a summary of the conclusions of a paper on "Relazioni fra costo e quantita prodotta" published in Vol. II of the *Annali di Economia*.

not furnish any "settled conclusions immediately applicable to policy."[2] It is essentially a pedagogic instrument, somewhat like the study of the classics, and, unlike the study of the exact sciences and law, its purposes are exclusively those of training the mind, for which reason it is hardly apt to excite the passions of men, even academical men—a theory, in short, in respect to which it is not worth while departing from a tradition which is finally accepted. However this may be, the fact of the agreement remains.

In the tranquil view which the modern theory of value presents us there is one dark spot which disturbs the harmony of the whole. This is represented by the supply curve, based upon the laws of increasing and diminishing returns. That its foundations are less solid than those of the other portions of the structure is generally recognised. That they are actually so weak as to be unable to support the weight imposed upon them is a doubt which slumbers beneath the consciousness of many, but which most succeed in silently suppressing. From time to time someone is unable any longer to resist the pressure of his doubts and expresses them openly; then, in order to prevent the scandal spreading, he is promptly silenced, frequently with some concessions and partial admission of his objections, which, naturally, the theory had implicitly taken into account. And so, with the lapse of time, the qualifications, the restrictions and the exceptions have piled up, and have eaten up, if not all, certainly the greater part of the theory. If their aggregate effect is not at once apparent, this is because they are scattered about in footnotes and articles and carefully segregated from one another.

It is not the purpose of this article to add anything to the pile, but simply to attempt to co-ordinate certain materials, separating what is still alive from what is dead in the concept of the supply curve and of its effects on competitive price determination.

At present the laws of returns are of special importance owing to the part they play in the study of the problem of value. But they are naturally much older than the particular theory of value in which they are employed, and it is precisely from their secular age and their original applications that they derive both their prestige and their weakness in their modern application. We are

---

[2] Keynes: *Introduction to Cambridge Economic Handbooks.*

disposed to accept the laws of returns as a matter of course, because we have before our eyes the great and indisputable services rendered by them when performing their ancient function, and we often neglect to ask ourselves whether the old barrels are still able to hold the new wine.

The law of diminishing returns has long been associated mainly with the problem of rent, and from this point of view the law as formulated by the classical economists with reference to land was entirely adequate. It had always been perfectly obvious that its operation affected, not merely rent, but also the cost of the product; but this was not emphasised as a cause of variation in the relative price of the individual commodities produced, because the operation of diminishing returns increased in a like measure the cost of all. This remained true even when the English classical economists applied the law to the production of corn, for, as Marshall has shown, "the term 'corn' was used by them as short for agricultural produce in general" (*Principles*, VI, i, 2, note).

The position occupied in classical economics by the law of increasing returns was much less prominent, as it was regarded merely as an important aspect of the division of labour, and thus rather as a result of general economic progress than of an increase in the scale of production.

The result was that in the original laws of returns the general idea of a functional connection between cost and quantity produced was not given a conspicuous place; it appears, in fact, to have been present in the minds of the classical economists much less prominently than was the connection between demand and demand price.

The development which has emphasised the former aspect of the laws of returns is comparatively recent. At the same time it has removed both laws from the positions which, according to the traditional partition of political economy, they used to occupy, one under the heading of "distribution" and the other under "production," and has transferred them to the chapter of "exchange-value"; there, merging them in the single "law of non-proportional returns," it has derived from them a law of supply in a market such as can be co-ordinated with the corresponding law of demand; and on the symmetry of these two opposite forces it has based the modern theory of value.

In order to reach this result it was found necessary to introduce certain modifications into the form of the two laws. Very little was necessary as regards the law of diminishing returns, which merely required to be generalised from the particular case of land to every case in which there existed a factor of production of which only a constant quantity was available. The law of increasing returns, however, had to be subjected to a much more radical transformation: the part played in it by the division of labour—now limited to the case of independent subsidiary factories coming into existence as the production of an industry increases—was greatly restricted; while consideration of that greater internal division of labour, which is rendered possible by an increase in the dimensions of an individual firm, was entirely abandoned, as it was seen to be incompatible with competitive conditions. On the other hand, the importance of "external economies" was more and more emphasised—that is, of the advantage derived by individual producers from the growth, not of their own individual undertakings, but of the industry in its aggregate.

Even in their present form, however, the two laws have preserved the characteristic of originating from forces of profoundly diverse nature. Such heterogeneousness, while not constituting in itself an insurmountable obstacle when it is attempted to co-ordinate them and employ them conjointly in problems mainly relating, not to the causes, but to the effects of variations in cost, involves a fresh difficulty when it is sought to classify the various industries according as they belong to one or the other category. It is, in fact, in the very nature of the bases of the two laws that the wider the definition which we assume for "an industry"— that is, the more nearly it includes all the undertakings which employ a given *factor* of production, as, for example, agriculture or the iron industry—the more probable will it be that the forces which make for diminishing returns will play an important part in it; the more restrictive this definition—the more nearly it includes, therefore, only those undertakings which produce a given type of consumable *commodity,* as, for example, fruit or nails— the greater will be the probability that the forces which make for increasing returns will predominate in it. In its effects this difficulty is parallel to that which, as is well known, arises from the consideration of the element of time, whereby the shorter the period of time allowed for the adjustments, the greater is the likeli-hood of decreasing returns, while the longer that period is, the greater is the probability of increasing returns.

The really serious difficulties make their appearance when it is considered to what extent the supply curves based on the laws of returns satisfy the conditions necessary to enable them to be employed in the study of the equilibrium value of single com-modities produced under competitive conditions. This point of view assumes that the conditions of production and the demand for a commodity can be considered, in respect to small variations, as being practically independent, both in regard to each other and in relation to the supply and demand of all other commodities. It is well known that such an assumption would not be illegiti-mate merely because the independence may not be absolutely perfect, as, in fact, it never can be; and a slight degree of inter-dependence may be overlooked without disadvantage if it applies to quantities of the second order of smalls, as would be the case if the effect (for example, an increase of cost) of a variation in the industry which we propose to isolate were to react partially on the price of the products of other industries, and this latter effect were to influence the demand for the product of the first industry. But, of course, it is a very different matter, and the assumption becomes illegitimate, when a variation in the quantity produced by the industry under consideration sets up a force which acts directly, not merely upon its own costs, but also upon the costs of other industries; in such a case the conditions of the "particular equilibrium" which it was intended to isolate are upset, and it is no longer possible, without contradiction, to neglect collateral effects.

It unfortunately happens that it is precisely into this latter category that the applications of the laws of returns fall, in the great majority of cases. As regards diminishing returns, in fact, if in the production of a particular commodity a considerable part of a factor is employed, the total amount of which is fixed or can be increased only at a more than proportional cost, a small in-crease in the production of the commodity will necessitate a more intense utilisation of that factor, and this will affect in the same manner the cost of the commodity in question and the cost of the other commodities into the production of which that factor enters;

and since commodities into the production of which a common special factor enters are frequently, to a certain extent, substitutes for one another (for example, various kinds of agricultural produce), the modification in their price will not be without appreciable effects upon demand in the industry concerned. If we next take an industry which employs only a small part of the "constant factor" (which appears more appropriate for the study of the particular equilibrium of a single industry), we find that a (small) increase in its production is generally met much more by drawing "marginal doses" of the constant factor from other industries than by intensifying its own utilisation of it; thus the increase in cost will be practically negligible, and anyhow it will still operate in a like degree upon all the industries of the group. Excluding these cases, and excluding—if we take a point of view embracing long periods—the numerous cases in which the quantity of a means of production may be regarded as being only temporarily fixed in respect to an unexpected demand, very little remains: the imposing structure of diminishing returns is available only for the study of that minute class of commodities in the production of which the whole of a factor of production is employed. Here, of course, by "a commodity" is to be understood an article in regard to which it is possible to construct, or at least to conceive, a demand schedule which is tolerably homogeneous and independent of the conditions of supply, and not, as is frequently implied, a collection of diverse articles, such as agricultural products or ironware.

It is not by mere chance that, notwithstanding the profoundly diverse nature of the two laws of returns, the same difficulties also arise, in almost identical form, in connection with increasing returns. Here again we find that in reality the economies of production on a large scale are not suitable for the requirements of the supply curve: their field of action is either wider or more restricted than would be necessary. On the one hand, reductions in cost which are due to "those *external* economies which result from the general progress of industrial environment" to which Marshall refers (*Principles*, V, xi, 1) must, of course, be ignored, as they are clearly incompatible with the conditions of the particular equilibrium of a commodity. On the other hand, reductions in cost connected with an increase in a firm's scale of production, arising from internal economies or from the possibility of distributing the overhead charges over a larger number of product units, must be put aside as being incompatible with competitive conditions. The only economies which could be taken into consideration would be such as occupy an intermediate position between these two extremes; but it is just in the middle that nothing, or almost nothing, is to be found. Those economies which are external from the point of view of the individual firm, but internal as regards the industry in its aggregate, constitute precisely the class which is most seldom to be met with. As Marshall has said in the work in which he has intended to approach most closely the actual conditions of industry, "the economies of production on a large scale can seldom be allocated exactly to any one industry: they are in great measure attached to groups, often large groups, of correlated industries."[3] In any case, in so far as external economies of the kind in question exist, they are not likely to be called forth by *small* increases in production. Thus it appears that supply curves showing decreasing costs are not to be found more frequently than their opposite.

Reduced within such restricted limits, the supply schedule with variable costs cannot claim to be a general conception applicable to normal industries; it can prove a useful instrument only in regard to such exceptional industries as can reasonably satisfy its conditions. In normal cases the cost of production of commodities produced competitively—as we are not entitled to take into consideration the causes which may make it rise or fall—must be regarded as constant in respect of small variations in the quantity produced.[4] And so, as a simple way of approaching the

---

[3] *Industry and Trade*, p. 188.

[4] The absence of causes which tend to cause the cost either to increase or diminish appears to be the most obvious and plausible way from which constant costs can arise. But as these constitute the most dangerous enemy of the symmetry between demand and supply, those writers who accept this doctrine, in order to be able to relegate the constant costs to the category of theoretical limiting cases which in reality cannot exist, have persuaded themselves that they are something extremely complicated and improbable, since they "can only result from the accidental balancing of two opposite tendencies; the tendency to diminution of cost . . . and the tendency to increase of cost . . ." (Sidgwick, *Principles of Political Economy*, 1st ed., p. 207; to the same effect see, e.g., Marshall, *Principles*, IV, xiii, 2, and *Palgrave's Dictionary, sub voce*

problem of competitive value, the old and now obsolete theory which makes it dependent on the cost of production alone appears to hold its ground as the best available.

This first approximation, as far as it goes, is as important as it is useful: it emphasises the fundamental factor, namely, the predominant influence of cost of production in the determination of the normal value of commodities, while at the same time it does not lead us astray when we desire to study in greater detail the conditions under which exchange takes place in particular cases, for it does not conceal from us the fact that we cannot find the elements required for this purpose within the limits of its assumptions.

When we proceed to a further approximation, while keeping to the path of free competition, the complications do not arise gradually, as would be convenient; they present themselves simultaneously as a whole. If diminishing returns arising from a "constant factor" are taken into consideration, it becomes necessary to extend the field of investigation so as to examine the conditions of simultaneous equilibrium in numerous industries: a well-known conception, whose complexity, however, prevents it from bearing fruit, at least in the present state of our knowledge, which does not permit of even much simpler schemata being applied to the study of real conditions. If we pass to external economies, we find ourselves confronted by the same obstacle, and there is also the impossibility of confining within statical conditions the circumstances from which they originate.

It is necessary, therefore, to abandon the path of free competition and turn in the opposite direction, namely, towards monopoly. Here we find a well-defined theory in which variations of cost connected with changes in the dimensions of the individual undertaking play an important part. Of course, when we are supplied with theories in respect to the two extreme cases of monopoly and competition as part of the equipment required in order to

---

Law of Constant Return). The dictum of Edgeworth, that "to treat *variables* as *constants* is the characteristic vice of the unmathematical economist," might to-day be reversed: the mathematical economists have gone so far in correcting this vice that they can no longer conceive of a constant except as the result of the compensation of two equal and opposite variables.

undertake the study of the actual conditions in the different industries, we are warned that these generally do not fit exactly one or other of the categories, but will be found scattered along the intermediate zone, and that the nature of an industry will approximate more closely to the monopolist or the competitive system according to its particular circumstances, such as whether the number of autonomous undertakings in it is larger or smaller, or whether or not they are bound together by partial agreements, etc. We are thus led to believe that when production is in the hands of a large number of concerns entirely independent of one another as regards control, the conclusions proper to competition may be applied even if the market in which the goods are exchanged is not absolutely perfect, for its imperfections are in general constituted by frictions which may simply retard or slightly modify the effects of the active forces of competition, but which the latter ultimately succeed in substantially overcoming. This view appears to be fundamentally inadmissible. Many of the obstacles which break up that unity of the market which is the essential condition of competition are not of the nature of "frictions," but are themselves active forces which produce permanent and even cumulative effects. They are frequently, moreover, endowed with sufficient stability to enable them to be made the subject of analysis based on statical assumptions.

Of these effects two, which are closely interconnected, are of special importance because they are to be found with great frequency in industries in which competitive conditions appear to prevail; and they also possess a special interest because, as they relate to certain of the most characteristic features of the theoretical conception of competition, they show how seldom it is for these conditions to be realised in their integrity, and how a slight divergence from them suffices to render the manner in which equilibrium is attained extremely similar to that peculiar to monopoly. These two points in which the theory of competition differs radically from the actual state of things which is most general are: first, the idea that the competing producer cannot deliberately affect the market prices, and that he may therefore regard it as constant whatever the quantity of goods which he individually may throw on the market; second, the idea that each competing producer necessarily produces normally in circumstances of individual increasing costs.

Everyday experience shows that a very large number of undertakings—and the majority of those which produce manufactured consumers' goods—work under conditions of individual diminishing costs. Almost any producer of such goods, if he could rely upon the market in which he sells his products being prepared to take any quantity of them from him at the current price, without any trouble on his part except that of producing them, would extend his business enormously. It is not easy, in times of normal activity, to find an undertaking which systematically restricts its own production to an amount less than that which it could sell at the current price, and which is at the same time prevented by competition from exceeding that price. Business men, who regard themselves as being subject to competitive conditions, would consider absurd the assertion that the limit to their production is to be found in the internal conditions of production in their firm, which do not permit of the production of a greater quantity without an increase in cost. The chief obstacle against which they have to contend when they want gradually to increase their production does not lie in the cost of production—which, indeed, generally favours them in that direction—but in the difficulty of selling the larger quantity of goods without reducing the price, or without having to face increased marketing expenses. This necessity of reducing prices in order to sell a larger quantity of one's own product is only an aspect of the usual descending demand curve, with the difference that instead of concerning the whole of a commodity, whatever its origin, it relates only to the goods produced by a particular firm; and the marketing expenses necessary for the extension of its market are merely costly efforts (in the form of advertising, commercial travellers, facilities to customers, etc.) to increase the willingness of the market to buy from it—that is, to raise that demand curve artificially.

This method of regarding the matter appears the most natural, and that which adheres to the reality of things. No doubt it is possible, from the formal point of view, to reverse these relations and regard every purchaser as being perfectly indifferent in his choice between the different producers, provided the latter, in order to approach him, are prepared to incur marketing expenses varying greatly in different cases, and to reckon these increased marketing expenses in the cost of production of each. In this way increasing individual costs can be obtained to any desired extent and a perfect market in which there is an unlimited demand, at current prices, for the products of each. But the question of allocating the marketing expenses cannot be decided from the point of view of formal correctness, for on that basis the two methods are equivalent; nor can it be decided acccording to the fact that these charges are actually paid by the purchaser or the seller, as this does not affect their incidence or their effects in any way. What is important is to ascertain how the various forces at work can be grouped in the most homogeneous manner, so that the influence of each of them on the equilibrium resulting from their opposition may be more readily estimated. From this point of view the second of the methods mentioned must be rejected, since it entirely conceals the effects which the circumstances from which the marketing expenses originate exercise in disturbing the unity of the market. It alters in a misleading way, moreover, the customary and well defined significance of the expression "cost of production," with the result of rendering it dependent upon elements quite extraneous to the conditions under which the production of a given undertaking takes place. It consequently misrepresents the manner in which the actual process of determining the price and the quantity produced by each undertaking is affected.

By adhering to the first point of view, therefore, we are led to ascribe the correct measure of importance to the chief obstacle which hinders the free play of competition, even where this appears to predominate, and which at the same time renders a stable equilibrium possible even when the supply curve for the products of each individual firm is descending—that is, the absence of indifference on the part of the buyers of goods as between the different producers. The causes of the preference shown by any group of buyers for a particular firm are of the most diverse nature, and may range from long custom, personal acquaintance, confidence in the quality of the product, proximity, knowledge of particular requirements and the possibility of obtaining credit, to the reputation of a trade-mark, or sign, or a name with high traditions, or to such special features of modelling or design in the product as—without constituting it a distinct commodity intended for the satisfaction of particular needs—have for their principal purpose that of distinguishing it from the products of other firms. What these and the many other possible reasons for preference have in common is that they are expressed in a willingness (which may frequently be dictated by necessity) on the part of the group of buyers who constitute a firm's clientele to pay, if necessary, something extra in order to obtain the goods from a particular firm rather than from any other.

When each of the firms producing a commodity is in such a position the general market for the commodity is subdivided into a series of distinct markets. Any firm which endeavours to extend beyond its own market by invading those of its competitors must incur heavy marketing expenses in order to surmount the barriers by which they are surrounded; but, on the other hand, within its own market and under the protection of its own barrier each enjoys a privileged position whereby it obtains advantages which—if not in extent, at least in their nature—are equal to those enjoyed by the ordinary monopolist.

Nor is it necessary to stress the customary conception of monopoly to make this case fit into it. In it also, in fact, we find that the majority of the circumstances which affect the strength of a monopolist (such as the possession of unique natural resources, legal privileges, the control of a greater or less proportion of the total production, the existence of rival commodities, etc.) exercise their influence essentially by affecting the elasticity of the demand for the monopolised goods. Whatever the causes may be, this is the only decisive factor in estimating the degree of independence which a monopolist has in fixing prices: the less elastic the demand for his product, the greater is his hold on his market. The extreme case, which may properly be called "absolute monopoly," is that in which the elasticity of the demand for the products of a firm is equal to unity[5]; in that case, however much the monopolist raises

---

[5] The elasticity of demand for the products of a monopolist cannot, of course, be less than unity in respect to prices immediately above the equilibrium price—that is, in respect to that part of the demand curve which alone counts in regard to the determination of the power of a monopolist in his own market; a question which is quite distinct from that of the magnitude of the gains obtainable by the monopoly, as the latter is dependent, not so much on

his prices, the sums periodically expended in purchasing his goods are not even partially diverted into different channels of expenditure, and his price policy will not be affected at all by the fear of competition from other sources of supply. So soon as this elasticity increases, competition begins to make itself felt, and becomes ever more intense as the elasticity grows, until to infinite elasticity in the demand for the products of an individual undertaking a state of perfect competition corresponds. In the intermediate cases the significance of a moderate elasticity in the demand is that, although the monopolist has a certain freedom in fixing his prices, whenever he increases them he is forsaken by a portion of his purchasers, who prefer to spend their money in some other manner. It matters little to the monopolist if they spend it in purchasing goods very different from his own, or goods identical with them, but supplied by other producers who have not increased their price; in either case he must undergo—if only in a slight degree— actual competition from such goods, since it is precisely the possibility of buying them that leads the purchasers gradually to give up using his product as he increases the price. The direct effects are thus equal whether the sums set free as the result of an increase in price by an undertaking are expended on a large number of different commodities, or whether they are employed preponderatingly in the purchase of one or a few rival commodities which are more or less available for buyers, as occurs in the case of an undertaking which, while controlling only a small part of the total production of a commodity, has the advantage of possessing a particular market of its own. But the indirect effects in the two cases are substantially different.

The method indicated by Marshall in regard to manufactures designed for particular tastes is applicable for the study of this latter case. "When we are considering an individual producer," he writes, "we must couple his supply curve, not with the general demand curve for his commodity in a wide market, but with the particular demand curve of his own special market" (*Principles*, V, xii, 2). If we extend this method to those industries in which each firm has more or less a particular market, we must not

---

the ratio of change, as on the absolute measure of the demand and the demand price.

restrict its employment to the occasions when we are considering
the individual producer, but we must adhere to it also when we
examine the manner in which equilibrium is attained in the trade
as a whole; for it is clear that such particular curves can by no
means be compounded so as to form a single pair of collective
demand and supply curves. The method mentioned above is the
very same as that followed in cases of ordinary monopoly, and in
both cases, in fact, the individual producer determines his selling
price by the well-known method which makes his monopoly
revenue or his profits the maximum obtainable.

The peculiarity of the case of the firm which does not possess
an actual monopoly but has merely a particular market is that,
in the demand schedule for the goods produced by it, the possible
buyers are entered in descending order according to the price
which each of them is prepared to pay, not rather than go entirely
without, but rather than not buy it from that particular producer
instead of elsewhere. That is to say, that two elements enter into
the composition of such demand prices—the price at which the
goods can be purchased from those other producers who, in the
order of a purchaser's preference, immediately follow the producer
under consideration, and the monetary measure of the value (a
quantity which may be positive or negative) which the purchaser
puts on his preference for the products of the firm in question.

For convenience in discussion it may be assumed that initially,
in an industry in which like conditions prevail, each producer sells
at a price which barely covers his costs. The individual interest
of each producer will urge him to increase his price quickly so as to
obtain the maximum profit. But in proportion as this practice
spreads throughout the trade the various demand schedules will
be modified as a result; for, as each buyer finds that the prices
of the substitutes upon which he was able to reckon are increased,
he will be inclined to pay a higher price for the products of the
firm whose customer he is. So that, even before the first increase
in price has been completely carried into effect, the conditions
will be created which may permit every one of the concerns to
make a further increase—and so on in succession. Naturally this
process speedily reaches its limit. The customers lost by a firm
whenever it raises its prices have recourse in part to other suppliers,
and these will return to it when the others also have raised their

prices; but in part they entirely give up buying the goods and definitely drop out of the market. Thus, every business has two classes of marginal customers—those who are at the margin only from its own individual standpoint and fix a limit for the excess of its prices over the prices generally ruling, and those who are at the margin from the standpoint of the general market and fix a limit for the general increase in price of the product.

It is, of course, possible that a general rise in the prices of a product may affect the conditions of demand and supply of certain firms in such a way as to make it advantageous for them to lower their prices rather than conform with the rise. But in an industry which has attained a certain degree of stability in its general structure, in regard of its methods of production, the number of undertakings composing it, and its commercial customs—in respect to which, therefore, statical assumptions are more nearly justified—this alternative is much less likely to be adopted than its opposite. In the first place, it involves great elasticity in the demand for the products of an individual business and rapidly diminishing costs for it—that is to say, a state of things the almost inevitable and speedy result of which is complete monopolisation, and which, therefore, is not likely to be found in a trade operated normally by a number of independent firms. In the second place, the forces which impel producers to raise prices are much more effective than those which impel them to reduce them; and this not merely owing to the fear which every seller has of spoiling his market, but mainly because an increase of profit secured by means of a cut in price is obtained *at the cost* of the competing firms, and consequently it impels them to take such defensive action as may jeopardise the greater profits secured; whereas an increase of profit obtained by means of a rise in prices not only does not injure competitors but brings them a positive *gain,* and it may therefore be regarded as having been more durably acquired. An undertaking, therefore, when confronted with the dual possibility of increasing its profits by raising its selling prices, or by reducing them, will generally adopt the first alternative unless the additional profits expected from the second are considerably greater.

These same reasons may serve to dispel the doubt, which might at first sight arise, whether in the case considered above the equilibrium may be indeterminate, as it is generally considered to be in the analogous case of multiple monopoly. In the first place, even in this case, as Edgeworth has noticed, "the extent of indeterminateness diminishes with the diminution of the degree of correlation between the articles" produced by the different monopolists[6]; that is to say, in our case, with the diminution of the elasticity of demand for the products of the individual firm—a limitation, it may be added, the effectiveness of which is the greater in proportion as the rapidity of decrease in the individual cost with the increase in the quantity produced becomes less. Both these conditions, as has been said above, are generally present to a large extent in the case we are considering. Moreover, the indeterminateness of the equilibrium in the case of multiple monopoly is necessarily dependent upon the assumption that at any moment each of the monopolists is *equally* inclined either to raise or to reduce his price, according as one or the other may suit him best from the point of view of immediate gain—a supposition which, at least in our case, is not, as we have said, justified.[7]

The conclusion that the equilibrium is in general determinate does not mean that generalising statements can be made regarding the price corresponding to that equilibrium; it may be different in the case of each undertaking, and is dependent to a great extent upon the special conditions affecting it.

The only case in which it would be possible to speak of a general price would be that of a trade in which the productive organisation of the different undertakings was uniform, and in which their particular markets were alike as regards the nature and attachment of the customers. In that case, as may readily be seen, the general price of the product, through the independent action of a number of firms, each of which is prompted only by its individual interests, would tend to reach the same level as that

---

[6] *The Pure Theory of Monopoly,* in Papers Relating to P. E., Vol. I, p. 121.

[7] The determinateness of the equilibrium would be more evident if, instead of regarding the various units of the same goods produced by different undertakings as rival commodities, we had regarded each unit as being composed of two commodities having, within each particular market, a joint demand, one of which (the commodity itself) is sold under competitive conditions, and the other (the special services, or the distinguishing features added to it by each producer) is sold under monopolistic conditions. This point of view, however, is more artificial and less in conformity with the customary method of regarding the matter.

which would be fixed by a single monopolistic association in accordance with the ordinary principles of monopoly. This result, far from being conditioned by the existence of an almost complete isolation of the individual markets, requires only a very slight degree of preference for a particular firm in each of the groups of customers. In itself, this case is of no importance, because it is extremely unlikely that such uniformity would actually be found; but it is representative of a tendency, which prevails even in actual cases where the conditions of the various undertakings differ among each other, whereby the cumulative action of slight obstacles to competition produces on prices effects which approximate to those of monopoly.

It should be noted that in the foregoing the disturbing influence exercised by the competition of new firms attracted to an industry the conditions of which permit of high monopolist profits has been neglected. This appeared justified, in the first place because the entrance of new-comers is frequently hindered by the heavy expenses necessary for setting up a connection in a trade in which the existing firms have an established goodwill—expenses which may often exceed the capital value of the profits obtainable; in the second place, this element can acquire importance only when the monopoly profits in a trade are considerably above the normal level of profits in the trade in general, which, however, does not prevent the prices from being determined up to that point in the manner which has been indicated.

It might seem, moreover, that the importance of the marketing difficulties as a limit to the development of the productive unit has been over-estimated as compared with the effect in the same direction exercised by the more than proportionate increase in the expenditure which a firm must sometimes incur in order to furnish itself with the additional means of production which it requires; but it will generally be found that such increases in costs are an effect, and not a determining cause, of the market conditions which render it necessary or desirable for a firm to restrict its production. Thus, the limited credit of many firms, which does not permit any one of them to obtain more than a limited amount of capital at the current rate of interest, is often a direct consequence of its being known that a given firm is unable to increase its sales outside its own particular market without incurring heavy marketing expenses. If it were known that a firm which is in a position to produce an increased quantity of goods at a lower cost is also in a position to sell them without difficulty at a constant price, such a firm could encounter no obstacle in a free capital market. On the other hand, if a banker, or the owner of land on which a firm proposes to extend its own plant, or any other supplier of the firm's means of production, stands in a privileged position in respect to it, he can certainly exact from it a price higher than the current price for his supplies, but this possibility will still be a direct consequence of the fact that such a firm, being in its turn in a privileged position in regard to its particular market, also sells its products at prices above cost. What happens in such cases is that a portion of its monopoly profits are taken away from the firm, not that its cost of production is increased.

But these are mainly aspects of the process of diffusion of profits throughout the various stages of production and of the process of forming a normal level of profits throughout all the industries of a country. Their influence on the formation of the prices of single commodities is relatively unimportant, and their consideration is therefore beyond the scope of this article.

10

COST CURVES AND SUPPLY CURVES [*]

By Jacob Viner ||

It is the primary purpose of this article to develop a graphical exposition of the manner in which supply curves are dependent upon the different possible types of technological and pecuniary cost situations, under the usual assumptions of atomistic competition and of rational economic behavior on the part of the producers. No attempt is made here at realistic description of the actual types of relationship between costs and supply, and the purpose is the more modest one of presenting the formal types of relationship which can be conceived to exist under certain simplifying assumptions. Analysis of this kind derives obviously from the path-breaking contribution of Alfred Marshall in his Principles of Economics. Interest in this type of problem has been largely confined to the Anglo-Saxon countries, and in these countries there has been a tendency until recent years for economists to accept and reproduce the general lines of Marshall's analysis somewhat uncritically and without much further elaboration. I have no very serious fundamental criticism to make of Marshall's analysis of the supply side of the exchange value problem. But Marshall's treatment is highly elliptical. A striking illustration of his tendency to telescope his argument is his common practice in his graphs of labelling cost curves and supply curves alike with the symbols *ss*, conventionally used for supply curves, and thus diverting the attention of his readers, and perhaps also occasionally his own attention, from the necessity of selecting from among the many possible types of cost curve that one which in the given circumstances alone has claims to being considered as also a supply curve. Marshall, moreover, although he made valuable additions to the conceptual

[*] *Zeitschrift für Nationalökonomie*, Vol. III (1931), pp. 23–46. Reprinted, by the courtesy of the publisher and the author, without change from the original text, with the addition of a supplementary note.

|| Princeton University.

terminology necessary for analysis of this type, nevertheless worked with vocabulary lacking sufficient terms to distinguish clearly from each other all the significant types of cost phenomena, and here also the terminological poverty tended to lead to inadequate classification not only on the part of his followers but on his own part. Marshall's analysis was excessively simple even on the basis of his own simplifying assumptions, and inadequately precise in formulation, and his followers have standardized an even simpler type of exposition of the relationship of cost to price.

In recent years a number of English economists, notably Pigou, Sraffa, Shove, Harrod and Robertson, have presented in the Economic Journal a series of criticisms, elaborations, and refinements of the Marshallian analysis which, in my opinion, go a long way both towards bringing out clearly the contribution contained in its implications as well as in its explicit formulations, and towards completing and correcting it where that is necessary. The indebtedness of the present paper to their writings is considerable and is freely acknowledged. But I have been presenting charts such as those contained in this article to my students at the University of Chicago for a long period antedating the writings referred to above, and if in the course of years these charts have undergone substantial revision and, as I am convinced, correction, chief credit is due to the penetrating criticisms of my students.

The analysis which follows is based on the usual assumptions and presuppositions of the Marshallian type of economics. As compared to the Lausanne School type of analysis, it contents itself with examination of the conditions of a partial equilibrium of a special sort, and does not inquire into the repercussions of the postulated changes in cost or demand conditions on the general equilibrium situation. Like all partial equilibrium analysis, including the allegedly "general" equilibrium theories of the Lausanne School, it rests on assumptions of the *caeteris paribus* order which posit independence where in fact there is some degree of dependence. For such logically invalid assumptions there is the pragmatic defense that they permit of more detailed analysis of certain phases of economic interdependence than would be possible in their absence, and that to the extent that they are fictions uncompensated by counterbalancing fictions, it is reasonable to believe that the errors in the results obtained will be almost invariably quantitative rather than qualitative in character, and will generally be even quantitatively of minor importance. As compared to the Austrian School, there is, I believe, no need either for reconciliation or for apology. On the somewhat superficial level on which analysis of the present type is conducted the basic issue as between the English and the Austrian Schools does not enter explicitly into the picture, and in so far as it has any bearing on the conclusions, this bearing is again quantitative rather than qualitative in character. The Austrian School starts with the assumption, usually tacit, never emphasized, that the supplies of all the elementary factors of production are given and independent of their rates of remuneration. The English School emphasizes, perhaps overemphasizes, the dependence of the amounts of certain of the elementary factors, notably labor and waiting, on their rates of remuneration. The techniques of analysis of each school are in essentials identical, and each school, if it were to apply its techniques to the situation postulated by the other, would reach identical conclusions. The difference in the assumptions of the two schools has bearing on the quantitative but not on the qualitative behavior of the prices of the elementary factors and therefore also of the money costs of their products, as the demands for these factors and products change. The conflict between the two schools has greater significance for the theory of the value of the elementary factors of production, i.e., for the theory of distribution, than for the theory of particular commodity price determination. For the present analysis, where it is assumed either that the prices of the elementary factors remain unaltered or that they undergo changes of a kind consistent with the basic assumptions of either school, the differences between the two schools would not affect qualitatively the character of the findings. All of the propositions laid down in this paper should, I believe, be acceptable to, or else should be rejected by, both schools.

The procedure which will be followed, will be to begin in each case with the mode of adjustment of a particular concern to the given market situation when the industry as a whole is supposed to be in stable equilibrium. This particular concern is not to be regarded as having any close relationship to Marshall's "representative firm." It will not be assumed to be necessarily typical of its industry with respect to its size, its efficiency, or the rate of slope of its various cost curves, but it will be assumed to be typical, or at least to represent the prevailing situation, with respect to the general qualitative behavior of its costs as it varies its own output or, in certain situations, as the industry of which it is part varies its output. All long-run differences in efficiency as between concerns will be assumed, however, to be compensated for by differential rates of compensation to the factors responsible for such differences, and these differential rates will be treated as parts of the ordinary long-run money costs of production of the different concerns. In the long-run, therefore, every concern will be assumed to have the same total costs per unit, except where explicit statement to the contrary is made. It will be assumed, further, that for any industry, under long-run equilibrium conditions, the same relationships must exist for every concern between its average costs, its marginal costs, and market price, as for the particular concern under special examination. But the reasoning of this paper would still hold if the realistic concession were made that in every industry there may be a few concerns which are not typical of their industry with respect to the qualitative behavior of their costs as output is varied either by themselves or by the industry as a whole, and which therefore do not wholly conform to these assumptions. It may be conceded, for instance, that in an industry in which for most producers expansion of their output means lower unit costs there should be a few producers for whom the reverse is true.

Short-Run Equilibrium for an Individual Concern

Chart I, which represents the behavior of money costs in the short-run for a single concern with a plant of a given scale, is the fundamental graph, and is incorporated in or underlies all the succeeding ones.[1] It is assumed that this concern is not of sufficient importance to bring about any change in the prices of the factors as a result of a change in its output. Since unit money costs of

---

[1] The charts were drawn for me by Y. K. Wong of the University of Chicago. Where in any chart one curve is derived from another or a combination of other curves presented in the same chart, it is drawn mathematically to scale. No attempt has been made, however, to maintain the same scales as between different charts. An attempt has been made to use mnemonic symbols for the various curves, MC for instance indicating marginal cost, P indicating price, and so forth. It is hoped that this will facilitate reading of the charts.

production are the sum of the products of the amounts of the factors used in the production of one unit multiplied by the prices of the factors, any change in unit money costs as output varies must in this case be due, therefore, to changes in the amounts of the factors required for the production of one unit, or to use Walras' term, to changes in the "technological coefficients of production." The "short-run" is taken to be a period which is long enough to permit of any desired change of output technologically possible without altering the scale of plant, but which is not long enough to permit of any adjustment of scale of plant. It will be arbitrarily

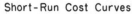

Short-Run Cost Curves

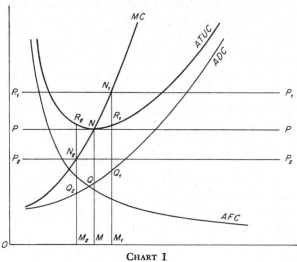

CHART I

assumed that all of the factors can for the short-run be sharply classified into two groups, those which are necessarily fixed in amount, and those which are freely variable. "Scale of plant" will be used as synonymous with the size of the group of factors which are fixed in amount in the short-run, and each scale will be quantitatively indicated by the amount of output which can be produced at the lowest average cost possible at that scale. The costs associated with the fixed factors will be referred to as the "fixed costs" and those associated with the variable factors will be called the "direct costs." It is to be noted that the "fixed costs" are fixed only in their aggregate amounts and vary with output in their amount per unit, while the "direct costs" are variable in their aggregate amount as output varies, as well as, ordinarily at least, in their amount per unit. Amounts of output are in this as in all the succeeding charts measured along the horizontal axis from O, and money costs and prices along the vertical axis from O.

The curve AFC represents the trend of the average fixed costs per unit as output is increased. Since these are the costs associated with the parts of the working combination which, by hypothesis, are absolutely fixed in their aggregate amount, this curve must be a rectangular hyperbola.[2] The curve ADC represents the trend of average direct costs per unit as output is increased. Since the increase in output is the result of the application, to a constant amount of "fixed" factors, of increased amounts of the variable factors, the law of diminishing returns, if it is operating, should make the output per unit of the variable factor employed diminish, i.e., should make the "direct" technical coefficients of production increase, as total output increases. As the prices of the factors by assumption remain constant, the average direct costs must also increase as output increases, if the law of diminishing returns is operative. It is assumed, not, I believe, without justification, that within the useful range of observation the law of diminishing returns is operative, and the average direct cost curve is therefore drawn positively inclined throughout.[3] The curve $ATUC$ represents the trend of average total (i.e., fixed plus direct) unit costs as output is increased, and is, of course, the sum of the ordinates of the ADC and AFC curves. It is necessarily U-shaped for all industries having any substantial fixed costs, and is in this respect a universal short-run curve qualitatively descriptive of the short-run behavior of average costs of practically all concerns and all industries which cannot quickly and completely adjust the amounts of all the factors they use to variations in their rates of output. But the relative lengths and the relative rates of inclination of the negatively inclined and the positively inclined portions of the curve will differ from concern to concern and from industry to industry, depending upon the relative importance of the fixed to the total costs and upon the degree of sharpness with which the

---

[2] I.e., the equation to the curve will be of the form $xy = c$.

[3] It is also drawn concave upward, to indicate the progressively sharper operation of the law of diminishing returns as the fixed factors are more intensively exploited.

law of diminishing returns is operative for the variable factors. The curve MC represents the trend of marginal costs as output is increased. Any point on it represents the increase in aggregate costs as output at that point is increased by one unit.[4]

The marginal cost curve must cut the average cost curve at the lowest point of the latter. At the point of intersection, average cost and marginal cost are of course equal. But average cost is equal to marginal cost only when average cost is constant, i.e., when the average cost curve is a horizontal line.[5] The point of intersection of the marginal cost curve with the average cost curve when the latter is concave upwards must therefore be at the lowest point of the latter, where its tangent is a horizontal line.[6]

If this particular producer is an insignificant factor in his industry, i.e., if atomistic competition prevails, he may reasonably assume that no change in his output, and especially no change consistent with the maintenance of the scale of plant at its original level, will have any appreciable effect on the price of his product. Under these conditions, the partial demand curve for his product may be taken as a horizontal line whose ordinate from the base is equal to the prevailing price.[7] It will be to his interest to carry production to the point where marginal cost equals price, i.e., his short-run MC curve will also be his rational short-run supply curve. If price is MN, this will mean an output of OM and no extra profit or loss on his operations, i.e., the quasi-rent on his fixed investment

---

[4] If y_a = average fixed cost per unit, y_b = average direct cost per unit, and x = output, then $ATUC = y_a + y_b$, and $MC = \dfrac{d[(y_a + y_b)x]}{dx}$. It is important to note that no consideration need be given to the fixed costs, if they really are absolutely fixed, in computing the marginal cost. Since $xy_a = c$, and $\dfrac{dc}{dx} = o, \ldots \dfrac{d[(y_a + y_b)x]}{dx} = \dfrac{d(xy_b)}{dx}$.

[5] If x = output, and y = average cost, marginal cost = $\dfrac{d(xy)}{dx}$. If $y = c$, then $\dfrac{d(xy)}{dx} = y$. If y is an increasing function of x then $\dfrac{d(xy)}{dx} > y$. If y is a decreasing function of x, then $\dfrac{d(xy)}{dx} < y$.

[6] For a mathematical proof, see Henry Schultz, "Marginal Productivity and the Pricing Process," *The Journal of Political Economy*, Vol. XXXVIII (1929), p. 537, note 33.

[7] This is equivalent to saying that the partial demand for his product has infinite elasticity.

per unit of output, NQ, would be equal to the fixed costs per unit. If price is P_1, output will be OM_1, and the quasi-rent per unit of output, N_1Q_1, will be in excess of the fixed costs per unit, R_1Q_1. If P_2 is the price, the output will be OM_2, and the quasi-rent per unit of output will be N_2Q_2, or less than the fixed costs per unit, R_2Q_2. All of these situations are consistent with short-run equilibrium, which, as far as individual producers are concerned, requires only that marginal cost equal price. The short-run supply curve for the industry as a whole is not shown in this chart, but is simply the sum of the abscissae of the individual short-run marginal cost ($=$ individual supply) curves.[8]

LONG-RUN EQUILIBRIUM

The long-run is taken to be a period long enough to permit each producer to make such technologically possible changes in the scale of his plant as he desires, and thus to vary his output either by a more or less intensive utilization of existing plant, or by varying the scale of his plant, or by some combination of these methods. There will therefore be no costs which are technologically fixed in the long-run,[9] and if in fact the scale of plant is not altered as long-run output alters, it will be the result of voluntary choice and not of absolute technological compulsion. For an industry as a whole long-run variations in output can result from more or less intensive use of existing plants, or from changes in the scale of plants, or from changes in the number of plants, or from some combination of these. Under long-run equilibrium conditions changes in output, whether by an individual producer or by the industry as a whole, will be brought about by the economically optimum method from the point of view of the individual producers, so that each producer will have the optimum scale of plant for his long-run output. To simplify the analysis, it will be assumed that in each industry the optimum type of adjustment to a long-run variation in output for that industry as a whole will not only be alike for all producers but will involve only one of the three possible methods of adjustment listed above; namely, change in intensity of use of existing plants, change in scale of plants, and change

---

[8] It is shown in Chart II.

[9] This is, of course, not inconsistent with the proposition that at any moment within the long-run there will be costs which from the short-run point of view are fixed.

in number of plants. The theoretical static long-run, it should be noted, is a sort of "timeless" long-run throughout which nothing new happens except the full mutual adjustment to each other of the primary factors existing at the beginning of the long-run period. It is more correct, therefore, to speak of long-run equilibrium in terms of the conditions which will prevail after a long-run, rather than during a long-run. Long-run equilibrium, once established, will continue only for an instant of time if some change in the primary conditions should occur immediately after equilibrium in terms of the pre-existing conditions had been reached. The only significance of the equilibrium concept for realistic price theory is that it offers a basis for prediction of the direction of change when equilibrium is not established. Long before a static equilibrium has actually been established, some dynamic change in the fundamental factors will ordinarily occur which will make quantitative changes in the conditions of equilibrium. The ordinary economic situation is one of disequilibrium moving in the direction of equilibrium rather than of realized equilibrium.

For long-run equilibrium not only must marginal cost of output from existent plant equal price for each individual producer, but it must also equal average cost. If this were not the case, there would be either abnormal profits or losses, which would operate either to attract capital into the industry or to induce withdrawal of capital from the industry, and in either case would tend to bring about a change in output. For long-run equilibrium it is further necessary not only that each producer shall be producing his portion of the total output by what is for him, under existing conditions, the optimum method, but that no other producer, whether already in the industry or not, shall be in a position to provide an equivalent amount of output, in addition to what he may already be contributing, at a lower cost. The relations of costs to supply in the long-run will depend on the technological conditions under which output can be most economically varied, and the succeeding discussion will consist in large part of a classification and analysis of these conceivable types of technological conditions.

"RICARDIAN" INCREASING COSTS

Chart II illustrates a special case corresponding to the Ricardian rent theory in its strictest form. Let us suppose that a given industry is already utilizing all of the supply available at any price of a necessary factor of production, so that the output of the industry as a whole can be increased only by the more intensive utilization of the absolutely limited factor. Suppose also that no appreciable economies are to be derived, whatever the output of the industry as a whole, by a combination into larger productive units, or a subdivision into smaller productive units, of the existing concerns. In order further to simplify the analysis, it is assumed that the identical portions of the working-combination which in this case remain technologically fixed in amount whatever may be

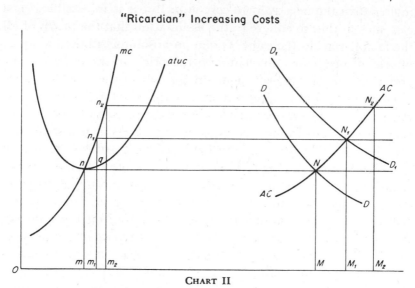

"Ricardian" Increasing Costs

CHART II

the short-run variations in output also remain economically fixed in amount whatever long-run variations in output may occur. If the particular concern whose costs are indicated in the left-hand portion of Chart II and the particular concern with which Chart I is concerned were identical, and if the two charts were drawn to the same scale, the MC curve in Chart I and the mc curve in Chart II would be identical, although the former represents the short-run trend and the latter represents the long-run trend of marginal costs as output is varied, i.e., for these assumptions, the short-run and the long-run marginal cost curves would be identical. The $atuc$ curve in Chart II, continuing these assumptions, would simply represent the short-run variations in average cost for this particular concern as output was varied, when long-run price was mn or MN,[10] and would be in all respects identical with the $ATUC$ curve of Chart I. When long-run price was MN, this concern would be in both short-run and long-run equilibrium when its output was Om, and its average cost, its marginal cost, and price were all equal.

Suppose now, that owing to a long-run increase of market demand from DD to D_1D_1, long-run price rises to M_1N_1. It will pay our producer to increase his output to Om_1, at which point the new marginal cost, m_1n_1, will be equal to the new price. If the prices of all the factors remain the same, the new price will be higher than the new average cost m_1q. But it is impossible, for a case such as this, to adhere to the assumption that the prices of all the factors remain the same. Given an absolutely limited amount of one of the factors, no change in the prices of the other factors, and a rise in the long-run demand for and in the long-run price of its product, and the long-run price of this absolutely scarce factor must rise. Let us suppose that the fixed factor is land. Its price or rent will rise until there ceases to be any excess of marginal over average cost. The $atuc$ curve in Chart II therefore has only short-run significance. A long-run increase in the price of the product will cause an increase in the price of land-use, and therefore a rise in the entire $atuc$ curve. The increase in land-rent, however, will have no effect on marginal costs, and therefore on the long-run mc curve, for it will be due to the increase in price of the product and not to the increase in output of this particular concern. Even if this producer maintained his output at Om, after long-run price had risen to M_1N_1, the $atuc$ curve would rise in the same manner and degree. It would always shift upward in such a way, however, that the mc curve would intersect it at its lowest point,[11] i.e., rent

---

[10] The qualifying phrase in italics is important. Its significance is explained in the next paragraph of the text.

[11] Each successive short-run $atuc$ curve of a particular producer, as the long-run price of his product rises, consists of the ordinates of his former $atuc$ curve plus a new rent charge fixed in total amount regardless of his output, and therefore of the form $xy = c$. As was pointed out in note 4, page 204, the vertical addition of a rectangular hyperbola to an average cost curve does not affect the marginal cost curve derivable from it. The same mc curve can, therefore, continue to be the short-run marginal cost curve, even when the short-run average cost curve is undergoing long-run changes consistently with the conditions assumed in this case.

for land would rise just sufficiently to make the new lowest average cost equal the new equilibrium marginal cost. When the long-run price was M_1N_1, therefore, average cost, marginal cost, and price would be equal for each producer under long-run equilibrium.

The AC curve in the right-hand portion of Chart II represents the long-run supply curve for the industry as a whole, and is simply the sum of the abscissas of the individual mc curves. It is also a long-run average cost curve for the industry as a whole inclusive of rent, and a long-run marginal cost curve for the industry as a whole exclusive of rent. For the individual producer, the changes in rent payments required as demand changes are due primarily to the changes in demand, secondarily to the changes in output of the industry as a whole, and only to an insignificant degree to his own changes in output. The individual producer will therefore not take the effect on his rent payments of increased output on his own part into account, and the supply curve for the industry as a whole will therefore be the marginal cost curve for the industry as a whole exclusive of rent.[12]

This appears to be the case usually designated in the textbooks as the case of "increasing costs." I have labelled it as "Ricardian increasing costs" to indicate its close relationship to the Ricardian rent theory. It is to be noted that as output increases the long-run average costs rise even if the increase of rents is disregarded and that there are increasing unit technological costs, therefore, whether the technical coefficients are weighted by the original or by the new prices of the factors. There are increasing marginal .costs in every possible sense of the term costs.

If mc were the short-run marginal cost curve for a scale adapted to a long-run equilibrium output of Om, and if not all the factors which were technologically fixed in the short-run remained economically fixed in the long-run as output was increased, then, since

---

[12] For the industry as a whole, however, the increase of output as demand increases will affect rent, on the one hand by influencing price and gross receipts, and on the other hand by influencing gross expenses. Depending upon the shift in position and the elasticity of the demand curve and upon the rate of slope of the industry marginal cost curve exclusive of rent, an increase of output when demand increases may make rent either greater or less than if output were kept constant. But under atomistic competition the possible results of keeping output constant when demand rises will play no part in the determination of output, of price, or of rent.

there would be less scope for the operation of the law of diminishing returns, the long-run marginal cost curve for the particular concern would be different from and less steeply inclined than the *mc* curve, and the new short-run $atuc_1$ curve for a long-run equilibrium scale of output of, for example, Om_1 would have no simple relationship to the *atuc* curve in Chart II. Similarly, the long-run supply curve for the industry as a whole, since it is the sum of the abscissas of the individual long-run marginal cost curves, would then also be less steeply inclined than the *AC* curve in Chart II, which would then be only a short-run supply curve for the industry as a whole, when the long-run equilibrium output of the industry was *OM*.

CONSTANT COSTS

In the short-run, for industries which have any fixed costs whatsoever, constant marginal costs as output is varied are wholly inconceivable if the law of diminishing returns is operative, and constant average costs are inconceivable if there are increasing marginal costs as required by the law of diminishing returns.[13]

In the long-run, however, constant costs are theoretically conceivable under two kinds of circumstances. The first case is when each producer can vary his scale of production without affecting his long-run average costs. The situation in this case for any individual concern will be as represented in Chart III. The curves $atuc_1$ and mc_1 represent, respectively, the short-run trends of average and marginal costs as output is varied from a plant of scale *OA*. The curves $atuc_2$ and mc_2, similarly represent, respectively, the short-run trends of average and marginal costs as output is varied from a plant of scale *OB*; and similarly, for scales *OC* and *OD*. In the long-run any output would be produced from the optimum scale for this output. The long-run average cost curve would therefore be the horizontal line *AC*, which passes through the lowest points of all the short-run *atuc* curves. Where average

---

[13] Let x = output, y_a = average fixed costs per unit, y_b = average direct costs per unit, and c and k be two different constants. Suppose that short-run average costs are constant, i.e., that $y_a + y_b = k$. But $xy_a = c$. Then $xy_b = kx - c$, and marginal cost, or $\dfrac{d(xy_b)}{dx} = \dfrac{d(kx - c)}{dx} = k$, which is inconsistent with the law of diminishing returns.

costs are constant as output varies, average cost and marginal cost are always identical.[14] This horizontal line would therefore also be the individual producer's long-run supply curve.

This case presents certain difficulties when perfect competition prevails which make it impossible to indicate graphically the relationship between the long-run supply curves of the individual concern and the industry as a whole. Read as an ordinary supply curve, the AC line indicates that in the long-run this concern would be unwilling to operate at any price under AN, would be

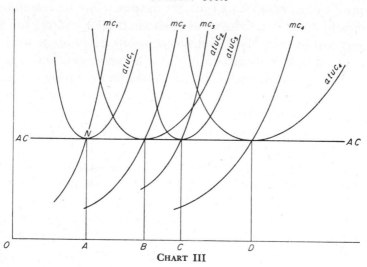

Constant Costs

CHART III

willing to produce any amount at a price AN, and would be anxious to produce unlimited quantities at any price over AN. If the costs of different producers in the industry are not uniform, then the lowest cost concern would tend to monopolize the industry. If the costs of different producers are uniform, the supply curve for the industry would be indefinite, and in the long-run there would be a constant tendency toward overproduction, with consequent losses and a reaction toward underproduction. Actual long-run price and output would be unstable, but would oscillate above and below stable points of equilibrium price and equilibrium output.

The second conceivable case of long-run constant costs, not

---

[14] See note 5, page 204.

illustrated graphically here, would be presented by a situation in which all of the concerns within the industry and an indefinite number of potential members of the industry can operate at long-run minimum average costs uniform as between the different concerns, but with average costs increasing for each as its output increases. The long-run output of the industry would then consist of the sum of the outputs of all the member concerns, each operating at that scale at which its costs are at the minimum common to all, and variations of output for the industry as a whole would result wholly from variations in the number of producers, each of whom would maintain a constant output while he remained in the industry. For the industry as a whole, therefore, long-run production would take place under conditions of constant long-run average and marginal cost, uniform for all producers and equal to each other, although each concern would be operating subject to short-run increasing average and marginal costs. Here also actual long-run price and output for the industry as a whole would tend to be unstable, but would oscillate above and below stable points of equilibrium price output.

The situation would in these two cases be somewhat analogous to that of a thermostatic control which aims at maintaining a uniform temperature, which is stimulated into operation only when there is a significant degree of variation from the desired temperature, and which succeeds only in keeping the ever-present variations from the desired temperature from exceeding narrow limits in either direction. Completely stable equilibrium under constant cost conditions is only conceivable on the assumption of some departure from perfect competition, in consequence of which variations in output by individual producers, or entrance into the industry by new producers or withdrawal of old, are subject to some difficulty even in the long-run after the equilibrium price and output have once been momentarily established.

Net Internal Economies of Large-Scale Production

We owe to Marshall the important distinction between the "internal" and the "external" economies resulting from increased output. For present purposes we will use the term "net internal economies of large-scale production" to mean net reductions in costs to a particular concern resulting from a long-run expansion in its output when each output is produced from a plant of the optimum scale for that output. The word "net" is introduced to make it clear that increase in output may result at the same time in economies and in diseconomies and that it is only the excess of the former over the latter to which reference is made here. Internal economies of large-scale production are primarily a long-run phenomenon, dependent upon appropriate adjustment of scale of plant to each successive output. They should not be confused with the economies resulting from "spreading of overhead," which are a short-run phenomenon, represented by the negative inclination of the average fixed cost curve in Chart I. Internal economies of large-scale production need not be relatively greater for those particular costs which in the short-run are the fixed costs than for those particular costs which in the short-run are the direct costs. In the long-run, in any case, there are no technologically fixed or overhead costs, if the definitions here followed of "long-run" and of "fixed costs" are adhered to. Internal economies of large-scale production are independent of the size of output of the industry as a whole, and may be accruing to a particular concern whose output is increasing at the same time that the output of the industry as a whole is undergoing a decline. It is for this reason that Marshall gave them the name of internal, to distinguish them from the external economies which are dependent on something outside the particular concerns themselves, namely, the size of output of the industry as a whole.

Internal economies may be either technological or pecuniary, that is, they may consist either in reductions of the technological coefficients of production or in reductions in the prices paid for the factors as the result of increases in the amounts thereof purchased. Illustrations of technological internal economies would be savings in the labor, materials, or equipment requirements per unit of output resulting from improved organization or methods of production made possible by a larger scale of operations. Pecuniary internal economies, on the other hand, would consist of advantages in buying, such as "quantity discounts" or the ability to hire labor at lower rates, resulting from an increase in the scale of purchases.[15]

---

[15] Pecuniary internal economies are, theoretically, as likely to result from expansion of output from a given plant as from expansion of output brought

Chart IV illustrates the behavior of the cost curves for a particular concern which enjoys net internal economies of large-scale production. As in Chart III the ac curves and the mc curves represent the short-run variations in average and marginal costs respectively, as output is varied from plants of each indicated scale. The AC curve represents the long-run trend of average costs, that is, the trend of average costs when each output is produced from a plant of the optimum scale for that output, and is drawn so as to connect the points of lowest average cost for each scale of plant.[16] The MC curve is the long-run marginal curve for this particular concern when the AC curve is interpreted as a continuous curve. It represents the increment in aggregate costs resulting from a unit increase in output, when each output is produced from a plant of the optimum scale for that output. It is to be noted that while the short-run marginal cost curves are positively inclined, the long-run marginal cost curve is negatively inclined.[17]

---

about by increase of scale of plant. But it is only the latter form of expansion of output which is likely to be great enough to result in significant pecuniary internal economies.

[16] The AC curve would represent a continuous trend only if it is assumed that scale of plant can be modified by small increments. If the curve is interpreted as a discontinuous one, then only the points N, N_1, N_2, . . . on it are significant, and the significant long-run costs for the intervals between are the lowest short-run average costs available for the indicated outputs. It may be noticed that at certain points the short-run ac curves are drawn so as to sink below the long-run AC curve. If the AC curve is interpreted as having significance only at the N points, this is of no consequence. But if the AC curve is interpreted as a continuous curve, this is an error. My instructions to the draftsman were to draw the AC curve so as never to be above any portion of any ac curve. He is a mathematician, however, not an economist, and he saw some mathematical objection to this procedure which I could not succeed in understanding. I could not persuade him to disregard his scruples as a craftsman and to follow my instructions, absurd though they might be.

[17] If y, y_1, y_2, are the short-run average costs for scales of plant, OM, OM_1, and OM_2, respectively, as indicated by the ac curves; $Y =$ long-run average cost, as indicated by the AC curve; $x =$ output; mc, mc_1, and mc_2 indicate the short-run marginal costs as represented by the mc curves; and MC indicates the long-run marginal cost, as represented by the MC curve, then:

$$mc = \frac{d(xy)}{dx}; \ mc_1 = \frac{d(xy_1)}{dx}; \ mc_2 = \frac{d(xy_2)}{dx}; \ \text{and} \ MC = \frac{d(xY)}{dx};$$
$$\text{and} \ \frac{d^2(xy)}{dx^2} > 0; \ \text{and} \ \frac{d^2(xY)}{dx^2} < 0.$$

The familiar proposition that net internal economies of large-scale production and long-run stable equilibrium are inconsistent under competitive conditions is clearly illustrated by this chart. When price is MN, this concern, if operating with the scale of plant represented by the short-run curves ac and mc, is in short-run equilibrium when its output is OM, for its short-run marginal cost is then equal to price. It will not be in long-run equilibrium, however, for its long-run marginal cost will then be only MQ, or less than price. Provided that no change in its output will affect market price, it will pay this concern to enlarge its plant whatever the price may

Net Internal Economies of Large-Scale Production

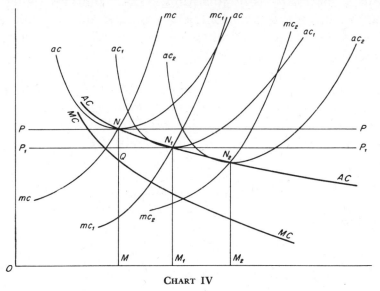

CHART IV

be, and whatever its existing scale of plant may be. If thereby it grows so large that its operations exert a significant influence on price, we pass out of the realm of atomistic competition and approach that of partial monopoly. Even then, however, it would still be profitable for this concern to enlarge its plant and increase its output as long as long-run marginal cost was lower than long-run marginal revenue, or the increment in aggregate receipts resulting from a unit increment in output, after allowance for any reduction in price.[18]

---

[18] If Y_p = long-run price, X = long-run output, and Y_c = long-run average cost, long-run marginal cost would be $\dfrac{d(XY_c)}{dX}$, long-run marginal revenue

For any particular concern operating under these conditions, and *a fortiori* for an industry as a whole consisting of such concerns, there is no definite long-run supply curve. At any price MN higher than the asymptote of the AC curve, this producer will be willing to produce any quantity not less than OM.

To negatively-inclined long-run cost curves such as the AC and MC curves in Chart IV, Marshall has denied the characteristic of "reversibility," i.e., of equal validity whether output is increasing or decreasing, on the ground that some of the economies accruing when the output of a concern, or of an industry as a whole, is increased will be retained if the output of the concern or of the industry returns to its original dimensions.[19] This reasoning appears to involve a confusion between static and dynamic cost curves. The reductions in costs as output is increased indicated by curves such as the AC and MC curves in Chart IV are purely functions of size of output when scale is adjusted to output and not of lapse of actual time during which improved processes may happen to be discovered. The economies associated with output OM are economies which are not available for any output less than OM. The only basis on which the irreversibility of these curves, as static curves, could logically be posited would be the existence of possible economies of a type adapted to any scale of output but discoverable only when output is great, where invention, but not its exploitation, was a function of scale of output.

---

would be $\dfrac{d(XY_p)}{dX}$, and it would pay to carry production to the point where long-run marginal cost equalled long-run marginal revenue, or $\dfrac{d(XY_c)}{dX} = \dfrac{d(XY_p)}{dX}$. Under atomistic competition, $\dfrac{d(XY_p)}{dX} = Y_p$, which is independent of this particular concern's output. Whatever the price, therefore, this concern would always have an incentive to increase its long-run output as long as long-run marginal cost remained less than that price. If partial monopoly resulted, however, marginal revenue, or $\dfrac{d(XY_p)}{dX}$, would become a function of market demand and of competitor's supply and would be smaller than Y_p, and a point of stable long-run equilibrium might exist, depending on how the other producers reacted to variations in output by this one. If complete monopoly resulted, there would probably be a definite point of stable equilibrium. These questions, however, are beyond the range of this paper.

[19] *Principles of Economics*, 8th ed., 1922, p. 808.

NET INTERNAL DISECONOMIES OF LARGE-SCALE PRODUCTION

Cases are clearly conceivable where increase of scale of plant would involve less efficient operation and consequently higher unit costs. The prevailing opinion in the United States that for most types of agriculture the one-family farm is still the optimum mode of agricultural organization would indicate that in this country at least agriculture was subject to net internal diseconomies of large-scale production after an early stage in the size of the farm-unit had been reached. But when increase of output by means of the increase of scale of existing plants involves a substantial increase in unit costs, it will always be possible for the industry as a whole to avoid the net internal diseconomies of large-scale production by increasing its output through increase in number of plants without increase in their scale.[20] This case has no practical importance, therefore, except as it represents an economic barrier against increase in scale of plants, and it is not worth while to illustrate it graphically.

NET EXTERNAL ECONOMIES OF LARGE PRODUCTION

External economies are those which accrue to particular concerns as the result of the expansion of output by their industry as a whole, and which are independent of their own individual outputs. If an industry which enjoys net external economies of large production increases its output—presumably through increase in number of plants—the average costs of the member concerns of that industry will fall even though each concern maintains a constant scale of plant and a constant output. Like internal economies, external economies may be either technological or pecuniary. Illustrations of technological external economies are difficult to find, but a better organization of the labor and raw materials markets with respect to the availability of laborers and materials when needed by any particular plant, and improvement

---

[20] Increase of scale should be distinguished from increase in output from the same scale of plant. In the former, all the factors are increased in about the same proportions; in the latter some factors remain fixed in amount. Whenever it is generally possible to increase all the factors in about the same proportion, i.e. to increase scale of plant, it is also possible, alternatively at least, to increase the number of plants.

in productive technique resulting from "cross-fertilization," or the exchange of ideas among the different producers, appear to be possible sources of technological external economies resulting from the increase in size of the industry as a whole. Illustrations of pecuniary external economies would be reductions in the prices of services and materials resulting from the increase in the amounts of such services and materials purchased by the industry as a whole. Pecuniary external economies to industry A are likely to be internal or external economies to some other industry B. If

Net External Economies of Large Production

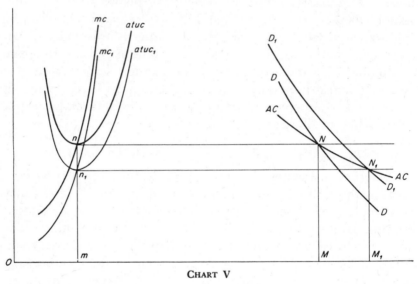

CHART V

industry A purchases materials in greater quantity, their price may fall because industry B can then produce them at lower unit cost. But cases are theoretically conceivable where pecuniary external economies to industry A may not be economies to any other industry, as, for instance, if laborers should have a preference, rational or irrational, for working in an important rather than in a minor industry, and should therefore be willing to accept lower wages as the industry expands.

  Chart V illustrates the case of net external economies of large production, irrespective of whether these economies are technological, or pecuniary, or both. As always, each concern will in the long-run tend to produce its output from the optimum scale

foɪ that output, and given that scale, to carry production to the
point where its average and marginal costs are both equal to price.
If Om represents the optimum scale of plant for the particular
producer, i.e., the scale at which he can produce at the lowest
average cost, if the long-run price is mn or MN, and if the long-
run output for the industry as a whole is OM, this producer will
be in long-run equilibrium when his output is om, and his average
and his marginal cost are both mn. Suppose now that long-run
demand rises from DD to D_1D_1, and that long-run output of the
industry as a whole increases, as the result of increase in the number of producers, from OM to OM_1. Since, by assumption, this
industry is subject to net external economies of large production,
the short-run average and marginal cost curves of each particular
concern will fall in the manner indicated in the left-hand portion
of Chart V. This particular concern will be in long-run equilib-
ɪium with the new situation when its output is om, as before,
but its long-run average and marginal costs will have fallen from
mn to mn_1. The AC curve represents the trend of the individual
average (and also marginal) costs as output of the industry as a
whole changes by the amounts indicated on the horizontal axis.
Any point on this curve represents the long-run average cost for
every individual producer, and therefore for the industry as a
whole, when the output of the industry as a whole is as indicated.
It is theoretically the same as the supply curve for the industry
as a whole. The long-run marginal cost curve for the industry as
a whole is not shown on the chart. It would fall below the AC
curve.[21] Its only relationship to the short-run marginal cost curves
of the individual concerns would be that it was a function of the
downward shifting of the lowest points on the individual short-run
atuc and *mc* curves as the output of the entire industry increased.
Under atomistic competition this marginal cost curve would have
no influence on supply, since individual producers would not
take it into account in deciding either upon their continuance in

---

[21] If $X =$ output of the industry as a whole, and $Y_a =$ long-run average
cost for the industry as a whole as represented by the AC curve, the MC curve
for the industry as a whole would be $\dfrac{d(XY_a)}{dX}, < Y_a$. If average cost for a particular producer $= y_a$, then $y_a = f(X)$, and at long-run equilibrium, $y_a = Y_a$.

or their entrance into the industry or upon their scale of output when in the industry.[22]

NET EXTERNAL DISECONOMIES OF LARGE PRODUCTION

Although it has not ordinarily been given consideration, the case of net external diseconomies of large production is of indisputable practical importance. Pecuniary diseconomies of this kind will always tend to result from the expansion of output of an industry because the increased purchases of primary factors and materials which this entails must tend to raise their unit prices. In order that pecuniary diseconomies shall not result from the expansion of an industry's output, it is necessary, for both primary factors of production and materials, that the increase in demand by this industry shall be accompanied by a corresponding and simultaneous decrease in demand by other industries or increase in supply of the factors and materials themselves, or, failing this, that the materials, because of net external or internal economies in the industries producing them, should have negatively inclined supply curves.[23] These pecuniary external diseconomies, however,

----

[22] Employing terminology resembling that used by Pigou in his *The Economics of Welfare,* the marginal private net cost would exceed the marginal industry net cost. If the output of an additional producer be represented by ΔX, and the average cost of his output and of the outputs of the other producers by $y_a = f(X)$, then the marginal private net cost would be y_a, and the marginal industry net cost would be $\dfrac{\Delta(XY_a)}{\Delta X}, < y_a$.

[23] It is worth pointing out that negative supply curves for the primary factors of production will not prevent an increased demand for them from a particular industry from resulting in an increase in their unit prices and therefore are not a barrier to pecuniary external diseconomies for that industry in so far as their primary factor costs are concerned. The negatively inclined supply curves of primary factors have a different meaning from the negatively inclined supply curves for commodities. If labor has a negatively inclined supply curve that means not that willingness to hire labor in greater quantities will result in a fall in the wage-rate, but, what is very different, that fewer units of labor will be offered for hire when a high rate of wages is offered than when a lower rate is offered. In the case of commodities, any point on a negatively inclined supply curve must be interpreted to mean that at the indicated price, the indicated quantity or more of the commodity can be purchased. In the case of labor, any point on a negatively inclined supply curve must be interpreted to mean that when the indicated wage-rate is obtainable, the indicated quantity of labor, but no more, will be available for

may be more than counterbalanced by technological external
economies, and need not necessarily result therefore in net external diseconomies. External technological diseconomies, or increasing technical coefficients of production as output of the
industry as a whole is increased, can be theoretically conceived,
but it is hard to find convincing illustrations. One possible in-

Net External Diseconomies of Large Production

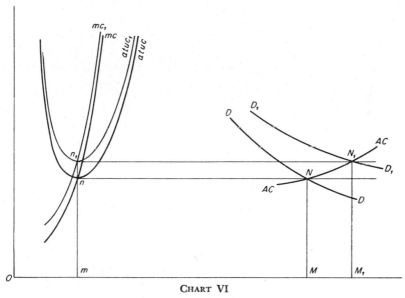

CHART VI

stance might be higher unit highway transportation costs when
an industry which provides its own transportation for materials
and products expands its output and thereby brings about traffic
congestion on the roads.

Chart VI illustrates the case of net external diseconomies of
large production, whether technological or pecuniary. When the
long-run equilibrium outputs of the industry as a whole are OM
and OM_1, respectively, the $atuc$ and $atuc_1$ curves represent the
respective trends of short-run average costs, the mc and mc_1 curves

hire. If the negatively inclined supply curve for labor has an elasticity of less
than unity, as seems probable, it must be assumed that labor will prefer a
high wage rate and partial employment to a low wage rate and fuller employment, and therefore will resist any movement toward the lower points on its
supply curve.

represent the trends of short-run marginal costs and mn and mn_1 represent the long-run equilibrium average and marginal costs, for one individual producer. The reverse of the conditions when net external economies of large production are present, in this case the long-run equilibrium average and marginal costs of the individual concern rise as the output of the industry as a whole increases. The AC curve represents the trend of the individual average (and also marginal) long-run costs and therefore also of the industry long-run average cost as the industry as a whole varies its output. This is also the long-run supply curve for the industry as a whole. The long-run marginal cost curve for the industry as a whole is not shown on the chart. It would rise above the AC curve.[24] Since the individual producers will not concern themselves with the effect on the costs of other producers of their own withdrawal from or entrance into the industry, and since in this case it is assumed that variation in output takes place only through variation in number of producers, the marginal cost curve for the industry as a whole will, under competitive conditions, have no influence on output.[25]

PARTICULAR EXPENSES CURVES

In the foregoing analysis of the relation of cost to supply, it has been throughout maintained, explicitly or implicitly, that under long-run static competitive equilibrium marginal costs and average costs must be uniform for all producers. If there are particular units of the factors which retain permanently advantages in value productivity over other units of similar factors, these units, if hired, will have to be paid for in the long-run at differential rates proportional to their value productivity, and if em-

---

[24] As for Chart V, if $X =$ output of industry as a whole and $Y_a =$ long-run average cost for industry as a whole, as represented by the AC curve, the marginal cost curve for the industry as a whole would be $\dfrac{d(XY_a)}{dX}$. If for the individual concern, $y_a =$ average cost, then $y_a = f(X)$, and at long-run equilibrium $y_a = Y_a$.

[25] In Pigou's terminology, the marginal industry net cost would exceed the marginal private net cost. If the output of an additional concern be represented by ΔX, and his average cost by $y_a = f(X)$, then the marginal private net cost would be y_a, and the marginal industry net cost would be $\dfrac{\Delta(XY_a)}{\Delta X}, > y_a$.

ployed by their owner should be charged for costing purposes with the rates which could be obtained for them in the open market and should be capitalized accordingly. In the short-run, the situation is different. There may be transitory fluctuations in the efficiency of particular entrepreneurs or of particular units of the factors, and it would neither be practicable nor sensible to recapitalize every unit of invested resources with every fluctuation in their rate of yield. Even in the short-run, there must be equality as between the marginal costs of different producers under equilibrium conditions,[26] but there may be substantial variations as between the average costs, and therefore as between the net rates of return on original investment, of different producers.

Statistical investigations of individual costs in the United States, based in the main on unrevised cost accounting records, have shown that the variations in average costs as between different producers in the same industry at the same time are very substantial, and that ordinarily a significant proportion of the total output of an industry appears to be produced at an average cost in excess of the prevailing price. To some extent these variations in cost can be explained away as due (1) to different and, from the point of view of economic theory unsatisfactory, methods of measuring costs, and especially the costs associated with the relatively fixed factors of production, (2) to regional differences in f.o.b. factory costs and in prices which, in an area as large as the United States, can be very substantial for bulky commodities without implying the absence of keen competition and (3), to the absence of atomistic competition. But even aside from such considerations, it should be obvious that such findings are in no way inconsistent with the propositions of equilibrium price theory as outlined above. Under short-run equilibrium the average costs,

---

[26] Since a time-interval is always present between the sale contract and at least some of the stages of hiring of factors and of actual production, there is opportunity under short-run equilibrium for some divergence between price and marginal cost, and therefore, between the marginal costs of different producers. It would be a more precise way of formulating the short-run theory to say that since all producers, if acting rationally, carry production to the point where anticipated marginal cost will equal anticipated price, and since price, in a perfect market, is uniform for all, marginal cost tends to be uniform for all producers, and variations as between different producers result only from errors in anticipation.

including the fixed costs, of any particular producer need bear no necessary relationship to price, except that the average direct costs must not exceed price. These statistical costs, moreover, are not the equilibrium costs of the theoretical short-run, but are the costs as they exist at an actual moment of time when short-run equilibrium with the fundamental conditions as they exist at the moment may not have been attained, and when these fundamental conditions are themselves liable to change at any moment.

It may be worth while, however, to show the relationship of the distribution of particular average costs within an industry at particular actual moments of time to the general supply conditions of the industry under assumptions of long-run equilibrium. To a curve representing the array of actual average costs of the different producers in an industry when the total output of the industry was a given amount, these individual costs being arranged in increasing order of size from left to right, Marshall gave the name of "particular expenses curve,"[27] and American economists have called such curves "bulk-line cost curves,"[28] "accountants' cost curves," and "statistical cost curves." In Chart VII, the curves AN, BN_1, and CN_2, are supposed to be the appropriate particular expenses curves for an industry subject to net external economies of large production, when the output of the industry as a whole is OM, OM_1, and OM_2, respectively. Because the industry is subject to net external economies, the entire particular expenses curves are made to shift downward as the output of the industry expands. (If the industry were subject to net external diseconomies of production, the particular expenses curves would shift upwards as the output of the industry expands. Corresponding modifications

---

[27] See *Principles,* 8th ed., Appendix *H,* p. 911. It will be noticed that his particular expenses curve, SS is drawn so as to project somewhat beyond the point of total output for the industry as a whole A. This is an error, and no significance can be given to the part of the curve projecting beyond the point of total output of the industry as a whole. If the output of the industry were to increase up to the terminal point of this curve, the entire curve would acquire a different locus.

[28] "Bulk-line cost curves" because if a perpendicular is dropped to the horizontal axis from the point of intersection of the price-line and the curve, the greater part or the "bulk" of the output would be to the left of this "bulk-line." See F. W. Taussig, "Price-Fixing as seen by a Price-Fixer," *The Quarterly Journal of Economics,* Vol. XXXIII.

in the chart would have to be made as other assumptions with respect to the conditions under which the industry can expand its output were introduced.) It is to be understood also that no dynamic changes in prices of the factors or in average technological cost conditions for the industry as a whole are occurring except such as are associated with variations in output of the industry as a whole.

The *HC* curve is a curve connecting the points of highest-cost for each successive output. These highest-costs, though often so designated, are not marginal costs in the strict sense of the term,

Particular Expenses Curves

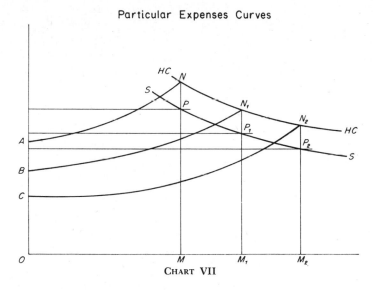

CHART VII

but are in each case simply the average costs of that producer whose average costs are the highest in the industry. If the statistical indications and also certain *a priori* considerations are to be followed, these highest average costs are likely to be, except in "boom years," distinctly higher than the true marginal costs,[29] and are

---

[29] If the *AN*, *BN₁*, and *CN₂* curves were the actual particular expenses curves when the actual outputs of the industry as a whole were *OM*, *OM₁* and *OM₂* respectively, the actual marginal cost curve for the industry as a whole would be a curve representing the differences per unit increase of output between the aggregate costs represented by the successive areas, *AOMN*, *BOM₁N₁*, *COM₂N₂*, . . . as output was increased from *OM* to *OM₁*, to *OM₂*, to . . . It would be negatively inclined, and would be much below the *HC* curve.

so drawn in this graph. The P, P_1, P_2 lines represent price, and are drawn to intersect the particular expenses curves below their highest points, in conformity with the statistical findings. The curve SS, drawn through the P, P_1, P_2 points representing actual prices prevailing when the outputs are OM, OM_1 and OM_2, respectively, is a sort of actual semi-dynamic[30] supply curve.

What is the ordinary relationship between the HC curve and the SS curve under fully dynamic conditions cannot be postulated on *a priori* grounds, and only statistical investigation can throw much light on it. American investigators of particular expenses curves believe that they have already demonstrated stable and predictable relations between them and price, but a reasonable degree of scepticism still seems to be justified. One point, however, is clear on *a priori* even more than on inductive grounds. If the SS curve in Chart VII were not ordinarily below, and substantially below, the HC curve, the familiar and continuously present phenomenon of bankruptcy would be inexplicable.

It is possible, moreover, to devise a theory of even long-run static equilibrium which still leaves room for an excess of the HC over the SS curves, and therefore for bankruptcy as a phenomenon consistent with long-run equilibrium. For such a theory, however, long-run equilibrium would apply only to the industry as a whole, and would be a sort of statistical equilibrium between rate of output and rate of consumption. None of the individual producers under this theory need be in long-run equilibrium at any time. At any moment, some producers would be enjoying exceptional profits, and others incurring heavy losses. The particular expenses curve could remain positive in its inclination and fixed in its locus, but there would be necessarily a constant process of shifting of their position on that curve on the part of the individual producers, and an equality in rate of withdrawal of producers from the industry through bankruptcy or otherwise, on the one hand, and of entrance of new producers into the industry, on the other hand. A theory of this sort would leave room for pure profits even in a static state.

––––––––

[30] "Semi-dynamic" because certain types of dynamic changes have been assumed not to occur.

SUPPLEMENTARY NOTE (1950) *

I do not take advantage of the opportunity to revise my 1931 article. Even the error in Chart IV (page 215) is left uncorrected, so that future teachers and students may share the pleasure of many of their predecessors of pointing out that if I had known what an "envelope" was I would not have given my excellent draftsman the technically impossible and economically inappropriate assignment of drawing an AC curve which would pass through the lowest cost points of all the ac curves and yet not rise above any ac curve at any point. It is left also to the reader to modify the general contour of the ATUC curve of Chart I in conformity with the evidence which inductive studies seem to provide that the trough of this curve has a negative inclination throughout almost all of its possible course.

I feel it incumbent upon me, however, so as to avoid propagating serious error, to carry the analysis of costs a stage further in one respect by departing here from the traditional Marshallian pattern of assumptions to which the article adheres. The partial-equilibrium nature of the Marshallian assumptions leaves a wider range of possibilities to the long-run tendencies of costs for an expanding industry than is consistent with general-equilibrium analysis. I first saw this in 1938, and thereafter pointed it out to my students at the University of Chicago. But the first, and, to my knowledge, still the only, analysis in print similar to what I have in mind[31] is in Joan Robinson's excellent article, "Rising Supply Price," *Economica*, VIII, February, 1941 (see page 241 of the present volume), which has not attracted the attention which in my opinion it eminently deserves. What follows is, I think, in substantial harmony with her argument, but is so presented as to provide a link with the analysis in my 1931 article.

The most significant long-run behavior of costs for many appli-

---

* Reprinted from *Readings in Economic Analysis*, ed. by R. V. Clemence, Addison-Wesley Press, Cambridge, 1950, Vol. II, pp. 31–35, by the courtesy of the publisher and the author, with an additional note.

[31] I have since found the same doctrine expounded in an earlier article by R. F. Harrod, "Notes on Supply," *The Economic Journal*, Vol. XL (1930), pp. 232–241, especially pp. 240–241. [Note added in 1951.]

cations of value theory to concrete economic issues is the trend
of unit costs, average or marginal, for a particular commodity (or
group of commodities) as the total output of such commodity
expands while the economy as a whole remains stable (or relatively stable), so that the expansion of output of this commodity
is of necessity simultaneous with a corresponding contraction of
output of all other commodities considered in the aggregate. Let
us assume that in an otherwise stable economy a shift of wants
occurs from other commodities to cloth, with a consequent expansion in the output of cloth. Except by coincidence, and even that
conceivable only at a "point" rather than over a substantial range,
the cloth industry will be using the various "factors" (or "ingre-
dients," or "resources," or "input items") in proportions somewhat
different from those in which the economy as a whole, and the
contracting section of it, uses them. As the cloth industry expands,
therefore, and bids for more factors, the contracting industries
will not, at prevailing prices for the factors, be releasing factors
in the same proportions in which the cloth industry is trying to
acquire them; at prevailing prices for the factors, those which the
woolen industry uses relatively heavily will be in short supply
while those which it uses relatively lightly will be in excess supply.
There will consequently occur a realignment of the prices of the
factors, with those used relatively heavily by the cloth industry
rising in price and those used relatively lightly by it falling in price.

Thus all industries must tend to be subject to "external net
pecuniary diseconomies of large production" when they expand
relative to the economy of which they are a part. The entrepreneurs in an expanding industry, to lessen the impact of these
pecuniary diseconomies, will endeavor to reduce the ratio of their
use of the factors which have risen in price to their use of the
factors which have fallen in price. But the extent to which such
change in the proportions in which the factors are combined is
technically feasible and economically profitable is limited by the
operation of the law of diminishing returns, i.e., increase in the
relative use of the cheaper factors results in decreased ratios of
output to input of these factors. It is not possible therefore completely to escape the pecuniary diseconomies resulting from the
relative changes in the prices of the factors by altering the proportions in which the factors are used, if it is assumed, as I do here,

that the law of diminishing returns is operating in the long run.

There is presented on page 231 an arithmetical illustration of the conclusions derivable from this reasoning with respect to money costs per unit of product and allocation of resources as between different industries when in an economy of stable size a shift of wants of given extent in favor of cloth results in an expansion of the cloth industry. Case I represents what are for present purposes the essential characteristics of the assumed original equilibrium of the economy as a whole, and Case II represents a possible new equilibrium, consistent with all the assumptions made, after there has been full adjustment to the shift in wants. It is assumed in Case II that all the factors are fixed in amount, and also that the total national income remains at $320. There are in Case II as compared to Case I: an increase in the output of cloth; a rise in the price of factor B used relatively heavily by the cloth industry and decreases in the prices of other factors; a relative decrease in the use of factor B as compared to other factors for each industry (although not for all industry in the aggregate); a rise in the average cost and in the price of cloth (there would also be a rise in the marginal cost of cloth but this is not brought out explicitly in the illustration) and falls in the average costs and prices of all other commodities taken as a whole. The degrees of change from Case I indicated in the illustration are in every instance arbitrary, though consistent with equilibrium for the economy as a whole, but the directions of change are in every instance necessary ones.

The assumption that the factors are fixed in amount, i.e., that the amounts offered for hire are independent of their rates of remuneration, is an unnecessary one; though for fortuitous historical reasons it is a popular assumption in economic theory and even sometimes presented as dogma which it is not respectable to depart from, it is in fact wholly arbitrary and unrealistic. It is easy to modify the arithmetical illustration, however, to adapt it to other types of assumptions as to the character of the supply functions of the factors. I will not take the space required to do this here, but will confine myself to a summary account of the character of the necessary changes in the results which follow changes in the assumptions as to the supply functions of the factors, all other assumptions remaining as before.

Case III. Assume that each of the factors has a supply function such that the quantity offered for hire is an increasing function of the rate of remuneration. All price and cost changes as compared to Case I will be the same in direction as in Case II, but less in degree. The total quantity of factor B used by the economy as a whole will be greater and of factors B and C will be less than in Case I or Case II.

Case IV. Assume that factor B has a fixed supply, while the amounts offered of factors A and C are increasing functions of their rates of remuneration. The cost and price of cloth will rise more than in Cases II or III and the cost and prices of other commodities will fall less than in Cases II or III.

Case V. Assume that the quantity of factor B offered for hire is an increasing function of its rate of remuneration, while the supplies of factors A and C are fixed. The cost and price of cloth will rise, but less than in Cases II, III, or IV, while the prices of other commodities will fall more than in Cases II, III, or IV.

Case VI. Assume that the supply functions of all of the factors of production can be represented graphically by "rising-backward" curves, i.e., that as higher rates of remuneration are offered for them smaller quantities are supplied.[32] The rise in the cost and the price of cloth would be greater and the fall in the costs and prices of other commodities would also be greater than in any of the preceding Cases II to V.

In all these cases an increase in the long-run output of cloth can occur only at higher cost, and these or allied cases cover all the assumptions as to the supply functions of the factors which seem to me to be conceivable as realities if the possibility of migration of factors to or from the economy in question is excluded. If the reasoning here presented is valid, there is therefore a universal long-run "law" of increasing money costs as output changes in response to shifts in wants in an economy of constant national

---

[32] "Rising-backward" supply curves need to be interpreted differently from ordinary negatively-inclined Marshallian supply curves, even when they are geometrically identical. In the former case each point on the curve represents a maximum quantity; in the latter case each point on the curve represents a minimum quantity. Negatively-inclined supply curves of the second type for basic factors of production seem to me so improbable as to make analysis of their consequences pedantic.

Factor	Rate of Remuneration Per Unit	Total Quantity of Factors Used			Total Payments to Factors	Industry	Output: Units	Input per Unit of Output ("Technical Coefficients")			Average Cost = Price
		By Cloth Industry	By Other Industries	By All Industries				A	B	C	
						Case I					
A	$4.00	1	29	30	$120	Cloth	4	$\frac{1}{4}$	$\frac{5}{4}$	$\frac{2}{4}$	$8.00
B	4.00	5	15	20	80	Other	36	$\frac{29}{36}$	$\frac{15}{36}$	$\frac{28}{36}$	8.00
C	4.00	2	28	30	120	All	40				8.00
				80	$320						
						Case II					
A	$3.40	6	24	30	$102	Cloth	8	$\frac{6}{8}$	$\frac{8}{8}$	$\frac{5}{8}$	$10.30
B	5.50	8	12	20	110	Other	30	$\frac{24}{20}$	$\frac{12}{30}$	$\frac{25}{30}$	7.92
C	3.60	5	25	30	108	All	38				8.42+
				80	$320						

money income. The "law" will operate unambiguously, however, only after the expanding industry has reached the stage beyond which there are no net technological or efficiency advantages of increasing the scale of plants in order to increase output of the particular commodities concerned as compared to increasing the number of plants, i.e., where there are no "net technological economies of large-scale production." When this stage is ordinarily reached is a question of fact, but I know of no convincing evidence that the optimum-efficiency size, as measured by the ratio of optimum-plant-capacity to total output of the industry, is not quite moderate for any industry of appreciable size outside the fields of transportation and communication, where "plant" is difficult to define.

11

RISING SUPPLY PRICE *

By Joan Robinson ||

Confusion in the discussion of the law of diminishing returns has mainly arisen from a failure to make clear what question is being discussed. When that has been decided the rest of the argument follows without difficulty. The classical analysis, which gave rise to the Ricardian theory of rent, dealt with the question of what happens when the supplies of labour and capital increase, and land remains fixed. This clearly has nothing to do with rising supply price for a particular commodity.[1] It belongs to the department of output as a whole. Then there is diminishing returns as it appears in the theory of employment. This is essentially a short-period problem—what happens to the prices of commodities in general when effective demand increases, organisation and capital resources being given, and the amount of employment being free to increase. This also belongs to the analysis of output as a whole.

The problem of the long-period supply curve of a particular commodity belongs to the department of the theory of value, which treats of relative prices of commodities. Marshall's analysis appears to be a cross between the theory of value and the theory of output as a whole. For he seems most often to be discussing the problem of the change in the supply of a particular commodity which occurs in response to a *net* increase in demand.

---

* *Economica*, New Series, Vol. VIII (1941), pp. 1–8. Reprinted, by the courtesy of the publisher and the author, with indicated changes by the author. It was prefaced by the following introductory paragraph:

"It may seem strange at this time of day to reopen the old familiar subject of diminishing returns and rising supply price. My purpose is frankly escapist, and what follows has no relevance to any problem of importance in the real world."

|| Cambridge University, England.

[1] Cf. Sraffa, "The Laws of Returns under Competitive Conditions," *The Economic Journal*, December, 1926 (reprinted in the present volume, page 180).

The demand for one commodity increases, but the demand for the rest does not decline. The additional factors, apart from land, employed in increasing the supply of the commodity are called into existence by the increase in demand. "While the supplies of all other agents of production respond in various degrees and various ways to the demand for their services, land makes no such response. Thus an exceptional rise in the earnings of any class of labour, tends to increase its numbers, or efficiency, or both . . . And the same is true as regards capital."[2]

"The building an additional floor on one factory or putting an extra plough on one farm does not generally take a floor from another factory or a plough from another farm; the nation adds a floor or a plough to its business as the individual does to his. There is thus a larger national dividend which is to be shared out. . . . In contrast to this the stock of land (in an old country) at any time is the stock for *all* time; and when a manufacturer decides to take in a little more land to his business, he decides in effect to take it away from someone else's business."[3]

Marshall's supply curve therefore relates to a rather queer problem. The demand for one commodity, say boots, is increased, the demand for all others remaining the same, so that there is an increase in total expenditure, devoted entirely to boots. The problem is too artificial to be interesting. But supposing we do want to discuss the problem, it is putting the cart before the horse to look at it in this way. Full employment of resources is always assumed, therefore a net increase in demand presupposes an increase in resources. And we cannot begin to discuss whether there will be diminishing returns or not until we know what factors of production have increased in supply.

The problem which belongs properly to the theory of value is the problem of how supply reacts to a transfer of demand. And when we are considering a transfer of demand, say, to boots from commodities in general, it is not at all obvious that Marshall's distinction between land and other factors has any relevance. Factors are released by the decline in demand for things in general, which are available to be employed in making boots, and land

---

[2] *Principles* (7th ed.), p. 534.

[3] *Ibid.*, pp. 535–536.

will be released as well as labour, capital and entrepreneurship.

Professor Hicks comes nearer to discussing the proper problem.[4] But he also presents it in a peculiar form. There is an increase in the demand for commodity X at the expense of commodity Y. The price of X, according to Professor Hicks, must rise. But to this there is an obvious objection. Before we know what happens to the price of X we must know what factors are released from the industry producing Y.[5] Professor Hicks merely relies upon the assumption of perfect competition.[6] Under perfect competition, it is true, marginal cost to the firm must be rising. But this is nothing to do with the case. We are discussing the supply of a particular commodity in long-period equilibrium, and it is both unnatural to assume that the number of firms producing that commodity is fixed, and unfair not to inform the reader that that assumption has been made. Further, we must notice that Professor Hicks's view that a rise in the general level of prices must accompany the rise in price of X is the result of an optical illusion, due to the fact that Y has been chosen as the *numéraire*. In a later passage Y is imperceptibly transmuted into money, and the increase in demand for X comes about through dis-hoarding.[7] The problem has thus become the issue of a cross between the theory of value and the theory of employment, comparable to that produced by Marshall's cross between the theory of value and the classical theory of output as a whole.

Let us now turn to the problem of a transfer of demand to one commodity, from commodities in general. We will assume (1) full employment, (2) perfect competition, (3) no economies of large-scale industry. The discussion is confined to conditions of full long-period equilibrium. In assuming perfect competition we have already begged the question of the definition of a commodity, for universal perfect competition is possible only in a world in which all consumption goods can be divided into groups (each group being called a commodity) such that within each group

---

[4] *Value and Capital,* p. 73.

[5] Production has not yet been introduced at this stage of Professor Hicks's argument, but in later chapters its conclusions are taken to be valid for a system with production.

[6] *Value and Capital,* p. 83.

[7] *Ibid.,* p. 108.

there is perfect substitutability, from the consumer's point of view, between any unit of the commodity and any other, while between commodities substitutability is less than perfect. Each group must be large enough to cover the output of a great number of firms. If the world were such that perfect competition were possible, it would be such that the demarcation of commodities would present no difficulty.

At the first stage of our argument we will further assume fixed supplies of all factors. In the real world the demarcation of factors is just as teasing a problem as the demarcation of commodities.[8] But since we are assuming perfect competition we may as well be hung for a sheep as a lamb, and assume that productive resources, as well as consumers' goods, exist in nature in groups (each group being called a factor) such that within each group the elasticity of substitution between units is infinite, while between factors it is finite or zero. By assuming no economies of large scale we have postulated that factors are divisible into units which are small relative to the supply of each factor.

Now to tackle our problem: the demand for a certain commodity, say alpha, increases while the demand for other commodities is reduced, the reduction in demand for any one commodity other than alpha being very small in relation to the increase in demand for alpha. Factors of production are transferred from industry in general to the alpha industry. If alpha employs factors in the same proportions as factors are released, the increase in output of alpha is produced under constant returns, and there is no change in relative prices.

But industries are idiosyncratic, and it is natural to suppose that alpha requires factors, not in the proportions in which they are employed in the average of all industries, but in proportions peculiar to itself. A relative increase in demand for alpha therefore entails an increase in the total demand for those factors which it employs in more than the average proportions and a decline in demand for those factors it employs in less than the average proportions. The relative prices of factors therefore alter.

---

[8] My own attempt to provide a "corrected natural unit" for the measurement of factors (*Economics of Imperfect Competition,* p. 332) was a mere aberration, and no genuine solution is possible which treats non-homogeneous factors as though they were homogeneous.

We are then confronted with the question: in what terms are we to measure the resources employed in alpha? We cannot say whether or not the supply price of alpna rises with an increase in its output until we know how prices are to be reckoned.[9] The obvious solution is to measure prices in terms of a composite unit of resources, the factors being weighted by the proportions in which they are found in industry as a whole. So long as we are assuming a fixed supply of each factor this measurement is quite unambiguous.

Now, the factors which alpha requires, or requires most, have risen in price in terms of the composite unit, while the factors which it does not require, or requires least, have fallen in price. Thus the supply price of alpha rises in terms of the composite unit, while the supply price of all other commodities falls, each a little.[10] Thus, for any commodity considered separately there is rising supply price, because an increase in the output of any commodity turns the relative factor prices against itself.[11]

The strength of the tendency to rising supply price will depend upon three considerations.

(1) The larger the proportion of all factors absorbed by alpha, the greater will be the effect upon relative factor prices of a given proportionate increase in the output of alpha. This expresses the familiar proposition that a widely defined industry is more likely to show rising supply price than a narrow one—there is more likely to be rising supply price for the products of engineering in general than for drawing-pins, and for agricultural produce than for Brussels sprouts.

(2) The more idiosyncratic alpha is in respect to the factors which it requires, the further will it be from employing factors in the average proportions, and the more will it raise the price of

---

[9] Cf. Pigou, "Laws of Diminishing and Increasing Cost," *The Economic Journal,* June 1927.

[10] Cf. Robbins, "Certain Aspects of the Theory of Costs," *The Economic Journal,* March 1934, p. 5, note.

[11] It is curious to observe that it is not necessary that there should be any change in the proportions in which factors are employed in alpha. It might happen that all the factors employed in alpha rose equally in terms of the composite unit, so that their prices relative to each other were unchanged. Thus rising supply price might occur without any appearance of diminishing returns in the ordinary sense.

the factors which it requires in terms of the composite unit. This also is familiar; indeed, the whole theory of diminishing returns in particular industries has developed round the case of the industry employing a rare factor, such as special soil, a particular mineral, or an unusual human skill. In such a case the industry employs the whole of a factor which is not used in other industries at all, so that its selection of factors is very far from the average.

(3) The more obstinately alpha adheres to a special selection of factors, that is, the more rigid the technical conditions, and the lower the elasticity of substitution between the factors which it employs, and between those other factors which it might employ, the greater will be the change in relative factor prices when alpha expands. For if the elasticity of substitution is high alpha will alter its employment of factors in the direction of the average employment of all factors, in response to a rise in the relative price of the factors it happened to be employing in the first position, and the change in relative factor prices will thus be kept in check.[12]

A markedly unaverage selection of factors and a low elasticity of substitution between factors are necessary conditions for an appreciable degree of rising supply price. Even a very large industry will show a small rise in supply price if its selection of factors is near the average, or if it is nearly indifferent as to what factors it employs. On the other hand, a very small industry may enjoy sharply rising supply price if it has very specialised requirements.

Let us now remove the assumption that the supply of each factor is fixed. Within the conditions of the problem total primary resources—for instance the population—must be assumed constant, but the supply of any particular factor—for instance a special type

---

[12] Keynes, in a letter dated April 20, 1941, made the following comment on this point: "I should have thought that the elasticity of substitution between factors which a employs was merely a particular case of the much more important question of the elasticity of substitution between the factors which β, γ, etc. employ. If there is easy substitution between the factors employed by other commodities, so that a small change in their relative prices releases the factor which a requires, a will not rise much in price, however particular it may be in its choice of factors. Generally speaking, much the biggest influence on price is, I should have thought, the question of the ease with which the *other* commodities can be persuaded to substitute one factor for another." This criticism is undoubtedly correct, but it does not apply to the case where alpha employs the whole of a specialized factor. [Note added, 1950.]

of skill—may be assumed to vary in response to its price. On this assumption, when alpha expands and all other industries contract there is an increase in the supply of the factors which alpha employs in more than the average proportions, and a contraction in supply of factors which it does not employ, or employs in less than the average proportions. Our unit of measurement is no longer unambiguous, since the proportions of factors in industry as a whole are now altered. We may measure price either in terms of the composite unit appropriate to the first position, or in terms of the composite unit after the change has taken place. In either terms, the prices of the factors employed by alpha rise by less than they would have done if all supplies of factors were fixed. The change alters the composite unit in such a way as to bring it closer to the proportions of factors employed in the alpha industry; the rise in the price of the alpha factors is therefore less in terms of the new unit than of the old.

We must now add a fourth to the influences governing rising supply price. The tendency to rising supply price will be stronger the less elastic the total supplies of those factors required by the expanding industry.

When a change in the total supplies of factors is admitted, it is no longer a universal rule that each industry (unless it employs factors in the average proportions) is working in conditions of rising supply price. Falling supply price may also occur, quite apart from economies of large scale industry. To take the extreme case—suppose that all the factors which alpha employs in more than the average proportions are in perfectly elastic supply, while others, which it employs, but employs in less than the average proportions, are in perfectly inelastic supply. Then an expansion in alpha leads to a fall in the price of the bundle of factors which it employs, in whichever composite unit the price is measured.[13] In less extreme cases there may be a fall in terms of the new composite unit when there is a rise in terms of the original com-

---

[13] If each factor is in perfectly elastic supply constant returns must always prevail, for relative factor prices cannot alter. The departure from constant supply price, in either direction, will be greater (other things equal) the greater the difference between the elasticities of supply of those factors which the expanding industry uses in more than the average proportions and of those factors which it employs in less than the average proportions.

posite unit. This type of falling supply price, due solely to changes in relative factor prices, is Professor Pigou's case of "decreasing supply price *simpliciter*" which is not "decreasing supply price from the standpoint of the community."[14] Where falling supply price occurs, it will work more strongly the larger is the industry; for, the bigger the industry, the greater the effect of a given proportionate increase in its output in altering the supplies of factors favourably to its own requirements.

On the above analysis it is possible to support Marshall's contention that rising supply price is more likely to be found in agriculture and mining than in manufacturing industry. The primary industries are highly idiosyncratic in the factors which they require, elasticity of substitution is often zero between certain factors which they employ and any possible alternative, and the total supply of their factors is highly inelastic. Marshall's distinction between the natural factors, which give rise to diminishing returns, and man-made factors, which do not, can therefore be justified. The logical distinction is not between natural and man-made factors, but between rare and common factors, between cranky and adaptable factors, and between factors in less or more elastic supply. But when the distinctions are drawn on this basis the natural factors are clearly more likely to qualify, in respect of rarity, crankiness and inelastic supply, than human factors. For the general run of manufactured commodities, on the other hand, in the perfectly competitive world postulated by our assumptions, almost constant supply price would be the general rule.

The question which we have chosen to discuss is of very limited interest. No actual change in demand comes about in the form of an increase in demand for one commodity accompanied by a small reduction in demand at the margin for each other commodity. In reality the same causes which produce an increase in taste for one thing will reduce the taste for some particular other

---

[14] *The Economics of Welfare,* 3rd ed., p. 224. Professor Hicks must surely be in error in supposing that the "stability conditions" cannot survive the faintest appearance of falling supply price, *Value and Capital,* p. 83. If he had provided himself with stability conditions of tougher morale he would not have been so appalled by the problem of monopoly.

things. Thus even granted the extreme assumptions of perfect competition and full equilibrium, the question which we have been discussing is an unnatural one. When the increase in demand for alpha comes about at the expense, not of things in general, but of other particular commodities, say beta and gamma, we must know what factors are employed by beta and gamma before we can say what happens to the supply price of alpha. And we must know how the changes in price of beta and gamma react on the demands for delta and omega. The analysis can be extended to any degree of refinement, but the more complicated the question the more cumbersome the analysis. In order to know anything it is necessary to know everything, but in order to talk about anything it is necessary to neglect a great deal.

12

EXTERNAL ECONOMIES AND DISECONOMIES [*]

By Howard S. Ellis and William Fellner [||]

I. Introduction

Along with its answer to the principal problem which it set for itself as to how competition allocates resources amongst various uses, neo-classical economics bequeathed to the present generation the much debated proposition that competition causes output under "diminishing returns" to exceed, and under "increasing returns" to fall short of, an output corresponding to the social optimum. Since this issue involves only negligibly any disagreement as to the economic facts, since it is indeed almost a purely quantitative problem not complicated by ethical or other preconceptions, one may find difficulty in understanding how theorists such as Marshall, Pigou, Viner, Graham, Hicks, and Lange could be ranged squarely against Allyn Young, Knight, and Stigler. The answer seems to be that apparently simple technical concepts are often fraught with confusing ambiguities; and the extensive discussion of this subject over a period of years[1] reveals that these ambiguities have already become perennial.

The effort to resolve the issues disputed amongst such distinguished protagonists is in itself an interesting undertaking in the development of theoretical ideas, but there is also no lack of pragmatic justification. The interpretation of certain commonly employed cost functions, of opportunity cost, and of marginal versus average cost can not be purely "academic" matters. Furthermore, the Marshall-Pigou proposals of taxes upon "industries of diminishing returns" and bounties upon those of "increasing re-

[*] *The American Economic Review,* Vol. XXXIII (1943), pp. 493–511. Reprinted, by the courtesy of the publisher and the authors, with typograpical corrections.

[||] University of California.

[1] The footnotes, including n. 22, p. 254, supply a fairly complete bibliography on the subject.

turn," and the Pigou-Graham proposals of a protective tariff in
certain instances upon much the same theoretical argument, lead
directly to important questions of fiscal and commercial policy.
Finally the recent descriptions of price systems under socialism
show that the present issues intimately affect not only the formulation of policies in a private enterprise economy but the very
concept of the socially optimum employment of resources under
(a more or less ideal form of) socialism.

The advocates of the tax-bounty thesis have mostly referred
Throughout the period of classical political economy it was
a settled but vaguely supported conviction that the price of agricultural produce tends to increase under the influence of diminishing returns, but that "it is the natural effect of improvements
to diminish gradually the real price of almost all manufactures."[2]
This bad mixture of a dubious "law" of economic history on the
one hand, and a truncated part of the static principle of combining proportions on the other may have been engendered originally out of resentment against the Corn Laws and the landed
gentry; but it seems to have been perpetuated to the present day
through simple confusion. Marshall attempted to give quantitative precision to the notion that "diminishing returns" somehow
represent a less favorable application of economic resources than
"increasing returns."[3] His demonstration, which ran in terms of
the effect of taxes and bounties upon consumers' surpluses in the
two cases, is sorely limited by the author's admission that it requires quite special elasticities of demand and supply and that
it assumes that marginal utility of money to be constant; and it is
entirely destroyed by the failure of the author to include producers'
surpluses into the social surplus to be maximized.[4]

The advocates of the tax-bounty thesis have mostly referred
to Pigou rather than to the original Marshallian version of the
thesis. We turn first to Pigou's analysis so far as it pertains to
"diminishing returns" (in his own terminology), which includes

[2] Adam Smith, *The Wealth of Nations,* Cannan ed., (New York, 1937)
Book I, Chap. 9, p. 242 *et passim*; cf. also J. S. Mill, *Principles of Political
Economy,* Gonner ed., (London, 1909), Book I, Chap. 12, p. 184 *et passim*.

[3] Alfred Marshall, *Principles of Economics,* 3rd ed. (London, ·1895), pp.
518–531; and in the corresponding chapter (Book V, Chap. 12) in later editions.

[4] Cf. J. R. Hicks, "The Rehabilitation of Consumers' Surplus," *The Review
of Economic Studies,* Vol. 8 (Feb. 1941), pp. 112–115.

also rising transfer costs, leaving until later the case of "increasing returns" (in his terminology), which actually means external economies.

II. DIMINISHING RETURNS AND RISING TRANSFER COSTS ("EXTERNAL DISECONOMIES"), WITHOUT EXTERNAL ECONOMIES

In *Wealth and Welfare*,[5] the first edition of the work later to be more widely known as *The Economics of Welfare,* Pigou draws two positively inclined cost functions (as in Fig. 1), the lower of which, labeled S_1, he calls "a supply curve of the ordinary type,"

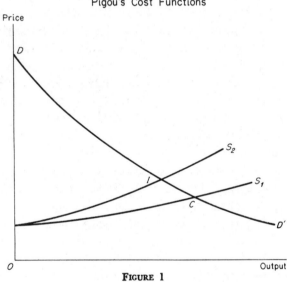

Pigou's Cost Functions

FIGURE 1

and the upper, labeled S_2, "a curve of marginal supply prices." The function S_1 is further described as showing at each point the cost or price at which the corresponding output on the abscissa can be maintained in the long run, and function S_2 as showing at each point "the difference made to *aggregate* expenses"[6] by the production of one more unit. With austere brevity, Pigou concludes directly from the description of the two functions that the intersection of S_1 with the demand schedule at C corresponds to output and price under competition, whereas the intersection of

---

[5] A. C. Pigou, *Wealth and Welfare* (London, 1912), pp. 172–179.

[6] Our italics.

S_2 with the demand schedule at I represents the correct output[7] under an ideal allocation of social resources.

In the universe of discourse of Pigou's problem, economic theory now operates with a number of cost functions presently to be described; but from the exposition of *Wealth and Welfare* it is impossible to discover which of three mathematical functions Pigou intended to employ. Retrospectively, in answer to criticisms, Pigou acknowledged one possible interpretation but denied that he had intended to draw his conclusions on this basis, proposed another interpretation, and finally, even upon this interpretation, limited his thesis to a special argument concerning international trade.

In a review of *Wealth and Welfare* appearing about a year after the publication of the book, Allyn Young hailed Pigou's S_2 curve as a "new and powerful instrument of economic analysis" especially as applied to monopoly, but denied that it proved a divergence of competitive from the ideal output.[8] Young's criticism also did not distinguish the three interpretations we shall point out. In fact it did not need to do so, as it is equally valid upon any of them; but Pigou did not believe this to be the case, and so we must examine the merits of each separately.

The three possible interpretations of Pigou's functions arise from the fact that increasing costs in an industry may come from (1) diminishing returns due to the presence of a factor which is fixed in supply for the industry; (2) rising transfer costs due to the presence of a factor which can be drawn in greater amounts from other industries only by a rise in its price; or (3) a combination of (1) and (2). In 1920 Pigou focused attention upon the *first* interpretation by admitting it as a legitimate reading of his cost curves but not what he had intended.[9] This interpretation permits

---

[7] By implication also the ideal price, but Pigou does not stress this.

[8] Allyn A. Young, "Pigou's Wealth and Welfare," *The Quarterly Journal of Economics*, Vol. 27 (Aug. 1913), pp. 672–686. Edgeworth also called the function "the marginal increment of cost from the viewpoint of a monopolist"; cf. F. Y. Edgeworth, "Contributions to the Theory of Railroad Rates, IV: A Digression on Professor Pigou's Thesis," *The Economic Journal*, Vol. 23 (June 1913), p. 211.

[9] A. C. Pigou, *The Economics of Welfare*, 1st ed. (London, 1920), pp. 934–936.

us to give unambiguous definitions to the S_1 and S_2 curves of Fig. 1 and to trace out the reasoning on this basis. The "supply curve of the ordinary type," S_1, in Pigou's language is the usual "marginal cost curve," that is, the curve indicating the cost of production of the marginal unit of output; and S_2 a function which adds to S_1 at each point the *aggregate* increment of costs on all intramarginal units of output.[10] Thus, if an expansion of output from 50,000 to 51,000 units involves a rise of cost at the margin from \$1.00 to

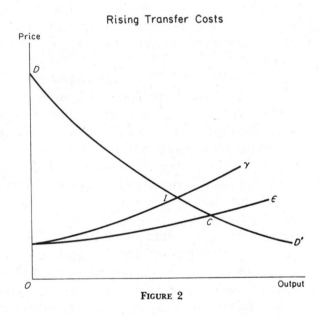

Rising Transfer Costs

Figure 2

\$1.01, the ordinate of S_1 at 51,000 units is \$1.01, and the ordinate of S_2 is the difference between 50,000 times \$1.00 and 51,000 times \$1.01, or \$1,510, divided by 1000, or \$1.51.

On the present interpretation of Pigou (which he acknowledged as a possibility) increasing costs arise solely from rising transfer costs; and to make this interpretation explicit, in Fig. 2 we give to S_1 and S_2, respectively, the distinctive labels of ϵ and γ. Pigou's S_1 (our ϵ) shows the cost of the marginal unit in isolation, or more explicitly: marginal cost excluding all increments of trans-

---

[10] If the n-th unit of the output is produced at a cost of $f(n)$, then $S_1 = f(n)$, and $S_2 = \dfrac{d[nf(n)]}{dn} = f(n) + nf'(n)$.

fer cost; alternatively ϵ shows also *average cost* per unit of output, including transfer rent. Pigou's S_2 (our γ) shows "marginal costs" also but in a different sense—marginal cost including the *total* increment to transfer costs *on all units.*

Pigou originally maintained that the intersection at C represents competitive equilibrium, but that the ideal allocation of resources would be given by reducing output through appropriate taxation to a magnitude given by the intersection at I. Allyn Young accepted this description of competitive equilibrium (as do all parties to the dispute) but denied that the *total* increment of cost to the industry could be regarded as a cost to society. In Pigou's excellent paraphrase, "In other words, according to Professor Young's view, the excess of marginal supply prices [our γ] in industries of diminishing returns [read: increasing costs'] over the corresponding supply prices [our ϵ] is merely a nominal excess of money paid, and not a real excess representing resources employed."[11]

If Young had spoken the magical word "rent," it seems probable that Pigou would have capitulated completely. For Young could have put his proposition in these words: "If the expansion of an industry gives a factor a higher per unit remuneration, whether or not that higher price induces a greater aggregate [social] supply of the factor, the units already being supplied earn producers' rents [or increase the previous rent]; and rent is not a cost in social resources." Consequently if the output of a commodity expands, the rise in transfer costs (i.e., in the value) of the intramarginal units of the transferred resource is not part of the marginal social cost of producing the commodity under consideration. The marginal social (opportunity) cost of transferring resources yielding n units is merely the cost of transferring the resources required for the production of the n-th unit. This cost is expressed by ϵ not by γ. The γ function is not a social cost curve because it includes increments to rent.

Pigou accepted this criticism without reservation so far as concerns transfer costs; and, we may add, he accepted it gracefully and without seeing, at that time, its full import. For he proceeded to

---

[11] Pigou, *op. cit.,* p. 935.

argue in the sentences immediately following that his conclusions are valid for diminishing returns, although not for rising transfer costs:

The reason why diminishing returns in terms of money [read: "increasing costs"] appear when they do appear is, in general, not that the money price of factors employed is increased, but that that proportionate combination of different factors, which it is most economical to employ when $(x + \Delta x)$ units of commodities are being produced is a less efficient proportionate combina-

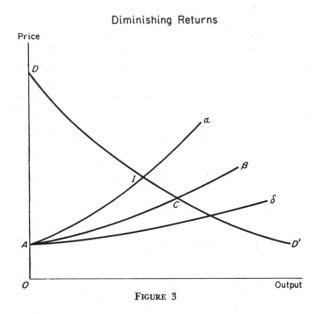

Diminishing Returns

FIGURE 3

tion than that which it is most economical to employ when x units are being produced; and the extra cost involved in this fact is real, not merely nominal. For these reasons Professor Young's objection, as a general objection, fails.[12]

Employing a useful notation introduced by Mrs. Joan Robinson,[13] we show in Fig. 3 the functions germane to diminishing returns, transfer costs assumed constant.

Mathematically the definitions of a and β, respectively, are

---

[12] Pigou, *op. cit.*, p. 936.

[13] Joan Robinson, *The Economics of Imperfect Competition* (London, 1933), Chap. 10, "A Digression on the Four Cost Curves." While her chapter fails to distinguish ϵ and restricts the concept of rent to "Ricardian" surplus on the fixed factor, it is in general accurate and illuminating, and has contributed indirectly very much toward the present analysis.

precisely the same as for γ and ϵ, since both a and γ satisfy the requirements of Pigou's S_2 and β and ϵ the requirements of S_1. Only the economic implication is changed: a refers to marginal cost including the total increment of Ricardian rent, and β to marginal cost excluding Ricardian rent or average cost including average Ricardian rent. The function δ, to which there is no counterpart in the case of rising transfer costs, is the familiar curve of average cost excluding rent. According to the first edition of *The Economics of Welfare,* the intersection at C shows the competitive solution, as before; and the intersection at I again is held to represent the socially ideal output, though this time on the grounds that less efficient combinations of factors signify a social "extra cost."[14]

However real the "extra cost" from these grounds, the application of Young's reasoning proves it to be adequately included in β, the cost *at the margin,* i.e., the incremental cost in the variable factor. Unless rent is a social cost, it is erroneous to envisage the social marginal cost as including the increment to rent as in the function a.

To maximize the aggregate of producers' and consumers' surpluses, the relevant magnitude is DCA, not DIA, if the marginal utility of money is assumed to be constant. Dropping the assumption of constant marginal utility for money renders it impossible to express the aggregate surplus of consumers and producers by areas lying between demand and supply curves. It still remains

---

[14] Pigou's contention (cf. 1st ed., p. 194) that of two roads connecting the same two points the one, assumed to be superior but narrow and therefore subject to diminishing returns, is overexploited in competition unless taxed differentially, seems to have rested on the notion that competitive output is determined by the δ function. The contention was proven to be fallacious by Professor Knight, who has shown that the owner of the good road will charge a toll that will raise costs to users to the β level. Cf. F. H. Knight, "Some Fallacies in the Interpretation of Social Cost," *The Quarterly Journal of Economics,* Vol. 38 (Aug. 1924), pp. 582–606, reprinted as Chap. VIII in *idem, The Ethics of Competition* (New York, 1935), pp. 217–236 (see pages 160–179 of the present volume). Pigou omitted the "two roads" example from the second edition of his book which happened to appear almost simultaneously with Knight's criticism, and does not refer to the latter. No special significance should be attributed to Pigou's recantation of the "two roads" proposition because it was inconsistent with his own position and should have been dropped even if his position had not been modified.

true, however, that the optimum output will be reached at the intersection of the demand curve with β, not α. The price will still express for each consumer the value of the change in total utility occasioned by the marginal unit of the commodity, although it will express this change in terms of the variable marginal utility of money rather than in a constant unit of measurement.

If marginal social cost equals price, it also equals the value of the marginal addition to the utility of each consumer as expressed in terms of the marginal utility of the money stock actually owned by him. This, however, implies that, given the distribution of wealth and income, the β intersection is optimal. If resources were to be shifted out of the industry in question, each consumer would lose more utility, as expressed in terms of money, than the saving in social cost; and if further resources were to be shifted into the industry, the addition to social cost would outweigh the gain in utility.

That his reply to Young was inadequate, Pigou admitted four years later in *The Economic Journal*,[15] adumbrating a revised statement in the second edition of *The Economics of Welfare*. The revision consisted in the abandonment of the general thesis that, under increasing cost, output under competition exceeds the ideal, and the adoption of the very limited proposition that a divergence occurs only from the viewpoint of one nation against another when it pays agricultural rents to foreign owners in the price of imports.[16]

This limited version of the proposition, retained in the later editions of *The Economics of Welfare*, requires the use of functions which express the effects of rising transfer costs as well as those of Ricardian diminishing returns. In Fig. 4, average costs as affected by diminishing returns but not by rising transfer costs[17] are shown by β; average costs as affected by rising transfer costs but not by diminishing returns[18] are shown by ϵ; and average costs as

---

[15] A. C. Pigou, "Comment," *The Economic Journal*, Vol. 34 (Mar. 1924), p. 31.

[16] A. C. Pigou, *The Economics of Welfare*, 2nd ed. (London, 1924), pp. 194–195. The third edition (London, 1929), p. 225, made no change. F. Y. Edgeworth, "The Revised Doctrine of Marginal Social Product," *The Economic Journal*, Vol. 35 (Mar. 1925), p. 35, agreed with this version of Pigou.

[17] I.e., calculated at constant transfer costs.

[18] I.e., calculated as though constant returns prevailed.

affected by both forces in conjunction are shown by ϕ. The function ϕ may be described further as marginal cost excluding all Ricardian rent and all increments to transfer rent, or as average cost including average Ricardian and average transfer rent. To this magnitude, at each point, θ adds the *total* increment of transfer rent on the intramarginal transferred units, and the *total* increment of Ricardian rent.[19] Pigou's argument with respect to foreign trade would then mean that rents transferred abroad, whether

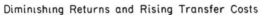

Diminishing Returns and Rising Transfer Costs

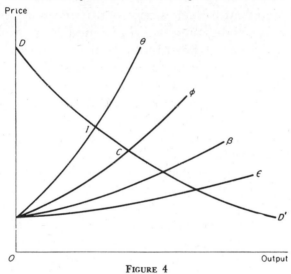

FIGURE 4

those rents originated in diminishing returns or rising transfer costs, are costs to the domestic economy; the competitive purchases of such imports would run to the foreign output as determined by ϕ, whereas ideally the importing country should buy only the foreign output as determined by θ.

But even the foreign trade argument, which had been adum-

---

[19] Mrs. Robinson makes α do double duty as a designation for marginal cost including only the total increment of Ricardian rent and as a designation for our θ. This is an undesirable ambiguity. Furthermore, since she omitted to distinguish ϵ, she has no function corresponding to our ϕ, which adds ϵ and β.

The functions α, lying between θ and β, and γ, lying between θ and ϵ have been omitted in Fig. 4; δ has likewise not been drawn.

brated by Graham a year [20] previous to Pigou's decision to restrict the argument to rents disbursed to foreign owners, is subject to rather severe limitation if not complete rejection. After all, the doctrine of optimum allocation in all of the versions here considered is a "cosmopolitan" doctrine in that it does not distinguish between surpluses accruing to domestic owners *and consumers* on the one hand and surpluses accruing to foreigners on the other. The qualifications required to allow for policies distinguishing between the interests of domestic economic subjects and foreigners are much more extensive than would be suggested by the limitation of Pigou's argument to such increases in rents as are included in the value of commodity imports. One would have to exclude from the aggregate to be maximized all consumers' surpluses accruing to foreigners; and also all producers' surpluses accruing to foreign stockholders or other foreign owners of domestic enterprise.

The Pigou doctrine in the latest and narrowest version would lead one to believe that in a competitive world the "national"—as opposed to the "cosmopolitan"—aggregate of surpluses is increased by a tax reducing the output of industries which, by importing raw materials, increase the value of foreign resources. The cosmopolitan net surplus is surely reduced by such a tax; whether the "national" net surplus is increased or reduced depends on how the aggregate of consumers' and producers' rents accruing to domestic economic subjects changes when other industrial activities are partly substituted for those connected with raw material imports.

To replace the "cosmopolitan" approach with the "national" would require a reinterpretation of the entire doctrine no less fundamental than that which would be required if the distribution of wealth within the economy were not to be accepted as "given." In both cases the "votes" of the consumers and of the producers whose behavior determines the allocation of resources is held to be weighted incorrectly. The important qualifications arising from this consideration must either be disregarded, which means accept-

---

[20] F. D. Graham, "Some Aspects of Protection Further Considered," *The Quarterly Journal of Economics,* Vol. 37 (Feb. 1923), pp. 199–227; "The Theory of International Values Re-examined," *ibid.,* Vol. 38 (Nov. 1923), pp. 54–86; "Some Fallacies in the Interpretation of Social Costs; a Reply" (to F. H. Knight), *ibid.,* Vol. 39 (Feb. 1925), pp. 324–330.

ing the cosmopolitan point of view and taking the distribution of wealth and income as given, or they must be dealt with in the framework of a broad sociological approach extending to questions such as reprisals in international relations, the potential stability of different patterns of distribution within social communities, etc. In no event does it seem satisfactory to confine the reinterpretation of the "cosmopolitan" doctrine to industries which, by importing raw materials, give rise to foreign producers' rents.

The preceding analysis is not concerned with the genuine diseconomies arising from phenomena such as the smoke nuisance, the wasteful exploitation of natural resources, etc.

So far as concerns the present heading—diminishing returns and rising transfer costs—we have found: (1) There is no divergence between the ideal and competitive outputs. (2) Pigou originally believed that output under competition is excessive because the total increment to rent is not included as cost. (3) Under the force of Allyn Young's criticism that rents are not social costs, Pigou gradually attenuated his thesis to the case of imports produced under rising supply price. (4) Writers who invoked the authority of Pigou after 1924 on what had once been his *general* thesis did so unjustifiably.[21] (5) Even the restricted foreign trade thesis has little or no validity as a single qualification because the entire problem would have to be reformulated if this qualification, in conjunction with more important ones, were to become valid. (6) Since rents are not social costs, the relevant cost function—one which maximizes the total of consumers' and producers' surpluses —is marginal cost in the sense of costs of the marginal unit of output alone (= average cost including average rent), that is, ϵ or β, and *not* marginal cost including the total increment of rent, that is, γ or a. (7) The atomistic single seller notices and acts correctly upon the costs of ϵ or β; he does not notice and should ignore the additional costs incorporated in γ or a.

III. External Economies

Economists upholding the special tax in the diminishing re-

[21] Oscar Lange (and F. M. Taylor), *On the Economic Theory of Socialism* (Minneapolis, 1938), pp. 98–99; Jacob Viner, "Cost Curves and Supply Curves," *Zeitschrift für Nationalokonomie,* Vol. 3 (Sept. 1931), p. 42 (reprinted in the present volume, page 198).

turns case also maintain the necessity of a bounty for the realization of external economies. One of the most debated issues in the entire discussion of the tax-bounty thesis has always been the reality of external economies.[22] Many supposed examples have proved to be spurious or far-fetched; but we do not propose to begin upon the painstaking inquiries into techniques and economic history which would be necessary to appraise the possibilities. Among the many difficulties and complexities, however, there are a few certainties.

One is that if an "external economy" is an internal economy to another *industry,* the outcome is either monopoly in the second industry, or else the complete exploitation of the internal and hence the disappearance of the external economies.[23] If the outcome is monopoly in the second industry, costs are very unlikely to decline in the first, since a monopolist will respond to a rise in demand with a reduction of price only (1) in case he is operating in the downward range of his *marginal* cost curve (and the elasticity of the new demand curve is not *sufficiently smaller* than was that of the old one to offset the downward slope of the marginal cost curve); or (2) if the new demand curve is *more* elastic than was the old one (and the upward slope of the marginal cost curve in the revelant range is insufficient to offset this circumstance).

Usually the monopolist will raise his price if demand increases, in which case such economies as are internal economies in the "second" industry will not lead to the realization of economies in the "first" industry. As Mr. Sraffa has suggested, the concept of external economies may, however, be rescued by illustrations not

---

[22] In addition to the literature elsewhere cited in these pages, see the following: J. H. Clapham, "Of Empty Economic Boxes," *The Economic Journal,* Vol. 32 (Sept. 1922), pp. 305–314 (reprinted in the present volume, page 119); A. C. Pigou, "Empty Economic Boxes: A Reply," *ibid.,* Vol. 34 (Dec. 1922), pp. 458–465 (reprinted in the present volume, page 131); *idem* and D. H. Robertson, "Those Empty Boxes," *ibid.,* Vol. 34 (Mar. 1924), pp. 16–31 (reprinted in the present volume, page 143); G. J. Stigler, *The Theory of Competitive Price* (New York, 1942), pp. 106, 142–144; K. E. Boulding, *Economic Analysis* (New York, 1941), p. 194; Joan Robinson, *op. cit.,* Appendix, pp. 337–343.

[23] Thus Knight, *op. cit.,* p. 229, and "On Decreasing Cost and Comparative Costs," *The Quarterly Journal of Economics,* Vol. 39 (Feb. 1925), pp. 331–333; and Joan Robinson, *op. cit.,* p. 340.

depending upon lowering the price of a commodity supplied by
another *industry*, but upon the better rendering of *services*.[24] The
development of a skilled labor force, the migration of suitable
labor, the appearance and progress of professional and trade associations and journals, and the like, are not to be dismissed as unrelated to output in every case.

When and if external economies exist, they must be incorporated into the structure of economic theory; but it must be
confessed that the theoretical treatment of this subject still leaves

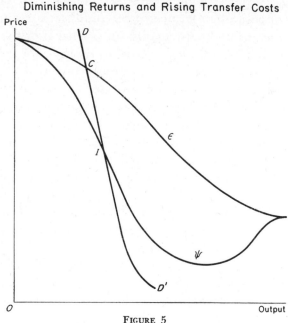

External Economies in the Absence of
Diminishing Returns and Rising Transfer Costs

FIGURE 5

much to be desired. The first step in reconstruction is a clear
description of the cost functions and of competitive equilibrium.

In Fig. 5 we assume that there is no "scarce" factor for this
particular industry, and that its demand for factors is atomistic
so that an extension of output does not cause rising transfer costs.
The function ϵ signifies, as in earlier contexts, average cost, or

[24] Piero Sraffa, "The Laws of Returns under Competitive Conditions," *The
Economic Journal,* Vol. 37 (Dec. 1926), pp. 535–550 (reprinted in the present
volume, page 180).

marginal cost in the sense of costs for the marginal output in contrast to smaller outputs.[25] The function ψ is defined somewhat analogously to γ and α as the total cost difference on *all* units (marginal and intramarginal). If there are no external economies (or none exploited), ϵ and ψ coincide in a horizontal line; if there are, ψ lies below ϵ. Thus without economies the per unit cost might be \$4.00 for all outputs. With economies the first "unit" costs \$4.00 if only one unit is produced; if "two units" are produced the second unit costs \$3.00 and the costs of the first unit also decline to \$3.00. At an output of two units $\epsilon = \$3.00$, $\psi = \$2.00$.

We employ the symbol ϵ because external economies have exactly the opposite significance *to the industry* as rising transfer costs. One must be on guard against an extension of the meaning of ϵ from the behavior of *output* costs to the price of the variable factor; if ϵ declines because of external economies, factor price almost necessarily rises. This probable rise, however, is disregarded in the graphic representation and in the foregoing example, where the industry in question is assumed to be atomistic and consequently constant factor prices are assumed.

The equilibrium to be expected from competition is determined by the intersection of DD' and ϵ. The costs of production at the margin will be equated to price. The circumstance that further expansion of the industry would reduce intramarginal costs will not produce such an expansion, since to the right of C costs at the margin fall short of price. Now it has been argued that optimum allocation in these circumstances requires subsidizing the industry under consideration in such a manner as to make its output expand to I, corresponding to the intersection of DD' with ψ (instead of ϵ).

This argument was presented by Pigou at the time when he first attempted to establish the proposition that increasing cost industries tend to overexpand in free competition. But while the proposition relating to increasing cost industries was gradually limited to the foreign trade proposition previously discussed, the thesis that decreasing cost industries do not expand sufficiently was and is maintained by him and other authors.[26] It is worth pointing

---

[25] On the assumption of free competition, costs to all firms are the same for their equilibrium outputs.

[26] A recent exposition of the thesis is found in Hicks, *op. cit.*

out that shifting resources into decreasing cost industries is not the same thing as shifting resources out of competitive increasing cost industries, since competitive industries may also operate under constant costs, not to speak of industries operating under monopoly and monopolistic competition. Besides, the proposition that the social optimum output of increasing cost industries is determined by S_2 functions (rather than S_1 functions)[27] would be basically different from the proposition that the social optimum output of decreasing cost industries is determined by S_2 functions (rather than S_1 functions), even if subsidizing decreasing-cost industries could be carried out only by taxing increasing-cost industries. We shall now be concerned with the second of these two propositions.

The reasoning by which it can be shown that the argument relating to increasing cost industries is faulty does not affect the validity of the argument relating to decreasing cost industries. The crucial point here is that, while in conditions of increasing supply price, the *rise* in intramarginal costs is rent rather than social cost, the *decline* in intramarginal costs attending the expansion of decreasing cost industries is a social economy, i.e., social cost with a negative sign. One might therefore conclude that in conditions of decreasing supply price the ψ function expresses marginal social cost; and that the social optimum output is I instead of C.[28] The competitive output, one might conclude, is determined by the socially "incorrect" cost function ϵ, which fails to express the marginal saving in intramarginal social cost, that is, the saving in social cost on intramarginal units of the resource attending the increase in total output by a marginal unit. The ψ function contains the necessary correction; and a permanent bounty inducing the production of I is required to achieve optimum allocation. It would have to be added that a two-dimensional presentation, like that in Fig. 5, overstates the deviation from the optimum in case the industry is not atomistic. In this event the ψ curve shifts upward as output expands, since opportunity costs rise as resources are shifted away from other employments.

------

[27] Cf. Fig. 1.

[28] We mean, of course, the corresponding distances along the abscissa. In the event of more than one intersection the optimum is reached at the intersection maximizing the expression $\int [D(x) - \Psi(x)]dx$, where $D(x)$ is the demand curve.

This conclusion is correct if the external economies are "reversible": the ψ function actually expresses marginal social cost in case the economies appear with an expansion of output, but *disappear* if and when output subsequently contracts.[29] In the event of irreversibility the problem acquires different characteristics, however. It may be suggested that irreversible external economies are much more significant than are reversible ones. Certain industries must usually reach some stage of growth before a geographical region starts to develop significantly and also before human and material resources become more specialized. But it is rarely true in these cases that a contraction of the output of any one industry would lead to a loss of the economies in question.

If irreversible external economies are potentially present, competitive equilibrium fails to achieve optimum allocation; at the same time I ceases to be the optimum output and the bounty required to achieve optimum allocation is temporary.

In the circumstances now considered the ψ function loses its significance. What happens in conditions like these can best be expressed by the statement that the ϵ function shifts permanently as we move downward along the curve.

Assuming that transfer costs remain unaffected by the output of the industry in question and that the industry does not give rise to Ricardian rents, there will be a point (D) on the ϵ curve to which an output (OM) corresponds that exhausts all potential external economies. Once that output is reached, the ϵ curve will intersect with the ordinates at Ad and it will be horizontal throughout its course. Before any output whatsoever is produced, the path of the function is marked by the points $A, B, C, D;$ the curve is horizontal only to the right of D. If a point lying along the curve (such as A or B) has already been realized, a movement backward, toward the ordinate, occurs along a horizontal line (such as AA_a or BA_b); whereas a movement forward, toward D occurs along the still unused portion of the original function (such as $ACBD$ or BCD).

To say that external economies are mostly of this kind, instead

---

[29] As was pointed out in the preceding paragraph, the function ceases to be a *curve* if the industry is not atomistic. In this event Ψ is a function of more than one variable. The "curve" shifts upward when output expands, and downward when it contracts.

of being "reversible," may be interpreted to mean that they are typically *dynamic* phenomena. Whether shifts like these should be excluded from equilibrium analysis as Knight suggests and then relegated to "dynamic theory" is clearly a matter of convenience. The opinion may be expressed, however, that, so long as certain shifts of functions are on the same level of predictability as are movements along the functions, it is not very fruitful to distinguish between two types of theory dealing with these two kinds of changes respectively. The shifts reflecting irreversible external

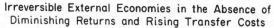

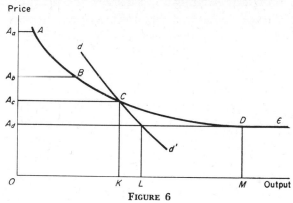

FIGURE 6

economies surely are not always on the same level of predictability as movements along given supply curves. But the difference may in some cases be insufficient to warrant the exclusion of the phenomenon from the type of theory we are concerned with at present.

Returning now to Fig. 6, we observe that the conditions sketched there would, in the first approximation, justify a temporary bounty raising the output of the industry from *OK* to *OM* and thereby producing the lowest obtainable social cost curve for the commodity. After the discontinuation of the bounty the output of the industry drops to *OL* and social net output is higher than it was prior to the interference and higher than it would be if the bounty were continued. We said this conclusion was justified only "in the first approximation" because it disregards the waste involved in moving temporarily an excessive stock of resources into the industry under consideration. The perpetual income stream yielded by the capital value of the temporary excess of resources is a loss to be counted against the decline in social cost if the excess of resources (corresponding to the temporary excess output OM minus OL) is completely immobile. The more mobile the excess is, the smaller does the loss become.

Moreover, by directly subsidizing certain processes, such as migration or the specialization of resources, it may be possible to induce, at the "permanent" output level OL, the economies that would develop automatically at the output level OM, and thus to avoid the detour over the excessive output OM. Such temporary subsidies, raising the output of the industry from OK directly to OL, might in certain circumstances achieve the maximum obtainable saving in social cost, with no sinking of an excessive stock of specialized resources into the subsidized industry. The detour over OM does involve costs of this character. If the costs of a detour are unavoidable the true optimum output which takes account of these costs may be different from OL since the temporary excess of output is not the same for the different potential final outputs.[30]

In the preceding pages we considered external economies in isolation, disregarding diminishing returns and rising transfer costs. If, as seems plausible to assume, external economies occur in conjunction with the two cost-raising forces functionally related to industry output, the fundamentals of the preceding analysis are not altered. For a comparison of competitive output with social optimum output it is not necessary to divorce the two *cost-raising* forces from one another, since neither of them upsets the identity of the two outputs in question. But it is necessary to divorce the *cost-diminishing* forces from those *raising* cost, because the divergence of social optimum output from competitive output is determined by the *cost-diminishing* forces, regardless of whether the interaction of all forces makes for increasing, constant or declining supply price.

It should be repeated in this connection that statements like the foregoing one imply that it is fruitful to include in equilibrium theory the analysis of certain phenomena that in a sense are "dynamic," i.e., that reflect themselves in shifts of the curves used in traditional equilibrium theory. Reversible external economies, not

---

[30] If the distance between the demand curve and the original curve increases monotonously to the right of OK, then the temporary excess will be smaller for final outputs smaller than OL.

implying shifts of the curves, are in all probability unimportant. Whether it is fruitful to take account of "dynamic"—that is, irreversible—external economies in this type of approach depends on the degree of predictability, or, as it may be expressed alternatively, on the "regularity" of the phenomenon called external economies. Inclusion into the body of equilibrium theory may be warranted in some cases, but certainly not in all cases in which costs are declining "historically."

IV. Summary

We have found that diminishing returns and external diseconomies (rising transfer costs) do not result in a divergence between social and competitive costs. Social cost equals resource (opportunity) costs, i.e., the cost of production of additional or marginal units. If this cost advances because of diminishing returns or rising transfer costs, the higher cost to society is completely exhausted by a price covering the increment to costs on marginal units. The increment to rents on intramarginal units are not social costs; they do not enter into competitive supply prices and they should not. The statement made by certain writers[31] that an ideal allocation of resources requires that production be guided by "marginal cost," and not by "average cost" as it is under competition is either meaningless or erroneous. It is meaningless because cost *including* the total increment to rent on intramarginal units (γ, a, and θ) is "marginal cost" in one sense; and cost on the marginal units excluding these rents (ϵ, β, and ϕ) are also "marginal costs" in another sense; and because the second set of functions, forming the supply curves under competition, are both "marginal" and "average," according as the cost is computed incrementally without rent, or averaged including *average* rent. The statement is wrong if it means that functions such as γ, a, and θ represent social costs.

When unexploited external economies exist, competitive output falls short of the optimum. But again this can not be expressed for all cases as a divergence of "average" and "marginal" cost, the former being represented as the correct guide. In the case of "reversible" external economies—those which disappear when the subsidy

---

[31] Lange, *op. cit.*, pp. 98–99, n. 2; A. P. Lerner, "Statics and Dynamics in Socialist Economies," *The Economic Journal*, Vol. 47 (June 1937), pp. 253–270.

is terminated—a marginal function such as ψ, which subtracts from the increment to costs attributable to the marginal unit in isolation the decrement to costs on intramarginal units occasioned by the external economies, should be regarded as the true social costs function.[32] But in the case of "irreversible" economies, the contrast of average and marginal costs can not be used to indicate the divergence of competitive from social costs, inasmuch as the economies simply cause a downward shift of average costs as a horizontal function up to each realized output; "marginal," as anything distinct from this successive lowering of average costs, has no meaning.

Retrospectively, it is also worth remarking that the "atomistic" character of one producer's output under competition, frequently thought to be crucial in the eternal economies—diseconomies context, is not decisive of itself. In the "diseconomies" case, as we have seen, the private calculus of the single competitive producer results in no divergence of competitive and ideal output, for rents are not social costs. Where there are *genuine* diseconomies ignored by the competitive producer—smoke nuisance, wasteful exploitation of resources, etc.—these results follow not from the atomistic character of production, but from technical or institutional circumstances as a consequence of which scarce goods are treated as though they were free; and the divorce of scarcity from effective ownership may be equally complete for atomistic, oligopolistic, and monopolistic private enterprise.

The divergence of competitive from ideal output under external economies is more closely related to the atomistic position of the single competitor because, to the monopolist, ψ functions are the marginal cost functions if the economies are reversible; and he may take account of the downward shift of the ϵ functions if the economies are irreversible but predictable. It must not be overlooked however, that, on the demand side, precisely the same circumstance—the non-atomistic position of the single producer—leads to the determination of output by marginal revenue which falls short of demand price. This in and of itself always tends to reduce output below the competitive level.

We have found theoretical possibilities of achieving by state interference more external economies than are given by competi-

---

[32] Ψ, as was shown, is a function of more than one variable, and hence not a curve, if the industry in question is not atomistic.

tion; but it is, to say the least, doubtful whether frequent or extensive interference would be justified in practice upon this basis. Where economies are such as to be permanent (irreversible) once the requisite output is developed, we have an almost perfect analogy with the infant industry argument for tariffs, and little more need be said to emphasize the pitfalls.

The departure of the economist's *free* competition from the ideal of social costs is in fact negligible for external economies and non-existent for the cost-increasing forces. The departures of *actual* competition and the manifold other market forces from free competition are striking, just as the departures of actual forms of the corporate state, socialism, and planning from more or less ideal prototypes might also be striking.

13

THE MEASUREMENT
OF STATISTICAL COST FUNCTIONS:
AN APPRAISAL OF SOME |RECENT |CONTRIBUTIONS* [1]

By Hans Staehle||

"When you cannot measure, your knowledge is of a meager and unsatisfactory kind." This famous statement of Lord Kelvin's may be paraphrased to the effect that, whenever attempts at measurement of previously unmeasured quantities and relationships are made, understanding and knowledge, if only of the complexities of the subject, are certain to be furthered. I shall pass in review, and appraise, a recent newcomer in the long series of efforts at quantification in economics, the literature on statistical cost functions.

The subject invites comparison with a closely associated development, the measurement of demand functions. From Gregory King to Marschak's most recent contribution, the process has been one of ever closer interpenetration of facts and theory. It is typical, for instance, that even to Marshall, aware though he was of the influence of factors other than price, elasticity of demand exclusively meant elasticity with respect to price, all other factors expressing their influence through either shifts or distortions in that price-quantity function. Marshall never used the concept of income-elasticity of demand. It was for H. L. Moore, the econometrician, to develop the idea of generalized partial elasticity coefficients of demand. As to the particular dependence of demand upon income and its elasticity, a relatively recent, and essentially measurement-inspired addition to the economist's toolbox, its possibilities for the further development of theoretical reasoning have already been exploited by Bowley and Allen, and have certainly

* *The American Economic Review*, Vol. XXXII (1942), pp. 321–333. Reprinted, by the courtesy of the publisher and the author, without change from the original text.

|| Economic Commission for Europe (UN).

[1] A paper presented at a joint meeting of the American Economic Association and the Econometric Society, held in New York, December 29, 1941.

contributed to shape Hicks's ideas. In other words, Marshall, the theorist, could afford to be content with stating *the* "law of demand" *ceteris paribus*. But attempts at measurement very soon made it necessary to find out what exactly the more important ones among the "other things" really were. For measurement of the price-quantity function is possible only if the influence of the *cetera* is successfully eliminated, and in order to eliminate we must know *what* and *how much*. The devices invented for the purpose of isolating what to Marshall was *the* law of demand have in turn proved stimulating to reasoning of a purely theoretical kind.

Later I shall examine whether a similar development can be expected in consequence of past and present endeavors in the field of cost measurements.

Similar in this respect to the theory of consumers' choices, the theory of short-run producers' behavior proceeds on the basis of a simple postulate of rationality. As Cournot put it in 1838, "the producer [he was speaking of a monopolist] will always stop [expanding his output] when the increase in expense exceeds the increase in receipts"; or, as we would say today, when marginal cost (increasing or constant) equals marginal revenue (constant or decreasing). Cournot then goes on to say that he will scarcely have occasion to consider directly the total-cost function, but only its derivative, i.e., marginal costs, the shape of which exercises the largest influence upon the solution of the principal problem of the science of economics.[2]

It is not idle to quote these remarks, not only because it never *can* be idle to read and quote Cournot; they also directly apply to all the statistical work which has been done in our field. Although each one of the authors finds it necessary to start out by measuring the total-cost function, all their work aims in the end at determining short-run marginal costs as a function of output. All these studies, in other words, by endeavoring to find a numerical expression for the function connecting marginal costs with output, are in fact, if not in intention, attempting to throw light upon the rationality of entrepreneurs' behavior. It would indeed be difficult to see why, if not for that reason, the measurements are undertaken.

[2] A. Cournot, *Principes Mathématiques de la Théorie des Richesses* (Paris, 1838), p. 65; Bacon's translation, p. 59.

In reviewing the literature on the subject I cannot hope to be complete. I shall therefore first list what appear to be the main contributions, and then briefly consider what methods were used to construct the relationship between output and costs; what concrete results have been reached, and what significance these results possess in relation to (1) the goal of the measurement itself, (2) business practice, and (3) cost theory. In a final section I shall try to speculate as to future possibilities.

I

Every field has its pioneers. With due reservation regarding the probability that Professor Viner will soon discover, if he has not already done so, a still earlier contribution, I wish to discuss as the first item in my list a brief article by an Austrian writer, Wilhelm von Nördling, on "Le Prix de Revient des Transports par Chemin de Fer" ("Cost of Production of Transportation by Railroad").[3] That article must not be considered as a *curiosum* only. Its scientific value, even for the present day, will become apparent in the summary that I shall give of it later. May I merely mention that I found it quoted in an important lecture delivered by Emile Cheysson, the well-known French social reformer and pupil of Le Play, under the title of *La Statistique Géométrique, Méthode pour la Solution des Problèmes Commerciaux et Industriels* ("Geometrical Statistics, A Method for the Solution of Commercial and Industrial Problems")[4] in which Cheysson not only evolves a scientific program which sounds very much like Frisch's introductory address at the first meeting of the Econometric Society at Lausanne in 1931,[5] but also attempts to determine the Cournot point in a con-

---

[3] Published in the *Annales des Ponts et Chaussées* for 1886 (1er semestre), pp. 292–303.

In the *Annales,* the author's name is, with typically French neglect for "umlaut," given as "W. Nordling, ancien directeur général des chemins de fer au Ministère du Commerce à Vienne." There is no doubt, however, that W. Nordling is identical with Wilhelm von Nördling, k.k. Sectionschef und General-Director des österr. Eisenbahnwesens a.D., who in 1885 published a book *Die Selbstkosten des Eisenbahn-Transportes und die Wasserstrassen-Frage in Frankreich, Preussen und Oesterreich,* Vienna. This book, though full of statistical data, contains no study of cost functions.

[4] Paris, Publications du Journal Le Génie Civil, 1887.

[5] *Econometrica,* Vol. 1, No. 1, pp. 74–76.

crete statistical case. It is of interest to note that, in the article devoted to Cheysson in the *Encyclopaedia of the Social Sciences*[6] it is said that he "contributed nothing new to sociology or economics."

My second item is a contribution by Ehrke and Schneider published in 1933, in the former's book on *Overproduction in the Cement Industry.*[7]

I shall further consider the studies by Yntema,[8] and Ezekiel and Wylie,[9] on the United States Steel Corporation, both published in 1940, and, of course, Dean's various studies, the first of which appeared in 1936.[10]

I shall have no time to consider the various studies dealing with farm management problems,[11] nor the so-called break-even charts developed by, e.g., Bolza[12] and Rautenstrauch,[13] nor finally the important work of Schmalenbach[14] and his school.[15] I also shall have to omit consideration of one attempt to measure a long-run cost curve (or envelope function) which Dean has produced but not yet published.

---

[6] Vol. 3, p. 371.

[7] Kurt Ehrke, *Die Uebererzeugung in der Zementindustrie von 1858–1913* (Jena, 1933), especially pp. 276–310.

[8] United States Steel Corporation, *T.N.E.C. Papers,* Vol. I, pp. 223–302, also printed in Hearings before the Temporary National Economic Committee, Pt. 26, *Iron and Steel Industry,* pp. 14032–14082.

[9] Kathryn H. Wylie and Mordecai Ezekiel, "The Cost Curve for Steel Production," *The Journal of Political Economy,* Vol. XLVIII, Dec. 1940, pp. 777–821. See also by the same authors "Cost Functions for the Steel Industry," *Journal of the American Statistical Association,* Vol. 36, March 1941, pp. 91–99.

[10] Joel Dean, *Statistical Determination of Costs, With Special Reference to Marginal Costs* (Chicago, 1936); and *Statistical Cost Functions of a Hosiery Mill* (Chicago, 1941); and *The Relation of Cost to Output for a Leather Belt Shop* (New York, National Bureau Economic Research, 1941). See also *The American Economic Review,* Suppl. Vol. XXX, March 1940, pp. 400–403.

[11] See, e.g., the studies quoted by E. H. Phelps Brown, *Econometrica,* Vol. 4, pp. 123–137.

[12] Hans Bolza, "Kostenstudien mit Erfahrungszahlen aus der Praxis," *Nordisk Tidsskrift for Teknisk Økonomi,* June 1937, pp. 97–109.

[13] Walter Rautenstrauch, *The Economics of Business Enterprise* (New York, 1939), pp. 303–309.

[14] E. Schmalenbach, *Selbstkostenrechnung und Preispolitik* (Leipzig, 1934).

[15] Reinhard Hildebrandt, Herbert Peiser, and others.

II

Granting these limitations of the subject, the great similarity in the problems encountered by the various authors, and in the methods they chose to solve them, suggests something of a necessity inherent in their task.

It is the aim of each one of these writers to isolate, from among the many factors that influence costs, the *net* influence of changes in the rate of output. In order to do this, each one attacks the problem by studying total costs, though they all are also, if not mainly, interested in marginal costs. Each one (with the exception of Ezekiel-Wylie and Ehrke-Schneider) runs up against the problem of measuring the volume of a diversified output. Each one has to face the problem of "technological change," and of possible change in the size of equipment, as one of the major factors to be eliminated. Finally, each one is compelled to consider the separation of costs which are not in the most immediate sense direct ones into those which depend on the lapse of time, and those which depend on utilization.

Von Nördling definitely sets out to obtain the relationship between costs and output when equipment is given. He carefully points out that what matters is not average cost, but only "the increment in expenditure necessary to transport one ton-kilometre *more* or, which amounts to the same thing, the saving that would be consequent upon the transportation of one ton-kilometre *less*." "Interest on invested capital," he goes on to say, "will not be part of costs thus understood, for interest is a permanent, invariable charge, independent of tonnage." He is aware of the problem involved in measuring output, consisting as it does of both passenger and merchandise traffic, and he adopts, after detailed justification, the convention of giving equal weight to a ton-kilometre of merchandise and a passenger-kilometre. Among the reasons for the adoption of this weighting system are considerations of the relative variable costs per unit. He then chooses from among the various railway systems existing in Austria at that time those for which in at least two, not necessarily consecutive, years the length of line operated remained as nearly constant as possible while at the same time large variations in the volume of transportation occurred;[16] and from the cost information available for the years thus chosen he then determines the total number of ton-kilometres supplied during the year (x) and the total variable costs (i.e., other than interest on bonds) (y) per kilometre operated. He shows himself surprised and delighted—and both these emotions are fully justified—to find that these points, though relating to various different enterprises, when plotted in a single graph, very closely approximated a continuous function, showing when extrapolated a small intercept with the cost axis, and a constantly decreasing slope. He correctly identifies the slope of the radius vector as average cost per unit (y/x), and the slope of the tangent to his function as marginal cost (dy/dx). And then he does something very surprising: he writes the ratio of marginal and average cost thus: $\dfrac{x}{y}\dfrac{dy}{dx}$

Though unwittingly, von Nördling thus seems to be the first man to have printed the celebrated elasticity formula. For although Marshall found it on a Palermo hotel roof in 1881,[17] he did not publish it until 1890, in the first edition of the *Principles*. As to von Nördling, he merely uses it to study the fluctuation of the ratio of marginal to average costs over the observed range of output (where he finds it to be consistently less than unity) and to predict that it would increase to unity if observations for larger output rates were available.

This brief summary of von Nördling's article is far from exhausting all that is of interest in it. But it is sufficient to show that his results are far from negligible, that he saw and successfully solved each one of the major problems above listed, and that in at least one important respect he went beyond what has since been done in this field: he attempted a comparison of cost conditions in firms belonging to the same industry, a suggestion

---

[16] Compare this to Dean's *Leather Belt Shop* study, p. 11: "The period . . . was chosen because it fulfilled the following conditions most satisfactorily: (1) The rate of output and other measurable cost determinants varied sufficiently to yield observations over a wide range. . . . (3) The plant and equipment remained unchanged during the analysis period, permitting the observation of short-run adjustments uninfluenced by long-run changes. . . ."

[17] A. C. Pigou, ed., *Memorials of Alfred Marshall* (London, 1925), p. 45.

which seems full of promise, as I shall mention in my concluding section.[18]

It is now necessary to pass to a brief consideration of later contributions. A detailed description, however, seems unnecessary, since the relevant publications are easily available and I therefore assume that they are known.

The common basic material seems to consist of data taken from the accounting records either as published, or directly. In some cases, adjustments were made to redistribute depreciation charges in what seemed to be a more rational way. Efforts were also made to ensure that costs and output data related to the same unit period. Finally, wherever possible and necessary, the cost data were corrected for changes in factor prices, a practice on which I shall make some comments later. All this, however, though obviously of great consequence for the results, is neither very startling nor very interesting. I have nothing worthy of mention to offer in these respects and had better refer for a thorough treatment of some of them to a recent article by C. Reinold Noyes.[19] The two real *problems* in all this seem to be the measurement of output when production is diversified, and the elimination of technological change, and/or of changing size of the firm when that sort of thing occurs.

First, as regards measuring output (a problem absent in Ehrke-Schneider's case, but present everywhere else), the tendency often is toward solving it by weighting the quantity ratios relating to the various commodities by the relative direct, or variable, costs to which they respectively give rise. This practice seems highly objectionable, though it is difficult to see what other solution could be suggested. It indeed amounts to determining output by costs, i.e., to introducing a spurious dependence where measurement of an independent relationship is really wanted. Nor could that problem easily be solved, as far as I can see, by any sort of correlation set-up.

---

[18] The only other attempt in this direction, though seriously imperfect in other respects, is a hitherto unpublished paper by Ernest M. Doblin who investigated costs in different steel companies.

[19] "Certain Problems in the Empirical Study of Costs," *The American Economic Review,* Vol. XXXI, Sept. 1941, pp. 473–492. The same study also appeared as a "Memorandum on Costs in Relation to Output" as an appendix to Joel Dean's study of a leather belt shop, above quoted.

Secondly, concerning technological change, the difficulties are truly insurmountable. There comes into being, of course, a new cost, if not a new production function, whenever such change occurs, and no amount of assuming, or fitting of trends to residuals will really do. Yntema has attempted the latter, and, without now going into a detailed criticism of his procedure, I merely wish to announce the appearance in a forthcoming number of the *Review of Economic Statistics* of a very thorough appraisal of both this and other aspects of Yntema's study by Caleb Smith.

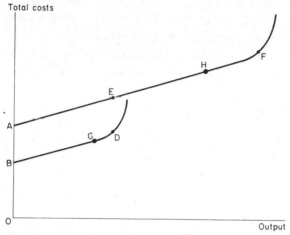

Similarly embarrassing is the problem of changes in the size of the firm. Yntema, as well as Ezekiel-Wylie, did not do much, if anything, about it. And yet it is important. For, even though technique may remain constant, Schneider's "law of harmony"[20] will apply. That law states that full harmony in the structure of the enterprise only exists if an increase in fixed costs produces no more than a proportional increase in the rate of output possible without running into increasing average costs. Or, in other words, minimum average costs may still be lowered, given marginal costs, as long as full harmony is not realized. Graphically, if in the adjoining diagram $AB/BO < EF/BD$, where $BD = AE$, harmony has not been reached. Yntema, to the extent that he failed

[20] See Ehrke, *loc. cit.*, where Schneider (p. 290, footnote) attributes the first formulation of this law to Ivar Jantzen. A German translation of the most relevant parts of Jantzen's original article is available in Erich Schneider, *Theorie der Produktion* (Vienna, 1934), pp. 83–92.

to take account of variations in the size of U. S. Steel during his period of observation, thus obviously runs the risk of overstating his marginal costs. Whether U. S. Steel during the relevant years was increasing or decreasing, Yntema's results may well be of the nature of points G and H in the graph.

As to Ezekiel-Wylie, they mostly have used percentage of capacity as the independent variable. But though satisfactory in that it *seems* to settle everything, this device is very doubtful, in the light of Terborgh's excellent remarks[21] on the measurement of capacity even in ordinary plants. His reasons apply *a fortiori* to U. S. Steel. Moreover, the device does not do away with the point mentioned in the previous paragraph.

Most other authors solve this problem by carefully avoiding it, i.e., by choosing their firms and periods such that both technological change and variations in size are absent, which indeed also is a solution, though not a very satisfying one.

I may conclude this very sketchy review by mentioning the very high quality of the statistical work done by Dean. This, however, by no means exempts his results from the criticism which I shall later direct against the significance of all these studies.

Now as regards the results, I already mentioned von Nördling's. Yntema, Dean, and Ehrke-Schneider end up with linear total-cost functions, Ezekiel-Wylie with a function which exhibits a decreasing rate of increase. The latter result, I would not take too seriously. As Mosak[22] and others[23] have pointed out, plausibility is not one of its outstanding features.

It is, finally, worth mentioning that Ehrke-Schneider are the only ones to have secured observations on those extreme reaches of the total cost curve where average costs decidedly increase. But it took the *maximum maximorum* in relative cyclical position to make that possible. Their cement factory worked beyond optimum capacity during two months out of a period of about fifty years,

---

[21] George Terborgh, "The Problem of Manufacturing Capacity." *Federal Reserve Bulletin,* July 1940, pp. 639–646.

[22] J. L. Mosak, "Some Theoretical Implications of the Statistical Analysis of Demand and Cost Functions for Steel," *The Journal of the American Statistical Association,* Vol. 36, pp. 100–109, especially p. 104.

[23] E.g., G. J. Stigler, *The American Economic Review,* Suppl., Vol. XXX, March 1940, p. 402.

at the top not only of the Juglar, but also of the Kondratieff, in 1873.

III

There is no reason, on grounds of theory, to be particularly upset by the conclusion which several of our authors have reached, namely, that marginal costs, instead of being U-shaped, seem to be constant over the whole of the observed range which, however, admittedly stops short of the probable point of optimum utilization of plant. All that this means is that an economic system in which such a condition holds rather generally, will be less stable than another in which U-shaped marginal costs predominate. And not one of the more competent theorists would need more than a moment's notice to invent and build into a "model" the compensating stabilizers required to approximate that model ever more intimately to "reality" which (as is well known) does not show uninterrupted series of explosions but some sort of stability. From under *that* old top-hat we may, to use Hicks's own image, confidently expect to be blessed with many more generations of lively rabbits. Economic theory, in short, cannot, quite apart from the Mises position, so easily be uprooted by any facts. In the particular case of constant marginal costs we are, thanks to Stigler,[24] in a position to look with equanimity upon any case of total-cost linearity that future measurements may grind out.

This, however, does not exempt us entirely from a consideration of the validity of the results so far presented. In fact, there is considerable room for doubting precisely their linearity aspect. An impressive array of arguments may be marshalled in this connection. I shall mention only a few points.

1. As Ruggles[25] has shown, very slight deviations from linearity in the total-cost function would be sufficient to impinge curvature upon the marginal cost curve.

2. Such deviations from linearity may easily occur for a number of reasons. For instance, the practice of straight-line depreciation fails to allow for the dependence of physical wear and tear

---

[24] G. J. Stigler, "Production and Distribution in the Short Run," *The Journal of Political Economy*, Vol. XLVII, June 1939, pp. 305–327.

[25] R. Ruggles, "The Concept of Linear Cost-Output Regressions," *The American Economic Review*, Vol. XXXI, June 1941, pp. 332–335.

upon output, thus understating costs at high, and overstating them at low, output levels. And negligible though that may appear, it might be just enough to confer upon the total-cost function that small amount of inverted S-shapedness which would suffice to bend marginal costs into their conventional U-shapes.

Furthermore, as Smith brings out in his forthcoming paper already quoted, in the event of a fairly long, say one-year, unit period, if the output is not spread evenly over each unit period, the use of the average rate of output during the period assumes a linear cost function and by this assumption biases the statistically determined cost function toward linearity, since the midpoint of a secant connecting any two points on a curve whose second derivative does not change sign lies closer to a straight line connecting the endpoints of the curve than does the corresponding point of the curve itself.

As Smith also shows, if costs are adjusted for changes in factor prices to any given period, this runs counter to the fundamental assumption of rationality in entrepreneurs' behavior and indeed destroys what evidence there may be of it in this important respect. If, in other words, the combination of factors used in the given period (to the prices of which the adjustment is made) was the most efficient one possible at the prices of that period, then costs in all other periods, when relative factor prices were different, would be overstated. This point of Smith's is, I believe, quite realistic in that, in addition to Stigler's type of flexibility built into a plant which would flatten out the average cost curve, possibly at the price of a higher minimum level, there may be present another sort of flexibility by which an identical output may be obtainable with different factor combinations, choice between which would be guided by the relative factor prices. This would, after revaluation of the real cost elements at constant factor prices, lead to a maximum and a minimum level of costs for each level of output, thus making for a zone, rather than a single-valued cost function, in the statistical results. The width of that zone would depend upon (1) the "flexibility" of this special sort of which the plant was capable, and (2) the amount of variation in relative factor prices that occurred during the period of observations.

3. If the total-cost function, even after allowance for the above and any other conceivable points, should still insist upon being

linear, it would not yet follow that marginal costs must be con stant. For, as Barone[26] remarks in connection with Pareto's law of income distributions, "it is not safe to draw, by means of analytical transformations, other laws from an empirical law obtained by interpolations because one may in so doing end up with results completely divergent from reality." To his unsophisticated mind that still seemed to matter. This point of Barone's has been elucidated by Haavelmo in a recent paper.[27]

Arguments of the above type are plentiful and to be found in almost any treatment of our subject. To the extent that they apply to any special case they, of course, damage not only the linearity of the function derived but also the function itself. More particularly with respect to theory, this whole situation is very interesting. On the one hand, many reasons may be given why the statistical results, however carefully elaborated, may be spurious. On the other hand, however, there is also the tendency on the part of theorists, exemplified by Stigler, to build up a defense against possible future confirmation and consolidation of what, though itself still but shakily established, seems to contradict an assumption conventionally made in non-statistical reasoning. It is an interesting example of the inner workings of scientific progress.

IV

The discussion so far has been in terms of the reliability of the statistical results in relation to the functions which they claim to represent, and also in relation to the conventional representation of such functions in non-statistical reasoning. The following remarks will bear upon the significance of these results in a somewhat wider sense.

The final aim of both cost theory and measurement is, of course, and could not be anything else but a better understanding of entrepreneurs' behavior. There is no room for doubting that every entrepreneur perfectly realizes that, as long as he can increase his receipts more than he increases his costs by expanding his rate of output, it will be in his interest to do so under any

---

[26] Enrico Barone, "Principi di Economia Finanziaria," now available as Vol. III of *Le Opere Economiche* (Bologna, 1937), p. 55.

[27] Trygve Haavelmo, *On the Theory and Measurement of Economic Relations* (Cambridge, 1941, multigraphed), especially pp. 19 *ff*.

given set of conditions which is likely to remain unchanged for some time to come. There is, however, considerable room for suspecting in the first place that, even abstracting from expected changes, entrepreneurs do not use marginal costs as *we* measure them in the application of that rationality principle. If that were so, it would not take long and painstaking research to discover marginal costs.

In the second place, even if actual objective marginal costs were known to entrepreneurs (as they quite probably are not), it might not be good policy to work at a rate of output which would maximize profits in the classical short-run fashion. For, although it is quite true that "in the long run we are all dead," that strictly applies to the long run only, and the likelihood of relief from duty through death does not normally enter an entrepreneur's business calculations. Provision must therefore be made for the period of time which presumably lies between the present and the date of death. There is, for instance, the question of overhead costs. We tell our imaginary enterprisers not to worry about overhead costs in making current business decisions. But real entrepreneurs know that overhead cannot all be handled by mere balance sheet adjustments: interest must be paid in hard cash at stated dates. And although to economists it may appear as perfectly obstinate to refuse to accept so obvious a distinction as that between costs which are a function of output and costs which depend only on the lapse of time, there is *some* wisdom in a policy which attempts to keep cash ready for the moment interest charges are due. So much wisdom, indeed, that even the venerable principle that no production really ought to take place unless at least variable costs are covered by expected receipts might break down under the stress of its weight.

I should not, however, if I were asked for it, give the advice to handle the problem by a mathematical analysis of the conditions that would maximize profits over time (*pace* Tintner). I would rather be inclined, in this particular respect as well as more generally in relation to the determination of cost functions, to look for another type of solution. I often wonder if statistical theories and techniques whose admirable development cannot fail to impress anybody *qua* intellectual exploit have not brought about a propensity to employ refined methods of inference where direct and complete knowledge would be readily available. Why go to all the trouble of measuring cost functions for an individual firm when it would be quite feasible to obtain from entrepreneurs (at any rate from those who open their books to the econometricians) the very best of information concerning the reasons for their decisions? Why not ask them directly, with all the caution required to avoid suggested answers, rather than try to infer in a most clever, but certainly roundabout, and probably incomplete way from dead records what probably is going to be a result irrelevant to actual business men's decisions?

I am not overlooking that the whole distinction between objective and subjective marginal costs and rationality would vanish in the event that private business men were replaced by government managers. The latter, being, I presume, less urgently concerned with the making of profits and the avoiding of losses, may possibly find the necessary leisure and be possessed of sufficient detachment to study marginal costs as they *really* are. And it is quite conceivable that the possibility of hinging price policies upon actual objective marginal costs would represent one of the major trumps in favor of socialism.

V

In this section, I wish to say a few words as to possibilities for future development in this line of inquiry.

In the study of demand, actual individual behavior is the deepest-lying level to which we can dig. Everything beyond is largely in the nature of speculation. I say largely, and not completely, remembering Thurstone's valiant attempt[28] to measure indifference curves by means of psychological experimentation. Nevertheless, it remains true that in that field, where the basic postulate of rationality is strictly analogous to the one which underlies supply theory, the greater part of the operation of this rationality takes place in regions where direct measurement is at least difficult. And being in a position to measure, so to speak, only one end of it, we are free to reconstruct the rest in agreement with any desired schema, e.g., our own conventional consumers' equilibrium, without much fear of contradiction.

[28] L. L. Thurstone, "The Indifference Function," *Journal of Social Psychology*, Vol. II, 1931, pp. 139–167.

The situation is *not* the same in the theory of supply. Costs here, as expenditures there, represent only one of two pillars of the short-run rationality principle. But the other, receipts, or revenues, is observable, at least in principle. And being observable, it has to be observed if we wish to avoid the absurdity of results obtained through application of our rationality principle to information on costs alone, a point which has so strikingly been shown by Leontief.[29]

Now I do not mean to say that any *statistical* approach to total, average, or marginal revenue functions for the firm is advisable. On the contrary, the doubts above uttered as to the significance of statistical cost functions fully apply to similar analyses of receipts. In addition, there are excellent reasons on the theoretical level which speak against any such venture. I am referring to the articles by Hall and Hitch[30] and Sweezy,[31] the simultaneous appearance of which again offers an example of ideas which are *in the air* and find independent and similar expression. And Sweezy's contribution in particular has the virtue of not being written in adaptation to, or in defense against, any previous findings which more or less explicitly claimed to disable preëxisting theoretical expectations. In consequence it may safely be said that there are excellent reasons why the subjective, i.e., actually operative, demand curves should have a kink at the level of the current price. I should therefore again advocate some method of inquiry similar to that used by the Oxford economists, and be inclined to expect significant results. These results might be even more valuable if they could be expanded horizontally, following von Nördling's suggestion, so as to cover conditions, both of cost and revenue, for firms operating in the same or immediately related markets.

Finally, there are no reasons why at the cost end of the matter we should stop at the cost function. Two years ago, Stigler[32] pro-

---

[29] W. Leontief, "Elasticity of Demand Computed from Cost Data," *The American Economic Review*, Vol. XXX, Dec. 1940, pp. 814–817.

[30] R. L. Hall and C. J. Hitch, "Price Theory and Business Behaviour," *Oxford Economic Papers*, No. 2, May 1939, pp. 12–45.

[31] P. M. Sweezy, "Demand under Conditions of Oligopoly," *The Journal of Political Economy*, Vol. XLVII, Aug. 1939, pp. 568–573.

[32] *The American Economic Review*, Suppl., March 1940, Vol. XXX, pp. 402–403.

posed another approach to cost functions, i.e., via production functions, such as might be established by engineers. While that still remains a useful suggestion, there are reasons to hope that another type of production function, more diversified than Douglas's, may soon become available, and from these it would be possible to derive cost functions typical for particular industries. The literature on statistical cost functions so far produced has certainly, as all measurements are bound to do, enhanced understanding and awareness of the complexity of the subject. But I cannot help thinking that it also represents a case which bears out just that, and not much else.

III. STOCKS IN THE THEORY OF PRICES

14

ASSETS, PRICES AND MONETARY THEORY [*]

BY HELEN MAKOWER [||] AND JACOB MARSCHAK [|||]

1. INTRODUCTION.[1] In order to understand what determines people's cash holdings and the prices of goods in terms of cash, we have to discuss more generally the causes making people hold idle stocks—of which cash balances are a particular case. This necessitates the application of Equilibrium Theory generalised to take account of time, imperfect competition and uncertainty. Our procedure is as follows.

§§ 2–7 give the theory of prices and quantities of assets generalised to take account of time. The case of joint demand together with joint supply[2] is presented: a number of consumption goods or *yields* are produced by the combination of a number of production goods, or *assets*. This takes us rather far back into the theory of marginal productivity and utility: we have to give a broader version of that theory, since the usual versions treat of joint demand without joint supply or vice versa.[3] It has seemed

[*] *Economica*, New Series, Vol. V (1938), pp. 261–288. Reprinted, by the courtesy of the publisher and the author, with typographical corrections.

[||] The London School of Economics and Political Science, England.

[|||] The University of Chicago.

[1] This article reconsiders certain ideas which were treated by one of the present authors in a memorandum on Investment circulated privately in 1935 and in a paper read at the 1935 Meeting of the Econometric Society. A mathematical version of the article is to appear shortly in *Econometrica;* see also the Report of the Colorado Springs Conference for Research in Economics, 1937. The subject was also treated by the writers in an unpublished thesis called *The Theory of Value on the Capital Market.* It will be noticed that in the present discussion of Value and the Capital Market, neither the word Capital nor the word Value appears. It was found better to base the discussion on prices and assets, which are measurable quantities.

[2] In Marshall's sense. *Principles,* Book V, Chap. VI.

[3] Loans repayable in a lump sum and stocks of consumers' goods represent as nearly as possible cases where there is no element of joint supply or joint demand. The theory of prices and quantities in an economy where one asset

worth while to do this spade-work deep down in the foundations
of equilibrium theory; for it enables us to build the theory of
asset prices upon something less uncanny than a sheep producing
quite on its own supplies of meat and wool ready for consumption; or a combination of assets producing an output (with no
by-products) at one blow, and then collapsing instantly on to the
scrap-heap.

The generalisation of the theory from one which is applicable
to a riskless economy only, to one which applies also to a hazardous world, is given in §§ 8–10. §§ 11–14 order assets according to
some fundamental characteristics, such as safety and future saleability, etc. In §§ 15–18 the theory is applied to cash holdings,
and a link is forged between the Quantity Theory of Money, the
Theory of Interest, and the Theory of Asset Prices.

We may distinguish the following types of *data* for each
individual:

Tastes;

Initial resources;

Transformation conditions;

Market conditions.

It will be shown that these data determine the following *unknown quantities* (also called equilibrium[4] quantities):

Prices of assets;

Quantities of assets exchanged and possessed by each individual in equilibrium;

Quantities of yields consumed in the future.

I. CERTAINTY

2. ASSETS AND YIELDS. Yields are *flows* while assets are *stocks*.
Yields are consumed but not exchanged; assets are exchanged but
not consumed.[5] Yields may differ not only in quality but also in
the time at which they accrue.

---

always produces one yield is given by Irving Fisher *(Theory of Interest)*. For
most items in a balance sheet, however, this simplification breaks down. Even
the marginal productivity theory of prices of factors of production is a special
case, because it assumes only one yield jointly produced by many factors.

[4] See, however, below § 7.

[5] Instead of contrasting production goods and consumption goods we shall
for the purpose of our analysis contrast assets and yields, the former being

Assets are physical goods or claims which give rise to yields. Debts are negative assets. There are only present assets, not future assets. Dealings in futures can be treated as dealings in pr·sent claims. Futures are present claims on future yields. We shall call a collection of assets a *property*, or balance sheet. The problem is, what property will each individual possess after having exchanged on the market, given the initial property with which he comes to the market, and given also his tastes and the transformation and market conditions.

It must be borne in mind that yields are here defined as amounts consumed. In the particular case where there is only one quality of yield, or else a bundle of fixed composition, we might define "investment" during a year as the discounted value of the yield series expected from a property as it is at the year's end *minus* the discounted value of the yield series expected from the property as it is at the year's beginning (the term discounted will be defined below, § 3). Investment thus defined may be negative; it is then usually called disinvestment or wear and tear. "Net yield," or income, would then be the sum of consumption and investment (or consumption *minus* wear and tear), and therefore consumption, or gross yield, is net yield *minus* investment (or *plus* wear and tear). In reality, however, there are many qualities of yield. Consequently it is not in general possible to define either investment or net yield without recourse to some artificial index numbers which break down whenever relative quantities change considerably. However, it is not necessary for us to use these concepts here: the quantities fundamental for our discussion are the various yields—by which we always mean *gross* yields—and the various assets.

Thus in the case of a loan the lender's yield in a given year is his consumption of the amount repaid to him, irrespective of how much represents "interest" (or net yield) and how much "amortisation" (or disinvestment). Or, if the share is sold, the yield is the ultimate consumption of the proceeds from the sale.

---

stocks, the latter consumed flows. The treatment of what might appear to be cross cases presents no serious difficulty: the service "dwelling accommodation" is a consumption flow, or yield. On the other hand labour is regarded as the stock of services of the labourer over the period for which the worker is signed on, that is as an asset.

Hence yields depend not only on physical transformation but also on future exchange. The appreciation of an asset which is to be sold must affect the yield in some year or years.

3. TASTES. Individuals' tastes refer to consumption. They are expressed by indicating the order of preference for all conceivable combinations of yields. Each individual tries to maximise the satisfaction he gets from the consumption of all the yields derived from all his assets. His satisfaction, or "utility," depends upon the size, physical quality and time distribution of his yields.

For each individual enjoying given quantities of yields there are definite rates at which he would be willing to substitute a small amount of any one yield (say milk in the first year) for any other yield (milk in the second or third year, or meat in the first, second or third year, etc.). These *rates of preference* are ratios between marginal utilities. They vary with the quantities of yields enjoyed (so-called "law of decreasing marginal utility"). The rates of preference enable us to express any bundle of yields—certain amounts of milk and meat in the first and second year—in terms of an equivalent amount of a single yield, say milk in the first year. If two yields differ not in quality but in time only, the rates of preference are called *time preference rates* (impatient people have high time preference rates). The translation of any future yield into an equivalent amount of present yield will be called *discounting*. It will be convenient to use this term in a wide sense, to describe the translation of any kind of yield at any time into some kind of present yield, by means of the time and quality preference rates. The yield selected as *standard yield* (e.g., present consumption of 1 lb. of bread) is, of course, arbitrary. By discounting a bundle of future yields we obtain the present value of the bundle.

People do not exchange yields, they exchange assets. Prices are exchange ratios between assets. Yet people have no direct preferences for assets, but only for things consumed. The link between yields and assets is provided by the *Transformation Conditions*.

4. TRANSFORMATION CONDITIONS. By a *bundle of yields* we mean a series of yields of various qualities in different intervals of time. Transformation conditions tell us all the possible bundles of yields which can be got in the future from any given property, either by physical transformation or by exchange.

In general there is no meaning in the phrase "productivity of an asset" independently of other assets. The increase of yields due to the addition of an asset depends upon the other assets with which it is combined. If a coal-washing plant is brought into a sugar factory it will make less difference to the yield than if the same plant is installed in connection with a coal mine.

The ratio at which it would be possible to substitute one asset for another while keeping yields unaltered, we shall call the *rate of transformation of assets*. This rate usually changes with the quantity of the asset that is substituted (the so-called "law of varying returns"). The larger the decrease in the rate of transformation accompanying a given change in the quantity transformed, the less transformable is the one asset into the other. (In the limiting case where the rate is constant, there would be perfect transformability.)

Similarly, the rate at which it would be possible to substitute one yield for another, without altering the assets, we shall call the *rate of transformation of yields*.

The transformation conditions are subjective in the sense that they are people's estimates. They need not be correct nor need they be the same for different individuals. Yet their being subjective does not mean that we are already concerned with an uncertain economy. Until § 8 we shall assume that every individual thinks he knows exactly the yields accruing from given properties.

5. THE INDIVIDUAL'S EQUILIBRIUM: (*a*) *Crusoe*. Since an isolated individual cannot exchange, he cannot alter his initial property, which is therefore identical with his equilibrium property. But he can choose between various bundles of yields which can be produced from his property. His satisfaction will only be at a maximum when his preference rate for yields is equal to the transformation rate for yields. Thus the condition of equilibrium is that the rate at which he is *willing* to substitute yields must be equal to the rate at which he is *able* to substitute them.

(*b*) *A Producer in a Perfect Market*. The individual in a perfect market regards prices as given to him and as uninfluenced by the quantities he sells. In equilibrium he will choose such a combination of assets, and with this combination he will produce such a bundle of yields, as will make (*i*) his rate of preference equal to the transformation rate for yields, (*ii*) the rate of transformation of assets equal to the ratio of market prices. The first condition also applies to Crusoe, but the second does not.

The equilibrium requirement can be put in the familiar way, in terms of marginal productivity, provided only that we define marginal productivity more generally than is done in the usual marginal productivity theory, where it is assumed that there is only one product. As has been seen, an asset may contribute a variety of alternative bundles of yields. The marginal productivity of an asset is the most preferred bundle of yields (properly discounted by using preference rates and thus expressed in terms of standard yield) of all those bundles which may result from the addition of one unit of an asset to the existing property. When we say that in equilibrium the price of each asset is proportionate to its marginal productivity, we mean that it is proportionate to the utility of its most preferred bundle of yields.

One asset—say £1 cash—may be chosen as a numéraire, i.e., its price taken as unity. The numéraire must not be confused with the standard yield—say present consumption of 1 lb. of bread—which is the yield (not an asset!) the marginal utility of which is taken as unity.

Since the future yields contributed at the margin by an asset depend not only on production, but also on the proceeds of future sales, the term marginal productivity is employed in a more general sense than usual.

(c) *A Producer in an Imperfect Market.* In the present passage and in § 6 (b) we give the analysis of equilibrium in an imperfect market.[6] This makes the theory more realistic. But it is not essential to the main argument and may be omitted by the reader. Only the concept of market imperfection is required for the later discussion, when we deal with future saleability as a property of cash.

We can generalise the analysis of the individual's equilibrium in a perfect market so as to cover also imperfect markets, by introducing the concept of *market conditions.* Market conditions describe the way in which price varies as the individual increases the quantity he sells. The "initial price" is the price obtained if

---

[6] Pietri-Tonelli (*La Spéculation de Bourse*) also treats imperfect competition in the capital market. Our method seems, however, to be more in tune with the General Equilibrium approach.

he sells a very small quantity. The ratio between total quantities exchanged is the *average price*. The *marginal price* is the exchange ratio between small quantities in the neighbourhood of the equilibrium point. Prices actually charged on the market are in general average, not marginal, prices. Only in a perfect market is the average price equal to the initial (and also to the marginal) price. Thus the case where the market is perfect represents one special market condition. The individual in an imperfect market regards the way in which prices vary with quantity sold, as given to him. Once the initial price is given, his equilibrium is fixed by his initial resources, his tastes, and his transformation conditions. He will sell that quantity which makes the ratio of the marginal prices equal to the ratio of the marginal transformation rates.[7]

6. THE MARKET IN EQUILIBRIUM: (a) *A Perfect Market*. When in the preceding section we assumed perfect markets, that is, dealt with an individual who regarded prices as uninfluenced by his own sales, we took the prices as given. Maintaining, to begin with, the restricting assumption of a perfect market, we shall now see how prices themselves are determined by the tastes, transformation conditions and initial resources of every individual.

---

[7] Geometrically, the relationship between the price of an asset and the quantity sold by an individual can be represented in the Marshallian way, as a Demand curve drawn in a system of co-ordinates measuring horizontally the quantity of an asset sold and vertically its price in terms of another asset. The initial price is given by the intercept of the curve on the vertical axis. When market conditions are given, the initial price fixes the whole curve.

The alternative way of representing graphically the relationship between prices and quantities sold is Pareto's (and Fisher's) way. Here each co-ordinate measures the quantity of one asset retained after exchange. The line connecting the point representing the initial quantities with other points accessible by exchange is called the market line (or surface) and the marginal price at any point is given by the slope of the line. The initial price is the slope at the point representing the initial quantities. If market conditions are given, the initial price fixes the whole *allure* of the market line.

In a Marshallian figure a perfect market is shown by a horizontal straight line, an imperfect market by a falling curve. In the Paretian system a perfect market is shown by a straight line (always falling), an imperfect one by a curve (always falling and concave downwards). The degree of perfection of the market can be roughly measured by the elasticity of the demand curve confronting an individual or firm, or by the curvature of the market line. Strictly, this concept of measurable perfection of the market only applies i the elasticity is constant all along the line.

For each conceivable exchange ratio between a pair of assets (goods or claims), there are definite quantities of each asset which each individual would be willing to buy or sell. Only that exchange ratio can obtain in the market for which the double condition is satisfied: that, for each asset, the total quantity people are willing to buy equals the total quantity other people are willing to sell (clearing of the market); and that each person's receipts, expressed in terms of any one asset, equal his expenditure.

(b) *An Imperfect Market.*[8] This statement of the way in which prices are determined can be generalised, so as to make it applicable also to the case where the market conditions of each individual are not perfect, but instead some other market conditions are given, in general different for each person. For each conceivable initial price, there are definite quantities which each individual would be willing to exchange—namely those which equalise the ratio of marginal prices to the ratio of transformation rates. These quantities imply also definite average prices. As in the case of the perfect market, the quantities and prices which each individual spends must be compatible with the quantities and prices selected by all other individuals. This gives the same double condition as before: total quantities bought and sold must be equal for each asset; expenditure must equal receipts for each individual.[9]

Suppose we add to our property an asset, some quantity of which is going to be sold at some definite time in the future. If

---

[8] As mentioned above, this passage may be omitted by the more impatient reader.

[9] We may now give the geometrical interpretation of the way in which prices themselves, as well as quantities of assets, are determined. Each market line (or demand curve) corresponds to the series of marginal prices, starting with the initial price, which may confront the individual as he proceeds to exchange increasing quantities. Only one line, for each individual, is eligible when initial resources, transformation conditions and tastes are given. Which line is thus eligible is determined by the double condition given in the text. Thus market conditions are a whole bundle or family of curves, going through the initial point, and having some given property. In the special case of perfect competition they degenerate into a bundle of straight market lines (or a set of horizontal linear demand curves). Constant (finite) elasticity is an example of an imperfect market condition. But a market condition is a more general property than elasticity. Any other property common to a family of curves can give a market condition.

the market is imperfect (few buyers) the future selling price and therefore the discounted yield from the present property is lower than if the market were perfect. We may compare the asset's discounted marginal contribution to the yield of the property with what this marginal contribution would be if the market for the asset were perfect. This difference between the two can be reduced, i.e., the market can be made more perfect, by advertising (in the wide sense of the word including, e.g., brokerage). Advertising will be pushed to the point where its cost equals the gain from perfecting the market.

In general the extent to which the imperfection of the market is reduced by advertisement depends on how long the seller waits between advertising and selling. By waiting longer he gets in touch with more buyers. But on the other hand the yields will have to be discounted more heavily for time (see § 3). He will select that waiting interval which maximises the sum of his discounted yields.[10]

7. INTEREST RATE, DETERMINACY AND EQUILIBRIUM. We have shown how the quantities of assets exchanged and possessed, together with their prices, are determined. It may be asked why no mention has been made of the rate of interest. As yields are not in general exchanged in the market, no "price of present yield in terms of future yield" can be found in the market. Individuals' subjective time preference rates refer to yields; they are not equalised in the market.

Instead of saying that a one-year loan of £100 with guaranteed interest of £7 p.a. costs to-day £104, we may, if we like, say that the rate of interest is 3 per cent. This is an application of the

---

[10] An interesting unpublished paper on this subject by Mr. Hasler was mimeographed for the London, Cambridge and Oxford Joint Seminar. Mr. Hasler depicts the equilibrium time for the seller to wait in a diagram, where the axes measure time and price. Equilibrium is shown as the point of tangency between an indifference line (for present and future yields) and the schedule connecting time and price.

The schedule of the prices that can be fetched after various waiting intervals depicts the ease with which an asset can be sold. But it does not help to explain the size of cash-holdings. We shall therefore not apply the term saleability to it. Saleability, in the sense in which this term will be used here to explain cash-holdings and other idle stocks, is a property which, although connected with market conditions, only arises in an uncertain world.

formula (§ 5 (*b*)): price is proportionate to the discounted value of the marginal gross yield.[11] Only it should be remembered that this "rate of interest" refers simply to the price of one asset (cash) in terms of another (one-year loan). If the loan runs for more than a year we can still define the rate of interest as that percentage which, given the yields, would, if used to discount yields in all years, give the actual price of the loan in terms of cash. It is in this sense that "the market rate of interest" is sometimes calculated from the yield and the price of consols. Clearly this calculated interest rate is quite distinct from individuals' preference rates. It is a function (a kind of mean) of the various preference rates for different years, for each individual. Obviously this mean may be the same for all individuals although no two individuals have the same time-preference rate for any given pair of years.

The data of our analysis—tastes, transformation conditions, initial resources and market conditions—are subjective, in the sense that they are estimates made by individuals. On the other hand the prices of assets and the quantities exchanged, which are unknowns of our system, are objective. At any given moment there are definite prices and quantities of assets which are consistent with the set of data. We sometimes call these the equilibrium prices and quantities. But it must be understood that by equilibrium we merely mean determinacy. There is absolutely no guarantee that the prices and quantities will persist through time. Suppose even that the data do not change, i.e., that people do not revise their estimates. Then, in the first place, the quantities and prices as determined in the first moment of time will in general not persist in the later moments, because people's plans for the future will usually incorporate quantities which vary through time. In the second place, even if we could assume that people plan for unvarying quantities, the fact that the plans of the various individuals need not be compatible will mean that quantities which had been planned in the past are not maintained; for the market for assets

---

[11] The present price of 100 units of the loan is: $£104 = 0 + \dfrac{107}{(1.03)^1}$.

The present price of 100 units of cash is: $£100 = 100 + \dfrac{0}{(1.03)^1}$.

Therefore the price ratio is $\dfrac{104}{100}$.

must always be cleared. Finally, the data usually do change: people continually revise their estimates in the light of experience. Thus prices and quantities tend to change continually, although they are determinate at each moment.

To talk of a "natural rate of interest" is an over-simplification. But we could define a natural system of prices in a way which might correspond to the situation that economists have in mind when they talk of the natural rate of interest. A natural system of asset prices would be a system which can remain stable through time. We have just shown that the data at any given time, though fixing equilibrium in the sense of a determinate system of prices, do not by any means imply a stable system either of prices or of quantities. The question of conditions of stability is essentially dynamic and requires a study of the causes determining the data themselves.

II. UNCERTAINTY

8. DEFINITIONS. We have assumed so far that there is certainty. We have now to enquire what are the data in an uncertain world.[12]

People do not know, they can only guess at, the yields they will be able to get from their properties, whether by productive activity or by future exchange. The yields must be expressed as an array of more or less probable quantities, that is as a frequency distribu-

---

[12] We appreciate the importance of Professor Knight's distinction between risk and uncertainty. It seems that we may interpret Professor Knight's "risk" as the dispersion of the frequency distribution of alternative future events, and his "uncertainty" as the degree of ignorance about this frequency distribution. For the first concept we too shall use the term *risk;* as to the second, we find it more convenient to call it *degree of ignorance.*

This enables us to reserve the term *uncertainty* to denote the fact that risk exists, i.e., that no event is assigned the probability 1 (and therefore the dispersion is greater than zero). This seems consistent with the ordinary use of the word "uncertainty." In the roulette room we are not ignorant about the probabilities which are to be assigned to the various alternative events; yet there is uncertainty even there about each single event.

On the other hand the fact that in ordinary life, outside games of chance, the frequency distributions are not exactly known, we denote as *ignorance.* A discussion of how, in the light of the Theory of Inference, we may measure the degree of ignorance, and how it affects the prices and holdings of assets, must be left for another occasion.

tion,[13] or more strictly a system of yields must be expressed by a joint frequency distribution.

At least two characteristics are usually used to describe approximately a frequency distribution: some measure of average and some measure of variability or dispersion. Measures of average are, for instance, the most probable value (mode), the mathematical expectation (mean or actuarial value), the mid-point between the extreme values, etc. As a measure of dispersion the difference between the extreme possible values (range) divided by the average may be used, or alternatively the coefficient of variation (i.e., the standard deviation divided by the mean).[14] Thus for example, an investor may think that a security will most probably yield £5; but that it may yield £6 and it may yield nothing. The mode is then

---

[13] Compare I. Fisher, *Capital and Interest*, 1906, App. to Chap. XVI, p. 10.

    A. C. Pigou, *Economics of Welfare*, 1920, App. I.

    P. S. Florence, *Statistical Methods in Economics and Political Science*, 1929, Chap. XVIII, p. 4.

    J. R. Hicks, *Economica*, May 1931 and February 1935. Leyden meeting of Econometric Society, 1933 (reported in *Econometrica*, 1934).

    K. Menger, *Zeitschrift für Nationalökonomie*, 1934.

[14] Our analysis is not dependent upon any particular measures selected to represent the probability distributions. Mode and range are less accurate than, for instance, the moments used in statistical work. But perhaps they correspond better to the vague way people think about expected yields.

We might, further, introduce a third characteristic of the frequency curve, its asymmetry. The economic relevance of this is mentioned in the next footnote. It may be measured by the difference between mean and mode, or between midpoint and mode (−2 in the first example cited at the end of § 8).

The analysis need not be confined to two or three characteristics, or parameters, but can be extended to any number (e.g., any number of moments). And instead of using a finite number of parameters we could use the full description of the probability distribution, stating the probabilities ascribed to each infinitely small range of values, or using the form of the function as a whole. The analysis would be unaltered in principle.

Further, as mentioned in the text, it is, strictly, the joint distribution of all yields rather than distributions of the separate yields which matter. This would mean using, in addition to the parameters attached to each variable (mean, dispersion, etc.), the parameters connecting them, such as correlation coefficients. In fact people are not indifferent as to whether there is association between simultaneous plenty and scarcity of different types of yields produced by the property in any one year (or any given quality of yields in successive years). However we shall not pursue this refinement here.

£5, the range £6. Or he may think it equally probable that a security will yield £2 and £8. The actuarial value or mean is then £4, the standard deviation is £2, and the coefficient of variation, 5.

9. TASTES IN AN UNCERTAIN WORLD. It was assumed earlier that a person's satisfaction depends upon the size, quality and time-distribution of his yields. But for "size" we must now substitute the two characteristics of the frequency distribution. People like yields with a high actuarial value—they like *lucrativity*.[15] And further, the dispersion of yields is relevant. If two expected yields of a given quality accruing in a given year have the same mean (or actuarial) value, most people prefer the one whose values do not usually deviate strongly from the mean. That is, people usually prefer safe yields and dislike risky ones. The *risk*, a disutility, may be measured by the coefficient of variation of yield; or alternatively, the *safety*, a utility, can be measured by the coefficient of variation taken with a negative sign.

Just as there are rates of preference between any two yields differing in time or quality, so also there are rates of preference between the mean and the dispersion of yield: we may call these rates *safety preferences*. "Audacious" people have a low safety preference. They would give up a lot of safety in exchange for a small increase in mean or lucrativity.[16] Using the individual's safety preference rate, in addition to his quality and time preference rates, we can express any expected bundle of yields in terms of a standard unit of yield, namely present lucrativity of a given quality. We can again, as in § 2, call this process discounting—in this case, discounting for risk.

10. MARGINAL LUCRATIVITY AND SAFETY. Our previous results can now be applied to the world of uncertainty. For this generalisation we simply have to substitute for the word "yields" the words "lucrativities and safeties of yields." An investor with a given

---

[15] In a world of certainty there is only one possible value for the yield which is therefore its own actuarial value.

[16] It seems also (cf. Professor Pigou, Professor Sargant Florence, Dr. Hicks) that people are not indifferent about the asymmetry of the probability distribution: of two equally lucrative and equally safe properties, the one offering a small chance of a very large gain is often preferred. Football pools are popular. "Long-odds enthusiasts" are willing to accept a considerably lower average in order to get a slightly more (positively) skew distribution.

property can choose between various bundles of lucrativities and safeties of yields. This is the generalised way of stating the transformation conditions. As before, an asset's contribution to yield is in general not independent of other assets. This is illustrated by Investment Trusts. The object of an Investment Trust is to increase the safety of the whole property by properly mixing the risks attached to various assets. A gas share added to a holding of electricity shares has a greater marginal safety than if it is added to a holding of gas shares.

It is now possible to extend the concept of marginal productivity so as to make it apply to an uncertain economy. We shall call this generalised concept *marginal contribution:* an asset's marginal contribution is the most preferred bundle of lucrativities and safeties, properly discounted, resulting from the addition of one unit of the asset to a given property. Asset prices are proportionate to marginal contributions. The price of the asset chosen as numéraire is unity. The lucrativity of one unit of the standard yield is also unity.

As an illustration, suppose a person's property consists mainly of plant. Let us first consider in what way the addition of more plant will affect expected yields. Let the most preferred contribution of the added plant be: nine units of lucrativity (discounted for time) and an amount of safety which, discounted for time and risk, is one unit of lucrativity. Suppose now that, instead of more plant, a house is added to the property and that the best yield-bundle consists of a smaller amount of lucrativity, 3, together with a larger amount of safety, say 7. The two assets then make contributions of equal value, viz., 10 lucrativity units. Therefore their present prices must be equal: the higher lucrativity of the plant is offset by its lower safety.

It now becomes clear why changes in interest rates do not materially affect investment plans, even long-term investment plans, except in the cases of housing and public utilities. The increase in lucrativity due to saving on interest payments is only one of the considerations relevant to the borrower: there is also the effect on safety. Whereas in the case of housing and public utilities the latter effect may be very small, in the case of industrial investments there may be such a large unfavorable effect on the safety of the yields from the whole property that the gain in lucrativity is outweighed by the loss in safety.

We have shown that the interest rate can be defined as the result of an arithmetical operation on the price and gross yield of a (safe) loan, like consols. The situation is analogous if we consider discounting for risk instead of for time. "The risk premium" would be that quantity which, if used to discount each successive unit of risk, would give the actual price of a (non-durable) asset. If, however, the asset is both durable and risky, the definition collapses: there is an indefinite number of pairs of interest and risk premia which, if applied in discounting a given yield series, will result in a given price. Asset prices are still perfectly determinate; but the interest rate and the risk premium are now indeterminate—we must abandon them, and we do so without regret. The fact that "interest rate" and "risk premium" vaguely suggest to us time-preference and safety-preference does not constitute a recommendation for them. The interest rate is not in general identical with any time-preference rate (see § 7) and, for analogous reasons, the risk premium is not identical with any safety-preference rate.

11. CLASSIFICATION OF ASSETS. We may group together familiar types of actual assets—like money, shares, plant—according to the ways in which they contribute to lucrativities and safeties. We shall start with simplified conditions and then introduce imperfection of the market and uncertainty.

(a) *Certainty with a Perfect Market.* In a certain world with a perfect market the marginal contributions of assets are simply their marginal productivities. All stocks are *productive* stocks. Asset prices are proportionate to these productivities. The quantities of stocks of each kind of asset held are such as to make asset prices proportionate to their marginal productivities.

It may appear that some stocks would be held in a world of certainty without contributing to productivity. For instance, an ounce of crude tin may be held simply because it is not worth while blowing-in the blast furnace. This, however, does not constitute any exception to our rule. Because of the high costs of melting small quantities, the marginal product of tin under process would be less than the marginal product of the idle stock of crude tin. What may be called *discontinuity stocks* are only an extreme case of this same phenomenon: they are therefore also a variety of productive stock. Crops ripen at a definite season. The reason why wheat is held over winter is that it is extremely expensive to grow wheat out of season, in hothouses. Ore from overseas arrives discontinuously in big ship-loads. It is cheaper to keep some ore in stock than to have it delivered in small canoes whenever it is wanted.

Thus, in a world of certainty with perfect market conditions all stocks are lucrative stocks or, more specifically, productive stocks.

(b) *Certainty with an Imperfect Market.* With an imperfect market some stocks may be acquired because their price is expected to rise in the future. Such stocks will be called *speculative.* Their acquisition contributes to lucrativity through exchange. In the absence of uncertainty speculative stocks can only exist if the market is imperfect. For in a perfect market with full certainty (§ 4) speculation would defeat its own end: any investor who, on going to the market, saw a possibility of speculative gains, would, by his own purchases, push up the present price to that level which he expected the future price to reach. Therefore in equilibrium no one could be expecting speculative gains. In an imperfect market, however, the investor would not push his purchases so far. He would take into account the effect of his own purchases upon price.

As a common term for speculative and productive stocks we may use the expression "lucrative stocks." As in the case of a perfect market, stocks may also be held owing to the high costs of investing small quantities—where by "investing" we now mean not only transforming physically but also exchanging in the market. Such stocks are merely a kind of lucrative stocks. In an imperfect market advertising costs arise. High brokerage charges may make the marginal product of a share with a low dividend greater than that of a share with a higher dividend.

This kind of consideration would explain the existence of some minimum stocks of cash even in the absence of uncertainty. Provided income does not accrue exactly at the same times and in the same quantities as expenditures are made, people will keep cash balances; for the cost of investing very small balances is prohibitive.

(c) *Uncertainty with a Perfect Market.* In a certain world, then, assets are valued in proportion to their marginal productivities. With the introduction of uncertainty the price-relations become different. Assets are valued in proportion to what we have defined as their marginal contributions. Some assets become more highly valued, and are acquired in larger quantities, than they would be in a world of certainty. Those parts of stocks which would not have been acquired in a certain economy are usually called non-productive. Some kinds of assets which are familiar in the world as we know it would hardly be held at all in the absence of un-certainty. The considerations determining people's asset-holdings in an uncertain world are reviewed below.

(i) *Lucrative Stocks.* Assets can contribute to lucrativity either by physical transformation or by exchange. Those assets acquired because of their contribution to lucrativity without recourse to the market are *productive stocks*. They would exist in a certain as well as in an uncertain world.

Assets may be acquired because they are expected to contribute to lucrativity through future exchange. Such assets are *speculative*. They may always exist in an uncertain world; in a certain world they can only exist if the market is imperfect.

(ii) *Safe Stocks.* Some assets are acquired because, without fu-ture exchange, they contribute to safety (i.e., reduce the dispersion of yields) more than others. Such assets may be called *safe in pro-duction*.

Further, there are assets which are acquired because their fu-ture prices are more certain than those of others (i.e., have a smaller dispersion). The small dispersion of price will make their yields after sale (consumed proceeds) less dispersed than those of other assets. Such assets may be called *safe in exchange*; they are sometimes described by the phrase "store of value." Thus money has often been called a store of value by economists who abstract from the experiences of inflation.

In so far as the yield-expectations of the various persons are based partly on the same objective facts and are therefore to some extent similar, assets with certain prices are usually those whose yield is known with some precision. Therefore assets which are safe in production are usually also safe in exchange and can be kept as stores of value. For instance the yield, and hence the price, of a bond is not subject to large dispersion; so that bonds are partly kept as a store of value.

(d) *An Uncertain Economy with an Imperfect Market.* The introduction of market imperfection into an uncertain economy gives rise to a distinction between assets which will be more and those which will be less *saleable*.

12. FUTURE SALEABILITY. The future saleability of any asset to a given investor depends upon two factors: the estimated degree of imperfection of the future market and the frequency distribution of expected future sales.[17]

A picture will be difficult to sell—it will be hard to find buyers; advertising costs will be high. On the other hand it will be easy to sell a single Imperial Chemicals Share of similar value. To meet a contingency, it will be easier to manœuvre if the future market is perfect.

When an investor adds an asset of the kind A to his property, he does not know exactly how much of it he will sell out later. If it should turn out that his best policy is to sell a small quantity, say a, of A, he would get a small quantity, say β, of B in exchange. But if he should sell $2a$, $3a$, or $4a$, etc., then he would get 2β, 3β, 4β, etc., *only if* the future market is perfect (if the A's are single shares, for instance). In an imperfect market, like that for pictures or for whole blocks of shares, he would get less than 2β, 3β, 4β, etc. It follows that for any given amount of A retained the seller will have less of B, the less perfect the market. He will therefore get smaller yields from the whole property the less perfect the market. The investor assigns probabilities to each event: selling none of A; selling a of A; selling $2a$ of A, etc. To this frequency distribution of amounts of A sold there corresponds a frequency distribution of yields from the property. The actuarial value of the expected yields from the property (its lucrativity) is evidently higher the less imperfect the market. An asset's marginal contribution is thus highest in a perfect market. The reduction in its marginal contribution—and hence in its price in terms of the numéraire—due to future market imperfection depends both on the degree of imperfection and on the form of the frequency distribution of expected sales. This reduction may be called the asset's future unsaleability, and the reciprocal its future saleability.

Our definition of saleability does not imply that an asset is exchanged against one other asset only; it may, of course, be ex-

---

[17] We speak of "future" saleability simply in order to emphasise that we are concerned only with *future* contingent exchanges. In our terminology there is no such thing as "present saleability." The ease with which an asset can be sold in the present market (§ 5 (c)) is not relevant to saleability in our sense. This will become clear in the present section.

changed against a number of assets. The rate at which different quantities of A will in the future be exchanged against other assets, taken in conjunction with the probabilities of the respective exchanges, determines the asset's marginal contribution and hence also its saleability.

It follows from our definition that saleability depends not only upon future market conditions but also on the frequency distribution of the quantities which the individual thinks it possible he may sell. The smaller the dispersion of these quantities, the greater is the asset's saleability. When times become more uncertain the dispersion increases. This, by introducing the possibility of large sales which entail large price-reductions, not only increases the dispersion of future yields, but also reduces their actuarial value. Therefore increased uncertainty will decrease the marginal contributions of assets with future imperfect markets. As uncertainty increases people try to reduce their holdings of such assets, with the result that their prices fall relatively to those of other assets: a phenomenon known as hoarding of liquid[18] assets takes place.

It should be clear from the above that saleability is not a new kind of utility additional to lucrativity and safety. Saleability is a reduction in price due to reductions in lucrativity caused by uncertainty and the imperfection of the future market.

In § 10 we considered for illustration two assets having the same price but differing in respect to the ways in which this price was built up. The table on p. 302 extends this illustration. As before, the safety preference rate has been used to express safety in lucrativity units. The table refers to a single investor.

Let us compare first the figures under the heading "With Perfect Market." There, plant appears more lucrative than shares and both are more lucrative than cash. The lucrativity may be derived via production or speculation (see § 11). On the other hand houses, bonds and cash have the highest safety, either because of stable yields or stable prices. They are stores of value. Consider now also the figures under the heading "Actual": we see that the fact that certain markets are more perfect than others increases the lucrativity of easily saleable assets—namely shares, bonds and cash—relatively to others.

---

[18] We should say "saleable" (§ 15 *sub finem*).

	Lucrativity		Safety (Discounted)		Asset's Marginal Contribution (Lucrativity + Safety)		Differ- ence
	Actual	With Perfect Market	Actual	With Perfect Market	Actual	With Perfect Market	
Plant	9	20	1	3	10	23	13
House	3	12	7	11	10	23	13
Shares	9	9	1	1	10	10	0
Bonds	3	3	7	7	10	10	0
Cash	1	1	9	9	10	10	0

It may be worth recalling again that the saleability or unsaleability of an asset must be distinguished from its appreciation (or depreciation). Depreciation is the excess of the future price over the present price. Saleability is the reciprocal of the difference between an asset's actual present price and the price which it would have at present if the market in which it may be sold in the future were perfect. Speculative stocks are thus distinct from saleable stocks.[19] Further, saleability is sometimes described as the relationship between the selling price and the time which the seller must wait in order to get it. If an example is chosen where "the selling price" includes appreciation (or depreciation) saleability and speculation will again be confused. If, however, an example is chosen where there is no appreciation or depreciation, the influence of time on the selling price is due to the seller's finding more buyers (compare the concluding paragraph of § 6). In this case the price-time schedule describes the imperfection of the market and therefore, *given the frequency distribution of expected sales,* it determines the degree of saleability.

13. FUTURE PLASTICITY.[20] The investor can meet an emergency either by exchanging or by physical transformation. In the first case manœuvring is easier the more perfect the future market for the asset, i.e., the less the rate of exchange will vary with the quantity exchanged. Analogously, manœuvring by physical transforma-

---

[19] This distinction is not always clearly made. See, for instance, "The Concept of Liquidity," A. M. Neumann, *Review of Economic Studies,* 1935.

[20] This section deals with physical transformation of assets and is therefore irrelevant to monetary theory. It is, however, important for the general theory of assets.

tion is easier the more substitutable the asset, i.e., the less the rate
of transformation will vary with the quantity transformed. The
investor does not know exactly what quantities of assets he will
substitute by physical transformation. If he should substitute a
small amount, a, of an asset A for another asset B, he would get
a small quantity, say β, of B. If, however, he should substitute $2a$,
$3a$, $4a$, etc., of A he will generally get less than 2β, 3β, 4β respectively of B. The rate at which he will be able to increase the
quantity of one asset at the expense of another is not generally
constant; it will depend on the quantity substituted (§ 4). If the
rate of substitution varies strongly with the quantity substituted,
the elasticity of substitution is small; if the ratio varies little the
elasticity of substitution is large. In the limiting case, where the
rate is constant, the elasticity of substitution is infinite. Just as we
found when dealing with saleability, so here an asset's marginal
contribution is found by assigning to each possible amount of A
substituted, the probability that this amount will be substituted.
With a given set of contingencies, the less the rate of substitution
is expected to vary with the amount substituted, the greater the
asset's marginal contribution—because the investor reckons to be
able to manœuvre with a smaller sacrifice of yields. An asset's
future "unplasticity" can be measured by the difference between
what its price would be if its elasticity of substitution were infinite,
and its actual price. The reciprocal of this quantity is the asset's
future *plasticity*.[21]

The fact that an asset has a relatively perfect market and high
elasticity of substitution for all other assets would not, in itself,
be sufficient to cause people to hold stocks of this asset if there were
no uncertainty about the future. But if there is uncertainty then,
for every given frequency distribution of contingencies, future
saleability is greater the more perfect the market, and future plasticity is greater the greater the elasticity of substitution.[22]

The reason why producers find it profitable to hold large stocks

---

[21] In our terminology there is no such thing as present plasticity. The
reason why we sometimes use the adjective "future" is the same as in the case
of saleability. (See footnote 17.)

[22] In geometrical terms, given the frequency distribution of expected sales
or transformation, saleability depends on the curvature of the market line,
and plasticity, in an exactly analogous way, on the curvature of the transformation line.

of raw cotton, but not to hold large stocks of finished cotton goods, is that it is easier to transform raw cotton into a large range of alternative products. It must of course be remembered that an asset's marginal contribution, and therefore its plasticity, depends on the other assets possessed by the investor. Even raw cotton has no particular advantages of high plasticity to a tin-smelting firm.

We could now add the assets raw cotton and cotton goods to our table in § 12, as follows:

	Lucrativity		Safety (Discounted)		Asset's Marginal Contribution (Lucrativity + Safety)		Difference
	Actual	With Perfect Market or Substitutability	Actual	With Perfect Market or Substitutability	Actual	With Perfect Market or Substitutability	
Raw Cotton	2	2	8	8	10	10	0
Cotton Goods	2	3	8	9	10	12	2

14. TYPES OF ASSET: SUMMARY. Assets may be classified according to the reasons which make people acquire and keep them. These reasons, which also determine the asset prices, may be different in perfect and imperfect markets, and, again, in certain and uncertain economies; also, of course, an asset may be kept for several reasons at a time.

In a world of certainty with a perfect market, assets are kept only for their productivity. If the market is imperfect they may also be kept as speculative stocks. In both cases they are kept for lucrativity. What we have called "discontinuity stocks" are a special case of lucrative stocks; they arise from the prohibitive costs of investing small quantities, i.e., transforming them into other assets either physically or by exchange.

In an uncertain economy stocks are held not only for their lucrativity (in production or exchange) but also for their safety: and again, stocks may be safe in production or in exchange. In an uncertain world, with a given set of contingencies, prices and/or quantities are lower the less perfect the market and the less physically transformable the asset is expected to be in the future.

III. MONEY AND OTHER ASSETS

15. CASH-HOLDINGS. Let us consider, in the light of the preceding discussion, what determines people's cash-holdings.

Cash cannot be held for productivity. It may be held speculatively, if prices are expected to fall: postponed expenditure may be expected to add more to the utility derived from the property than the utility obtainable by present expenditure on consumption.

Owing to the high cost of investing small quantities, cash may also be held without expectation of a fall in prices. This is important because of the intervals which usually exist between an investor's receipt of income and his various expenditures. Thus cash-holdings due to such intervals appear as a special—and important—case of lucrative stocks.

The two above reasons for holding cash might exist even in the absence of uncertainty. They are, however, not the most important or characteristic reasons for holding cash. In fact many other assets are kept for the same reasons to at least as large an extent as cash. People frequently hold goods for appreciation in terms of other goods. Also raw materials often lie in stock because of the high cost of investing small quantities; whenever delivery is made discontinuously and does not exactly synchronise with outgoings, there will be stocks.

There are, however, two qualities which, in the eyes of investors, cash possesses in an especially high degree. These are safety and future saleability.

In times of monetary stability cash is held because it is safe in exchange—at least it is believed to be so by those who forget the experiences of inflation. This is the quality of money which economists have often described as a "store of value."

Second, cash possesses in a high degree the property of future saleability. This may be illustrated by contrasting cash with houses. When an investor sells out his house-property, he is likely by his own action to depress the price of houses in terms of other goods, because there are relatively few buyers of houses. When he "sells out" his cash he does not noticeably depress its price in terms of other goods, because there are many buyers of cash. The saleability of cash is presumably what was meant by economists when they praised it as a "good medium of exchange" owing to its universal, or almost universal, acceptability.[23] It does not matter, of course, whether the saleability of cash is due to law or custom. The market for cash is more nearly perfect than that for other assets.

It is clear that the future saleability of cash has nothing to do with appreciation (§ 12). Cash may still be saleable even when it is depreciating.

These two properties, safety and future saleability, which money possesses in a higher degree than many other assets, are often lumped together under the name of "liquidity." Those assets are said to be liquid which are in some way like cash. Thus liquidity is used to denote "being like cash." But since the two properties do not necessarily go together, two terms are required in order to avoid ambiguity.

It may occur to the reader that the term liquidity might be chosen to denote future saleability:[24] the word would indeed suggest the fact that money is easily transformable (on the market) into other assets and is thus an effective instrument for manœuvring. This terminology would be justified by the metaphorical allusion conveyed by the word "liquid" and its opposite "frozen": liquids change shape more easily than solids. However, "liquidity" has so often been used to cover all properties of money indiscriminately that it seems better not to use it for any of the separate properties of money. We thus resign ourselves to giving up "liquidity" as a measurable concept: it is, like the price level, a bundle of measurable properties.

16. "THE VELOCITY OF CIRCULATION." "THE LIQUIDITY POSITION." Once the factors determining cash-holdings have been analysed it would be mere arithmetic to take the ratio of cash-holdings to income—the well-known Cambridge k; or its reciprocal—the notorious Income Velocity of Circulation; or the proportion of cash-holdings to other items in the balance sheet—the so-called liquidity position of firms.

In fact these derived magnitudes become unnecessary tools if

---

[23] See Jevons, *Money*, 1875.
       Wicksell, *Lectures on Political Economy*, Vol. 2, Introduction.
       Marshall, *Money, Credit and Commerce*, Book I, Chap. 1.
       Mises, *The Theory of Money and Credit*, Part I, Chap. I, etc.
[24] As in *Kapitalbildung* (by J. Marschak and W. Lederer), pp. 8–10.

we have direct access to the fundamental variables: asset holdings of all kinds including cash; prices; yields (i.e., quantities consumed). In order to explain prices it is not necessary to bring cash-holdings into relation with income. The very concept of income can be dispensed with and has not been used here. The quantities we need are the amounts of various commodities and services consumed in various time intervals, and the asset holdings. To introduce the concept income would be merely to reduce the amounts consumed, and the changes in asset holdings, to a single quantity by the use of some ill-defined index-numbers. This would again be mere arithmetic, and not even very sound arithmetic. For certain purposes the reduction of the multiplicity of yields and assets to imaginary entities like consumption and investment is a useful statistical approximation; but it is an approximation which is inapplicable in practice whenever there are any considerable changes in relative prices or quantities. Such an approximation ought therefore not to be fundamental to our theory.

Similarly, the liquidity position can be described as the ratio of cash to total wealth only at the cost of neglecting important qualitative distinctions between various assets, both positive and negative.

Short-hand measures, however essential for statistical purposes, are no substitute for the causal analysis undertaken here.

17. THE RATIONALE OF "THE INTEREST RATE" AND "THE PRICE LEVEL." To have first explicitly approached money as one among many assets is an important service rendered by Dr. Hicks to modern economic theory.[25] The present analysis shows the connection between two aspects of monetary theory which textbooks usually put into watertight compartments: the theory of the price-level of commodities in terms of money, and the theory of the interest rate. The first aspect is treated under captions such as "The Quantity Theory of Money," "The Equation of Exchange," "The Velocity of Circulation," and "The Value of Money." The second compartment works with concepts like "The Price of Loans," "The Price of Waiting," "Liquidity Premium," and sometimes—rather unclearly related to "The Value of Money" of the first compartment—"The Price of Money." But in fact one and

---

[25] *Economica,* 1935. "A Suggestion for Simplifying the Theory of Money."

the same thing is treated in the two compartments. Given tastes, transformation conditions and market conditions, as defined above, the quantity of cash held, and its price in terms of each of the other assets, are simultaneously determined. These other assets may be commodities bought for immediate consumption, goods bought as a source of future consumption, or claims. In discussing the value or money one or other of these groups of assets has been isolated by writers. The prices of immediate consumption goods have been singled out and submitted to arithmetical operations of index-number computation; prices of other goods like raw materials, houses and land being sometimes added in, sometimes excluded, the so-called price level was obtained. On the other hand claims were bundled together—with or without an admixture of houses and land—and their prices described under the rubric "Interest Rate." Or sometimes separate bundles of claims, classified according to their duration, were made up, and a kind of average "short-term interest rate" and average "long-term interest rate" were calculated. The difference between the short- and long-term rate was vaguely associated with the risk premium, although the measurement of the price of risk obviously presupposes the fixing of a unit of risk, which was not done.

Strictly speaking, there is a multiplicity of asset prices. We may, however, depart from this purist standpoint and venture out into approximations, grouping or ranking assets in whatever way is relevant to the problem in hand; but then we must always remember that this procedure implies the use of the concept of a "representative investor" with given expectations and tastes. Bearing this in mind we may, for instance, isolate the influence of risk on price by comparing two asset-groups which differ from each other little except in respect to their (marginal) safety. Similarly, if we can find two asset-groups differing little except in respect to the year in which their yield accrues, we can roughly isolate the influence of the time of yield upon price—always assuming that investors' expectations are sufficiently uniform to allow us to interpret them as the expectations of the "representative investor." This is the rationale of the market rate of interest and the market risk premium.

Similarly, indices of "real income" are used as approximate measures of total utilities. Assets have no utilities, and there is, strictly, no market price which expresses the ratio of utilities of two yields. Yields are not traded, and assets, which are traded, give rise in general to bundles of yields. However, an approximation to the ratio of the utilities of two yields is given by the relative prices of two assets with negligible future yields and negligible risk—i.e., of two so-called non-durable consumption goods. Still assuming that all investors have the same expectations and tastes, and that gross yields do not vary very much in time or quality, an approximate measure of the relative utilities of the yields from two properties, or from all the properties in two economies could be obtained. We could then take as our measure simply the annual yield or (as yields are not traded) the annual quantity of consumption goods bought. This measure is probably at the back of economists' minds when they say that in order to measure real income we must use, not some general index, but an index of the cost of living. All indices are, however, only simplifications which are more or less liable to become unusable in the real world, owing to the non-uniformity of tastes and expectations, the inconstancy of the yield-flow through time and its variability in composition. We must therefore have a theory which does not collapse at the introduction of a touch of realism.

18. CHANGING DATA. Changes in (relative) prices and in quantities of assets, including cash, may be due to changes in any of the data, viz., to changes in tastes, changes in transformation conditions or changes in market conditions. It will be remembered that all these data are subjective, and changes in them may be due to mere changes in mood. Individuals' tastes may shift—for instance, safety preferences may decline. People will then reduce their reserves of cash and other safe assets; they will dishoard and drive up prices of, say, shares in terms of bonds and cash. On the other hand, a revision of the estimates of transformation conditions will cause the choice of yield-bundles which the investors regard as open to them, to change. For example, they may reduce their estimate of the difference in safety between, say, cash, bank notes, call money, bonds, on the one hand, and houses, durable plant, shares, on the other. In this case again the price of cash and the other assets in the first group will fall relatively to the prices of the second group. Further, if for any reason people's estimates of the degree of perfection in the market for, say, houses, increases, the price of

houses will rise; there will be dishoarding of cash, etc. If all yields become less safe the prices of saleable and plastic assets will rise relatively to those of others. Empirically, it is very difficult to ascribe dishoarding to a change in one particular type of data.

We can regard banks as individuals, and consider an increase in the note issue or in bank deposits as a result of decreased safety preference, or revision of estimated data, on the part of the banks. As before, there will result a rise in the price of other assets in terms of money. These considerations provide a link between the Quantity Theory of Money and the Theory of Asset Prices.

We have described how prices and quantities of assets at any given moment are determined by the data at that moment. In particular we have tried to show how the explanation of money prices and cash balances is to be found in the general theory of asset prices and quantities. A dynamic analysis, which is an explanation of the time sequence of prices or quantities, has not been attempted. Dynamic analysis implies additional hypotheses about how the data at one moment depend upon prices and quantities in preceding moments. It presupposes an inquiry, of the kind undertaken here, into the mechanism by which prices and quantities at each moment are determined by the data at that moment.

15

A LIQUIDITY PREFERENCE THEORY
OF MARKET PRICES*

By K. E. Boulding ||

The ultimate "causes of price"—to use a Classical term—lie
deeply embedded in the psychology and techniques of mankind
and his environment, and are as manifold as the sands of the sea.
All economic analysis is an attempt to classify these manifold
causes, to sort them out into categories of discourse that our limited
minds can handle, and so to perceive the unity of structural relationship which both unites and separates the manifoldness. Our
concepts of "demand" and "supply" are such broad categories. In
whatever sense they are used, they are not ultimate determinants
of anything, but they are convenient channels through which we
can classify and describe the effects of the multitude of determinants of the system of economic magnitudes. These ultimate determinants are, on the one hand, the patterns of choice between
alternatives of all individuals, and on the other, the pattern of technical limitation of resources such as labour time and raw materials
and the transformation functions of these resources into commodities and services. It is possible to show, algebraically, how these
billions of determinants operate to create and to change the structure of economic quantities (prices, volumes, etc.). Such algebraic
demonstration, after the manner of the Lausanne school, though
logically necessary, is not practically valuable in the solution of
particular problems.[1] For this task we need to be able to divide the
multitude of causes into a few broad workable categories, of which
the Marshallian demand and supply analysis is an admirable ex-

---

* *Economica*, New Series, Vol. IX (1944), pp. 55–63. Reprinted, by the
courtesy of the publisher and the author, with typographical corrections.

   || University of Michigan.

[1] The brilliant work of Professor Leontief *(The Structure of American
Economy, 1919–1929)* might seem at first sight to disprove this assertion. But
even Professor Leontief has to simplify his system of simultaneous equations
radically in order to obtain any results.

ample. It is not the purpose of this paper to overthrow the Marshallian methods, or to question their limited validity. Rather is it to suggest a new dichotomy of forces in the special case of market price in a competitive market, not into "demand" and "supply," but into "price determining factors" and "quantity determining factors." For many purposes it would seem that this new dichotomy is much more useful than the old, and leads to results which could not have been attained with the demand and supply apparatus.

It should be noted carefully that the situation discussed in this paper is that of the determination of market price in a perfectly competitive market on a single "day," the "day," of course, being as short as we wish to make it and being defined by the condition that the market is cleared and that all transactions which can be accomplished under existing conditions have been accomplished. This itself, of course, is a fiction, though a useful and necessary one: our mind finds it difficult to grasp the slippery and continuous processes of the actual world without first "fixing" each position in our mind before proceeding to the next. The simplest approach to dynamic economics is through a succession of static pictures, just as the representation of movement on the screen is obtained through a rapid succession of stationary projections. In the "market day" therefore we make the following assumptions: (i) the quantity of exchangeables (goods and money) possessed by all people in the market does not change during the course of the "day." All that happens is exchange, in the simplest and most literal sense of the word—i.e., a *rearrangement of ownership* of the goods and money in the market. At the end of the day some people have more money, some less; some have more commodity, some less, but the increases must be exactly balanced by the declines as the total quantities possessed by all marketers have not changed. (ii) We will assume that the price that clears the market is discovered immediately and prevails all through the "day," and that all transactions made during the "day" are made at that price. This assumption does not quite correspond to reality: nevertheless if the "day" is sufficiently short no serious errors are likely to be introduced by it, and it enables us to sidestep a number of highly difficult problems of secondary importance concerning the effect of transactions on the market.[2]

---

[2] Marshall, we may note, avoided the same set of problems in his discus-

The situation envisaged above must be distinguished sharply from the analysis of normal price by means of long-run demand and supply curves. In the normal price analysis we are considering an equilibrium of *flows* of commodity on and off the market. The demand curve in this case shows the average rate of consumption, and the supply curve the average rate of production, that would prevail at each price. It is dangerously easy to carry over habits of thought from the long-run analysis into the analysis of the market, yet the two are very distinct, and it must constantly be borne in mind in the following analysis that the quantities refer to *stocks*, both of commodity and money, that are shifted around in ownership, and do not refer to *flows* of production, consumption, .or income.

We will begin the analysis by considering the situation of a single marketer in a one-commodity market, possessing a quantity of money m_1 and a quantity of commodity a_1. His willingness to buy or sell can be described by his individual market demand-supply curve or function, showing what quantities of the commodity he will buy or sell at each price. This will normally be a continuous function: at high prices he will sell, at low prices he will buy, and at some intermediate price, which may be called the "null price" he will neither buy nor sell, being satisfied with the quantity in his possession. It is convenient to adopt the convention that purchases (because they add to the stocks of the purchaser) are positive in sign, and that sales are negative. We can then express the individual market demand-supply function by a single equation,

(1) $$q_1 = f_1(p)$$

A negative value of q_1 here represents an offer to sell, and a positive value an offer to buy.

In the market there will be a number of individuals, 1 to N, each having his own demand-supply function, $q_1 = f_1(p)$, $q_2 = f_2(p)$ ......$q_n = f_n(p)$. Knowing these functions we can immediately derive the market demand and market supply schedules by adding, for each value of p, the positive q's to get the total quantity demanded, Q_d, and the negative q's to get the total quantity supplied, Q_s. Thus we obtain the demand function, $Q_d = F_d(p)$ and the

---

sion of the "corn market" by assuming that the marginal utility of money remained constant.

supply function $Q_s = F_s(p)$, and the condition that the price must equate the quantity demanded and the quantity offered—i.e., $Q_d = Q_s$, gives us a third equation from which we can now derive the three unknowns, Q_d, Q_s, and p. This is the usual demand and supply market analysis.

There is, however, another way to approach the problem. If we add, algebraically, all the individual q's at each price we get a figure $Q_e = (Q_d - Q_s)$ which represents the excess demand or excess supply, according as it happens to be positive or negative. Thus by simple addition we derive from the individual demand-supply functions, an excess demand-supply function, $Q_e = F_e(p) = \Sigma f(p)$. Then at the equilibrium price we know that $Q_e = O$, i.e.,

(2) $$\Sigma f(p) = O$$

What has been done here is to separate out that element in the market situation which is responsible purely for the determination of price. Graphically, the price is given by the point at which the excess demand-supply curve (which I have elsewhere called the "total market curve"[3]) cuts the vertical (price) axis. The "height" of the excess demand-supply curve is in some sense an "average" of the heights of all the individual demand-supply curves from which it is derived. That is to say, the market price will be some kind of weighted average (the weight, of course, depending on the type of individual demand-supply function) of the "null prices" of the various marketers.[4] The "null price" of an individual's demand-supply curve is a measure of his willingness to buy, or what is the same thing, his unwillingness to sell. Any increase in

---

[3] Boulding, *Economic Analysis*, p. 73. See also Hicks, *Value and Capital*, p. 63.

[4] It is easy to show that when the individual demand-supply functions are linear the market price is the weighted average of the null prices of all the marketers, weighted by the slopes of each individual demand-supply curve. Thus let the individual demand-supply functions be $p_1 = h_1 q_1 + c_1$, $p_2 = h_2 q_2 + c_2$, ... $p_n = h_n q_n + c_n$. Then $c_1, c_2, \ldots c_n$ are the null prices of the various marketers. The equilibrium price p is given by equation (2), i.e.,

$$\frac{p}{h_1} - \frac{c_1}{h_1} + \frac{p}{h_2} - \frac{c_2}{h_2} + \ldots\ldots + \frac{p}{h_n} - \frac{c_n}{h_n} = 0$$

$$\text{i.e., } p = \frac{\dfrac{c_1}{h_1} + \dfrac{c_2}{h_2} + \ldots\ldots + \dfrac{c_n}{h_n}}{\dfrac{1}{h_1} + \dfrac{1}{h_2} + \ldots\ldots + \dfrac{1}{h_n}}$$

his willingness to buy raises his whole demand-supply schedule, and with it raises his null price. A rise in the market price therefore can only result from a general net increase in the willingness to buy the commodity in question. It is this, and no other factor, that determines price.

It is possible also to separate out those elements in the total market situation which determine the quantity exchanged. If all the demand-supply curves of the individual marketers passed through the same point on the price axis—i.e., if all the marketers had the same null price—the demand and supply curves would intersect on the price axis and there would be no exchanges on the market at all. There might be a market price quoted, but as this would of necessity be equal to the null prices of all the marketers, nothing would be bought or sold at that price. It is only because the different marketers have different degrees of willingness to buy or sell that transactions can take place at all. This property of the market we may call its "divergence," and it is this, and this alone, which determines the quantity exchanged. The greater the divergence of the individual demand-supply curves—i.e., the greater the spread of the null prices of the various marketers about the market price, the greater will be the quantity exchanged.[5]

We have now effected our new dichotomy of the forces in the

---

[5] Where the individual demand-supply functions are linear an algebraic formula for the quantity exchanged can be derived as follows, using the notation of footnote 4, p. 314. Let $c_1, c_2 \ldots c_k$ be the null prices of all those marketers whose null prices are greater than the market price, p. These are the buyers. The amount that buyer K will buy at the price p is $\dfrac{c_k - p}{h}$, and the total amount bought is

$$Q_d = \frac{c_1 - p}{h_1} + \frac{c_2 - p}{h_2} + \cdots + \frac{c_k - p}{h_k}$$

Similarly the marketers whose null prices are greater than p, $c_{k+1}, c_{k+2} \ldots c_n$, are the sellers, and the quantity sold, Q_s, is given by:

$$Q_s = \frac{c_{k+1} - p}{h_{k+1}} + \frac{c_{k+2} - p}{h_{k+2}} + \cdots + \frac{c_n - p}{h_n}$$

Q_s, of course, is equal to Q_d. The quantity exchanged, therefore, is equal to the weighted sum of either the positive or the negative deviations of the null prices from the market price weighted according to the reciprocal of the slope of the individual demand-supply curve. The greater these deviations—i.e., the greater the "divergence" in the market, the greater the quantity exchanged. If all the null prices were the same, then we should have $c_1 = c_2 = \cdots = c_k = \cdots = c_n = p$, and both Q_d and Q_s would be zero.

market, dividing them not into "supply" and "demand," but into "price determining" and "quantity determining" factors. The descriptive advantages of such a division are obvious, and it is interesting to compare the description of various changes under our analysis and under the old supply and demand analysis. Suppose, for instance, that we have a "pure" price-raising movement, through a uniform increase in the height of *all* the individual demand-supply curves. That is, there is a uniform increase in the willingness to buy, or what is the same thing, a uniform decrease in the willingness to sell. This is reflected merely in the price, the quantity exchanged remaining as before. In our analysis it is represented simply by a rise in the total market demand-supply curve, which now cuts the price axis at a higher price than before. In the demand and supply analysis this same movement would be represented by a rise in the market demand curve coupled with a fall in the market supply curve, the new point of intersection being at a higher price, but at the same quantity as before. These movements in the demand and supply curves, however, are not independent; they are both the result of a single force, the increase in the willingness to buy or unwillingness to sell expressed by the rise in the individual demand-supply curves. Indeed, a situation is hardly conceivable in which a change in market demand does not go hand in hand with a change in market supply. It is this interdependence of market demand and supply curves that makes them rather unsuitable for market analysis.

Similarly, when we have a "pure" change in market divergence, resulting in a change in the quantity bought without change in the price, the result is a change in *both* supply and demand curves, proceeding from the same course. Suppose that the divergence of the various individual null prices becomes wider, without any change in the market price. The quantity exchanged will increase. The market demand and supply curves will both move to the right, intersecting at a point representing a larger quantity, but the same price as before. The movement of both demand and supply curves thus follows from exactly the same cause: viz., the increase in market divergence. It is evident that the division of the market situation into "demand" on the one hand, and "supply" on the other, does not correspond to any very significant distinction within the structure of the market. The reason for this is clear: in a competitive market "buyers" and "sellers" are not distinct groups of people, separate from each other. Any marketer may be a buyer at one price and a seller at a higher price: every rise in prices induces some who were previously in the buyer's camp to cross over into the seller's, and every fall in prices has the reverse effect. Hence the demand and supply curves cannot be independent: they represent only a momentary division of the market, and will invariably move together except in the unlikely case of exactly counterbalancing changes in eagerness to buy and in market divergence. This is not the case, it should be noticed, in the case of the long-run demand and supply analysis: the producers and consumers of a single commodity are usually different groups of people, with only a little overlapping. In this case it is reasonable to assume that demand and supply curves are independent of each other and of the price, and hence they have much more individual meaning and validity.

We can now take yet another step in the analysis, and actually define an equation for the individual demand-supply curve on a simple and plausible assumption. From this we shall go on to derive a simple yet revolutionary formula which gives us the market price itself. The assumption is that each marketer wishes to hold a certain proportion of his total capital resources in the form of money, which we will call the *preferred liquidity ratio, r,* or his "liquidity preference," and that this proportion is independent of the absolute level of the price of the commodity. As we shall see, the preferred liquidity ratio is by no means independent of anticipated changes in prices, but there seems to be no reason to suppose that it would be affected by the actual level of absolute prices. This assumption alone is sufficient to give us an equation for the individual demand-supply curve and a simple formula for market price.

Let an individual marketer possess a quantity of money m_1, a quantity of commodity a_1, and suppose that his preferred liquidity ratio is r_1. Let q_1 be the quantity of commodity that he exchanges in the "day": q_1 if positive will represent a purchase, if negative, a sale. Let the price be p_1. Then we will assume to begin with that he possesses only commodity A and money, and that no other commodities enter into the market, or, what is perhaps more realistic, that his other possessions and transactions do not affect his transactions in commodity A. Then after he has completed his transactions the total amount of commodity he possesses is $a_1 + q_1$, and the total amount of money is $m_1 - p_1 q_1$. The total value of commodity possessed by him is $p_1 a_1 + p_1 q_1$. The total value of his holdings of money and commodity combined is therefore $(p_1 a_1 + p_1 q_1) + (m_1 - p_1 q_1) = p_1 a_1 + m_1$. It will be noticed that the total value of his holdings is not affected by the exchanges he makes, as what he receives is always equal in value to what he gives up. After his exchanges have been completed the ratio of the money he now possesses to the value of his total holdings should equal his preferred liquidity ratio, r_1, for presumably the *object* of his transactions was to rearrange the form of his possessions into the desired liquidity ratio. We have, therefore,

$$(3a) \qquad r_1 = \frac{m_1 - p_1 q_1}{m_1 + p_1 a_1}$$

This equation can also be written:

$$(3b) \qquad p_1 = \frac{m_1(1 - r_1)}{r_1 a_1 + q_1}$$

or

$$(3c) \qquad q_1 = \frac{m_1(1 - r_1)}{p_1} - r_1 a_1$$

This is the equation of the individual's demand-supply curve, for it shows what quantity of the commodity he will buy or sell at each price in order to achieve his preferred liquidity ratio. It is a rectangular hyperbola, asymptotic to the quantity axis at $q = \infty$, and to the line $q_1 = - r_1 a_1$ at $p_1 = \infty$. This expresses the fact that an individual will never sell a greater proportion of the commodity that he possesses than his liquidity ratio, and will only sell all the commodity he possesses if he wants to have all his holdings in the form of money (i.e., if $r = 1$). The asymmetry between buying and selling is interesting: no matter how high the price rises the amount an individual is willing to sell cannot go beyond a certain point. There is no limit, however, to the increase in the amount that an individual is willing to buy as the price falls, for with each fall in price the purchasing power of his money increases.

    It is now easy to obtain a formula for the market price, knowing the quantities of money and of commodity possessed by each marketer, and knowing the preferred liquidity ratio of each. Denoting the quantities associated with the various marketers by suffixes 1, 2, ... n, and applying equation 2 we have immediately the market price, p, given by equation (4):

$$(4) \quad p = \frac{m_1(1 - r_1) + m_2(1 - r_2) + \cdots + m_n(1 - r_n)}{r_1 a_1 + r_2 a_2 + \cdots + r_n a_n}$$

This is a most instructive equation. It shows at once that an increase in the quantity of money, or a decrease in the quantity of commodity, possessed by any marketer, or a decrease in the preferred liquidity ratio of any marketer, will raise the price. It shows also that the effect on the price produced by a change in the quantity of money or of commodity possessed by any marketer depends on his preferred liquidity ratio. A change in the stock of commodity will have a larger effect on price if it is felt by those marketers with the higher liquidity preference. A change in the stock of money will have a larger effect on price if it is felt by those with a lower liquidity preference. Thus if new money gets into the hands of "hoarders" with high liquidity preference it will have less effect on price than if it gets into the hands of individuals with small liquidity preference (spenders). The equation also shows two interesting extreme cases. that if the preferred liquidity ratio is zero—i.e., if people do not wish to hold any money—the price will be infinite; if the preferred liquidity ratio is 1, so that people wish to hold all their resources in the form of money and none in the form of commodities, then the price will fall to zero. It also shows that when liquidity preference is high, a change in the stocks of commodity produces a greater effect on price than a change in the stocks of money. On the other hand, when liquidity preference is low, changes in the stocks of money produce more effect than changes in stocks of commodities.

If the preferred liquidity ratio of all individuals is the same and equal to r, equation (4) reduces to the very simple form

$$(5) \quad p = \frac{M(1 - r)}{Ar}$$

where M is the total stock of money in the market and A is the total stock of commodity. Even if the preferred liquidity ratios of the various individuals differ, equation (5) is still highly significant: r then means the "average" or "market" liquidity ratio. It is the proportion of the value of liquid property to the value of all property which the market as a whole feels is most desirable. The market liquidity ratio, r, is not a simple average of the individual ratios, however, but a complex weighted average.[6]

The important equation (5) can easily be derived directly, without reference back to individual preferences. The total value of goods and money owned by marketers is $pA + M$. If r is the preferred liquidity ratio for the market as a whole, therefore, we have

$$r = \frac{M}{pA + M,}$$

which when transposed immediately gives equation (5). This equation should be compared with Fisher's equation of exchange, to which it bears some resemblance. The liquidity preference concept and the concept of velocity of circulation are at bottom different ways of expressing the same phenomenon. It would be quite possible to apply equation (5) to the general price level. In that case p would represent the price level, M the total quantity

---

[6] We have, combining equations (4) and (5)

$$\frac{M(1 - r)}{Ar} = \frac{m_1(1 - r_1) + m_2(1 - r_2) + \ldots + m_n(1 - r_n)}{a_1 r_1 + a_2 r_2 + \ldots + a_n r_n}$$

(6)   whence $r = \dfrac{M \Sigma a_i r_i}{AM + M \Sigma a_i r_i - A \Sigma r_i m_i}$

If money and commodity were equally distributed among all the marketers this equation would reduce to the simple average of the individual r's—i.e., $r = \dfrac{\Sigma r_i}{n}$. Where there is not this equal division it should be noticed that the market liquidity ratio, r, could change somewhat even if the individual preferred ratios, r_1, r_2, etc., did not change, through a change in the a's and m's. It is not, therefore, a wholly satisfactory measure of liquidity preference, but the same difficulty is encountered in any weighted average. Yet another simplification can be made: if it is assumed that the ratio of the amount of commodity to the amount of money possessed by each marketer is the same—i.e. $\dfrac{a_1}{m_1} = \dfrac{a_2}{m_2} = \ldots = \dfrac{a_n}{m_n} = K$, then equation (6) reduces to $r = \dfrac{\Sigma a_i r_i}{A}$, i.c., the market ratio is the weighted average of the individual ratio, weighted by the amount of commodity possessed by each marketer. In such a case a decline in the amount of commodity possessed by a marketer with a liquidity preference, above the average, would tend to lower the market ratio even if the individual ratios did not change. Such an interpretation of the market ratio, however, is not unreasonable, and the assumption on which it is based is not likely to be far from the truth.

of money, A the total quantity of commodities and other valuta not including money, and r would be the general liquidity preference ratio. An increase in liquidity preference is the same thing as a decline in the velocity of circulation—i.e., it represents an increased desire for money and therefore a decreased willingness to spend it. The ratio $\dfrac{(1 - r)}{r}$ may therefore be called the "velocity ratio," v: it rises and falls, along with the velocity of circulation of money, as r falls and rises. The differences between equation (5)—which may perhaps be called the "equation of price determination" and Fisher's equation of exchange are, however, highly significant. Equation (5) interprets prices in terms of *stocks* of commodities and of money, coupled with a preference factor. Fisher's equation describes simply an identity of *flows*: of money on the one hand and of the value of goods on the other. Although useful in many ways, it fails to give any causal explanations of the determination of price, for price and the quantity exchanged are always determined together; hence an equation which includes the volume of transactions is useless as an explanation of prices, for the volume of transactions is one of the unknowns which has to be determined along with price. Equation (5) has the advantage that all its components, except price, are historically determined or are given as data: the stock of money, the stock of goods, and the preferred liquidity ratios are objective facts at any moment of time, and may truly be described as the only short-run determinants of market price. There still remains the question "what determines the stocks and the preferences": that, however, is a long-run problem of normal price.

From the stocks and preferences data we can also derive a formula which gives the quantity exchanged, or the volume of transactions in the "day." The null price of marketer I, c_1, is found by putting $q_1 = O$ in equation 3b, whence

$$(7) \qquad\qquad c_1 = \frac{m_1(1 - r_1)}{r_1 a_1}$$

Substituting the value of $m_1(1 - r_1)$ from equation 7 into equation (3c) we have:

$$q_1 = \frac{r_1 a_1}{p}\,(c_1 - p_1)$$

If the subscripts 1 to k represent the buyers in the market—i.e., those individuals whose null prices are greater than the market price, then the total volume of transactions, Q, is given by:

$$(8) \qquad Q = \Sigma_1^k q_i = \Sigma_1^k \frac{r_i a_i}{p} (c_1 - p)$$

The volume of transactions is again seen to depend on the divergence of the null prices of the various marketers from the market price.

Substituting the value of p from equation 4 in equation 3c, summing $\Sigma_1^k q_1$ and simplifying, we arrive at the general formula for the quantity exchanged,

$$(9)$$
$$Q = \frac{M_d \Sigma_{k+i}^n r_i a_i - M_s \Sigma_i^k r_i a_i + (\Sigma_i^k r_i a_i)(\Sigma_{k+i}^n r_i m_i) - (\Sigma_{k+i}^n r_i a_i)(\Sigma_i^k r_i m_i)}{M - \Sigma_i^n m_i r_i}$$

If the liquidity preference of each marketer was equal to r, the formula simplifies to:

$$(10) \qquad Q = \frac{r(A_s M_d - A_d M_s)}{M}$$

where A_d and A_s respectively signify the amounts of commodity possessed by buyers and by sellers, and M_d and M_s represent the quantity of money possessed by buyers and sellers. Although this formula is suggestive, it is not as useful as might at first sight appear, for as we have seen there is no clear distinction in the market between buyers and sellers. Nevertheless the formula suggests roughly that a rise in the quantity of commodity, or a fall in the quantity of money held by the "sellers" side of the market will tend to raise the volume of transactions, while a rise in the quantity of commodity or a fall in the quantity of money held by the "buyers" side of the market will have the opposite effect. It also suggests that a rise in liquidity preference, or a fall in the total quantity of money held in the market will have a general tendency to increase the volume of transactions, though this result is not necessary.

The analysis can now be extended without much difficulty to include any number of commodities. Suppose that there are Z commodities, A, B, C, ... Z. Let the total value of all these commodities, plus the money held by the marketers be v. By "commodity" we here mean anything that has monetary value: it therefore includes securities and other valuta. We can now express the "commodity preference" for each commodity as the preferred ratio of the value of the commodity to the total value of all things, including money, held in the market. Thus if p_a is the price of commodity A, and A is the amount held by the marketers, the "commodity preference ratio" for commodity A, r_a, is given by the equation:

$$(11) \qquad r_a = \frac{Ap_a}{v}$$

If M is the total quantity of money held in the market, and r_m is the liquidity preference ratio, we have:

$$(12) \qquad r_m = \frac{M}{v}$$

Eliminating V between these two equations we have:

$$(13) \qquad p_a = \frac{Mr_a}{Ar}$$

Similarly for the other commodities we have:

$$(13) \qquad p_b = \frac{Mr_b}{Br} , \; p_c = \frac{Mr_c}{Cr} \; \cdots \; p_z = \frac{Mr_z}{Zr}$$

It follows that an increase in the quantity of money, or a decrease in liquidity preference, will raise *all* prices. An increase in the quantity of any one commodity will lower the price of that commodity; if the preferences of the market do not change, however, an increase in the quantity of one commodity will not change the prices of any other commodity.[7] This will only be true where the commodity is neither a substitute for nor a complement of any other commodity: i.e., where $\frac{\delta r_b}{\delta a} = \frac{\delta r_c}{\delta a,} = \cdots = \frac{\delta r_z}{\delta a} = 0$. If the commodity A has a substitute, B, then an increased quantity of A in the hands of the marketers will cause a decrease in the preference for B: i.e., $\frac{\delta r_b}{\delta a}$ is negative. If the commodity A has a *comple-ment*, C, then an increased quantity of A will cause an *increase* in the preference for C—i.e., $\frac{\delta r_c}{\delta a}$ is positive. In such a case an

---

[7] It will, of course, lower the price level in so far as its own price is lowered.

increase in the quantity of A will cause a decrease in the price of the substitute, B, and an increase in the price of the complement, C, according to equations (13). We see therefore that this method provides an easy solution for the problem of relatedness in demand.

It must be observed that there cannot be a change in one preference ratio without there being an equal compensating change in the sum of all other preference ratios, for the sum of all the preference ratios must be equal to unity: i.e.,

$$(14) \qquad r_a + r_b + \ldots + r_z + r_m = 1$$

It follows that a change in price which is due to a change in *preference*, as opposed to a change in the quantities of goods or money, must be accompanied by opposite changes in other prices, unless it is counterbalanced by an equal and opposite change in liquidity preference or in quantities. Thus if the *preference* of the market for commodity A increases, without there being any change in the preference for money or in the quantities held, there must be not only a rise in the price of A but also a fall in the price of other commodities.

The mathematically inclined reader will not find it difficult to derive the general formulæ relating the price of each commodity to the individual preference ratios of each marketer for each commodity and for money. A general formula for the quantities exchanged can also be developed for the many-commodity case. As these formulæ involve complex and unresolvable determinants, however, they are of no practical value that I can discover, and are omitted.

The implications of the above analysis for economic theory are, I believe, profound. It is, in the first place, a powerful instrument for the unification of many parts of our existing theoretical structure which hitherto have been rather unrelated. It unifies, for instance, the theory of general prices and the theory of particular prices. As we have seen, if P is the general price level, W the total stock of all valuta, excluding money, R_w is the general commodity preference ratio and R_m the liquidity or money preference ratio, we have a formula for the general price level exactly analogous to equations (13) and (5):

$$(15) \qquad P = \frac{MR_w}{WR_m} = \frac{M(1 - R_m)}{WR_m}$$

This price-level formula has an important contribution to make to the understanding of the crisis of late capitalism in which we seem to be living. The most striking feature of the past twenty years has been the strength of the deflationary forces in the western world. Equation (15) gives an important clue to this mystery. We see immediately that the total *value* of the stock of goods (PW) is equal to the quantity of money, M, multiplied by the "preference factor," R_w/R_m. It follows that if the quantity of money and the preference factor are constant, the total value of the stock of goods cannot change, for every increase in the quantity of goods will result in a proportionate decline in their price. In such a case investment, in the financial sense, is absolutely impossible, for by investment we mean the *increase* through time of the total value of goods. (By "goods," of course, we mean all physical capital.) Investment is only possible if either the quantity of money increases or liquidity preference declines, no matter how rapid the accumulation of physical capital. The rate of investment therefore depends, paradoxically enough, directly on the monetary situation, and only indirectly on the rate of accumulation of goods. It follows immediately that if there is no change in the preference ratios the rate of investment is equal to the rate of growth of the monetary stock. In the absence of a growth of the monetary stock or a fall in liquidity preference the accumulation of physical capital must inevitably result in a deflationary movement of prices.

The commodity preference ratio is likely to fall and the liquidity preference ratio to rise on the expectation of falling prices, for when prices are falling the purchasing power of stocks of money is continually increasing while the money value of a given stock of commodities is declining. This in itself is sufficient to account for the self-justifying nature of price anticipations: if people expect a fall in prices, R_m will rise and R_w will fall and P will fall in the absence of counterbalancing changes, whereas if people expect a rise in prices R_m will fall and R_w will rise and a rise in prices will ensue.

There is no reason to suppose also that commodity preference will decline and liquidity preference increase as the total stock of goods increases. There is no point in piling up stocks for ever, and in the course of accumulation the time must come when further accumulation becomes less and less desirable. This will be reflected in a declining rate of profit, which will make the holding of goods less attractive relative to the holding of money. When accumulation has proceeded to the point where stocks of most physical goods are large there will be a deflationary force operating due to the decline in commodity preference. This will be re-inforced by the expectation of declining prices; hence even if money stocks keep pace with stocks of goods, there will still be a powerful deflationary force operating. In such a period a rapid increase in money stocks will be necessary to keep the price level constant. The equilibrium of the price system, however, will be difficult to maintain because of the expectational factor.

The present analysis also enables us to see the so-called "liquid-ity preference" theory of interest as merely a special case of equa-tion (13). The true money rate of interest to be expected from a security is determined at any moment by the price of that security. The higher the price of the security, the lower the rate of interest assuming that the future payments accruing to the owner of the security do not change. There is no such thing, strictly, as a "market rate of interest"—it is not the rate of interest that is determined in the market, but the price of securities—i.e., of expected future payments-series. The rate of interest itself is not a price, like the price of wheat: it does not have the dimensions of price. It is merely a certain mathematical property of a series of expected payments and their present price. The price of securities is not determined by the rate of interest; the expected rate of interest (and all rates of interest are expected) is determined by the secu-rity's present price. The price of a security is determined by the same factors that determine the price of any commodity—the quan-tity of money in the market, the quantity of the security in the market, the liquidity preference ratio and the security preference ratio (the proportion of total resources which the market wishes to hold in the form of the particular security). Thus if S is the quantity of the security held, R_s the security preference ratio, the price of the security is given by equation (13): $P_s = \dfrac{MR_s}{SR_m}$. We see therefore that the price of a security will be increased, and the rate of interest will therefore be lowered, by an increase in the quantity of money, by a decrease in the quantity of the security, by an increase in security preference or by a decrease in liquidity preference.

A formal explanation of the difference in apparent yields of various classes and terms of securities can be given in terms of the "security preference" concept. Where a security or other item of property has certain desirable qualities apart from its monetary return—such as, for instance voting privileges, or a high degree of salability, or a certain prestige value, its "security preference" will be high, its price high and the rate of return correspondingly low.

The extension of the principles of this paper to the theory of the firm, to the labour market, and to the theory of monopoly and imperfect competition must wait for another paper. Instead of treating the firm primarily as a profit and loss account, as is done in the usual marginal analysis, it can be treated as a balance sheet, and its decisions described in terms of their effects on the balance sheet rather than on the income account. Thus a purchase of anything, whether it be raw materials, equipment, or labour, involves an asset transfer—a reduction in liquid assets and an increase in illiquid assets. Similarly a sale involves a reduction in illiquid assets and a gain in liquid assets. The willingness of firms to buy and sell can therefore be explained partly in terms of their preferred liquidity ratio. This aspect of a firm's behaviour is strictly analogous to the type of analysis we have employed in this paper. There is, of course, an additional complication that firms buy and sell not merely to change the form of their assets, but to increase their net worth. This is the sole assumption behind the refined marginal analysis. Thus it is assumed that a firm will extend its purchases of each factor of production until the discounted marginal productivity of the factor is equal to its marginal cost. The discounted marginal productivity, however, is what the purchase of the factor adds to the illiquid assets of the firm; its marginal cost is what the purchase of the factor subtracts from the liquid assets. We can rephrase the marginal productivity condition, therefore, and say that a firm will extend its purchases of any factor as long as there is a net addition to its assets. It will be seen immediately that the marginal productivity analysis assumes that the firm is quite indifferent as to the *form* of its assets—i.e., has an infinite number of preferred liquidity ratios. This assumption is very far from the truth, and changes in the liquidity preference of firms, as well as the composition of their assets, may have profound effects on their demand for factors of production. This is a factor that has been largely neglected in the theory of the firm, although it is implicit in much recent monetary analysis. The effects of an increase in liquid balances on the demand for labour and on the level of employment can hardly be explained without some reference to the liquidity preference factors in the demand for input.

This "asset-transfer" type of analysis provides, I believe, the most useful stepping-stone to the analysis of dynamic problems. Not only does it provide us with an "instantaneous" picture of price determination which can then serve as a basis for the "moving picture" technique of describing dynamic changes, but it also gives us a parameter which can reflect all the forces operating from the side of the future: viz., the preference ratios. Not only, therefore, have we separated out of the chaos of causes the price-determining and the quantity-determining factors; in the price-determining factors themselves we have distinguished between those that operate from the results of the past and those that operate from the expectations of the future. The quantity of money and of goods are given to us as a result of past events. The preference ratios are in part determined by future expectations. It would be difficult to devise a more suitable dichotomy for the analysis of the well-nigh inconceivable fluxes of reality.

IV. THE RATIONALE OF THE FIRM

16

THE NATURE OF THE FIRM *

By R. H. Coase ||

Economic theory has suffered in the past from a failure to state clearly its assumptions. Economists in building up a theory have often omitted to examine the foundations on which it was erected. This examination is, however, essential not only to prevent the misunderstanding and needless controversy which arise from a lack of knowledge of the assumptions on which a theory is based, but also because of the extreme importance for economics of good judgment in choosing between rival sets of assumptions. For instance, it is suggested that the use of the word "firm" in economics may be different from the use of the term by the "plain man."[1] Since there is apparently a trend in economic theory towards starting analysis with the individual firm and not with the industry,[2] it is all the more necessary not only that a clear definition of the word "firm" should be given but that its difference from a firm in the "real world," if it exists, should be made clear. Mrs. Robinson has said that "the two questions to be asked of a set of assumptions in economics are: Are they tractable? and: Do they correspond with the real world?"[3] Though, as Mrs. Robinson points out, "more often one set will be manageable and the other realistic," yet there may well be branches of theory where assumptions may be both manageable and realistic. It is hoped to show in the following paper that a definition of a firm may be obtained which is not only realistic in that it corresponds to what is meant by a firm in the real world, but is tractable by two of the most

* *Economica*, New Series, Vol. IV (1937), pp. 386–405. Reprinted, by the courtesy of the publisher and the author, without change from the original text.

|| University of Buffalo.

[1] Joan Robinson, *Economics is a Serious Subject,* p. 12.

[2] See N. Kaldor, "The Equilibrium of the Firm," *The Economic Journal,* March 1934.

[3] *Op. cit.,* p. 6.

powerful instruments of economic analysis developed by Marshall, the idea of the margin and that of substitution, together giving the idea of substitution at the margin.[4] Our definition must, of course, "relate to formal relations which are capable of being *conceived* exactly."[5]

I

It is convenient if, in searching for a definition of a firm, we first consider the economic system as it is normally treated by the economist. Let us consider the description of the economic system given by Sir Arthur Salter.[6] "The normal economic system works itself. For its current operation it is under no central control, it needs no central survey. Over the whole range of human activity and human need, supply is adjusted to demand, and production to consumption, by a process that is automatic, elastic and responsive." An economist thinks of the economic system as being co-ordinated by the price mechanism and society becomes not an organisation but an organism.[7] The economic system "works itself." This does not mean that there is no planning by individuals. These exercise foresight and choose between alternatives. This is necessarily so if there is to be order in the system. But this theory assumes that the direction of resources is dependent directly on the price mechanism. Indeed, it is often considered to be an objection to economic planning that it merely tries to do what is already done by the price mechanism.[8] Sir Arthur Salter's description, however, gives a very incomplete picture of our economic system. Within a firm, the description does not fit at all. For instance, in economic theory we find that the allocation of factors of production between different uses is determined by the price mechanism. The price of factor A becomes higher in X than in Y. As a result, A moves from Y to X until the difference be-

---

[4] J. M. Keynes, *Essays in Biography*, pp. 223–224.

[5] L. Robbins, *Nature and Significance of Economic Science*, p. 63.

[6] This description is quoted with approval by D. H. Robertson, *Control of Industry*, p. 85, and by Professor Arnold Plant, "Trends in Business Administration," *Economica*, February 1932. It appears in *Allied Shipping Control*, pp. 16–17.

[7] See F. A. Hayek, "The Trend of Economic Thinking," *Economica*, May 1933.

[8] See F. A. Hayek, *op. cit.*

tween the prices in X and Y, except in so far as it compensates for other differential advantages, disappears. Yet in the real world, we find that there are many areas where this does not apply. If a workman moves from department Y to department X, he does not go because of a change in relative prices, but because he is ordered to do so. Those who object to economic planning on the grounds that the problem is solved by price movements can be answered by pointing out that there is planning within our economic system which is quite different from the individual planning mentioned above and which is akin to what is normally called economic planning. The example given above is typical of a large sphere in our modern economic system. Of course, this fact has not been ignored by economists. Marshall introduces organisation as a fourth factor of production; J. B. Clark gives the co-ordinating function to the entrepreneur; Professor Knight introduces managers who co-ordinate. As D. H. Robertson points out, we find "islands of conscious power in this ocean of unconscious co-operation like lumps of butter coagulating in a pail of buttermilk."[9] But in view of the fact that it is usually argued that co-ordination will be done by the price mechanism, why is such organisation necessary? Why are there these "islands of conscious power"? Outside the firm, price movements direct production, which is co-ordinated through a series of exchange transactions on the market. Within a firm, these market transactions are eliminated and in place of the complicated market structure with exchange transactions is substituted the entrepreneur-co-ordinator, who directs production.[10] It is clear that these are alternative methods of co-ordinating production. Yet, having regard to the fact that if production is regulated by price movements, production could be carried on without any organisation at all, well might we ask, why is there any organisation?

Of course, the degree to which the price mechanism is superseded varies greatly. In a department store, the allocation of the different sections to the various locations in the building may be done by the controlling authority or it may be the result of

---

[9] *Op. cit.*, p. 85.

[10] In the rest of this paper I shall use the term entrepreneur to refer to the person or persons who, in a competitive system, take the place of the price mechanism in the direction of resources.

competitive price bidding for space. In the Lancashire cotton industry, a weaver can rent power and shop-room and can obtain looms and yarn on credit.[11] This co-ordination of the various factors of production is, however, normally carried out without the intervention of the price mechanism. As is evident, the amount of "vertical" integration, involving as it does the supersession of the price mechanism, varies greatly from industry to industry and from firm to firm.

It can, I think, be assumed that the distinguishing mark of the firm is the supersession of the price mechanism. It is, of course, as Professor Robbins points out, "related to an outside network of relative prices and costs,"[12] but it is important to discover the exact nature of this relationship. This distinction between the allocation of resources in a firm and the allocation in the economic system has been very vividly described by Mr. Maurice Dobb when discussing Adam Smith's conception of the capitalist: "It began to be seen that there was something more important than the relations inside each factory or unit captained by an undertaker; there were the relations of the undertaker with the rest of the economic world outside his immediate sphere . . . . the undertaker busies himself with the division of labour inside each firm and he plans and organises consciously," but "he is related to the much larger economic specialisation, of which he himself is merely one specialised unit. Here, he plays his part as a single cell in a larger organism, mainly unconscious of the wider rôle he fills."[13]

In view of the fact that while economists treat the price mechanism as a co-ordinating instrument, they also admit the co-ordinating function of the "entrepreneur," it is surely important to enquire why co-ordination is the work of the price mechanism in one case and of the entrepreneur in another. The purpose of this paper is to bridge what appears to be a gap in economic theory between the assumption (made for some purposes) that resources are allocated by means of the price mechanism and the

---

[11] *Survey of Textile Industries*, p. 26.

[12] *Op. cit.*, p. 71.

[13] *Capitalist Enterprise and Social Progress*, p. 20. Cf., also, Henderson. *Supply and Demand*, pp. 3–5.

assumption (made for other purposes) that this allocation is dependent on the entrepreneur-co-ordinator. We have to explain the basis on which, in practice, this choice between alternatives is effected.[14]

II

Our task is to attempt to discover why a firm emerges at all in a specialised exchange economy. The price mechanism (considered purely from the side of the direction of resources) might be superseded if the relationship which replaced it was desired for its own sake. This would be the case, for example, if some people preferred to work under the direction of some other person. Such individuals would accept less in order to work under someone, and firms would arise naturally from this. But it would appear that this cannot be a very important reason, for it would rather seem that the opposite tendency is operating if one judges from the stress normally laid on the advantage of "being one's own master."[15] Of course, if the desire was not to be controlled but to control, to exercise power over others, then people might be willing to give up something in order to direct others; that is, they would be willing to pay others more than they could get under the price mechanism in order to be able to direct them. But this implies that those who direct pay in order to be able to

---

[14] It is easy to see when the State takes over the direction of an industry that, in planning it, it is doing something which was previously done by the price mechanism. What is usually not realised is that any business man in organising the relations between his departments is also doing something which could be organised through the price mechanism. There is therefore point in Mr. Durbin's answer to those who emphasise the problems involved in economic planning that the same problems have to be solved by business men in the competitive system. (See "Economic Calculus in a Planned Economy," *The Economic Journal*, December 1936.) The important difference between these two cases is that economic planning is imposed on industry while firms arise voluntarily because they represent a more efficient method of organising production. In a competitive system, there is an "optimum" amount of planning!

[15] Cf. Harry Dawes, "Labour Mobility in the Steel Industry," *The Economic Journal*, March 1934, who instances "the trek to retail shopkeeping and insurance work by the better paid of skilled men due to the desire (often the main aim in life of a worker) to be independent" (p. 86).

do this and are not paid to direct, which is clearly not true in the majority of cases.[16] Firms might also exist if purchasers preferred commodities which are produced by firms to those not so produced; but even in spheres where one would expect such preferences (if they exist) to be of negligible importance, firms are to be found in the real world.[17] Therefore there must be other elements involved.

The main reason why it is profitable to establish a firm would seem to be that there is a cost of using the price mechanism. The most obvious cost of "organising" production through the price mechanism is that of discovering what the relevant prices are.[18] This cost may be reduced but it will not be eliminated by the emergence of specialists who will sell this information. The costs of negotiating and concluding a separate contract for each exchange transaction which takes place on a market must also be taken into account.[19] Again, in certain markets, e.g., produce exchanges, a technique is devised for minimising these contract costs; but they are not eliminated. It is true that contracts are not eliminated when there is a firm but they are greatly reduced. A factor of production (or the owner thereof) does not have to make a series of contracts with the factors with whom he is co-operating within the firm, as would be necessary, of course, if this co-operation were as a direct result of the working of the price mechanism. For this series of contracts is substituted one. At this stage, it is important to note the character of the contract into which a factor enters that is employed within a firm. The contract is one whereby

---

[16] None the less, this is not altogether fanciful. Some small shopkeepers are said to earn less than their assistants.

[17] G. F. Shove, "The Imperfection of the Market: a Further Note," *The Economic Journal,* March 1933, p. 116, note 1, points out that such preferences may exist, although the example he gives is almost the reverse of the instance given in the text.

[18] According to N. Kaldor, "A Classificatory Note of the Determinateness of Equilibrium," *The Review of Economic Studies,* February 1934, it is one of the assumptions of static theory that "All the relevant prices are known to all individuals." But this is clearly not true of the real world.

[19] This influence was noted by Professor Usher when discussing the development of capitalism. He says: "The successive buying and selling of partly finished products were sheer waste of energy." (*Introduction to the Industrial History of England,* p. 13). But he does not develop the idea nor consider why it is that buying and selling operations still exist.

the factor, for a certain remuneration (which may be fixed or fluctuating), agrees to obey the directions of an entrepreneur *within
certain limits*.[20] The essence of the contract is that it should only
state the limits to the powers of the entrepreneur. Within these
limits, he can therefore direct the other factors of production.

There are, however, other disadvantages—or costs—of using
the price mechanism. It may be desired to make a long-term contract for the supply of some article or service. This may be due
to the fact that if one contract is made for a longer period, instead
of several shorter ones, then certain costs of making each contract
will be avoided. Or, owing to the risk attitude of the people concerned, they may prefer to make a long rather than a short-term
contract. Now, owing to the difficulty of forecasting, the longer
the period of the contract is for the supply of the commodity or
service, the less possible, and indeed, the less desirable it is for
the person purchasing to specify what the other contracting party
is expected to do. It may well be a matter of indifference to the
person supplying the service or commodity which of several courses
of action is taken, but not to the purchaser of that service or
commodity. But the purchaser will not know which of these several courses he will want the supplier to take. Therefore, the
service which is being provided is expressed in general terms,
the exact details being left until a later date. All that is stated
in the contract is the limits to what the persons supplying the
commodity or service is expected to do. The details of what the
supplier is expected to do is not stated in the contract but is
decided later by the purchaser. When the direction of resources
(within the limits of the contract) becomes dependent on the buyer
in this way, that relationship which I term a "firm" may be
obtained.[21] A firm is likely therefore to emerge in those cases
where a very short term contract would be unsatisfactory. It is

---

[20] It would be possible for no limits to the powers of the entrepreneur to
be fixed. This would be voluntary slavery. According to Professor Batt, *The
Law of Master and Servant*, p. 18, such a contract would be void and un-
enforceable.

[21] Of course, it is not possible to draw a hard and fast line which determines whether there is a firm or not. There may be more or less direction. It
is similar to the legal question of whether there is the relationship of master
and servant or principal and agent. See the discussion of this problem below.

obviously of more importance in the case of services—labour—than it is in the case of the buying of commodities. In the case of commodities, the main items can be stated in advance and the details which will be decided later will be of minor significance.

We may sum up this section of the argument by saying that the operation of a market costs something and by forming an organisation and allowing some authority (an "entrepreneur") to direct the resources, certain marketing costs are saved. The entrepreneur has to carry out his function at less cost, taking into account the fact that he may get factors of production at a lower price than the market transactions which he supersedes, because it is always possible to revert to the open market if he fails to do this.

The question of uncertainty is one which is often considered to be very relevant to the study of the equilibrium of the firm. It seems improbable that a firm would emerge without the existence of uncertainty. But those, for instance, Professor Knight, who make the *mode of payment* the distinguishing mark of the firm—fixed incomes being guaranteed to some of those engaged in production by a person who takes the residual, and fluctuating, income—would appear to be introducing a point which is irrelevant to the problem we are considering. One entrepreneur may sell his services to another for a certain sum of money, while the payment to his employees may be mainly or wholly a share in profits.[22] The significant question would appear to be why the allocation of resources is not done directly by the price mechanism.

Another factor that should be noted is that exchange transactions on a market and the same transactions organised within a firm are often treated differently by Governments or other bodies with regulatory powers. If we consider the operation of a sales tax, it is clear that it is a tax on market transactions and not on the same transactions organised within the firm. Now since these are alternative methods of "organisation"—by the price mechanism or by the entrepreneur—such a regulation would bring into existence firms which otherwise would have no *raison d'être*. It would furnish a reason for the emergence of a firm in a specialised exchange economy. Of course, to the extent that firms already

---

[22] The views of Professor Knight are examined below in more detail.

exist, such a measure as a sales tax would merely tend to make them larger than they would otherwise be. Similarly, quota schemes, and methods of price control which imply that there is rationing, and which do not apply to firms producing such products for themselves, by allowing advantages to those who organise within the firm and not through the market, necessarily encourage the growth of firms. But it is difficult to believe that it is measures such as have been mentioned in this paragraph which have brought firms into existence. Such measures would, however, tend to have this result if they did not exist for other reasons.

These, then, are the reasons why organisations such as firms exist in a specialised exchange economy in which it is generally assumed that the distribution of resources is "organised" by the price mechanism. A firm, therefore, consists of the system of relationships which comes into existence when the direction of resources is dependent on an entrepreneur.

The approach which has just been sketched would appear to offer an advantage in that it is possible to give a scientific meaning to what is meant by saying that a firm gets larger or smaller. A firm becomes larger as additional transactions (which could be exchange transactions co-ordinated through the price mechanism) are organised by the entrepreneur and becomes smaller as he abandons the organisation of such transactions. The question which arises is whether it is possible to study the forces which determine the size of the firm. Why does the entrepreneur not organise one less transaction or one more? It is interesting to note that Professor Knight considers that:

the relation between efficiency and size is one of the most serious problems of theory, being, in contrast with the relation for a plant, largely a matter of personality and historical accident rather than of intelligible general principles. But the question is peculiarly vital because the possibility of monopoly gain offers a powerful incentive to *continuous and unlimited* expansion of the firm, which force must be offset by some equally powerful one making for decreased efficiency (in the production of money income) with growth in size, if even boundary competition is to exist.[23]

Professor Knight would appear to consider that it is impossible to treat scientifically the determinants of the size of the firm. On

---

[23] *Risk, Uncertainty and Profit*, Preface to the Re-issue, London School of Economics Series of Reprints, No. 16, 1933.

the basis of the concept of the firm developed above, this task will now be attempted.

It was suggested that the introduction of the firm was due primarily to the existence of marketing costs. A pertinent question to ask would appear to be (quite apart from the monopoly considerations raised by Professor Knight), why, if by organising one can eliminate certain costs and in fact reduce the cost of production, are there any market transactions at all?[24] Why is not all production carried on by one big firm? There would appear to be certain possible explanations.

First, as a firm gets larger, there may be decreasing returns to the entrepreneur function, that is, the costs of organising additional transactions within the firm may rise.[25] Naturally, a point must be reached where the costs of organising an extra transaction within the firm are equal to the costs involved in carrying out the transaction in the open market, or, to the costs of organising by another entrepreneur. Secondly, it may be that as the transactions which are organised increase, the entrepreneur fails to place the factors of production in the uses where their value is greatest, that is, fails to make the best use of the factors of production. Again, a point must be reached where the loss through the waste of resources is equal to the marketing costs of the exchange transaction in the open market or to the loss if the transaction was organised by another entrepreneur. Finally, the supply price of one or more of the factors of production may rise, because the "other advantages" of a small firm are greater than those of a large firm.[26] Of course, the actual point where the expansion

---

[24] There are certain marketing costs which could only be eliminated by the abolition of "consumers' choice" and these are the costs of retailing. It is conceivable that these costs might be so high that people would be willing to accept rations because the extra product obtained was worth the loss of their choice.

[25] This argument assumes that exchange transactions on a market can be considered as homogeneous; which is clearly untrue in fact. This complication is taken into account below.

[26] For a discussion of the variation of the supply price of factors of production to firms of varying size, see E. A. G. Robinson, *The Structure of Competitive Industry*. It is sometimes said that the supply price of organising ability increases as the size of the firm increases because men prefer to be the heads of small independent businesses rather than the heads of departments

of the firm ceases might be determined by a combination of the factors mentioned above. The first two reasons given most probably correspond to the economists' phrase of "diminishing returns to management."[27]

The point has been made in the previous paragraph that a firm will tend to expand until the costs of organising an extra transaction within the firm become equal to the costs of carrying out the same transaction by means of an exchange on the open market or the costs of organising in another firm. But if the firm stops its expansion at a point below the costs of marketing in the open market and at a point equal to the costs of organising in another firm, in most cases (excluding the case of "combination"[28]), this will imply that there is a market transaction between these two producers, each of whom could organise it at less than the actual marketing costs. How is the paradox to be resolved? If we consider an example the reason for this will become clear. Suppose A is buying a product from B and that both A and B could organise this marketing transaction at less than its present cost. B, we can assume, is not organising one process or stage of production, but several. If A therefore wishes to avoid a market transaction, he will have to take over all the processes of production controlled by B. Unless A takes over all the processes of production, a market transaction will still remain, although it is a different product that is bought. But we have previously assumed that as each producer expands he becomes less efficient; the additional costs of organising extra transactions increase. It is probable that A's cost of organising the transactions previously organised by B will be greater than B's cost of doing the same thing. A

---

in a large business. See Jones, *The Trust Problem*, p. 531, and Macgregor, *Industrial Combination*, p. 63. This is a common argument of those who advocate Rationalisation. It is said that larger units would be more efficient, but owing to the individualistic spirit of the smaller entrepreneurs, they prefer to remain independent, apparently in spite of the higher income which their increased efficiency under Rationalisation makes possible.

[27] This discussion is, of course, brief and incomplete. For a more thorough discussion of this particular problem, see N. Kaldor, "The Equilibrium of the Firm," *The Economic Journal*, March 1934, and E. A. G. Robinson, "The Problem of Management and the Size of the Firm," *The Economic Journal*, June 1934.

[28] A definition of this term is given below.

therefore will take over the whole of B's organisation only if his cost of organising B's work is not greater than B's cost by an amount equal to the costs of carrying out an exchange transaction on the open market. But once it becomes economical to have a market transaction, it also pays to divide production in such a way that the cost of organising an extra transaction in each firm is the same.

Up to now it has been assumed that the exchange transactions which take place through the price mechanism are homogeneous. In fact, nothing could be more diverse than the actual transactions which take place in our modern world. This would seem to imply that the costs of carrying out exchange transactions through the price mechanism will vary considerably as will also the costs of organising these transactions within the firm. It seems therefore possible that quite apart from the question of diminishing returns the costs of organising certain transactions within the firm may be greater than the costs of carrying out the exchange transactions in the open market. This would necessarily imply that there were exchange transactions carried out through the price mechanism, but would it mean that there would have to be more than one firm? Clearly not, for all those areas in the economic system where the direction of resources was not dependent directly on the price mechanism could be organised within one firm. The factors which were discussed earlier would seem to be the important ones, though it is difficult to say whether "diminishing returns to management" or the rising supply price of factors is likely to be the more important.

Other things being equal, therefore, a firm will tend to be larger:

(a) the less the costs of organising and the slower these costs rise with an increase in the transactions organised.

(b) the less likely the entrepreneur is to make mistakes and the smaller the increase in mistakes with an increase in the transactions organised.

(c) the greater the lowering (or the less the rise) in the supply price of factors of production to firms of larger size.

Apart from variations in the supply price of factors of production to firms of different sizes, it would appear that the costs of organising and the losses through mistakes will increase with an increase in the spatial distribution of the transactions organised, in the dissimilarity of the transactions, and in the probability of changes in the relevant prices.[29] As more transactions are organised by an entrepreneur, it would appear that the transactions would tend to be either different in kind or in different places. This furnishes an additional reason why efficiency will tend to decrease as the firm gets larger. Inventions which tend to bring factors of production nearer together, by lessening spatial distribution, tend to increase the size of the firm.[30] Changes like the telephone and the telegraph which tend to reduce the cost of organising spatially will tend to increase the size of the firm. All changes which improve managerial technique will tend to increase the size of the firm.[31-32]

It should be noted that the definition of a firm which was

---

[29] This aspect of the problem is emphasised by N. Kaldor, *op. cit.* Its importance in this connection had been previously noted by E. A. G. Robinson, *The Structure of Competitive Industry*, pp. 83–106. This assumes that an increase in the probability of price movements increases the costs of organising within a firm more than it increases the cost of carrying out an exchange transaction on the market—which is probable.

[30] This would appear to be the importance of the treatment of the technical unit by E. A. G. Robinson, *op. cit.*, pp. 27–33. The larger the technical unit, the greater the concentration of factors and therefore the firm is likely to be larger.

[31] It should be noted that most inventions will change both the costs of organising and the costs of using the price mechanism. In such cases, whether the invention tends to make firms larger or smaller will depend on the relative effect on these two sets of costs. For instance, if the telephone reduces the costs of using the price mechanism more than it reduces the costs of organising, then it will have the effect of reducing the size of the firm.

[32] An illustration of these dynamic forces is furnished by Maurice Dobb, *Russian Economic Development*, p. 68. "With the passing of bonded labour the factory, as an establishment where work was organised under the whip of the overseer, lost its *raison d'être* until this was restored to it with the introduction of power machinery after 1846." It seems important to realise that the passage from the domestic system to the factory system is not a mere historical accident, but is conditioned by economic forces. This is shown by the fact that it is possible to move from the factory system to the domestic system, as in the Russian example, as well as vice versa. It is the essence of serfdom that the price mechanism is not allowed to operate. Therefore, there has to be direction from some organiser. When, however, serfdom passed, the price mechanism was allowed to operate. It was not until machinery drew workers into one locality that it paid to supersede the price mechanism and the firm again emerged.

given above can be used to give more precise meanings to the terms "combination" and "integration."[33] There is a combination when transactions which were previously organised by two or more entrepreneurs become organised by one. This becomes integration when it involves the organisation of transactions which were previously carried out between the entrepreneurs on a market. A firm can expand in either or both of these two ways. The whole of the "structure of competitive industry" becomes tractable by the ordinary technique of economic analysis.

III

The problem which has been investigated in the previous section has not been entirely neglected by economists and it is now necessary to consider why the reasons given above for the emergence of a firm in a specialised exchange economy are to be preferred to the other explanations which have been offered.

It is sometimes said that the reason for the existence of a firm is to be found in the division of labour. This is the view of Professor Usher, a view which has been adopted and expanded by Mr. Maurice Dobb. The firm becomes "the result of an increasing complexity of the division of labour . . . . The growth of this economic differentiation creates the need for some integrating force without which differentiation would collapse into chaos; and it is as the integrating force in a differentiated economy that industrial forms are chiefly significant."[34] The answer to this argument is an obvious one. The "integrating force in a differentiated economy" already exists in the form of the price mechanism. It is perhaps the main achievement of economic science that it has shown that there is no reason to suppose that specialisation must lead to chaos.[35] The reason given by Mr. Maurice Dobb is therefore inadmissible. What has to be explained is why one integrating force (the entrepreneur) should be substituted for another integrating force (the price mechanism).

The most interesting reasons (and probably the most widely

---

[33] This is often called "vertical integration," combination being termed "lateral integration."

[34] *Op. cit.*, p. 10. Professor Usher's views are to be found in his *Introduction to the Industrial History of England*, pp. 1–18.

[35] Cf. J. B. Clark, *Distribution of Wealth*, p. 19, who speaks of the theory of exchange as being the "theory of the organisation of industrial society."

accepted) which have been given to explain this fact are those to be found in Professor Knight's *Risk, Uncertainty and Profit.* His views will be examined in some detail.

Professor Knight starts with a system in which there is no uncertainty:

acting as individuals under absolute freedom but without collusion men are supposed to have organised economic life with the primary and secondary division of labour, the use of capital, etc., developed to the point familiar in present-day America. The principal fact which calls for the exercise of the imagination is the internal organisation of the productive groups or establishments. With uncertainty entirely absent, every individual being in possession of perfect knowledge of the situation, there would be no occasion for anything of the nature of responsible management or control of productive activity. Even marketing transactions in any realistic sense would not be found. The flow of raw materials and productive services to the consumer would be entirely automatic.[36]

Professor Knight says that we can imagine this adjustment as being "the result of a long process of experimentation worked out by trial-and-error methods alone," while it is not necessary "to imagine every worker doing exactly the right thing at the right time in a sort of 'pre-established harmony' with the work of others. There might be managers, superintendents, etc., for the purpose of co-ordinating the activities of individuals," though these managers would be performing a purely routine function, "without responsibility of any sort."[37]

Professor Knight then continues:

With the introduction of uncertainty—the fact of ignorance and the necessity of acting upon opinion rather than knowledge—into this Eden-like situation, its character is entirely changed . . . . With uncertainty present doing things, the actual execution of activity, becomes in a real sense a secondary part of life; the primary problem or function is deciding what to do and how to do it.[38]

This fact of uncertainty brings about the two most important characteristics of social organisation.

In the first place, goods are produced for a market, on the basis of entirely impersonal prediction of wants, not for the satisfaction of the wants of the producers themselves. The producer takes the responsibility of forecasting the consumers' wants. In the second place, the work of forecasting and at the

---

[36] *Risk, Uncertainty and Profit,* p. 267.

[37] *Op. cit.,* pp. 267–268.

[38] *Op. cit.,* p. 268.

same time a large part of the technological direction and control of production are still further concentrated upon a very narrow class of the producers, and we meet with a new economic functionary, the entrepreneur. . . . . When uncertainty is present and the task of deciding what to do and how to do it takes the ascendancy over that of execution the internal organisation of the productive groups is no longer a matter of indifference or a mechanical detail. Centralisation of this deciding and controlling function is imperative, a process of "cephalisation" is inevitable.[39]

The most fundamental change is:

the system under which the confident and venturesome assume the risk or insure the doubtful and timid by guaranteeing to the latter a specified income in return for an assignment of the actual results. . . . With human nature as we know it it would be impracticable or very unusual for one man to guarantee to another a definite result of the latter's actions without being given power to direct his work. And on the other hand the second party would not place himself under the direction of the first without such a guarantee. . . . The result of this manifold specialisation of function is the enterprise and wage system of industry. Its existence in the world is the direct result of the fact of uncertainty.[40]

These quotations give the essence of Professor Knight's theory. The fact of uncertainty means that people have to forecast future wants. Therefore, you get a special class springing up who direct the activities of others to whom they give guaranteed wages. It acts because good judgment is generally associated with confidence in one's judgment.[41]

Professor Knight would appear to leave himself open to criticism on several grounds. First of all, as he himself points out, the fact that certain people have better judgment or better knowledge does not mean that they can only get an income from it by themselves actively taking part in production. They can sell advice or knowledge. Every business buys the services of a host of advisers. We can imagine a system where all advice or knowledge was bought as required. Again, it is possible to get a reward from better knowledge or judgment not by actively taking part in production but by making contracts with people who are producing. A merchant buying for future delivery represents an example of this. But this merely illustrates the point that it is quite possible to give a guaranteed reward providing that certain acts are per-

---

[39] *Op. cit.*, pp. 268–295.
[40] *Op. cit.*, pp. 269–270.
[41] *Op. cit.*, p. 270.

formed without directing the performance of those acts. Professor Knight says that "with human nature as we know it it would be impracticable or very unusual for one man to guarantee to another a definite result of the latter's actions without being given power to direct his work." This is surely incorrect. A large proportion of jobs are done to contract, that is, the contractor is guaranteed a certain sum providing he performs certain acts. But this does not involve any direction. It does mean, however, that the system of relative prices has been changed and that there will be a new arrangement of the factors of production.[42] The fact that Professor Knight mentions that the "second party would not place himself under the direction of the first without such a guarantee" is irrelevant to the problem we are considering. Finally, it seems important to notice that even in the case of an economic system where there is no uncertainty Professor Knight considers that there would be co-ordinators, though they would perform only a routine function. He immediately adds that they would be "without responsibility of any sort," which raises the question by whom are they paid and why? It seems that nowhere does Professor Knight give a reason why the price mechanism should be superseded.

IV

It would seem important to examine one further point and that is to consider the relevance of this discussion to the general question of the "cost-curve of the firm."

It has sometimes been assumed that a firm is limited in size under perfect competition if its cost curve slopes upward,[43] while under imperfect competition, it is limited in size because it will not pay to produce more than the output at which marginal cost is equal to marginal revenue.[44] But it is clear that a firm may

---

[42] This shows that it is possible to have a private enterprise system without the existence of firms. Though, in practice, the two functions of enterprise, which actually influences the system of relative prices by forecasting wants and acting in accordance with such forecasts, and management, which accepts the system of relative prices as being given, are normally carried out by the same persons, yet it seems important to keep them separate in theory. This point is further discussed below.

[43] See Kaldor, *op cit.*, and Robinson, *The Problem of Management and the Size of the Firm.*

[44] Mr. Robinson calls this the Imperfect Competition solution for the survival of the small firm.

produce more than one product and, therefore, there appears to be no *prima facie* reason why this upward slope of the cost curve in the case of perfect competition or the fact that marginal cost will not always be below marginal revenue in the case of imperfect competition should limit the size of the firm.[45] Mrs. Robinson[46] makes the simplifying assumption that only one product is being produced. But it is clearly important to investigate how the number of products produced by a firm is determined, while no theory which assumes that only one product is in fact produced can have very great practical significance.

It might be replied that under perfect competition, since everything that is produced can be sold at the prevailing price, then there is no need for any other product to be produced. But this argument ignores the fact that there may be a point where it is less costly to organise the exchange transactions of a new product than to organise further exchange transactions of the old product. This point can be illustrated in the following way. Imagine, following von Thunen, that there is a town, the consuming centre, and that industries are located around this central point in rings. These conditions are illustrated in the following diagram in which *A*, *B* and *C* represent different industries.

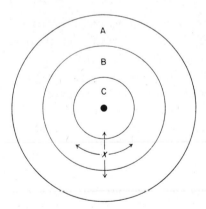

Imagine an entrepreneur who starts controlling exchange trans-

---

[45] Mr. Robinson's conclusion, *op. cit.,* p. 249, note 1, would appear to be definitely wrong. He is followed by Horace J. White, Jr., "Monopolistic and Perfect Competition," *The American Economic Review,* December 1936, p. 645, note 27. Mr. White states "It is obvious that the size of the firm is limited in conditions of monopolistic competition."

[46] *Economics of Imperfect Competition.*

actions from *x*. Now as he extends his activities in the same product (*B*), the cost of organising increases until at some point it becomes equal to that of a dissimilar product which is nearer. As the firm expands, it will therefore from this point include more than one product (*A* and *C*). This treatment of the problem is obviously incomplete,[47] but it is necessary to show that merely proving that the cost curve turns upwards does not give a limitation to the size of the firm. So far we have only considered the case of perfect competition; the case of imperfect competition would appear to be obvious.

To determine the size of the firm, we have to consider the marketing costs (that is, the costs of using the price mechanism), and the costs of organising of different entrepreneurs and then we can determine how many products will be produced by each firm and how much of each it will produce. It would, therefore, appear that Mr. Shove[48] in his article on "Imperfect Competition" was asking questions which Mrs. Robinson's cost curve apparatus cannot answer. The factors mentioned above would seem to be the relevant ones.

V

Only one task now remains; and that is, to see whether the concept of a firm which has been developed fits in with that existing in the real world. We can best approach the question of what constitutes a firm in practice by considering the legal relationship normally called that of "master and servant" or "employer and employee."[49] The essentials of this relationship have been given as follows:

(1) the servant must be under the duty of rendering personal services to

---

[47] As has been shown above, location is only one of the factors influencing the cost of organising.

[48] G. F. Shove, "The Imperfection of the Market," *The Economic Journal*, March 1933, p. 115. In connection with an increase in demand in the suburbs and the effect on the price charged by suppliers, Mr. Shove asks ". . . . why do not the old firms open branches in the suburbs?" If the argument in the text is correct, this is a question which Mrs. Robinson's apparatus cannot answer.

[49] The legal concept of "employer and employee" and the economic concept of a firm are not identical, in that the firm may imply control over another person's property as well as over their labour. But the identity of these two concepts is sufficiently close for an examination of the legal concept to be of value in appraising the worth of the economic concept.

the master or to others on behalf of the master, otherwise the contract is a contract for sale of goods or the like.

(2) The master must have the right to control the servant's work, either personally or by another servant or agent. It is this right of control or inter-ference, of being entitled to tell the servant when to work (within the hours of service) and when not to work, and what work to do and how to do it (within the terms of such service) which is the dominant characteristic in this relation and marks off the servant from an independent contractor, or from one employed merely to give to his employer the fruits of his labour. In the latter case, the contractor or performer is not under the employer's control in doing the work or effecting the service; he has to shape and manage his work so as to give the result he has contracted to effect.[50]

We thus see that it is the fact of direction which is the essence of the legal concept of "employer and employee," just as it was in the economic concept which was developed above. It is inter-esting to note that Professor Batt says further:

That which distinguishes an agent from a servant is not the absence or presence of a fixed wage or the payment only of commission on business done, but rather the freedom with which an agent may carry out his employment.[51]

We can therefore conclude that the definition we have given is one which approximates closely to the firm as it is considered in the real world.

Our definition is, therefore, realistic. Is it manageable? This ought to be clear. When we are considering how large a firm will be the principle of marginalism works smoothly. The question always is, will it pay to bring an extra exchange transaction under the organising authority? At the margin, the costs of organising within the firm will be equal either to the costs of organising in another firm or to the costs involved in leaving the transaction to be "organised" by the price mechanism. Business men will be constantly experimenting, controlling more or less, and in this way, equilibrium will be maintained. This gives the position of equilibrium for static analysis. But it is clear that the dynamic factors are also of considerable importance, and an investigation of the effect changes have on the cost of organising within the firm and on marketing costs generally will enable one to explain why firms get larger and smaller. We thus have a theory of moving

---

[50] Batt, *The Law of Master and Servant*, p. 6.
[51] *Op. cit.*, p. 7.

equilibrium. The above analysis would also appear to have clarified the relationship between initiative or enterprise and management. Initiative means forecasting and operates through the price mechanism by the making of new contracts. Management proper merely reacts to price changes, rearranging the factors of production under its control. That the business man normally combines both functions is an obvious result of the marketing costs which were discussed above. Finally, this analysis enables us to state more exactly what is meant by the "marginal product" of the entrepreneur. But an elaboration of this point would take us far from our comparatively simple task of definition and clarification.

17

A NOTE ON PROFIT MAXIMISATION
AND ITS IMPLICATIONS *

By T. Scitovsky ||

That the entrepreneur aims at maximising his profits is one of the most fundamental assumptions of economic theory. So much so that it has almost come to be regarded as equivalent to rational behaviour, and as an axiom, which is self-evident and needs no proof or justification. Doubts have been raised by several writers whether maximising his profits is always the entrepreneur's best policy.[1] But such doubts were few and have died away without reverberation; mainly, I think, because it has never been made clear what exactly profit maximisation implies; and perhaps also because we have a vested interest in maintaining this assumption—it makes economic analysis so much simpler. In the following we set out to show that by attributing to the entrepreneur the desire to maximise his profits we also attribute to him a particular psychology, which, though very plausible, is rather special.

Let us draw the entrepreneur's indifference map between money income, m, and entrepreneurial inactivity, i[2] (Fig. 1)[3]. Entrepreneurial activity is the negative of i and is measured from right to left along the horizontal axis. Assume next that entre-

---

* *The Review of Economic Studies,* Vol. XI (1943), pp. 57–60. Reprinted, by the courtesy of the publisher and the author, without change from the original text.

|| Stanford University.

[1] Cf. J. R. Hicks: "Annual Survey of Economic Theory: The Theory of Monopoly," *Econometrica,* Vol. 3 (1935), p. 8; B. Higgins: "Elements of Indeterminacy in the Theory of Non-Perfect Competition," *The American Economic Review,* Vol. 29 (1939), pp. 468–479. See also E. S. Lynch's comment on the latter article and Professor Higgins' reply in *The American Economic Review,* Vol. 30 (1940), pp. 347–350.

[2] This term is somewhat inelegant but it is more accurate than the usual term, leisure.

[3] I am indebted to Mr. D. E. McCoy for drawing the original diagrams.

preneurial activity is a limitational factor in the manufacture of the entrepreneur's produce and can, therefore, be measured in terms of output.[4] Point ω represents zero output or total entrepreneurial inactivity.

Since the unit of measurement along the horizontal axis is the unit of output, we can draw the entrepreneur's total receipts curve and total outlays curve in this diagram. The vertical difference of the two curves shows, for each level of output, the entrepreneur's total net income from operating his firm. Taking these differences

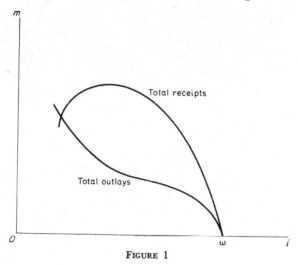

FIGURE 1

as ordinates we can draw the entrepreneur's net income curve (Fig. 2). The point at which the net income curve is tangential to an indifference curve is the entrepreneur's point of maximum satisfaction and determines his optimum rate of output. This optimum rate of output may or may not maximise his profits; and our problem is to find out under what conditions (i.e., for what shape of the indifference map) it does.

The entrepreneur's net income would be highest at point h. But for an indifference curve to be tangential to the income curve at this point, it would have to be horizontal or even upward-sloping over part of its range. This is very unlikely and conflicts with our general notions of the shape of indifference curves.

---

[4] A limitational factor is a factor of production whose quantity per unit of output is fixed and cannot be varied.

We must bear in mind, however, that what the entrepreneur is supposed to maximise is not his total net income. He is assumed to maximise the difference between his total receipts and total costs; and total costs are always assumed to comprise, not only the entrepreneur's outlays, but also the wages of routine management and supervision, which he is supposed to pay to himself and include in his regular cost calculations. In other words, the entrepreneur's income consists of two elements. The wages of routine management, which form part of costs; and the profits of entrepreneurship

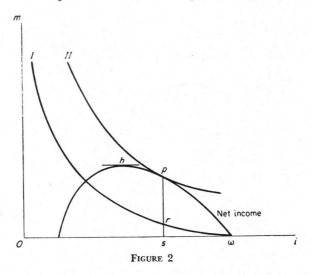

FIGURE 2

proper, which are his residual income. Marshall called both elements profits: the one normal, the other extraordinary, profits. For our purposes it will be more convenient to refer to the former as the entrepreneur's wages, and to apply the term profit only to his residual income. But irrespectively of terminology, it is always his residual income only that the entrepreneur is supposed to maximise. That this dichotomy of the entrepreneur's income is always implied in the orthodox theory will become plain to the reader when he recalls the full equilibrium conditions of perfect competition: the equality of price with marginal and average costs. While the latter condition eliminates the entrepreneur's residual income completely, he is still supposed to earn wages for supervision (normal profits) in this situation. These must consequently be included in costs; and they are supposed to represent the entrepreneur's minimum (i.e., marginal) income. Profits, therefore, the entrepreneur's residual income, are of the nature of a rent.[5]

In our diagram (Fig. 2) we can separate the two elements of the entrepreneur's income by drawing the indifference curve that goes through the point ω. This indifference curve represents the minimum satisfaction that will keep the entrepreneur in his profession. If his satisfaction were to fall below this level he would cease being an entrepreneur and do something else. That part of his income, therefore, which brings the entrepreneur to this level of satisfaction is his minimum income, the wage of routine management.[6] Only the part of his income that brings his satisfaction above the indifference curve I can be regarded as profit proper. In Fig 2, therefore, of ps, the entrepreneur's total net income, pr is profit, and rs is wages.

We are now in a position to answer the question, under what conditions does the maximising of profits lead to the maximisation of the entrepreneur's satisfaction. Profit, the vertical distance between the net income curve and the difference curve I, is greatest at the level of output where the tangents to the two curves are parallel. The entrepreneur's satisfaction is greatest at the level of output where the net income curve is tangential to an indifference curve. It is clear that the two levels of output need not coincide For we used one indifference curve to determine maximum profits another one for determining maximum satisfaction: and as long as we make no special assumption about the individual's psychology or behaviour, there is no definite relationship between the shape or position of the various indifference curves in his indifference map. In order, therefore, that maximum profits should maximise his satisfaction, the entrepreneur must have a special type of psychology, and, corresponding to it, a special type of indifference map.

The geometrical nature of this condition will be immediately

---

[5] Cf. Alfred Marshall: *Principles of Economics,* definitive edition, pp. 618–619; Joan Robinson: *The Economics of Imperfect Competition,* London, 1933, Chaps. 7, 8 and 9; B. Higgins: *op. cit.*

[6] Since this part of the entrepreneur's remuneration enters into cost, the indifference curve I must be added vertically to the total outlays curve (Fig. 1) to give the entrepreneur's total cost curve. We have not drawn this curve, since it is not needed for our argument.

obvious to the reader. For the net income curve to be tangential to an indifference curve at the same level of output at which its slope equals that of indifference curve I, the tangents to the two indifference curves at that level of output must be parallel. In order that this condition may be satisfied for any and every kind of net income curve, *all* indifference curves must have the same slope for *each* abscissa. In other words, the several indifference curves must be vertical displacements of each other.

The economic meaning of the above geometrical condition is that the entrepreneur's choice between more and less activity— or between more income and more leisure—must be independent of his income. This is equivalent to Marshall's familiar assumption of a constant marginal utility of money; or, to use more up-to-date terminology, to a zero income elasticity of supply of entre-preneurship.

At first sight it may seem strange and unrealistic to attribute to the entrepreneur a type of behaviour that would fulfil this condition. For, if his aim is to make money, it seems natural that the amount he is already making should affect the ardour and energy with which he seeks to make more. But the assumption that the entrepreneur's willingness to work is independent of his income need not imply that he is not interested in the material rewards of his work. It may also mean that he is so keen on making money that his ambition cannot be damped by a rising income. The latter interpretation seems to be the more realistic one of the two. Businessmen regard the income they earn as an index of their success and efficiency; and their ambition of excelling in their profession manifests itself in the desire to make more money. We claim that a businessman's entrepreneurial activity will remain unaffected by a rise in his income if he makes money, not in order to have more to spend, but for its own sake, because it is an index and token of his success in life.

The man who aims at raising his standard of living tends to relax his efforts when they meet with success. This is so, not only because material demands are satiable, but also because leisure is an essential ingredient of a good life. He, however, who wants success for its own sake, and measures it in terms of money, is likely to keep working unabated even after his income has risen. This is likely to be the case, partly because the desire for success is more insatiable than the demand for material goods, and partly because it is not a high but a rising income that is a sign of business success.[7]

For the supply of entrepreneurship to be independent of income it is not necessary that the entrepreneur's psychology should be such that he save the total increment of a rise in his income. He may devote part or all of it to raising his standard of living, provided that he regards this as no more than a by-product of his business success and its outward manifestation. As long as raising his standard of living does not become the entrepreneur's primary aim, the amount of work and energy expended by him will remain independent of his income and be limited only by considerations of age and health, habit and temperament; by family and social obligations; by competing (e.g., political) ambitions; and the like. In such a case, therefore, the assumption of a zero income elasticity of supply of entrepreneurship will be perfectly justified, and it will be correct to ascribe to the entrepreneur the desire to maximise his profits. Only when he is more susceptible to the attractions of leisure than to those of his work and is consequently induced by a higher income to take life easier, will the entrepreneur's optimum behaviour be, not to maximise profits, but to keep his exertions and output below the point at which profits would be at a maximum.

The puritan psychology of valuing money for its own sake, and not for the enjoyments and comforts it might yield, is that of the ideal entrepreneur as he was conceived of in the early days of capitalism. The combination of frugality and industry, the entrepreneurial virtues, is calculated to insure the independence of the entrepreneur's willingness to work from the level of his income. The classical economists, therefore, were perfectly justified in assuming that the entrepreneur aims at maximising his profits. They were concerned with a type of businessman whose psychology happened to be such that for him maximising profits was identical with maximising satisfaction.

The entrepreneur of to-day may have lost some of the frugality and industry of his forefathers; nevertheless, the assumption that he aims at maximising his profits is still quite likely to apply to

---

[7] A high but constant level of income can be a sign of past business success.

him—at least as a first approximation. For this assumption is patently untrue only about people who regard work as plain drudgery: a necessary evil, with which they have to put up in order to earn their living and the comforts of life. The person who derives satisfaction from his work—other than that yielded by the income he receives for it—will to a large extent be governed by ambition, a spirit of emulation and rivalry, pride in his work, and similar considerations, when he plans his activity. We believe that the entrepreneur usually belongs to this latter category.

However, we set out, not to justify or criticise the assumption that entrepreneurs aim at maximising profits, but to make its implications explicit. Many of us have been in the habit of regarding this assumption as similar in every respect to the assumption that the individual maximises his satisfaction. We have shown above that this is not so. For to say that the individual maximises his satisfaction is a perfectly general statement. It says nothing about the individual's psychology or behaviour, is, therefore, devoid of empirical content, and is true by definition. As against this, the assumption that the entrepreneur maximises his profits is based on observation and implies a special hypothesis concerning the businessman's psychology. It is, therefore, an empirical law, which need not apply to every businessman, and may conceivably be untrue even about the representative entrepreneur. Its justification lies in its usefulness, which should be enhanced by a better understanding of its exact meaning and limitations.

V. IMPERFECT COMPETITION

18

ANNUAL SURVEY OF ECONOMIC THEORY:
THE THEORY OF MONOPOLY*

By J. R. Hicks

I propose in this survey to confine attention to the progress which has recently been made in one particular part of economic theory. Such a limitation has obvious advantages in facilitating more detailed discussion; and when one has decided to confine oneself to a particular field, it is obvious that monopoly has the best claim to be chosen. The last five or six years have seen the appearance of at least four important works specially devoted to this subject—those of Dr. Zeuthen, Dr. Schneider, Professor Chamberlin, and Mrs. Robinson;[1] while there is, I think, no theoretical subject which has received more attention in the recent volumes of most of the chief economic journals than the theory of monopoly and imperfect competition. To most of these articles we shall refer as we proceed; but the names of Mr. Harrod, Mr. Shove, Dr. v. Stackelberg, and Professor Hotelling, cannot be omitted from even a preliminary bibliography.[2]

The preoccupation of contemporary theorists with problems of monopoly does not appear to be due, as might perhaps be expected, to their consciousness of the increased urgency of these problems in the modern world. It may very well be that monopoly is more important today than it was fifty years ago, though it is not so

---

* *Econometrica*, Vol. III (1935), pp. 1–20. Reprinted, by the courtesy of the publisher and the author, with additional notes and a typographical correction.

‖ Nuffield College, Oxford University, England.

[1] F. Zeuthen, *Problems of Monopoly and Economic Warfare*, London, 1930; Schneider, *Reine Theorie monopolistischer Wirtschaftsformen*, Tübingen, 1932; E. H. Chamberlin, *Theory of Monopolistic Competition*, Harvard, 1933; J. Robinson, *Economics of Imperfect Competition*, London, 1933.

[2] R. F. Harrod, "Notes on Supply," *The Economic Journal*, 1930; "Law of Decreasing Costs," *The Economic Journal*, 1931; "Doctrines of Imperfect Competition," *The Quarterly Journal of Economics*, 1934; G. F. Shove, "The Imperfection of the Market," *The Economic Journal*, 1933; H. Hotelling, "Stability in Competition," *The Economic Journal*, 1929.

obvious as it appears at first sight. It is certain, however, that the phenomena of monopolistic competition to which attention has so particularly been directed are not new phenomena; they were observed and analyzed, however imperfectly, by older economists, by Cairnes and Wicksell, if by no others.[3]

The widespread interest in monopoly theory is much easier to account for on grounds inherent in the development of economic theory itself, though here an element of coincidence is present. On the one hand, the generally increased interest in mathematical economics during the last few years (of which this journal is itself a symptom) has naturally turned attention back to the work of Cournot, the great founder of the subject, and still one of its best teachers. It was Cournot's creation of elementary monopoly theory which was the first great triumph of mathematical economics; yet Cournot had left much undone, and it is not surprising that the endeavor to complete his work should have been an attractive occupation for his successors.

But if some modern monopoly theorists have been seeking to fill the gaps in Cournot, others have been more concerned with the gaps in the work of Marshall. These gaps were more skilfully pasted over, and it was not until after many years' criticism that they were clearly discerned. But the controversy on the "Laws of Returns," begun by Mr. Sraffa in 1926, and carried on more or less continuously in *The Economic Journal* for some years afterwards,[4] made it increasingly evident to the most convinced Marshallians that the device of "external economies," by which Marshall sought to reconcile the postulate of perfect competition with the observed facts of increasing returns, would not bear the weight that had been imposed upon it. A tendency therefore developed away from the postulate of perfect competition. The participants in the discussion began to assume as the normal case that a firm can influence to some extent the prices at which it sells, that it is confronted with a downward sloping demand curve for its products, though this demand curve may have a high elasticity. With this assumption, the cardinal difficulty of increasing returns disappeared, since a firm might still be in equilibrium under conditions of diminishing cost. But numerous other difficulties started up, and it became

---

[3] Cairnes, *Political Economy*, pp. 115–116 (quoted Chamberlin, *op. cit.*, p. 106); Wicksell, *Lectures on Political Economy*, Vol. I, pp. 87–88.

[4] See bibliography in *The Economic Journal*, 1930, p. 79.

necessary for these writers, like those mentioned before, to make a detailed examination of the theory of monopoly.

From each line of approach a substantially similar theory has emerged, though there are important points which still remain controversial. It remains convenient for us to discuss the modern theory under the old headings: (1) *Simple Monopoly,* where the individual firm is confronted with given demand functions for its products, and given supply functions for its factors; (2) *Monopolistic Competition,* the relations of a group of firms producing similar products, i.e., an industry; (3) *Bilateral Monopoly,* where one firm is selling to another.

I. Simple Monopoly

As far as simple monopoly is concerned, the improvement on Cournot is mainly a matter of exposition, although there has been some further enquiry into the effect of monopoly on the demand for factors of production.

1. If the prices at which the monopolist hires his factors are fixed, his cost of production can be taken as a simple function of output. Let $\phi(x)$ be the total cost of producing an output x.

If the monopolist's selling price is p, and $p = f(x)$ is the demand curve confronting him, his profit on selling an output x will be

$$xf(x) - \phi(x)$$

which is maximized when

$$xf'(x) + f(x) = \phi'(x).$$

So much has been familiar since Cournot; the principal recent innovation has been to give the expression on the left of the last equation a name "Marginal Revenue."[5] The equation can then be written

$$\text{Marginal Revenue} = \text{Marginal Cost}$$

which is certainly a convenient way of expressing the first condition of monopolistic equilibrium.

Since the elasticity of the demand curve $= \eta = \dfrac{f(x)}{xf'(x)}$, marginal revenue

$$= \text{price} \left(1 - \frac{1}{\eta}\right)$$

---

[5] So Mrs. Robinson. It seems the most convenient of the names which have been suggested.

The second condition of maximum profits is that

$$\frac{d}{dx}\{xf'(x) + f(x) - \phi'(x)\}$$

should be negative. This can be written

$$\frac{d}{dx}(MR) < \frac{d}{dx}(MC).$$

Monopolistic equilibrium is therefore stable, so long as the marginal revenue curve slopes downwards more steeply than the marginal cost curve. All cases where the marginal revenue curve slopes downwards and the marginal cost curve upwards are therefore stable, but instability may occur if either of these conditions is not fulfilled. Upward sloping marginal revenue curves, though possible, are unlikely to be very important, since the demand curve from which a marginal revenue curve is derived may be taken to be always downward sloping. Much more important is the fact that stable equilibrium with a downward sloping marginal cost curve is possible, so long as the downward slope is less than that of the marginal revenue curve, and so long, also, as total receipts exceed total costs by an amount sufficient to keep the monopolist in business.

The question of stability once settled, it becomes possible to apply the apparatus in the ordinary manner, familiar in elementary theory, to simple problems of change. A rise in the marginal cost curve will reduce output, a rise in the marginal revenue curve will increase it; but a rise in the demand (average revenue) curve may not increase output, unless it is such as to cause a rise in the marginal revenue curve. Similarly a rise in average costs will not contract output, unless it is associated with a rise in marginal costs, or is otherwise large enough to drive the monopolist out of business.

2. THE MONOPOLIST AND THE FACTORS OF PRODUCTION.[6] It is convenient, for the analysis of this problem, to conceive of the monopolist as owning certain factors of production (his *private factors*, we may call them) and hiring others. If he is unable to vary the supply of these private factors, then it is strictly correct to suppose him endeavouring to maximize his profits, that is to say,

---

[6] Robinson, *op. cit.*, Books VII–IX; Schneider, "Bemerkungen zur Grenzproductivitätstheorie," *Zeitschrift für Nationalökonomie*, 1933. See also Dr. Schneider's *Theorie der Produktion* (1934); pp. 57, 76.

to maximise the net earnings of these private factors. If this assumption cannot be made, difficulties emerge, which had better be examined later.

If the quantities of factors hired are $a, b, c, \cdots$, their prices π_a, $\pi_b, \pi_c, \cdots$, and their supply curves to the monopolist are given. then

$$\text{Monopoly profit} = xp - a\pi_a - b\pi_b - c\pi_c - \cdots.$$

This is maximised when

$$\left(p + x\,\frac{dp}{dx}\right) dx - \left(\pi_a + a\,\frac{d\pi_a}{da}\right) da -$$

$$\left(\pi_b + b\,\frac{d\pi_b}{db}\right) db - \cdots = 0$$

which becomes

$$MR dx - MC_a da - MC_b db - \cdots = 0,$$

if we write MC_a for $\pi_a + a\,\dfrac{d\pi_a}{da}$, and so on.

Taking $x = \phi(a, b, c, \cdots)$ as the production function, technically given, then

$$dx = \frac{\partial x}{\partial a}\,da + \frac{\partial x}{\partial b}\,db + \cdots.$$

Substituting in the above, we have

$$\left(MR\,\frac{\partial x}{\partial a} - MC_a\right) da + \left(MR\,\frac{\partial x}{\partial b} - MC_b\right) db + \cdots = 0.$$

Since this equation must hold for all values of $da, db, \cdots$, it follows that

$$MR\,\frac{\partial x}{\partial a} = MC_a,\ MR\,\frac{\partial x}{\partial b} = MC_b,\ \cdots$$

for all factors.

$MC_a, MC_b, \cdots$, are the *marginal costs to the monopolist* of hiring an additional unit of the factors, $a, b, \cdots$. If the supply curves of the factors slope upwards, these marginal costs will exceed the prices of the factors by $a\,\dfrac{d\pi_a}{da}$ etc., respectively, that is to say, by the additional amounts which have to be paid on earlier units in order to keep their prices on a level with that of the marginal unit of the factor. $MR\,\dfrac{\partial x}{\partial a}$ is conveniently described as the "marginal value product" of the factor a, it is the increment in the total value of the product which results from the application of an additional unit of *a*. The condition of factor equilibrium is thus that the marginal value product of a factor should equal its marginal cost.

The stability conditions for factor equilibrium do not appear to have been fully investigated; but a cursory examination suggests that there are several ways in which the presence of monopoly brings into the possible range of stable equilibria positions which would not be stable under perfect competition.

If the supply curve of any factor to the monopolist is horizontal, so that the monopolist is unable to affect the price of that factor, then even so his demand for that factor will be reduced below what it might have been, if the product demand curve confronting him is imperfectly elastic. Monopolistic exploitation of the consumer therefore brings about a directly consequent reduction in the demand for factors. And if a number of monopolists are employing a particular factor, they may each be unable by isolated action to influence the price of the factor; and yet, in their efforts to exploit the consumer, they will each reduce their demand for the factor, and the price of the factor may, in consequence, be reduced. But this is a different thing from the additional reduction in demand which comes about if a monopolist is able to influence the price of a factor directly, so that he takes into account the saving on other units which he gets by reducing his demand at the margin. The first type of reduction would be called by Mrs. Robinson "monopolistic exploitation" of the factor, while she has invented the term "monopsonistic" to describe exploitation of the second type.

3. SIMPLE MONOPOLY AND JOINT PRODUCTION. Nearly all the writers here discussed have confined their analysis of simply monopoly to the case where the monopolist produces only one product.[7] For reasons which will appear later, this limitation seems rather unfortunate. A brief but illuminating discussion of the problem has, however, been given by Dr. von Stackelberg, which we may here reproduce.[8]

It is convenient, in order to isolate the problem, to assume

---

[7] Professor Chamberlin gives us an interesting account of the factors which determine what that one product shall be (*op. cit.*, Chaps. 4 and 5).

[8] H. von Stackelberg, *Grundlagen einer reinen Kostentheorie* (Vienna, 1932), p. 68. See also Hotelling, "Edgeworth's Taxation Paradox," *The Journal of Political Economy*, 1932.

that the prices of the factors are now given to the monopolist; we can then introduce a cost function expressing the total cost of production of quantities x_1, x_2, $\cdots$, of the different products. Let $\phi(x_1, x_2, \cdots)$ be the cost function.

Then Monopoly profit $= p_1x_1 + p_2x_2 + p_3x_3 + \cdots - \phi(x_1, x_2, \cdots)$.

If we assume that the demand curves for the various products are independent, so that p_1 depends upon x_1 only, not on x_2, $x_3 \cdots$, then the conditions of equilibrium are

$$\frac{d}{dx_1}(p_1x_1) = \frac{\partial \phi}{\partial x_1}, \frac{d}{dx_2}(p_2x_2) = \frac{\partial \phi}{\partial x_2}, \cdots .$$

The ordinary "marginal revenue marginal cost" condition still holds.

If, however, the demand curves are not independent, then the conditions become

$$p_1 + x_1 \frac{\partial p_1}{\partial x_1} + x_2 \frac{\partial p_2}{\partial x_1} + \cdots = \frac{\partial \phi}{\partial x_1}$$

$$p_2 + x_1 \frac{\partial p_1}{\partial x_2} + x_2 \frac{\partial p_2}{\partial x_2} + \cdots = \frac{\partial \phi}{\partial x_2}$$

and so on. That is to say, the monopolist has to take into account, when fixing the output of any particular product, not only the reaction of an increased supply upon the price of that product, but also its reaction upon the prices of all other products which he is selling. If the cross-coefficients $\left(\frac{\partial p_2}{\partial x_1} \text{ etc.}\right)$ are negative (roughly speaking, the case when the different products are competitive in consumption),[9] these reactions will lower the marginal revenue curve for any particular product, and so tend to restrict output. But in the opposite case, when the cross-coefficients are positive, the marginal revenue curve will be raised; so that here the restriction of output under monopoly will be less than we should have at first expected.

If $x_2 \dfrac{\partial p_2}{\partial x_1} + x_3 \dfrac{\partial p_3}{\partial x_1} + \cdots$ is positive, and greater than $\dfrac{\partial \phi}{\partial x_1}$, it

[9] I say "roughly speaking," for it is becoming apparent that the terms *competitive* and *complementary* conceal a great many ambiguities. (See Hicks and Allen, "A Reconsideration of the Theory of Value," *Economica*, 1934.)

may pay the monopolist to produce a finite output of x_1, even if he has to give it away. And such a phenomenon is surely not uncommon; a very considerable part of what are usually described as "selling costs" comes very conveniently under this head. The subject of selling costs has been analyzed at considerable length and with much insight by Professor Chamberlin, who maintains, however, the single-product firm as the foundation of his analysis. It may be suggested that the subject could be further illuminated, and brought closer into relation with fundamentally analogous cases where the "bait" is not actually given away, if a start had been made from Dr. von Stackelberg's more general case.[10]

4. DISCRIMINATION. From one point of view, discrimination is a limiting case of joint production. When we say that a single commodity is sold by a monopolist at various different prices, the singleness of the commodity consists solely in its various units being perfect substitutes on the supply side. We can introduce this condition of being perfect substitutes in production, and so go over from joint production to discrimination.

But this line of approach, although it has conveniences, and brings discrimination into a very satisfactory relation with general monopoly theory, is not that which has traditionally been adopted. Of recent writers, Mrs. Robinson is the only one who has added anything substantial to the traditional theory of discrimination. She has devoted to it what is probably the best, as it is certainly the most ingenious, part of her book; there can be no question that these chapters will find their place along with Dupuit and Pigou on the very select bibliography of discrimination theory.

5. THE "PRIVATE" FACTORS. Most modern writing on monopoly, as we have said, has been content to assume a monopolist simply seeking to maximise his profits, that is to say, it neglects possible changes in the supply of private factors. This omission seems to me unfortunate, though it must be confessed that the subject presents grave difficulties.[11] On the one hand, unless we assume that the marginal utility of money to the monopolist is constant, we cannot unambiguously express in monetary terms

---

[10] The same foundation might be used for an analysis of monopolistic exploitation by "compulsory joint supply."

[11] Cf. Robinson, "Euler's Theorem and the Problem of Distribution," (*The Economic Journal,* 1934).

the subjective cost to the monopolist of producing additional units of output; we are therefore unable to introduce the private factors into the "marginal revenue = marginal cost" equation, and are obliged to fall back upon Paretian indifference curves, more cumbrous, and in this case decidedly less informative. The second difficulty is even more formidable. Under conditions of monopoly, there is no reason to suppose any particular connection between subjective cost and *output*, since it is probable that a considerable part of the monopolist's efforts and sacrifices will be devoted, not to increasing his output, but finding to what precise point he should restrict it. Now, as Professor Bowley[12] and others have pointed out, the variation in monopoly profit for some way on either side of the highest profit output may often be small (in the general case, it will depend on the difference between the slopes of the marginal revenue and marginal cost curves); and if this is so, the subjective costs involved in securing a close adaptation to the most profitable output may well outweigh the meagre gains offered. It seems not at all unlikely that people in monopolistic positions will very often be people with sharply rising subjective costs; if this is so, they are likely to exploit their advantage much more by not bothering to get very near the position of maximum profit, than by straining themselves to get very close to it. The best of all monopoly profits is a quiet life.

II. Monopolistic Competition

1. We come now to the "group problem," the equilibrium of a group of firms producing similar but not identical products. The treatment of this problem by Professor Chamberlin and by Mrs. Robinson (the same applies, though with some qualification, to Mr. Harrod) is based upon a very neat geometrical proposition.[13] Since the products of the various firms are not identical, the demand curve which confronts each individual firm will not be horizontal, but will slope downwards.[14] On the other hand, if

---

[12] *Mathematical Groundwork of Economics,* pp. 25, 60.

[13] Chamberlin, *op. cit.,* p. 84; Robinson, pp. 94–95; Harrod, "Doctrines of Imperfect Competition," *The Quarterly Journal of Economics,* 1934, p. 457.

[14] Professor Chamberlin constructs this individual demand curve on the assumption that the prices of the rival commodities remain unchanged (p. 75). Mrs. Robinson's formulation seems distinctly ambiguous (p. 21).

entry into the industry is free, it will be impossible for the firms in the industry to earn more than "normal profits." On the basis of the first assumption, it is concluded that the output of each firm will have to satisfy the condition of monopolistic equilibrium, marginal revenue = marginal cost. On the basis of the second, it is concluded that the price of each product will have to equal average cost, when average cost is calculated in such a way as to include "normal profits."

If then we write π_x = average cost (in the above sense) of producing an output x, and p_x = the price at which the firm can sell that output, the second condition gives us

(1) $$p_x = \pi_x$$

while we have from the first condition

$$\frac{d}{dx}(xp_x) = \frac{d}{dx}(x\pi_x)$$

$$\therefore \quad p_x + x\frac{dp_x}{dx} = \pi_x + x\frac{d\pi_x}{dx}$$

(2) $$\therefore \text{ from (1), } \frac{dp_x}{dx} = \frac{d\pi_x}{dx}.$$

From (1) and (2) it follows that the demand curve and the average cost curve must touch at a point of equilibrium.

Since the demand curve is downward sloping, the average cost curve must also be downward sloping at the equilibrium point. Equilibrium under monopolistic competition is only possible when average costs are diminishing; that is to say, the equilibrium output of a firm will be less than the output which would give minimum average costs—the output which would actually be reached under conditions of perfect competition. From this Professor Chamberlin proceeds to the conclusion that analysis based on perfect competition makes "the price always too low, the cost of production too low, the scale of production too large, and the number of producers too small."

In order for us to estimate the importance of this result, we must begin by examining the premises on which it is based. To take first the "average cost curve." When Walras and Pareto reckoned profits into costs, they were thinking of conditions of perfect competition, and their conclusion that price = average cost, so that the entrepreneur makes "ni bénéfice ni perte," meant nothing else than that the private factors of the entrepreneur could get no other return in the static equilibrium of perfect competition than would have accrued to them if they had been directly hired out on the market. But is it possible to transfer this conception to the theory of monopolistic competition? So far as the private factors are to some extent unique, so that there are no perfect substitutes for them (and this seems the most likely case in which monopolistic competition might arise), they can have no market price which is not to some extent monopolistically determined. If there are perfect substitutes for them, why are those perfect substitutes not being employed in making perfect substitutes for the product?

There is only one way out of this dilemma, and I can only suppose that it is this which the writers in question have in mind. The factors of production, private or hired, may be sufficiently divisible, and sufficiently scattered in ownership, to ensure that there is a perfect market for them, or something sufficiently perfect for the imperfections to be negligible. But there may still be a range of increasing returns in the production of any particular product, due to indivisibilities in the production function, not in the factors themselves.[15] If this is the case, substantially homogeneous factors may be put together by a limited number of firms into a limited number of different products, each of which is unique, and the demand curve for each of which is downward sloping.

This is the only state of affairs of which the Chamberlin-Robinson apparatus seems to be an exact description; it is probable that it does correspond with a certain region of reality. But I cannot help feeling that the application of the apparatus is implicitly much exaggerated. This is only partly because of the actual heterogeneity of factors—both writers accept this difficulty, and at the worst it only means that the technical apparatus is over-rigid. They can still claim to have shown that monopolistic restriction of output is compatible with earnings in no way out of the ordinary. A much more serious objection arises from the variability of the product.

---

[15] Kaldor, "The Equilibrium of the Firm," *The Economic Journal*, March 1934, p. 65n. On the general question of indivisibilities and costs, see also the appendix to Mrs. Robinson's book; also Schneider, *Theorie der Production*, Chap. 1.

There are two relevant sorts of product variation. One, the only kind which has been much discussed, is where each firm produces a single product, but the nature of that product is capable of being changed. This problem has been dealt with mostly in terms of location; a product available in a different place is economically a different product, and a change in the location of the firm is one of the ways of varying the product. (Professor Chamberlin's discussion of location is, however, reinforced by a discussion of the same problem in more general terms.)

In his paper, "Stability in Competition,"[16] Professor Hotelling had demonstrated that there is a tendency, when two firms are competing for a given market, for them to get together in the centre of the market. This tendency in itself would thus be favorable to the establishment of conditions of approximately perfect competition, if it could be shown to hold for more firms than two.

Unfortunately, as Professor Chamberlin shows, this is not so.[17] Once there are more than two firms in the market, they will tend to scatter, since any firm will try to avoid being caught between a pair of others. It seems evident that this general tendency to dispersion will be present when it is a question of quality competition as well as of competition in location, though of course the possible kinds of variation are even more complex.

Thus, so long as we retain the "one firm, one product" assumption, variability of the product is not sufficient to prevent an appreciable degree of imperfection in the elasticity of the demand curve confronting any particular firm. The position seems, however, to be different once we drop this assumption.

In fact, when "product" is interpreted in the strict economic sense of a collection of articles that are to the consumer perfect substitutes, almost every firm does produce a considerable range of different products. It does so largely because there are economies to be got from producing them together,[18] and these economies consist largely in the fact that the different products require much the same overheads. Further, at any time the products it is actually

---

[16] *Op. cit.* See also Zeuthen, "Theoretical Remarks on Price Policy," *The Quarterly Journal of Economics,* 1933.

[17] *Theory of Monopolistic Competition,* Appendix C.

[18] In the sense that it costs less to produce outputs x_1 and x_2 in a single firm, than it would cost (in total) to produce output x_1 in one firm and output x_2 in another.

producing will probably not exhaust the list of products it could produce from approximately the same plant. Thus it will have various potential products which it could produce in small quantities at quite a low marginal cost.

Now when other producers are able to supply small quantities of highly competitive products at low prices, this is at last an effective force tending to keep the demand curve for a particular product of a particular firm very highly elastic. Of course, it will probably not be perfectly elastic; for in fact any degree of specialization on a particular line offers a *prima facie* case that the specializing firm has some particular facilities for that line, and it may be able to carry out a certain degree of restriction before it tempts other firms to follow it. Further, a firm is always likely to be on the lookout for a line in which it is relatively safe from such competition. Nevertheless, this consideration does seem to go a good way to justify the traditional practice of economists in treating the assumption of perfect competition as a satisfactory approximation over a very wide field.[19]

A considerable degree of the sort of market imperfection we have been discussing seems likely to arise in two cases only: (1) where the producer has command of some specialized "factor," such as patent, legal privilege, site, or business capacity, for which no clear substitute is available; (2) where economies of scale are narrowly specialized, so that it would be impossible for another firm to produce commodities highly competitive with these produced by the first firm excepting at much greater marginal cost. There is no doubt that such conditions as these are fairly frequent, but they are, after all, precisely the cases which have been traditionally treated under the heading of monopoly.

2. DUOPOLY. There is, however, one further difficulty of great

---

[19] Cf. Shove, "The Imperfection of the Market," *The Economic Journal,* 1933, pp. 115–116. [Note added in 1950: The above passage has been much criticized. I myself should not have written it in this form if I had absorbed the message of Mr. Kaldor's "Market Imperfection and Excess Capacity," *Economica,* 1935 (reprinted in the present volume, pages 384–403), which he was writing almost at the same time as I was writing this paper. My present view is more nearly expressed on p. 116 of "The Rehabilitation of Consumers' Surplus," *The Review of Economic Studies,* 1941. It is certainly not true that the argument in the text can be used as a justification of the perfect competition hypothesis; but it is not wholly valueless as a criticism of the formal theory of imperfect competition.]

importance. We have suggested that the demand curve for a particular product of a particular firm will usually be kept highly elastic by the incursion of other producers selling small quantities of highly competitive products, if the first firm raises its price, But if they do so, will not the first firm retaliate on them?

Two cases have thus to be distinguished. The first is when the other potential producers are fairly numerous. In this case, they are not likely to be much deterred by the fear of retaliation. For although the first firm may find it profitable to turn its attention to some other product if it meets with competition in the line it had first chosen, the chance of that other product being highly competitive with the products of any particular other producer is small.

In the other case, when the other potential producers are few, the fear of retaliation is likely to be more serious, and it may very well stop poaching.

The difficult problem which arises from the relations of a very small number of competing firms has been much studied in recent years, but there has not yet developed any very close agreement on the solution. Largely owing to the difficulty of the problem, it has been chiefly studied in its most simple case, that of two firms producing an identical product—duopoly.[20]

The theory of duopoly has a long history; and here we can do no more than allude to the classical theory of Cournot, and the displacement of Cournot's theory by the criticisms of Bertrand and Edgeworth, which form the ancient history of the subject. Edgeworth's solution, based on "the characteristic freedom of the monopolist to vary price," involved such peculiar assumptions about costs that it could hardly have held the field forever. The post-war period therefore saw a renaissance of Cournotism, led by Amoroso and Wicksell;[21] this movement is represented also by the chapter on "Mehrfaches Monopol" in Dr. Schneider's book.[22] In the next stage, criticisms of both the Cournot and Edgeworth

---

[20] Chamberlin, however, has made at any rate a preliminary investigation of the more complex cases where several firms are involved. See his sections on "oligopoly" (*Theory*, pp. 100, 170).

[21] Amoroso, *Lezioni d'economia matematica;* Wicksell, Review of Bowley's *Mathematical Groundwork, Archiv für Sozialwissenschaft,* 1927.

[22] Schneider, *Reine Theorie,* Chap. 4.

solutions were offered by Dr. Zeuthen and by Professor Chamberlin;[23] it then became clear that each of the rivals had pointed the way towards a possible solution, but that even together they did not exhaust the list.

A very convenient line of approach, which sets these alternative solutions in their places, and so opens a path towards a general theory, can be developed from a hint given in Professor Bowley's *Mathematical Groundwork*.[24] It is this approach which appears to be gaining ground at present. Its main principle can be expressed as follows.[25]

The marginal revenue, which a duopolist endeavors to equate to his marginal cost,

$$= \frac{d}{dx_1} (px_1)$$

where x_1 is his output, and $p = f(x_1 + x_2)$, x_2 being the output of his rival. Thus

$$MR_1 = \frac{d}{dx_1} (px_1) = p + x_1 f'(x_1 + x_2) + x_1 f'(x_1 + x_2) \frac{\delta x_2}{\delta x_1}.$$

The marginal revenue curve which confronts the duopolist is thus in part dependent upon a quantity $\frac{\delta x_2}{\delta x_1}$, which we can only interpret as the degree to which the duopolist expects his rival to expand (or contract) output, if he himself expands his output by an increment dx_1. Since $f'(x_1 + x_2)$ is negative, a negative value of $\frac{\delta x_2}{\delta x_1}$ will raise the adjusted marginal revenue curve of the duopolist, and thus be favorable to an expansion of output; a positive value will favor a contraction.

The conception of these "conjectural variations," $\frac{\delta x_2}{\delta x_1}$ etc., has been analysed in very general terms by Professor Frisch.[26] There is, in the short period, no need for any particular degree of con-

---

[23] Zeuthen, *Problems of Monopoly*, Chap. 2; Chamberlin, *Theory*, Chap. 3, which substantially reproduces his article on "Duopoly," *The Quarterly Journal of Economics*, 1929.

[24] P. 38.

[25] The following owes much to some yet unpublished work by Mr. W. M. Allen, of Oxford.

[26] "Monopole—Polypole—La Notion de Force dans l'économie," *Nationaløkonomisk Tidsskrift*, 1933.

sistency[26a] between the conjecture of the first duopolist $\frac{\delta x_2}{\delta x_1}$, and that of the second $\frac{\delta x_1}{\delta x_2}$.

The equation of marginal revenue and marginal cost thus determines the output of the first duopolist, once the output of the second duopolist, and the first duopolist's conjecture as to the variation of this output are given. For any particular type of conjecture, we can thus construct a "reaction curve," similar to that employed by Cournot, giving the preferred output of the first duopolist, corresponding to each possible output of the second. A similar reaction curve can be constructed for the second duopolist, and the intersection of the two will give the point of equilibrium.

In the majority of cases, these reaction curves will be negatively inclined;[27] and in the majority of these cases, the inclination will be such that an increased output by the other duopolist will react on the first in such a way as to increase the total output of both together. If we confine our attention to these *normal* cases, which are much the most likely to yield stable solutions, the more interesting assumptions about conjectures which have been made by recent writers fall into their places very simply.

[26a] [Note added in 1950: This can only be true in the *very* short period. The most important work in duopoly, since the present article was written, has consisted in the superimposition of a consistency postulate on the above theory. See R. F. Kahn, "The Problem of Duopoly," *The Economic Journal*, 1937.]

[27] The condition for negative inclination is that $1 + \frac{hx_1}{x}\left(1 + \frac{\delta x_2}{\delta x_1}\right)$ should be positive; where h is the "adjusted concavity" of the market demand curve. (That is to say, $h = \frac{(x_1 + x_2)f''(x_1 + x_2)}{f'(x_1 + x_2)}$. Cf. Robinson, *Economics of Imperfect Competition*, p. 40.) Since we may assume that in all sensible cases, $1 + \frac{\delta x_2}{\delta x_1}$ is positive, it follows that the reaction curve will be negatively inclined in all cases when h is positive (when the demand curve is convex upwards) and also for a considerable number of cases when h is negative. It has been further shown by Mr. Allen that in such cases of negative inclination, the slope of the reaction curve will also (for reasons of stability) be numerically less than 1, excepting when there is a high degree of asymmetry between the positions of the two duopolists. "Normal cases" are defined as satisfying these two conditions, so that dx_1/dx_2, taken along the reaction curve of the first duopolist, lies between 0 and -1.

(1) If the conjectural variations are both zero, we have of course the Cournot case. (2) If one of the conjectural variations is zero, but the other duopolist takes as his conjectural variation the actual slope of the reaction curve of his rival, we have the case of an "active" policy by one duopolist.[28] In *normal* conditions, this will make the conjectural variation of the active duopolist negative; thus, as compared with the Cournot case, it will raise his marginal revenue curve, increase his output, and (again in normal conditions) lead to an increased total output, and so a lower price. (3) If both duopolists act in this manner, each calculating conjectural variations from the other's Cournotian reaction curve, we have a curious case which has been investigated by Dr. von Stackelberg and Mr. Harrod.[29] In normal conditions, once more, this will lead to a further expansion of total output, and a further fall in price. (4) There does not seem to be any reason why we should stop here. One duopolist may become doubly "active," and calculate a conjectural variation from the reaction curve of his rival on the assumption that the rival is active. In most, though not (it appears) quite all, *normal* cases, this would lead to a further fall in price. The process becomes similar to one of price-cutting.

But once we are on the road of competitive price-cutting, it is reasonable to suppose that, sooner or later, one duopolist or the other would perceive that his conjecture that an increase in his output was leading to a contraction of his rival's was proving wrong. Once he acted on this, and constructed a conjectural variation based on this experience (and consequently a *positive* variation) the whole situation would be transformed. Price-cutting would give place to "tacit combination"; positive conjectures, again in normal conditions, would give a higher price than that given by the Cournot equilibrium.[30]

The method just described is capable of extension to the case

[28] v. Stackelberg, "Sulla teoria del duopolio e del polipolio," *Rivista italiana di statistica,* June 1933. This article also contains an important and ingenious extension of the theory to the case of several producers.

[29] v. Stackelberg, *ibid.* Harrod, "The Equilibrium of Duopoly," *The Economic Journal,* June 1934.

[30] Nicoll, "Professor Chamberlin's Theory of Limited Competition," *The Quarterly Journal of Economics,* February 1934. Mr. Nicoll's case of tacit combination emerges if we write $\dfrac{\delta x_2}{\delta x_1} = \dfrac{x_2}{x_1}, \dfrac{\delta x_1}{\delta x_2} = \dfrac{x_1}{x_2}.$

where the product of one duopolist is not a perfect substitute for that of the other. We have only to write $p_1 = f_1(x_1, x_2)$, $p_2 = f_2(x_1, x_2)$; the two sellers will now of course usually sell at different prices. We then have

Adjusted marginal reve-
nue of first seller $= \dfrac{d}{dx_1}(p_1 x_1) = p_1 + x_1 \dfrac{\partial p_1}{\partial x_1} + x_1 \dfrac{\partial p_1}{\partial x_2}\left(\dfrac{\delta x_2}{\delta x_1}\right),$

from which we proceed much as before. This highly general solution can be applied whatever is the relation between the demands for the products; it can thus be applied to cases where the products are complementary instead of competitive.[31] Here $\dfrac{\partial p_1}{\partial x_2}$ will probably be positive, so that it is an anticipated consequential expansion of the other's output which will raise the marginal revenue curve of the first duopolist, and *vice versa*.[32]

III. BILATERAL MONOPOLY

"Bilateral Monopoly" is a phrase which has been applied to two different problems, and it is well to keep them distinct. The first is the case of isolated exchange, or of exchange between a group of buyers and a group of sellers, each acting in combination. Now so far as this problem is concerned, when the exchange is studied *in vacuo*, without reference to other people (outside the two groups) who may be indirectly concerned, I think one may say that there is complete agreement among economists. It has been evident since the days of Edgeworth that isolated exchange leads to "undecidable opposition of interests,"[33] and that therefore the problem is indeterminate, in the sense that the mere condition of each party seeking its maximum advantage is not sufficient to define an equilibrium.

The second problem is a more complex one. It arises when the commodity sold is a raw material or factor of production; so that we have also to take into account the relation of the buyer of the raw material to another market—that in which he sells his

[31] Cf. Edgeworth, "The Pure Theory of Monopoly," *Papers* II, pp. 122–126.

[32] See further, on the subject of duopoly, Professor Divisia's paper to the Leyden meeting of the Econometric Society, summarized in *Econometrica*, June 1934, and also in the *Revue d'Économie politique*, May 1934.

[33] *Mathematical Psychics*, p. 29.

finished product. For this problem there existed a solution alternative to Edgeworth's, that of Cournot; Cournot had concluded that
this more general problem is determinate. Here, as in the question of duopoly, Cournot has his modern followers; his position
is defended by Dr. Schneider, and also, though with considerable
qualifications, by Dr. Zeuthen.[34]

It must be confessed, however, that the reader of their works
finds it very difficult to see just how the presence of a consumers'
market makes any difference to the opposition of interests deduced
by Edgeworth; and we have the authority of Professor Bowley in

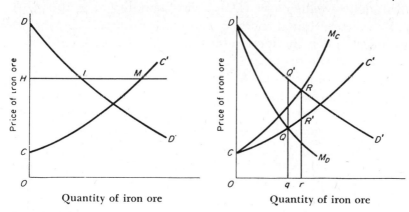

support of the view that there is indeterminateness also in the
more general case.[35] Personally, I find myself in agreement with
Professor Bowley; but I think it may be worth while to restate
Professor Bowley's argument in terms of the *marginal revenue*
concept, since this seems to make the crux of the dispute clearer
than it has been made up to the present.

A, a monopolist producer of raw material (iron ore), is selling
to B, a monopolist producer of finished product (steel). Now, as
we have seen, B's demand curve for iron ore (DD') is given by
the marginal value product of iron ore (i.e., marginal physical
product of iron ore in steel production $\times$ marginal revenue from
the sale of steel); while A's supply curve of iron ore will be given
by his ordinary marginal cost curve (CC'). That is to say, if a

[34] Schneider, *Reine Theorie*, Chap. 2; Zeuthen, *Problems of Monopoly*,
pp. 65 ff.

[35] "Bilateral Monopoly," *The Economic Journal*, 1928.

particular price OH is fixed by some external authority, A would be willing to supply HM units, B would be willing to take HL units; the amount actually sold will be whichever of these is the less. Now, within limits, the higher the price fixed, the greater will be A's profits, the lower the price fixed, the greater will be the profit of B. There is thus an opposition of interests. But this only within limits; for after a point it would not pay A to push up the price any further. The output which maximizes A's profits will be given by the intersection of the curve marginal to DD' with CC'. DD' is the demand curve confronting A; we can draw a marginal revenue curve (DM_D) corresponding to it, to cut CC' at Q. A vertical line through Q cuts the horizontal axis in q, and DD' in Q'. Then the most profitable position for A is when his output is Oq and his price $Q'q$.

If on the other hand, B can fix the price, what is the point where his profits are maximized? This is found by drawing a curve marginal to CC' (CM_C), to intersect DD' in R. Draw $RR'r$ perpendicular to the horizontal axis. The output most favourable to B will then be Or, and the price $R'r$.

Thus there does seem to be an "opposition of interests"; how did Cournot and his followers come to an opposite view? They would hold that there is an equilibrium with the price at $Q'q$, for in this case both producers are earning a maximum monopoly profit, B from the consumers of steel, A from B. That is perfectly true; no monopoly action by A can stop B earning a monopoly profit from the consumers. But 𝔅 is not only a monopoly seller with regard to the consumers; he is also a monopoly buyer with respect to A. If he is allowed to do so, he will also extract a monopsony profit from A; it was this that Cournot left out of account.

As we have said, this indeterminateness does not mean that the law of causality is suspended; it only means that the static assumptions of fixed demand and cost curves do not suffice to determine the price. Attempts have been made by Dr. Zeuthen and myself to reach a determinate solution by introducing more "dynamic" factors.[36] Dr. Zeuthen's solution proceeds by examin-

---

[36] Zeuthen, *op. cit.*, Chap. 4; "du Monopole Bilatéral," *Revue d'Économie politique*, 1933; Hicks, *Theory of Wages*, Chap. 7; A treatment somewhat similar to Dr. Zeuthen's is to be found in G. di Nardi, "L'Indeterminazione nel Monopolio bilaterale," *Archivo Scientifico*, Bari, 1934.

ing the probability of each side breaking off relations, which correspond to each set of terms; mine by considering the length of time for which either party would be willing to "strike" in order to get any particular price. The two methods appear to be complementary.

IV. Conclusion

I have so far confined my remarks to the purely formal aspect of recent work on monopoly; but in conclusion something ought to be said about the applicability of this now well-developed technique. It is evidently the opinion of some of the writers under discussion that the modern theory of monopoly is not only capable of throwing considerable light on the general principles underlying an individualistic economic structure, but that it is also capable of extensive use in the analysis of particular practical economic problems, that is to say, in applied economics. Personally, I cannot but feel sceptical about this.

We have already seen, in the case of duopoly, that the marginal revenue of a duopolist depends upon a term which can properly be called "conjectural." It is not the actual degree to which the second seller's output would change—it is the estimate of this degree on the part of the first seller. But once we have seen this, why mark this term only as conjectural? Is not the slope of the individual demand curve confronting a simple monopolist conjectural too? There does not seem to be any reason why a monopolist should not make a mistake in estimating the slope of the demand curve confronting him, and should maintain a certain output, thinking it was the position which maximized his profit, although he could actually have increased his profit by expanding or contracting.[37]

It is this subjective character of the individual demand curve which leads one to scepticism about the applicability of the apparatus. For what are the objective grounds from which we can deduce the existence of a significant degree of imperfect competition? It may be said that as soon as we find firms concerning themselves with a price policy, or undertaking selling costs, some degree of imperfect competition must be present. This may be

---

[37] This argument is fortified if the demand curve is interpreted (as for most purposes it probably ought to be) as a fairly "long-period" demand curve.

granted;[38] but what degree? Is it important or negligible? There is no means of finding out but to ask the monopolist, and it will be kind of him to tell us.

Whether competition is perfect or imperfect, the expansion of the individual firm will be stopped by factors which are purely subjective estimates; in the one case by rising subjective costs or costs of organization;[39] in the other by an estimated downward slope of the marginal revenue curve. Objective facts give us no means of distinguishing between them.

The new theories seem to make little difference to the laws of change as they are exhibited in the traditional analysis; usually they do no more than suggest new reasons why we should get certain familiar effects, and there is very little means of distinguishing between the new reasons and the old. Whether an industry is monopolized, or duopolized, or polypolized, or operates under conditions of perfect competition, we shall expect a rise in demand to lead to a rise in output (though in all cases there are possible, but highly improbable, exceptions); and it is still likely that the rise in demand will be accompanied either by no change in price, or by a rise. New reasons are indeed adduced why a rise in output may be accompanied by a fall in price; it may be due to a rise in the elasticity of demand to the individual firm, rather than to economies of the Marshallian type. But the new explanation is not overwhelmingly convincing, and does not drive the Marshallian from the field.[40]

---

[38] Professor W. H. Hutt, "Economic Method and the Concept of Competition," *Economic Journal of South Africa,* June 1934, disputes this as far as selling costs are concerned. His argument would appear to be valid so long as advertisement and product are sold in fixed proportions, but it ceases to be so if the "coefficients of consumption" are variable.

[39] Cf. E. A. G. Robinson, "The problem of management and the size of firms," *The Economic Journal,* June 1934, and the same author's *Structure of Competitive Industry.* Also Kaldor, *op. cit.*

[40] It is tempting to propose a rehabilitation of Marshall on the basis of these recent developments. Since it has become clear that "increasing returns" are mainly a matter of indivisibilities and discontinuities, it is very possible that a firm may be in perfect competitive equilibrium with its (conjectured) demand curve horizontal, at the point of equilibrium, although it knows that a considerable increase in output would enable it to diminish average costs (of hired factors) considerably. But it is uncertain whether so large an increase

It does indeed now become possible that a rise in supply—if it takes the form of an influx of new firms—may actually lead to a rise in price, as would not be possible under perfect competition. Yet the conditions for this to happen, that the influx of firms should make the demand curve confronting each firm in the industry *less elastic,* is so peculiar, that it is hard to attach very much importance to this case—at least, as analyzed.

It is therefore hard to see that the new analysis does much to displace Marshallian methods. Marshall's assumptions are simpler, and if we are unable to tell which of two hypotheses is more appropriate, the simpler has the obvious claim to be chosen. But of course this is not to say that in strong cases—cases, for example, where discrimination is practiced—we are not obliged to assume monopoly conditions, and to make what use we can of the elaborations here described.

From this point of view, substantial gains have certainly been made; we are now in the possession of a much more complete theory of monopoly than was the case a very few years ago. If, when we have it, it seems less use than had been hoped, this is not an uncommon experience in the history of human thought.[41]

---

in sales could be brought about without a considerable reduction in price, and refrains from expansion because it is unwilling to take the risk. This seems at least as plausible a construction as the other, and better suited to a world of very imperfect knowledge.

On the general question of discontinuity in cost, see M. Joseph, "A Discontinuous Cost Curve," *The Economic Journal,* Sept. 1933.

[41] [Note added in 1950: The great weakness of this article, running all through it, but particularly evident in the last section, is its failure to perceive that the significance of monopoly theory lies in the direction of welfare economics. When the theory is conceived of as a branch of positive economics, the above strictures remain fully justified; but they are not at all so well justified when the theory is looked at the other way round.]

19

MARKET IMPERFECTION AND EXCESS CAPACITY *

BY NICHOLAS KALDOR ‖

Of all the doctrines emerging from recent work on the economics of imperfect competition, none appears more intellectually striking or more significant from a practical point of view than the doctrine of "excess capacity." It is intellectually striking, because it admits possibilities which the traditional "laws of economics" seem to have excluded: e.g., that an increase in "supply" may be followed by a rise in price.[1] And it is practically significant, because if the main contentions of the theory are found to be correct, it affords some reasons for interfering with the "free play of competitive forces" on grounds upon which traditional economic theory would have dismissed the case for interference. The theory envisages a situation, where, on the one hand the market facing a group of competing firms is, for one reason or another, not absolutely "perfect," while on the other hand the entry of resources into the "industry" is free, and it shows that under such conditions "competition" (i.e., the free flow of resources into uses where they expect to obtain the largest net remuneration) will drive each producer to a situation in which it is not using its resources to the best advantage; and it will thus lead to a reduction of the physical productivity of resources all round. In a sense, it thus reverses the old argument about "increasing returns" and monopoly; it not only says that falling costs will lead to monopoly

---

*Economica, New Series, Vol. II (1935), pp. 33–50. Reprinted, by the courtesy of the publisher and the author, without change from the original text.

‖ King's College, Cambridge University, England.

[1] Since Marshall, we are aware of the fact that given certain cost conditions an increase in demand may be followed by a fall in price. But neither the Marshallian, nor, so far as the present writer is aware, any other theoretical system left room for the possibility that under certain market conditions, an increase in the number of sources of supply (an inflow of resources into the "industry") could lead to a rise in prices.

but that a monopolistic or rather a pseudo-monopolistic situation[2] will automatically lead each firm to a position where it is faced with falling average costs.[3] It is a highly ingenious and one might almost say revolutionary doctrine: it shows up "free competition" (i.e., the freedom of entry into any trade or industry) not in the traditional and respectable role as the eliminator of the unfit but in the much more dubious role as the creator of excess capacity. It affords an excellent theoretical background for the age-old cry of business men about the "wastes of competition"—so far completely neglected by the economists. It is worth while therefore to examine this theory in some detail.

The theory is put forward both in Professor Chamberlin's recent work and also in Mrs. Robinson's book.[4] Closer inspection reveals, however, that Mrs. Robinson's version possesses a merely formal similarity with Professor Chamberlin's theory. For Mrs. Robinson includes in her "cost curves" such profits which are not competed away by the entry of new producers; and under the circumstances, her statement that "demand curves will be tangential to cost curves" and that firms will be of "less than their

---

[2] We shall see later what precisely the term "monopolistic" implies in this connection.

[3] "Falling average costs," if they are to be regarded as the criterion of "excess capacity," should be interpreted that in the relevant output, costs are falling *in a state of long-period equilibrium* (after *all* adjustments have been made to that output), which also implies that *variable costs* are falling (since in the long run the supply of all factors—even the resources supplied by the entrepreneur himself—can be assumed variable and consequently there are no "fixed" costs). Since in a state of full equilibrium "short-run" cost curves must be tangential to the long-run cost curve: falling long-period costs also imply that short-run total costs are falling. But the converse is not necessarily true; falling short-run total costs (the "fixed costs" being calculated on a "historic" basis) need not involve falling long-run costs, for the same output, and consequently these are no safe criteria for the prevalence of excess capacity.

[4] Chamberlin, *The Theory of Monopolistic Competition,* Chap. V. Mrs. Robinson, *The Economics of Imperfect Competition,* Chap. 7. The theory, of course, is by no means completely new. Wicksell already stated it (*Lectures,* p. 86) and it is also to be found, in essentials, in Cairnes' *Political Economy,* p. 115. It was outlined in P. Sraffa's well-known article ("The Laws of Returns under Competitive Conditions," *The Economic Journal,* 1926, reprinted in the present volume, page 180). The first systematic exposition is, however, Chamberlin's.

optimum size" is merely a statement of a tautology.[5] It does not imply "excess capacity" or anything of that sort. In the subsequent analysis we shall follow therefore mainly Professor Chamberlin's statement of the theory.

II

The main argument can be stated briefly. Although not stated so explicitly, it is really based on four assumptions. Firstly, it is assumed that there are a large number of independent producers, each selling one product only, which is "slightly different" from the products of the rest of the producers. The words "slightly different" imply, that while the demand for the product of any of the producers is highly sensitive to the prices charged by the others, yet this sensitiveness is never so great as to compel all producers to sell at the same price. It implies that a producer, by lowering his price relatively to his competitors' prices, will attract away some, but not *all* their customers; or alternatively, that he will lose some, but not all of his own customers, if he raises his price relatively to the rest.[6] It is assumed, secondly, that *"consumers' preferences are fairly evenly distributed among the different varieties,"*[7] and since there are a large number of them "any adjustment of price or of 'product' by a single producer spreads its influence over so many of his competitors that the impact felt by any one is negligible and does not lead him to any readjust-

---

[5] Cf. on this point G. F. Shove, "The Imperfection of the Market" (*The Economic Journal,* March 1933), an article, which in the present writer's view, contains one of the most penetrating analyses so far published on this whole subject.

[6] In technical terms this implies that the consumer's "elasticity of substitution" between the different producers' products is large, but not infinite; which is the same thing as saying that the "cross-elasticities of demand" (the elasticity of demand for one producer's product with respect to another producer's price) are considerable but not infinite. Looking at it in this way, "monopoly" and "perfect competition" appear as the two limiting cases, where the "cross-elasticities" are zero or infinite, respectively; and there can be little doubt that the large majority of industrial producers in the real world are faced with imperfect markets in this sense.

[7] Which implies, in the above terminology, that the cross-elasticity of the demand for the product of any producer is of the same order of magnitude with respect to the price of *any* of his competitors. Cf. my article, "Mrs. Robinson's Economics of Imperfect Competition," *Economica,* August 1934, p. 339

ment of his own situation."[8] Thus, given the prices of all the others, a "demand curve" can be drawn up with respect to the product of each.[9] Thirdly, it is assumed that no producer possesses an "institutional monopoly" over any of the varieties produced and thus the entry of new producers "into the field in general and every portion of it in particular is free and unimpeded." Fourthly, the long-run cost curves of all producers are assumed to be falling up to a certain rate of output; in other words, it is assumed that up to a certain output, there are "economics of scale" (Professor Chamberlin's cost curves are U-shaped, i.e., they begin to rise after a certain point. But while the legitimacy of the latter assumption in the case of long-run curves appears doubtful,[10] it does not affect his argument, which merely requires that costs should be falling over a certain range.) The elasticities of the demand curve and the cost curves of each producer are also assumed to be the same, but this, as I shall try to show, is not essential to the main argument so long as "institutional monopolies" are assumed to be absent. Now, given these two curves each producer will try to produce that output which will maximise his own profits, i.e., equate marginal revenue with marginal cost. But since marginal revenue is less than price, price will be higher than average cost (including under the latter the displacement cost of the resources supplied by the entrepreneur himself) unless average cost is also, and to a corresponding degree, higher than marginal cost (which it can only be if average costs are falling). Let us assume that this is not the case initially. Entrepreneurs in the industry will then make "monopoly profits," i.e., remuneration for their own resources will be higher than that which similar resources could earn elsewhere. This will attract such resources into the "industry"; new firms will come in, producing new sub-

---

[8] Chamberlin, p. 83. Mrs. Robinson does not state this so definitely, but her analysis is implicitly based on the same assumptions. Professor Chamberlin states (pp. 82–83) that he only makes these assumptions temporarily in order to facilitate the exposition, and removes them later on (pp. 100–111). But, as I shall try to show, the theory, in its rigid form at any rate, really stands or falls with these assumptions.

[9] In the absence of these assumptions one can speak of a demand curve only in the sense of an "imagined demand curve," cf. below.

[10] Cf. my article, "The Equilibrium of the Firm," *The Economic Journal*, March 1934, p. 70.

stitutes, which will reduce the demand for all existing producers; and this process will continue, until profits are reduced to normal, i.e., the difference between the actual earnings and the displacement costs of the entrepreneur's own resources is eliminated. In the position of final equilibrium not only will marginal cost be equal to marginal revenue, but average cost will also be equal to price. The demand curve will thus be "tangential" to the cost curve. The effect of the entry of new competitors will not necessarily reduce the price of existing products; it may even raise them. The profits which the entrepreneur no longer earns will thus not be passed on to the consumer in the form of lower prices but are mainly absorbed in lower productive efficiency. The producers, *as a body,* could of course prevent this from occurring by reducing their prices *in anticipation* of the entry of new competitors. But since the appearance of any *single* new producer will only affect the demand of a *single* existing producer very slightly, while similarly the reduction of price of a *single* existing producer will only slightly affect the profits which a potential producer can expect, no producer could take these indirect effects on his own price policy into consideration.

There can be little doubt that given these assumptions the theory is unassailable. Any criticism therefore must be directed against the usefulness and the consistency of the assumptions selected.

III

1. The first of these concerns the assumptions made about the interrelations of the demand for the products of various producers (which are substantially the same as those underlying Mrs. Robinson's conception of an "imperfectly competitive industry"[11]). No doubt, in most cases, the products of various producers selling the same sort of goods are not "perfect substitutes" to each other in the sense that the slightest price difference would eliminate all demand for the products of higher-price producers. The reasons for such "market imperfection" may be classed under one of three headings. There may either be slight differences in the products

---

[11] Cf. *The Economics of Imperfect Competition,* Chap. 1. Cf. on this point my review, *op. cit.,* p. 339.

themselves (as in the case of motor cars, wireless sets, etc., the absence of "standardisation"); or differences in the geographical location of producers in cases where the consumers themselves are distributed over an area; or finally, there may exist a certain "inertia" on behalf of the buyers themselves who will require either some time, or a certain magnitude in the price-difference, before they make up their minds to buy from another seller— even if they are quite indifferent as between the products of different sellers.[12] Whatever the cause, the effect, from the analytical point of view, will be the same: the "cross elasticities" of demand will have a positive finite value. But is there any justification for the further assumption that they will also be of the same order of magnitude with respect to the prices of *any* group of rival products? Can we say that any adjustment of price or of "product" by a single producer will spread its influence evenly over all his competitors? No doubt, cases are conceivable when it would. When the "imperfection of the market" is due to sheer buyers' inertia *and nothing else*, we could invoke the law of large numbers and say that the buyers who no longer buy from A, will pair themselves more or less evenly with B, C, D. . . . But buyers' inertia, though an important factor in practice, is rarely found in isolation as a cause of market-imperfection. It is generally coupled with either or both of the other causes.[13] And in these cases, it is clear that the different producers' products will never

---

[12] It might be objected that anything which causes a lack of indifference between buyers will make the products "imperfect substitutes" in relation to each other (since the consumers' attitude is the final criterion for classifying "products") and consequently no distinction can be made out between "buyers' inertia" and "product-differentiation" as causes of market imperfection. There is, however, a very good reason for keeping them separate. Whereas in the ordinary case of imperfectly substitutable commodities the consumers' "elasticity of substitution" between two products is symmetrical (i.e., a given change in the price ratio will cause a given change in the relative quantities demanded, whichever of the two prices has moved relatively to the other) this is by no means the case when the lack of indifference is merely due to the inertia of buyers. In the latter case, one cannot even speak of a given "marginal rate of substitution," since this rate will be different according to the direction of the change.

[13] Moreover, the case where market-imperfection is *merely* due to buyers' inertia is not a very good one from the point of view of this theory: since it always implies the presence of "institutional monopoly" as well. Cf. p. 45.

possess the same degree of substitutability in relation to any particular product. Any particular producer will always be faced with rivals who are nearer to him, and others who are "farther off." In fact, he should be able to class his rivals, *from his own point of view*, in a certain order, according to the influence of their prices upon his own demand (which will not be necessarily the same order as that applying to any particular rival of his). This is clear in the case where "market imperfection" is merely due to differences in the geographical location of producers. It is equally true in cases of "product-differentiation." Savile Row tailors will be most influenced by Savile Row prices; they will be less concerned with fluctuations in the price of East-end clothes.[14]

"Pseudo-monopolists"—distinguished from the old-fashioned "real monopolists" merely by the fact that the "cross-elasticities of demand" for their product is large—thus cannot be grouped together in a lump but can at best be placed into a series. Each "product" can be conceived as occupying a certain position on a "scale"; the scale being so constructed that those products are neighbouring each other between which the consumers' elasticity of substitution is the greatest (a "product" itself can be defined as a collection of objects between which the elasticity of substitution of all relevant consumers is infinite). Each producer then is faced on each side with his nearest rivals; the demand for his own product will be most sensitive with respect to the prices of these; less and less sensitive as one moves further away from him. "Product variation" by an individual producer can then itself be represented as a movement *along* the scale; and, given the position of all other producers, each producer will tend to settle at that point on the scale where his anticipated profits are the greatest. New entrants must also occupy a position on that scale, and will thus necessarily make the chain of substitutes "tighter."

The idea of such a "scale" can best be envisaged in the case

---

[14] It is conceivable that the "scale of preferences" of different consumers should differ in just that degree as to eliminate the differences in the degree of substitutability of different products for the body of consumers as a whole. (If individual X regards product B as a nearer substitute to A than either C or D, but Y regards C as a nearer substitute than either B or D, while Z regards D as the nearest substitute to A, then the prices B, C, D may have the same influence on the demand for A.) But this is a rather improbable supposition.

of the simplest type of market-imperfection: the distribution of consumers over an area. Let us assume that all consumers are situated along a road (a kind of "ribbon development"), they are of an even degree of density, and all of them have an equal desire to buy. They are completely indifferent as between the products of different sellers; or rather the only difference consists in respect to transport costs (which can be equally regarded to be borne either by the buyers or the sellers). Under such conditions, sellers will tend to settle at equidistant points from each other along the road,[15] and thus they are all "pseudo-monopolists," since no two producers sell from the same spot.[16] Looked at from the point of view of any seller, a change of price by any other particular seller (the prices of the rest being assumed as given) is less and less important for him, the further away that particular seller is situated.

It follows from this, first, that even when the number of producers is large (the chain of substitutes tight) it cannot be assumed that the effect of a single producer's action will spread itself *evenly* over a large number of his rivals and will be negligible for each of them individually. The other producers' prices and "products" thus cannot be assumed as "given" in drawing up the demand schedule for the first; and the real demand curve for a single producer's product is thus indeterminate (depending on any of the large numbers of possible reactions in which his rivals might indulge).[17] The problems of "duopoly" are thus not merely con-

---

[15] If only there are more than two of them, cf. Chamberlin, p. 196, where Professor Hotelling's relevant theorem is corrected.

[16] The assumption that "institutional monopolies" are absent, implies in this case, that any seller *could,* if he wanted to, move to the same spot as that occupied by any other seller (or so near to it as to eliminate differences in transport costs) and thus make his own product "indistinguishable" from that of the other. Neglect to distinguish between these two cases of "monopolies" has been the source of much confusion in the past.

[17] Which does not imply that each producer will not base his policy upon certain ideas concerning the relation between the demand of his product and its price. But this "imagined demand curve" is based on certain expectations concerning his rivals' behaviour as a result of changes in his own policy; irrespectively whether these expectations are correct or not. Such an "imagined demand curve" is always determinate (since something must always exist in the producer's own mind). But it is a different sort of thing from the "demand

comitants of a situation where there are a "small number of producers" but arise in all cases where producers are selling substitute products, since the fact of "imperfect substitutability" necessarily involves the presence of the "scale" and thus of the "small number." "Duopoly" is thus seen not as a special class by itself but rather as "the leading species of a large genus."

Secondly, it can just as little be assumed that "new products" (the products of new or prospective entrants) will stand in the same or similar relation with *all* existing products. A new product must necessarily be placed in between two existing products; and will thus make considerable inroads into the markets of his nearest neighbours. Thus a producer, if far-sighted, will take the effect of his own actions not merely on his existing competitors into consideration but also on his *potential competitors.*[18] He will act on the basis of an "imagined demand curve" which shows the amount he can sell at different prices in *the long run,* under the assumption that his competitors' products, prices, and the number of his competitors are all adjusted to his price. If a producer knows that if he charges a high price to-day a competitor will appear to-morrow whose mere existence will put him in a *permanently worse position,* he will charge a price which will afford him only a low profit, if only he hopes to secure this profit permanently; i.e., he will act in a manner *as if* his own demand curve were very much more elastic than it is. And this "foresight" will, or at any rate may, prevent him from being driven to a state of "excess capacity."[19]

---

curves" of traditional analysis which always implied an *objective* relationship between price and the quantity demanded. For a fuller treatment of the distinction between a real and an imagined demand curve, cf. my previous article quoted above (*Economica,* August 1934, p. 340).

[18] If a producer takes into account the consequences of his own policy on his *existing* competitors, this will probably induce him to charge a higher price than otherwise (will make his "imagined demand curve" less elastic). But if he takes *potential competition* into account, this will probably induce him to charge a price lower than otherwise (make his imagined demand curve more elastic). "Potential competition" implies both (*a*) the appearance of a new rival, (*b*) the possibility of "product-adjustment" rather than price-adjustment by an existing rival.

[19] Whether it will do so or not, will depend on the relative willingness and ability of bearing losses—on behalf of the "existing producer" and the "new

2. Moreover, it can be shown that even if none of the producers takes the indirect effects of his own policy into consideration[20] "potential competition" will never succeed in making the individual demand and cost curves tangential, if "economies of scale" exist; while the possibility of "product-differentiation" will by itself never prevent the establishment of "perfect competition" if "economies of scale" are completely absent. Demand curves and cost curves therefore will only become necessarily "tangential" to each other when "demand curves" have also become horizontal.

In order to prove this, let us again take the simplest case of market imperfection which is at the same time the one most favourable to the "excess capacity" theory: when it exists solely on account of the spreading of consumers over a large area. Let us again assume that consumers are evenly distributed over the whole area; that they have no preferences whatever as between the different sellers; and that the cost functions of all producers are identical. The demand curves of individual sellers will be "downward sloping" solely on account of the increase in transport costs as more is sold. Let us assume that producers are situated at equal distances from each other and that they all make "profits" (sell at prices which more than cover average displacement costs). Let us assume that new producers enter the field. Each producer's market will be smaller; the elasticity of demand, at any price, higher than before. But if we assume that economies of scale are completely absent (i.e., long-run cost curves are horizontal) profits will never be eliminated altogether so long as the elasticity of demand is less than infinite.

---

entrant." For let us assume that a producer reduces his price in anticipation of the entrance of new competitors. If the "new producer" comes in nevertheless, *at the ruling price,* both will be involved in losses. But there will be some higher price at which both will make some profits; and if the new entrant can induce the old producer to raise his price to that level he can thereby secure his place on the "scale" permanently. If on the other hand, the old producer persists in charging the low price, one of them will have to drop out. (In so far as "buyers' inertia" is present at all, there is always a presumption that such a price-war will cost less to the old producer than the new one.)

[20] I.e., they all act on the basis of an "imagined demand curve" which corresponds to a "real demand curve" drawn on the assumption that the prices and "products" of all other producers remain the same, irrespectively of what the first producer is doing (which is the assumption underlying Professor Chamberlin's demand curves).

For each producer can always recover some of his lost profits by reducing output up to the point where marginal revenue equals marginal cost (which in this case, also equals average cost). The inflow of new producers will continue, leading to a continuous reduction in the output of existing producers and a continuous increase in the elasticities of their demand until the latter becomes infinite and prices will equal "average costs." There the movement will stop. But each "firm" will have reduced his output to such an extent that he has completely lost his hold over the market.

We see therefore that the mathematical economists in making "perfect competition" as their starting point, weren't such fools after all. For they assumed perfect divisibility of everything; and where everything is perfectly divisible, and consequently economies of scale completely absent, "perfect competition" must necessarily establish itself solely as a result of the "free play of economic forces." No degree of "product-differentiation" and no possibility of further and further "product-variation" will be sufficient to prevent this result, so long as all kinds of "institutional monopolies" and all kinds of indivisibilities are completely absent.

Let us now introduce indivisibilities and economies of scale. The movement of new "firms" into the field will then not continue until the elasticities of demand for individual producers become infinite; it will be stopped long before that by the increase in costs as the output of producers is reduced. *But there is no reason to assume that it will stop precisely at the point where the demand and cost curves are tangential.* For, on account of the very reason of "economies of scale" the potential producer cannot hope to enter the field profitably with less than a certain magnitude of output; and that additional output may reduce demand, both to his nearest neighbours and to him, to such an extent that the demand curves will lie *below* the cost curves and all will be involved in losses. The interpolation of a third producer in between any two producers may thus transform "profits" into "losses." *The same reason therefore which prevents competition from becoming "perfect"—i.e. indivisibles—will also prevent the complete elimination of "profits."* It will secure a "monopolistic advantage" to anybody who is first in the field and merely by virtue of priority. The ultimate reason for this being that it is not the original resources themselves, but the various uses to which they are put that are indivisible—you can divide "free capital" but you cannot invest *less* than a certain amount of it in a machine—and consequently the investment of resources cannot be so finely distributed as to equalise the level of marginal productivities.[21]

The above argument does not hold, if we assume as Professor Chamberlin assumed at the start, that consumers' preferences are *evenly distributed* over the whole field; and consequently the entry of a new firm affects *all* existing firms to an equal degree. Then the demand for each is only reduced by an insignificant amount by a single new entrant; and consequently the number of firms could increase with impunity until profits are completely wiped out and the demand curves become "tangential."

That Professor Chamberlin is aware of our first objection is clear from his analysis of chain-relationships on pp. 102–104 of his book. That he is also aware of the second is clear from certain remarks in connection with spatial competition on p. 199. It would be most unfair therefore to criticise him on a point of logic—since the logic of Professor Chamberlin's analysis is indeed excellent. What he does not seem to be aware of is the degree of unreality involved in his initial assumptions; and the extent to which his main conclusions are dependent on those assumptions.

3. So far we have not mentioned the most frequent and conspicuous objection against the "excess capacity" theory: that it assumes "identical cost and demand curves" for the different producers. In our view, this is no valid criticism on Professor Chamberlin's assumptions. The identity of the demand curves merely ensures that the *prices* of different producers will be identical. But since producers are free to vary the quality of their product as well as their price, differences in elasticity will not save producers from being driven to a position of "tangency"—although they may reach this position by selling at different prices. The identity of the cost curves—*in the required sense*—follows on the other hand from the

---

[21] This brings out clearly also the objection against Mrs. Robinson's "normal profits." We see how the level of profits in each firm—the difference between its actual remuneration and the displacement cost of its earnings—is determined by the degree of indivisibility which acts as a "protective shield" against intruders. There is no more reason to assume these profits to tend to a "normal" level than there is to assume that the extent of indivisibilities is the same in all cases.

assumption of the absence of any "institutional monopoly." It is assumed, that is to say, that every producer, *could,* if he wanted to, produce commodities completely identical to those of any other producer—if he does not, this is merely because he would not find it profitable to do so.[22, 23] Such "institutional monopolies" may consist of patents, copyrights, trade-marks or even a trade-name. They may be conferred by law, by ownership, or merely by the will of the public. If the public *prefers* to buy from Messrs. Smith and Robinson and thus the name of the seller becomes part of the "quality of the product," then Messrs. Smith and Robinson have an "instiutional monopoly" of their products. They possess something which others cannot possess. Similarly, if the entrepreneur *owns* resources which are *relatively* better fitted for the production of some varieties than the resources over which other entrepreneurs have command, he has exclusive control over resources which to that extent are unique: and this also implies the presence of some "institutional monopoly."[24] Consequently, in the absence of these, since the relative costs of producing different varieties must be the same for the different producers, their cost curves, *for each single variety,* must also be identical.

It might be objected, that "institutional monopoly" thus defined, covers a much larger number of cases than what is generally understood by this term. Indeed, one could make out a nice distinction between the possession of an "absolute" monopoly (when no other producer is able to produce a completely identical product at *any* cost) or a comparative or "partial" monopoly (when no other producer is able to produce the same product at the same relative cost). But as all "products" are more or less close substitutes for one another, this distinction becomes analytically unim-

---

[22] Professor Chamberlin does not state this explicitly; but this is the only logically consistent interpretation one can give to his assumption that "the entry of new producers into the field in general and every portion of it in particular is free and unimpeded."

[23] This implies in our terminology that every producer is free to move along and settle at any point of the "scale," he can get therefore "as near to" the products of any other producer as he wants without incurring higher *relative* costs.

[24] In order to avoid misunderstanding it must be pointed out that the absence of "institutional monopoly" does not imply that the abilities of each entrepreneur, and consequently the *absolute level* of their costs, are identical.

portant since it comes to the same thing whether producer B can produce merely a "more or less close substitute" to A—or whether he can produce the *same* product but only at a higher cost than A.[25] Anything therefore which imposes higher costs on one producer than another (whether it is due to the possession of "unique" resources by one entrepreneur or whether it is merely due to "buyers' inertia"[26] imposing a special "cost of entry" on new producers) implies, to that extent, the presence of "institutional monopoly."

Such "institutional monopolies" of course are never completely absent. Their presence—though as we have seen in the last section, is by no means essential—may even be directly responsible for a large part of market imperfection—as Professor Chamberlin himself so convincingly shows in his appendix in favour of "unfair trading." They cannot therefore usefully be assumed absent when a situation is analysed which is often largely bound up with them. And what does the situation look like when they are not absent?

If the "scale of differentiation" of the consumers can be regarded as given (as e.g. in the previous example, when the degree of substitutability of different "products" was rigidly determined by the level of transport costs) institutional monopoly, to the extent to which it is present, will prevent the generation of "excess capacity"—since to that extent, "profits" earned by one producer cannot be competed away by another producer. Many types of "institutional monopolies," however, by themselves increase the degree of market imperfection, and to that extent are favourable to the generation of "excess capacity."[27] The sudden appearance of

---

[25] In both cases producer B will obtain smaller total receipts for the same total outlay.

[26] What we designated above as "sheer buyers' inertia" (i.e., that consumers require either a certain lapse of time, or a certain minimum of price-difference before they change over from one seller to another, even if they are otherwise completely indifferent between the different sellers' products) is merely a special case of "institutional monopoly"; since it always imposes a differential advantage on the existing producer relative to the new entrant. The mere existence of specialised durable plant, however, does not imply such a differential advantage in the long run, although it may prevent adjustments being undertaken in the short run.

[27] The difference between these two types of "institutional monopolies" (the one which affects merely the relative costs of different producers, and the other which affects the elasticities of the demand curves for products as well)

buyers' inertia, for example, has the double effect of reducing the elasticity of demand for the individual products and of imposing a cost of entry on potential competitors; these two opposing tendencies may cancel out, or the net effect may go in either direction.

To sum up the results of the above argument. The extent to which "excess capacity" may be generated as a result of "free competition" (under the assumption that the existence of "economies of scale" will prevent this competition from becoming "perfect") will depend: (i) On the degree of "short-sightedness" or "far-sightedness" of producers (how far they take potential competition into account in deciding upon their price- and product-policy). This is a question of business psychology rather than economics. (ii) The extent to which "institutional monopolies" are present. This, as we have seen, will tend to prevent the generation of "excess capacity" if it leaves the scale of differentiation unaffected; while it will have an uncertain effect if it increases the scale of differentiation as well. (iii) The extent to which the market-situation resembles a "chain relationship" (in Professor Chamberlin's terminology), i.e. the extent to which the various "cross-elasticities" of demand differ in order of magnitude. Only in the special case when they are all of the same order of magnitude will Professor Chamberlin's conclusion (that demand curves will be tangential to cost curves) necessarily follow. At the same time, there is a presumption that some degree of "excess capacity" will be generated even if profits will not be completely competed away: since "indivisibilities," by themselves, will not offer a strong enough shield to prevent *some* rise in costs as a consequence of the intrusion of new competitors. Many of the objections therefore which can be brought against the theory if put forward in its *rigid* form (that demand curves will tend to become "tangential" with the cost curves), do not affect the fundamental proposition that the effect

---

can best be elucidated by examples. A legal patent for a certain cheap process of producing ordinary window glass will not lead the consumers to differentiate between glass produced by one process or another. It will merely have the effect of imposing higher costs upon anybody who does not possess the patent. A trade-mark protecting a certain soap or medicine may lead, however, the consumers to differentiate between different soaps or medicines; and thus reduce the elasticity of demand for the products of each producer.

of the competition of "new entrants" and consequent reduction of the level of profits earned may take the form of a rise in costs rather than a reduction of prices.[28]

4. So far we have not touched upon another abstract assumption which Professor Chamberlin has made, i.e. that each producer produces only a single "product." In reality the majority of producers produce a series of different products, if products are to be defined by the same rigid market-criteria as were applied in the earlier parts of this article. And at first sight at any rate, it does appear as if the spreading of production over a series of different products is the way in which producers can overcome the effect of those "indivisibilities" which form the *conditio sine qua non* of imperfect competition. If there is not a sufficiently great demand to produce one product on an "optimal scale," the producer may still utilise his plant fully by producing two or more products, rather than building a smaller, sub-optimal plant or leaving his existing plant under-employed. In this way, "indivisibilities" will be overcome; and consequently "excess capacity" will not make its appearance either. The effect of "competition from outside" will be to induce producers to produce a larger series of products, rather than to reduce the scale of output as a whole.

In our view this line of reasoning is not strictly accurate; for even if it is admitted that varying the number of different kinds of products produced provides one line of adjustment for the entrepreneur, this does not imply that the essential consequences of this type of situation (that increased competition will lead to an

---

[28] Professor Chamberlin's analysis is most valuable also in throwing light upon the probable consequences of all monopolistic agreements which refer to selling prices rather than quantities produced. It explains why, if a uniform taxi-fare is imposed, one will find too many empty taxis about. Or if the code of "professional etiquette" prevents doctors and lawyers from undercutting each other, sooner or later they will all complain that they are "under-employed." Or if manufacturers' cartels or trade associations impose a uniform price or a uniform "profit-margin" on retailers, one will find too many tobacco-shops round the streets. It should also make us very sceptical about any remedying of the evils of "imperfect competition" by compulsory rationalisation, cartellisation, or any type of interference with price-competition. For measures which intend to prevent the alleged evils of "price-cutting" not infrequently tend to aggravate the real evils which they are supposed to remedy.

increase in costs) can thereby be avoided. Whether they will or not, will depend on the nature of the cost-function of the jointly produced products.

Commodities, of course, will only be produced jointly if it is cheaper to produce them jointly than separately. For certain commodities (such as wheat and straw) this is always the case: whatever is the amount produced of each (or rather whatever is the amount of resources engaged in producing them); irrespectively therefore whether the economies due to scale are attained or not. These are the cases of "by-products"; where more than one commodity emerges as a result of single productive process. Certain other commodities, however, may be jointly produced simply because the demand for any of them is not large enough to be produced on a scale which should enable the realisation of the economies of scale; while some of these economies can be retained by utilising a larger "plant" for the production of several commodities. For such commodities "joint production" will only be profitable as certain outputs, and will become unprofitable as soon as the demand for each or any of them is sufficiently large to enable the "economies of scale" to be secured in case of separate production. This is the case simply because the "indivisible factors" (buildings, machinery, etc.) which are responsible for these economies, are never completely specialised; and can be used, more or less effectively, for the production of several things simultaneously.

Since, however, in most cases, "indivisible factors" are not completely unspecialised either, such a "spreading of production" is always attended with some cost; i.e. the physical productivity of a *given* quantity of resources calculated in terms of *any* of the products will always be less, the greater the number of separate commodities they are required simultaneously to produce. That this is the case for a large proportion of jointly produced commodities is shown by the fact that the development of an "industry" is always attended by "specialisation" or "disintegration," i.e. the reduction of the number of commodities produced by single firms.[29]

Assuming that the cost-functions of jointly produced commodities are of this nature, how does the equilibrating process work

---

[29] Cf. Allyn Young, "Increasing Returns and Economic Progress," *The Economic Journal,* 1929.

itself out under our previous assumptions? For simplicity, we can postulate that there are a given number of firms, and initially each of them produces only one product and all are making profits (not necessarily to the same degree). Let us suppose that one of them finds it profitable to produce another commodity, highly competitive with the products of some other producers. These latter producers will now find the demand for their products reduced; and *this* may make it profitable for them to engage in the production of a second, or even a third, commodity—even if this was not profitable before. This in turn will induce other producers (possibly our "first" producer) to do the same, which in turn will lead to a further "spreading of production" by competing producers. Assuming always that producers merely take the *direct* effects of their actions into consideration (i.e. act upon an "imagined demand curve" which regards the prices and the "products" of all other producers as given[30]) this process will continue, so long as producers continue to make some profits; and so long as the loss caused by a reduction in the amount of resources engaged (if the reduction in the output of one commodity were not compensated by an increase in the output of another) is greater than the loss caused by a further "spreading of output." A precise formulation of this process would require either some very cumbrous language or some rather involved mathematics; but without resorting to either, it is easy to see what conditions the final equilibrium will involve. The demand curve for each single "product," will have become very much more elastic[31] (since each producer now produces a very much smaller share of each product, or "type of product"); profits will have been wiped out and the general level of costs for each product, or type of product; will have become higher. There will not be much "excess capacity" in the sense, that

---

[30] This implies in this case that producers ignore not only any adjustment of price or of product by other producers as a result of their own policy, but also any effect upon the demand for some of the other commodities produced by themselves.

[31] It can become infinitely elastic only when the "spreading of output" involves *no* additional cost at all. In this case the "economies of scale" refer to the amount of resources used by single firms rather than those engaged in the production of certain products; and for each single product, conditions of perfect competition might be brought about even if the total number of firms is small.

given the *number* of different products produced simultaneously by each firm, an increase in the output of all of them would reduce costs per unit. Yet there will be a "technical wastage," since the physical productivity of resources will be less than what it would be if each producer produced a smaller number of products and a large proportion of the total output of each; a policy they undoubtedly would prefer, if all of them would foresee the ultimate, as distinct from the immediate, consequences of their actions.[32]

IV

We have seen therefore that in all cases where economies of scale are present over certain ranges of output and where market imperfection exists (in the sense that highly and yet imperfectly substitutable commodities are on sale), "increased competition" (i.e. an increase in the number of firms in a particular industrial field) might lead to a reduction of technical efficiency rather than to a reduction in price or an increase in aggregate output; while in cases where firms can vary the number of different products produced, this might come about even without an inflow of "new firms." In both cases this result was seen to depend on a certain "short-sightedness" of producers who act on the basis of the immediate industrial situation confronting them rather than follow out the further consequences of their own policy. The prevalence of such short-sightedness can be sufficiently accounted for, however, partly by the producers' ignorance of those further consequences and partly by the uncertainty as to the extent of far-sightedness with which their actual and potential competitions are endowed.

It is extremely difficult to deduce any general conclusions from the above analysis as to the effect of the generation of "excess capacity" upon economic welfare in general—in whatever arbitrary way this concept may be defined. If the money-value of the National Dividend is to be made its criterion (calculated on the basis of some *given* price-level), then no doubt, it could be increased, in some fields quite considerably, by compulsory "standardisation,"

---

[32] There may be another reason, apart from this type of "short-sightedness," why producers would prefer a policy of many-product production: and this is the reduction of risk, especially important in cases of "fashionable" articles, where they cannot calculate with any precision how the public will take any particular "variety."

cartel-agreements, the restriction of entry or any similar measure enabling producers to realise more fully the "economies of scale." The recognition of this fact, however, as yet far from warrants the advocacy of such measures. Apart from the ill-effects on distribution (and in a world of wage-rigidities, upon employment) which such processes of monopolisation inevitably involve, the public would be offered finally larger amounts of a smaller number of commodities; and it is impossible to tell how far people prefer quantity to diversity or vice versa.

Neither is it permissible to argue, on the other hand, that the generation of "excess capacity" is itself the result of consumers' choice; since it only comes about by creating a greater diversity of commodities: and consequently its emergence is evidence that the public, to that extent, prefer "variety" to "cheapness." This line of reasoning would only be permissible if consumers were actually confronted with the choice of having *either* a smaller range of commodities at lower prices *or* a larger range at higher prices. In fact, they never are in a position to choose between these alternatives: they are offered either the one or the other, but never both. To expect the consumers to be so "far-sighted" as to concentrate on the purchase of a few varieties merely in the hope of thereby reducing prices in the future, is an assumption which even the highest level of abstraction should avoid.

20

DEMAND UNDER CONDITIONS OF OLIGOPOLY*

By Paul M. Sweezy

It is pretty well agreed among economists that the ordinary concept of a demand curve is inapplicable to the study of oligopoly. What would be sold at various prices if everything else remained unchanged does not concern an entrepreneur when he knows that everything else, and in particular the prices charged by his rivals, is most unlikely to remain unchanged. What does concern him is his own estimate of what can be sold at various prices, making the best allowance he can for the probable reactions of his rivals. These estimates can conveniently be arranged in the form of a demand schedule, but the result must not, of course, be confused with the type of demand schedule which is commonly used in economic discussion. Mr. Nicholas Kaldor has suggested the name "imagined demand curve" for the concept which is applicable to the oligopoly case, and in this article I propose to follow this usage.[1]

So far as I know no attempt has yet been made to investigate the characteristics of imagined demand curves, though it should be obvious that such an investigation is desirable. Oligopoly is probably the typical case throughout a large part of the modern economy, and yet the theory of oligopoly can scarcely be said to be in a very advanced state, consisting as it does of a number of special cases which allow of little generalization. My purpose in this note is to show that a very considerable degree of clarification might be introduced into the study of this subject by a systematic inquiry into the nature of imagined demand curves.

The most important consideration in this connection seems to me to be the obvious fact that rivals react differently according

---

* The Journal of Political Economy, Vol. XLVII (1939), pp. 568–573. Reprinted, by the courtesy of The University of Chicago Press and the author, without change from the original text.

[1] See Mr. Kaldor's review of Mrs. Joan Robinson's Economics of Imperfect Competition, in Economica, August 1934, pp. 340–341.

to whether a price change is upward or downward. If producer A raises his price, his rival producer B will acquire new customers. If, on the other hand, A lowers his price, B will lose customers. Ordinarily the reaction to a gain in business is a pleasurable feeling calling for no particular action; the reaction to a loss in business, however, is likely to be some viewing with alarm accompanied by measures designed to recoup the loss. If the cause of the loss is obviously a rival's price cut, the natural retaliation is a similar cut. From the point of view of any particular producer this means simply that if he raises his price he must expect to lose business to his rivals (his demand curve tends to be elastic going up), while if

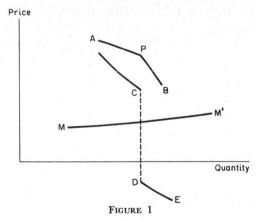

FIGURE 1

he cuts his price he has no reason to believe he will succeed in taking business away from his rivals (his demand curve tends to be inelastic going down). In other words, the imagined demand curve has a "corner" at the current price. Fig. 1 depicts such a curve, *APB,* where *P* is the current price.

That many producers do think of their demand curves as having this shape I think will be evident to anyone who sets out to investigate the subject by interviewing businessmen. They frequently explain that they would lose their customers by raising prices but would sell very little more by lowering prices. Economists who are accustomed to thinking in terms of traditional demand-curve analysis are likely to attribute this kind of answer to ignorance or perversity. Actually, it has a sound rational foundation which becomes readily intelligible when the analysis is cast in terms of imagined demand curves.

The marginal revenue curve which is derived from the demand curve in Fig. 1 is shown by the broken line $ACDE$. Where the demand curve has a corner, the marginal revenue curve, of course, has a discontinuity. The marginal cost curve MM' passes between the two parts of the marginal revenue curve.[2] Certain interesting corollaries follow from this. The first is that the conditions for short-run equilibrium are not at all precise. It is not possible to apply the condition that marginal cost must equal marginal revenue; all we can say is that marginal cost must certainly not be greater than marginal revenue. It may, however, be less. Second, it is not permissible to speak of the factors' remunerations' being equal to their marginal value productivities. And, third, any disturbance which affects only the position of the marginal cost curve may leave the short-run equilibrium of price and output entirely unaffected. Thus, for example, a successful strike for higher wages may be without influence on either price or output. Trade-unionists who believe that the only effect of higher wages is lower profits may have more truth on their side than economists have been willing to grant.

The imagined demand curve need not, of course, have the shape depicted in Fig. 1. Fig. 2 shows the most important variants both for downward and for upward movements of price. The stretch labeled PM indicates the expected reaction to price reductions, assuming that rivals will not retaliate in kind. Such an assumption is ordinarily likely to be justified only if rivals are not aware of the price reduction, that is, if the reduction takes the form of secret concessions from the list price. This consideration allows us to bring within the purview of theory a widely recognized phenomenon of actual business practice, namely, the practice of departing from quoted prices. We should, however, be fully aware of the fact that a full analysis of this practice in theoretical terms would be much more complex than these few remarks might lead one to believe. For example, there is a very high degree of probability that secret price cutting will be accompanied by a certain amount of discrimination between different customers or groups

---

[2] This does not necessarily mean that profits are being made. Whether they are or not, of course, depends upon the position of the average cost curve, which is not shown in the diagram.

of customers. From a formal point of view it would be more satisfactory to describe the stretch *PM* in Fig. 2 as a discriminating
average revenue curve for downward movements in the average
price charged all customers.

In Fig. 2, *LP* depicts the expected reaction to price increases,
assuming that rivals will also raise their prices. This type of curve
for upward movements of price is particularly relevant for producers who occupy the position of price leader.

So far nothing has been said of the effect of shifts in demand,
from the point of view of buyers, on the shape of imagined demand

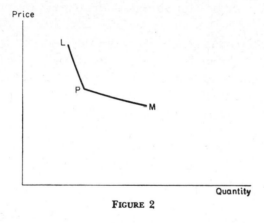

FIGURE 2

curves. It seems clear that any such shift will first make itself felt
in a change in the quantity sold at the current price. But ordinarily
it will also cause producers to revise their ideas about the probable
reactions to alterations in their prices. It may be suggested that
an increase in demand leading to a fuller use of capacity, more
difficulty in getting quick delivery, etc., will make the imagined
demand curve less elastic for upward movements in price. For
downward movements in price the result is likely to be a more
elastic curve, since it may be assumed that rivals are less worried
about losses in business and hence less ready to retaliate against
a price cut. In terms of the marginal revenue curve the effect is
thus to bring the two sections closer together and to decrease the
gap between them. This may or may not induce the producer to
change his price. Much depends upon the location of the marginal
cost curve, as a little experimentation with pencil and paper will
show. Since, however, the presumption is that marginal cost curves

are likely to be shifting upward in a time of increasing demand, because of higher wage and raw material costs, it is perhaps legitimate to conclude that an increase in demand is more likely to lead to a price increase than to a price cut.

A decrease in demand, for reasons analogous to those just set forth, can be expected to have the opposite effect on the shape of imagined demand curves, making them more elastic for upward movements in price and less elastic for downward movements. In terms of the marginal revenue curve the two sections will be farther separated than they were before. The result will be that the producer will be more anxious than ever to hold his price where it is.

It is an interesting conclusion from this type of reasoning that an expansion in demand is likely to lead to an increase in oligopoly prices; whereas a contraction in demand sets up strong resistance to any reduction in oligopoly prices. At the same time, however, a contraction puts a premium on successful secret price cutting. As far as the cyclical behavior of oligopoly prices is concerned we might expect to find (1) that prices go up easily and openly in time of upswing; (2) that prices resist downward pressure in times of recession and depression; and (3) that list prices become less trustworthy guides to real prices the longer bad times last. I think this analysis can be developed in such a way as to throw valuable light on the much-debated problem of rigid prices, but to do so would be beyond the scope of this paper.[3]

It should be noted that the analysis suggested here runs in terms of movements in price from a currently existing situation. No attempt is made to explain how the current price and output situation came about except as it may be explained by reference to a

---

[3] There are many relevant considerations which are not even touched upon here. For example, the effects of building up or whittling down inventories, actions which are due to producers' ideas about future demand and cost conditions, are evidently important and may lead to results quite unpredictable by reasoning such as that set forth above. Illustration: an oligopolist caught with large inventory at the beginning of a decline in demand may cut price and drastically curtail output in order to work down his stocks, even though he would maintain price unchanged if he had only current output to think of. This consideration is particularly likely to be important in the case of commodities which take a relatively long time to process but which are not made to special order, e.g., metals such as copper.

previously existing situation. This is unavoidable since imagined demand curves, unlike the ordinary demand curves of economic analysis, can only be thought of with reference to a given starting-point. That starting-point itself cannot, of course, be explained in terms of the expectations to which it gives rise. Once this is realized, it becomes very doubtful whether the traditional search for "the" equilibrium solution to a problem in oligopoly has very much meaning. Generally speaking, there may be any number of price-output combinations which constitute equilibriums in the sense that, *ceteris paribus,* there is no tendency for the oligopolist to move away from them. But which of these combinations will be actually established in practice depends upon the previous history of the case. Looking at the problem in this way the theorist should attempt to develop an analysis which will enable him to understand the processes of change which characterize the real world rather than waste his time in chasing the will-o'-the-wisp of equilibrium.

The suggestions thrown out in this paper on the problems of oligopoly analysis are, of course, not intended to exhaust the subject. They are rather offered as raw material for further processing by those who, unlike the author, make a business of studying prices and price policies.

21

THE KINKY OLIGOPOLY DEMAND CURVE AND RIGID PRICES*

By George J. Stigler ||

Just before World War II, the theory was advanced that there exists a kink in the demand curve for the product of an oligopolist and that this kink goes far to explain observed price rigidities in oligopolistic industries. The theory has rapidly gained wide acceptance: many economists give it some place in their theoretical system, and some economists make it *the* theory of oligopoly price.

The theory is an ingenious rationalization of the price rigidities that were reported in many statistical studies of prices during the thirties, and no doubt this explains its popularity. But no one, so far as I know, has examined in detail either the pure theory of the kinky demand curve or the degree of correspondence between the price patterns implied by the theory and the observed price patterns in oligopolistic industries. These two tasks will be undertaken in Parts I and II, respectively, of this paper.

I. The Formal Theory

1. The Received Theory

The theory of the kinky demand curve was advanced independently and almost simultaneously by R. L. Hall and C. J. Hitch in England and Paul M. Sweezy in America.[1] The latter's version will be summarized first.

---

* *The Journal of Political Economy*, Vol. LV (1947), pp. 432–449. Reprinted, by the courtesy of the publisher and the author, with typographical corrections.

|| Columbia University.

[1] Hall and Hitch, "Price Theory and Business Behavior," *Oxford Economic Papers*, No. 2 (May 1939), pp. 12–45; and Sweezy, "Demand under Conditions of Oligopoly," *The Journal of Political Economy*, Vol. XLVII (August 1939), pp. 568–573 (reprinted in the present volume, pages 404–409).

410

The Sweezy Version

The market situation contemplated by Sweezy is one in which rivals will quickly match price reductions but only hesitantly and incompletely (if at all) follow price increases. This pattern of expected behavior produces a kink at the existing price ($= p_0$ in Fig. 1) in the demand curve for the product of an oligopolist,[2] and the corresponding marginal revenue curve will possess a discontinuity the length of which is proportional to the difference be-

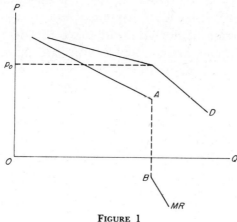

FIGURE 1

tween the slopes of the upper and lower segments of the demand curve at the kink.[3] Sweezy assumes that "the marginal cost curve

---

[2] The demand curve for the product of an oligopolist can be defined only if the reactions of rivals to price changes are known. The upper branch of the demand curve in Fig. 1 represents the quantities that consumers will buy from one oligopolist at various prices if rival producers set a price of p_0; the lower branch represents the quantities that consumers will buy if the rivals charge identical prices. This demand curve is objective in the sense that it is consistent with the facts of the market if rivals behave in the specified manner. Sweezy appears to view it as subjective because it is based upon beliefs concerning rivals' price reactions which may have to be revised (although no occasions for revision of beliefs are treated in his article).

[3] With reference to Fig. 1, if $f(x)$ is the demand curve, x_0 the output at the kink, and subscripts 1 and 2 refer to the upper and lower segments of the demand curve respectively,

$$A - B = x_0[f'(x_0 - O) - f'(x_0 + O)]$$
$$= p_0\left(\frac{1}{\eta_1} - \frac{1}{\eta_2}\right).$$

passes between the two parts of the marginal revenue curve," so
that fluctuations in marginal cost are not likely to affect output
and price.

He considers also two other possibilities. An oligopolist may
believe that secret price cuts will remain secret, in which case the
demand curve becomes elastic throughout and the kink disappears.
Or the oligopolist may be a price leader, so that price increases
will be followed and the kink again disappears.[4]

Sweezy assumes that shifts in demand will not affect the price
at which the kink occurs and argues that the results of increases
and decreases of demand are asymmetrical:

1. An increase of demand will make the demand curve less
elastic in its upper branch, since rivals are operating closer to
capacity,[5] and more elastic in the lower branch because rivals "are
less worried about losses in [of?] business." If marginal costs are
also shifting upward as demand increases, "an increase in demand
is more likely to lead to a price increase than to a price cut."

2. A decrease in demand will have the converse effects—increased elasticity of the upper branch and decreased elasticity of
the lower branch—so the discontinuity of marginal revenue will be
increased and the oligopolists will be "more anxious than ever"
to hold to the existing price.

Except where price leaders exist or secret price concessions are
possible, therefore, oligopoly price may rise in good times and will
not be reduced in bad times.[6]

The Oxford Version

Hall and Hitch conclude, after reporting interviews with some
thirty-eight entrepreneurs on price policy, that businessmen seek

---

[4] These possibilities, which are obviously mutually exclusive, are illustrated
in the same diagram (Sweezy, *op. cit.*, p. 407, Fig. 2). If the upper branch (for
the price leader) and the lower branch (for the secret price cutter) were nevertheless joined, the resulting marginal revenue curve would again be discontinuous, but then maximum profits would never be secured at the price at
which the kink arises.

[5] *Ibid.*, p. 407. Presumably the rivals' higher rates of production lead them
to follow the price increase (although this reaction causes trouble; see below),
or, if they maintain prices, the buyers are rationed.

[6] The implications of Sweezy's theory for price rigidity were emphasized by
M. Bronfenbrenner in "Applications of the Discontinuous Oligopoly Demand
Curve," *The Journal of Political Economy*, Vol. XLVIII (1940), pp. 420–427.

prices that cover average cost, regardless of marginal revenue and marginal cost (which they seldom know).[7] This "full-cost" principle is apparently the result of tacit or open collusion, consideration of long-run demand and costs, moral conviction of fairness, and uncertainty of effects of price increases and decreases.[8] The particular results of the interviews need not be discussed here.[9]

The entrepreneur therefore sets a price that covers average cost (including "profits") at the expected or some conventional

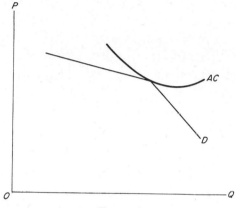

FIGURE 2

output (see Fig. 2). Increases or decreases of demand will usually shift the kink to the right or left and leave price unchanged, but there are two exceptions to this rule, as enumerated on p. 414.

---

[7] The treatment of entrepreneurial knowledge is contradictory. On the one hand, Hall and Hitch state that "most of our informants were vague about anything so precise as elasticity. . . . . In addition, many, perhaps most, apparently made no effort, even implicitly, to estimate elasticities of demand . . . . and of those who do, the majority considered the information of little or no relevance to the pricing process save perhaps in very exceptional conditions" (Hall and Hitch, *op. cit.*, p. 18). But, on the other hand, a majority of the entrepreneurs believed that price cuts would be matched and price increases would not be matched by rivals (*ibid.*, p. 21, Tables 3 and 4) so they did act rationally on marginal principles (within a certain framework).

[8] Several of these factors contradict the existence of a kink in the demand curve.

[9] The questioning was not persistent and resourceful, nor were ambiguous answers clarified; for example, three entrepreneurs did not charge more than average cost because "buyers technically informed about costs" (*ibid.*, p. 21). Does this mean that buyers would otherwise enter into production of the article? Why was the same answer not given for unwillingness to sell below cost?

1. If the demand decreases greatly and remains small for some time, the price is likely to be cut in the hope of maintaining output. The chief explanation for this price cut is that one rival becomes panicky and his irrational behavior forces the others to cut prices.

2. If the average cost curves of all firms shift by similar amounts, due perhaps to changes in factor prices or technology, this is "likely to lead to a revaluation of the 'full cost' price" (*ibid.*, p. 25). However, ". . . . there will be no tendency for [prices] to fall or rise more than the wage and raw material costs" (*ibid.*, p. 32).

The full-cost principle would suggest also that prices will vary inversely with output, i.e., that high prices are necessary to cover the high average costs of small outputs. This price pattern is not followed, apparently, because the oligopolists (1) place a value on price stability, (2) are influenced by the kink, and (3) wish to "keep plant running as full as possible, giving rise to a general feeling in favour of price concessions."[10]

Comparison of the Versions

The Sweezy version is a consistent application of the kinky demand curve to price determination, without conflicting principles to modify its workings. The Oxford version embraces also the "full-cost" principle (and apparently also the "large-output" principle), although the possibilities of conflict between the two are manifold. Hall and Hitch resolve some of the conflicts by abandoning the kink (e.g., when prices follow production costs) and some by abandoning the "full-cost" principle (e.g., when entrepreneurs do not raise prices in depression). They take no account of the difficulties raised by differences among the average costs of various oligopolists or of many other troublesome features of the "full-cost" principle. Their thesis that the kink follows changes in wage rates and material prices implies a degree of collusion—or at least such beautiful rapport—among the oligopolists that it is hard to see why a kink should appear at all (see below). Their fluid version can explain any pattern of prices, and therefore forecast none, and accordingly I shall henceforth devote primary attention to the Sweezy version.

---

[10] *Ibid.*, p. 28.

2. *Elaboration of the Theory*

The discussions of the kinky demand curve have been rather laconic. Certain implications of the theory must be elaborated in order to derive specific price patterns for the subsequent empirical tests.

The Length of the Discontinuity in Marginal Revenue

The length of the discontinuity in marginal revenue is proportional to the difference between the slopes of the demand curve on the two sides of the kink. The longer this discontinuity, the greater the fluctuations in marginal cost (and in demand, if the kink stays at the same price) that are compatible with price stability and therefore the greater the probability of rigid prices in any interval of time. Some of the factors that affect the length of this discontinuity are:

A) THE NUMBER OF RIVALS (OF A GIVEN DEGREE OF CLOSENESS, MEASURED BY THE CROSS-ELASTICITY OF DEMAND). We should expect that a price increase is more likely to be followed if there are few rivals than if there are many, because the rivals will realize that the temporary gains from holding down their prices will soon be erased. If this is so, the discontinuity will be short (in time) or nonexistent when there are few rivals. The larger the number of rivals, the less likely are they to follow one oligopolist's price increases; on the other hand, the less likely are they also to match his price reductions, at least immediately. It seems probable, therefore, that the discontinuity is longest with an intermediate number of rivals, say, five to ten.

B) THE RELATIVE SIZE OF RIVALS (OF A GIVEN DEGREE OF CLOSENESS). When one firm (or an inner clique) is dominant in size, it will presumably be the price leader. When this firm increases its price, rivals are likely to follow (for individually they can sell as much as they wish at the ruling price); when the firm cuts prices the rivals must follow. Hence the dominant firm will have no kink in its demand curve. The smaller firms cannot raise their prices above the leader's unless he is rationing buyers but can shade prices without being followed immediately or perhaps at all.[11] Again there will be no kink.

---

[11] These conclusions can also be reached by a more mechanical application

c) The Differences Among the Rivals' Products. The discontinuity will be longer, the more homogeneous the products, because customers will shift more rapidly to the low-price firm.

d) The Extent of Collusion. Should explicit collusion replace the stand-offish attitude visualized by the theory, the kink will vanish; there is no kink in a monopolist's demand curve.

Other factors affecting the length of the discontinuity in marginal revenue could be mentioned, for example, the number of buyers.[12] But these factors do not lend themselves to the type of empirical tests that will be employed in Part II and will not be discussed.

The Workings of the Kink

In order to study the workings of the kinky demand curve, let us consider two producers (of equal size) of similar, but not identical, commodities. The initial demand and marginal revenue

---

of kink theory. A rise of the dominant firm's price will so increase the demand of each small firm that marginal cost will intersect marginal revenue at an output less than that at which the kink occurs, so the small firm will also increase price. A reduction in price by a small firm will decrease the demand for the output of the dominant firm by so small an amount that probably no price change will be induced.

[12] Fewness of buyers is difficult to fit into the kink theory. If few buyers face a competitive supply, each will presumably believe that, if he raises his buying price, rivals will follow and the quantity supplied to him will not increase much; and, if he lowers his buying price, rivals will not follow and the quantity supplied to him will decrease greatly. Hence there will be a kink in the supply curve to the firm (which is illustrated by Bronfenbrenner, *op. cit.*). Combining this with oligopoly of sellers, presumably both supply and demand curves have a kink at the same price, which will be especially rigid.

But the whole argument is very elusive. If one buyer offered a higher price to a seller who assumed that his rivals would not follow a price increase, the seller would of course offer his entire output to the buyer, whose supply curve might therefore be extremely elastic for higher prices—the opposite of the above argument. And, conversely, if one seller offered a lower price to one buyer, who assumed that his rivals would be unwilling to reduce their buying prices, the buyer would snatch at the bargain so the seller's demand curve would be elastic for lower prices—again the opposite of the above argument. The difficulty is that the assumptions are inconsistent: if sellers believe that price reductions will be matched but price increases will not be matched and buyers believe the opposite, someone is likely to be wrong.

curves of duopolist A are given in Fig. 3; they are denoted by the subscript 1. Assume now that the aggregate demand for the two commodities increases so that A's demand curve shifts to D_2, but marginal costs do not change. Then A will increase his price to p_2. What will duopolist B do?

If B's costs and demand are similar to A's, the former will simultaneously raise his price to p_2. But then D_2 must be redrawn above p_0 because this branch was drawn on the assumption that the rival's price was p_0. The situation becomes classical duopoly—with the usual wide range of possible patterns of behavior. It would be foolish to put a new kink in D_2 (as redrawn) at the level p_2. Experience has shown that the rival will follow a price increase, and businessmen will learn from this experience that there is no kink.

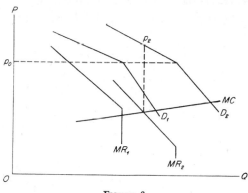

FIGURE 3

On the other hand, B may still find it profitable to stay at price p_0. But then his demand curve must shift to the right, for it was drawn on the assumption that A set a price of p_0 or less. If this demand shift leads B to set a new price, then A's demand curve must be redrawn. Again the existence of the kink is contradicted by experience.

The theory of the kinky demand curve explains why prices that have been stable should continue to be stable despite certain changes in demand or costs. But the theory does not explain why prices that have once changed should settle down, again acquire stability, and gradually produce a new kink. One possible explanation might be that a period of stability of demand and costs has created a tradition of stable prices, so that, when demand or cost conditions change materially, the kink has emerged to preserve price stability.

Other Kinks and Discontinuities

For present purposes it is not necessary to discuss additional implications of the theory of kinky demand curves, but two are of sufficient interest to deserve brief mention.

The pattern of oligopolistic behavior underlying the kinky demand curve will also produce a discontinuous marginal cost curve. If one firm reduces its wage rate, for example, other firms will not follow, but these other firms will match wage increases. At the output corresponding to this input kink, there will be a discontinuity in marginal cost. A good part of the appeal of the kinky demand curve theory is that it is easy to draw demand and cost curves that lead to price stability. This appeal is definitely weakened if the marginal cost curve is also discontinuous, as the reader can readily verify.

The same general line of reasoning leads to kinks in the curves of other variables of policy—advertising, quality changes, etc. Indeed, the logic of the theory requires only that there be one variable—output—against which the discontinuities in the other variables may be displayed.

3. *Alternative Theories of Price Stability*

Explanations of price stability are not common or prominent in the neoclassical price theory of Marshall's era. (Part II of this paper contains some evidence that bears on the question whether this is a cause for commendation or condemnation.) Of course it would be a grotesque caricature to describe this theory as requiring a change of price in response to every quiver of the demand or the cost curve. Three factors making for price stability were generally incorporated (without emphasis) into the neoclassical theory.

Long-run Considerations

In the long run the demand curve is usually more elastic because buyers can make changes in technology, commitments, and habits that permit use of substitutes and because new rivals will be attracted at certain prices. Therefore an exorbitant current price may lose more (discounted) revenue in the future than it adds in the present. This type of consideration argues against raising prices greatly in short-run periods of inelastic demand but does not imply price rigidity.[13]

Administrative Weaknesses in Collusion

When a group of producers arrives at a mutually agreeable or tolerable price by collusion, this price will have a strong tendency to persist. When some of the firms will be injured by a price change (which must often occur when their costs, market areas, and product structures differ), they will naturally oppose change. When all will gain from a price change, they will usually wish different amounts of change. Opening the question of prices may therefore lead to a pitched battle, and one can seldom be sure that things will stay in hand. Frequent resort to this area of political-economic determination must be avoided, so changes are postponed as long as possible. If they are postponed long enough, the need for them will pass.

Cost of Price Changes

The nature of the product and market may be such that small or frequent price changes cost more than they yield. There are costs of informing buyers of price changes: new lists, advertising, etc. If long-term contracts contain provisions that the buyer will receive any price reductions during the life of the contract, the short-run marginal revenue from a price reduction may be small or negative. Even when there are no contracts, price reductions may incur the ill will of early buyers of a "style" good.

4. A Comparison of the Implications of the Theories of Price Stability

There is no reason why the kinky demand curve cannot be joined with the other explanations of price stability. But there is also no purpose in adding it to the neoclassical theory unless it

---

[13] Marshall also had the doctrine that prices will not fall to prime costs in depression because of a fear of "spoiling the market" (*Principles of Economics* [8th ed.; London, Macmillan & Co., 1920], pp. 374–376). He apparently assumed, in addition to oligopoly, that the long-run demand curve was inelastic for price reductions.

explains price behavior in areas where the other explanation is silent or contradicts the implications of the neoclassical theory in areas where both apply. For the empirical tests in Part II, the following differences between the implications of the kinky demand curve and the neoclassical theory will be used:

A) The kinky demand curve theory is silent on monopolies, for the essential feature of retaliation by rivals is absent. Should monopoly prices be rigid, the forces that explain this rigidity (say cost of price changes) may suffice to explain an equal amount of price rigidity under oligopoly. Unless the factors making for monopoly price rigidity do not operate under oligopoly, we can dispense with the kink unless greater rigidity is found in the oligopolistic industries.

B) The discontinuity in marginal revenue will disappear, and with it the reason for price rigidity, if formerly independent firms enter into collusion. The neoclassical theory emphasizes the administrative weaknesses in collusion, on the other hand, and this argues for greater price rigidity.

C) Prices will be relatively flexible with very few and with many firms in the industry, and relatively rigid with a moderate number of firms (say, five to ten), according to the kink theory. The neoclassical theories of oligopoly are neither outspoken nor unanimous on this question, but there is a general suggestion that price flexibility increases continuously with the number of firms.

D) When there is a dominant firm or set of firms (acting together) in the role of price leader, prices should be more flexible than if there is no price leader, on the kink theory. The neoclassical theory is silent on this point.

E) Given the number and size configuration of firms, prices should be more flexible the more heterogeneous the products, under the kinky demand curve theory. The neoclassical theory has no such implication.

II. Empirical Tests of the Theory

One may submit to empirical tests either the assumption of entrepreneurial behavior underlying the theory of the kinky demand curve or the implications of the kink for price behavior. The former alternative requires an analysis of the sequence of price changes made by oligopolists in an industry; the latter alternative can be developed by a comparison of observed price rigidity with that prophesied by the theory.

1. The Validity of the Assumption

If price increases of one firm are not followed by rivals, but price reductions are followed, the oligopolists have a basis in experience for believing that there is a kink in their demand curves. If price reductions are not followed by rivals, or price increases are as closely followed, no such objective basis for a kink exists.

The cigarette industry (with three large firms) offers a good example of the type of experience that would create a belief in the existence of a kink. On September 28, 1918, the American Tobacco Company raised the list price of Lucky Strikes from $6.00 to $7.50 per thousand, but the rivals continued to charge the lower price. The sales of Lucky Strikes fell 31 per cent from September to November, when the price was reduced to $6.00, and continued to decline for several months.[14] The later price history in this industry, however, is not such as to create a belief in the existence of a kink:

April 20, 1928: Reynolds (Camels) announced a reduction from $6.40 to $6 per thousand, effective April 21. American Tobacco followed on April 21 and Liggett and Myers on April 23.

October 4, 1929: Reynolds announced an increase to $6.40, effective October 5, and both rivals followed on that day.

June 23, 1931: Reynolds announced an increase to $6.85, effective June 24, and both rivals followed that day.

January 1, 1933: American Tobacco reduced its price to $6, effective January 3, and both rivals followed that day.

February 11, 1933: American Tobacco reduced its price to $5.50, and both rivals followed the same day.

January 9, 1934: Reynolds increased its price to $6.10, and both rivals followed the same day.[15]

These price changes, incidentally, were relatively larger than they

---

[14] This episode is reported in detail in the forthcoming study of the American tobacco industry by William H. Nicholls.

[15] Federal Trade Commission, *Agricultural Income Inquiry* (Washington, 1937), Vol. I, p. 448. The history of prices after 1934 follows essentially the same pattern, although Nicholls reports an unmatched and unsuccessful price increase by Liggett and Myers on July 30, 1946—followed by a general increase on October 14, 1946, with American Tobacco the price leader.

appear: the manufacturer's net was smaller by a three-dollar tax and trade discounts.

The more complicated pattern of price changes for automobiles is illustrated for two leading firms in Fig. 4. The prices of the two firms changed at different dates and by different amounts, and price increases were more nearly simultaneous than price reductions. Price experience in this field should not lead a firm to believe

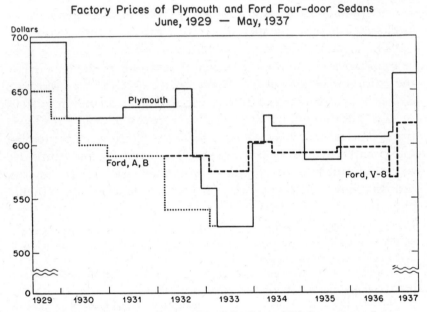

Factory Prices of Plymouth and Ford Four-door Sedans
June, 1929 — May, 1937

Source Federal Trade Commission, *Report on Motor Vehicle Industry* (76th Cong., 1st sess., House Doc. 468 [Washington, 1940]), pp. 894-95, 896.

FIGURE 4

that price reductions will be matched immediately or wholly nor that in a period of business recovery rivals will fail to increase prices.

Six anthracite companies produced 62.5 per cent of the aggregate output in 1930, and eight companies usually produce 70 to 80 per cent of aggregate output.[16] The prices of seven companies, for each size of coal, are listed (in very large type) every week in the *Coal and Coal Trade Journal*. These prices are identical and they

---

[16] C. E. Fraser and G. F. Doriot, *Analysing Our Industries* (New York, McGraw-Hill Book Co., 1932), pp. 400, 401.

almost invariably change on the same day.[17] There is no evidence of a kink: prices change often in a marked, but by no means rigid, seasonal pattern.

Some direct evidence argues against the existence of a kink in the demand curve for steel produced by United States Steel: Bethlehem, for example, has faithfully followed the price increases.[18] But the important evidence is indirect: there is no evidence of price rigidity within this industry. The official price lists and trade-journal quotations have been honored almost exclusively in the breach, and the transactions take place at prices that appear to be fairly sensitive to demand conditions.[19] It is debatable whether the steel industry, with its price leader, should have rigid prices on the kinky demand curve theory, and it is also debatable whether the price leader often leads the industry in lowering prices.

Three firms produce most of the dynamite used in mining, quarrying, and construction in the United States. The wholesale prices for 40 per cent ammonium dynamite, per 50-pound bag, moved as follows during the thirties:

February 27, 1933: All firms reduced the price from $12.25 to $10.50.

March 12, 1934: Du Pont and Hercules reduced the price to $10; Atlas followed 17 days later.

January 14, 1935: All firms increased the price to $10.50.

May 7, 1936: Du Pont and Hercules reduced the price to $9.50; Atlas followed the next day.

May 8, 1937: Du Pont and Atlas increased the price to $10.50; Hercules followed 3 days later.[20]

Again there is no empirical basis for believing the kink exists.

---

[17] Occasionally there is a temporary discrepancy. For example, six companies announced prices of $4.70 per ton for pea-size coal in the July 4, 1929, issue; one company retained the previous price of $4.60. A week later the exception disappeared.

[18] Temporary National Economic Committee, *Hearings,* Part 19: *Iron and Steel Industry* (Washington, 1940), pp. 10587 ff.

[19] See especially the study made by the Bureau of Labor Statistics, "Labor Department Examines Consumers' Prices of Steel Products," *Iron Age,* April 25, 1946. United States Steel officials testified before the T.N.E.C. that the Birmingham quotation had not been realized between 1932 and 1939 and that the general reduction in 1938 was merely a formal recognition of ruling prices (*Hearings,* Part 19, pp. 10546, 10505 ff.). See also *Hearings,* Part 27: *Iron and Steel Industry* (Washington, 1940), pp. 14141 f., 14172 f.

[20] I am indebted to Mr. Edward W. Proctor of Brown University for the

Socony-Vacuum and Atlantic Refining are two important sellers of gasoline in the Boston area. Aside from three periods in 1934 and 1935 when Socony-Vacuum's price was less than Atlantic's, the prices of the two firms changed as shown in the accompanying list in the period 1929–37.

Simultaneous price changes....................................... 40
    Increases 22
    Opposite 1
    Decreases 17
Delay in following price increases............................ 12
    Days
      1 9
      2 1
      3 1
      4 1
Delay in following price decreases............................ 10
    Days
      1 1
      2 3
      3 1
     10 1
     21 1
     23 1
     28 1
     47 1

It appears, then, that price increases are more nearly simultaneous than price decreases—the opposite of the kinky demand curve assumption.[21]

The most striking case of contradiction of the assumption of the theory, however, is provided by potash. On June 1, 1934, the American Potash and Chemical Corporation issued a price list that carried about 26 per cent reductions from the prices in the previous year. The other firms failed to follow. On June 26 the lower prices were withdrawn, and the company lamented: "It was expected that other potash producers would likewise announce

---

information in this paragraph, which was secured by correspondence with Du Pont, Atlas Powder, and Hercules Powder. The three companies have headquarters in Wilmington; the latter two were created in 1912 by an antitrust action.

[21] I am indebted to Mr. Melvin D. Sargent of Brown University for the information on gasoline prices. The price quotations are from *Oil Price Handbook, 1929–37* (Cleveland, National Petroleum News, 1938).

their prices in accordance with long prevailing custom. No such announcements have been forthcoming. Under the circumstances this Company is compelled to withdraw the schedule of prices and terms referred to."[22]

In these seven industries there is little historical basis for a firm to believe that price increases will not be matched by rivals and that price decreases will be matched. This indicates only that not every oligopoly has reason to believe that it has a kinky demand curve, and most adherents of the theory would readily concede this.[23] On the other hand, here are seven industries in which the existence of the kinky demand curve is questionable— a list that is longer by seven than the list of industries for which a prima facie case has been made for the existence of the kink.[24]

2. The Validity of the Implications

The kinky demand curve would prove to be an incorrect or unimportant construction if oligopoly prices were as flexible as monopoly and/or competitive prices. It is not possible to make a direct test for price rigidity, in part, because the prices at which the products of oligopolists sell are not generally known. For the purpose of such a test we need transaction prices; instead, we have quoted prices on a temporal basis, and they are deficient in two respects.

The first deficiency is notorious: Nominal price quotations may be stable although the prices at which sales are taking place fluctuate often and widely. The disparity may be due to a failure to take account of quality, "extras," freight, guaranties, discounts, etc.; or the price collector may be deceived merely to strengthen

---

[22] *Chemical Industries* (July 1934), p. 49.

[23] But apparently not all. O. Lange treats only of kinky demand curves in his theory of oligopoly (see *Price Flexibility and Employment* [Bloomington, Principia Press, 1944], Chap. VII); and L. Tarshis has recently done the same in his *The Elements of Economics* (New York, Houghton Mifflin Co., 1947), pp. 139 ff.

[24] In the Conference on Price Research study, *Cost Behavior and Price Policy* (New York, National Bureau of Economic Research, 1943), it is stated: "There is rather strong reason for believing that leading firms in the automobile, steel, agricultural implement, and many other industries act upon approximately this view of the situation [i.e., that there is a kink in the demand curve]" (*ibid.*, p. 278). The reason is not given. We have discussed automobiles and steel; agricultural implements will be taken up subsequently.

morale within the industry. The various studies of steel prices, already referred to, contain striking examples of this disparity, and others can be cited.[25] We cannot infer that all nominally rigid prices are really flexible, but there is also very little evidence that they are really rigid.

The second deficiency is that published prices are on a temporal basis. If nine-tenths of annual sales occur at fluctuating prices within a month (as is true of some types of tobacco), and the remainder at a fixed price during the rest of the year, the nominal price rigidity for eleven months is trivial. With each price we ought to have the corresponding quantities sold: for a study of price rigidity, "April" would better be the fourth one-twelfth of the year's sales than the fourth month of the year.

Despite these shortcomings, a comparison of the implications of the kinky demand curve for price behavior with observable behavior (even if observable only in bulletins of the Bureau of Labor Statistics) has some value. If the theory cannot explain the pattern of rigidity of quoted prices among industries, there is no presumption that it would explain the pattern of transaction price rigidity among industries.

Our tests are made by comparing observed price rigidity in a group of industries with the relative rigidities forecast by the theory for industries with these market structures. We choose the period, June, 1929, through May, 1937, which embraces both a complete business cycle and the periods used in most empirical studies of price rigidity. We require three types of information:

A) A LIST OF OLIGOPOLISTIC INDUSTRIES. The two basic criteria are (1) a fairly precise knowledge of the industry structure, and (2) continuous price and output series. The industries are described briefly in the Appendix.[26]

---

[25] See the industry studies of the Division of Research of N.R.A.; the prices revealed in prosecutions under the Robinson-Patman Act; Saul Nelson, "A Consideration of the Validity of the Bureau of Labor Statistics Price Indexes," in *The Structure of the American Economy* (Washington, National Resources Committee, 1939), pp. 173–184.

[26] More specifically, the oligopolies discussed by Clair Wilcox in *Competition and Monopoly in American Industry* ("T.N.E.C. Monographs," No. 21 [Washington, 1940]) formed the basic list. An industry was excluded if (1) necessary information was not available, (2) the industry was analyzed in the preceding section, or (3) the firms were in known collusion throughout the

b) Some Measure of Expected Price Changes in the Absence of Restrictions on Price Changes. Shifts in demand are of primary (although far from exclusive) importance, and we measure them roughly by the coefficient of variation of production (or some related series) in 1929, 1931, 1933, 1935, and 1937.

c) A Measure of Price Rigidity. The basic test used is frequency of change in the monthly price quotations; for the theory under examination implies that there will be *no* changes—not merely that the price changes will be small. This test is supplemented by the coefficient of variation of monthly prices for two reasons. First, the price series have technical features that lead to more numerous price changes than actually occur. They are often averages of weekly quotations, and hence show two changes in the monthly averages when a price change occurs within a month.[27] They are often averages of prices of several firms, and if each firm makes one price change the average can display as many changes as there are firms. Second, it can be argued that the kink is an exaggeration—that actually there is a sharp bend in the demand curve of the firm so that small price changes are what the theory prophesies.[28] But frequent small price changes would still be improbable because of the cost of making price changes.

The basic data that are used in the tests are summarized in Table 1; fuller information is given in the Appendix. It will be observed that the two tests of price rigidity differ substantially: the coefficient of rank correlation between number of price changes and coefficient of variation of prices is +.69 for the nineteen oligopolies listed in Table 1, on p. 429.

Monopolies Versus Oligopolies

The monopolies listed in Table 1 are unsurpassed for price rigidity, despite the fact that their outputs varied more than those

---

period. In addition, many chemicals were excluded because of ignorance of substitution relationships.

[27] Thus the B.L.S. reports as eight changes the six changes made by Pittsburgh Plate Glass during the period.

[28] To secure a sharp bend, we must assume that rivals will partly follow price increases and decreases that are small but fail to follow large increases and completely follow large decreases.

of most oligopolistic industries. This finding, which could be supported by more cases,[29] suggests the possibility that the forces that make for price rigidity in monopolies are sufficiently strong to account for the lesser rigidity in oligopolies. One might argue that special factors are at work in monopoly, but the only two that come to mind are fear of governmental attention or action and the conservatism that comes with size. The former, however, is even more effective against oligopolies because of the importance of conspiracy in the antitrust laws, and the latter is presumably also a function of absolute size. It should be added that the neoclassical theory does not provide a satisfactory explanation for this extraordinary rigidity of monopoly prices.

According to the kink theory, there will be no kink when the oligopolists enter into explicit collusion; and hence prices would be expected to become more flexible. All empirical evidence contradicts this implication. Of our industries, at least two had periods of collusion. There was a combination of rayon producers to fix prices between October 21, 1931, and May 23, 1932:[30] There were no price changes during this period, none in the preceding period of equal length, and four in the subsequent period of equal length. There are only two periods of protracted rigidity in the price series for copper: the first occurs under Copper Exporters (a Webb-Pomerene cartel), the second under N.R.A.

A number of examples are also provided by other industries. On August 30, 1932, the six important growers and canners of pineapple entered a ten-year agreement to restrict output and market through the Pineapple Producers Cooperative Association.[31] In the thirty-nine months preceding this date there were

---

[29] Thus, the price of magnesium was very rigid; the rentals of the International Business Machines Corporation have not varied (Wilcox, *op. cit.*, p. 106); the retail price of incandescent lamps of common sizes changed once or twice (United States Tariff Commission, *Incandescent Electric Lamps* [Report No. 133 (2d ser., Washington, 1939)], p. 47); this was virtually a General Electric monopoly because of its licensing provisions.

[30] "Viscose Company *et al.*," *Federal Trade Commission Decisions*, Vol. XXV (Washington, 1939), p. 425.

[31] "The move brought all the island packers into complete accord and cooperation for the first time in history" (*New York Times*, August 31, 1932, p. 10); see also J. A. Shoemaker, "Labor Conditions in Hawaii," *Monthly Labor Review*, January 1941, pp. 30 ff.

TABLE 1

MEASURES OF MARKET STRUCTURE FOR TWENTY-ONE PRODUCTS
AND OF THEIR PRICE FLEXIBILITY AND OUTPUT VARIABILITY
JUNE, 1929—MAY, 1937

Product	Number of Firms in Industry	Price Leader	Price Flexibility		Coefficient of Variation of Output
			Number of Price Changes	Coefficient of Variation	
Oligopolies:					
Bananas	2	Yes	46	16	17
Boric acid	3	No	7	17	16
Cans	4	Yes	6	5	27
Cement	12	No	14	11	41
Copper	4	No	63	37	43
Gasoline*	11	No	84	22	16
Grain-binder	2	Yes	5	3	63
Linoleum	2	No?	12	9	30
Newsprint	9	No	6	16	16
Plaster	3	Yes	4	5	29
Plate glass	2	No	8	13	34
Plows	6	No	25	6	50
Rayon	8	No	26	30	34
Soap	3	No	9	12	7
Starch	4	Yes	20	12	13
Sulphur	2	Yes	0	0	24
Tires	8	No	36	9	16
Tractors	4	Yes	6	6	76
Window glass	3	No	20	21	24
Monopolies:					
Aluminum	1	....	2	6	47
Nickel	1	....	0	0	35

* In Pennsylvania and Delaware.

seventeen price changes in canned pineapples; in the subsequent
fifty-seven months, eight changes. Prices of typewriters were very
rigid during a period when the four important producers were
charged with colluding.[32] During the period of operation of the

---

[32] Wilcox, *op. cit.*, p. 140.

midwestern oil pool (Madison Oil Case), prices "displayed a rigidity without parallel in the history of the industry."[33]

If the disappearance of the kink through collusion has a tendency to increase price flexibility, this tendency is completely submerged by the opposite effects of administrative limitations on cartel price policy.

The Number of Firms

The number of firms that enters into the formation of price policy is difficult to determine; a completely satisfactory determination would require knowledge of cross-elasticities of demand, the entrepreneur's knowledge and objectives, and similar data.

TABLE 2

| Number of Firms in Industry | Number of Industries in Sample | Price Flexibility | | Average of Coefficients of Variation of Outputs |
		Number of Price Changes	Coefficient of Variation	
2	5	14.2	8.2	33.6
3, 4	8	16.8	14.4	29.4
6, 8	3	29.0	15.0	33.3
9, 11, 12	3	34.7	16.3	24.3

As an unsatisfactory substitute for this information, we have been guided by two criteria: that sufficient firms be included to account for two-thirds to three-quarters of the output of the product and that the largest firm omitted from the count sell less than a tenth of the amount sold by the largest firm in the industry. Although these rules are arbitrary, they focus attention on relevant variables: if we do not include enough firms to account for a predominant share of output, the firms will not be able to control prices (attenuated oligopoly); and if we exclude firms large relative to those that are included, we may be omitting firms that are in the oligopolistic relationship. The precise number of firms, even by these arbitrary criteria, is in doubt in more than half the industries listed in Table 1, but it was thought better to give a

[33] *Ibid.*, p. 136.

single number than a range that invites mechanical averaging to secure a single number.

Our expectation, on the kink theory, is that a very few rivals will have relatively flexible prices because the impossibility of maintaining a price lower than a rival's will be evident. On the other hand, with many rivals the fear that price cuts will be matched is reduced, and again the kink disappears. We do not test this latter implication because it is identical with that of the neoclassical theory.

If the data in Table 1 are summarized by number of firms, we find a definite tendency for price flexibility to increase with the number of firms in the industry (Table 2). The coefficient of rank correlation between number of firms and number of price changes is +.41, that between number of firms and coefficient of variation of prices is +.31. There is virtually no relationship between fluctuations of output and number of firms, nor is the strength or direction of relationship between number of firms and price flexibility affected if industries with price leaders are segregated.[34] Thus there is a weak tendency for a greater number of firms to be associated with a greater frequency and amplitude of price changes, the contrary of the implications of the kinky demand curve.

Price Leadership

The term, "price leadership," is used in two very different senses in economic literature. In the one sense it refers to a dominant firm that sets the price, allows the minor firms to sell what they wish at this price (subject perhaps to nonprice competition), and supplies the remainder of the quantity demanded. In the other sense, price leadership refers to the existence of a firm that conventionally first announces price changes that are usually followed by the remainder of the industry, even though this firm may not occupy a dominant position. For example, International Paper was for a long period the price leader in newsprint although it produced less than one-seventh of the output, and it was succeeded in this role by Great Northern, a smaller firm. This

---

[34] The coefficient of rank correlation between number of firms and number of price changes is .37 for seven products with price leaders and .39 for twelve products without price leaders.

latter type of price leadership has been illuminatingly described by S. A. Swensrud of Standard Oil of Ohio:

> In any territory all suppliers are watching the same things. They watch the statistical position of the industry as a whole, that is, production of crude oil and gasoline, sales of petroleum products, and stocks of crude oil and gasoline. . . . . They watch the ambitions of competitors to increase their share of the business in the territory. They gage these ambitions by reports of salesmen on price concessions to commercial customers, by observations of the amount of business done by trackside operators and sellers of unbranded and locally branded gasoline, by the reports of salesmen as to competitive offers being made to dealers, and by reports of salesmen as to the extent of secret price cuts, discounts, and the like being offered by retailers. All these facts are constantly before local managers and central organizations.
>
> Now suppose that secret price cutting by dealers in some particular area breaks out into the open in the form of a cut in the posted price because some dealer becomes disgusted with the uncertainty as to how much business he is losing to competitors granting secret discounts. As the openly admitted price reduction operates, the local officers of all suppliers are assailed with demands from dealers, relayed and in some instances emphasized by salesmen, for a reduction in the tank-wagon price. . . . . The local manager of the leading marketer of course faces more demands than any other manager. He attempts to gage the permanence of the retail cut. Frequently local managers elect to make no change in the tank-wagon price. Ordinarily this decision springs from the conclusion that the local price war will soon run its course because it is not supported by weakness in basic markets. On other occasions the local manager concludes that the causes of the retail price cutting rest primarily on the availability of sufficient low-price gasoline so that the condition may be considered deep-seated, and he therefore authorizes or recommends a local reduction in the tank-wagon price. . . . . Thus the particular local territory becomes a subnormal territory, that is, one in which prices are out of line with those generally prevailing in the marketing area.
>
> The major sales executives of all companies watch carefully the number and size of subnormal markets. . . . . If the number of local price cuts increases, if the number and amount of secret concessions to commercial consumers increase, if the secret unpublicized concessions to dealers increase, it becomes more and more difficult to maintain the higher prices. . . . . Finally, some company, usually the largest marketer in the territory, recognizes that the subnormal price has become the normal price and announces a general price reduction throughout the territory. . . . .
>
> In summary, therefore, the so-called price leadership in the petroleum industry boils down to the fact that some company in each territory most of the time bears the onus of formally recognizing current conditions. . . . . In short, unless the so-called price leader accurately interprets basic conditions and local conditions, it soon will not be the leading marketer. Price leadership

does not mean that the price leader can set prices to get the maximum profit and force other marketers to conform.[35]

The difference between these two types of price leadership from the viewpoint of the theory of kinky demand curves is basic. The dominant firm has no kink in its demand curve because rivals have no reason for charging a lower price: they are permitted to sell as much as they wish at the leader's price.[36] The

TABLE 3

	Industries with Leader	Industries without Leader
Two-firm industries:		
Number in sample	3	2
Average number of price changes	17	10
Average coefficient of variation of prices	6.3	11.0
Average coefficient of variation of outputs	34.7	32.0
Three- and four-firm industries:		
Number in sample	4	4
Average number of price changes	9	24.8
Average coefficient of variation of prices	7.0	21.8
Average coefficient of variation of outputs	36.2	22.5

second type of leader, the barometric firm, commands adherence of rivals to his price only because, and to the extent that, his price reflects market conditions with tolerable promptness. The widespread development of barometric firms is therefore explicitly a device to insure that there will be no kink, or that the kink will not prevent readjustment of price to important changes in cost or demand conditions.

Only the price leadership exercised by dominant firms, therefore, is relevant in testing the implication of the kinky demand curve theory that there will be no kink when there is price leadership. Accordingly, we classify as industries with price leaders only those in which there is a relatively large firm, producing, say, 40

[35] W. S. Farish and J. H. Pew, *Review and Criticism . . . . of Monograph No. 39* ("T.N.E.C. Monographs," No. 39A [Washington, 1941]), pp. 47–49.

[36] For the details of price determination in this situation see my "Notes on the Theory of Duopoly," *The Journal of Political Economy*, Vol. XLVIII (1940), p. 523 ff.

per cent of the output of the industry at a minimum, and more if the second largest firm is large (because otherwise the situation approaches classical duopoly). On this basis there are seven leaders among our nineteen industries (see Table 1), and they are compared with the remaining twelve industries in Table 3. Except for the number of price changes of two-firm industries (where bananas dominate the result), the prices of industries with price leaders are less flexible than those of industries without price leaders, despite the larger fluctuations of output of the former

TABLE 4

	Homogeneous Products	Heterogeneous Products
Number of products........................	13	6
Average number of price changes.............	23.4	15.5
Average coefficient of variation of prices.......	15.8	7.5
Average coefficient of variation of outputs	25.7	40.3

group. This is contrary to Sweezy's conjecture and is in keeping with the price rigidity found in monopolistic industries.

Goodness of Substitutes

It is almost inherent in the methods of quotation of price statistics that most of the commodities examined in this article are nearly homogeneous. If products are rather heterogeneous, the significance of an average price becomes doubtful and the B.L.S. does not report it. Of our nineteen industries, only six have products whose prices appear to differ significantly and persistently among firms: soap, tractors, grain-binders, plows, tires, and linoleum. Their prices appear to change less often and less widely, on average, than those of homogeneous products as shown in Table 4. It should be noted that we might, with some justification, have designated our monopolies (aluminum and nickel) as oligopolies with differentiated products.

3. Conclusion

The empirical evidence reveals neither price experiences that would lead oligopolists to believe in the existence of a kink nor the pattern of changes of price quotations that the theory leads us to expect. The industries included in these tests are not very numerous, but they are sufficiently varied and important to suggest that similar adverse results would be secured from a larger sample.

But is this adverse conclusion really surprising? The kink is a barrier to changes in prices that will increase profits, and business is the collection of devices for circumventing barriers to profits. That this barrier should thwart businessmen—especially when it is wholly of their own fabrication—is unbelievable. There are many ways in which it can be circumvented. We have had occasion to notice the development of price leadership of the barometric variety as one device, and the old-fashioned solution of collusion is not always overlooked. In addition there is the whole range of tactical maneuvers that Neumann and Morgenstern's theory of games has uncovered. In the multi-dimensional real world there are many ways to teach a lesson, especially when the pupil is eager to learn.

Appendix

The summary descriptions of the industries used in Part II are based upon indicated references and C. L. James, *Industrial Concentration and Tariffs*, T.N.E.C. Monograph No. 10 (Washington, 1940); *The Structure of Industry*, T.N.E.C. Monograph No. 27 (Washington, 1941); and C. Wilcox, *Competition and Monopoly in American Industry*, Monograph No. 21 (Washington, 1940), which may be referred to for information on imports, concentration ratios, and general market structures, respectively. Price quotations are from the Bureau of Labor Statistics bulletins, *Wholesale Prices*. In the few cases where price quotations begin in 1931, the number of price quotations reported in Table 1 is 96/77 of the actual number. Unless otherwise noted, quantity data are from S. Fabricant's *The Output of Manufacturing Industries, 1899–1937* (New York, National Bureau of Economic Research, 1940).

Aluminum:
    The Aluminum Company of America produced all new aluminum during the period and also dominated the scrap market.
    Quantity: production *(Minerals Yearbook)*
    D. H. Wallace, *Market Control in the Aluminum Industry* (Cambridge, Harvard University Press, 1937)

Bananas:
    In 1936 United Fruit handled 60 per cent, and Standard Fruit and Steamship 30 per cent, of the bananas imported.

Prices: Jamaica 9's to July 1931, then Honduras (spliced for continuity)

Quantities: imports *(Statistical Abstract)*

BORIC ACID:

In 1937 there were only three producers. Pacific Coast Borax produced half of the total, American Potash and Chemical about 40 per cent, and Stauffer Chemical the remainder.

C. L. James, *op. cit.,* chap. V

CANS:

In 1937 American Can produced about half, and Continental Can about one-quarter, of total output. The latter company also produced cans for Campbell Soup on a fixed-fee basis. McKeesport Tin Plate was third, with about 10 per cent of output, and Owens-Illinois Can was fourth, with less than 5 per cent. There were also fourteen smaller companies.

Standard Statistics Company, *Standard Corporation Reports*

CEMENT:

In 1931 the leading companies in the northeastern section and their percentages of sales were Lehigh, 19.1; Universal Atlas, 15.2; International, 8.1; Penn-Dixie, 7.9; Alpha, 6.7; a total of 57.0 per cent. The next seven mills (it is not clear that each was separately owned), with individual percentages ranging from 3.6 down to 2.4, totaled another 20.3 per cent.

Prices: Northampton

Quantities: production, northeastern section *(Minerals Yearbook)*

Federal Trade Commission, *Cement Industry* (73d Cong., 1st sess., Senate Doc. 71 [Washington, 1933])

COPPER:

In 1947 the leading companies and their percentages of total production were Kennecott Copper, 35.9; Anaconda, 22.9; Phelps Dodge, 18.8; Calumet and Hecla, 4.5.

Quantities: production *(Minerals Yearbook)*

The Structure of Industry, pp. 248–249

GASOLINE:

In 1938 the leading companies in the Pennsylvania-Delaware area and their percentages of sales were Atlantic Refining, 21.9; Standard Oil of New Jersey, 14.5; Gulf Oil, 10.2; Sun Oil, 9.8; Standard Oil of Indiana, 8.5; Consolidated Oil, 7.6; Socony-Vacuum, 6.8; Texas, 4.8; Tide Water, 3.4; Pure Oil, 2.1; and Cities Service, 2.3. In 1926 Atlantic's percentage was 44.5 and Gulf Oil's, 20.8.

Prices: Pennsylvania

Quantities: consumption in Pennsylvania and Delaware *(Minerals Yearbook)*

Federal Trade Commission, *Report on Distribution Methods and Costs,* Part IV (Washington, 1944), p. 52

GRAIN-BINDER:

In 1935 the leading companies and their percentages of total sales were International Harvester, 67.2; Deere, 24.7; and there were also four other companies.

Quantities: production (1933 estimated from *Census of Manufactures*)

Federal Trade Commission, *Report on the Agricultural Implement and Machinery Business* (75th Cong., 3d sess., House Doc. 702 [Washington, 1938]), p. 153

LINOLEUM:

In 1937 there were only four producers of inlaid linoleum. Armstrong Cork and Congoleum Nairn supplied most of the output.

Prices: 1931 on

Quantities: production, 1931 on

Standard Statistics Company, *Standard Corporation Reports*

NEWSPRINT:

In 1928 the leading firms and their percentages of the total production in Canada and the United States were International Paper, 14; Canadian Power and Paper, 12; Abitibi, 11; Great Northern, 9; Crown Zellerbach, 8; Minnesota and Ontario, 5; Price, 5; and Powell River, 4. Crown Zellerbach operated only on the Pacific Coast, where it supplied 70 per cent of the total.

Quantities: domestic production plus imports (the latter from *Statistical Abstract*)

Federal Trade Commission, *Newsprint Paper Industry* (71st Cong., spec. sess., Senate Doc. 214 [Washington, 1930]), pp. 18 ff.

NICKEL:

The International Nickel Company produces about 90 per cent of the output of North America, and its leading rival, Falconbridge Nickel Mines, sells chiefly in Europe.

Quantities: domestic production plus imports minus exports *(Minerals Yearbook)*

A. Skelton in *International Control in the Non-ferrous Metals,* ed. W. Y. Elliott (New York: Macmillan Co., 1937), Part II, chap. V

Report of Commissioner, Combines Investigation Act, *Canada and International Cartels* (Ottawa, 1945), p. 31

PLASTER:

In 1937 United States Gypsum produced almost half the output. National Gypsum and Certain-teed Products and Celotex are other large producers of gypsum products and together account for almost 40 per cent of 1937 output of plaster. The four firms produced 83.4 per cent of total output.

Quantities: production (1933 estimated from *Minerals Yearbook*)

PLATE GLASS:

In 1935 Libby-Owens-Ford and Pittsburgh Plate Glass produced 95 per cent of the output of plate glass; their outputs were about equal. The remainder of the industry consisted of three firms, of which one (Ford Motor) produced for its own use.

Prices: 3–5 square feet

Quantities: production (United States Tariff Commission study [cited below], p. 91; 1936 used in lieu of unknown 1937 data)

United States Tariff Commission, *Flat Glass and Related Glass Products* (2d ser.; Rept. No. 123 [Washington, 1937]), p. 24

"Life Goes On," *Fortune*, January 1934, p. 43

PLOWS:

In 1936 the leading firms and their percentages of total sales were International Harvester, 17.5; Oliver, 16.7; Unknown, 15 to 20 (judging from the 1937 concentration ratio of 65.7); Deere, 12.2; Avery, 3.5; and Minneapolis-Moline, 2.5. It is not certain that the latter two are fifth and sixth in size.

Prices: walking, two-horse

Federal Trade Commission, *Agricultural Implements* (73d Cong., 1st sess., Senate Doc. 71 [Washington, 1933]), p. 151

RAYON:

In 1935 the capacities of the leading firms for producing yarn were American Viscose, 34.8; Du Pont Rayon, 17.6; Celanese, 12.8; North American, 7.3; Industrial Rayon, 6.1. Four smaller firms had an additional 14.9 per cent of capacity. Output was fairly close to capacity in this year.

Prices: 300 denier, first quality

Quantities: production of yarn (*Chemical and Metallurgical Engineering*, February 1943, p. 116)

The Structure of Industry, pp. 263–264

SOAP:

In 1931 Procter and Gamble sold about 40 per cent, Colgate-Palmolive-Peet about 24 per cent, and Lever Brothers about 14 per cent of total soap. In 1935 the four largest firms produced 73.5 per cent of all soap (which is believed to be less concentrated than hand soap) and the eight largest firms 83.1 per cent.

Prices: 1931 on, toilet soap

Quantities: production, 1931 on

"Procter and Gamble," *Fortune*, December 1931, p. 97

STARCH:

In 1937 Corn Products Refining Company made more than half of the total sales. The other large firms are A. E. Staley Manufacturing, Penick and Ford, and American Maize Products, with about one-third of total sales. There were also seven smaller companies.

C. L. James, *op. cit.*, p. 15

SULPHUR:

In 1937 Texas Gulf Sulphur supplied 64 per cent of total output, Freeport Sulphur, 26 per cent, and two other companies another 9 per cent.
Minerals Yearbook

TIRES:

In 1933 the leading companies and their percentages of the industry's capacity were Goodyear, 26.4; Firestone, 13.6; United States, 12.3; Goodrich, 12.0; Fisk, 9.1; Kelly-Springfield, 3.5; Mansfield, 2.8; General Tire, 2.6.
Prices: balloon (spliced for continuity)
W. H. Gross, *Evidence Study No. 36 of the Rubber Tire Manufacturing Industry* (Washington, N.R.A. Division of Review [October 1935]), p. 5

TRACTORS:

In 1935 the leading companies and their percentages of total sales were International Harvester, 49.5; Deere, 24.5; Allis-Chalmers, 9.5; J. I. Case, 7.1. In 1929 International Harvester's percentage was 59.9 and Deere's, 21.1.
Prices: 10–20 horse-power
Federal Trade Commission, *Agricultural Implements*, p. 153

WINDOW GLASS:

In 1935 the industry was composed of twelve companies with twenty-one plants, of which thirteen were in operation. Libby-Owens-Ford, Pittsburgh Plate Glass, and American Window Glass produced more than 75 per cent of total output. In 1936 four other companies organized a common sales company (Fourco Glass Company) which bought up several idle plants. These four companies comprised virtually the entire industry thereafter.
Price: Single B
United States Tariff Commission, *Flat Glass*, p. 24.

22

PRICE THEORY AND OLIGOPOLY *

By K. W. Rothschild ||

I

In the theory of a capitalist market economy price has always been one of the central problems, if not *the* problem. And, indeed, for a long time it seemed as if this problem at least had found a methodological approach and a solution which might require refinements, but which by and large could provide the main answers for the purposes of interpretation, economic policy and economic forecasting. Then, with more and more refinements and reconsiderations taking place in the 'twenties, doubts with regard to the general validity of the fundamentals of price theory began to grow and spread, until finally the theory of imperfect and monopolistic competition opened new paths for the treatment of the price problem.

These new developments were and are rightly hailed as great advances, which have enabled us to get a more realistic view of the pricing process and to include in our theoretical scheme a number of cases which could only be fitted into the competitive theory by making special assumptions, such as "friction," "irrationality," "non-economic factors," etc. But, great and important as was the advance, it soon turned out that even the new theory did not provide the tools that would cover satisfactorily all major aspects of the price-making process. Within a few years from the publication of Joan Robinson's and Edward Chamberlin's standard works, descriptive economists and economic field-workers complained that the new theory did not provide a sufficiently useful frame of reference for the factual material they had to investigate

* *The Economic Journal*, Vol. LVII (1947), pp. 299–320. Reprinted, by the courtesy of the publisher and the author, without change from the original text.

|| Österreichisches Institut für Wirtschaftsforschung (Austrian Institute for Economic Research).

and to interpret.[1] The purpose of the present article is to investigate the reasons for these shortcomings and to indicate some steps which might help price theory to cover some of the "irregular" cases more successfully and more systematically.

II

The great power and attraction of the neo-classical competitive price theory lay in its simplicity and determinateness. This determinateness was due to the fact that in a market of competitive small-scale enterprise, price is the outcome of impersonal forces. Demand and cost conditions could be assumed as given—at least for a single industry—and outside the control of any single firm. If, in addition, the assumption was made that firms could enter and leave the industry freely, and would try to maximise profits, then a point of price equilibrium followed with the logical necessity of a physical law. And, indeed, it was the natural sciences which provided the main signposts for the choice of terminology (stable and unstable equilibrium, the pull of the market forces, elasticity of demand and supply) and of method (mathematical approach, predominantly mechanistic and static cause—effect relationships). Quite rightly, therefore, this theoretical approach has been characterised as "value mechanics."[2]

There is no doubt that this theory was a satisfactory approach to an explanation of the price problem in the typical mid-nine-

---

[1] Thus, for instance, R. L. Hall and C. J. Hitch, after discussing the results of an inquiry into the pricing methods of thirty-eight firms, came to the conclusion that "these considerations seem to vitiate any attempts to analyse normal entrepreneurial behaviour in the short period in terms of marginal curves" ("Price Theory and Business Behaviour," *Oxford Economic Papers,* May 1939, p. 32). Or, Professor Walton Hamilton, in introducing several industrial case studies carried out for the U. S. Cabinet Committee on Price Policy, says: "As the world is not all black and white, so industry cannot be set down in terms of an antithesis between competition and monopoly. . . . To set cases down along a straight line that moves from monopoly through duopoly and oligopoly to competition pure and undefiled, and to measure competitive forces by the relative number and size of sellers and buyers, is to make hypothetical economic phenomena the subject of mathematical exercises . . . the result is not a picture of pragmatic reality called industry" (Walton Hamilton and others, *Price and Price Policies,* New York, 1938, pp. 22–23).

[2] E. G. Nourse, "The Meaning of 'Price Policy,'" *The Quarterly Journal of Economics,* Feb. 1941, p. 205.

teenth century market. There is also no doubt that it is still a very useful model for some of the present-day markets. But at the same time it became increasingly clear that with modern trends towards large-scale enterprise, product differentiation, advertising and trade agreements, the competitive price analysis lost much of its force. Of course, Marshall, Edgeworth and their contemporaries were aware of the existence of imperfect competition, but they treated such cases largely as exceptions. And the one case they really dealt with in detail—the pure monopoly case—is to some extent an economic monstrosity, because, strictly speaking, a pure monopoly never exists in a world full of substitutes.

Thus it was not until the early 'thirties that a new theoretical framework was created which allowed for the inclusion of the now typical non-competitive markets. The main methodological change was that price was no longer regarded as the sole outcome of impersonal market forces dictating a unique solution to the individual firms, but that it was realised that under imperfect competition the firms themselves had a certain amount of freedom of action with regard to price, the nature of the product and selling expenditure. The consequence was that analysis shifted from the industrial supply and demand curves to the cost and demand conditions of the individual firms, and that price—or rather a price structure—was explained in terms of the adjustment of the firms to different and changing market situations. This meant that the analogies drawn from the world of mechanics became less applicable. Some of the new ideas, such as the "organic growth" of a firm or the survival of the most suitable business form, rather pointed to a certain affinity with biological thinking, and indeed biological reasoning and biological terminology (price environment, conditioning, ecology) found their way into economic theory.[3]

This change in price theory meant a great advance, in so far as it included a vast number of cases in the main theoretical body, which were formerly regarded as "exceptions" and had to be explained by additional factors. At the same time, with its greater scope, price theory lost some of the simplicity and determinate-

---

[3] See E. G. Nourse, *op. cit.*, p. 182.

ness which it possessed under the competitive approach. With the consideration of product differentiation, price discrimination, and advertising, "industry," "commodity," "cost" and "price" lost their exactly definable meanings, and it seemed as if the new theory would no longer be able to offer any exact solution of an "equilibrium price." This in itself need not be very tragic if the loss in simple determinateness is compensated by a greater relevance of the theory.[4] Nevertheless the strong tradition of price theory centring round a definite long-term "equilibrium price" made any idea of indeterminateness so abhorrent to the "father," and even more to the "mother," of imperfect competition theory[5] that most of their analysis was centred on those cases where determinate solutions in the mechanistic–biological sense could be most easily achieved. That is, their typical case deals with the market situation characterised by many small producers, product differentiation and free entry, which sets very definite limits to the freedom of action of the individual firm. A determinate solution is achieved by making the impersonal market forces the very powerful factor, and restricting the independent action of the firm to an adjustment to these forces—an adjustment which will be unique on the basis of profit maximisation (and survival in the case of the marginal firm).

This is, of course, a very important addition to the perfect competition model, and a useful frame of reference when we try to explain price in many of the present-day markets, particularly in retailing, but also in some small-scale industries. But, again, what can be regarded as the established body of "monopolistic competition theory" does not cover the whole field of price formation. In particular, it badly neglects the case where a small number of powerful firms compete with each other, the action of each exerting a marked influence on the position of all the others, and each of them not only adjusting itself passively to a "given" market

---

[4] Not all economists will subscribe to this view. Thus, for instance, J. R. Hicks, in his *Value and Capital,* justifies his unrealistic assumption of perfect competition by pointing out that this is the only way of saving something from the threatened wreckage of economic theory (p. 84).

[5] I hope Professor Chamberlin and Mrs. Robinson will not object to this spiritual relationship.

situation, but capable of actively changing that market situation. This neglect of duopoly and oligopoly problems[6] is the more regrettable as recent investigations have shown that oligopoly is by no means an exception, but that the most typical case in industry is probably monopolistic competition, with a considerable admixture of oligopoly.[7] Indeed, the reader of the classics of monopolistic competition must be left with the impression that the problem of monopoly with which our society is faced is predominantly created by the small grocer down the street rather than by the big steel firms.

III

To say that duopoly and oligopoly problems have been neglected does not mean that there have not been frequent attempts towards their theoretical solution. But it seems to the writer that these attempts—in contrast to much of the descriptive literature on this subject—have been hampered by being too much influenced by the models of perfect and monopolistic competition, and "pure" monopoly. Yet neither of these theories can be expected to form a sound basis for the study of duopoly and oligopoly prices.

On the whole, we can divide the theories dealing with duopoly and oligopoly into two groups:[8] those presenting a determinate solution and those stressing the indeterminateness of the problem. The determinate solution, in turn, can be reached in two ways. Either it is assumed that the oligopolists do not take into account the effects of their action on the policy of their rivals, as in the famous Cournot and Bertrand solutions; or these effects

---

[6] The neglect is particularly noticeable in Mrs. Robinson's book. Professor Chamberlin devotes some space to these problems, but they are definitely relegated to a secondary place, and he tries hard to formulate his additional assumptions for the oligopolistic case in such a way as to obtain a determinate equilibrium price similar to that of "pure" monopolistic competition. A good critical review of the unsatisfactory treatment of the oligopoly problem in Robinson's and Chamberlin's works can be found in R. Triffin, *Monopolistic Competition and General Equilibrium Theory*, Chaps. I and II.

[7] See R. L. Hall and C. J. Hitch, *op. cit.*, p. 29.

[8] A good summary of the more important theories can be found in E. H. Chamberlin, *The Theory of Monopolistic Competition*, Chap. III and Appendix A.

are recognised, but a determinate solution is reached with the help of additional assumptions. The first type of approach is absolutely valueless, because it only solves the oligopoly problem by removing from the analysis its most essential differentiating aspect: the oligopolists' consciousness of their interdependence.

Those who take into account this interdependence are free from this fundamental mistake. But in spite of this, their theories do not advance much towards a better explanation of reality, because in their desire to reach determinate solutions within the traditional framework of price theory they adopt additional assumptions which are too artificial.[9] In particular, these theories are all based on the assumption that the oligopolists—while recognising that their price activities will call forth reactions from their rivals—acquiesce in the permanent nature of the industry's structure. But since it is doubtless one of the distinguishing characteristics of duopoly and oligopoly that the rival firms can *actively* influence and change the market situation, these theories, too, fail to provide a theoretical framework for the interpretation of reality.[10]

In a certain way, therefore, the writers who stressed the indeterminateness of the problem made an important step in the right direction. For they recognised that the reduction of producers to a small number meant that the market situation was no longer the "natural" price determining force of perfect competition theory nor the strictly limiting price environment of monopolistic competition. They realised that under such condi-

---

[9] "The unreal atmosphere which surrounds our current theories of oligopoly may be ascribed to the fact that the assumptions are too often chosen for their analytical convenience, rather than for their actual relevance to the real world of to-day" (R. Triffin, *op. cit.*, p. 78).

[10] Thus R. F. Kahn, who amongst this group of writers makes perhaps the most serious attempt to get away from the unrealistic flavour of earlier theories, has still to depend for his solution on a qualifying statement of this sort: "I imagine my firms to be searching, by means of experiment or of trial and error, for the most profitable price and output—but not for more than that, not for the most profitable line of reaction to a change in a competitor's behaviour" ("The Problem of Duopoly," *The Economic Journal*, March 1937, p. 14). In this way the important problem of major changes in price and output policy directed towards a fundamental change in the market situation simply drops out of the picture.

tions the firms become active agents which have the power to change those very market factors on which the determinate theories had to rely for their solution.

But while thus the increasing acceptance of the indeterminateness of the problem was an advance towards a more realistic treatment of the subject, it was also a retreat from the former belief that price theory could be sufficiently developed to deal with all possible market phenomena. Indeed, the majority of these writers, once they have shown the inadequacy of the determinate solutions, take up an almost nihilistic attitude towards the theory of duopoly and oligopoly. They may, like Chamberlin, just add a short list of "uncertainties" to an artificial, determinate solution;[11] or they may deny the possibility of a general theory covering industry under oligopolistic conditions and substitute for it voluminous case-studies describing the behaviour pattern of particular industries;[12] or oligopolistic industry is just viewed as a chaotic mess where practically anything may happen, and about which economic analysis has very little to say.[13]

But, surely, the recognition of indeterminateness should have been only the first step towards building up a more adequate price theory for duopoly and oligopoly conditions. For the statement that there is no determinate solution to the problem can only be a relative one. It can only mean that the question cannot be suitably solved *within the framework of existing price theory,* just as the question of the monopolistic competition price could not have been suitably solved with the industrial demand and supply curves of perfect competition theory. But there can be no absolute and inherent indeterminateness in this problem, any more than in any other of the questions facing natural or social science. It has been said quite rightly:

---

[11] *The Theory of Monopolistic Competition,* 5th ed., pp. 52–53.

[12] See, for instance, Walton Hamilton, *op. cit.,* p. 22: "There exists to-day a competition of big business as well as a competition of petty trade; but the ways by which the battles for custom go on are quite different. . . . As industry becomes the concern of human beings and of public policy, the way of its control descends from the absolute and the imponderable *to the concrete and specific.*" (Italics mine.)

[13] This view is most forcefully represented by H. von Stackelberg's *Marktform und Gleichgewicht.*

No doubt, there is a sense in which the solution is always determinate; it all depends on the number of variables that are considered. But it is clear that the variables that would have to be added to determine the solution might be of a very different type from the ones generally used by pure economics of the equilibrium brand. Such considerations as financial backing, political influence, prestige psychology, optimistsic or pessimistic slant, enterprise or routine-like attitude in business, etc. may well play an overwhelming role in determining the solution.[14]

Economists have on the whole shied away from this problem of drawing up a wider and different framework which could deal with the oligopolistic cases, because the concepts and methods used for the other market situations would be of little use. In particular, the influence of analogies drawn from mechanics and biology—so fruitful in the fields of perfect and monopolistic competition respectively—must be discarded when we deal with powerful active agents like duopolists and oligopolists. If analogies have to be used (and they may be of considerable heuristic value), then they will have to be drawn from those spheres where writers deal with moves and counter-moves, with struggles for power and position—in short, from books dealing with the general aspects of politics, and military strategy and tactics.

This is by no means a new discovery. Not only has a military terminology found increasing acceptance in price theory (e.g., economic warfare, price strategy, aggressive and non-aggressive price policies), but both theoretical and descriptive economists have

---

[14] R. Triffin, op. cit., p. 71. It is a pity that Mr. Triffin, after thus recognising the necessity for a different approach to the oligopoly problem, and after a very able criticism of the shortcomings of the leading oligopoly theories, does nothing to advance towards the formulation of a theory of price under such conditions. He restricts himself to a refined re-classification of market situations, making extensive use of cross-elasticities of demand which completely neglect those factors which are mentioned in the above quotation. The consequence is that in the Conclusion the reader is left uncertain whether, after all, economic theory, has anything to contribute to the problem of oligopoly. (". . . The way is now open for a different type of economics. Instead of drawing its substance from arbitrary assumptions, chosen for their simplicity and unduly extended to the whole field of economic activity, our theory may turn to more pedestrian, but more fruitful methods. It will recognise the richness and variety of all concrete cases, and tackle each problem with due respect for its individual aspects. More advantage will be taken of all relevant factual information, and less reliance will be placed on a mere resort to the pass-key of general theoretical assumptions"—p. 189.)

pointed out the appropriateness of comparing oligopolistic price behaviour with this field of human activity. Thus, Professor Pigou, in his *Economics of Welfare*, refers to the resemblance between the mutual bluff under oligopolistic conditions and a game of chess.[15] Speaking of the motives influencing the actions of big corporations, Berle and Means come to the conclusion that "it is probable that more could be learned regarding them by studying the motives of an Alexander the Great, seeking new worlds to conquer, than by considering the motives of a petty tradesman of the days of Adam Smith."[16] The matter is put still more definitely in a recent article by Nourse:

> While, of course, the conditioning environment imposes rigorous limitations on the price administrator's freedom of action in a capitalist society dedicated to "free enterprise," he devises and implements business plans in ways broadly similar to those of military command. A general must operate within the limitations of the terrain on which he fights and of the personnel and material at his disposal—to say nothing of meteorological conditions. But at the same time, much depends too on the strategy which he and the high command devise and the specific tactics by which he and his officers seek to carry it out. It seems appropriate, therefore, to discuss price policy in terms of business strategy and tactics.[17]

But while thus the need for a new methodological and conceptual framework for oligopolistic price theory is clearly recognised, no attempt is made to lay the foundation for such a theory. Nourse, in particular, after stating the necessity of a new approach in the clear way illustrated by the above quotation, largely spoils his case by urging more research into the thinking, prejudices, etc., of the entrepreneur in order to make possible a more proper analytical treatment of price policy.[18] But, surely, the peculiarities of price behaviour under oligopolistic conditions are not due to any peculiarities in the psychology of duopolists and oligopolists, but to the different economic environment in which they work. By all means let us have more research into the psychology of the business-man in all the various market situations, but the *distinguishing* feature of oligopolistic price theory cannot lie in addi-

---

[15] *Op. cit.*, 1st ed., p. 233.
[16] *The Modern Corporation and Private Property*, p. 350.
[17] *Op. cit.*, pp. 189–190.
[18] *Op. cit.*, p. 199.

tional psychological investigations, but in the provision of a framework which will show the actions of a "normal" business-man under the specific conditions of an oligopolistic environment.[19]

---

[19] A completely novel and highly ingenious general theoretical apparatus for such a solution of the oligopoly problem has been recently created by John von Neumann and Oskar Morgenstern in their book *Theories of Games and Economic Behaviour*. Unfortunately, at the time of writing this article I had no opportunity of obtaining a copy of this important book, and I had to rely on the very capable summaries given in the review articles by Leonid Hurwicz and Jacob Marschak in *The American Economic Review* (Vol. 35, 1945) and *The Journal of Political Economy* (Vol. 54, 1946), respectively (republished as No. 13 in the Cowles Commission Papers, New Series). Like this article, the book starts from the recognition of the inadequacy of the calculus and similar methods when dealing with the complex interdependence in oligopolistic situations. A completely new mathematical and conceptual apparatus is then constructed, which makes this interdependence, the possibility of coalitions and collusion, of bribery, etc., an integral part of the general theory. As the title indicates, the analogy from which inspiration is drawn is that of games. But it is recognised that the techniques developed in the book have also a bearing on optimum military and diplomatic strategies (which to me seem to have a closer resemblance to oligopolistic situations than chess, poker and similar games).

There is no doubt that Neumann's and Morgenstern's approach surpasses in generality, rigour and elegance of treatment by far anything that could be achieved on the lines suggested in the following section of this article. At the same time, this very generality and rigour set, at the present stage of development of their theory, very serious limitations to the application of their theory to the price problems of the oligopolistic world. Not only are certain assumptions introduced for the sake of obtaining a more determinate solution rather than for their relevance to the real world (e.g., the introduction of "mixed strategies," and the neglect of the influence which *variations* in profits may have on price policy), but it also seems that considerable difficulties present themselves when an attempt is made to deal with cases that involve more than three persons. And, above all, the theory is, at present, exclusively static. But in no market situation is the dynamic aspect, the timing of price and output decisions, so important for an understanding of "what's going on" as in the case of oligopoly.

It seems to me, therefore, that while the further development of the "pure" theory expounded in *The Theory of Games and Economic Behaviour* may some day yield a very powerful tool for treating oligopolistic price problems, its present stage justifies the simultaneous exploration of the more modest and pedestrian paths indicated in this article. Their greater concreteness and their allowance for dynamic factors may give them a greater usefulness than a more general, "pure" theory can at present provide.

The oligopoly-theorist's classical literature can neither be Newton and Darwin, nor can it be Freud; he will have to turn to Clausewitz's *Principles of War*. There he will not only find numerous striking parallels between military and (oligopolistic) business strategy, but also a method of a *general* approach which— while far less elegant than traditional price theory—promises a more realistic treatment of the oligopoly problem. To write a short manual on the *Principles of Oligopolistic War* would be a very important attempt towards a new approach to this aspect of price theory; and the large amount of descriptive material that has been forthcoming in recent years should provide a sufficient basis for a start.

Any such attempt would, of course, go beyond the limits of a single article. All that can be done in this context, therefore, is to outline some considerations to which this approach gives rise.

IV

The first point that requires reconsideration when dealing with duopoly and oligopoly situations is the motive force behind price decisions. Profit maximisation has up till now served as the wonderful master-key that opened all the doors leading to an understanding of the entrepreneur's behaviour. True, it was always realised that family pride, moral and ethical considerations, poor intelligence and similar factors may modify the results built on the maximum profits assumption; but it was rightly assumed that these "disturbing" phenomena are sufficiently exceptional to justify their exclusion from the main body of price theory.

But there is another motive which cannot be so lightly dismissed, and which is probably of a similar order of magnitude as the desire for maximum profits: the desire for *secure* profits.[20] This motive has, of course, not completely escaped the attention of economists. But they usually thought they could subordinate this aspect of entrepreneurial behaviour to that of profit maximisation by simply postulating that it is *long-term* profits he is trying to maximise.[21] Since, however, uncertainty is an essential

---

[20] See A. G. B. Fisher, *The Clash of Progress and Security*, p. 159 and *passim*.

[21] An even more careful formulation of profit maximisation is "maximisa-

feature in this changing world, it is clear that the vague knowledge a firm possesses of its demand and cost schedules cannot extend far into the future. Any theory, therefore, which tries to explain price behaviour in terms of marginal curves derived from *long-term* demand and cost curves really by-passes the problem of uncertainty, and thus the very factor which gives rise to that desire for security which the theory tries to explain.

In fact, the reasons for the neglect of the security motive are not difficult to find. They are again due to the preoccupation of price theory with the cases where numbers are large—be it a perfectly or monopolistically competitive market—or where a complete monopoly exists; because in these cases the problem of security does not arise. For the absolute monopolist security against competitors is part of the definition; and for the small competitor, for whom the security question is a very urgent one, the market conditions are such an overwhelming force that he alone cannot do anything to safeguard his position. All he can do is to try to make full use of every opportunity as it comes up. Maximisation of (short-term) profits is, therefore, a legitimate generalisation for an explanation of price behaviour in the large-number cases.

But once we enter the field of duopoly and oligopoly this assumption is no longer sufficient. For here we find neither the safety of the single monopolist nor the impotence *vis-à-vis* his environment of the small competitor. Here is both the desire for achieving a secure position as well as the power to act on this desire. How is it, then, that in spite of the growth of oligopolistic elements, economic theory has been able to neglect this additional motive from its basic assumptions and to rely exclusively on the maximisation principle? The reason for this lies in the fact that some of the most conspicuous actions motivated by the desire for maximum security are identical with actions aiming at maximum profits. Thus, above all, the outstanding trend towards monopolistic agreements can and does serve both ends, as has been clearly shown in the New Deal and other Government pol-

tion of the current value of the proprietorship interest in the firm" (*Cost Behaviour and Price Policy, A Study Prepared by the Committee on Price Determination for the Conference on Price Research,* National Bureau of Economic Research, 1943, p. 275).

icies which, while aiming at increasing the stability of certain industries, soon enabled these industries to increase their monopoly profits.

There are other examples where the desire for profit maximisation and security maximisation converge on one type of action —e.g., the pressure for tariffs, the desire for direct access to the political machine, etc. In all these cases the behaviour of firms could be (so it seemed) satisfactorily explained by the "monistic" profit maximisation approach. But there are other cases where the two motives lead to conflicting patterns of behaviour. Where profit maximisation demands prices fluctuating with every change in revenue and cost conditions, security maximisation may demand rigid prices; while profit maximisation should tend to create firms of optimum size, security considerations will favour the oversized firm; again, where we should expect reserve funds to be invested in response to expected returns, we may find their practically unconditional reinvestment in their own firm.

All these divergences from "expected" behaviour have, of course, been noticed, not only by descriptive, but also by theoretical economists. But the latter have usually tended to relegate such "exceptions" into footnotes with a passing remark on security and long-term considerations, or simply to dismiss them as irrational behaviour.[22] This *impasse* can only be overcome, and oligopolistic price theory can only be developed, if we recognise that under this market situation the security motive must be given the same pride of place as has been occupied by the profit maximisation principle for such a long time.

As soon as we acknowledge that a "struggle for position" is taking place side by side with the attempt to make the best of

---

[22] Thus, for instance, R. F. Harrod seems to regard the widespread adoption of the full cost principle, as revealed by Hitch's and Hall's investigation, as at least "to some extent irrational" ("Price and Cost in Entrepreneur's Policy," *Oxford Economic Papers,* May 1939, p. 3). But, as we shall see below, this principle loses its irrational flavour once we recognise the importance of the security motive. Of course, even if business behaviour were *really* irrational, this would not serve as an excuse for the neglect of such behaviour. Irrationality would then have to become one of the premises of oligopolistic price theory. But the writer believes that the existing evidence does not point towards such a necessity.

every position that is held at any special moment,[23] many price
phenomena which proved awkward in the past will readily fall
into an appropriate niche. It will also mean that we have to consider price as a dynamic phenomenon. To say this does not, of
course, mean that we must expect oligopolistic price to fluctuate
more than the competitive static equilibrium price. On the contrary, as we shall see presently, oligopoly more than any other
market situation makes for rigid prices. But what it does mean
is that even the most wildly fluctuating competitive price reaches
at every given moment a static equilibrium, determined by the
then existing supply and demand conditions; while oligopoly
prices have to be interpreted not only in terms of factors that
are co-existing with them, but also in relation to future changes
at which the price policy aims. Thus care has to be taken to see
such price policies in their proper setting, past, present and future
each given their proper weight.[24]

The background to oligopoly, then, is—as we said—a struggle.
But this is, of course, not a continuous struggle. On the contrary,
most oligopolists will try to keep such struggles, costly as they are,
at a minimum. Their normal desire will be to entrench themselves in as secure a position as possible which will enable them
"to hold what they hold," and—should an opportunity arise—to
launch an offensive into rival territory. Price policy will take a
pivotal place in this entrenchment policy. A price will have to be
quoted that will allow the oligopolist to hold his own both *vis-à-vis*
existing and potential rivals and *vis-à-vis* the consumers. This
means that in "normal" periods the price must not be so low that

---

[23] That is, within the limits set by the strategic plan, short-term profits will
be maximised at any given time according to the principles worked out by the
current theory of value. Atomistic competition (both perfect and monopolistic), becomes then a special case of the oligopoly theory—viz. where the individual firm has no powers of strategic planning, and where the action of the
firm is reduced to pure profit maximisation.

Since the principles of profit maximisation have been fully developed elsewhere, and will be known to the reader, this article restricts itself to a discussion of the strategic aspects of the oligopolist's behaviour.

[24] "There is usually some element in the prices ruling at any time which
can only be explained in the light of the history of the industry" (Hall and
Hitch, *op. cit.*, p. 33).

it provokes retaliations from the competitors, nor so high that it encourages new entrants,[25] and it must be within the range which will maintain the goodwill of the customers[26]—i.e., will maintain a protection against aggressive policies of the rivals.

Within these limits, and the minimum which he regards as essential for his continued stay in the industry, the oligopolist will try to quote that price which will promise him maximum profits. The freedom he has in the choice of his base price will depend on the relative strength of the factors mentioned above. In order to make his continued existence possible and worth-while, he will at least aim at a price which will cover his expected costs. Thus cost calculations become the basis from which oligopolistic price-fixing starts. To these costs will be added a profit which will be largely determined by the strength of the oligopolist's position.

If this position is weak and the obstacles for newcomers fairly small—i.e., if we have monopolistic competition with oligopolistic elements—then the percentage added to costs will be determined by "normal" or "conventional" profits, because the fear of encouraging new entry will be predominant. Thus the "full-cost principle" which so startled Hall and Hitch in their inquiry, because it seemed so opposed to the principle of profit maximisation,[27] is a perfectly logical outcome of the market situation with which they were primarily concerned—monopolistic competition with an admixture of oligopoly—once we give due weight to the security considerations. When, however, the position of the oligopolists or duopolists is more powerful and not easily invaded they will not keep to the full-cost principle, but will add varying and "abnormal" profit percentages to their costs[28] in proportion to their assumed strength, or they will fix prices without reference to costs altogether.[29]

---

[25] These are the dominant considerations in the conservative price policies of the oligopolists. See Hall and Hitch, *op. cit.*, p. 21.

[26] This will set a definite limit in the case of the so-called "conventional" or "charm" prices. See C. Clive Saxton, *The Economics of Price Determination*, p. 19.

[27] *Op. cit.*, pp. 18–19.

[28] Saxton, *op. cit.*, p. 125.

[29] See, for instance, the price strategy of the American tobacco industry's giants in A. R. Burns, *The Decline of Competition*, pp. 225–229.

Since, therefore, the quoted price is not the mechanic result of impersonal market forces nor the essential adjustment to a constantly changing environment, but the expression of a strategic policy, it is clear that there will be a tendency for its rigid maintenance. The propagandistic value of declaring a position as a stronghold will soon evaporate if this stronghold is constantly shifted. The existence of a stable price instead of a fluctuating one will deter rivals from starting panicky price-reduction campaigns, and it will not induce newcomers to enter a booming market; consumers, too, are often supposed to prefer fixed prices.[30] Thus, the desire for building up a strategic stronghold will—within certain limits—neutralise the profit maximising principle of changing price with every change in demand or costs.[31] Even a price change of one's rivals may be ignored as long as one's *relative* position in the industry is not affected.[32]

It follows: *Price rigidity is an essential aspect of "normal" oligopolistic price strategy.*

Since, however, this attempt towards a price rigidly fixed for a longish period takes place in a world where changes are constantly taking place, there is a danger that inflexibility may ultimately lead to the disaster which the price maintenance policy tried to avoid. If one holds too uncompromisingly to a fortification, however important it may seem, while circumstances change, not only that fortification, but many more strategic advantages may come down. In order, therefore, to reduce the rigidity, which the decision to stick to the fortress of the quoted price introduces, this price is surrounded by a variety of minor weapons which permit a more elastic policy without giving up the basic position. These additional weapons, such as changes in quality, credit and discount arrangements, salesmanship, etc.,[33] can be used to adjust the firm to some extent to changes in the "external circumstances" particularly in demand and costs. They also serve as tools for tactical manoeuvres in the enemy's territory, testing his strength

---

[30] Saxton, *op. cit.*, p. 139.

[31] See Hall and Hitch, p. 33; Burns, *op. cit.*, Chap. V; and the growing literature on price rigidity.

[32] *Cost Behaviour and Price Policy*, p. 278.

[33] See Nourse, *op. cit.*, pp. 193–194; and the chapter on "Non-price Competition" in Burns, *op. cit.*

without provoking a major conflict; or to provide a "defence in depth" against inroads from the rivals, if it is deemed possible to hold the basic position.

It follows: *Oligopolistic circumstances lead to a multitude of conditions surrounding the quoted price.*

As long as profit maximisation is regarded as the sole motive force, price can indeed be regarded as a unique expression of this desire. But the struggle for a safe position has many different aspects, which often conflict with each other, and the oligopolistic price can therefore often only be understood as a compromise between conflicting tendencies.

The struggle for position involves not only the sales and costing departments—which alone are considered in traditional price theory—but also the legal, technical (patent rights), advertising, labour (very often the oligopolist will also be an oligopsonist), and other departments. They all will desire certain price-output decisions which would help them to establish a situation which from their different points of view seems to promise greater security. Prices are therefore increasingly the outcome of the different pulls of the conflicting interests of various departments.[34] And just as in the age of "combined operations" the actions of the infantry cannot be properly understood if one does not take into account the complementary actions of naval and air forces, so in oligopolistic circumstances the picture of the "price-fixing entrepreneur" has to give place to that of the price-fixing board of the heads of several departments.

It follows: *Under oligopoly the price tends to be the outcome of a variety of conflicting tendencies within the firm, which have all to be taken into account if a full explanation is aimed at.*

It will have become apparent from the discussion up to this point that the idea of a struggle is a vital aspect of the oligopoly problem. Yet all the time we have talked of a tendency towards rigid prices and rigid relative positions as the characteristics of the "normal" oligopoly situation. But there is no contradiction between these two aspects. It is the continuous existence of a *potential* struggle for a "new order" which induces the oligopolistic firm to follow the peculiar "normal" price policy which we have out-

---

[34] See *Cost Behaviour and Price Policy*, p. 43.

lined in previous paragraphs.[35] The "normal" periods may then extend for very long stretches of time, and actual price wars—violent changes in price policy—may occur only at rare intervals. But because their possibility really dominates the situation, they must take an important place in the study of oligopoly price.

A "quiescent" price policy[36] may come to an end either through external circumstances—what we might call "changes in terrain"—or through internal stresses, i.e., attempts towards a redistribution of relative shares among the rival firms. "Changes in terrain" refers to alterations in costs, demand or other conditions (affecting all the oligopolistic firms) of such decisive importance that even after full use has been made of the price-surrounding weapons (discounts, retarded delivery, etc.) the habitual price policy becomes obviously untenable. Two cases become at once apparent: one, where the terrain becomes less favourable and "closes in" on the quoted price, and the other, where new territory opens up offering room for expansion. Each of these cases will lead to a different pattern of price policy.

Take first the case of a deterioration in circumstances, such as a considerable rise in cost or a sharp fall in demand. Soon it would become obvious for several firms that a significant upward or downward revision in the base price would be in the best interests of profit maximisation. At the same time, the fear that rivals will not follow suit (in case of an upward change), or will more than follow suit (in case of a downward change),[37] and that thus the readjustment may deteriorate into a price-war for changed relative positions, will tend to prevent the revision from taking place. Ultimately, however, the external stresses may prove too strong for such a stubborn hold-on policy. The outcome may then be an inter-rival price war, if some of them feel prepared for such a trial of strength. With this case we shall deal below. More frequently, however, the desire for a show-down is not very strong in hard times, and the withdrawal to new, more appropriate price

---

[35] As an American oil producer put it: "If you start real competition . . . you are up against a system of reprisals that rather deprive you of a desire to try the experiment more than once." (Quoted in F. A. Fetter, *The Masquerade of Monopoly*, p. 52.)

[36] This term is taken from Saxton, *op. cit.* See pp. 129 and 133.

[37] See Hall and Hitch, p. 22.

positions is likely to take place concurrently, co-ordinated by tacit or open agreement. Therefore the well-known growth of price-fixing agreements in depressions.

A widening of the terrain for all the oligopolists within an industry will occur when technical progress opens up revolutionary changes in cost through large-scale production methods and/or when by a significant change in price sales can be pushed forward to large numbers of previously untouched customers. This is a situation which is typical for new and expanding industries, producing semi-luxuries (e.g., motor-cars), after the first stage of technical and sales pioneering has been passed. Here the desire to proceed to new, lower price positions—induced by the profit maximisation principle—will not be held back by the fear of an internal war. For here it is not a question of invading the rival's territory, but of rushing into new, unoccupied territory before the others have taken possession of it. Thus the action demanded by the maxim of maximum profits is in this case reinforced by strategic considerations, and the price pattern for such new, expanding industries is in fact one of strong price competition, followed by a rigid price policy after the new territory has been divided up and further expansion would involve an attack on rival strongholds.[38]

Finally, a quiescent price policy may come to an end, and an aggressive policy take its place, because some of the oligopolists may attempt to improve their position at the expense of their rivals. The desire for this will always be present. For such a move would not only reduce insecurity—the danger of an attack from the others—but it would also increase future profit opportunities, even though immediate profits would be reduced. But the cost of such a struggle, the uncertainty of its outcome, and the harmful effects it may have on other aspects of the security drive (e.g., public opinion), will make the actual outbreak of hostilities the exception rather than the rule. Nevertheless, such struggles are bound to occur from time to time. They may develop automatically, wanted by nobody in particular, out of the unsettling influences of the external factors mentioned before; or they may be the outcome of a well-prepared strategic plan of an "aggressive" firm.

---

[38] See *Cost Behaviour and Price Policy*, p. 281.

In any case, whether a firm has aggressive designs or just wants to be prepared against an attack, the oligopolistic situation will force considerations on the firms which do not arise under either atomistic competition or pure monopoly. These considerations will not be predominantly concerned with price policy, but since they have an influence on the structure and costs of the firm, they, too, have to be brought in when oligopolistic price is examined.

Preparedness for a price war means above all to be able to continue in existence as long as possible in circumstances where price has no relation whatsoever to the realities of a situation, but is exclusively used as a weapon. To survive such a period demands a powerful position with plentiful resources. The actions taken to obtain such a position will again often conflict with those which we would expect if profit maximisation alone were taken into account. The first and foremost aim will be financial strength. Thus size will be desired for its own sake, independent of technical considerations. The indications in American studies that mergers have sometimes led to over-sized firms would be quite intelligible on these grounds. Indeed, once we add the security motive to the profit maximum motive, the "optimum size" of the firm—as seen from the entrepreneur—will usually be larger than that indicated by current-value theory. Again, the reinvestment of profits in the concern irrespective of the yields obtainable elsewhere, while being "irrational" from the maximum point of view, are easily explained as a security measure.

But size and reserves are not enough. Security must be carried forward and backward. Forward, by "immunising" consumers more and more against rival invasion through massive advertising. Oligopolists fail to adjust their arvertising expenditure nicely to the marginal equilibria expected by the text-books, not because they lack the necessary information (this is, of course, also important), but because their advertisement is just as much a preparation for the great battle as it is an attempt at higher immediate profits.

Security is carried backward by the attempt to reduce the pressure which may threaten one's position in dangerous times from raw material and finance supply sources. The bigger oligopolists will guard against this danger either by vertical integration or at least by interlocking directorates and shareholdings. The enormous growth of interlocking directorates in recent decades—

so conveniently overlooked by current theory—is indeed an essential outcome of the spreading of oligopolistic market situations. Here, again, it should be noted that our framework gives a logical explanation for developments which run counter to the principles of current theory, in this case the principle of growing specialisation.

In these and other ways[39] the fear of the coming price war or the wish to provoke one will *all the time* impress a behaviour pattern on oligopolistic firms which cannot be understood by interpreting it in terms of profit maximisation only. The actual price wars, as has been mentioned before, are not likely to occur very frequently. But when they occur, they can take on very violent forms, and price-cutting may be carried to extremes. The lower limit of short-term marginal prime costs of perfect competition fame will not be active, because here again we do not witness a maximisation of short-term profits, but a struggle for position— a fundamentally altered position in this case. The tactics and the duration of such a war will be decided predominantly by objective circumstances—i.e., the strength and position of the rivals— but also to a minor extent by subjective considerations, such as their expectations with regard to each other's actions and their resistance to wars of nerves.

The "ideal" aim of a price war is, of course, complete victory— the annihilation of the adversaries. Very often, however, this may prove impossible or too costly. In such cases the superior power may be satisfied with a position which will allow him in the future to decide his strategic policy without having to pay too much attention to the reactions amongst his rivals.[40] Needless to say that this pattern of price leadership will not only occur after a

---

[39] As one should expect in a warlike atmosphere, the desire to know what is happening in the hostile camp is often very strong. As one business-man put it in an answer to a questionnaire: "No agreement in this trade, but firms were all anxious to know what their rivals were doing" (Hall and Hitch, p. 43). This, too, may sometimes lead to interlocking directorates.

[40] "The typical situation in British industry seems to be one where oligopolistic elements are of most importance, although there may be a large number of smaller firms engaged within or upon the fringes of the industry, whose price-policy is entirely dependent upon that of the price-leader" (Saxton, *op. cit.*, p. 168). For American conditions, see Burns, *op. cit.*, Chap. III.

price war. The mere fear of such hostilities may bring about the same result.[41]

It follows: *Price wars, while tending to occur infrequently, are a dominant feature of the oligopolistic situation. They may be caused by external or internal factors. The preparation for them, aggressive or defensive, leads to the adoption of measures which are peculiar to oligopoly. The outcome of a successful price war or the mere threat of one may be the complete annihilation of a rival's independence or the reduction of his status to that of a price follower.*

But the quest for more secure and more advantageous positions does not confine itself to the traditional field of economic theory. The water-tight separation of the business-man's personality into that of an "economic man," a "political man" and probably several other men, is a legitimate simplification under atomistic competition and even for small oligopolists, where any isolated political action they may take cannot possibly have any appreciable effect on their market position. The market situation and the price of the commodity can, therefore, be quite well explained by concentrating attention on the purely economic activities of the firm.

But when we come to the big oligopolists, who *do* have the power to change the market situation by their own political action, then the separation of the economic from the political must necessarily result in a very incomplete picture, which will not suffice for giving us a reasonable explanation of oligopoly price. Indeed, what is, for instance, the logic of some of the recent American economic literature which tries to evaluate in great detail the effects on price and output of the huge selling expenditure of big corporations, and yet never even mentions the sums spent for exactly the same aims in the lobbies?[42] For the gap that divides

---

[41] "A 'follow-the-leader policy' takes the place of the older, cruder, cut-throat competition and works just as effectively. . . . This docility of all the so-called independents in following the leader may be seen, on more careful scrutiny, to be the result of competitors' fear of cut-throat competition, more artfully and sparingly exercised than in the old days. . . ." (Frank A. Fetter, *The Masquerade of Monopoly*, p. 51).

[42] See Anna Rochester, *Rulers of America*, Chap. VIII, and the literature quoted there.

selling expenditure from political activities is methodologically much smaller than the one that divides the former from production costs proper.[43]

The fact is that when we enter the field of rivalry between oligopolistic giants, the traditional separation of the political from the economic can no longer be maintained. Once we have recognised that the desire for a strong position ranks equally with the desire for immediate maximum profits we must follow this new dual approach to its logical end, if we want to construct a relevant theory. Only by acknowledging the importance of the political factor can we account for such trends as the increasing appointments of people who have "good connections with the government," of first-rate experts as political advisers to great concerns, etc., trends, which on a purely economic interpretation can only be regarded as "irrational" and inexcusable waste. Explicit recognition of the political aspects of the oligopolistic struggle will also help applied economists to make their advice more significant and more immediately useful. It will help them to recognise the absurdity of the conclusions of a theorist like Stackelberg, who, as an apologist of the Fascist corporate State, regards this political form as the only means of bringing order into the chaos of oligopolistic indeterminateness.[44] For they would realise at once that Fascism, far from being an independent arbiter in the oligopolistic struggle, has been largely brought into power by this very struggle in an attempt of the most powerful oligopolists to strengthen, through political action, their position in the labour market and vis-à-vis their smaller competitors, and finally to strike out in order to change the world market situation in their favour.[45]

And this brings us, finally, to the most violent aspect of the oligopolistic struggle: the attempts of the biggest oligopolistic groupings to regroup their forces on a world scale. It is now more

---

[43] I wonder how some of the "pure" economic theorists would deal with the advertisements now appearing in the press against the nationalisation of certain industries. Are they to be included in selling costs—for advertisements they obviously are—or are they to be neglected because they represent political action?

[44] See his *Marktform und Gleichgewicht*.

[45] The autobiography of the big German industrialist Fritz Thyssen will be found very revealing on this point.

than thirty years since Hobson and Lenin drew attention to the necessary growth of imperialism with the increase in the friction between huge oligopolies (or "rival monopolies" as they called it). Yet in spite of the large amount of factual material that has been accumulating giving empirical support to this view,[46] nine out of ten writers on the oligopolistic market situation manage to avoid any reference whatsoever to imperialism. The consequence is not only that a full explanation of oligopoly prices—generally or in particular cases—becomes impossible, but also that students of modern monopoly theory tend to become enormously worried about the excess capacity of the small oligopolistic shop, while they do not even realise the danger of a clash between the big world oligopolies.

We have, therefore, to conclude that a theory of oligopoly can be complete and relevant only if its framework includes *all* the main aspects of the struggle for security and position. Like price wars, open imperialist conflicts will not be the daily routine of the oligopolistic market. But, like price wars, their possibility and the preparation for them will be a constantly existing background against which current actions have to be understood. And the imperialistic aspects of modern wars or armed interventions must be seen as part of a dynamic oligopoly theory just as much as the more traditional "economic" activities like cut-throat pricing, full-line forcing, boycotting, etc. For there is no fundamental difference between the two.

It follows: *The oligopolistic struggle for position and security includes political action of all sorts right up to imperialism. The inclusion of these "non-economic" elements is essential for a full explanation of oligopoly behaviour and price.*

V

In an interesting article, written on the occasion of the cente-

---

[46] There is a lot of useful information in the reports of United States Senate Commissions and of the Temporary National Economic Committee. (See for instance, the Report of the Nye Committee on the Munitions Industry, or the T.N.E.C. Monograph No. 26 on *Economic Power and Political Pressure.*) This, and a large amount of other relevant material, has been admirably presented by Robert A. Brady in his *Business as a System of Power* (Columbia University Press, 1943).

nary of Marshall's birth,[47] Mr. Shove pointed out how modern conditions have largely destroyed the applicability of Marshall's price analysis to the world of to-day.

It is the territory between atomic competition and absolute monopoly that the pure theory of the book (the *Principles*) does not cover at all satisfactorily. And it is precisely this territory which has been so greatly enlarged by the development of the joint-stock company and the advantages (or necessity) of large-scale control. The conflicts of interest within the firm; the interpenetration of interests between firms through interlocking directorates, shareholdings, subsidiary concerns and the like; the domination of an industry by a few large units; the intermixture of public and private control as seen in the various types of semi-public corporation and of regulating boards and devices; these are the features of modern industrial structure which find little or no place in the analytical framework of the *Principles*.[48]

The newer developments in price theory have on the whole kept to this Marshallian tradition. Though they have introduced a large number of theoretical refinements it is nevertheless true that "the general theory of value and distribution as a whole has scarcely advanced at all into that part of the field at which the *Principles* stopped short. It is still concerned almost exclusively with the case of pure monopoly on the one side and on the other with atomic competition, 'perfect' or 'imperfect.' "[49]

That the gap has not been filled is partly due to the force of tradition; partly, as Shove points out, to the increasing separation of analytical and descriptive work and the itch for precise results. But the undiscovered territory must be entered by economic theory if it is not to lose all touch with reality. The tentative first step outlined in the previous section certainly looks very crude and pedestrian when compared with the polished elegance of modern value theory. But it is tentative steps of this sort which economic analysis must undertake to-day. For "it is better to be vaguely right than precisely wrong."[50]

---

[47] "The Place of Marshall's *Principles* in the Development of Economic Theory," *The Economic Journal*, December 1942. It was that essay which provided the first stimulus for the present article.

[48] *Ibid.*, p. 320.

[49] *Ibid.*, p. 322.

[50] Professor Wildon Carr, quoted by G. F. Shove, *op. cit.*, p. 323.

VI. SPATIAL COMPETITION

23

STABILITY IN COMPETITION [*][1]

By Harold Hotelling ||

After the work of the late Professor F. Y. Edgeworth one may doubt that anything further can be said on the theory of competition among a small number of entrepreneurs. However, one important feature of actual business seems until recently to have escaped scrutiny. This is the fact that of all the purchasers of a commodity, some buy from one seller, some from another, in spite of moderate differences of price. If the purveyor of an article gradually increases his price while his rivals keep theirs fixed, the diminution in volume of his sales will in general take place continuously rather than in the abrupt way which has tacitly been assumed.

A profound difference in the nature of the stability of a competitive situation results from this fact. We shall examine it with the help of some simple mathematics. The form of the solution will serve also to bring out a number of aspects of a competitive situation whose importance warrants more attention than they have received. Among these features, all illustrated by the same simple case, we find (1) the existence of incomes not properly belonging to any of the categories usually discussed, but resulting from the discontinuity in the increase in the number of sellers with the demand; (2) a socially uneconomical system of prices, leading to needless shipment of goods and kindred deviations from optimum activities; (3) an undue tendency for competitors to imitate each other in quality of goods, in location, and in other essential ways.

---

[*] *The Economic Journal*, Vol. XXXIX (1929), pp. 41–57. Reprinted, by the courtesy of the publisher and the author, without change from the original text.

|| The University of North Carolina.

[1] Presented before the American Mathematical Society at New York, April 6, 1928, and subsequently revised.

Piero Sraffa has discussed[2] the neglected fact that a market is commonly subdivided into regions within each of which one seller is in a quasi-monopolistic position. The consequences of this phenomenon are here considered further. In passing we remark that the asymmetry between supply and demand, between buyer and seller, which Professor Sraffa emphasises is due to the condition that the seller sets the price and the buyers the quantities they will buy. This condition in turn results from the large number of the buyers of a particular commodity as compared with the sellers. Where, as in new oil-fields and in agricultural villages, a few buyers set prices at which they will take all that is offered and exert themselves to induce producers to sell, the situation is reversed. If in the following pages the words "buy" and "sell" be everywhere interchanged, the argument remains equally valid, though applicable to a different class of businesses.

Extensive and difficult applications of the Calculus of Variations in economics have recently been made, sometimes to problems of competition among a small number of entrepreneurs.[3] For this and other reasons a re-examination of stability and related questions, using only elementary mathematics, seems timely.

Duopoly, the condition in which there are two competing merchants, was treated by A. Cournot in 1838.[4] His book went apparently without comment or review for forty-five years until Walras produced his *Théorie Mathématique de la Richesse Sociale,* and Bertrand published a caustic review of both works.[5] Bertrand's criticisms were modified and extended by Edgeworth in his treatment of duopoly in the *Giornale degli Economisti* for

---

[2] "The Laws of Returns Under Competitive Conditions," *The Economic Journal,* Vol. XXXVI, pp. 535–550, especially pp. 544 ff. (December 1926).

[3] For references to the work of C. F. Roos and G. C. Evans on this subject see the paper by Dr. Roos, "A Dynamical Theory of Economics," in *The Journal of Political Economy,* Vol. XXXV (1927), or that in the *Transactions of the American Mathematical Society,* Vol. XXX (1928), p. 360. There is also an application of the Calculus of Variations to depreciation by Dr. Roos in the *Bulletin of the American Mathematical Society,* Vol. XXXIV (1928), p. 218.

[4] *Recherches sur les Principes Mathématiques de la Théorie des Richesses,* Paris (Hachette), Chap. VII. English translation by N. T. Bacon, with introduction and bibliography by Irving Fisher (New York, Macmillan, 1897 and 1927).

[5] *Journal des Savants* (1883), pp. 499–508.

1897,[6] in his criticism of Amoroso,[7] and elsewhere. Indeed all writers since Cournot, except Sraffa and Amoroso,[8] seem to hold that even apart from the likelihood of combination there is an essential instability in duopoly. Now it is true that such competition lacks complete stability; but we shall see that in a very general class of cases the independent actions of two competitors not in collusion lead to a type of equilibrium much less fragile than in the examples of Cournot, Edgeworth and Amoroso. The solution which we shall obtain can break down only in case of an express or tacit understanding which converts the supposed competitors into something like a monopoly, or in case of a price war aimed at eliminating one of them altogether.

Cournot's example was of two proprietors of mineral springs equally available to the market and producing, without cost, mineral water of identical quality. The demand is elastic, and the price is determined by the total amount put on the market. If the respective quantities produced are q_1 and q_2 the price p will be given by a function

$$p = f(q_1 + q_2).$$

The profits of the proprietors are respectively

$$\pi_1 = q_1 f(q_1 + q_2)$$

and

$$\pi_2 = q_2 f(q_1 + q_2).$$

The first proprietor adjusts q_1 so that, when q_2 has its current value, his own profit will be as great as possible. This value of q_1 may be obtained by differentiating π_1, putting

$$f(q_1 + q_2) + q_1 f(q_1 + q_2) = 0.$$

In like manner the second proprietor adjusts q_2 so that

$$f(q_1 + q_2) + q_2 f(q_1 + q_2) = 0.$$

There can be no equilibrium unless these equations are satisfied simultaneously. Together they determine a definite (and equal) pair of values of q_1 and q_2. Cournot showed graphically how, if a different pair of q's should obtain, each competitor in turn

---

[6] Republished in English in Edgeworth's *Papers Relating to Political Economy* (London, Macmillan, 1925), Vol. I, pp. 116–126.

[7] *The Economic Journal*, Vol. XXXII (1922), pp. 400–407.

[8] *Lezioni di Economia Mathematica* (Bologna, Zanichelli, 1921).

would readjust his production so as to approach as a limit the value given by the solution of the simultaneous equations. He concluded that the actual state of affairs will be given by the common solution, and proceeded to generalise to the case of n competitors.

Against this conclusion Bertrand brought an "objection péremptoire." The solution does not represent equilibrium, for either proprietor can by a slight reduction in price take away all his opponent's business and nearly double his own profits. The other will respond with a still lower price. Only by the use of the quantities as independent variables instead of the prices is the fallacy concealed.

Bertrand's objection was amplified by Edgeworth, who maintained that in the more general case of two monopolists controlling commodities having correlated demand, even though not identical, there is no determinate solution. Edgeworth gave a variety of examples, but nowhere took account of the stabilising effect of masses of consumers placed so as to have a natural preference for one seller or the other. In all his illustrations of competition one merchant can take away his rival's entire business by undercutting his price ever so slightly. Thus discontinuities appear, though a discontinuity, like a vacuum, is abhorred by nature. More typical of real situations is the case in which the quantity sold by each merchant is a continuous function of two variables, his own price and his competitor's. Quite commonly a tiny increase in price by one seller will send only a few customers to the other.

I

The feature of actual business to which, like Professor Sraffa, we draw attention, and which does not seem to have been generally taken account of in economic theory, is the existence with reference to each seller of groups of buyers who will deal with him instead of with his competitors in spite of a difference in price. If a seller increases his price too far he will gradually lose business to his rivals, but he does not lose all his trade instantly when he raises his price only a trifle. Many customers will still prefer to trade with him because they live nearer to his store than to the others, or because they have less freight to pay from his warehouse to their own, or because his mode of doing business is more to their liking, or because he sells other articles which they desire, or because he is a relative or a fellow Elk or Baptist, or on account of some difference in service or quality, or for a combination of reasons. Such circles of customers may be said to make every entrepreneur a monopolist within a limited class and region—and there is no monopoly which is not confined to a limited class and region. The difference between the Standard Oil Company in its prime and the little corner grocery is quantitative rather than qualitative. Between the perfect competition and monopoly of theory lie the actual cases.

It is the gradualness in the shifting of customers from one merchant to another as their prices vary independently which is ignored in the examples worked out by Cournot, Amoroso and Edgeworth. The assumption, implicit in their work, that all buyers deal with the cheapest seller leads to a type of instability which disappears when the quantity sold by each is considered as a continuous function of the differences in price. The use of such a continuous function does, to be sure, seem to violate the doctrine that in one market there can at one time be only one price. But this doctrine is only valid when the commodity in question is absolutely standardised in all respects and when the "market" is a point, without length, breadth or thickness. It is, in fact, analogous to the physical principle that at one point in a body there can at one time be only one temperature. This principle does not prevent different temperatures from existing in different parts of a body at the same time. If it were supposed that any temperature difference, however slight, necessitates a sudden transfer of all the heat in the warmer portion of the body to the colder portion—a transfer which by the same principle would immediately be reversed—then we should have a thermal instability somewhat resembling the instability of the cases of duopoly which have been discussed. To take another physical analogy, the earth is often in astronomical calculations considered as a point, and with substantially accurate results. But the precession of the equinoxes becomes explicable only when account is taken of the ellipsoidal bulge of the earth. So in the theory of value a market is usually considered as a point in which only one price can obtain; but for some purposes it is better to consider a market as an extended region.

Consider the following illustration. The buyers of a commodity will be supposed uniformly distributed along a line of length l, which may be Main Street in a town or a transcontinental railroad. At distances a and b respectively from the two ends of this line are the places of business of A and B (Fig. 1). Each buyer transports his purchases home at a cost c per unit distance. Without effect upon the generality of our conclusions we shall suppose that the cost of production to A and B is zero, and that unit quantity of the commodity is consumed in each unit of time in each unit of length of line. The demand is thus at the extreme of inelasticity. No customer has any preference for either seller except on the ground of price plus transportation cost. In general there will be many causes leading particular classes of buyers to prefer one seller to another, but the ensemble of such considera-

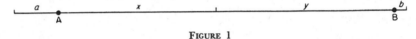

FIGURE 1

Market of length $l = 35$. In this example $a = 4$, $b = 1$, $x = 14$, $y = 16$.

tion is here symbolised by transportation cost. Denote A's price by p_1, B's by p_2, and let q_1 and q_2 be the respective quantities sold.

Now B's price may be higher than A's, but if B is to sell anything at all he must not let his price exceed A's by more than the cost of transportation from A's place of business to his own. In fact he will keep his price p_2 somewhat below the figure $p_1 - c(l - a - b)$ at which A's goods can be brought to him. Thus he will obtain all the business in the segment of length b at the right of Fig. 1, and in addition will sell to all the customers in a segment of length y depending on the difference of prices and lying between himself and A. Likewise A will, if he sells anything, sell to all the buyers in the strips of length a at the left and of length x to the right of A, where x diminishes as $p_1 - p_2$ increases.

The point of division between the regions served by the two entrepreneurs is determined by the condition that at this place it is a matter of indifference whether one buys from A or from B. Equating the delivered prices we have

$$p_1 + cx = p_2 + cy.$$

Another equation between x and y is

$$a + x + y + b = l.$$

Solving we find

$$x = \tfrac{1}{2}\left(1 - a - b + \frac{p_2 - p_1}{c}\right),$$

$$y = \tfrac{1}{2}\left(1 - a - b + \frac{p_1 - p_2}{c}\right),$$

so that the profits are

$$\pi_1 = p_1 q_1 = p_1(a + x) = \tfrac{1}{2}(1 + a - b)p_1 - \frac{p_1^2}{2c} + \frac{p_1 p_2}{2c},$$

and $$\pi_2 = p_2 q_2 = p_2(b + y) = \tfrac{1}{2}(1 - a + b)p_2 - \frac{p_2^2}{2c} + \frac{p_1 p_2}{2c}.$$

If p_1 and p_2 be taken as rectangular co-ordinates, each of the last equations represents a family of hyperbolas having identical asymptotes, one hyperbola for each value of π_1 or π_2. Some of these curves are shown in Fig. 2, where (as also in Fig. 1) we have taken $l = 35$, $a = 4$, $b = 1$, $c = 1$.

Each competitor adjusts his price so that, with the existing value of the other price, his own profit will be a maximum. This gives the equations

$$\frac{\partial \pi_1}{\partial p_1} = \tfrac{1}{2}(1 + a - b) - \frac{p_1}{c} + \frac{p_2}{2c} = 0,$$

$$\frac{\partial \pi_2}{\partial p_2} = \tfrac{1}{2}(1 - a + b) + \frac{p_1}{2c} - \frac{p_2}{c} = 0,$$

from which we obtain

$$p_1 = c\left(1 + \frac{a - b}{3}\right),$$

$$p_2 = c\left(1 - \frac{a - b}{3}\right);$$

and $$q_1 = a + x = \tfrac{1}{2}\left(1 + \frac{a - b}{3}\right),$$

$$q_2 = b + y = \tfrac{1}{2}\left(1 - \frac{a - b}{3}\right).$$

The conditions $\partial^2 \pi_1 / \partial p_1^2 < 0$ and $\partial^2 \pi_2 / \partial p_2^2 < 0$, sufficient for a maximum of each of the functions π_1 and π_2, are obviously satisfied.

If the two prices are originally the co-ordinates of the point Q in Fig. 2, and if A is the more alert business man of the two, he will change his price so as to make his profit a maximum. This is represented graphically by a horizontal motion to the point R on the line $\partial\pi_1/\partial p_1 = 0$. This line has the property that every point on it represents a greater profit for A than any other point having the same ordinate. But presently B discovers that his profits can be increased by a vertical motion to the point S on his own line of maximum profit. A now moves horizontally to T. Thus there is a gradual approach to the point E at the intersection of the two lines; its co-ordinates are given by the values of p_1 and p_2 found above. At E there is equilibrium, since neither merchant can now increase his profit by changing his price. The same result is reached if instead of Q the starting point is any on the figure.[9]

Now it is true that prices other than the co-ordinates of the equilibrium point may obtain for a considerable time. Even at this point one merchant may sacrifice his immediate income to raise his price, driving away customers, in the hope that his rival will do likewise and thus increase both profits. Indeed if A moves to the right from E in Fig. 2 he may reasonably expect that B will go up to his line of maximum profit. This will make A's profit larger than at E, provided the representing point has not gone so far to the right as K. Without this proviso, A's position will be improved (and so will B's as compared with E) if only B will sufficiently increase p_2. In fact, since the demand is inelastic, we may imagine the two alleged competitors to be ami-

---

[9] The solution given above is subject to the limitation that the difference between the prices must not exceed the cost of transportation from A to B. This means that E must lie between the lines $p_1 - p_2 = \pm c(l - a - b)$ on which the hyperbolic arcs shown in Fig. 2 terminate. It is easy to find values of the constants for which this condition is not satisfied (for example, $l = 20$, $a = 11$, $b = 8$, $c = 1$). In such a case the equilibrium point will not be E and the expressions for the p's, q's and π's will be different; but there is no essential difference either in the stability of the system or in the essential validity of the subsequent remarks. A's locus of maximum profit no longer coincides with the line $\partial\pi_1/\partial p_1 = 0$, but consists of the portion of this line above its intersection with $p_1 - p_2 = c(l - a - b)$, and of the latter line below this point. Likewise B's locus of maximum profit consists of the part of the line $\partial\pi_2/\partial p_2 = 0$ to the right of its intersection with $p_2 - p_1 = c(l - a - b)$, together with the part of the last line to the left of this point. These two loci intersect at the point whose co-ordinates are, for $a > b$,
$$p_1 = c(3l - 3a - b), \quad p_2 = 2c(l - a),$$
and the type of stability is the same as before.

cably exploiting the consumers without limit by raising their prices. The increases need not be agreed upon in advance but may proceed by alternate steps, each seller in turn making his price higher than the other's, but not high enough to drive away all business. Thus without a formal agreement the rivals may succeed in making themselves virtually a monopoly. Something of a tacit understanding will exist that prices are to be maintained above the level immediately profitable in order to keep profits high in the long run.

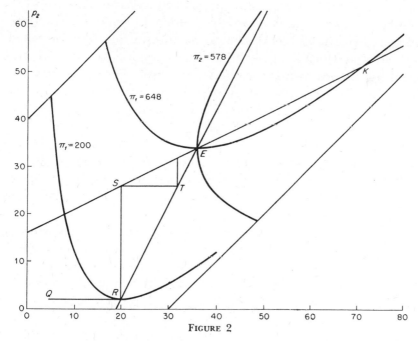

FIGURE 2

Conditions of competition for the market of Fig. 1. The co-ordinates represent the prices at A's and B's shops for the same article. The straight lines through E are the two lines of maximum profit. On one of the curves through E, A's profit is everywhere 648; on the other, B's is 578. The lower curve is the locus on which A's profit is 200.

But understandings between competitors are notoriously fragile. Let one of these business men, say B, find himself suddenly in need of cash. Immediately at hand he will have a resource: Let him lower his price a little, increasing his sales. His profits will be larger until A decides to stop sacrificing business and lowers his price to the point of maximum profit. B will now be likely to go further in an attempt to recoup, and so the system will descend to the equilibrium position E. Here neither competitor will have any incentive to lower his price further, since the increased business obtainable would fail to compensate him.

Indeed the difficulties of maintaining a price-fixing agreement have often been remarked. Not only may the short-sighted cupidity of one party send the whole system crashing through price-cutting; the very fear of a price cut will bring on a cut. Moreover, a price agreement cannot be made once for all; where conditions of cost or of demand are changing the price needs constant revision. The result is a constant jarring, an always obvious conflict of interests. As a child's pile of blocks falls to its equilibrium position when the table on which it stands is moved, so a movement of economic conditions tends to upset quasi-monopolistic schemes for staying above the point E. For two independent merchants to come to an agreement of any sort is notoriously difficult, but when the agreement must be made all over again at frequent intervals, when each has an incentive for breaking it, and when it is frowned upon by public opinion and must be secret and perhaps illegal, then the pact is not likely to be very durable. The difficulties are, of course, more marked if the competitors are more numerous, but they decidedly are present when there are only two.

The details of the interaction of the prices and sales will, of course, vary widely in different cases. Much will depend upon such market conditions as the degree of secrecy which can be maintained, the degree of possible discrimination among customers, the force of habit and character as affecting the reliance which each competitor feels he can put in the promises of the other, the frequency with which it is feasible to change a price or a rate of production, the relative value to the entrepreneur of immediate and remote profits, and so on. But always there is an insecurity at any point other than the point E which represents equilibrium. Without some agreement, express or tacit, the value of p_1 will be less than or equal to the abscissa of K in Fig. 2; and in the absence of a willingness on the part of one of the competitors to forgo immediate profits in order to maintain prices, the prices will become the co-ordinates of E.

One important item should be noticed. The prices may be maintained in a somewhat insecure way *above* their equilibrium values but will never remain *below* them. For if either A or B has a price which is less than that satisfying the simultaneous equations it will pay him *at once* to raise it. This is evident from the figure. Strikingly in contrast with the situation pictured by Bertrand, where prices were for ever being cut below their calculated values, the stabilising effect of the intermediate customers who shift their purchases gradually with changing prices makes itself felt in the existence of a pair of minimum prices. For a prudent investor the difference is all-important.

It is, of course, possible that A, feeling stronger than his opponent and desiring to get rid of him once for all, may reduce his price so far that B will give up the struggle and retire from the business. But during the continuance of this sort of price war A's income will be curtailed more than B's. In any case its possibility does not affect the argument that there is stability, since stability is by definition merely the tendency to return after *small* displacements. A box standing on end is in stable equilibrium, even though it can be tipped over.

II

Having found a solution and acquired some confidence in it, we push the analysis further and draw a number of inferences regarding a competitive situation.

When the values of the p's and q's obtained on page 473 are substituted in the previously found expressions for the profits we have

$$\pi_1 = \frac{c}{2}\left(1 + \frac{a - b}{3}\right)^2, \quad \pi_2 = \frac{c}{2}\left(1 - \frac{a - b}{3}\right)^2.$$

The profits as well as the prices depend directly upon c, the unit cost of transportation. These particular merchants would do well, instead of organising improvement clubs and booster associations to better the roads, to make transportation as difficult as possible. Still better would be their situation if they could obtain a protective tariff to hinder the transportation of their commodity between them. Of course they will not want to impede the transportation of the supplies which come to them; the object of each is merely to attain something approaching a monopoly.

Another observation on the situation is that incomes exist

which do not fall strictly within any of the commonly recognised categories. The quantities π_1 and π_2 just determined may be classified as monopoly profits, but only if we are ready to extend the term "monopoly" to include such cases as have been considered, involving the most outright competition for the marginal customer but without discrimination in his favour, and with no sort of open or tacit agreement between the sellers. These profits certainly do not consist of wages, interest or rent, since we have assumed no cost of production. This condition of no cost is not essential to the existence of such profits. If a constant cost of production per unit had been introduced into the calculations above, it would simply have been added to the prices without affecting the profits. Fixed overhead charges are to be subtracted from π_1 and π_2, but may leave a substantial residuum. These gains are not compensation for risk, since they represent a minimum return. They do not belong to the generalised type of "rent," which consists of the advantage of a producer over the marginal producer, since each makes a profit, and since, moreover, we may suppose a and b equal so as to make the situation symmetrical. Indeed π_1 and π_2 represent a special though common sort of profit which results from the fact that the number of sellers is finite. If there are three or more sellers, income of this kind will still exist, but as the number increases it will decline, to be replaced by generalised "rent" for the better-placed producers and poverty for the less fortunate. The number of sellers may be thought of as increasing as a result of a gradual increase in the number of buyers. Profits of the type we have described will exist at all stages of growth excepting those at which a new seller is just entering the field.

As a further problem, suppose that A's location has been fixed but that B is free to choose his place of business. Where will he set up shop? Evidently he will choose b so as to make

$$\pi_2 = \frac{c}{2}\left(1 + \frac{b - a}{3}\right)^2$$

as large as possible. This value of b cannot be found by differentiation, as the value thus determined exceeds 1 and, besides, yields a minimum for π_2 instead of a maximum. But for all smaller values of b, and so for all values of b within the conditions of the problem, π_2 increases with b. Consequently B will seek to make b as large as possible. This means that he will come just as close to A as other conditions permit. Naturally, if A is not exactly in the centre of the line, B will choose the side of A towards the more extensive section of the market, making b greater than a.[10]

This gravitation of B towards A increases B's profit at the expense of A. Indeed, as appears from the expressions on page 473, if b increases so that B approaches A, both q_2 and p_2 increase while q_1 and p_1 diminish. From B's standpoint the sharper competition with A due to proximity is offset by the greater body of buyers with whom he has an advantage. But the danger that the system will be overturned by the elimination of one competitor is increased. The intermediate segment of the market acts as a cushion as well as a bone of contention; when it disappears we have Cournot's case, and Bertrand's objection applies. Or, returning to the analogy of the box in stable equilibrium though standing on end, the approach of B to A corresponds to a diminution in size of the end of the box.

It has become common for real-estate subdividers in the United States to impose restrictions which tend more or less to fix the character of future businesses in particular locations. Now we find from the calculations above that the total profits of A and B amount to

$$\pi_1 + \pi_2 = c\left[l^2 + \left(\frac{a - b}{3}\right)^2 \right].$$

---

[10] The conclusion that B will tend to gravitate *infinitesimally* close to A requires a slight modification in the particular case before us, but not in general. In the footnote on p. 474 it was seen that when A and B are sufficiently close together, the analytic expressions for the prices, and consequently the profits, are different. By a simple algebraic calculation which will not here be reproduced it is found that B's profits π_2 will increase as B moves from the centre towards A, only if the distance between them is more than four-fifths of the distance from A to the centre. If B approaches more closely his profit is given by $\pi_2 = bc(3l - a - 3b)$, and diminishes with increasing b. This optimum distance from A is, however, an adventitious feature of our problem resulting from a discontinuity which is necessary for simplicity. In general we should consider q_1 and q_2 as continuous functions of p_1 and p_2, instead of supposing, as here, that as $p_2 - p_1$ falls below a certain limit, a great mass of buyers shift suddenly from B to A.

Thus a landlord or realtor who can determine the location of future stores, expecting to absorb their profits in the sales value of the land, has a motive for making the situation as unsymmetrical as possible; for, the more the lack of symmetry, the greater is $(a - b)^2$, which appears in the expression above for $\pi_1 + \pi_2$.

Our example has also an application to the question of capitalism *v.* socialism, and contributes an argument to the socialist side. Let us consider the efficiency of our pair of merchants in serving the public by calculating the total of transportation charges paid by consumers. These charges for the strip of length a amount to

$$c \int_0^a t \, dt, \text{ or } \tfrac{1}{2}ca^2.$$ Altogether the sum is

$$\tfrac{1}{2}c(a^2 + b^2 + x^2 + y^2).$$

Now if the places of business are both fixed, the quantities a, b and $x + y$ are all determined. The minimum total cost for transportation will be achieved if, for the given value of $x + y$, the expression $x^2 + y^2$ is a minimum. This will be the case if x and y are equal.

But x and y will not be equal unless the prices p_1 and p_2 are equal, and under competition this is not likely to be the case. If we bar the improbable case of A and B having taken up symmetrical positions on the line, the prices which will result from each seeking his own gain have been seen to be different. If the segment a in which A has a clear advantage is greater than b, then A's price will be greater than B's. Consequently some buyers will ship their purchases from B's store, though they are closer to A's, and socially it would be more economical for them to buy from A. If the stores were conducted for public service rather than for profit their prices would be identical in spite of the asymmetry of demand.

If the stores be thought of as movable, the wastefulness of private profit seeking management becomes even more striking. There are now four variables, a, b, x and y, instead of two. Their sum is the fixed length l, and to minimise the social cost of transportation found above we must make the sum of their squares as small as possible. As before, the variables must be equal. This requires A and B to occupy symmetrical positions at the quartiles of the market. But instead of doing so they crowd together as closely as possible. Even if A, the first in the field, should settle at one of these points, we have seen that B upon his arrival will not go to the other, but will fix upon a location between A and the centre and as near A as possible.[11] Thus some customers will have to transport their goods a distance of more than $\frac{1}{2}l$, whereas with two stores run in the public interest no shipment should be for a greater distance than $\frac{1}{4}l$.

If a third seller C appears, his desire for as large a market as possible will prompt him likewise to take up a position close to A or B, but not between them. By an argument similar to that just used, it may be shown that regard only for the public interest would require A, B and C each to occupy one of the points at distances one-sixth, one-half and five-sixths of the way from one end of the line to the other. As more and more sellers of the same commodity arise, the tendency is not to become distributed in the socially optimum manner but to cluster unduly.

The importance and variety of such agglomerative tendencies become apparent when it is remembered that distance, as we have used it for illustration, is only a figurative term for a great congeries of qualities. Instead of sellers of an identical commodity separated geographically we might have considered two competing cider merchants side by side, one selling a sweeter liquid than the other. If the consumers of cider be thought of as varying by infinitesimal degrees in the sourness they desire, we have much the same situation as before. The measure of sourness now replaces distance, while instead of transportation costs there are the degrees of disutility resulting from a consumer getting cider more or less different from what he wants. The foregoing considerations apply, particularly the conclusion that competing sellers tend to become too much alike.

The mathematical analysis thus leads to an observation of wide generality. Buyers are confronted everywhere with an excessive sameness. When a new merchant or manufacturer sets up shop he must not produce something exactly like what is already on the market or he will risk a price war of the type discussed by Bertrand in connection with Cournot's mineral springs. But there is an incentive to make the new product very much like the old,

---

[11] With the unimportant qualification mentioned in the footnote on p. 474.

applying some slight change which will seem an improvement to as many buyers as possible without ever going far in this direction. The tremendous standardisation of our furniture, our houses, our clothing, our automobiles and our education are due in part to the economies of large-scale production, in part to fashion and imitation. But over and above these forces is the effect we have been discussing, the tendency to make only slight deviations in order to have for the new commodity as many buyers of the old as possible, to get, so to speak, *between* one's competitors and a mass of customers.

So general is this tendency that it appears in the most diverse fields of competitive activity, even quite apart from what is called economic life. In politics it is strikingly exemplified. The competition for votes between the Republican and Democratic parties does not lead to a clear drawing of issues, an adoption of two strongly contrasted positions between which the voter may choose. Instead, each party strives to make its platform as much like the other's as possible. Any radical departure would lose many votes, even though it might lead to stronger commendation of the party by some who would vote for it anyhow. Each candidate "pussyfoots," replies ambiguously to questions, refuses to take a definite stand in any controversy for fear of losing votes. Real differences, if they ever exist, fade gradually with time though the issues may be as important as ever. The Democratic party, once opposed to protective tariffs, moves gradually to a position almost, but not quite, identical with that of the Republicans. It need have no fear of fanatical free-traders, since they will still prefer it to the Republican party, and its advocacy of a continued high tariff will bring it the money and votes of some intermediate groups.

The reasoning, of course, requires modification when applied to the varied conditions of actual life. Our example might have been more complicated. Instead of a uniform distribution of customers along a line we might have assumed a varying density, but with no essential change in conclusions. Instead of a linear market we might suppose the buyers spread out on a plane. Then the customers from one region will patronise A, those from another B. The boundary between the two regions is the locus of points for which the difference of transportation costs from the two shops equals the difference of prices, i.e., for which the delivered price is the same whether the goods are bought from A or from B. If transportation is in straight lines (perhaps by aeroplane) at a cost proportional to the distance, the boundary will be a hyperbola, since a hyperbola is the locus of points such that the difference of distances from the foci is constant. If there are three or more sellers, their regions will be separated from each other by arcs of hyperbolas. If the transportation is not in straight lines, or if its cost is given by such a complicated function as a railroad freight schedule, the boundaries will be of another kind; but we might generalise the term hyperbola (as is done in the differential geometry of curved surfaces) to include these curves also.

The number of dimensions of our picture is increased to three or more when we represent geometrically such characters as sweetness of cider, and instead of transportation costs consider more generally the decrement of utility resulting from the actual commodity being in a different place and condition than the buyer would prefer. Each homogeneous commodity or service or entrepreneur in a competing system can be thought of as a point serving a region separated from other such regions by portions of generalised hyperboloids. The density of demand in this space is in general not uniform, and is restricted to a finite region. It is not necessary that each point representing a service or commodity shall be under the control of a different entrepreneur from every other. On the other hand, everyone who sells an article in different places or who sells different articles in the same place may be said to control the prices at several points of the symbolic space. The mutual gravitation will now take the form of a tendency of the outermost entrepreneurs to approach the cluster.

Two further modifications are important. One arises when it is possible to discriminate among customers, or to sell goods at a delivered price instead of a fixed price at store or factory plus transportation. In such cases, even without an agreement between sellers, a monopoly profit can be collected from some consumers while fierce competition is favouring others. This seems to have been the condition in the cement industry about which a controversy raged a few years ago, and was certainly involved in the railroad rebate scandals.

The other important modification has to do with the elasticity of demand. The problem of the two merchants on a linear market might be varied by supposing that each consumer buys an amount of the commodity in question which depends on the delivered price. If one tries a particular demand function the mathematical complications will now be considerable, but for the most general problems elasticity must be assumed. The difficulty as to whether prices or quantities should be used as independent variables can now be cleared up. This question has troubled many readers of Cournot. The answer is that either set of variables may be used; that the q's may be expressed in terms of the p's, and the p's in terms of the q's. This was not possible in Cournot's example of duopoly, nor heretofore in ours. The sum of our q's was constrained to have the fixed value 1, so that they could not be independent, but when the demand is made elastic the constraint vanishes.

With elastic demand the observations we have made on the solution will still for the most part be qualitatively true; but the tendency for B to establish his business excessively close to A will be less marked. The increment in B's sales to his more remote customers when he moves nearer them may be more than compensation to him for abandoning some of his nearer business to A. In this case B will definitely and apart from extraneous circumstances choose a location at some distance from A. But he will not go as far from A as the public welfare would require. The tempting intermediate market will still have an influence.

In the more general problem in which the commodities purveyed differ in many dimensions the situation is the same. The elasticity of demand of particular groups does mitigate the tendency to excessive similarity of competing commodities, but not enough. It leads some factories to make cheap shoes for the poor and others to make expensive shoes for the rich, but all the shoes are too much alike. Our cities become uneconomically large and the business districts within them are too concentrated. Methodist and Presbyterian churches are too much alike; cider is too homogeneous.

24

OPTIMUM LOCATION IN SPATIAL COMPETITION [*]

By Arthur Smithies [||]

I. Introductory

The purpose of this paper is to take some further steps in the direction of generalizing the theory of spatial competition. The very fact that Professor Harold Hotelling's pioneer article[1] explained so successfully the close similarity of the Republican and Democratic platforms in 1928 indicates that something more was needed in 1936. It was probably true to say in 1928 that by moving to the center of electoral opinion neither party risked losing its peripheral support. The situation at the present time requires no elaboration; suffice it to say that neither party feels itself free to compete with the other for the undecided vote at the center, in full confidence that it will retain its support from the extremes of political opinion. Leaving the political analogy, Hotelling's assumption of completely inelastic demand means that neither competitor makes sacrifices at the ends of the market when he invades his rival's territory; thus there is no check on the two competitors' moving together. Actually, elastic demands do impose such a check and do account for the fact that equilibrium is frequently established, with the competitors free to move but spatially separated. I do not dispute Hotelling's conclusion that there is a tendency for two competitors to cluster nearer to the center than to the quartiles of a linear market; I suggest, however, that it is important to analyze not only the forces that tend to bring them together but also those that keep them apart. An

* The Journal of Political Economy, Vol. XLIX (1941), pp. 423–439. Reprinted, by the courtesy of The University of Chicago Press and the author, without change from the original text.

|| Harvard University.

[1] "Stability in Competition," The Economic Journal, March 1929, p. 41 (reprinted in the present volume, page 467).

important step in this direction was made by A. P. Lerner and H. W. Singer,[2] who modified Hotelling's assumption of complete inelasticity by postulating that demand was inelastic over a price range extending from zero to a finite upper limit. However, it seems desirable to go further and assume an elastic demand function at every point of the market. This I shall do in this paper, to the modest extent of assuming an identical linear demand function at every point of a linear market.

Hotelling and Lerner and Singer have confined themselves substantially[3] to the extreme competitive assumption that each competitor fixes his price and location, assuming that the price and location of his rival remain unaffected by his action. In this paper I shall consider, in addition, cases where each competitor makes his adjustments expecting reactions from his rival.

Finally, a considerable part of this paper will be concerned with the effects of the magnitude of the freight rates[4] and of changes in marginal costs for one or both producers.

The analysis of these problems can be carried out rigorously only by mathematical methods. Although the methods are elementary, their application is complicated.[5] For this reason and also for the reason that the mathematics do not bring out clearly the economic principles involved, I have attempted to present

---

[2] "Some Notes on Duopoly and Spatial Competition," *The Journal of Political Economy*, April 1937, p. 145.

[3] Lerner and Singer do modify this assumption in cases where one competitor attempts to cut out his rival entirely. I shall deal with this point later.

[4] Hotelling's simple result (*op. cit.*, p. 50; see also page 477 of the, present volume), that profits depend directly on freight rates, is true only in the special-demand situation he has examined. Lerner and Singer's treatment of freight rates (*op. cit.*) depend on the setup of their particular problem, and no general principles are developed. I know of no treatment of the problem of changes in marginal costs.

[5] G. H. Orcutt of the University of Michigan has constructed a mechanical model for solving this problem with a greater degree of generality than is possible by analytic methods. The principle of the machine is to represent, for each competitor, price, quantity per unit distance, and distance by voltage drops along linear resistance wires. These resistance wires are included in an electric circuit such that the product of these three voltages, i.e., total profits, can be read off a voltmeter. The machine is operated by varying price and distance for each competitor, in accordance with the assumptions of the problem, until a simultaneous maximum is achieved.

the whole argument in purely verbal form and to indicate in an appendix the general mathematical methods.[6]

Considerations of space suggest that the discussion should be confined to cases where the producers are free to shift their locations at will. However, some indication of the solution of the fixed-location problem[7] in its relation to freight rates will be given in footnotes.

II. Assumptions

We have now to formulate two sets of assumptions—the structural assumptions which limit the problem as a whole and the assumptions as to the character of the competition.

The structural assumptions are as follows:

1. There is a linear market bounded at both ends.

2. At every point of the market there can be only one price, and there are identical linear demand functions relating price to quantity sold per unit of time at that point. Thus, the total amount sold at any point is supplied by the competitor charging the lower delivered price at that point.

3. There are two competitors, A and B, having single locations. We can, without loss of generality, assume that A is located to the left of B.

4. The competitors are subject to constant marginal costs. Except where we are considering the effects of (small) changes in the costs of one or both competitors, marginal costs for both competitors will be assumed equal and zero. Fixed costs will be ignored throughout.

5. There is a uniform freight rate per unit of distance for both competitors, which is independent of distance and of the price and quantity of the goods transported.

6. Each competitor will sell on an f.o.b. mill basis.[8] That is, he

---

[6] The need to return to Marshallian orthodoxy in this problem has been impressed on me equally by Lerner and Singer's geometry and by my own algebra.

[7] For a discussion of equilibrium in the fixed-location problem see Erich Schneider, "Bermerkungen zu einer Theorie der Raümwirtschaft," *Econometrica*, January 1935, p. 79. Schneider does not deal with the freight-rate problem.

[8] I am restricting this paper to f.o.b. mill selling entirely for reasons of space. The analysis of the case where each producer attempts to maximize his

will fix a mill-price to prevail at the point where he is located, and his delivered price will be computed by adding to the mill-price the freight cost from his mill to the point of delivery.

7. Each competitor is free to move his location instantaneously and without cost.[9]

8. Each competitor will attempt to fix his mill-price and his location so as to maximize his instantaneous rate of profits in respect of his total sales.

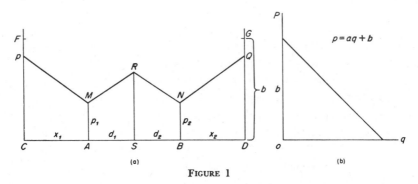

FIGURE 1

9. The relation of freight rates to demand conditions is such that, in all the cases under examination, there are sales at every point of the market.[10]

---

expected profits at every point of his sections of the market is very similar to the f.o.b. case. Whereas in the f.o.b. case delivered price, by definition, exceeds mill-price by the full amount of freight costs from the mill to the point of delivery, in this case, given the linear demand conditions we have assumed, delivered price will be equal to mill-price *plus* half the freight costs from the mill to the point of delivery. Thus, since in both cases we have a linear relation between mill-prices and delivered prices, the qualitative results of the argument will be the same.

[9] Although these assumptions are quite unrealistic in many cases, I feel— and I take it that Lerner and Singer also feel—that they are useful for demonstrating clearly certain fundamental economic tendencies that have a wider application than merely to the problem at present in hand. I need only refer once more to Hotelling's brilliant analogies and to the use made by Chamberlin (*Theory of Monopolistic Competition* [Harvard University Press, 1933]) of the theory of spatial competition to illustrate the theory of product differentiation.

[10] This assumption avoids the necessity of considering the possibility of locational indeterminateness. This question has been adequately dealt with by Lerner and Singer (*op. cit.*, p. 150).

The setup described by the above assumptions can be illustrated by Fig. 1. CD represents the linear market of length l, and A and B the positions of producers A and B, respectively. AM and BN are their respective mill-prices, denoted by p_1 and p_2. The lines MP and MR show delivered prices for A, while NR and NQ show delivered prices for B. The slopes of these delivered-price lines will depend on the freight rate. It is evident that A will not be able to sell to the right of S, or B to the left of it. The vertical lines CF and DG are drawn for reference, of height $b-b$ being the price intercept of the demand curve—shown in Fig. 1 (b), which is assumed to be of the form $p = aq + b$,[11] where p denotes the delivered price charged at any point in the market and q the quantity sold at that point, and $a<o$, $b>o$. The distances AC and BD of the competitors from their respective ends of the market are denoted by x_1 and x_2, respectively, while their distances from S are denoted by d_1 and d_2. It is worth emphasizing that x_1 and x_2 are within the complete control of the competitors, whereas d_1 and d_2 depend on the mutual interactions of their price policy and their location policy. We shall term the regions AC and BD the "hinterlands" of A and B, while AB will be called their "competitive region."

Our next problem is to consider the conjectural hypotheses made by the competitors as to each other's behavior. In contrast to the nonspatial problem of imperfect competition, each competitor's policy will depend on his estimate of his rival's reactions in respect both of price and of location. We shall be concerned with the following three cases.

1. Each competitor in making an adjustment assumes that his rival will set a price equal to his own and will adopt a location symmetrical with his own. By this is meant that A in fixing his location will assume that B will fix his location so as to make $BD = AC$ in Fig. 1. Our analysis will show that if the competitors behave in this way the equilibrium position they will achieve will be the same as if they had acted jointly as a monopolist. Thus, for want of a better term, I shall describe this situation as "full quasi-co-operation."

---

[11] Although in our present problem price is the independent variable, the demand function is written in this form for the sake of convenience in the mathematical analysis.

2. Each competitor assumes that his rival will have the same price reactions as above but will keep his location unchanged. This situation may be termed "quasi-co-operative as to prices and competitive as to locations."

3. Lastly,[12] we have the case which is substantially that examined by Hotelling and Lerner and Singer, where each competitor assumed that both the price and the location of his rival will be fixed independently of his own. That is, there is competition both as to prices and as to location. This we may term "full competition." However, I shall not assume, as Lerner and Singer do originally,[13] that this assumption holds where one competitor adopts a price and location policy designed to cut his rival out of the market entirely; such credulity as this implies is fantastic—as Lerner and Singer realize. Nor shall I consider their amendment[14]—that a competitor adopts such a price and location, not with the hopes of cutting his rival out entirely, but with the strategic purpose of forcing him into a disadvantageous location. It seems to me that such action is virtually a declaration of economic war which is likely to be reciprocated and that the competitors will try to achieve *Lebensräume* satisfactory to both before resorting to policies of extermination. However, we shall see that in some conditions no such equilibrium is possible—and in those cases the possibilities of economic warfare must be considered.

The three cases proposed for examination are, of course, extreme, and in general the situation would be somewhere between quasi-co-operation and full competition. I have elsewhere[15] used generalized methods of formulating the problem so as to cover such intermediate cases, but in the present problem the complexity involved is too great to make that procedure worth while. Examination of the extreme cases indicates, at any rate, the qualitative results for the intermediate cases.[16]

---

[12] Considerations of symmetry would seem to suggest that we should consider also competition as to prices and quasi-co-operation as to location. However, since such a situation seems of little importance, it is omitted for the sake of brevity.

[13] *Op. cit.,* p. 151.   [14] *Ibid.,* p. 161.

[15] A. Smithies, "Equilibrium in Monopolistic Competition," *The Quarterly Journal of Economics,* November 1940, p. 95; and A. Smithies and L. J. Savage, "A Dynamic Problem in Duopoly," *Econometrica,* April 1940, p. 130.

[16] The foregoing statement of the problem has ignored (for the sake of

III. Verbal Argument

The attempt to solve our problem by purely verbal argument will involve little more than an appeal to informed common sense, but it seems worth while to make it in order to establish some general principles which will help to indicate the solution to problems that are too complex to be treated by rigorous methods. Our first problem is to determine the equilibrium position under our various competitive hypotheses. However, it seems pedagogically helpful to begin with a discussion of the (well-known) equilibrium position of a monopolist in the type of market and subject to the cost and f.o.b. selling conditions we have postulated for competitors. Second, we shall consider the dependence of equilibrium on the level of freight rates and, third, determine the effects of changes in marginal costs for one or both competitors.

1. Conditions for Equilibrium

A. Monopolist. A monopolist will be free from the asymmetry of having a hinterland on one side of him and a competitive region on the other. His markets on both sides of his mill will be equally exploitable. Assuming the monopolist has one plant, then, if he had no freight to consider, it would be indifferent to him where he located, and he would charge a price of $b/2$ at every point in the market in order to maximize his profits. Now, how will the existence of a freight rate affect him? It will mean, first, that he is unable to charge a uniform price at every point and, second, that he must decide how much of the freight to absorb himself and how much to "pass on" to consumers. Both of these exigencies will adversely affect his profits, so that his third problem is to locate himself at the point where their burden is minimized. It requires no argument to answer the third question; obviously, the monopolist will locate at the center of the market. Turning to the second question, the imposition of a freight rate is precisely analogous to the imposition of an excise tax per unit of commodity, uniform at every point of the market but, for any one point, linearly dependent on its distance from the mill of the producer. Now,

---

simplicity) the possibility that a competitor expects his rival to react to a price or location change by adjusting, respectively, his location or price.

for the cost and demand conditions assumed it is well known that a monopolist will absorb part of the tax himself and will pass some on to consumers in the form of a higher price. These considerations apply to the present case, and when the requirement of f.o.b. selling is introduced it can be adduced that at his mill (located at the center) he will charge a price which is less than $b/2$ by a determinate amount which is less than the cost of transporting a unit of commodity over half the length of the market, while at the ends of the market he will charge a price which is greater than $b/2$ by another such amount.

If a monopolist should have two plants instead of one,[17] the considerations of the foregoing paragraph make it evident that in order to maximize profits he will locate one plant at each quartile of the market, and in respect of each plant he will behave, in respect of its own half of the market, in the same way as the monopolist with the single plant behaved in respect of the whole market.

  B. FULL QUASI-CO-OPERATION. The essential difference between two competitors and a two-plant monopolist is that each competitor strives to occupy more than half the market whereas the monopolist aims at maximizing profits in each half of the market. Successful invasion on the part of one competitor involves both enlarging his hinterland and occupying a greater fraction of the competitive region. The essential limitation on such incursions is that every move to add new territory is accompanied by less successful exploitation of the original hinterland (because of the higher freight charges involved).

Now, in this case of full quasi-co-operation we are, in effect, postulating that there are no profits to be gained from invasion— for each competitor assumes that any price he sets and any location he adopts will be identically met by his rival. Then, no matter what he does, neither competitor can expect to occupy more than half the market. Hence, he will not be prepared to make any sacrifices in his hinterland, and his efforts will be directed to exploiting half the market so as to maximize profits. It is evident that in this case the mutual actions of both competitors will result in an equi-

---

  [17] I am not here concerned with the interesting theoretical problem of the optimum number of plants for a monopolist. I merely assume that the optimum number is two.

librium position that is identical with that of the two-plant monopolist.

C. QUASI-CO-OPERATION AS TO PRICES; COMPETITION AS TO LOCATIONS. In this case each competitor believes to an equal degree that he has one effective strategy for increasing his territory—namely, moving closer to the center while expecting that his rival will not change his location but will meet price competition. We can thus expect (except in the limiting cases to be dealt with) that equilibrium will be achieved with each competitor at an equal distance from the center of the market and closer to it than the quartiles. Although each competitor will be disappointed in his hopes for territorial expansion, neither will retire toward the quartile position because he believes that any gains he may make in his hinterland will be more than offset by losses to his rival, whom he does not expect to retreat.

Although we have excluded competitive price-cutting from this case, the (equal) equilibrium mill-prices for the competitors will be lower than in Case B. This is due to the fact that average freight charges to the hinterland of each producer will be higher than if he were situated at his quartile, and in order to maximize his profits he will charge a price lower than $b/2$ by an amount greater than that in Case A.[18]

D. FULL COMPETITION. Here each producer thinks he can increase his territory both by moving toward the center and by price-cutting. And, what is more, he believes that these strategies

---

[18] In discussing the process of adjustment in this and the following case, I am implicitly assuming that the starting-point of each competitor is farther from the center of the market than his ultimate equilibrium position. This is not necessary; the equilibrium position is independent of the starting-points. Suppose (in Fig. 1) B is located as a monopolist at the center. Then A, assuming B will remain there, will locate at the optimum position between C and B. Producer B will then find it profitable, to some extent, to sacrifice some of the competitive region in order the more effectively to exploit his hinterland. This retirement of B will encourage further advance of A, and so on. The process of adjustment will involve successive advances by A and successive strategic retirements by B, until each reaches his equilibrium position. It is also evident from this example that if B is originally located at the center we have lost no generality by assuming that A locates to the left of B. Also, once A has located to the left of B, B will move to his right; and A will have no inducement to move to the right of B, since the greater segment of the market lies to the left of B, where A already is.

are not independent of each other in their effectiveness. Price-cutting increases the advantages of territorial advance and vice versa.[19] And, as before, he has to make hinterland sacrifices in respect of both strategies. Again equilibrium will be achieved, with equal prices and equal territories, closer to the center than to the quartiles. The prospects of gain from price-cutting and of loss from price-raising will result in a lower equilibrium price than in Case B, while the complementary relationship of price-cutting and locational advance will mean that the latter policy will be carried further than in Case C and equilibrium will be established closer to the center of the market.

In the light of our analysis we can now see the implications of Hotelling's assumption of zero elasticity of demand. This means that a producer by altering his position does not affect his position in the hinterland, since he can always pass on to the consumer his entire freight charges without affecting profits. Thus, there are no restraints to territorial advance, so that the competitors, if both are free to move, will inevitably both move to the center of the market.

2. Dependence on Freight Rates

The argument of the preceding paragraphs has clearly indicated that the relation of freight charges to demand conditions is of critical importance in the quantitative determination of equilibrium. In our present problem our special assumptions make it possible to say that the critical relation is the ratio of the cost of transporting a unit of commodity the whole length of the market to the price intercept of the demand curve, i.e., b. For brevity, I shall denote this ratio by s. Our present purpose, then, is to supplement the description of the four equilibrium positions we have determined by considering specifically their dependence on s.

CASES A AND B (TWO-PLANT MONOPOLY AND FULL QUASI-CO-OPERATION). In these cases we have seen that the equilibrium location is uniquely determined—at the quartiles. The magnitude of s is therefore relevant only in so far as it affects the equilibrium

---

[19] This proposition can be proved mathematically. It is to be noted that this complementary relationship also obtains in Case C, but since in that case price-cutting is not undertaken, the relation in that case will be inoperative in inducing the competitors to move nearer the center than they otherwise would.

price and profits. We have already seen that if the freight rate approaches zero the equilibrium price will be $b/2$, and as freight rate increases it will be profitable for the producers to absorb some of the increase in the form of a lower mill-price. Hence, the greater the value of s, the smaller will be the equilibrium mill-price. Also, it follows from general principles that profits will decrease as s increases.

It remains to determine the conditions under which the whole market will be supplied. Clearly, s can have a value in excess of which it will be unprofitable for each producer to supply the outlying parts of his market. This critical value of s is determined by finding the value for s for which the delivered price both at the ends and at the center of the market is b; and sales at these points, consequently, are zero. A simple calculation shows that this is the case if $s = 8/3$, and at that point the equilibrium mill-price $p = p_1 = p_2 = b/3$.

CASES C AND D. In both these cases it follows from our previous argument that hinterland sacrifices will be greater and prospective gains from territorial expansion toward the center will be less, the greater the value of s. This suggests, first, that s may be sufficiently high to force the competitors to establish equilibrium at the quartiles and, second, that s may be sufficiently low for the hinterland deterrents to be inoperative, so that the competitors will both move to the center.

Such is the case. If we determine the conditions under which the competitors are charging a price b and selling zero quantity at the ends of the market, we find that they will be located at the quartiles and will also be charging price b and selling zero quantity at the center. The necessary and sufficient conditions are again $s = 8/3$, and again we have $p = b/3$. Hence we can say that in the cases examined, for $s = 8/3$, the equilibrium price and location of the competitors is independent of the nature of the competition.

Let us next consider the effect of low values of s. We have seen that the tendency to move toward the center of the market is stronger in Case D than in Case C, so that we should expect the minimum value of s necessary to keep the competitors apart to be greater in the latter case than in the former. Our calculations confirm this inference; we find that d_1 and d_2 in Fig. 1 will be zero if $s = 4/7$ in Case C, and $8/11$ in Case D. The corresponding prices are $3b/7$ and $3b/11$, respectively. If s is less than $4/7$ in the one case and $8/11$ in the other, the competitors will still move to the center and remain there in their efforts to maximize profits, although a maximum in the mathematical sense will not have been attained.

Hotelling[20] recognizes the instability of this situation; and this implies that in his case the stability in competition depends on the difficulties of shifting location, which may be overcome in the

TABLE 1

Situation	s	Prices	Profits	Location $x_1 = x_2$
		b Multiplied by	b^2l Multiplied by	l Multiplied by
Case C:				
Equilibrium at the center...	4/7 (0.57)	3/7 (0.43)	9/98 (0.092)	1/2 (0.50)
Maximum profits	0.72	0.44	0.094	0.43
Maximum price	0.72	0.44	0.094	0.43
....	2.00	0.37	0.072	0.27
Equilibrium at the quartiles	8/3 (2.67)	1/3 (0.33)	1/18 (0.056)	1/4 (0.25)
Case D:				
Equilibrium at the center...	8/11 (0.73)	3/11 (0.26)	9/121 (0.074)	1/2 (0.50)
Maximum profits	1.00	0.33	0.084	0.39
Maximum price	1.70	0.36	0.077	0.29
....	2.00	0.36	0.070	0.27
Equilibrium at the quartiles	8/3 (2.67)	1/3 (0.33)	1/18 (0.056)	1/4 (0.25)

long run. Equilibrium at the center would be stable only if one assumes that each competitor sells only in his own hinterland and does not attempt to invade the hinterland of his rival. I prefer to say that the forces of competition that eliminate the competitive region also destroy the inviolability of the hinterlands, and that once the competitors have come together they compete as duopolists in the entire market; and that the whole question must then be reopened and examined from the point of view of the theory of duopoly in a nonspatial market, which theory can be applied to the present case with but trivial modifications and upon which I shall not attempt to embark here.

---

[20] *Op. cit.*, p. 52 (p. 479 of the present volume).

Our next problem is the somewhat more complicated one of determining the general relations between s and the equilibrium price and profits. We have seen that forces of competition drive the competitors nearer to the center of the market than in the case of full quasi-co-operation, in futile endeavors to increase their territory; and the deterrent to these activities is the magnitude of s with which they are faced. In this case it is by no means clear that maximum profits are associated with the lowest possible freight rates or that, as freight rates increase, equilibrium mill-prices decrease. In fact, for Case D, we have already seen that where $s = 8/3$ the mill-price is greater than where $s = 8/11$. One is led to believe that there are values of s between these extrems which will maximize prices and profits, respectively. In other words, up to a certain level freight rates will serve to protect the competitors from their own self-destructive instincts. (This point may be readily apprehended by imagining the extreme case of an insuperable wall erected at the center of the market. This would undoubtedly increase profits for both producers, since they would then be forced to act as monopolists.) Our previous argument has shown that in Case C the competitors need less protection against themselves than in Case D. This suggests that the optimum value of s is lower in Case C than in Case D. The effect of higher freight rates is to make the behavior of the competitors more monopolistic; this has the effect initially of increasing both prices and profits. But in the cases under examination the rise of prices under the influence of increasing freight rates will persist longer than the rise of profits—appreciably longer in Case D and inappreciably longer in Case C. Eventually, however, the competitors will find it profitable to absorb part of the increase of freight rates by charging lower mill-prices.

The results of this argument can now be summarized by giving the results of the numerical calculations in Table 1.[21]

---

[21] It is worth recording that the analysis of the section applies also to the fixed-location problem dealt with by Hotelling in the first part of his paper (pp. 45–47; see also pp. 472–473 of the present volume), where locations are fixed and each competitor assumes his rival will keep his price unchanged. If the freight rate is zero, it is obvious that the competitors will cut prices to zero on these assumptions. Also, if we assume that the fixed locations are at the quartiles, the situation where the whole market is only just being supplied will be

3. Changes in Marginal Costs

In this section we shall consider the effects on the equilibrium situation of (a) a small change in marginal costs equal for both producers (i.e., we shall consider the effects of marginal costs rising above the zero level that we have hitherto assumed) and (b) a small increase in the level of marginal costs for one producer alone. We shall also, as before, consider the case of the monopolist for the sake of comparison.

a) This case offers no difficulty; the general reasoning from nonspatial markets indicates that in all the cases examined, including the monopolist, it will be profitable to pass on part, but only part, of the increased costs to the consumer in the shape of higher prices. In Cases A and B, where equilibrium is established at the quartiles, this rise of price will have no effect on location. In Cases C and D, where the equilibrium positions of the competitors are, in general, closer to the center than to the quartiles, they will find it profitable to move back toward the quartiles in order to reduce the incidence of higher prices on sales in their hinterlands, which constitute the greater part of their respective markets. In fact, if marginal costs rise sufficiently we shall have a case analogous to that examined in the last section, where the competitors will not

---

identical with the cases already examined; namely, we shall have $s = 8/3$ and $p = b/3$. In the same way as before, freight rates up to a certain level will protect competitors against the destructive effects of price competition; up to that level a rise of freight rates will increase profits, while prices will continue to rise somewhat longer. Table 2, analogous to Table 1, summarizes the numerical results.

TABLE 2

Situation	s	Prices b Multi-plied by	Profits b²l Multi-plied by
Zero freight rates..............	0.00	0.00	0.00
Maximum profits	0.50	0.375	0.110
Maximum prices	1.00	0.40	0.095
Zero quantities at the ends and center of the market...........	8/3 (2.66)	1/3 (0.33)	1/18 (0.056)

move from the quartiles, no matter what competitive assumptions are made.

b) This case is more complicated, and we must consider the various cases separately.

CASE A: If the costs rise for one plant of a monopolist, it will be profitable for him to raise the price charged in that plant, but it will also be profitable for him to use his low-cost plant to supply more than half the market. Further, as we have seen, it is profitable for him to locate each plant at the center of the part of the market that it supplies. Hence, the monopolist will move his high-cost plant nearer to its end of the market than to the quartile and his low-cost plant nearer the center. This readjustment will also involve reducing the mill-price charged by the latter plant.

CASE B: The case of full quasi-co-operation is now somewhat different from that of the monopolist. For the small rise of marginal costs for one competitor is assumed not to alter either producer's expectation that he will continue to supply half the market. The competitors will continue to locate at the quartiles. Producer A, whose marginal costs have risen, will raise his price in order to charge the monopoly price appropriate to his new cost situation for half the market, while Producer B, whose costs have not changed, will continue to charge his old price. Although A will be disappointed with the results and B will be pleasantly surprised, we are still entitled to regard the situation as one of equilibrium. However, this equilibrium will contain the germs of instability. Depending on the size of the rise of A's marginal costs, B's joy and A's consternation will tend to make them revise their assumptions in the direction of B's expecting A to charge a higher price than his own and vice versa. Our analysis must, therefore, be confined strictly to small changes of marginal costs.

CASES C AND D: In both these cases A, whose marginal costs have risen, will charge a higher mill-price and move back toward his quartile. A's retreat will improve B's position in the competitive region. This opens up to B the possibilities of charging higher prices and of moving toward the center, except that the more he moves toward the center, the less profitable will it be for him to charge a higher price. In fact, it may be profitable for him to charge a lower price, depending on the extent of his move. What he actually does depends on the freight rate or, more accurately, on s. The smaller the value of s, the greater will be the tendency for him to move toward the center and charge lower prices, while for larger values of s he will move less toward the center and will raise his price. The critical values of s are approximately 0.65 in Case C and 1.70 in Case D.

This concludes the verbal argument. It should be pointed out that in this type of argument it is impossible to do justice to the essential character of the adjustment as one of mutual determination, and in this respect the arguments of this part sin more than once.

IV. MATHEMATICAL APPENDIX

In this appendix I shall merely indicate the general methods used to reach the conclusions arrived at by verbal argument in Part III.[22]

We shall make use of the following symbols. Geometrical references are to Fig. 1. Let $l =$ the length of the market; r the freight rate per unit of distance; x_1 and x_2 the distances of A from D and B from C, respectively; d_1 and d_2 the distances from S of A and B, respectively; p_1 and p_2 their mill-prices; and c_1 and c_2 their marginal costs.

The variables within the control of the competitors are p_1 and x_1 for A and p_2 and x_2 for B. The quantities d_1 and d_2 are dependent variables and may be expressed in terms of the four independent variables. Then letting π_1 and π_2 be the profits of A and B, respectively, we may write

$$\pi_1 = \pi_1 (p_1, x_1, p_2, x_2, r, c_1, l),$$
$$\pi_2 = \pi_2 (p_2, x_2, p_1, x_1, r, c_2, l).$$

The producers aim at maximizing not their actual profits but their expected profits. Expected profits for A may be obtained from these functions by substituting for p_2 and x_2 the values that A expects these variables to take on as the result of his own action. Thus, in Case A he will expect $p_1 = p_2$ and $x_1 = x_2$, while in Case B he will expect $p_1 = p_2$ and x_2 to remain unchanged by his action. In Case C he will expect both p_2 and x_2 to remain unaffected by his action.

---

[22] A detailed presentation of the mathematical argument is available in mimeographed form on application to the author.

Now, for A and B simultaneously to maximize their expected profits, the following conditions are necessary:

$$\frac{\partial \pi_1}{\partial x_1} = \frac{\partial \pi_2}{\partial p_1} = \frac{\partial \pi_2}{\partial x_2} = \frac{\partial \pi_2}{\partial p_2} = 0.$$

In order to obtain manageable solutions to these four equations, it was necessary to assume $c_1 = c_2$ and to assume a linear demand function at every point of the market. The solutions then express the optimum values of p_1, p_2, x_1, x_2; π_1 and π_2 as functions of r, l, and c.

By investigating the behavior of these functions with respect to r the results given in Table 1 can be obtained. The results given in Table 2 are obtained by imposing the restriction $x_1 = x_2 = 1/4$.

The effects of a change in marginal costs for both producers are found by determining the effects of a small change in c, while the effects of a change in the marginal costs of one producer are found by taking as our starting-point $c_1 = c_2$ and determining the effects of a small change in c_1, c_2 remaining unchanged.

VII. THEORY OF GAMES

25

THE THEORY OF ECONOMIC BEHAVIOR[*][1]

By Leonid Hurwicz ‖

Had it merely called to our attention the existence and exact nature of certain fundamental gaps in economic theory, the *Theory of Games and Economic Behavior* by von Neumann and Morgenstern would have been a book of outstanding importance. But it does more than that It is essentially constructive: where existing theory is considered to be inadequate, the authors put in its place a highly novel analytical apparatus designed to cope with the problem.

It would be doing the authors an injustice to say that theirs is a contribution to economics only. The scope of the book is much broader. The techniques applied by the authors in tackling economic problems are of sufficient generality to be valid in political science, sociology, or even military strategy. The applicability to games proper (chess and poker) is obvious from the title. Moreover, the book is of considerable interest from a purely mathematical point of view. This review, however, is in the main confined to the purely economic aspects of the *Theory of Games and Economic Behavior*.

To a considerable extent this review is of an expository[2] nature. This seems justified by the importance of the book, its use of new and unfamiliar concepts and its very length which some may find a serious obstacle.

---

[*] *The American Economic Review,* Vol. XXXV (1945), pp. 909–925. Reprinted, by the courtesy of the publisher and the author, with a typographical correction. The tables and figures used in this article were originally drawn by Mrs. D. Friedlander of the University of Chicago.

‖ University of Minnesota.

[1] *Theory of Games and Economic Behavior.* By John von Neumann and Oskar Morgenstern. (Princeton: Princeton University Press, 1944, pp. xviii, 625.)

[2] The exposition is mostly carried out by means of comparatively simple numerical examples. This involves loss of generality and rigor, but it may be hoped that it will make the presentation more accessible.

The existence of the gap which the book attempts to fill has been known to the economic theorists at least since Cournot's work on duopoly, although even now many do not seem to realize its seriousness. There is no adequate solution of the problem of defining "rational economic behavior" on the part of an individual when the very rationality of his actions depends on the probable behavior of other individuals: in the case of oligopoly, other sellers. Cournot and many after him have attempted to sidetrack the difficulty by assuming that every individual has a definite idea as to what others will do under given conditions. Depending on the nature of this expected behavior of other individuals, we have the special, well-known solutions of Bertrand and Cournot, as well as the more general Bowley concept of the "conjectural variation."[3] Thus, the individual's "rational behavior" is determinate *if* the pattern of behavior of "others" can be assumed *a priori* known. But the behavior of "others" cannot be known *a priori* if the "others," too, are to behave rationally! Thus a logical *impasse* is reached.

The way, or at least *a* way,[4] out of this difficulty had been pointed out by one of the authors[5] over a decade ago. It lies in the rejection of a narrowly interpreted maximization principle as synonymous with rational behavior. Not that maximization (of utility[6] or profits) would not be desirable if it were feasible, but

---

[3] More recent investigations have led to the idea of a kinked demand curve. This, however, is a special—though very interesting—case of the conjectural variation.

[4] Cf. reference to von Stackelberg in footnote 17 and some of the work quoted by von Stackelberg, *op. cit.*

[5] J. von Neumann, "Zur Theorie der Gesellschaftsspiele," *Mathematik Annalen* (1928).

[6] A side-issue of considerable interest discussed in the *Theory of Games* is that of measurability of the utility function. The authors need measurability in order to be able to set up tables of the type to be presented later in the case where utility rather than profit is being maximized. The proof of measurability is not given; however, an article giving the proof is promised for the near future and it seems advisable to postpone comment until the proof appears. But it should be emphasized that the validity of the core of the *Theory of Games* is by no means dependent on measurability or transferability of the utilities and those who feel strongly on the subject would perhaps do best to substitute "profits" for "utility" in most of the book in order to avoid judging the achievements of the *Theory of Games* from the point of view of an unessential assumption.

there can be no true maximization when only one of the several factors which decide the outcome (of, say, oligopolistic competition) is controlled by the given individual.

Consider, for instance, a duopolistic situation[7] where each one of the duopolists A and B is *trying* to maximize his profits. A's profits will depend not only on his behavior ("strategy") but on B's strategy as well. Thus, *if* A could control (directly or indirectly) the strategy to be adopted by B, he would select a strategy for himself and one for B so as to maximize his own profits. But he cannot select B's strategy. Therefore, he can in no way make sure that by a proper choice of his own strategy his profits will actually be unconditionally maximized.

It might seem that in such a situation there is no possibility of defining rational behavior on the part of the two duopolists. But it is here that the novel solution proposed by the authors comes in. An example will illustrate this.

Suppose each of the duopolists has three possible strategies at his disposal.[8] Denote the strategies open to duopolist A by A_1, A_2, and A_3, and those open to duopolist B by B_1, B_2, and B_3. The profit made by A, to be denoted by a, obviously is determined by the choices of strategy made by the two duopolists. This dependence will be indicated by subscripts attached to a, with the first subscript referring to A's strategy and the second subscript to that of B; thus, e.g., a_{13} is the profit which will be made by A if he chooses strategy A_1 while B chooses the strategy B_3. Similarly, b_{13} would denote the profits by B under the same circumstances. The possible outcomes of the "duopolistic competition" may be -represented in the two tables shown on p. 508.

Table 1a shows the profits A will make depending on his own and B's choice of strategies. The first row corresponds to the choice of A_1, etc.; columns correspond to B's strategies. Table 1b gives analogous information regarding B's profits.

In order to show how A and B will make decisions concerning strategies we shall avail ourselves of a numerical example given in Tables 2a and 2b.

Now let us watch A's thinking processes as he considers his choice of strategy. First of all, he will notice that by choosing

---

[7] It is assumed that the buyers' behavior may be regarded as known.

[8] Actually the number of strategies could be very high, perhaps infinite.

strategy A_3 he will be sure that his profits cannot go down below 5, while either of the remaining alternatives would expose him to the danger of going down to 3 or even to 1. But there is another

A's Profits

B's choice of strategies / A's choice of strategies	B_1	B_2	B_3
A_1	a_{11}	a_{12}	a_{13}
A_2	a_{21}	a_{22}	a_{23}
A_3	a_{31}	a_{32}	a_{33}

TABLE 1A

B's Profits

B's choice of strategies / A's choice of strategies	B_1	B_2	B_3
A_1	b_{11}	b_{12}	b_{13}
A_2	b_{21}	b_{22}	b_{23}
A_3	b_{31}	b_{32}	b_{33}

TABLE 1B

A's Profits

B's choice of strategies / A's choice of strategies	B_1	B_2	B_3
A_1	2	8	1
A_2	4	3	9
A_3	5	6	7

TABLE 2A

B's Profits

B's choice of strategies / A's choice of strategies	B_1	B_2	B_3
A_1	11	2	20
A_2	9	15	3
A_3	8	7	6

TABLE 2B

reason for his choosing A_3. Suppose there is a danger of a "leak": B might learn what A's decision is before he makes his own. Had A chosen, say, A_1, B—if he knew about this—would obviously choose B_3 so as to maximize his own profits; this would leave A with a profit of only 1. Had A chosen A_2, B would respond by selecting B_2, which again would leave A with a profit below 5 which he could be sure of getting if he chose A_3.

One might perhaps argue whether A's choice of A_3 under such circumstances is the only way of defining rational behavior, but it certainly is *a* way of accomplishing this and, as will be seen later, a very fruitful one. The reader will verify without difficulty that similar reasoning on B's part will make him choose B_1 as the optimal strategy. Thus, the outcome of the duopolistic competition is determinate and can be described as follows: A will choose A_3, B will choose B_1, A's profit will be 5, B's 8.

An interesting property of this solution is that neither duopolist would be inclined to alter his decision, even if he were able to do so, after he found out what the other man's strategy was.

To see this, suppose B has found out that A's decision was in favor of strategy A_3. Looking at the third row of Table 2b, he will immediately see that in no case could he do better than by choosing B_1, which gives him the highest profit consistent with A's choice of A_3. The solution arrived at is of a very stable nature, independent of finding out the other man's strategy.

But the above example is artificial in several important respects. For one thing, it ignores the possibility of a "collusion" or, to use a more neutral term, coalition between A and B. In our solution, yielding the strategy combination (A_3, B_1), the joint profits of the two duopolists amount to 13; they could do better than that by acting together. By agreeing to choose the strategies A_1 and B_3 respectively, they would bring their joint profits up to 21; this sum could then be so divided that both would be better off than under the previous solution.

A major achievement of the *Theory of Games* is the analysis of the conditions and nature of coalition formation. How that is done will be shown below. But, for the moment, let us eliminate the problem of coalitions by considering a case which is somewhat special but nevertheless of great theoretical interest: the case of *constant sum* profits. An example of such a case is given in Tables 3a and 3b.

Table 3a is identical with Table 2a. But figures in Table 3b have been selected in such a manner that the joint profits of the two duopolists always amount to the same (10), no matter what strategies have been chosen. In such a case, A's gain is B's loss and vice versa. Hence, it is intuitively obvious (although the authors take great pains to show it rigorously) that no coalition will be formed.

The solution can again be obtained by reasoning used in the previous case and it will again turn out to be (A_3, B_1) with the respective profits 5 and 5 adding up to 10. What was said above about stability of solution and absence of advantage in finding the opponent[9] out still applies.

There is, however, an element of artificiality in the example chosen that is responsible for the determinateness of the solution. To see this it will suffice to interchange 5 and 6 in Table 3a. The changed situation is portrayed in Table 4 which gives A's profits for different choices of strategies.[10]

A's Profits

B's choice of strategies / A's choice of strategies	B_1	B_2	B_3
A_1	2	8	1
A_2	4	3	9
A_3	5	6	7

TABLE 3A

B's Profits

B's choice of strategies / A's choice of strategies	B_1	B_2	B_3
A_1	8	2	9
A_2	6	7	1
A_3	5	4	3

TABLE 3B

There is no solution now which would possess the kind of stability found in the earlier example. For suppose A again chooses A_3; then if B should find that out, he would obviously "play" B_2 which gives him the highest possible profit consistent with A_3. But then A_3 would no longer be A's optimum strategy: he could do much better by choosing A_1; but if he does so, B's optimum strategy is B_3, not B_2, etc. There is no solution which would not give at least one of the opponents an incentive to change his

---

[9] In this case the interests of the two duopolists are diametrically opposed and the term "opponents" is fully justified; in the previous example it would not have been.

[10] The table for B's profits is omitted because of the constant sum assumption. Clearly, in the constant sum case, B may be regarded as minimizing A's profits since this implies maximization of his own.

decision if he found the other man out! There is no stability.[11]

What is it in the construction of the table that insured determinateness in the case of Table 3 and made it impossible in
Table 4? The answer is that Table 3 has a *saddle point* ("mini-
max") while Table 4 does not.

The saddle point has the following two properties: it is the
highest of all the row minima and at the same time it is lowest
of the column maxima. Thus, in Table 3a the row minima are
respectively 1, 3, and 5, the last one being highest among them
(*Maximum Minimorum*); on the other hand, the column maxima

A's Profits

B's choice of strot-egies A's choice of strotegies	B_1	B_2	B_3
A_1	2	8	1
A_2	4	3	9
A_3	6	5	7

TABLE 4

are respectively 5, 8, and 9 with 5 as the lowest (*Minimum Maximorum*). Hence the combination (A_3, B_1) yields both the highest
row minimum and the lowest column maximum, and, therefore,
constitutes a saddle point. It is easy to see that Table 4 does *not*
possess a saddle point. Here 5 is still the *Maximum Minimorum*,
but the *Minimum Maximorum* is given by 6; the two do not
coincide, and it is the absence of the saddle point that makes for
indeterminateness in Table 4.

Why is the existence of a unique saddle point necessary (as
well as sufficient) to insure the determinateness of the solution?
The answer is inherent in the reasoning used in connection with

---

[11] There is, however, a certain amount of determinateness, at least in the
negative sense, since certain strategy combinations are excluded: e.g. (A_2, B_1);
A would never choose A_2 if he knew B had chosen B_1, and vice versa.

the earlier examples: if A chooses his strategy so as to be protected in case of any leakage of information concerning his decision, he will choose the strategy whose row in the table has the highest minimum value, i.e., the row corresponding to the *Maximum Minimorum*—A_3 in case of Table 4—for then he is sure he will not get less than 5, even if B should learn of this decision. B, following the same principle, will choose the column (i.e., strategy) corresponding to the *Minimum Maximorum*—B_1 in Table 4—thus making sure he will get at least 4, even if the information does leak out.

In this fashion both duopolists are sure of a certain minimum of profit—5 and 4, respectively. But this adds up to only 9. The residual—1—is still to be allocated and this allocation depends on outguessing the opponent. It is this residual that provides an explanation, as well as a measure, of the extent of indeterminacy. Its presence will not surprise economists familiar with this type of phenomenon from the theory of bilateral monopoly. But there are cases when this residual does equal zero, that is, when the *Minimum Maximorum* equals the *Maximum Minimorum,* which (by definition) implies the existence of the saddle point and complete determinacy.

At this stage the authors of the *Theory of Games* had to make a choice. They could have accepted the fact that saddle points do not always exist so that a certain amount of indeterminacy would, in general, be present. They preferred, however, to get rid of the indeterminacy by a highly ingenious modification of the process which leads to the choice of appropriate strategy.

So far our picture of the duopolist making a decision on strategy was that of a man reasoning out which of the several possible courses of action is most favorable *("pure strategy")*. We now change this picture and put in his hands a set of dice which he will throw to determine the strategy to be chosen. Thus, an element of chance is introduced into decision making ("mixed strategy").[12] But not everything is left to chance. The duopolist A must in advance formulate a rule as to what results of the throw—

---

[12] The authors' justification for introducing "mixed strategies" is that leaving one's decision to chance is an effective way of preventing "leakage" of information since the individual making the decision does not himself know which strategy he will choose.

assume that just one die is thrown—would make him choose a given strategy. In order to illustrate this we shall use a table that is somewhat simpler, even if less interesting than those used previously. In this new table (Table 5)[13] each duopolist has only two strategies at his disposal.

A's Profits

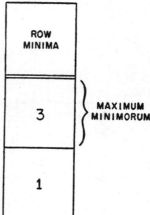

B's choice of strategies / A's choice of strategies	B₁	B₂		ROW MINIMA	
A₁	5	3		3	} MAXIMUM MINIMORUM
A₂	1	5		1	

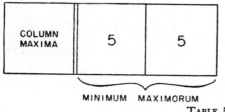

COLUMN MAXIMA	5	5

MINIMUM MAXIMORUM

TABLE 5

An example of a rule A might adopt would be:

If the result of the throw is 1 or 2, choose A₁;
if the result of the throw is 3, 4, 5, or 6, choose A₂.

If this rule were followed, the probability that A will choose A₁ is 1/3, that of his choosing A₂ is 2/3. If a different rule had been decided upon (say, one of choosing A₁ whenever the result of the throw is 1, 2, or 3), the probability of choosing A₁ would have

---

[13] In Table 5 there is no saddle point.

been 1/2. Let us call the fraction giving the probability of choosing A_1 A's *chance coefficient*; in the two examples, A's chance coefficients were 1/3 and 1/2 respectively.[14]

As a special case the value of the chance coefficient might be zero (meaning, that is, definitely choosing strategy A_2) or one

Mathematical Expectations : of A's Profits

B's chance coefficients / A's chance coefficients	0	$\frac{1}{3}$	$\frac{2}{3}$	1	ROW MINIMA
0	5	$3\frac{2}{3}$	$2\frac{1}{3}$	1	1
$\frac{1}{3}$	$4\frac{1}{3}$	$3\frac{2}{3}$	3	$2\frac{1}{3}$	$2\frac{1}{3}$
$\frac{2}{3}$	$3\frac{2}{3}$	$3\frac{2}{3}$	$3\frac{2}{3}$	$3\frac{2}{3}$	$3\frac{2}{3}$ } MAXIMUM MINIMORUM
1	3	$3\frac{2}{3}$	$4\frac{1}{3}$	5	3
COLUMN MAXIMA	5	$3\frac{2}{3}$	$4\frac{1}{3}$	5	

MINIMUM MAXIMORUM

TABLE 6

(meaning that A is definitely choosing strategy A_1); thus in a sense "pure strategies" may be regarded as a special case of mixed strategics. However, this last statement is subject to rather important qualifications which are of a complex nature and will not be given here.

---

[14] Since the probability of choosing A_2 is always equal to one minus that of choosing A_1, specification of the probability of choosing A_1 is sufficient to describe a given rule. However, when the number of available strategies exceeds two, there are several such chance coefficients to be specified.

Now instead of choosing one of the available strategies the duopolist A must choose the optimal (in a sense not yet defined) chance coefficient. How is the choice of the chance coefficient made? The answer lies in constructing a table which differs in two important respects from those used earlier. Table 6 provides an example. Each row in the table now corresponds to a possible value of A's chance coefficient; similarly, columns correspond to possible values of B's chance coefficient. Since the chance coefficient may assume any value between zero and one (including the latter two values), the table is to be regarded merely as a "sample." This is indicated by spaces between rows and between columns.

The numbers entered in the table are the average values (mathematical expectations) corresponding to the choice of chance coefficients indicated by the row and column.[15] (One should mention that Table 6 is only an expository device: the actual procedures used in the book are algebraic and much simpler computationally.)

If we now assume with the authors that each duopolist is trying to maximize the mathematical expectation of his profits (Table 6) rather than the profits themselves (Table 5), it might seem that the original source of difficulty remains if a saddle point does

------

[15] To see this we shall show how, e.g., we have obtained the value in the second row and third column of Table 5 (viz. 3).

We construct an auxiliary table valid only for this particular combination of chance coefficients (A's 1/3, B's 2/3).

This table differs from Table 5 only by the omission of row maxima and column minima and by the insertion of the probabilities of choosing the available strategies corresponding to the second row, third column of Table 6. The computation of the mathematical expectation is indicated in Table 6.

COMPUTATION OF THE MATHEMATICAL EXPECTATION FOR THE 2ND ROW, 3RD COLUMN IN TABLE 6

B's choice of strategies		B_1	B_2
A's choice of strategies	B's chance coefficients / A's chance coefficients	$\frac{2}{3}$	$\frac{1}{3}$
A_1	$\frac{1}{3}$	5	3
A_2	$\frac{2}{3}$	1	5

$$\tfrac{1}{3} \times \tfrac{2}{3} \times 5 + \tfrac{1}{3} \times \tfrac{1}{3} \times 3$$
$$+ \tfrac{2}{3} \times \tfrac{2}{3} \times 1 + \tfrac{2}{3} \times \tfrac{1}{3} \times 5$$
$$= 2\tfrac{7}{9} = 3$$

not happen to exist. But the mixed strategies were not introduced in vain! It is shown (the theorem was originally proved by von Neumann in 1928) that in the table of mathematical expectations (like Table 6) a saddle point *must* exist; the problem is always determinate.[16]

The reader who may have viewed the introduction of dice into the decision-making process with a certain amount of suspicion will probably agree that this is a rather spectacular result. Contrary to the initial impression, it *is* possible to render the problem determinate. But there is a price to be paid: acceptance of mixed strategies, assumption that only the mathematical expectation of profit (not its variance, for instance) matters, seem to be necessary. Many an economist will consider the price too high. Moreover, one might question the need for introducing determinateness into a problem of this nature. Perhaps we should consider as the "solution" the interval of indeterminacy given by the two critical points: the *Minimum Maximorum* and *Maximum Minimorum*.

As indicated earlier in this review, one should not ignore, in general, the possibility of a collusion. This is especially evident when more complex economic situations are considered.

We might, for instance, have a situation where there are two sellers facing two buyers. Here a "coalition" of buyers, as well as one of sellers, may be formed. But it is also conceivable that a buyer would bribe a seller into some sort of coöperation against the other two participants. Several other combinations of this type can easily be found.

When only *two* persons enter the picture, as in the case of duopoly (where the rôle of buyers was ignored), it was seen that a coalition would not be formed if the sum of the two persons' profits remained constant. But when the number of participants is *three* or more, subcoalitions can profitably be formed even if the sum of all participants' profits is constant; in the above four-person example it might pay the sellers to combine against the buyers even if (or, perhaps, especially if) the profits of all four always add to the same amount.

---

[16] In Table 6 the saddle point is in the third row, second column; it is to be stressed that Table 5 has no saddle point.

Hence, the formation of coalitions may be adequately treated without abandoning the highly convenient constant-sum assumption. In fact, when the sum is known to be non-constant, it is possible to introduce (conceptually) an additional fictitious participant who, by definition, loses what all the real participants gain and vice versa. In this fashion a non-constant sum situation involving, say, three persons may be considered as a special case of a constant-sum four-person situation. This is an additional justification for confining most of the discussion (both in the book and in the review) to the constant-sum case despite the fact that economic problems are as a rule of the non-constant sum variety.

We shall now proceed to study the simplest constant-sum case which admits coalition formation, that involving three participants. The technique of analysis presented earlier in the two-person case is no longer adequate. The number of possibilities increases rapidly. Each of the participants may be acting independently; or else, one of the three possible two-person coalitions (A and B *vs.* C, A and C *vs.* B, B and C *vs.* A) may be formed. Were it not for the constant-sum restriction, there would be the additional possibility of the coalition comprising all three participants.

Here again we realize the novel character of the authors' approach to the problem. In most[17] of traditional economic theory the formation—or absence—of specific coalitions is *postulated*. Thus, for instance, we discuss the economics of a cartel without rigorously investigating the necessary and sufficient conditions for its formation. Moreover, we tend to exclude *a priori* such phenomena as collusion between buyers and sellers even if these phenomena are known to occur in practice. The *Theory of Games*, though seemingly more abstract than economic theory known to us, approaches reality much more closely on points of this nature. A complete solution to the problems of economic theory requires

---

[17] In his *Grundlagen einer reinen Kostentheorie* (Vienna, 1932) H. von Stackelberg does point out (p. 89) that "the competitors [duopolists] must somehow unite; they must . . . supplement the economic mechanics, which in this case is inadequate, by economic politics." But no rigorous theory is developed for such situations (although an outline of possible developments is given). This is where the *Theory of Games* has made real progress.

an answer to the question of coalition formation, bribery, collusion, etc. This answer is now provided, even though it is of a somewhat formal nature in the more complex cases; and even though it does not always give sufficient insight into the actual workings of the market.

Let us now return to the case of three participants. Suppose two of them are sellers, one a buyer. Traditional theory would tell us the quantity sold by each seller and the price. But we know that in the process of bargaining one of the sellers might bribe the other one into staying out of the competition. Hence the seller who refrained from market operations would make a profit; on the other hand, the nominal profit made by the man who did make the sale would exceed (by the amount of bribe) the actual gain made.

It is convenient, therefore, to introduce the concept of *gain*: the bribed man's gain is the amount of the bribe, the seller's gain is the profit made on a sale minus the bribe, etc. A given distribution of gains among the participants is called an *imputation*. The imputation is not a number: it is a set of numbers. For instance, if the gains of the participants in a given situation were g_A, g_B, g_C, it is the set of these three g's that is called the imputation. The imputation summarizes the outcome of the economic process. In any given situation there are a great many possible imputations. Therefore, one of the chief objectives of economic theory is that of finding those among all the possible imputations which will actually be observed under rational behavior.

In a situation such as that described (three participants, constant-sum) each man will start by asking himself how much he could get acting independently, even if the worst should happen and the other two formed a coalition against him. He can determine this by treating the situation as a two-person case (the opposing coalition regarded as one person) and finding the relevant *Maximum Minimorum*, or the saddle point, if that point does exist; the saddle point would, of course, exist if "mixed strategies" are used. Next, the participant will consider the possibility of forming a coalition with one of the other two men. Now comes the crucial question: under what conditions might such a coalition be formed?

Before discussing this in detail, let us summarize, in Table 8, all the relevant information.

TABLE 8

I. If A acts alone, he can get	5
If B acts alone, he can get	7
If C acts alone, he can get	10.
II. If A and B form a coalition, they can get	15
If A and C form a coalition, they can get	18
If B and C form a coalition, they can get	20.
III. If A, B, and C act together, they can get	25.

Among the many possible imputations, let us now consider the three given in Table 9.

TABLE 9

	A	B	C
#1	6.5	8.3	10.2
#2	5.0	9.5	10.5
#3	4.0	10.0	11.0

It will be noted that under imputation #1, B and C are each better off than if they had been acting individually: they get respectively 8.3 and 10.2 instead of 7 and 10. Hence, there is an incentive for B and C to form a coalition since without such a coalition imputation #1 would not be possible. But once the coalition is formed, they can do better than under #1; viz., under #2, where each gets more (9.5 and 10.5 instead of 8.3 and 10.2, respectively). In such a case we say that imputation #2 *dominates* imputation #1. It might seem that #3, in turn, dominates #2 since it promises still more to both B and C. But it promises too much: the sum of B's and C's gains under #3 is 21, which is more than their coalition could get (cf. Table 8)! Thus #3 is ruled out as unrealistic and cannot be said to dominate any other imputation.

Domination is an exceptionally interesting type of relation. For one thing, it is not transitive: we may have an imputation i_1 dominating the imputation i_2 and i_2 dominating i_3, without thereby implying that i_1 dominates i_3; in fact, i_1 might be dominated by

i_s.[18] Moreover, it is easy to construct examples of, say, two imputations, neither of which dominates the other one.[19]

To get a geometric picture of this somewhat unusual situation one may turn to Fig. 1, where points on the circle represent
different possible imputations. (The reader must be cautioned
that this is merely a geometrical analogy, though a helpful one.)
Let us now say that point #1 dominates point #2 if #2 is less
than 90° (clockwise) from #1. It is easy to see in Fig. 1 that #1

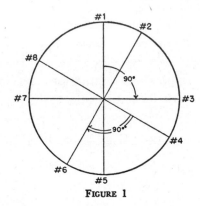

FIGURE 1

dominates #2 and #2 dominates #3, but in spite of that, #1 does
not dominate #3.

This geometrical picture will help define the very fundamental
concept of a *solution*.

Consider the points (imputations) #1, 3, 5, and 7 in Fig. 1.
None of them dominates any other since any two are either *exactly*
or more than 90° apart. But any other point on the circle is
dominated by at least (in this case: exactly) one of them: all
points between #1 and #3 are dominated by #1, etc. There is no
point on the circle which is not dominated by one of the above

---

[18] I.e., domination may be a *cyclic* relation. For instance, consider the following three imputations in the above problem: #1 and #2 as in Table 9,
and #4, where

	A	B	C
#4	6.0	7.0	12.0

Here #2 (as shown before) dominates #1 (for the coalition B, C), #4 dominates #2 (for coalition A, C), but at the same time #1 dominates #4 (for the
coalition A, B): the cycle is completed.

[19] For instance, #2 and #3 in Table 9.

four points. Now we *define* a solution as a set of points (imputations) with two properties: (1) no element of the set dominates any other element of the set, and (2) any point outside the set must be dominated by at least one element within the set.

We have seen that the points #1, 3, 5, 7 do have both of these properties; hence, the four points together form a solution. It is important to see that none of the individual points by itself can be regarded as a solution. In fact, if we tried to leave out any one

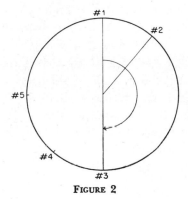

FIGURE 2

of the four points of the set, the remaining three would no longer form a solution; for instance, if #1 were left out, the points between #1 and #3 are not dominated by any of the points #3, 5, 7. This violates the second property required of a solution and the three points by themselves are not a solution. On the other hand, if a fifth point were added to #1, 3, 5, 7, the resulting five element set would not form a solution either; suppose #2 is the fifth point chosen; we note that #2 is dominated by #1 and it also dominates #3. Thus, the first property of a solution is absent.

Contrary to what would be one's intuitive guess, an element of the solution may be dominated by points outside the solution: #1 is dominated by #8, etc.

There can easily be more than one solution. The reader should have no trouble verifying the fact that #2, 4, 6, 8 also form a solution, and it is clear that infinitely many other solutions exist.

Does there always exist at least one solution? So far this question remains unanswered. Among the cases examined by the authors none has been found without at least one solution. But it has not yet been proved that there must always be a solution.

To see the theoretical possibility of a case without a solution we shall redefine slightly our concept of domination (cf. Fig. 2): #1 dominates #2 if the angle between them (measured clockwise) does not exceed 180°.

Hence, in Fig. 2 point #1 dominates #3, but not #4, etc. It can now be shown that in this case *no* solution exists. For suppose there is one; then we may, without loss of generality, choose #1 as one of its points. Clearly, #1 by itself does not constitute a solution, for there are points on the circle (e.g., #4) not dominated by #1; thus the solution must have at least two points. But any other point on the circle either is dominated by #1 (e.g., #2), or it dominates #1 (e.g., #4), or both (#3), which contradicts the first requirement for the elements of a solution. Hence there is no solution consisting of two points either. *A fortiori,* there are no solutions containing more than two points. Hence we have been able to construct an example without a solution. But whether this type of situation could arise in economics (or in games, for that matter) is still an open question.

Now for the economic interpretation of the concept of solution. Within the solution there is no reason for switching from one imputation to another since they do not dominate each other. Moreover, there is never a good reason for going outside a given solution: any imputation outside the solution can be "discredited" by an imputation within the solution which dominates the one outside. But, as we have seen, the reverse is also usually true: imputations within the solution may be dominated by those outside. If we are to assume that the latter consideration is ignored, the given solution acquires an institutional, if not accidental, character. According to the authors, a solution may be equivalent to what one would call the "standards of behavior" which are accepted by a given community.

The multiplicity of solutions can then be considered as corresponding to alternative institutional setups; for a given institutional framework only one solution would be relevant. But even then a large number of possibilities remains since, in general, a solution contains more than one imputation. More indeterminacy yet would be present if we had refrained from introducing mixed strategies.

It would be surprising, therefore, if in their applications von Neumann and Morgenstern should get no more than the classical results without discovering imputations hitherto neglected or ignored. And there are some rather interesting "unorthodox" results pointed out, especially in the last chapter of the book.

In one case, at least, the authors' claim to generality exceeding that of economic theory is not altogether justified in view of the more recent literature. That is the case of what essentially corresponds to bilateral monopoly (p. 564, proposition 61:C). The authors obtain (by using their newly developed methods) a certain interval of indeterminacy for the price; this interval is wider than that indicated by Böhm-Bawerk, because (as the authors themselves point out) of the dropping of Böhm-Bawerk's assumption of a unique price. But this assumption has been abandoned, to give only one example, in the theories of consumer's surplus, with analogous extension of the price interval.

It will stand repeating, however, that the *Theory of Games* does offer a greater generality of approach than could be attained otherwise. The existence of "discriminatory" solutions, discovered by purely analytical methods, is an instance of this. Also, the possibility of accounting for various types of deals and collusions mentioned earlier in connection with the three-person and four-person cases go far beyond results usually obtained by customarily used methods and techniques of economic theory.

The potentialities of von Neumann's and Morgenstern's new approach seem tremendous and may, one hopes, lead to revamping, and enriching in realism, a good deal of economic theory. But to a large extent they are only potentialities: results are still largely a matter of future developments.

The difficulties encountered in handling, even by the more powerful mathematical methods, the situations involving more than three persons are quite formidable. Even the problems of monopoly and monopsony are beyond reach at the present stage of investigation. The same is true of perfect competition, though it may turn out that the latter is not a "legitimate" solution since it excludes the formation of coalitions which may dominate the competitive imputations. A good deal of light has been thrown on the problem of oligopoly, but there again the results are far from the degree of concreteness desired by the economic theorist.

The reviewer therefore regards as somewhat regrettable some of the statements made in the initial chapter of the book attacking (rather indiscriminately) the analytical techniques at present used by the economic theorists. True enough, the deficiencies of economic theory pointed out in the *Theory of Games* are very real; nothing would be more welcome than a model giving the general properties of a system with, say, m sellers and n buyers, so that monopoly, duopoly, or perfect competition could simply be treated as special cases of the general analysis. Unfortunately, however, such a model is not yet in sight. In its absence less satisfactory, but still highly useful, models have been and no doubt will continue to be used by economic theorists. One can hardly afford to ignore the social need for the results of economic theory even if the best is rather crude. The fact that the theory of economic fluctuations has been studied as much as it has is not a proof of "how much the attendant difficulties have been underestimated" (p. 5). Rather it shows that economics cannot afford the luxury of developing in the theoretically most "logical" manner when the need for the results is as strong as it happens to be in the case of the ups and downs of the employment level!

Nor is it quite certain, though of course conceivable, that, when a rigorous theory developed along the lines suggested by von Neumann and Morgenstern is available, the results obtained in the important problems will be sufficiently remote from those obtained with the help of the current (admittedly imperfect) tools to justify some of the harsher accusations to be found in the opening chapter of the book. It must not be forgotten, for instance, that, while theoretical derivation of coalitions to be formed is of great value, we do have empirical knowledge which can be used as a substitute (again imperfect) for theory. For example, cartel formation may be so clearly "in the cards" in a given situation that the economic theorist will simply include it as one of his assumptions while von Neumann and Morgenstern would (at least in principle) be able to *prove* the formation of the cartel without making it an additional (and logically unnecessary) assumption.

The authors criticize applications of the mathematical methods to economics in a way which might almost, in spite of protests to the contrary, mislead some readers into thinking that von Neumann and Morgenstern are not aware of the amount of recent progress in many fields of economic theory due largely to the use of mathematical tools. They also seem to ignore the fact that economics developed in literary form is, implicitly, based on the mathematical techniques which the authors criticize. (Thus it is not the methods of mathematical economics they are really questioning, but rather those elements of economic theory which literary and mathematical economics have in common.) While it is true that even mathematical treatment is not always sufficiently rigorous, it is as a rule more so than the corresponding literary form, even though the latter is not infrequently more realistic in important respects.

There is little doubt in the reviewer's mind that nothing could have been further from the authors' intentions than to give aid and comfort to the opponents of rigorous thinking in economics or to increase their complacency. Yet such may be the effect of some of the vague criticisms contained in the first chapter; they hardly seem worthy of the constructive achievements of the rest of the book.

Economists will probably be surprised to find so few references to more recent economic writings. One might almost form the impression that economics is synonymous with Böhm-Bawerk plus Pareto. Neither the nineteenth century pioneers (such as Cournot) nor the writers of the last few decades (Chamberlin, Joan Robinson, Frisch, Stackelberg) are even alluded to. But, perhaps, the authors are entitled to claim exemption from the task of relating their work to that of their predecessors by virtue of the tremendous amount of constructive effort they put into their opus. One cannot but admire the audacity of vision, the perseverance in details, and the depth of thought displayed on almost every page of the book.

The exposition is remarkably lucid and fascinating, no matter how involved the argument happens to be. The authors made an effort to avoid the assumption that the reader is familiar with any but the more elementary parts of mathematics; more refined tools are forged "on the spot" whenever needed.

One should also mention, though this transcends the scope of the review, that in the realm of strategic games proper (chess, poker) the results obtained are more specific than some of the economic applications. Those interested in the nature of determinacy of chess, in the theory of "bluffing" in poker, or in the proper strategy for Sherlock Holmes in his famous encounter with Professor Moriarty, will enjoy reading the sections of the book which have no direct bearing on economics. The reader's views on optimum military or diplomatic strategies are also likely to be affected.

Thus, the reading of the book is a treat as well as a stage in one's intellectual development. The great majority of economists should be able to go through the book even if the going is slow at times; it is well worth the effort. The appearance of a book of the caliber of the *Theory of Games* is indeed a rare event.

BIBLIOGRAPHY OF ARTICLES ON PRICE THEORY

Price theory is the theory of the determination of relative prices and of their effects on the allocation and combination of productive services and the output and distribution of goods. Economists need not be reminded that price theory is pervasive: that price enters into an enormous variety of economic phenomena and that price theory enters into every branch of economic analysis. Nor need they be pressed to admit that the literature of price behavior and its analysis receives stupendous literary recognition, not merely in the writings of professional economists but also in the pages of almost every trade journal. The difficulties raised for a bibliography of price theory by this popularity of prices is somewhat reduced by the fact that parts of the literature are referred to in previous volumes in the Blakiston Series of Republished Articles on Economics, particularly in *Readings in the Theory of Income Distribution*, and *Readings in Business Cycle Theory*, and it is further reduced by the decision of the editors to exclude from this volume certain closely related fields, such as welfare economics. Even with these exclusions, however, the literature is enormous.

Since a reasonably comprehensive bibliography was impossible simply on grounds of length, several restrictions were imposed on the following compilation. First, the bibliography was restricted to periodical literature. Few books or *Festschriften* on economics fail to touch on some facet of price theory, and it would be difficult and invidious to include only a few of these volumes. Second, the bibliography was restricted to the general professional journals. Many important articles have appeared in the more specialized journals, such as those in marketing, taxation, and public utilities, but it would be difficult to draw any line as to where they become too specialized for inclusion in our list, and even the inclusion of a selected list would (because of space limitations) force exclusion of items now included. Third, the foreign language periodicals are excluded because of their inaccessibility to many economists. As some token of the importance of this literature, however, short lists of important articles have been added. The German list was compiled by Professor Oskar Morgenstern, the Italian list by Professor Giorgio Fuà, the Swedish list by Professor Eric Lundberg, and the French list by Professor François Perroux. Finally, the bibliography is restricted to the period 1920 through 1949, with the first of these three decades covered more selectively than the later two.

ROSE FRIEDMAN

OUTLINE OF THE BIBLIOGRAPHY

ENGLISH ARTICLES

I. UTILITY AND DEMAND

ADARKAR, B., Interpersonal comparisons of utility, *Indian Journal of Economics,* XX (1939–40), 513–30.

ALLEN, R. G. D., The nature of indifference curves, *Review of Economic Studies,* I (1933–4), 110–21.

———, A reconsideration of the theory of value, *Economica* (NS), I (1934), 196–219.

———, A comparison between different definitions of complementary and competitive goods, *Econometrica,* II (1934), 168–75.

———, A critical examination of Professor Pigou's method of deriving demand elasticity, *Econometrica,* II (1934), 249–57.

———, Professor Slutsky's theory of consumers' choice, *Review of Economic Studies,* III (1935–6), 120–9.

ANGELL, J. W., Consumers' demand, *Quarterly Journal of Economics,* XXXIX (1924–5), 584–611.

ARMSTRONG, W. E., Determinateness of the utility function, *Economic Journal,* XLIX (1939), 453–67.

———, Uncertainty and the utility function, *Economic Journal,* LVIII (1948), 1–10.

BERNARDELLI, H., The end of the marginal utility theory, *Economica* (NS), V (1938), 192–212.

BISHOP, R. L., Consumer's surplus and cardinal utility, *Quarterly Journal of Economics,* LVII (1942–3), 421–49.

———, Professor Knight and the theory of demand, *Journal of Political Economy,* LIV (1946), 141–69.
    Comment by F. H. KNIGHT, *ibid.,* 170–6.

BLACK, R. P., Trinity College, Dublin and the theory of value, 1832–1863, *Economica* (NS), XII (1945), 140–8.

BOULDING, K. E., Quantitative Economics, *Canadian Journal of Economics and Political Science,* V (1939), 521–8.

————, The concept of economic surplus, *American Economic Review*, XXXV (1945), 851–69.

BRAY, F. S., An accountant's comments on the subjective theory of value and accounting cost, *Economica* (NS), XIII (1946), 295–9.

BROSTER, E. J., A simple method of deriving demand curves, *Journal of the Royal Statistical Society*, C (1937), 625–41.

————, Elasticities of demand for tea and price fixing policy, *Review of Economic Studies*, VI (1938–9), 165–76.

BROWN, E. H. P., Demand functions and utility functions: a critical examination of their meaning, *Econometrica*, II (1934), 51–8.

BROWN, T. H., The law of demand and the theory of probability, *Journal of the American Statistical Association*, XX (1925), 223–30.

BURK (BERGSON), A., Real income, expenditure proportionality, and Frisch's "new methods of measuring marginal utility," *Review of Economic Studies*, IV (1936–7), 33–52.

CANNAN, E., "Total utility" and "consumer's surplus," *Economica* (OS), IV (1924), 21–6.

Reply by D. H. MACGREGOR, *ibid.*, 131–4.

A note by A. L. BOWLEY, *ibid.*, 135–9.

CASSELS, J. M., A critical consideration of Professor Pigou's method for deriving demand curves, *Economic Journal*, XLIII (1933), 575–86.

Note by PIGOU, *ibid.*, 586–7.

CLARK, J. M., Realism and relevance in the theory of demand, *Journal of Political Economy*, LIV (1946), 347–53.

CLAWSON, M., Demand interrelations for selected agricultural products, *Quarterly Journal of Economics*, LVII (1942–3), 265–302.

COPPOCK, J. D., Indifference curve analysis applied to the food stamp plan, *American Economic Review*, XXXV (1945), 99–110.

COURT, L. M., Entrepreneurial and consumer demand theories for commodity spectra, *Econometrica*, IX (1941), 135–62, 241–97.

DANIELS, G. W., The objective basis of economics, *Manchester School*, III (1932), 1–14.

FERGER, W. F., The static and the dynamic in statistical demand curves, *Quarterly Journal of Economics*, XLVII (1932–3), 36–62.

————, Notes on Pigou's method of deriving demand curves, *Economic Journal*, XLII (1932), 17–26.

FRIEDMAN, M., Professor Pigou's method for measuring elasticities of demand from budgetary data, *Quarterly Journal of Economics*, L (1935–6), 151–63.

Notes by PIGOU, *ibid.*, 532.

FRIEDMAN, *ibid.*, 532–3.

GEORGESCU-ROEGEN, *ibid.*, 533–9.

————, Mr. Broster on demand curves, *Journal of the Royal Statistical Society*, CI (1938), 450–4.

*————, and SAVAGE, L. J., The utility analysis of choices involving risk, *Journal of Political Economy*, LVI (1948), 279–304.

————, The Marshallian demand curve, *Journal of Political Economy*, LVII (1949), 463–95.

GEORGESCU-ROEGEN, N., Note on a proposition of Pareto, *Quarterly Journal of Economics*, XLIX (1934–5), 706–14.

* Reprinted in the present volume.

GEORGESCU-ROEGEN, N., The pure theory of consumer's behavior, *Quarterly Journal of Economics*, L (1935–6), 545–93.

GILBOY, E. W., Demand curves in theory and practice, *Quarterly Journal of Economics*, XLIV (1929–30), 601–20.

——, The Leontieff and Schultz methods of deriving "demand" curves, *Quarterly Journal of Economics*, XLV (1930–1), 218–61.

——, Studies in demand: milk and butter, *Quarterly Journal of Economics*, XLVI (1931–2), 671–97.

——, Demand curves by personal estimate, *Quarterly Journal of Economics*, XLVI (1931–2), 376–84.

——, Methods of measuring demand and consumption, *Review of Economics and Statistics*, XXI (1939), 69–74.

GIRSHICK, M. A., and HAAVELMO, T., Statistical analysis of the demand for food—examples of simultaneous estimation of structural equations, *Econometrica*, XV (1947), 79–110.

HAAVELMO, T., Family expenditures and the marginal propensity to consume, *Econometrica*, XV (1947), 335–41.

HENDERSON, A. M., Consumer's surplus and the compensating variation, *Review of Economic Studies*, VIII (1940–1), 117–21.

HICKS, J. R., A reconsideration of the theory of value, *Economica* (NS), I (1934), 52–76.

——, The rehabilitation of consumers' surplus, *Review of Economic Studies*, VIII (1940–1), 108–16.

——, Consumers' surplus and index numbers, *Review of Economic Studies*, IX–X (1941–3), 126–37.

——, The four consumer's surpluses, *Review of Economic Studies*, XI–XII (1943–5), 31–41.

——, The generalized theory of consumer's surplus, *Review of Economic Studies*, XIII (1945–6), 68–74.

HOBSON, J. A., Neo-classical economics in Britain, *Political Science Quarterly*, XL (1925), 337–83.

HOLT, C. C., and SAMUELSON, P. A., The graphic depiction of elasticity of demand, *Journal of Political Economy*, LIV (1946), 354–7.

HOTELLING, H., Demand functions with limited budgets, *Econometrica*, III (1935), 66–78.

KNIGHT, F. H., Realism and relevance in the theory of demand, *Journal of Political Economy*, LII (1944), 289–318.

KOZLIK, A., Conditions for demand curves whose curves of total revenue, consumer's surplus, total benefit, and compromise benefit are convex, *Econometrica*, VIII (1940), 263–71.

——, Note on consumer's surplus, *Journal of Political Economy*, XLIX (1941), 754–62.

——, The use of per capita figures for demand curves, *Journal of the American Statistical Association*, XXXVI (1941), 417–22.

LANGE, O., The determinateness of the utility function, *Review of Economic Studies*, I (1933–4), 218–25.

——, Theoretical derivations of elasticities of demand and supply: the direct method, *Econometrica*, X (1942), 193–214.

LEONTIEFF, W. W., Pitfalls in the construction of demand and supply curves: a reply, *Quarterly Journal of Economics*, XLVIII (1933–4), 355–61.

LERNER, A. P., The diagrammatical representation of elasticity of demand, *Review of Economic Studies*, I (1933–4), 39–44.

LESER, C. E. V., Family budget data and price elasticities of demand, *Review of Economic Studies*, IX–X (1941–3), 40–56.

LEWIS, E. E., Note on inter-commodity relationships in demand, *Review of Economic Studies*, V (1937–8), 53–9.

———, The relation of commodities in demand, *American Economic Review*, XXVIII (1938), 488–96.

———, Intercommodity relationships in stable demand, *Econometrica*, VI (1938), 130–42.

LITTLE, I. M. D., A reformulation of the theory of consumer's behavior, *Oxford Economic Papers* (NS), I (1949), 90–9.

McGOUN, A. F., Higher and lower desires, *Quarterly Journal of Economics*, XXXVII (1922–3), 291–301.

MAKOWER, H., Elasticity of demand and stabilization, *Review of Economic Studies*, IV (1936–7), 25–32.

MARSCHAK, J., Demand elasticities reviewed, *Econometrica*, XI (1943), 25–34.

METZLER, L. A., The assumptions implied in least squares demand techniques, *Review of Economics and Statistics*, XXII (1940), 138–49.

MIGHELL, R. L., and ALLEN, R. H., Demand schedules—"normal" and instantaneous, *Journal of Farm Economics*, XXI (1939), 555–69.

MILLER, H. E., Utility curves, total utility, and consumer's surplus, *Quarterly Journal of Economics*, XLI (1927), 292–316.

MOORE, H. L., Elasticity of demand and flexibility of prices, *Journal of the American Statistical Association*, XVIII (1922), 8–19.

———, Partial elasticity of demand, *Quarterly Journal of Economics*, XL (1925–6), 393–401.

MORGENSTERN, O., Demand theory reconsidered, *Quarterly Journal of Economics*, LXII (1947–8), 165–201.

NICHOL, A. J., Measures of average elasticity of demand, *Journal of Political Economy*, XXXIX (1931), 249–55.
A further note, *ibid.*, 658–61.

———, Probability analysis in the theory of demand, net revenue and price, *Journal of Political Economy*, XLIX (1941), 637–61.

NORRIS, R. T., The analysis of demand, *Quarterly Journal of Economics*, LIV (1939–40), 131–42.

PANKRAZ, O., Sur la loi de la demande, *Econometrica*, IV (1936), 153–6.

PARIMAL, R., On elasticity of demand, *Indian Journal of Economics*, XX (1939–40), 151–60.

PIGOU, A. C., The statistical derivation of demand curves, *Economic Journal*, XL (1930), 384–400.

PRESCOTT, R. B., Law of growth in forecasting demand, *Journal of the American Statistical Association*, XVIII (1922), 471–9.

PREST, A. R., Some experiments in demand analysis, *Review of Economics and Statistics*, XXXI (1949), 33–49.

REILLY, E. E., The use of the elastic concept in economic theory (with special reference to some economic effects of a commodity tax), *Canadian Journal of Economics and Political Science*, VI (1940), 39–55.

RICCI, U., The psychological foundation of the law of demand, *Journal of Political Economy*, XL (1932), 145–85.

———, Pareto and pure economics, *Review of Economic Studies*, I (1933–4), 3–21.

———, On the demand for rival (or substitute) commodities, *Econometrica*, I (1933), 181–9.

RICCI, U., The modification of the utility curve for money in the case of indivisible goods and goods of increasing utility, *Economica* (NS), II (1935), 168–97.

ROBBINS, L. C., Interpersonal comparisons of utility: a comment, *Economic Journal*, XLVIII (1938), 635–41.

ROBERTSON, R. M., Mathematical economics before Cournot, *Journal of Political Economy*, LVII (1949), 523–36.

ROOS, C. F., Theoretical studies of demand, *Econometrica*, II (1934), 73–90.

———, and VON SZELISKI, V., The concept of demand and price elasticity—the dynamics of automobile demand, *Journal of the American Statistical Association*, XXXIV (1939), 652–64.

ROY, R., La hiérarchie des besoins et la notion de groupes dans l'économie de choix, *Econometrica*, XI (1943), 13–24.

SAMUELSON, P. A., A note on measurement of utility, *Review of Economic Studies*, IV (1936–7), 155–61.

———, A note on the pure theory of consumer's behavior, *Economica* (NS), V (1938), 61–71.

An addendum, *ibid.*, 353–4.

———, The empirical implications of utility analysis, *Econometrica*, VI (1938), 344–56.

———, The numerical representation of ordered classifications and the concept of utility, *Review of Economic Studies*, VI (1938–9), 65–70.

———, Consumption theory in terms of revealed preference, *Economica* (NS), XV (1948), 243–53.

SCHULTZ, H., The statistical law of demand as illustrated by the demand for sugar, *Journal of Political Economy*, XXXIII (1925), 481–503; 577–637.

———, The shifting demand for selected agricultural commodities, 1875–1929, *Journal of Farm Economics*, XIV (1932), 201–27.

———, Interrelations of demand, *Journal of Political Economy*, XLI (1933), 468–512.

———, A comparison of elasticities of demand obtained by different methods, *Econometrica*, I (1933), 274–302.

———, Interrelations of demand, price and income, *Journal of Political Economy*, XLIII (1935), 433–81.

SHAUL, J. R. H., The demand curve for beef and veal in Great Britain, *Economic Journal*, XLV (1935), 493–500.

SHEPHERD, G., Vertical and horizontal shifts in demand curves, *Journal of Farm Economics*, XV (1933), 723–9.

SMITH, H., A note on time elasticity of demand, *Economica* (NS), IV (1937), 309–22.

STAEHLE, H., Annual survey of statistical information: family budgets, *Econometrica*, II (1934), 349–62.

STIGLER, G. J., The limitations of statistical demand curves, *Journal of the American Statistical Association*, XXXIV (1939), 469–81.

———, Notes on the history of the Giffen paradox, *Journal of Political Economy*, LV (1947), 152–6.

Comment by A. R. PREST, *ibid.*, LVI (1948), 58–60.

Reply by STIGLER, *ibid.*, 61–2.

STONE, R., The analysis of market demand, *Journal of the Royal Statistical Society*, CVIII (1945), 286–382.

SWEEZY, A. R., The interpretation of subjective value theory in the writings of the Austrian economists, *Review of Economic Studies*, I (1933–4), 176–85.

SZATROWSKI, Z., Time series correlated with the beef-pork consumption ratio, *Econometrica*, XIII (1945), 60–78.

SZELISKI, V. S., and PARADISO, L. I., Demand for boots and shoes as affected by price levels and national income, *Econometrica*, IV (1936), 338–55.

THARAKAN, K. J. M., The theory of consumer's surplus, a defense, *Indian Journal of Economics*, XIX (1938–9), 413–20.

Reply by M. H. GOPAL, *ibid.*, XX, 161–72.

Rejoinder by THARAKAN, *ibid.*, XXI, 307–19.

THOMPSON, C. D., A special type of utility function, *Indian Journal of Economics*, XIII (1932–3), 133–48.

TINTNER, G., The theoretical derivation of dynamic demand curves, *Econometrica*, VI (1938), 375–80.

———, The maximization of utility over time, *Econometrica*, VI (1938), 154–8.

———, Elasticities of expenditure in the dynamic theory of demand, *Econometrica*, VII (1939), 266–70.

———, A contribution to the non-static theory of choice, *Quarterly Journal of Economics*, LVI (1941–2), 274–306.

———, The theory of choice under subjective risk and uncertainty, *Econometrica*, IX (1941), 298–304.

VICKREY, W., Measuring marginal utility by reaction to risk, *Econometrica*, XIII (1945), 319–33.

VINER, J., The utility concept in value theory and its critics, *Journal of Political Economy*, XXXIII (1925), 369–87; 638–59.

WALD, A., The approximate determination of indifference surfaces by means of Engel curves, *Econometrica*, VIII (1940), 144–75.

WAUGH, A. E., Elasticity of demand, from Budget studies, *Quarterly Journal of Economics*, XLVII (1932–3), 134–7.

Note by PIGOU, *ibid.*, 342.

WEINTRAUB, S., The foundations of the demand curve, *American Economic Review*, XXXII (1942), 538–52.

WHITMAN, R. H., The problem of statistical demand techniques for producer's goods: an application to steel, *Journal of Political Economy*, XLII (1934), 577–94.

———, The statistical law of demand for a producer's good as illustrated by the demand for steel, *Econometrica*, IV (1936), 138–52.

WILLIAMS, F. M., The measurement of the demand for food, *Journal of the American Statistical Association*, XXIV (1929), 288–95.

WILSON, E. B., Generalization of Pareto's demand theorem, *Quarterly Journal of Economics*, XLIX (1934–5), 715–7.

———, On notation for utility theory, *Quarterly Journal of Economics*, LVIII (1943–4), 647–50.

———, Pareto on Marshall's demand curve, *Quarterly Journal of Economics*, LVIII (1943–4), 141–5.

———, Consumption in fixed proportions, *Quarterly Journal of Economics*, LIX (1944–5), 635–9.

———, Hicks on perfect substitutes, *Quarterly Journal of Economics*, LIX (1944–5), 134–40.

———, Notes on utility theory and demand equations, *Quarterly Journal of Economics*, LX (1945–6), 453–60.

WISNIEWSKI, J., Demand in relation to the income curve, *Econometrica*, III (1935), 411–5.

WOLD, H., A synthesis of pure demand analysis, *Skandinavisk Aktuarietidskrift*, XXVI (1943), 85–118; 220–63: *ibid.*, XXVII (1944), 69–120.

WOLFE, A. B., Three dimensional diagrams in illustration of consumers' demand and of interest rates and saver's surpluses, *American Economic Review*, XV (1925), 228–38.

Further discussion by J. M. CLARK, *ibid.*, 717–9.

DE WOLFF, P., The demand for passenger cars in the United States, *Econometrica*, VI (1938), 113–29.

Reply by R. SOLO, *ibid.*, VII (1939), 271–6.

Rejoinder by DE WOLFF, *ibid.*, 277–82.

———, Income elasticity of demand, *Economic Journal*, LI (1941), 140–5.

WOOLLEY, H. B., The general elasticity of demand, *Econometrica*, XV (1947), 226–30.

*WORKING, E. J., What do statistical "demand curves" show?, *Quarterly Journal of Economics*, XLI (1926–7), 212–35.

———, Indications of changes in the demand for agricultural products, *Journal of Farm Economics*, XIV (1932), 239–56.

WORKING, H., The statistical determination of demand curves, *Quarterly Journal of Economics*, XXXIX (1924–5), 503–39.

ZEUTHEN, F., On the determinateness of the utility function, *Review of Economic Studies*, IV (1936–7), 236–9.

ZIMMERMAN, C. C., Ernst Engel's law of expenditures for food, *Quarterly Journal of Economics*, XLVII (1932–3), 78–101.

II. COSTS AND PRICING

ABRAMOVITZ, M., Monopolistic selling in a changing economy, *Quarterly Journal of Economics*, LII (1937–8), 191–214.

ABRAMSON, A. G., Cost of production and normal supply price, *American Economic Review*, XXVII (1937), 468–78.

Note by A. C. NEAL, *ibid.*, XXIX (1939), 108–10.

Reply by ABRAMSON, *ibid.*, 110–1.

———, Price policies, *Southern Economic Journal*, XII (1945), 39–47.

ACKLEY, G., Spatial competition in a discontinuous market, *Quarterly Journal of Economics*, LVI (1941–2), 212–30.

ADELMAN, M. A., The A & P case: a study in applied economic theory, *Quarterly Journal of Economics*, LXIII (1949), 238–57.

———, The large firm and its suppliers, *Review of Economics and Statistics*, XXXI (1949), 113–8.

ALLEN, R. G. D., Decreasing costs: a mathematical note, *Economic Journal*, XLII (1932), 323–6.

———, The foundations of a mathematical theory of exchange, *Economica* (OS), XII (1932), 197–226.

———, A comparison between different definitions of complementary and competitive goods, *Econometrica*, II (1934), 168–75.

———, The mathematical foundations of economic theory, *Quarterly Journal of Economics*, LXIII (1949). 111–27.

ALSBERG, C. L., Economic aspects of adulteration and imitation, *Quarterly Journal of Economics*, XLVI (1931–2), 1–33.

ALT, R. M., Statistical measurement of price flexibility, *Quarterly Journal of Economics*, LVI (1941–2), 497–502.

———, The internal organization of the firm and price formation: an illustrative case, *Quarterly Journal of Economics*, LXIII (1949), 92–110.

---

* Reprinted in the present volume.

APEL, H., Marginal cost constancy and its implications, *American Economic Review*, XXXVIII (1948), 870–85.

ARNOLD, S., Forward shifting of a payroll tax under monopolistic competition, *Quarterly Journal of Economics*, LXI (1946–7), 267–84.

ASHTON, H., Railroad costs in relation to the volume of traffic, *American Economic Review*, XXX (1940), 324–32.

BACKMAN, J., The causes of price inflexibility, *Quarterly Journal of Economics*, LIV (1939–40), 474–89.

——, Price inflexibility and changes in production, *American Economic Review*, XXIX (1939), 480–6.

——, Price inflexibility—war and postwar, *Journal of Political Economy*, LVI (1948), 428–37.

BAIN, J. S., Market classifications in modern price theory, *Quarterly Journal of Economics*, LVI (1942), 560–74.

——, Output quotas in imperfect cartels, *Quarterly Journal of Economics*, LXII (1947–8), 617–22.

——, A note on pricing in monopoly and oligopoly, *American Economic Review*, XXXIX (1949), 448–64.

BALLAINE, W. C., How government purchasing procedures strengthen monopoly elements, *Journal of Political Economy*, LI (1943), 538–46.

BARKIN, S., The regional significance of the integration movement in the southern textile industry, *Southern Economic Journal*, XV (1948), 395–411.

BAUER, P. T., A note on monopoly, *Economica* (NS), VIII (1941), 194–202.

——, Rubber production costs during the great depression, *Economic Journal*, LIII (1943), 361–9.

——, Future competition between natural and synthetic rubber, *Manchester School*, XIV (1945–6), 40–64.

——, Notes on cost, *Economica* (NS), XII (1945), 90–100.

BEACH, E. F., Triffin's classification of market positions, *Canadian Journal of Economics and Political Science*, IX (1943), 69–74.

BELL, S., Size of plants in its relation to price control and price flexibility, *American Economic Review*, XXVI (1936, Proceedings), 46–61.
Discussions by F. C. MILLS, *ibid.*, 62–4; G. DICKINSON, *ibid.*, 64–6; and H. L. McCRACKEN, *ibid.*, 66–7.

BERGLUND, A., The United States Steel Corporation and price stabilization, *Quarterly Journal of Economics*, XXXVIII (1923–4), 1–30.

——, The United States Steel Corporation and industrial stabilization, *Quarterly Journal of Economics*, XXXVIII (1923–4), 607–30.

BISHOP, R. L., Cost discontinuities, declining costs and marginal analysis, *American Economic Review*, XXXVIII (1948), 607–17.

BITTERMAN, H. J., Elasticity of supply, *American Economic Review*, XXIV (1934), 417–29.

BLACK, D., On the rationale of group decision making, *Journal of Political Economy*, LVI (1948), 23–34.

BLADEN, V. W., The role of trade associations in the determination of prices, *Canadian Journal of Economics and Political Science*, IV (1938), 223–7.

BLAIR, J. M., The relation between size and efficiency of business, *Review of Economics and Statistics*, XXIV (1942), 125–35.

——, Technology and size, *American Economic Review*, XXXVIII (1948, Proceedings), 121–52.

BOBER, M. M., Price and production policies, *American Economic Review*, XXXII (1942, Proceedings), 23–52.

BOSLAND, C. C., Forecasting the price of wheat, *Journal of the American Statistical Association*, XXI (1926), 149–61.

BOULDING, K. E., Equilibrium and wealth: a word of encouragement to economists, *Canadian Journal of Economics and Political Science*, V (1939), 1–18.

——, The theory of the firm in the last ten years, *American Economic Review*, XXXII (1942), 791–802.

*——, A liquidity preference theory of market prices, *Economica* (NS), XI (1944), 55–63.

——, In defense of monopoly, *Quarterly Journal of Economics*, LIX (1944–5), 524–42.

——, Samuelson's foundations: the role of mathematics in economics, *Journal of Political Economy*, LVI (1948), 187–99.

——, Professor Tarshis and the state of economics, *American Economic Review*, XXXVIII (1948), 92–102.

BRAITHWAITE, D., The economic effects of advertisement, *Economic Journal*, XXXVIII (1928), 16–37.

BREMS, H., The interdependence of quality variations, selling effort and price, *Quarterly Journal of Economics*, LXII (1947–8), 418–40.

BRESSLER, R. G., JR., Research determination of economies of scale, *Journal of Farm Economics*, XXVII (1945), 526–39.

BRONFENBRENNER, M., Applications of the discontinuous oligopoly demand curve, *Journal of Political Economy*, XLVIII (1940), 420–7.

——, Price control under imperfect competition, *American Economic Review*, XXXVII (1947), 107–20.

BROSTER, E. J., Variability of railway operating costs, *Economic Journal*, XLVIII (1938), 674–84.

BROWN, E. C., Price competition in the commercial printing industry of Chicago, *Journal of Political Economy*, XXXVIII (1930), 194–212.

BUCHANAN, N. S., A reconsideration of the cobweb theorem, *Journal of Political Economy*, XLVII (1939), 67–81.

BURNS, A. R., The organization of industry and the theory of prices, *Journal of Political Economy*, XLV (1937), 662–80.

——, Bain's analysis of the Pacific coast petroleum industry, *Journal of Political Economy*, LVI (1948), 35–53.

CARVER, T. N., The incidence of costs, *Economic Journal*, XXXIV (1924), 576–88.

CASSADY, R., JR., Maintenance of resale prices by manufacturers, *Quarterly Journal of Economics*, LIII (1938–9), 454–64.

CASSELS, J. M., The nature of statistical supply curves, *Journal of Farm Economics*, XV (1933), 378–87.

——, Excess capacity and monopolistic competition, *Quarterly Journal of Economics*, LI (1936–7), 426–43.

——, Monopolistic competition and economic realism, *Canadian Journal of Economics and Political Science*, III (1937), 376–93.

CHAMBERLIN, E. H., Duopoly: value where sellers are few, *Quarterly Journal of Economics*, XLIV (1929–30), 63–100.

——, Monopolistic or imperfect competition?, *Quarterly Journal of Economics*, LI (1936–7), 557–80.

---

* Reprinted in the present volume.

——, Proportionality, divisibility and economies of scale, *Quarterly Journal of Economics*, LVII (1947–8), 229–62.

Comment by A. N. McCloud, *ibid.*, LXIII (1948–9), 128–31; by F. H. Hahn, *ibid.*, 131–7.

Reply by Chamberlin, *ibid.*, 137–43.

——, An experimental imperfect market, *Journal of Political Economy*, LVI (1948), 95–108.

——, Some final comments, *Review of Economics and Statistics*, XXXI (1949), 123–9.

Chenery, H. B., Engineering production functions, *Quarterly Journal of Economics*, LXIII (1948–9), 507–31.

Ciriacy-Wantrup, S., Economics of joint costs in agriculture, *Journal of Farm Economics*, XXIII (1941), 771–818.

*Clapham, J. H., Empty economic boxes, *Economic Journal*, XXXII (1922), 305–14.

Reply by A. C. Pigou, *ibid.*, 458–65.

Rejoinder by Clapham, *ibid.*, 560–3.

Clark, F. E., An appraisal of certain criticisms of advertising, *American Economic Review*, XV (1925, Proceedings), 5–13.

Clark, J. M., Overhead costs in modern industry, *Journal of Political Economy*, XXXI (1923), 47–64; 209–42; 606–36.

——, Basing-point methods of price quoting, *Canadian Journal of Economics and Political Science*, IV (1938), 477–89.

——, Toward a concept of workable competition, *American Economic Review*, XXX (1940), 241–56.

——, Imperfect competition theory and basing-point problems, *American Economic Review*, XXXIII (1943), 283–300.

Reply by V. E. Mund, *ibid.*, 612–6.

Rejoinder by Clark, *ibid.*, 616–9.

——, Machlup on the basing-point system, *Quarterly Journal of Economics*, LXIII (1948–9), 315–21.

——, The law and economics of basing points: appraisal and proposals, *American Economic Review*, XXXIX (1949), 430–47.

Clarke, R. W. B., Production, output per head, prices and costs in the iron and steel industry, 1924–1931, *Journal of the Royal Statistical Society*, XCVI (1933), 637–50.

Clemens, E. W., Price discrimination in decreasing cost industries, *American Economic Review*, XXXI (1941), 794–802.

Coase, R. H., The problem of duopoly reconsidered, *Review of Economic Studies*, II (1934–5), 137–43.

*——, The nature of the firm, *Economica* (NS), IV (1937), 386–405.

——, Some notes on monopoly price, *Review of Economic Studies*, V (1937–8), 17–31.

——, The marginal cost controversy, *Economica* (NS), XIII (1946), 169–82.

——, Monopoly pricing with interrelated costs and demands, *Economica* (NS), XIII (1946), 278–94.

——, The economics of uniform pricing systems, *Manchester School*, XV (1947), 138–56.

Colbert, M. R., Monopoly prices under joint costs fixed proportions, *Journal of Political Economy*, XLIX (1941), 103–10.

———————

* Reprinted in the present volume.

COMER, G. P., The outlook for effective competition, *American Economic Review*, XXXVI (1946, Proceedings), 154–71.

COMMONS, J. R., Delivered price practice in the steel market, *American Economic Review*, XIV (1924), 505–19.

COOPER, G., Econometric models and economic research, *Journal of Farm Economics*, XXX (1948), 101–16.

COOPER, W. W., Theory of the firm: some suggestions for revision, *American Economic Review*, XXXIX (1949), 120–4.

COPELAND, M. A., Economic theory and natural science theory, *American Economic Review*, XXI (1931), 67–79.

——, Professor Knight on psychology, *Quarterly Journal of Economics*, XLIX (1934–5), 134–51.

——, The theory of monopolistic competition, *Journal of Political Economy*, XLII (1934), 531–6.

——, Competing products and monopolistic competition, *Quarterly Journal of Economics*, LV (1940–41), 1–35.

COURT, L. M., Invariable classical stability of entrepreneurial demand and supply functions, *Quarterly Journal of Economics*, LVI (1941–2), 134–44.

——, and LEWIS, H. G., Production cost indices, *Review of Economic Studies*, IX–X (1941–3), 28–42.

CRUM, W. L., The statistical allocation of joint costs, *Journal of the American Statistical Association*, XXI (1926), 9–24.

CURTIS, C. A., Resale price maintenance, *Canadian Journal of Economics and Political Science*, IV (1938), 350–9.

DANIELS, G. W., The relevance of political economy, *Manchester School*, V (1934), 19–31.

DAS GUPTA, A. K., On the ultimate nature of costs, *Indian Journal of Economics*, XX (1939–40), 141–50.

——, On certain limitations of the theory of competitive equilibrium, *Indian Journal of Economics*, XX (1939–40), 61–74.

DAVIS, G. R., Pricing and price levels, *Econometrica*, XIV (1946), 219–26.

DEAN, J., Statistical cost curves, *Journal of the American Statistical Association*, XXXII (1937), 85–9.

——, Cost structure of enterprise and break-even charts, *American Economic Review*, XXXVIII (1948, Proceedings), 153–64.

DENNISON, S. R., The theory of industrial location, *Manchester School*, VIII (1937), 23–47.

DINGWALL, J., Equilibrium and process analysis in the traditional theory of the firm, *Canadian Journal of Economics and Political Science*, X (1944), 448–63.

DRUMMOND, G. F., Variations in cost, *Canadian Journal of Economics and Political Science*, V (1939), 479–91.

DUE, J. F., A theory of retail price determination, *Southern Economic Journal*, VII (1939), 380–97.

DUNCAN, A. J., Monopoly adjustments to shifts in demand, *Econometrica*, X (1942), 75–9.

DUNLOP, J. T., Price flexibility and the "degree of monopoly," *Quarterly Journal of Economics*, LIII (1938–9), 522–33.

EASTHAM, J. K., Rationalization in the tin industry, *Review of Economic Studies*, IV (1936–7), 13–32.

EDWARDS, C. D., The effect of recent basing point decisions upon business practices, *American Economic Review*, XXXVIII (1948), 828–42.

EFROYMSON, C. W., A note on kinked demand curves, *American Economic Review*, XXXIII (1943), 98–109.

EITEMAN, W. J., The equilibrium of the firm in multi-process industries, *Quarterly Journal of Economics*, LIX (1944–5), 280–6.

Comments by M. A. ADELMAN, *ibid.*, LX, 464–8.

——, Factors determining the location of the least cost point, *American Economic Review*, XXXVII (1947), 910–8.

*ELLIS, H. S., and FELLNER, W., External economies and diseconomies, *American Economic Review*, XXXIII (1943), 493–511.

ENKE, S., Profit maximization under monopolistic competition, *American Economic Review*, XXXI (1941), 317–26.

——, Space and value, *Quarterly Journal of Economics*, LVI (1941–2), 627–37.

——, Resource misallocation within firms, *Quarterly Journal of Economics*, LXIII (1949), 572–6.

EVANS, G. C., Maximum production studied in a simplified economic system, *Econometrica*, II (1934), 37–50.

EZEKIAL, M., Statistical analysis and the "laws of price," *Quarterly Journal of Economics*, XLII (1927–8), 199–227.

——, A statistical examination of factors related to lamb prices, *Journal of Political Economy*, XXXV (1927), 233–60.

——, Some considerations on the analysis of the prices of competing or substitute commodities, *Econometrica*, I (1933), 172–80.

——, The cobweb theorem, *Quarterly Journal of Economics*, LII (1937–8), 255–80.

——, and WYLIE, K. H., Cost functions for the steel industry, *Journal of the American Statistical Association*, XXXVI (1941), 91–9.

FAGAN, E. D., Tax shifting and laws of cost, *Quarterly Journal of Economics*, XLVII (1932–3), 680–710.

——, and JASTRAM, R. W., Tax shifting in the short-run, *Quarterly Journal of Economics*, LIII (1938–9), 562–89.

FANNO, M., Interrelations des prix et courbes statistiques de demande et d'offre, *Econometrica*, I (1934), 162–71.

FELLNER, W., Prices and wages under bilateral monopoly, *Quarterly Journal of Economics*, LXI (1946–7), 503–32.

——, Average cost pricing and the theory of uncertainty, *Journal of Political Economy*, LVI (1948), 249–52.

FETTER, F. A., Value and the larger economics, *Journal of Political Economy*, XXXI (1923), 587–605; 790–803.

——, The economic law of market areas, note, *Quarterly Journal of Economics*, XXXVIII (1923–4), 520–9.

——, Economics and Portland cement prices, *American Economic Review*, XIV (1924), 647–57.

Reply by G. S. BROWN, *ibid.*, XV (1925), 77–80.

Reply to Brown by FETTER, *ibid.*, 80–1.

——, The new plea for basing point monopoly, *Journal of Political Economy*, XLV (1937), 577–605.

——, Exit basing point pricing, *American Economic Review*, XXXVIII (1948), 814–27.

---

* Reprinted in the present volume.

FISHER, G., The nature of economic regions, *Southern Economic Journal,* V (1938), 71–8.

FOWLER, R. F., The diagrammatical representation of elasticity of supply, *Economica* (NS), V (1938), 213–29.

FOX, H. G., Patents in relation to monopoly, *Canadian Journal of Economics and Political Science,* XII (1946), 328–42.

Notes by I. M. KEIGAN, *ibid.,* 470–82.

Rejoinder by Fox, *ibid.,* XIII (1947), 68–80.

FRIEDMAN, M., Lange on price flexibility and employment: a methodological criticism, *American Economic Review,* XXXVI (1946), 613–31.

GALBRAITH, J. K., Monopoly power and price rigidities, *Quarterly Journal of Economics,* L (1935–6), 456–75.

GARFIELD, F. R., and HOOD, W. M., Construction costs and real property values, *Journal of the American Statistical Association,* XXXII (1937), 643–53.

GEORGESCU-ROEGEN, N., Fixed coefficients and the marginal productivity theory, *Review of Economic Studies,* III (1935–6), 40–9.

GOODWIN, R. M., Dynamical coupling with especial reference to markets having production lags, *Econometrica,* XV (1947), 181–204.

GORDON, R. A., Short period price determination in theory and practice, *American Economic Review,* XXXVIII (1948), 265–88.

GRANT, I. F., The survival of the small unit in industry, *Economic Journal,* XXXII (1922), 489–505.

GREGORY, P. M., Fashion and monopolistic competition, *Journal of Political Economy,* LVI (1948), 69–75.

GRUNWALD, K., On the law of returns in a growing industrial economy, *Journal of the Royal Statistical Society,* XCVIII (1935), 695–704.

GUILLEBAUD, C. W., Davenport on the economics of Alfred Marshall, *Economic Journal,* XLVII (1937), 21–43.

GUTHRIE, J. A., Price regulation in the paper industry, *Quarterly Journal of Economics,* LX (1945–6), 194–218.

HAGUE, D. C., Economic theory and business behavior, *Review of Economic Studies,* XVI (1949–50), 144–57.

HAINES, W. W., Capacity production and the least cost point, *American Economic Review,* XXXVIII (1948), 617–25.

Rejoinder, *ibid.,* 899–904.

HALL, R. J., and HITCH, C. J., Price theory and business behavior, *Oxford Economic Papers,* II (1939), 12–45.

HARROD, R. F., Notes on supply, *Economic Journal,* XL (1930), 232–41.

———, The law of decreasing costs, *Economic Journal,* XLI (1931), 566–76.

An addendum, *ibid.,* XLII (1932), 490–2.

A further note, *ibid.,* XLIII (1933), 337–41.

Reply by J. ROBINSON, *ibid.,* 531–2.

A note by R. F. KAHN, *ibid.,* XLII (1932), 657–61.

———, Doctrines of imperfect competition, *Quarterly Journal of Economics,* XLVIII (1933–4), 442–70.

———, The equilibrium of duopoly, *Economic Journal,* XLIV (1934), 355–7.

———, Price and cost in entrepreneurs' policy, *Oxford Economic Papers,* II (1939) 1–11.

HARTKEMEIER, H. P., Note on shifts in demand and supply curves, *Econometrica,* III (1935), 428–34.

HAWKINS, E. R., Marketing and the theory of monopolistic competition, *Journal of Marketing,* IV (1939–40), 382–9.

————, A note on Chamberlin's monopoly supply curve, *Quarterly Journal of Economics*, LIII (1938–9), 641–2.

Reply by CHAMBERLIN, *ibid.*, 642–4.

HAYES, H. G., Land, rent and prices of commodities, *American Economic Review*, XVII (1927), 217–29.

HAYES, S. P., JR., Potash prices and competition, *Quarterly Journal of Economics*, LVII (1942–3), 31–68.

HENDERSON, A. M., A further note on the problem of bilateral monopoly, *Journal of Political Economy*, XLVIII (1940), 238–43.

————, The pricing of public utility undertakings, *Manchester School*, XV (1947), 223–48.

HENDERSON, H. D., The price system, *Economic Journal*, LVIII (1948), 467–82.

HEYWARD, E. J. R., H. von Stackelberg's work on duopoly, *Economic Record*, XVII (1941), 99–106.

HICKS, J. R., Marginal productivity and the theory of variation, *Economica* (OS), XII (1932), 79–88.

————, A note on the elasticity of supply, *Review of Economic Studies*, II (1934–5), 31–7.

*————, Annual survey of economic theory: the theory of monopoly, *Econometrica*, III (1935), 1–20.

HIGGINS, B., W. S. Jevons—a centenary estimate, *Manchester School*, VI (1935), 103–11.

————, Elements of indeterminacy in the theory of non-perfect competition, *American Economic Review*, XXIX (1939), 168–79.

HILLMAN, H. C., Size of firms in the boot and shoe industry, *Economic Journal*, XLIX (1939), 276–93.

HOOD, W. C., Some aspects of the treatment of time in economic theory, *Canadian Journal of Economics and Political Science*, XIV (1948), 453–68.

HOOVER, E. M., JR., The location of the shoe industry in the United States, *Quarterly Journal of Economics*, XLVII (1932–3), 254–76.

————, Spatial price discrimination, *Review of Economic Studies*, IV (1936–7), 182–91.

HOPKINS, J. A., A theory of the variation of costs, *Journal of Farm Economics*, XV (1933), 621–32.

HOTCHKISS, G. B., An economic defense of advertising, *American Economic Review*, XV (1925, Proceedings), 14–22.

*HOTELLING, H., Stability in competition, *Economic Journal*, XXXIX (1929), 41–57.

————, Edgeworth's taxation paradox and the nature of demand and supply functions, *Journal of Political Economy*, XL (1932), 577–616.

HUMPHREY, D. D., The nature and meaning of rigid prices, *Journal of Political Economy*, XLV (1937), 651–61.

*HURWICZ, L., The theory of economic behavior, *American Economic Review*, XXXV (1945), 909–25.

————, Some problems arising in estimating economic relations, *Econometrica*, XV (1947), 236–40.

HUTT, W. H., Economic method and the concept of competition, *South African Journal of Economics*, II (1934), 3–23.

————, Co-ordination and the size of firm, *South African Journal of Economics*, II (1934), 383–402.

————, The nature of aggressive selling, *Economica* (NS), II (1935), 298–320.

————, Natural and contrived scarcities, *South African Journal of Economics*, III (1935), 345–53.

---

* Reprinted in the present volume.

HUTT, W. H., The price mechanism and economic immobility, *South African Journal of Economics*, IV (1936), 319–30.

HYSON, C. D., and SANDERSON, F. H., Monopolistic discrimination in the cranberry industry, *Quarterly Journal of Economics*, LIX (1944–5), 330–69.

INNIS, H. A., The penetrative powers of the price system, *Canadian Journal of Economics and Political Science*, IV (1938), 297–319.

ISARD, W., The general theory of location and space economy, *Quarterly Journal of Economics*, LXIII (1949), 476–506.

JAIN, P. C., Optimum production under imperfect competition, *Indian Journal of Economics*, XIX (1938–9), 405–11.

JAMES, L. M., Restrictive agreements and practices in the lumber industry, 1880–1939, *Southern Economic Journal*, XIII (1945), 115–25.

JASTRAM, R. W., Advertising aspect of the monopoly problem, *Review of Economics and Statistics*, XXXI (1949), 106–9.

JEWKES, J., Factors in industrial integration, *Quarterly Journal of Economics*, XLIV (1929–30), 621–38.

JOHNSTON, J., Price ratios in recent Irish agricultural experience, *Economic Journal*, XLVII (1937), 680–5.

JONES, EDGAR, Price leadership in the rayon industry, *Manchester School*, XII (1941), 80–96.

JONES, ELIOT, Is competition in industry ruinous?, *Quarterly Journal of Economics*, XXXIV (1938–9), 473–519.

JONES, J. H., Organized marketing in the coal industry, *Economic Journal*, XXXIX (1929), 157–71.

——, The present position of the British coal trade, *Journal of the Royal Statistical Society*, XCIII (1930), 1–53.

JOSEPH, M. F. W., A discontinuous cost curve and the tendency to increasing returns, *Economic Journal*, XLIII (1933), 390–8.

KAHN, R. F., Some notes on ideal output. *Economic Journal*, XLV (1935), 1–35.

——, Two applications of the concept of elasticity of substitution, *Economic Journal*, XLV (1935), 242–5.

——, The problem of duopoly, *Economic Journal*, XLVII (1937), 1–20.

KALDOR, N. A., A classificatory note on the determinateness of equilibrium, *Review of Economic Studies*, I (1933–4), 122–36.

——, The equilibrium of the firm, *Economic Journal*, XLIV (1934), 60–76.

——, Mrs. Robinson's "economics of imperfect competition," *Economica* (NS), 1 (1934), 335–41.

*——, Market imperfection and excess capacity, *Economica* (NS), II (1935), 33–50.

——, Limitational factors and the elasticity of substitution, *Review of Economic Studies*, IV (1936–7), 162–5.

——, Professor Chamberlin on monopolistic and imperfect competition, *Quarterly Journal of Economics*, LII (1937–8), 513–29.

KALECKI, M., The supply curve of an industry under imperfect competition, *Review of Economic Studies*, VII (1939–40), 91–112.

KAPP. K. W., Rational human conduct and modern industrial society, *Southern Economic Journal*, X (1942), 136–50.

KATONA, G., Psychological analysis of business decisions and expectations, *American Economic Review*, XXXVI (1946), 44–62.

* Reprinted in the present volume.

KAYSEN, C., A revolution in economic theory, *Review of Economic Studies*, XIV (1946–7), 1–15.

——, Basing point pricing and public policy, *Quarterly Journal of Economics*, LXIII (1949), 289–314.

——, A dynamic aspect of the monopoly problem, *Review of Economics and Statistics*, XXXI (1949), 109–13.

KEEZER, D. M., The effectiveness of the federal antitrust laws: a symposium, *American Economic Review*, XXXIX (1949), 689–724.

KILLOUGH, H. B., and KILLOUGH, L. W., Price making forces in cotton markets, *Journal of the American Statistical Association*, XXI (1926), 47–54.

KLEIN, L. R., Remarks on the theory of aggregation, *Econometrica*, XIV (1946), 303–12.

——, Macro economics and the theory of rational behavior, *Econometrica*, XIV (1946), 93–108.

KNAUTH, O., Monopoly reconsidered, *Political Science Quarterly*, LX (1945), 563–77.

KNIGHT, F. H., Ethics and the economic interpretation, *Quarterly Journal of Economics*, XXXVI (1921–2), 454–81.

——, Cost of production and price over long and short periods, *Journal of Political Economy*, XXIX (1921), 304–35.

——, The ethics of competition, *Quarterly Journal of Economics*, XXXVII (1922–3), 579–624.

——, Some books on fundamentals, *Journal of Political Economy*, XXXI (1923), 342–57.

*——, Some fallacies in the interpretation of social cost, *Quarterly Journal of Economics*, XXXVIII (1923–4), 582–606.

Reply by F. D. GRAHAM, *ibid.*, XXXIX (1924–5), 324–30.

Rejoinder by KNIGHT, *ibid.*, 331–3.

——, Economic psychology and the value problem, *Quarterly Journal of Economics*, XXXIX (1924–5), 372–409.

——, Fact and metaphysics in economic psychology, *American Economic Review*, XV (1925), 247–66.

——, A suggestion for simplifying the statement of the general theory of price, *Journal of Political Economy*, XXXVI (1928), 353–70.

——, The nature of economic science in some recent discussion, *American Economic Review*, XXIV (1934), 225–38.

——, The common sense of political economy (Wicksteed reprinted), *Journal of Political Economy*, XLII (1934), 660–73.

——, The Ricardian theory of production and distribution, *Canadian Journal of Economics and Political Science*, I (1935), 3–25; 171–96.

——, Issues in the economics of stationary states, *American Economic Review*, XXVI (1936), 393–411.

——, Immutable law in economics: its reality and limitations, *American Economic Review*, XXXVI (1946, Proceedings), 93–111.

KOOPMANS, T., Identification problems in economic model construction, *Econometrica*, XVII (1949), 125–43.

KREPS, T. J., Joint costs in the chemical industry, *Quarterly Journal of Economics*, XLIV (1929–30), 416–61.

KRISTENSON, T., A note on duopoly, *Review of Economic Studies*, VI (1938–9), 56–9.

---

* Reprinted in the present volume.

KRZYMOWSKI, R., Graphical presentation of Thuenen's theory of intensity, *Journal of Farm Economics*, X (1928), 461–82.

LACHMANN, L. M., A note on the elasticity of expectations, *Economica* (NS), XII (1945), 248–53.

LAMONTAGNE, M., Some French contributions to economic theory, *Canadian Journal of Economics and Political Science*, XIII (1947), 514–32.

LAVINGTON, F., Technical influences on vertical integration, *Economica* (OS), VII (1927), 27–36.

LEONTIEFF, W. W., Stackelberg on monopolistic competition, *Journal of Political Economy*, XLIV (1936), 554–9.

——, The theory of limited and unlimited discrimination, *Quarterly Journal of Economics*, LIV (1939–40), 490–501.

——, Elasticity of demand computed from cost data, *American Economic Review*, XXX (1940), 814–7.

——, The pure theory of the guaranteed annual wage contract, *Journal of Political Economy*, LIV (1946), 70–9.

——, Wages, profit, and prices, *Quarterly Journal of Economics*, LXI (1946–7), 26–39.

LERNER, A. P., The concept of monopoly and the measurement of monopoly power, *Review of Economic Studies*, I (1933–4), 157–75.

——, and SINGER, H. W., Some notes on duopoly and spatial competition, *Journal of Political Economy*, XLV (1937), 145–86.

LERNER, J., Constant proportions, fixed plant, and the optimum conditions of production, *Quarterly Journal of Economics*, LXIII (1949), 361–70.

LESTER, R. A., Shortcomings of marginal analysis for wage employment problems, *American Economic Review*, XXXVI (1946), 63–82.
   Comment by G. J. STIGLER, *ibid.*, XXXVII (1947), 154–7.

——, Equilibrium of the firm, *American Economic Review*, XXXIX (1949), 478–84.

LEVY, M. J., JR., Note on some Chamberlinian solutions, *American Economic Review*, XXX (1940), 344–6.

LEWIS, H. G., The nature of the demand for steel, *Journal of the American Statistical Association*, XXXVI (1941), 110–5.

——, Some observations on duopoly theory, *American Economic Review*, XXXVIII (1948), 1–9.

LEWIS, W. A., Competition in retail trade, *Economica* (NS), XII (1945), 202–34.

——, Fixed costs, *Economica* (NS), XIII (1946), 231–58.

LINDBLOOM, C., The union as a monopoly, *Quarterly Journal of Economics*, LXII (1947–8), 671–97.

LOMAX, K. S., Analysis of demand and supply in textiles, *Manchester School*, XVI (1948), 46–65.

LÖWE, A., Economic analysis and social structure, *Manchester School*, VII (1936), 18–37.

——, The social productivity of technical improvements, *Manchester School*, VIII (1937), 109–24.

——, A reconsideration of the law of supply and demand, *Social Research*, IX (1942), 431–57.

LYON, L. S., and RASSIEUR, T. E., The price responsiveness of wheat growers, *Journal of Political Economy*, XXXII (1924), 707–21.

MACDOUGALL, G. D. A., The definition of prime and supplementary costs, *Economic Journal*, XLVI (1936), 443–61.

McDougall, J. L., Motor competition and railway labour costs, *Canadian Journal of Economics and Political Science*, V (1939), 52–5.

MacGregor, D. H., Marshall and his book, *Economica* (NS), IX (1942), 313–24.

Machlup, F., A note on fixed costs, *Quarterly Journal of Economics*, XLVIII (1933–4), 559–64.

——, Monopoly and competition: a classification, *American Economic Review*, XXVII (1937), 445–51.

——, Evaluation of the practical significance of the theory of monopolistic competition, *American Economic Review*, XXIX (1939), 227–36.

——, Professor Hicks' statics, *Quarterly Journal of Economics*, LIV (1939–40), 277–97.

——, Competition, pliopoly and profits, *Economica* (NS), IX (1942), 1–23; 153–73.

——, Marginal analysis and empirical research, *American Economic Review*, XXXVI (1946), 519–54.

——, Rejoinder to an anti-marginalist, *American Economic Review*, XXXVII (1947), 148–54.

*Makower, H., and Marschak, J., Assets, prices and monetary theory, *Economica* (NS), V (1938), 261–88.

——, Rationing and value theory, *Review of Economic Studies*, XIII (1945–6), 75–80.

Maroni, Y. R., Discrimination under market interdependence, *Quarterly Journal of Economics*, LXII (1947–8), 95–117.

Marschak, J., Neumann's and Morgenstern's new approach to static economics, *Journal of Political Economy*, LIV (1946), 97–115.

Mason, E. S., Price and production policies of large scale enterprise, *American Economic Review*, XXIX (1939, Proceedings), 61–74.

Maxwell, J. A., Some Marshallian concepts, *American Economic Review*, XIX (1929), 626–37.

May, K., The aggregation problem for a one industry model, *Econometrica*, XIV (1946), 285–98.

Meade, J. E., Mr. Lerner on "the economics of control," *Economic Journal*, LV (1945), 47–69.

Mears, E. G., Wheat, wheat flour, and bread composite prices, *Economic Journal*, XXXIII (1923), 39–50.

Mehta, J. K., The concepts of static and dynamic equilibria in the general theory of value, *Indian Journal of Economics*, XXVI (1945–6), 1–10.

Meriam, R. S., Supply curves and maximum satisfaction, *Quarterly Journal of Economics*, XLII (1927–8), 169–98.

Mills, F. C., Industrial productivity and prices, *Journal of the American Statistical Association*, XXXII (1937), 247–62.

Monroe, A. E., Cost and its relation to value, *Quarterly Journal of Economics*, XLII (1927–8), 530–63.

Moore, H. L., A moving equilibrium of demand and supply, *Quarterly Journal of Economics*, XXXIX (1924–5), 357–71.

——, Pantaleoni's problem in the oscillation of prices, *Quarterly Journal of Economics*, XL (1925–6), 586–96.

——, A theory of economic oscillations, *Quarterly Journal of Economics*, XLI (1926–7), 1–29.

---

* Reprinted in the present volume.

Moos, S., Price formation and price maintenance on the aluminum market, *Manchester School*, XVI (1948), 60–93.

———, The structure of the British aluminum industry, *Economic Journal*, LVIII (1948), 522–37.

Morgan, J. N., Bilateral monopoly and the competitive output, *Quarterly Journal of Economics*, LXIII (1949), 371–91.

Morgan, T., A measure of monopoly in selling, *Quarterly Journal of Economics*, LX (1945–6), 461–3.

Morgenstern, O., Oligopoly, monopolistic competition, and the theory of games, *American Economic Review*, XXXVIII (1948), 10–8.

Moriarty, W. D., An appraisal of the present status of advertising, *American Economic Review*, XV (1925, Proceedings), 23–35.

Morice, E., Loi de la demande d'un service monopolisé, *Econometrica*, VI (1938), 291–310.

Mosak, J., Interrelations of production, price, and derived demand, *Journal of Political Economy*, XLVI (1938), 761–87.

———, Some theoretical implications of the statistical analysis of demand and cost functions for steel, *Journal of the American Statistical Association*, XXXVI (1941), 100–9.

Mund, V. A., Prices under competition and monopoly, *Quarterly Journal of Economics*, XLVIII (1933–4), 288–303.

———, The financial adjustment in the empirical law of cost, *American Economic Review*, XXVI (1936), 74–80.

———, The "freight allowed" method of price quotation, *Quarterly Journal of Economics*, LIV (1939–40), 232–45.

———, The application of economic analysis to anti-trust law policy, *Proceedings of the Pacific Coast Economics Association* (December, 1941), 25–81.

———, Monopolistic competition theory and public price policy, *American Economic Review*, XXXII (1942), 727–43.

Nataf, A., Sur la possibilité de construction de certains macromodèles, *Econometrica*, XVI (1948), 232–44.

Neal, A. C., Marginal cost and dynamic equilibrium of the firm, *Journal of Political Economy*, L (1942), 45–63.

Neumann, J. von, A model of general economic equilibrium, *Review of Economic Studies*, XIII (1945–6), 1–9.

Note by D. D. Champernowne, *ibid.*, 10–8.

Nichol, A. J., Professor Chamberlin's theory of limited competition, *Quarterly Journal of Economics*, XLVIII (1933–4), 317–37.

———, A re-appraisal of Cournot's theory of duopoly price, *Journal of Political Economy*, XLII (1934), 80–105.

———, The influence of marginal buyers on monopolistic competition, *Quarterly Journal of Economics*, XLIX (1934–5), 121–35.

Comments by Chamberlin, *ibid.*, 135.

———, Edgeworth's theory of duopoly price, *Economic Journal*, XLV (1935), 50–66.

———, Monopoly supply and monopsony demand, *Journal of Political Economy*, L (1942), 861–79.

———, Production and the probabilities of cost, *Quarterly Journal of Economics*, LVII (1942–3), 69–89.

Nicholls, W. H., Post-war concentration in the cheese industry, *Journal of Political Economy*, XLVII (1939), 823–45.

———, Social biases and recent theories of competition, *Quarterly Journal of Economics*, LVIII (1943–4), 1–26.

————, Imperfect competition in agricultural processing and distributing industries, *Canadian Journal of Economics and Political Science*, X (1944), 150–64.

————, The tobacco case of 1946, *American Economic Review*, XXXIX (1949), 284–96.

NICOLS, A., The rehabilitation of pure competition, *Quarterly Journal of Economics*, LXII (1947–8), 31–63.

————, The cement case, *American Economic Review*, XXXIX (1949), 297–310.

————, The development of monopolistic competition and the monopoly problem, *Review of Economics and Statistics*, XXXI (1949), 118–23.

NORDIN, J. A., Note on a light plant's cost curves, *Econometrica*, XV (1947), 231–5.

NORTHROP, F. S. C., The impossibility of a theoretical science of economic dynamics, *Quarterly Journal of Economics*, LVI (1941–2), 1–17.

NOURSE, E. G., The meaning of "price policy," *Quarterly Journal of Economics*, LV (1940–1), 175–209.

NOYES, C. R., Certain problems in the empirical study of costs, *American Economic Review*, XXXI (1941), 473–92.

OLIVER, H. M., JR., Average cost and long-run elasticity of demand, *Journal of Political Economy*, LV (1947), 212–21.

————, Marginal theory and business behavior, *American Economic Review*, XXXVII (1947), 375–83.

PABST, W. R., JR., Monopolistic expectations and shifting control in the anthracite industry, *Review of Economics and Statistics*, XXII (1940), 45–52.

————, Unstable conditions of competition and monopoly in exhaustible resource industries, *Journal of Political Economy*, L (1942), 739–49.

PAINE, C. L., Rationalization and the theory of excess capacity, *Economica* (NS), III (1936), 46–60.

————, Some aspects of discrimination by public utilities, *Economica* (NS), IV (1937), 425–39.

PANCOAST, O., Malthus versus Ricardo: the effects of distribution on production, *Political Science Quarterly*, LVIII (1943), 46–66.

PAPANDREOU, A. G., Market structure and monopoly power, *American Economic Review*, XXXIX (1949), 883–97.

PARSONS, T., The motivation of economic activities, *Canadian Journal of Economics and Political Science*, VI (1940), 187–202.

Note by F. H. KNIGHT, *ibid.*, 460–5.

Reply to Knight by PARSONS, *ibid.*, 466–72.

PATINKIN, D., Multiple-plant firms, cartels and imperfect competition, *Quarterly Journal of Economics*, LXI (1946–7), 173–205.

Comment by W. W. LEONTIEFF, *ibid.*, 650–1.

Note by PATINKIN, *ibid.*, 651–7.

————, The indeterminacy of absolute prices in classical economic theory, *Econometrica*, XVII (1949), 1–27.

PATTON, H. S., The market influence of the Canadian wheat pool, *Journal of the American Statistical Association*, XXIV (1929), 210–8.

PAULSON, W. E., Diagrammatic economics, *Journal of Farm Economics*, XXVIII (1946), 687–722.

————, Characteristics of the marginal cost curve, *Journal of Farm Economics*, XXX (1948), 467–99.

PIGOU, A. C., The laws of diminishing and increasing cost, *Economic Journal*, XXXVII (1927), 188–97.

————, An analysis of supply, *Economic Journal*, XXXVIII (1928), 238–57.

Pigou, A. C., A note on imperfect competition, *Economic Journal*, XLIII (1933), 108–12.

———, Models of short period equilibrium, *Economic Journal*, LII (1942), 250–7.

Comment by N. A. Kaldor, *ibid.*, 257–8.

———, A comment on duopoly, *Economica* (NS), XV (1948), 254–8.

Plant, A., The economic theory concerning patents for inventions, *Economica* (NS), I (1934), 30–51.

———, The economic aspects of copyright in books, *Economica* (NS), I (1934), 167–95.

———, and Fowler, R. F., The analysis of costs of retail distribution, *Economica* (NS), VI (1939), 121–55.

Ponsonby, G. J., An aspect of competition in transport, *Economica* (NS), II (1935), 448–59.

———, Freight charges by road in competition, *Economic Journal*, XLVIII (1938), 52–63.

Putnam, G. E., Joint costs in the packing industry, *Journal of Political Economy*, XXIX (1921), 293–303.

———, Unit costs as a guiding factor in buying operations, *Journal of Political Economy*, XXIX (1921), 663–75.

Reder, M. W., Monopolistic competition and the stability conditions, *Review of Economic Studies*, VIII (1940–1), 122–5.

———, Inter-temporal relations of demand and supply within the firm, *Canadian Journal of Economics and Political Science*, VII (1941), 25–38.

———, Professor Samuelson on the foundations of economic analysis, *Canadian Journal of Economics and Political Science*, XIV (1948), 516–30.

Reynolds, L. G., Some notes on the distributive trades in Canada, *Canadian Journal of Economics and Political Science*, IV (1938), 533–48.

———, Competition in the rubber-tire industry, *American Economic Review*, XXVIII (1938), 459–68.

———, Cut-throat competition, *American Economic Review*, XXX (1940), 736–47.

———, The supply of labor to the firm, *Quarterly Journal of Economics*, LX (1945–6), 390–411.

Rhodes, E. C., Output, labour, and machines in the coal mining industry in Great Britain, *Economica* (NS), XII (1945), 101–10.

Robbins, L. C., Dynamics of capitalism, *Economica* (OS), VI (1926), 31–9.

Reply by M. H. Dobb, *ibid.*, 214–7.

———, The representative firm, *Economic Journal*, XXXVIII (1928), 387–404.

———, On a certain ambiguity in the conception of stationary equilibrium, *Economic Journal*, XL (1930), 194–214.

———, Remarks on the relationship between economics and psychology, *Manchester School*, V (1934), 89–101.

Note by B. Higgins, *ibid.*, VI (1935), 59–61.

———, Certain aspects of the theory of costs, *Economic Journal*, XLIV (1934), 1–18.

———, The place of Jevons in the history of economic thought, *Manchester School*, VII (1936), 1–17.

Robertson, D. H., Economic incentive, *Economica* (OS), I (1921), 231–45.

*———, Those empty boxes, *Economic Journal*, XXXIV (1924), 16–31.

Robertson, D. H., Sraffa, P., and Shove, G. F. (Symposium), Increasing returns and the representative firm, *Economic Journal*, XL (1930), 79–116.

Robinson, E. A. G., The problem of management and the size of firms, *Economic Journal*, XLIV (1934), 242–57.

Reply by P. S. Florence, *ibid.*, 723–9.

———

* Reprinted in the present volume.

———, A problem in the theory of industrial location, *Economic Journal*, LI (1941), 270–5.

ROBINSON, H. W., The equilibrium price in a perfect intertemporal market, *Econometrica*, VI (1938), 48–62.

ROBINSON, J., Imperfect competition and falling supply price, *Economic Journal*, XLII (1932), 544–54.

———, What is perfect competition?, *Quarterly Journal of Economics*, XLIX (1934–5), 104–20.

*———, Rising supply price, *Economica* (NS), VIII (1941), 1–8.

ROLLITT, J. B., Competitive aspects of road and rail freight and passenger rates, *Canadian Journal of Economics and Political Science*, V (1939), 40–52.

ROOS, C. F., A dynamical theory of economics, *Journal of Political Economy*, XXXV (1927), 632–56.

ROSENSTEIN-RODAN, P. N., The role of time in economic theory, *Economica* (NS), I (1934), 77–97.

ROTHSCHILD, K. W., Monopsony, buying costs and welfare expenditure, *Review of Economic Studies*, IX–X (1941–3), 62–7.

———, The degree of monopoly, *Economica* (NS), IX (1942), 24–39.

Note by J. S. BAIN, *ibid.*, X (1943), 66–8.

A further note by ROTHSCHILD, *ibid.*, 69–70.

*———, Price theory and oligopoly, *Economic Journal*, LVII (1947), 299–320.

Round table on imperfect competition, *American Economic Review*, XXIV (1934, Proceedings), 21–32.

ROY, P., On Marshall's statics and dynamics, *Indian Journal of Economics*, XX (1939–40), 761–71.

RUDD, R. W., and MACFARLANE, D. L., The scale of operations in agriculture, *Journal of Farm Economics*, XXIV (1942), 420–33.

RUGGLES, R., The concept of linear cost-output regressions, *American Economic Review*, XXXI (1941), 332–5.

RYAN, J., Machinery replacement in the cotton trade, *Economic Journal*, XL (1930), 568–80.

SCHULTZ, H., Theoretical considerations relating to supply, *Journal of Political Economy*, XXXV (1927), 437–64.

———, Marginal productivity and the general pricing process, *Journal of Political Economy*, XXXVII (1929), 505–51.

SCHULTZ, T. W., Diminishing returns in view of progress in agricultural production, *Journal of Farm Economics*, XIV (1932), 640–9.

SCHUMPETER, J. A., Robinson's economics of imperfect competition, *Journal of Political Economy*, XLII (1934), 249–57.

SCITOVSKY, T., Prices under monopoly and competition, *Journal of Political Economy*, XLIX (1941), 663–85.

*———, A note on profit maximisation and its implications, *Review of Economic Studies*, XI (1943), 57–60.

———, Some consequences of the habit of judging quality by price, *Review of Economic Studies*, XI–XII (1943–5), 100–5.

SHACKLE, G. L. S., An analysis of speculative choice, *Economica* (NS), XII (1945), 10–21.

SHAW, E. S., Element of a theory of inventory, *Journal of Political Economy*, XLVIII (1940), 465–85.

---

* Reprinted in the present volume.

SHEPHERD, G., The burden of increased costs of distribution, *Journal of Farm Economics*, XIV (1932), 650–61.

SHONE, R., Selling costs, *Review of Economic Studies*, II (1935), 225–31.

SHOVE, G. F., Varying costs and marginal net products, *Economic Journal*, XXXVIII (1928), 258–66.

——, The representative firm and increasing returns, *Economic Journal*, XL (1930), 94–116.

——, The imperfection of the market: a further note, *Economic Journal*, XLII (1933), 113–25.

SIEGEL, I. H., The concept of productive activity, *Journal of the American Statistical Association*, XXXIV (1939), 218–28.

SILBERLING, N. J., Graphic illustration of the laws of price, *American Economic Review*, XIV (1924), 417–42.

SILCOCK, T. H., Some problems of price maintenance, *Economic Journal*, XLVIII (1938), 43–51.

——, Professor Chamberlin and Mr. Smith on advertising, *Review of Economic Studies*, XVI (1947–8), 34–9.

Reply by H. SMITH, *ibid.*, 40–1.

Rejoinder by CHAMBERLIN, *ibid.*, XVII, 226–30.

SILVERMAN, H. A., The optimum firm in the boot and shoe industry, *Oxford Economic Papers*, VI (1942), 95–111.

SIMKIN, G. G. F., Some aspects and generalizations of the theory of discrimination, *Review of Economic Studies*, XV (1947–8), 1–13.

SIMONS, H. C., The requisites of free competition, *American Economic Review*, XXVI (1936, Proceedings), 68–76.

SIMPSON, K., A statistical analysis of the relation between cost and price, *Quarterly Journal of Economics*, XXXV (1920–1), 264–87; XXXVII (1922–3), 476–90.

SMITH, C. A., The cost-output relation for the U. S. Steel Corporation, *Review of Economics and Statistics*, XXIV (1942), 166–76.

SMITH, H., Discontinuous demand curves and monopolistic competition: a special case, *Quarterly Journal of Economics*, XLIX (1934–5), 542–50.

——, Advertising costs and equilibrium, *Review of Economic Studies*, II (1934–5), 62–5.

——, The imputation of advertising costs, *Economic Journal*, XLV (1935), 682–99.

SMITH, R. H., A note on the meaning of the term "rationalization," *South African Journal of Economics*, XI (1943), 210–7.

SMITH, V. E., The statistical production function, *Quarterly Journal of Economics*, LIX (1944–5), 543–62.

——, Nonlinearity in the relation between input and output, *Econometrica*, XIII (1945), 260–72.

——, Note on the kinky oligopoly demand curve, *Southern Economic Journal*, XV (1947), 205–10.

SMITHIES, A., The theory of value applied to retail selling, *Review of Economic Studies*, VI (1938–9), 215–21.

——, The maximization of profits over time with changing cost and demand functions, *Econometrica*, VII (1939), 312–8.

——, and SAVAGE, L. J., A dynamic problem in duopoly, *Econometrica*, VIII (1940), 130–43.

——, Equilibrium in monopolistic competition, *Quarterly Journal of Economics*, LV (1940–1), 95–115.

An addendum, *ibid.*, LVI (1941–2), 332–6.

————, Monopolistic price policy in a spatial market, *Econometrica*, IX (1941), 63–73.

————, Optimum location in spatial competition, *Journal of Political Economy*, XLIX (1941), 423–39.

————, The stability of competitive equilibrium, *Econometrica*, X (1942), 258–74.

————, Aspects of the basing point system, *American Economic Review*, XXXII (1942), 705–26.

Comment by V. SALERA, *ibid.*, XXXIII (1943), 900–2.

Reply by SMITHIES, *ibid.*, 902.

SOLOMON, M. R., The structure of the market in undeveloped economies, *Quarterly Journal of Economics*, LXII (1947–8), 519–41.

SOUCEY, R. D., Group equilibrium with selling costs variable, *Review of Economic Studies*, VI (1938–9), 222–5.

SOUTER, R. W., Modern monopoly as the gentleman crook, *Political Science Quarterly*, XLVIII (1933), 240–54.

SPENGLER, J. J., Sociological presuppositions in economic theory, *Southern Economic Journal*, VII (1939), 131–57.

Comments by B. P. BECKWITH, *ibid.*, 398–9.

Reply by SPENGLER, *ibid.*, 399–401.

———— Monopolistic competition and the use and price of urban land service, *Journal of Political Economy*, LIV (1946), 385–412.

*SRAFFA, P., The laws of returns under competitive conditions, *Economic Journal*, XXXVI (1926), 535–50.

*STAEHLE, H., Statistical cost functions: appraisal of recent contributions, *American Economic Review*, XXXII (1942), 321–33.

STAFFORD, J., The problem of value, *Manchester School*, IV (1933), 30–40.

STIGLER, G. J., Production and distribution in the short run, *Journal of Political Economy*, XLVII (1939), 305–27.

————, A note on discontinuous cost curves, *American Economic Review*, XXX (1940), 833–5.

————, Notes on the theory of duopoly, *Journal of Political Economy*, XLVIII (1940), 521–41.

————, Extent and bases of monopoly, *American Economic Review*, XXXII (1942, Supplement Pt. 2), 1–22.

*————, The kinky oligopoly demand curve and rigid prices, *Journal of Political Economy*, LV (1947), 432–49.

————, A theory of delivered price systems, *American Economic Review*, XXXIX (1949), 1143–59.

STOCKING, C. A., Modern advertising and economic theory, *American Economic Review*, XXI (1931), 43–55.

A criticism by A. V. ABRAMSON, *ibid.*, 685–90.

STOLPER, W. F., The possibility of equilibrium under monopolistic competition, *Quarterly Journal of Economics*, LIV (1939–40), 519–26.

STONE, R., The theory of games, *Economic Journal*, LVIII (1948), 185–201.

SWAN, T. W., Price flexibility and employment, *Economic Record*, XXI (1945), 236–53.

*SWEEZY, P. M., Demand under conditions of oligopoly, *Journal of Political Economy*, XLVII (1939), 568–73.

---

* Reprinted in the present volume.

TAUSSIG, F. W., Is market price determinate?, *Quarterly Journal of Economics*, XXXV (1920–1), 394–411.

THIRLBY, G. F., The subjective theory of value and accounting "cost," *Economica* (NS), XIII (1946), 32–49.

———, The marginal cost controversy: a note on Mr. Coase's model, *Economica* (NS), XIV (1947), 48–53.

THORP, W. L., Price theories and market realities, *American Economic Review*, XXVI (1936, Proceedings), 15–22.

TINBERGEN, J., Annual survey of significant developments in general economic theory, *Econometrica*, II (1934), 13–36.

TINTNER, G., Monopoly over time, *Econometrica*, V (1937), 160–70.

———, Note on the problem of bilateral monopoly, *Journal of Political Economy*, XLVII (1939), 263–70.

———, Homogeneous systems in mathematical economics, *Econometrica*, XVI (1948), 273–94.

TRIFFIN, R., Monopoly in particular equilibrium and in general equilibrium economics, *Econometrica*, IX (1941), 121–34.

TUCKER, R. S., The reasons for price rigidity, *American Economic Review*, XXVIII (1938), 41–54.

Comments by R. C. WOOD, *ibid.*, 663–73.

———, The degree of monopoly, *Quarterly Journal of Economics*, LV (1940–1), 167–9.

TWEDDLE, W. A., and STONE, R., A study of costs, *Econometrica*, IV (1936), 226–41.

URWICK, E. J., The ethics of competition—review article, *Canadian Journal of Economics and Political Science*, III (1937), 250–63.

VANDERBLUE, H. B., Pricing policies in the automobile industry, *Harvard Business Review*, XVII (1938–9), 385–401.

VEBLEN, T., Economic theory in the calculable future, *American Economic Review*, XV (1925, Proceedings), 48–55.

VERHULST, M. J. J., The pure theory of production applied to the French gas industry, *Econometrica*, XVI (1948), 295–308.

VICKREY, W., Some objections to marginal-cost pricing, *Journal of Political Economy*, LVI (1948), 218–38.

VINER, J., Objective tests of competitive price applied to the cement industry, *Journal of Political Economy*, XXXIII (1925), 107–11.

*———, Cost curves and supply curves, *Zeitschrift für Nationalökonomie*, III (1931–2), 23–46.

WALKER, E. R., Limited competition, *Economic Record*, X (1934), 195–212.

WALKER, G., The economics of road and rail competition, *Economic Journal*, XLIII (1933), 217–36.

WARRINER, D., Schumpeter and the conception of static equilibrium, *Economic Journal*, XLI (1931), 38–50.

WEINTRAUB, S., The classification of market positions: comment, *Quarterly Journal of Economics*, LVI (1941–2), 663–73.

Reply by TRIFFIN, *ibid.*, 673–7.

———, Monopoly equilibrium and anticipated demand *Journal of Political Economy*, L (1942), 427–34.

———, Monopoly pricing and unemployment, *Quarterly Journal of Economics*, LXI (1946–7), 108–24.

---

* Reprinted in the present volume.

WEISS, E. D., Rail and road competition in Great Britain, *South African Journal of Economics*, V (1937), 28–37.

WELDON, J. C., The multi-product firm, *Canadian Journal of Economics and Political Science*, XIV (1948), 176–90.

WENDZEL, J. T., The mill demand for wool and inter-textile competition, *Review of Economics and Statistics*, XVIII (1935–6), 172–82.

WHITE, G. R., Live-stock by-products and by-product industries, *Journal of the Royal Statistical Society*, XCV (1932), 455–87.

WHITE, H. G., A review of monopolistic and imperfect competition theory, *American Economic Review*, XXVI (1936), 637–49.

WHITE, W. L., The situation in chain-store distribution, *Southern Economic Journal*, III (1935), 411–26.

WHITMAN, R. H., A note on the concept of "degree of monopoly," *Economic Journal*, LI (1941), 261–69.
Comment by M. KALECKI, *ibid.*, LII (1942), 121–7.

WHITNEY, S. N., Competition under secret and open prices, *Econometrica*, III (1935), 40–65.

WILLIS, H. P., The problem of competitive price, *American Economic Review*, XV (1925, Proceedings), 42–7.

WILSON, E. B., Pareto versus Marshall, *Quarterly Journal of Economics*, LIII (1938–9), 645–9.

WILSON, T., Private enterprise and the theory of value, *Manchester School*, XVI (1948), 164–91.

WOLFE, A. B., "Competitive" costs and the rent of business ability, *Quarterly Journal of Economics*, XXXIX (1924–5), 39–69.

―――, Cassel's theory of pricing, *American Economic Review*, XVI (1926), 59–73.

WOOLLEY, H. B., The anomalous case of the shifting cost curve, *Quarterly Journal of Economics*, LVII (1942–3), 646–56.

WORCESTER, D. A., JR., Justifiable price "discrimination" under conditions of natural monopoly: a diagrammatic representation, *American Economic Review*, XXXVIII (1948), 382–8.

WORKING, H., Differential price behavior as a subject for commodity price analysis, *Econometrica*, III (1935), 416–27.

WYLIE, K. H., and EZEKIAL, M., The cost curve for steel production, *Journal of Political Economy*, XLVIII (1940), 777–813.

YNTEMA, T. O., The influence of dumping on monopoly price, *Journal of Political Economy*, XXXVI (1928), 686–98.

―――, Competition as a norm of economic behavior, *Journal of Business*, XIV (1941), 270–83.

YOUNG, ALLYN A., Increasing returns and economic progress, *Economic Journal*, XXXVIII (1928), 527–42.

ZAPOLEON, L. B., International and domestic commodities and the theory of prices, *Quarterly Economic Journal*, XLV (1930–1), 409–59.

ZAWADSKI, W. L., Changes in the price level under the influence of maladjustment of supply and demand, *Economica* (NS), IV (1937), 119–36.

ZEUTHEN, F., Theoretical remarks on price policy; Hotelling's case with variations, *Quarterly Journal of Economics*, XLVII (1932–3), 231–53.

―――, Monopolistic competition and the homogeneity of the market, *Econometrica*, IV (1936), 193–209.

FRENCH ARTICLES

ANTONELLI, E., Les problèmes de la corrélation et de l'élasticité (étude théorique autour de la loi de King), *Revue d'Economie Politique*, LVI (1946), 354–8.

BALLANDE, L., Prix de cartels et prix de concurrence, *Activité Economique*, No. 13 (1938), 13–32.

BOITEUX, M., La tarification des demandes en pointe: application de la théorie de la vente au coût marginal, *Revue Générale d'Electricité*, LVIII (1949), 321–40.

DENUC, J., Mouvements différentiels des prix de gros des produits industriels en France de 1929 à 1937, *Activité Economique*, No. 13 (1938), 1–13.

DESSUS, G., and FLEURQUIN, M., Les tarifs du gaz et de l'électricité du l'orientation du consommateur, *Revue d'Economie Politique*, LVIII (1948), 513–46.

GUITTON, H., L'élasticité de la demande des produits agricoles, *Etudes agricoles d'Economie Corporative*, II (1942), 191–230.

———, Offre et demande et débit, *Revue d'Economie Politique*, LVI (1946), 135–77.

———, and GUILBAUD, G. T., Déterminisme et marché, *Revue d'Economie Politique*, LVI (1946), 409–35.

MARCHAL, J., Prix de gros et prix de détail, *Revue d'Economie Politique*, XLV (1931), 1219–50.

MARCY, G., Essai sur les prix différentiels, *Revue d'Economie Politique*, LII (1938), 1063–96.

MARJOLIN, R., La production des biens et les mouvements de prix de longue durée, *Activité Economique*, No. 12 (1938), 149–80.

ROY, R., La demande dans ses rapports avec la répartition des revenus, *Metron*, VIII (1930), 101–53.

———, Les lois de la demande, *Revue d'Economie Politique*, XLV (1931), 1190–1218.

———, L'élasticité de la demande, *Revue d'Economie Politique*, XLVIII (1934), 1179–1211.

———, De l'utilité, contribution à la théorie des choix, *Actualités scientifiques et industrielles*, No. 930 (Paris, Hermann, 1942).

———, La hiérarchie des besoins et la notion de groupes dans l'économie de choix, *Econometrica*, XI (1943), 13–24.

———, La distribution du revenu entre les divers biens, *Econometrica*, XV (1947), 205–25.

WOLFF, R., Liaison entre prix et monnaie, *Revue d'Economie Politique*, XLVIII (1934), 1691–1746.

GERMAN ARTICLES

AMONN, A., Cassel's System der Theoretischen Nationalökonomie, *Archiv für Sozialwissenschaft und Sozialpolitik*, LI (1923–4), 1–87; 322–61.

FRISCH, R., Einige Punkte einer Preistheorie mit Boden und Arbeit als Produktionsfaktoren, *Zeitschrift für Nationalökonomie*, III (1931–2), 62–104.

HAYEK, F. A., Das intertemporale Gleichgewichtssystem der Preise und die Bewegungen des "Geldwertes," *Weltwirtschaftliches Archiv*, XXVIII (1928, II), 33–76.

LACHMANN, L. M., Preiserwartungen und intertemporales Gleichgewicht, *Zeitschrift für Nationalökonomie*, VIII (1937), 33–46.

MENGER, K., Das Unsicherheitsmoment in der Wertlehre, *Zeitschrift für Nationalökonomie*, V (1934), 459–85.

———, Bemerkungen zu den Ertragsgesetzen, *Zeitschrift für Nationalökonomie*, VII (1936), 25–56.

————, Weitere Bemerkungen zu den Ertragsgesetzen, *Zeitschrift für Nationalökonomie*, VII (1936), 388–97.

MÖLLER, H., Die Formen der regionalen Preisdifferenzierung, *Weltwirtschaftliches Archiv*, LVII (1943), 81–112.

————, Grundlagen einer Theorie der regionalen Preisdifferenzierung, *Weltwirtschaftliches Archiv*, LVIII (1943), 335–91.

MORGENSTERN, O., Offene Probleme der Kosten—u. Ertragstheorie, *Zeitschrift für Nationalökonomie*, II (1931), 481–522.

————, Die drei Grundtypen der Theorie des subjektiven Wertes, *Schriften des Vereins für Sozialpolitik*, Vol. 183 (1931), 1–43.

————, Das Zeitmoment in der Wertlehre, *Zeitschrift für Nationalökonomie*, V (1934), 433–58.

————, Vollkommene Voraussicht und Wirtschaftliches Gleichgewicht, *Zeitschrift für Nationalökonomie*, VI (1935), 337–57.

SCHAMS, E., Die Casselschen Gleichungen und die mathematische Wirtschaftstheorie, *Jahrbücher für Nationalökonomie und Statistik*, CXXVII (1927), 385–400.

SCHNEIDER, E., Preisbildung und Preispolitik unter Berücksichtigung der geographischen Verteilung von Erzeugern und Verbrauchern, *Schmollers Jahrbuch*, LVIII (1934), 257–77.

————, Absatz, Produktion und Lagerhaltung bei einfacher Produktion, *Archiv für Mathematische Wirtschafts- und Sozialforschung*, IV (1938), 99–120.

————, Zur Konkurrenz und Preisbildung auf vollkommenen und unvollkommenen Märkten, *Weltwirtschaftliches Archiv*, XLVIII (1938), 399–419.

————, Zielsetzung, Verhaltensweise und Preisbildung, *Jahrbücher für Nationalökonomie und Statistik*, CLVII (1943), 405–34.

SCHUMPETER, J., Zur Einführung der folgenden Arbeit Knut Wicksells, *Archiv für Sozialwissenschaft und Sozialpolitik*, LVIII (1927), 238–51.

STACKELBERG, H. VON, Die grundlegenden Hypothesen der neueren Preisanalyse, *Archiv für Mathematische Wirtschafts- und Sozialforschung*, I (1935), 84–103.

————, Probleme der unvollkommenen Konkurrenz, *Weltwirtschaftliches Archiv*, XLVIII (1938), 95–141.

————, Angebot und Nachfrage in der Produktionswirtschaft, *Archiv für Mathematische Wirtschafts- und Sozialforschung*, IV (1938), 73–99.

ITALIAN ARTICLES

I. UTILITY AND DEMAND

AMOROSO, L., Intorno alla determinazione empirica delle leggi della domanda e offerta, *Giornale degli economisti*, LXX (1930), 941–4.

————, La teoria matematica del programma economico, *Rivista italiana di scienze economiche*, X (1939), 67–80.

ANGIOLINI, V., Alcune osservazioni su di un vecchio tema, *Giornale degli economisti* (NS), IX (1950), 372–9.

BORDIN, A., La legge della domanda dal punto di vista della statica e della dinamica, *Giornale degli economisti*, LXX (1930), 421–71.

————, Nota sui caratteri della curva dei baratti e su un criterio di indipendenza dei beni, *Economia*, XXV (1940), 355–69.

BORGATTA, G., La rendita del consumatore e le sue applicazioni finanziarie, *Giornale degli economisti*, LXI (1921), 157–74; 248–71.

BRAMBILLA, F., Curve di domanda della farina di frumento in Italia dal 1925 al 1942, Appendix to the *Gazzetta Ufficiale* (1949).

Bruguier, C., and Manià, B., Carattere costruttivo delle funzioni utilità nell'economia matematica, *Giornale degli economisti*, LXXVI (1936), 661–71.

Carli, F., Teoria sociologica dei bisogni, *Economia*, III (1925), 230–78.

Costanzo, A., Modificazioni della struttura qualitativa e quantitativa dei bilanci alimentari in funzione delle variazioni della spesa per il vitto, *Rivista internazionale di scienze sociali*, L (1942), 241–50.

D'Albergo, E., L'analisi Pareto-Slutsky sulla domanda e la teoria delle imposte sui consumi, *Giornale degli economisti* (NS), VIII (1949), 59–90.

De Finetti, B., Sui campi di ofelimità, *Rivista italiana di scienze economiche*, VII (1935), 523–32.

Del Vecchio, G., Ricerche sopra l'entrata e la spesa di famiglie operaie a Trieste, *Bollettino dell'Ufficio del Lavoro e della Statistica*, XLVII (1922), No. 4.

Demaria, G., Un nuovo metodo "obiettivo" per lo studio della dipendenza dei beni, *Acta Seminari* (Università Bocconi, Milano), I (1942), 83–92.

Dominedò, V., Considerazioni intorno alla teoria della domanda: rilievi critici sulla determinazione del prezzo, *Giornale degli economisti*, LXXIII (1933), 30–40.

———, Le principali premesse e caratteristiche delle curve statiche, *Giornale degli economisti*, LXXIII (1933), 765–807.

———, Ancora in tema di curve di domanda, *Giornale degli economisti*, LXXIV (1934), 115–6.

———, Quantità economiche oggettive e moventi edonistici, *Rendiconti del Seminario matematico e fisico di Milano* (1935).

———, Coerenza e stabilità nella condotta economica razionale, *Giornale degli economisti* (NS), VI (1947), 1–12.

Einaudi, L., La paternità della legge detta di King, *Rivista di storia economica*, VIII (1943), 33–8.

Fanno, M., Contributo alla teoria economica dei beni succedanei, *Annali di Economia* (Università Bocconi, Milano), II (1926), No. 2, 1–140.

Foà, B., In tema di curve di domanda, *Giornale degli economisti*, LXXIII (1933), 571–9.

———, Pellegrino Rossi e la teoria soggettiva del valore, *Rivista di storia economica*, I (1936), 309–16.

Fossati, E., Osservazioni sulla legge di Wieser per la determinazione del valore di una provvista di beni omogenei, *Studi in onore di Riccardo Dalla Volta*, Cya, Firenze, II (1936), 137–64.

Fuà, G., Schemi di calcolo economico su dati incerti, *Giornale degli economisti* (NS), VII (1948), 361–414.

Gambino, A., La raffigurazione della rendita del consumatore rispetto alle curve dei baratti, *Giornale degli economisti* (NS), V (1946), 63–75.

Gobbi, U., Ancora due parole sulla rendita del consumatore, *Giornale degli economisti*, LXIX (1929), 153–9.

———, La rendita del consumatore e i principi generali dell'economia, *Giornale degli economisti*, LXX (1930), 329–34.

———, Appunti critici sul massimo di utilità dato dalla libera concorrenza, *Giornale degli economisti* (NS), I (1939), 608–12.

Also G. Demaria, *ibid.*, 613–20.

Gobbi, *ibid.*, 621–3.

Graziani, A., Appunti sulla rendita del consumatore, *Giornale degli economisti*, LXX (1930), 46–51.

Griziotti-Kretschmann, J., Il valore nelle dottrine classica e subiettiva, *Giornale degli economisti*, LXXVIII (1938), 185–205.

————, Il valore nella dottrina moderna, *Giornale degli economisti*, LXXVIII (1938), 433–52.

MASCI, G., Sulla determinazione statistica della curva di domanda, *Rivista italiana di statistica economia e finanza*, IV (1932), 476–514.

MENGARINI, P., Formazione e trasformazione dei gusti, *Revista di politica economica*, XXVII (1937), 709–22.

PAPI, G. U., Uniformità nel piano di un consumatore, *Giornale degli economisti* (NS), IV (1942), 518–45.

PIETRANERA, G., Considerazioni sulla natura dell'atto economico, *Giornale degli economisti* (NS), I (1939), 692–707.

REPACI, F. A., Prezzi e consumi del tobacco in Italia, *La riforma sociale*, XLI (1930), 379–93.

RICCI, U., Elasticità dei bisogni, della domanda e dell'offerta, *Giornale degli economisti*, LXIV (1924), 413–31; 509–31.

Errata, *ibid.*, LXVII (1927), 503–4.

————, Se il sacrificio del contribuente sia maggiore, o minore con un'imposta diretta o di consumo, *Giornale degli economisti*, LXXVIII (1938), 722–37.

————, Eccezioni apparenti alla legge teorica di domanda, *Rivista internazionale di scienze sociali*, XLIX (1941), 306–30.

————, Una legge dinamica della domanda, *Studi economici*, I (1946), 18–49; first published in *Archiv für Mathematische Wirtschafts- und Sozialforschung*, VII (1941), 103–24.

ROSENSTEIN-RODAN, P. N., La complementarità, prima delle tre tappe della teoria economica, *La riforma sociale*, XLIV (1933), 257–308.

ROSSI, L., Del concetto di elasticità in economia, *Giornale degli economisti*, LXXII (1932), 18–26.

SENSINI, G., Gli studi di Vilfredo Pareto sulle funzioni di domanda e offerta, *Giornale degli economisti* (NS), VIII (1949), 1–18.

————, Ancora sugli studi di Vilfredo Pareto, *Giornale degli economisti* (NS), IX (1950), 67–86.

VIANELLI, S., Le tabelle di consumo in relazione alla dottrina paretiana, *Rivista italiana di scienze economiche*, XII (1940), 189–216.

————, Piano di consumo e teoria degli errori nella dinamica economica, *Giornale degli economisti* (NS), III (1941), 336–49.

VINCI, F., L'elasticità dei consumi, *Rivista italiana di statistica economia e finanza*, III (1931), 52–66.

————, I bilanci di famiglia nella prassi e nella teoria economica, *Rivista italiana di scienze economiche*, XI (1940), 171–88.

ZACCAGNINI, E., Razionalità della domanda e criteri d'indipendenza dei beni, *Giornale degli economisti* (NS), V (1946), 219–43.

ZACCHERINI, G., Determinatezza della funzione dell'ofelimità, *Giornale degli economisti* (NS), VIII (1948), 176–86.

II. COSTS AND PRICING

AMOROSO, L., La curva statica di offerta, *Giornale degli economisti*, LXX (1930), 1–26.

————, La produzione in regime di concentrazione industriale, *Rivista italiana di scienze economiche*, VII (1935), 157–63.

BARONE, E., I costi connessi e l'economia dei trasporti, *Giornale degli economisti*, LXI (1921), 56–84.

BERTOLINO, A., Prime linee di una teoria del costo, *Studi Senesi* (Università, Siena), XLII (1928), 191–227.

BORDIN, A., Un caso di monopolio bilaterale, *Rivista italiana di scienze economiche*, VIII (1936), 504–20.

――――, Alcune generalizzazioni di un caso di monopolio bilaterale, *Giornale degli economisti*, LXXVI (1936), 672–94.

――――, Il monopolio bilaterale in termini di ofelimità e gli accordi intersindacali dell'economia corporativa, *Rivista italiana di scienze economiche*, IX (1937), 147–88.

――――, L'equilibrio dell'impresa. La funzione Cobb-Douglas, *Giornale degli economisti* (NS), IV (1942), 151–68.

BREGLIA, A., Sul valore in regime di costi crescenti, *Giornale degli economisti*, LXX (1930), 554–66.

――――, Sul raggiungimento dell'ottima costituzione delle imprese, *Giornale degli economisti*, LXXI (1931), 706–14.

――――, Variazioni della richiesta di una merce prodotta in concorrenza e relative variazioni dell prezzo, *Giornale degli economisti*, LXXII (1932), 71–8.

――――, In tema di costi crescenti, *Giornale degli economisti*, LXXII (1932), 721–9.

――――, Prezzi in mercato corporativo, *La riforma sociale*, XLV (1934), 381–401.

BRESCIANI-TURRONI, C., La formazione dei prezzi delle azioni industriali durante l'inflazione cartacea, *Giornale degli economisti*, LXV (1925), 237–74.

――――, Alcune lezioni sulla teoria della produttività marginale, *Acta Seminari* (Università Bocconi, Milano), I (1942), 5–39.

CABIATI, A., Per riempire alcune "empty boxes" finanziarie, *Giornale degli economisti*, LXVIII (1928), 81–98.

――――, Sull'influenza dell'elasticità della domanda nella produttività decrescente, *Giornale degli economisti*, LXX (1930), 335–7.

CARLI, G., Aspetti della pianificazione economica tedesca: la disciplina dei prezzi, *Rivista italiana di scienze economiche*, XIV (1942), 321–39; 517–37.

CIANCI, E., La dinamica dei prezzi, in *Trattato elementare di statistica* (edited by C. Gini), Giuffré, Milano, Vol. V, Part I (1933), 57–82.

DA EMPOLI, A., Costi crescenti descrescenti e costanti nello studio degli effetti economici delle imposte, *Archivio Scientifico* (Università, Bari), VIII (1933–4), 357–400.

DAMI, C., A proposito di un suggerimento del Pareto al ministro della produzione in uno stato collettivista, *Giornale degli economisti* (NS), V (1946), 154–79.

DEL VECCHIO, G., Il costo quale elemento della teoria economica, *Giornale degli economisti*, LXVI (1926), 167–72.

――――, La dinamica economica di H. L. Moore, *Giornale degli economisti*, LXX (1930), 545–53.

DEMARIA, G., Commercio a termine, *Enciclopedia italiana*, istituto Giovanni Treccani, X (1931), 966–8.

――――, Oligopolio e azione corporativa, *Giornale degli economisti*, LXXIV (1934), 714–25.

DE PIETRI-TONELLI, A., Considerazioni intorno alla speculazione di borsa, *Giornale degli economisti*, LXXVI (1936), 65–81.

DI FENIZIO, F., Osservazioni sul controllo dei prezzi in Germania, *Giornale degli economisti*, LXXV (1935), 612–26.

――――, L'opera scientifica di Erich Schneider, preface to Schneider's *Teoria della produzione*, Cea, Milano (1942), 9–46.

DI NARDI, G., Studi sull'equilibrio dell'impresa e sulla rappresentazione grafica dell'offerta collettiva, *Annali della Facoltà di Economia e commercio* (Università, Bari), V (1943).

————, Contributo alla interpretazione della curva di offerta del mercato, *Studi in onore di Guglielmo Masci*, Giuffré, Milano, I (1943), 233–44.

DOMINEDÒ, V., Intorno al problema delle variazioni di quantità nel consumo e nella produzione, *Acta Seminari* (Università Bocconi, Milano), II (1943), 91–108.

EINAUDI, L., Il prezzo dell'energia elettrica, *La riforma sociale*, XLV (1934), 495–506; 615–8.

FANFANI, A., Review of Hauser's *Recherches et documents sur l'histoire des prix en France de 1500 à 1800* in *Rivista internazionale di scienze sociali*, XLV (1937), 357–9.

Comment by HAUSER, *ibid.*, 874–82.

Reply by FANFANI, *ibid.*, 883–90.

FANNO, M., Correlazioni tra prezzi e curve statistiche di domanda e offerta, *Rivista italiana di statistica economia e finanza*, IV (1932), 223–37.

FASIANI, M., Contributo ad alcuni punti della teoria della traslazione delle imposte sui "profitti" e sui "redditi," *Studi Sassaresi* (Università, Sassari), IX–X (1930–1).

————, Di un fenomeno di attrito, *Rivista italiana di statistica economia e finanza*, IV (1932), 248–81.

FEDERICI, L., Uno studio sulla teoria dei dazi d'importazione, *Giornale degli economisti* (NS), V (1946), 36–62.

FUBINI, R., Contributo allo studio degli effetti dell'imposta generale sul reddito, *Giornale degli economisti*, LXXII (1932), 365–404.

GRASSER-RESCHITZ, B., Note sul mercato del pesce fresco in Italia, *Giornale degli economisti*, LXXVII (1937), 178–83.

LUZZATTO-FEGIZ, P. P., Alimentazione e prezzi in tempo di guerra (1942–1943), *Annali Triestini* (Università, Trieste), XVIII (1948), Part 2, 1–208.

MASCI, G., Metodi statistici per lo studio dell'equilibrio generale dinamico, *Economia*, IX (1932), 375–97.

————, Costo di produzione, utilità marginale ed equilibrio generale economico, *Saggi critici di teoria e metodologia economica*, Studio Editoriale, Catania (1934), 61–87.

PAPI, G. U., Uniformità nel piano di un produttore, *Giornale degli economisti* (NS), VIII (1949), 239–64.

PARENTI, G., Considerazioni su recenti indagini intorno alla storia dei prezzi, *Annali di Statistica e di Economia* (Università, Genova), VI (1940), Issues 7–8, 253–82.

PORRI, V., Limiti e metodi nel controllo dei prezzi, *La riforma sociale*, XLV (1934), 249–54.

ROSSI, L., Dei prezzi di monopolio pubblico e in particolare delle tariffe viaggiatori nelle ferrovie, *Rivista italiana di statistica economia e finanza*, VI (1934), 837–58.

————, Il prezzo dell'energia elettrica e l'ordine corporativo, *Rivista italiana di scienze economiche*, VII (1938), 502–22.

SENSINI, G., Le equazioni della dinamica economica nel caso più semplice del regime di libera concorrenza completa, *Giornale degli economisti* (NS), VII (1948), 516–30.

————, Le equazioni della dinamica economica nel caso più semplice del regime di monopolio della produzione delle merci, *Giornale degli economisti* (NS), VIII (1949), 367–78.

SRAFFA, P., Sulle relazioni fra costo e quantità prodotta, *Annali di Economia* (Universita Bocconi, Milano), II (1925), 1o, 277–328.

STACKELBERG, H., Sulla teoria del duopolio e del polipolio, *Rivista italiana di statistica economia e finanza*, V (1933), 275–89.

STEVE, S., Sul concetto di imposta generale, *Giornale degli economisti* (NS), VI (1947), 573–626.

UGGÉ, A., Sul controllo dei prezzi, *Rivista internazionale di scienze sociali*, LV (1947), 22–37.

VIANELLI, S., Confronti internazionali tra prezzi delle merci e corsi delle azioni, *Rivista italiana di statistica economia e finanza*, V (1933), 679–710.

VILLANI, F., Di un caso di traslazione d'imposta in regime di monopolio e in regime di concorrenza monopolistica, *Rivista italiana di scienze economiche*, XIII (1941), 1039–62.

VINCI, F., Prezzi e scorte, *Rivista italiana di scienze economiche*, XI (1940), 1031–37.

SWEDISH ARTICLES

AIZSILNIEKS, A., Prisbildningsteorien och konsumtionsföreningsarnas prispolitik (Price theory and the pricing policy of consumers' cooperatives), *Ekonomisk Tidskrift*, IL (1947), 193–209; 259–71.

BAGGE, G., Den aftagande och den tilltagande afkastningens lagar (The laws of increasing and decreasing returns), *Ekonomisk Tidskrift*, XXII (1920), 193–228.

CARLSON, S., Prisövervakning och kostnadsberäkning under en avspärrningskris (Costing and supervision of prices in an isolated country under warfare conditions), *Ekonomisk Tidskrift*, XLI (1939), 325–332; XLII (1940), 105–116.

DAVIDSON, D., Varuvärde och penningvärde (The value of goods and the value of money), *Ekonomisk Tidskrift*, XXVIII (1926), 1–18.

DICKSON, H., and ÖSTLIND, A., Prisstabiliserande egenskaper hos en säljares efterfrågeforeställningar (Sellers' demand concepts: factors working for price stabilization), *Ekonomisk Tidskrift*, XLV (1943), 215–41.

HAMMARSKJÖLD, D., Utkast till en algebraisk metod för dynamisk prisanalys (An outline of an algebraic method of dynamic price analysis), *Ekonomisk Tidskrift*, XXXIV (1932), 157–76.

HECKSCHER, E., Intermittent fria nyttigheter (Entrepreneurial ubiquities), *Ekonomisk Tidskrift*, XXVI (1924), 41–54.

———, Forklaringen till konstanta priser (Explanation of constant prices), *Ekonomisk Tidskrift*, XXVII (1925), 47–56.

LINDAHL, E., Prisbildningsproblemets uppläggning från kapitalteoretisk synpunkt (The pricing problem from the point of view of capital theory), XXXI (1929), 31–81.

LUNDBERG, E., Om begreppet ekonomisk jämvikt (On the concept of economic equilibrium), *Ekonomisk Tidskrift*, XXXII (1930), 133–60.

———, Gränsen för prisstegring och prispolitik (Limits of price rise and price policy), *Ekonomisk Tidskrift*, XLIII (1941), 261–75.

MYRDAL, G., Om penningteoretisk jämvikt. En studie over den "normala räntan" i Wicksells penninglära (Monetary equilibrium. A study in Wicksell's "normal interest"), *Ekonomisk Tidskrift*, XXXIII (1931), 191–302.

ÖSTLIND, A., Realistiska inslag i den moderna nationalekonomiens uppfattning av enskilda företags prispolitik (Some realistic interpretations of business pricing policy), *Ekonomisk Tidskrift*, VLIII (1946), 184–96.

OHLIN, B., Till frågan om skogarnas omloppstid (The optimum investment period of Swedish forests): Nationalekonomiska studier tillägnade professor Knut Wicksell (Economic studies in honour of Professor Knut Wicksell), *Ekonomisk Tidskrift*, XXIII (1921), 89–113.

PALANDER, T., Konkurrens och marknadsjamvikt vid duopol och oligopol (Adjustments and market equilibrium under duopoly and oligopoly), *Ekonomisk Tidskrift*, XLI (1939), 123–45; 222–50.

———, Kan man uppställa enhetliga principer för kostnadsberäkning? (Are uniform costing principles possible?), *Affärsekonomi* (1949), 5–105.

SjÖBERG, A., Järnvägarnas godstariffsystem och des återverkningar på konkurrensen mellan järnvägar och bilar (Railway rates and their effects on the competition between railways and trucks), *Ekonomisk Tidskrift*, VLII (1945), 327–34.

SUNDBOM, I., Pris- och kostnadsdifferentiering (Price and cost differentiation), *Ekonomist Tidskrift*, XXXVII (1935), 135–52.

———, Marknadsformerna och förutsättningarna för monopolistisk samverkan mellan producenter (Market types and conditions for monopolistic cooperation between producers), *Ekonomisk Tidskrift*, VLI (1944), 21–39.

WICKSELL, K., Valutaspörsmålet i de skandinaviska länderna (Foreign exchange problems in the Scandinavian countries), *Ekonomisk Tidskrift*, XXVII (1925), 205–22.

INDEX OF NAMES